Bad Kids

STUDIES IN CRIME AND PUBLIC POLICY

Michael Tonry and Norval Morris, *General Editors*

Bad Kids

Race and the Transformation of the Juvenile Court

I I I I BARRY C. FELD

New York   Oxford • Oxford University Press • 1999

Oxford University Press

Oxford   New York
Athens   Auckland   Bangkok   Bogotá   Buenos Aires   Calcutta
Cape Town   Chennai   Dar es Salaam   Delhi   Florence   Hong Kong   Istanbul
Karachi   Kuala Lumpur   Madrid   Melbourne   Mexico City   Mumbai
Nairobi   Paris   São Paulo   Singapore   Taipei   Tokyo   Toronto   Warsaw

and associated companies in
Berlin   Ibadan

Copyright © 1999 by Oxford University Press, Inc.

Published by Oxford University Press, Inc.
198 Madison Avenue, New York, New York 10016

Oxford is a registered trademark of Oxford University Press.

Library of Congress Cataloging-in-Publication Data
Feld, Barry C.
Bad kids : race and the transformation of the juvenile court /
Barry C. Feld.
    p.   cm.—(Studies in crime and public policy)
Includes bibliographical references.
ISBN 0-19-509787-4; ISBN 0-19-509788-2 (pbk.)
1. Juvenile justice, Administration of—United States.   2. Juvenile courts—United States.
3. Discrimination in juvenile justice administration—United States.   I. Series.
HV9104.F43   1999
364.36'0973—dc21   98-7271

9 8 7 6 5 4 3 2 1

Printed in the United States of America
on acid-free paper

To
my mother, Flora Papier Feld,
and to the memory of
my father, Arthur Sidney Feld

Acknowledgments

I have studied and written about juvenile justice administration for more than twenty-five years, and I have incurred debts to many colleagues and organizations along the way. The Harry Frank Guggenheim Foundation and the University of Minnesota's Bush Sabbatical program provided generous support during my 1994–1995 sabbatical year, when I began to write this book in earnest. The University of Minnesota Law School's Partners in Excellence program provided additional support during several subsequent summers of writing. Deans Robert A. Stein and E. Thomas Sullivan at the University of Minnesota Law School supported and encouraged me throughout my career and assisted me in many ways with this project. I am especially grateful to Bob Stein who took an administrative risk a decade ago and enabled me to grow and flourish personally and professionally in ways that neither of us could anticipate then.

A number of colleagues and friends generously took time from their busy lives to read drafts of chapters or the entire manuscript and suggested many ways to improve this book. I am grateful to Tom Bernard, Donna Bishop, Jeffrey Fagan, Patricia Feld, James Jacobs, Kimberly Kempf-Leonard, Steven Morse, Roger Richards, Irene Rosenberg, Elizabeth Scott, Suzanna Sherry, Simon Singer, Michael Tonry, and Frank Zimring, who provided constructive critiques, pointed out my many errors, and tried to protect me from my own wrong-headedness. Despite their best efforts, they bear no responsibility for my failure to heed their wise advice. Howard Snyder and the National Center for Juvenile Justice provided invaluable assistance in assembling some of the data analyzed in this book. Several fine research assistants, Sheila T. Starkey, Melissa Weldon, and Stacey Drentlaw, deserve special recognition for the outstanding research assistance they provided when my attention focused directly on this project; they responded creatively and energetically to my outrageous research questions. My daughter, Julia Feld, suggested the title for this book, *Bad Kids*, a vast improvement over my earlier versions.

Because this book culminates several decades of research and writing about juvenile justice administration, I have published earlier versions of parts of several chapters in criminology journals and law reviews. Although I have substantially revised, rewritten, and changed those earlier articles almost beyond recognition, I am grateful to the following journals who have kindly allowed me to use those articles:

In chapter 4, University of Minnesota Law Review for "Criminalizing Juvenile Justice: Rules of Procedure for the Juvenile Court," *Minnesota Law Review* 69:141–276 (1984); Northwestern University School of Law for "The Right to Counsel in Juvenile Court: An Empirical Study of When Lawyers Appear and the Difference They Make," *Journal of Criminal Law and Criminology* 79 (1989):1185–1346; Sage Publications for "*In re Gault* Revisited: A Cross-State Comparison of the Right to Counsel in Juvenile Court," *Crime and Delinquency* 34 (1988):393–424; Northwestern University School of Law for "Justice by Geography: Urban, Suburban, and Rural Variations in Juvenile Justice Administration," *Journal of Criminal Law and Criminology* 82 (1991): 156–210.

In chapter 6, University of Minnesota Law Review for "Reference of Juvenile Offenders for Adult Prosecution: The Legislative Alternative to Asking Unanswerable Question," *Minnesota Law Review* 62:515–618 (1978); Northwestern University School of Law for "The Juvenile Court Meets the Principle of the Offense: Legislative Changes in Juvenile Waiver Statutes," *Journal of Criminal Law and Criminology* 78 (1987):471–533; University of Minnesota Law School for "Bad Law Makes Hard Cases: Reflections on Teen-Aged Axe-Murderers, Judicial Activism, and Legislative Default," *Journal of Law and Inequality* 8:1–101 (1990); University of Minnesota Law Review for "Violent Youth and Public Policy: A Case Study of Juvenile Justice Law Reform," *Minnesota Law Review* 79:965–1128 (1995); University of Chicago Press for "Juvenile and Criminal Justice Systems' Responses to Youth Violence," *Crime and Justice* 24:189–262 (1998).

In chapter 7, Boston University Law School for "The Juvenile Court Meets the Principle of Offense: Punishment, Treatment, and the Difference It Makes," *Boston University Law Review* 68:821–915 (1988); University of Chicago Press for "Juvenile and Criminal Justice Systems' Responses to Youth Violence," *Crime and Justice: A Review of Research* 24:189–262 (1998).

In chapter 8, University of Chicago Press for "Criminalizing the American Juvenile Court," *Crime and Justice: A Review of Research* 17:197–280 (1993); Northwestern University School of Law for "Abolish the Juvenile Court:

Youthfulness, Criminal Responsibility, and Sentencing Policy," *Journal of Criminal Law and Criminology* 88:68–136 (1998).

In addition, I must also thank the authors and copyright holders of the following works, who permitted the inclusion of excerpts from their work in this book:

American Bar Association Juvenile Justice Center for *A Call for Justice: An Assessment of Access to Counsel and Quality of Representation in Delinquency Proceedings* (copyright 1995, reprinted by permission).

American Civil Liberties Union for Martin A. Guggenheim, "A Call to Abolish the Juvenile Justice System," *Children's Rights Reporter* 2:7–19 (copyright 1978, reprinted by permission).

Basic Books for W. Norton Grubb and Marvin Lazerson, *Broken Promises: How Americans Fail Their Children* (copyright 1982, reprinted by permission of Basic Books, Inc.)

Basic Books for Joseph F. Kett, *Rites of Passage: Adolescence in America 1790 to the Present* (copyright 1977, reprinted by permission of Basic Books, Inc.).

Doubleday, a division of Bantam Doubleday Dell Publishing, Inc., for Peter L. Berger and Brigitte Berger, *The War Over the Family* (copyright 1983, reprinted by permission).

Elaine Markson Agency and Neil Postman for Neil Postman, *The Disappearance of Childhood*, published by Random House (copyright 1994, reprinted by permission).

Farrar, Straus and Giroux, for Ellen Ryerson, *The Best-Laid Plans: American's Juvenile Court Experiment* (copyright 1978, reprinted by permission).

Harvard Law Review Association for Julian Mack, "The Juvenile Court," *Harvard Law Review* 23:104–122 (copyright 1909, reprinted by permission of Harvard Law Review Association).

Little, Brown and Co. for David J. Rothman's *Conscience and Convenience: The Asylum and Its Alternatives in Progressive America* (copyright 1980 by David J. Rothman, reprinted by permission).

National Academy of Sciences for Alfred Blumstein, Jacqueline Cohen, Jeffrey A. Roth, and Christy Visher, *Criminal Careers and "Career Criminals"* (copyright 1986, reprinted by permission of National Academy Press).

National Academy of Sciences for Lee B. Sechrest, Susan O. White, and Elizabeth D. Brown, *The Rehabilitation of Criminal Offenders* (copyright 1979, reprinted by permission of National Academy Press).

National Council of Juvenile and Family Court Judges for Earl Warren, "Equal Justice for Juveniles," *Juvenile Court Judges Journal* (copyright 1964, reprinted by permission).

New York State Bar Association, Committee on Juvenile Justice and Child Welfare for Jane Knitzer and Merril Sobie's *Law Guardians in New York State: A Study of the Legal Representation of Children* (copyright 1988, reprinted by permission).

North Carolina Law Review Association for Janet E. Ainsworth's "Re-Imagining Childhood and Reconstructing the Legal Order: The Case for Abolishing the Juvenile Court," *North Carolina Law Review* 69:1083–1133 (copyright 1991, reprinted by permission of the North Carolina Law Review Association).

Office of Juvenile Justice and Delinquency Prevention and National Center for Juvenile Justice for Jeffrey A. Butts, Howard N. Snyder, Terrence A. Finnegan, Anne L. Aughenbaugh, and Rowen S. Poole, *Juvenile Court Statistics 1994* (copyright 1997, reprinted by permission).

Office of Juvenile Justice and Delinquency Prevention and National Center for Juvenile Justice for Melissa Sickmund, Anne Stahl, Terrence Finnegan, Howard Snyder, Rowen Poole and Jeffrey Butts. *Juvenile Court Statistics 1995* (copyright 1998, reprinted by permission).

Office of Juvenile Justice and Delinquency Prevention and National Center for Juvenile Justice for Melissa Sickmund, Howard Snyder, and Eileen Poe-Yamagata, *Juvenile Offenders and Victims: 1997 Update on Violence* (copyright 1997, reprinted by permission).

Office of Juvenile Justice and Deliquency Prevention and National Center for Juvenile Justice for Howard Snyder, *Juvenile Arrests 1996* (copyright 1997, reprinted by permission).

Oxford University Press for Thomas J. Bernard, *Cycle of Juvenile Justice* (copyright 1992, Reprinted by permission of Oxford University Press).

Oxford University Press for Joseph M. Hawes, *Children in Urban Society: Juvenile Delinquency in Nineteenth-Century America* (copyright 1971, reprinted by permission of Oxford University Press).

Pantheon Books, a division of Random House, for David Rothman, "The State as Parent: Social Policy in the Progressive Era," in *Doing Good: The Limits of Benevolence* (copyright 1978, reprinted by permission).

President and Fellows of Harvard College for Douglas S. Massey and Nancy A. Denton, *American Apartheid* (copyright 1993, reprinted by permission of Harvard University Press).

Random House for David J. Rothman, "The State as Parent: Social Policy in the Progressive Era," in *Doing Good: The Limits of Benevolence* (copyright 1978, reprinted by permission).

Regents of the University of California for John Sutton, *Stubborn Children: Controlling Delinquency in the United States, 1640–1981* (copyright 1988, reprinted by permission of University of California Press).

Regents of the University of California, the University of California Law Review, and Fred B. Rothman & Co., for Andrew Walkover, "The Infancy Defense in the New Juvenile Court," *U.C.L.A. Law Review* 31:503–562 (copyright 1984, reprinted by permission).

Simon & Schuster for Andrew Hacker, *Black and White: Separate, Hostile, and Unequal* (copyright 1992, reprinted by permission).

Simon & Schuster for Franklin E. Zimring, *The Changing Legal World of Adolescence* (copyright 1982, reprinted by permission).

Stanford University for Herbert L. Packer, *The Limits of the Criminal Sanction* (copyright 1968, reprinted by permission of Stanford University Press).

The Board of Trustees of Leland Stanford Junior University and Stanford

Law Review for Lois Weithorn, "Mental Hospitalization of Troublesome Youth," *Stanford Law Review* 40:773–838 (copyright 1988, reprinted by permission).

United States Department of Justice, Bureau of Justice Statistics, for Kathleen Maguire and Ann L. Pastore, eds., *Sourcebook for Criminal Justice Statistics—1993* (copyright 1994, reprinted by permission).

University of California Press and Society for the Study of Social Problems for Paul Colomy and Martin Kretzmann, "Projects and Institution Building: Judge Ben B. Lindsey and the Juvenile Court Movement," *Social Problems* 42: 191–215 (copyright 1995, reprinted by permission).

University of Chicago Press for David Garland, *Punishment and Modern Society* (copyright 1990, reprinted by permission of University of Chicago Press).

University of Chicago Press for Lee B. Sechrest, "Classification for Treatment," *Crime and Justice: A Review of Research*, vol. 9 pp. 293–322 (copyright 1987, reprinted by permission of University of Chicago Press).

University of Chicago Press for Steven Schlossman, *Love and the American Delinquent: The Theory and Practice of "Progressive" Juvenile Justice* (copyright 1977, reprinted by permission of University of Chicago Press).

University of Chicago Press for Patricia Wald, "Pretrial Detention for Juveniles" in *Pursuing Justice for the Child*, ed. Margaret Rosenheim (copyright 1976, reprinted by permission of University of Chicago Press).

University of Chicago Press for James S. Coleman, Robert H. Bremner, Burton R. Clar, John B. David, Dorothy H. Eichorn, Zvi Griliches, Joseph F. Kett, Norman B. Ryder, Zahava Blum Doering, and John M. Mays, *Youth: Transition to Adulthood* (copyright 1974, reprinted by permission of University of Chicago Press).

W. W. Norton and Co. for Burton J. Bledstein, *The Culture of Professionalism: The Middle Class and the Development of Higher Education in America* (copyright 1976, reprinted by permission of W. W. Norton and Co.).

The Yale Law Journal Co. and Fred B. Rothman and Co. for Marjan Da maska, "Structures of Authority and Comparative Criminal Procedure," *Yale Law Journal* 84:480–544 (reprinted by permission of Yale Law Journal Co.).

Yale University Press for Francis A. Allen, *The Decline of the Rehabilitative Ideal* (copyright 1981, reprinted by permission).

I have dedicated this book to my mother, Flora Papier Feld, and to the memory of my late father, Arthur Sidney Feld. My father practiced law honorably, brought a commitment to justice and fairness to his clients' causes, and represented the best of what the legal profession can be. My mother made a warm home and provided the "domestic haven" that nurtured their three sons. Together, they provided the warmth and love, material support, and emotional encouragement that enabled me to flourish and to develop into the person that I am becoming. Only now that I am an adult and a parent can I appreciate and understand the commitments and sacrifices that they made. I am grateful beyond words for all that they gave and taught me.

My wife, Patricia Feld, is the most important person in the world to me.

Her unconditional love and unstinting encouragement bring meaning, joy, and purpose to my life. Our children, Ari Daniel and Julia Elise, provide a special source of inspiration. Patty home-schooled Ari and Julia for the first decade of their "formal" education. As parents, we experienced the joy and pleasure of watching our children flourish and grow into spectacular young people. I write this book with the hope that every child will have an equal opportunity to realize a brighter future and to fully achieve his or her potential.

Effie, Minnesota   B. C. F.
July 1998

Contents

Figures and Tables

Figures

Tables

Bad Kids

Introduction

Within the past three decades, judicial decisions, legislative amendments, and administrative changes have transformed the juvenile court from a nominally rehabilitative social welfare agency into a scaled-down second-class criminal court for young people. Politicians and the public have repudiated the court's original rehabilitative premises and endorsed punishment of young offenders. Judicial opinions and statutory changes have rejected procedural informality and incorporated imperfectly many of the safeguards of criminal courts. These substantive and procedural reforms have converted the historical ideal of the juvenile court as a welfare agency into a quasi-penal system that provides young offenders with neither therapy nor justice.

The Progressive reformers who created the juvenile court conceived of it as an informal welfare system in which judges made dispositions in the "best interests" of the child, and the state functioned as *parens patriae*, as a surrogate parent. In 1967 the Supreme Court in *In re Gault* granted juveniles some constitutional procedural rights in delinquency hearings and provided the impetus to modify juvenile courts' procedures, jurisdiction, and purposes (387 U.S. 1[1967]). The ensuing procedural and substantive convergence between juvenile and criminal courts eliminated virtually all the conceptual and operational differences in strategies of social control for youths and adults. Even proponents reluctantly acknowledge that juvenile courts often fail either to "save" children or to reduce youth crime. In short, the contemporary juvenile court constitutes a conceptually and administratively bankrupt institution with neither a rationale nor a justification.

Social structural and cultural changes fostered both the initial creation and contemporary transformation of the juvenile court. Ideological changes in cultural conceptions of children and in strategies of social control during the nineteenth century led Progressive reformers to create the juvenile court in 1899. Rapid industrialization and modernization, immigration and urbanization, social change and intellectual ferment provided the impetus for the juvenile court. Reformers combined new theories of criminality, such as positivism, with new ideas about childhood and adolescence to construct a social welfare alternative to criminal courts. They designed juvenile courts to respond flexibly to youths' criminal and noncriminal misconduct, to assimilate and integrate poor and immigrant children, and to expand control and supervision of young people and their families. The juvenile court reformers removed children from the criminal justice and corrections systems, provided them with individualized treatment in a separate system, and substituted a scientific and preventive alternative to the criminal law's punitive policies. By separating children from adults and providing a rehabilitative alternative to punishment, juvenile courts also rejected criminal law's jurisprudence and its procedural safeguards, such as juries and lawyers. Juvenile courts' flexible and discretionary strategies enabled its personnel to differentiate and discriminate between their own children and "other people's children," those of the poor and immigrants.

A century later, social structural changes have modified the cultural conceptions of young people and the strategies of social control that juvenile courts employ. These changes leave the juvenile court, as an institution, searching for a new policy foundation and legal rationale. Since *Gault*, social structural, demographic, and legal changes have altered dramatically juvenile courts' structure and functions, the characteristics of their clientele, and the crime and social welfare issues that they confront. The internal migration of African Americans from the rural South to the urban North and West in the decades before and after World War II greatly increased the minority populations in urban ghettos and placed race on the national legal and public policy agendas. By the 1960s the Warren Court embarked upon its civil rights and due process revolutions in constitutional jurisprudence. Responding to the issues of race, the Supreme Court scrutinized and invalidated many discriminatory laws, biased public policies, and abusive law enforcement practices. The Court's decisions modified the practices of many criminal justice, administrative, and social service agencies, including juvenile courts. By the 1970s and 1980s, the structural transition from an industrial and manufacturing to an information and service economy and the migration of many white people and employment opportunities from cities to suburbs further increased the social isolation and concentration of poverty of the urban minority population. Macrostructural changes within the past two decades resulted in the deindustrialization of the urban cores in which most African Americans live, eroded the employment opportunities for lower skilled and less well educated young black males, and fostered the emergence of a structural "underclass." By the late 1980s, the "crack cocaine" epidemic exacerbated the historical relationships among urbanism, poverty, race, and youth crime. In inner-city areas of intense racial segregation, concentrated poverty, industrial decline, and weakened family and community social controls, young black men entered the violent drug economy and youth homicide rates soared. In media depictions and in the public mind, a close linkage exists between minority youths, escalating violence, and crime. Since the "baby boom" increases in youth crime that began in the late 1960s, "law-and-order" politicians have responded to these social structural and racial demographic changes with "get-tough" policies to "crack down" on crime. Increasingly, punitive juvenile justice policies impose harsh sanctions disproportionately on minority youths and foster the growing procedural and substantive convergence between juvenile and criminal courts.

Throughout these analyses, I trace the relationships between social changes and legal changes. In the language of the social sciences, the juvenile court constitutes the dependent variable, and social structural, economic, racial, demographic, and other legal changes constitute independent variables. A century ago, the processes of modernization and industrialization fostered a particular ideological conception of *childhood* and *positive criminology*, which, in turn, provided the impetus to create the "rehabilitative" juvenile court. More recent social structural and macroeconomic changes provide the catalyst to transform the juvenile court into a more punitive agency. From the juvenile court's inception, the social control of ethnic and racial minority offenders has constituted one of its most important functions. The Progressives created the juvenile court to assimilate, integrate, and control the children of the eastern European immigrants pouring into cities of the East and Midwest at the turn of the century. In postindustrial American cities today, juvenile courts function to maintain social control of minority youths, predominantly young black males. The current, more punitive juvenile justice policies reflect the changing character and complexion of juvenile courts' clientele. Fear of other people's children, especially minority youths charged with crimes, provides the impetus to transform the juvenile court from a welfare agency into a second-rate criminal court for young offenders.

Writing about race, crime, and social control policies produces intensely charged ideological debates about the causes of minority youths' demonstrable overrepresentation in the juvenile justice system. For example, does their disproportional presence reflect a subculture of violence or social structural inequality? Does it reflect differential involvement in criminal behavior or discriminatory decision making by justice system personnel? Unfortunately, even to pose these questions or to analyze the relationships between race, crime, and juvenile justice administration exposes one to the dangers of being misunderstood or labeled a racist. Despite these hazards, one cannot understand current juvenile justice policies and practices in isolation from their broader social context, especially the role of race in American society. The macro-structural transformation of cities—deindustrialization, racial segregation, and concentration of poverty—fostered an increase in youth violence and, especially, murders committed with guns by young black men. The visibility of young black men in media depictions of crime promoted public and political perceptions that juvenile courts deal primarily with violent minority delinquents. Public hostility toward other people's children, especially minority and poor children, provides the catalyst for more punitive juvenile justice policies. As African Americans became urban Americans and the public attributed increases in crime primarily to urban black youths, race and crime intersected to produce more punitive juvenile justice policies.

Public officials couch their get-tough policy changes in terms of "public safety" rather than racial repression. But, ambivalence about young people and conceptual contradictions embedded in the *ideas* of *childhood* and *social control* readily facilitated the rapid reformulation of juvenile justice practices from rehabilitation to retribution and from support to suppression. Policies toward young offenders balance precariously between America's century-old experiment with the paternalistic, rehabilitation-oriented juvenile court and the more modern movement to punish youthful offenders as if they were adults. Proponents of special procedures for young offenders argue that "kids are different" and less blameworthy than adults, that youth policies should protect and enhance troubled children's life chances, and that adult sentences are too harsh to inflict on young people. Others, by contrast, insist that serious youth crime and violence are just as harmful and damaging as serious adult crime and violence, and public protection requires harsh punishments even for younger offenders.

American cultural and legal conceptions of young people contain two competing images of youth that also facilitate the transformation of the juvenile court. On the one hand, the legal culture views young people as innocent, vulnerable, fragile, and dependent *children* whom their parents and the state should protect and nurture. On the other hand, the legal culture perceives young people as vigorous, autonomous and responsible *adultlike* people from whose criminal behavior the public needs protection. From its inception, the juvenile court attempted to reconcile the fundamental ambivalence and conflicted impulses engendered by these competing images when a child is a criminal and the criminal is a child.

Progressive reformers attempted to harmonize the dissonance created by the *child* and the *criminal* by constructing a binary opposition between the juvenile and criminal justice systems. They did so by situating the juvenile court on several unstable cultural and criminological fault lines that embodied the binary constructs of *childhood* and *social control*. They conceived of the juvenile court as a welfare agency to *treat children* rather than as a criminal court to *punish adults*. Thus, the *ideas* of the juvenile court implicate many cultural and criminological tensions: positivism versus classicism, determinism versus choice, child versus adult, dependence versus independence, treatment versus punishment, offender versus offense, forward-versus backward-looking responses to crime, welfare versus just deserts, discretion versus rules, procedural informality versus formality, social welfare versus social control, and the like. Across these various dimensions, Progressive reformers emphasized the first element of each juxtaposed pair, obscured its polar opposite with euphemisms and good intentions, but left the foundation of the juvenile court vulnerable and unstable.

The recent escalation of serious youth crime challenges these dichotomous constructs. Currently, juvenile justice jurisprudence, law, policy, and practice emphasize increasingly the second element of each binary pair, for example, punishment rather than treatment, rules rather than discretion, adult rather than child, and crime control rather than social welfare. These changes question and implicitly reject the traditional ideas of childhood and benevolent social control on which the Progressives founded the juvenile court. Characterizing delinquents as responsible young offenders rather than as misguided, troubled children abets juvenile courts' transformation from a rehabilitative to a punitive institution. Juvenile courts' reorientation from social welfare to crime control and reconfiguration of youths from being dependent to being responsible reflect broader cultural and legal changes. Progressive reformers asserted a public obligation to provide for the welfare and control of children. More recent punitive policies reduce the state's duty to intervene affirmatively and make youths more responsible and accountable for their own conduct regardless of their social circumstances.

Judicial decisions and legal policies selectively choose between these two competing cultural conceptions and legal formulations of young people—responsible and autonomous or vulnerable and dependent—in order to maximize their social control. From the juvenile court's inception, Progressive reformers designed juvenile courts to enable them to respond differently to other people's children than to their own. In the last three decades, this administrative flexibility enables juvenile courts to intervene disproportionally in the lives of minority youths.

Recent changes in juvenile courts—increase in procedural formality, diversion of status offenders, waiver of serious young offenders to the adult system, and harsher punishment of delinquents—constitute a form of criminological "triage" to distinguish between "our children" and "other people's children." In so doing, these policies erode the theoretical and practical differences between the juvenile and criminal justice systems. The triage strategy selectively manipulates the alternative conceptions of young people as dependent and vulnerable or as autonomous and responsible to remove many middle-class, white, and female noncriminal status offenders from the juvenile justice system to the private social service systems; to consign persistent, violent, and disproportionally minority youths to criminal court for prosecution as adults; and to impose increasingly punitive sanctions on those middle-range delinquents who remain within the jurisdiction of the juvenile court. By shedding the "soft" and "hard" ends of its client spectrum, these legal changes have transformed the juvenile court into a second-class criminal court. The macrostructural changes in urban America and the public and political linkages between race and serious youth crime coincide with these moves toward increased punitiveness in juvenile courts. The triage policies enacted by lawmakers and implemented by juvenile justice practitioners separate "our children" from "other people's children" and cull the salvageable from the hopeless. In short, the transformation of the juvenile court occurs within the broader structural context of the racial metamorphosis of urban America.

The shortcomings of the juvenile court stem from its conceptual bankruptcy, rather than simply from its failures of implementation, profound though they may be. Juvenile courts *do* lack adequate resources to address child welfare needs, at least in part because of the gender, socioeconomic class and racial characteristics of their clients. But even more fundamental obstacles prevent the juvenile court from successfully implementing its "rehabilitative ideal." The juvenile court's creators envisioned a social service agency in a judicial arena and attempted to fuse its social welfare mission with the power of state coercion. The *idea* that judicial clinicians successfully can combine social welfare and criminal social control in one agency constitutes the juvenile court's inherent conceptual flaw. Progressives created an irreconcilable conflict by asking the juvenile court simultaneously to enhance child welfare and to control youths' violations of criminal law. The hostile impulses people experience toward other people's threatening children undermine benevolent aspirations and elevate crime control concerns. Juvenile courts inevitably subordinate social welfare considerations to crime control concerns because of their built-in penal focus. Every state's juvenile code defines juvenile courts' jurisdiction based on a youth's committing a crime, a prerequisite that detracts from a compassionate response. Because juvenile courts define eligibility for "services" on the basis of criminality, they highlight those aspects of youth that rationally elicit the least sympathy and ignore social conditions that might evoke a greater desire to help. Recent changes in juvenile court waiver and sentencing laws to emphasize punishment, "accountability," and personal responsibility further reinforce juvenile courts' penal foundations and reduce support for humanitarian assistance.

If we separate social welfare from penal social control, then no need remains for a separate juvenile court for young offenders. Systematically uncoupling social welfare from criminal social control can lead to greater conceptual clarity, improved justice for young offenders, and broadened support for child welfare. If criminal social control is the "real" reason why states refer youths to juvenile courts, then we can abolish juvenile courts and try younger offenders in criminal courts alongside their adult counterparts. But if the criminal is a child, then states must modify their criminal justice system to accommodate the youthfulness of some defendants. The physical and psychological immaturity and lesser culpability of younger defendants require criminal courts to make certain substantive and procedural modifications. Developmental psychological research and jurisprudential policies provide rationale to grant greater procedural safeguards to youths and to sentence younger offenders less severely than older offenders for their misdeed simply because they are young. Trying and sentencing all offenders in one integrated court recognizes that adolescents do not differ from adults to nearly the degree that traditional legal dichotomies imply. Rather, young people mature and criminal careers emerge along a developmental continuum, and youths do not graduate from irresponsible childhood one day to responsible adulthood the next except as a matter of law. Taken in combination, these substantive and procedural modifications can avoid the "worst of both worlds," provide youths with protections functionally equivalent to those accorded adults, and do justice in sentencing. Uncoupling social welfare from social control also avoids many of the constraints that providing for child welfare through a juvenile court imposes. If we frame child welfare policy proposals in terms of child welfare rather than as a response to crime, then opportunities to intervene creatively and proactively in the lives of all young people expand greatly.

I critically analyze the *idea* of the juvenile court and its sustaining ideologies of *childhood* and *social control* for several purposes. The earlier *idea* of a rehabilitative juvenile court combined a theory of delinquency with a policy prescription, for example, troubled children required treatment. However, contemporary public and political pressures to get tough repudiate rehabilitation, foster the convergence between juvenile and criminal courts, and require a different rationale for the social control of youths. The *idea* of youthful partial responsibility provides a rationale and a policy prescription for sentencing young offenders in an integrated criminal justice; youthful reduced culpability deserves a mitigated sentence. Because states already sentence many youths as adults, the *idea* of youthfulness as a mitigating factor in sentencing has considerable contemporary salience whether or not states abolish juvenile courts in their entirety.

The transformation of the juvenile court also provides a metaphor of the changing social construction and legal status of youth. The current schizophrenic formulations of youth—dependent and vulnerable or independent and responsible—enable states to selectively choose between the two constructs to manipulate young people's legal status, to maximize their social control, and to subordinate their freedom and autonomy. Reexamining the social construction of adolescence through a lens of partial responsibility may facilitate the formulation of social policies that foster greater autonomy, equality, and realism in young people's transition to adulthood.

Finally, the transformation of the juvenile court forces us to confront the issue of race in American society. The increasing and explicit punitiveness of juvenile and criminal justice policies emerge against the backdrop of the structural transformation of cities, the deindustrialization of the urban core, and the emergence of a threatening black "underclass" living in racial isolation and concentrated poverty. A century ago, Progressive reformers had to choose between either initiating social structural reforms that would reduce inequality and ameliorate criminogenic forces or ministering to the young people damaged by those adverse conditions. "Child saving" satisfied Progressives' humanitarian impulses without engendering more fundamental social changes. A century later, we face similar choices between either rehabilitating "damaged" individuals in a criminal justice system or undertaking more fundamental changes that address the issues of racial and social inequality. Unfortunately, neither juvenile court judges nor any other criminal justice agencies realistically can ameliorate the social ills that afflict young people or significantly enhance their life chances. On the other hand, uncoupling criminal social control from social welfare enables us to make societal commitment to the welfare of all children regardless of their criminality and to expand the possibilities of positive intervention for all young people. Public policies to provide all young people with a hopeful future and to reduce racial and social inequality require a political commitment to the welfare of children that extends far beyond the resources or competencies of any juvenile justice system.

This book examines what went wrong with the juvenile court and proposes an alternative model of child welfare and youth crime social control. Chapter 1 traces the relationships between social structural changes and the social construction of childhood and adolescence in the nineteenth century. During the transition from an agricultural to an industrial economy, social changes associated with modernization such as urbanization and immigration posed problems of cohesion, social control, and assimilation. As informal social controls weakened, Progressive reformers placed increased reliance on formal organizations to govern, to maintain order, and to oversee social change. Modernization also affected families' structure and function, separated work from the home, and altered youths' economic value. Particularly within upper-and middle-class urban families, a new conception emerged of childhood and adolescence as an extended period of irresponsibility, dependency, and preparation for adulthood. Child-saving Progressive reformers used the newer imagery of childhood to advance a variety of legal and social reforms including compulsory school attendance laws, child labor laws, child welfare laws, and juvenile courts. These laws formally differentiated young people from adults, institutionalized the dependent status of children, isolated them within child-serving organizations, and restricted their autonomy.

Chapter 2 links changes in ideological assumptions about the causes of and responses to crime with the emergence of juvenile courts. Positivist criminology attributed crime and delinquency to deterministic forces rather than to freewill choices, and social pathologists sought to identify those causal features. Ascribing criminal behavior to antecedent forces reduced offenders' moral responsibility for their criminal behavior and focused on efforts to change them rather than to punish them. The rehabilitative juvenile court removed children from the adult criminal justice system, enforced the new conception of childhood with the state acting as *parens patriae*, and developed a judicial welfare alternative to criminal punishment. Reformers' benevolent aims, individualized solicitude, and "scientific" intervention led them to expand the power of the state. They maximized discretion to diagnose and treat youths and to focus on a child's character and lifestyle rather than her crimes. Juvenile courts provided Progressives a powerful tool with which to differentiate between their children and other people's children. Juvenile courts imposed indeterminate and nonproportional sentences to maximize the social control of poor and immigrant children.

Chapter 3 places *In re Gault* and the "constitutional domestication" of the juvenile court in the broader social and legal context of the Warren Court's civil rights decisions and "due process revolution" during the 1960s. The great black migration from the rural South to urban locales in the decades before World War II provided the impetus for the civil rights movement and subsequent constitutional law reform. The Supreme Court's procedural due process decisions provided a constitutional strategy by which to enhance the visibility, accountability, and evenhandedness of justice administration and to sever the connection between discretionary and discriminatory governmental decision making. The increased constitutional emphasis on procedural formality and individual rights in the 1960s also coincided with dramatic increases in youth crime. The children of the post–World War II baby-boom began to reach adolescence in the 1960s. As the baby-boom demographic bulge moved through the social structure, youth crime rates surged, college campuses erupted in protests, and urban race riots racked American cities. Public and political fears of social disorder, of the young, and of urban blacks exacerbated the crisis of law and order, provided fuel for advocates of repression, and led conservative critics to denounce juvenile courts for coddling young criminals.

The role of race in American society provides the crucial link between heightened concern about urban crime and violence, the invidious consequences of discretionary decision making, and the Warren Court's decisions that emphasized civil rights and procedural justice. The Court's opinions attempted to protect individual liberty and restrict and regulate decisions by state officials. The Supreme Court case of *In re Gault* in 1967 began to transform the juvenile court into a very different institution from the Progressives' vision of an informal social welfare agency. *Gault* mandated formal trial procedures in delinquency hearings and shifted the focus of juvenile courts from paternalistic assessments of a youth's "real needs" to proof that the youth committed a crime. By formalizing the connection between criminal conduct and coercive intervention, *Gault* made explicit the relationship between crime and consequences and revealed the nexus that Progressives refused to acknowledge and deliberately obscured. The Supreme Court attempted to rationalize juvenile courts' procedures and to reconcile their rehabilitative rhetoric and their punitive reality, but its efforts unintentionally provided the impetus to transform juvenile courts into scaled-down criminal courts. Ironically, *Gault*'s insistence on more elaborate procedural safeguards legitimated the imposition of more punitive sanctions that now fall disproportionately on minority offenders. The relationships between race, crime and violence, and punitive juvenile justice policies provide a recurring subtext for all subsequent judicial and legal reforms.

In the three decades since *Gault*, legislative, judicial, and administrative changes have modified juvenile justice administration and fostered the convergence with criminal courts. These procedural, jurisdictional, and jurisprudential reforms exemplify juvenile courts' changed strategies of social control and reformulated imagery of childhood. Although theoretically, juvenile courts' procedural safeguards closely resemble those of criminal courts, in practice, the procedural justice routinely afforded juveniles remains far lower than the minimum insisted upon for adults. The recognition that juvenile courts often failed to realize their benevolent purposes has led to two jurisdictional changes. First, recent reforms limit juvenile courts' dispositional authority or even jurisdiction over the noncriminal, status offenders. Second, courts and legislatures increasingly criminalize serious juvenile offenders and transfer them to criminal courts for prosecution as adults. As the juvenile court's jurisdiction contracts, its commitment to rehabilitating offenders diminishes. Courts sentence delinquents charged with crimes increasingly on the basis of their "just deserts" rather than on their "real needs." Proportional and determinate or mandatory minimum sentences based on the present offense and prior record, rather than on the "best interests" of the child, dictate the length, location, and intensity of intervention. These triage policies emerged against the backdrop of the structural transformation of cities and changes in patterns of crime and violence within the minority, urban underclass and reflect historical continuities in the differentiation between "our children" and "other people's children."

Chapters 4 through 7 examine four critical arenas of juvenile justice reforms since the 1970s that embody the policies of triage. These procedural, jurisdictional, and jurisprudential developments exemplify the "criminalizing" of juvenile justice: a shift from treatment to punishment, from "welfare" to "deserts," and from imagery of childhood innocence to criminal responsibility.

Chapter 4 analyzes juvenile courts' procedures and the substantial gulf that remains between "the law on the books" and "the law in action." In theory, *Gault* provided the impetus for a procedural convergence between juvenile courts and adult criminal courts. In reality, youths accused of crimes receive fewer procedural protections than do their adult criminal counterparts. In part, the continuing procedural disjunctions reflect juvenile courts' historical and ideological commitment to rehabilitation rather than to punishment. Crucially, however, the procedural disparities reflect the manipulation of the social and legal construction of adolescence to maximize the social control of young people. Chapter 4 examines several court procedures to demonstrate that most states provide neither special procedures to protect juveniles from their own immaturity nor the full panoply of adult procedural safeguards. Sometimes, states invoke the imagery of responsibility to treat juveniles just like adult criminal defendants when formal equality redounds to youths' disadvantage. In other instances, states invoke paternalistic, protectionist rationales to justify less-adequate juvenile court safeguards when those deficient procedures provide an advantage to the state. Chapter 4 analyzes juveniles' waivers of *Miranda* rights during pretrial interrogation and waivers of their right to counsel at trial as examples of formal equality that produces practical inequality. Despite *Gault*'s promise of counsel, for example, the continuing absence of lawyers in juvenile courts in many states calls into question the legitimacy of juvenile "justice." Chapter 4 also analyzes preventive detention and denial of jury trials and public trials as examples of special "protective" juvenile procedures that provide an advantage to the state. Although the right to a jury trial provides a critical procedural safeguard in an increasingly punitive juvenile system, states' denials of that right offer a symbolic example of the legal order placing youths at a systematic disadvantage relative to adult criminal defendants. Ultimately, juvenile courts convict youths in a procedural regime under which few adults charged with a crime and facing the prospect of confinement would consent to be tried.

Chapter 5 examines changes in juvenile courts' status jurisdiction. The noncriminal status jurisdiction encompasses misconduct, such as truancy, curfew, runaway, and incorrigibility, and other behaviors that would not be a crime if committed by an adult. It provided judges with the authority to enforce the normative conception of childhood dependency that emerged at the turn of the century and best exemplified juvenile courts' social welfare role. After *Gault*, critics objected that juvenile courts' status jurisdiction treated noncriminal offenders indiscriminately like criminal delinquents, disabled families and other sources of referral through one-sided intervention, and posed insuperable legal issues for the court. In the 1970s, judicial and legislative disillusionment with juvenile courts' responses to noncriminal youths prompted a variety of reforms—diversion, deinstitutionalization, and decriminalization of status offenders—that removed most of the "soft" end of the juvenile court clientele. These reforms represent a diminished prevention mission, an acknowledgment of the limits of coercion to provide child welfare, and a strategic retreat from the judicial role of enforcing normative concepts of childhood. These reforms have met with mixed successes: decarcerating some youths, widening the net of informal controls over others, and propelling an increased number of white, female, and middle-class youths into a "hidden system" of social control. The coercive, private sector treatment system, administered by mental health and chemical dependency service providers, affords youths even fewer legal protections than those available in juvenile courts. The ideology of childhood dependency and paternalistic impulses clash with the greater autonomy that many youths exercise and accounts for the legal preoccupation with noncriminal "problem" youths. Legislators and judges paternalistically manipulate the social construct of adolescence to provide the "troublesome" youths with fewer procedural safeguards in the "hidden system" and to maximize their social control. Finally, these changes at the "soft" end of the juvenile court reflect one element of a triage strategy that relegates poor and minority juveniles to punitive public correctional institutions and remits more privileged white youths to private-sector facilities.

Chapter 6 analyzes the criminalizing of serious young offenders. Jurisdictional waiver constitutes the criminological triage at the "hard" end of the juvenile court. Juvenile court judges, prosecutors, and legislators increasingly transfer violent and chronic young offenders to criminal courts for prosecution as adults. The various transfer laws represent alternative methods that states use to define the formal boundaries of childhood, illustrate changes in juvenile court sentencing philosophy, illuminate the complex and conflicting relationships between juvenile and criminal sentencing policies, and highlight our changing assumptions about young offenders' criminal responsibility. In the 1970s and 1980s the macrostructural transition from an industrial to an information economy, the migration of whites to the suburbs, and the segregation of blacks living in concentrated poverty in urban America coalesced and influenced patterns of youth crime. The deindustrialization of cities, the solidification of the structural underclass, the introduction of crack cocaine, and the proliferation of handguns within the youth culture produced a dramatic rise in minority youth homicide and gun violence. In response to the very visible escalation in this narrow segment of all youth crime, almost every state amended its waiver statutes and other provisions of its juvenile codes in a frantic effort to get tough and crack down. Recent changes in waiver statutes signal a fundamental inversion in juvenile court jurisprudence from treatment to punishment, from offender to offense, and from immature child to responsible adult. Within the past decades, waiver laws increasingly use age and offense criteria to redefine the boundaries of adulthood, to coordinate juvenile court transfer and criminal court sentencing practices, to integrate juvenile records with criminal records, and to reduce the "punishment gap" when young career offenders make the transition between the two systems. The common overarching legislative theme reflects a jurisprudential shift from the *principle of individualized justice* to the *principle of offense*, from rehabilitation to retribution, and from a clinical preoccupation with an offender's "amenability to treatment" to a focus on the seriousness of the offense. State legislative amendments use offense criteria either as dispositional guidelines to structure and limit judicial discretion, to guide prosecutorial charging decisions, or automatically to exclude certain youths from juvenile court jurisdiction. These get-tough strategies repudiate rehabilitation and judicial discretion, reflect a shift toward more-retributive sentencing policies, narrow juvenile courts' jurisdiction, and base youths' "adult" status increasingly on their offenses. Because minority juveniles commit violent crimes at higher rates than do white youths, facially neutral legislative policies to crack down on violent crime disproportionately expose minority youths to harsher penalties in the criminal justice system. Finally, while the *idea* of *childhood* that underlies the juvenile court conceives of children and adults as fundamentally different and dichotomous, waiver blurs that bifurcation and erodes those distinctions. Once youths make the transition to criminal courts, get tough policies—"old enough to do the crime, old enough to do the time"—disregard any remaining differences between children and adults. Judges typically sentence transferred youths under the same laws and to the same facilities as they sentence other adult offenders. In 1989 in *Stanford v. Kentucky* (492 U.S. 361 [1989]), the Supreme Court upheld the death penalty for for youths who committed murders at sixteen years of age or older. *Stanford* rejected any bright-line distinctions between youths and adults, affirmed youths' legal and criminal responsibility, and provided a striking illustration of changing legal and cultural imagery of children.

Chapter 7 examines the convergence between juvenile and criminal courts' sentencing policies and practices toward "ordinary" delinquents. Progressive reformers envisioned a broader and more encompassing social welfare system for youths and did not circumscribe narrowly the discretionary power of the state. Juvenile courts' *parens patriae* ideology combined social welfare and penal social control in one agency and maximized discretion to provide flexibility in diagnosis and treatment. The public and political pressures to transfer serious young offenders to criminal courts also provide the impetus to get tough and punish more severely the delinquents who remain in juvenile court, the residue of the triage process. Several legal and criminological indicators— legislative purpose clauses, court opinions, sentencing statutes, empirical evaluations of sentencing practices, assessments of conditions of confinement in institutions, and evaluations of treatment effectiveness—demonstrate that juvenile courts punish young offenders for their crimes rather than treat them based on their real needs. These legal changes eliminate most of the differences between juvenile and criminal courts' sentencing practices and consistently reveal that *treating* juveniles closely resembles *punishing* adults. Juvenile courts' legal theory and sentencing practices have shifted from treatment to punishment or incapacitation.

The procedural, jurisdictional, and jurisprudential changes have transformed the juvenile court from its original Progressive model as a social service agency into a deficient second-rate criminal court that provides young people with neither therapy nor justice. Neither the *ideas* of *childhood* nor *social control* distinguish juvenile and criminal justice policies and practices. Chapter 8 examines and rejects other policy options—rehabilitating the juvenile court to revive its social welfare mission and creating a juvenile version of a "criminal" court—and concludes that states should try all offenders in one integrated criminal court. Juvenile courts' fundamental shortcoming represents a failure in conception rather than simply a century-long failure of implementation. The Progressives attempted to combine social welfare and criminal social control in the juvenile court but produced an inherently unstable organization that inevitably subordinated social welfare to penal concerns.

Uncoupling social welfare from social control and recognizing the contradictory impulses provoked when the child is a criminal and the criminal is a child enables us to formulate a rationale for a justice system for young offenders. If the child is a criminal and social control provides the "real" reason that states refer youths to juvenile courts, then states could abolish juvenile courts and try young offenders in criminal courts alongside their adult counterparts. Abolishing juvenile courts does not constitute either an unqualified endorsement of punishment or a primitive throwback to an earlier view of young people as miniature adults. It does reflect a commitment to honesty. Young offenders appear in juvenile courts for criminal social control, regardless of the courts' ability to treat them. Because the criminal is also a child, however, states must modify their criminal justice systems to accommodate the youthfulness of some defendants. Younger offenders require both greater procedural safeguards and *deserve* less-severe sanctions for their misdeeds than do more mature offenders, *simply* because they are younger, less culpable, and have had limited opportunities to develop their capacity for self-control. Procedural justice requires giving to younger offenders all the safeguards that adults receive and additional protections to compensate for youthful immaturity and inexperience. Substantive justice requires a rationale for courts to sentence young offenders differently and *more leniently* than they sentence adult offenders and to recognize *youthfulness as a mitigating factor*. Certain characteristic developmental differences distinguish the quality of judgments that young people make from those of adults and justify a somewhat more protective stance. Adolescents and adults differ in their breadth of experience, short-term versus long-term temporal perspectives, attitudes toward risk, impulsivity, and the importance they attach to peer influences. These developmentally unique attributes of youth affect young people's qualities of judgment and capacity to exercise self-control in ways that distinguish them from adults and bear on their deserved criminal punishment. Developmental psychology, jurisprudence, and sentencing policy justify a more protective stance toward younger offenders because they *deserve* less-severe sentences than do adults. Explicitly punishing young offenders affirms their responsibilities and rests on the premise that they possess sufficient moral reasoning, cognitive capacity, and volitional controls to hold them accountable for their behavior, albeit not to the same degree as adults. But shorter sentences for reduced culpability provides a more modest and attainable reason to treat young offenders differently from adults than the rehabilitative claims of Progressive child savers. Trying all offenders in one integrated criminal court and sentencing them based on a sliding scale of criminal responsibility also addresses many of the crime control and administrative problems created by trying to maintain two separate, binary, and contradictory justice systems based on an arbitrary age classification of a youth as a child or as an adult.

The epilogue briefly examines some of the implications of uncoupling social welfare and social control for the social construction of adolescence and child welfare. The transition from an industrial to a postindustrial service and information economy poses problems akin to those that Progressive reformers confronted a century ago. Structural changes within the past quarter century have depressed the earnings of many middle-class wage earners, propelled more women into the workforce, increased unemployment and underemployment among many urban residents, decreased the rates of family formation, altered family composition, and increased the numbers and rates of children living in poverty. Child poverty, in turn, constitutes the biggest single risk factor to adolescents' successful development. Macroeconomic and social structural changes confront minority youth with even greater obstacles to a successful transition to adulthood. By separating social welfare from criminal social control, public officials can focus more clearly on policies to provide all young people with a more hopeful future, to achieve racial and social justice, to facilitate youth's transition to adulthood, and to improve the social conditions for the next generation.

I I I I ONE

The Social Construction
of Childhood and
Adolescence

The *ideas* of *childhood* and *adolescence* as distinct developmental stages and the *belief* that young people between about seven and seventeen years of age constitute a separate category with special needs represent relatively recent historical phenomena. While infants' and young children's biological or physical dependence may demarcate them from adults, to a much greater degree, social and cultural assumptions and legal strictures determine the status of adolescents. The variability of childhood and adolescence across cultures, time, and human experience greatly outweighs the universal and constant features attributable to innate biological development.

Childhood and adolescence constitute social constructs or cultural artifacts (Berger and Luckmann 1967). Social, historical, and cultural contingencies influence most of the properties and qualities that people attribute to the status of adolescence. Those characterizations tell us as much about how people in a particular culture think about a particular idea, for example, adolescence, as they do about the nature of the social "object" itself. Of course, people socialized into a certain social reality experience difficulty escaping from its seeming objectivity, universality, and immutability.

Before the Renaissance, people in western societies viewed young people after infancy as miniature adults, smaller versions of their parents, rather than as qualitatively different from their elders (Aries 1962). By the end of the nineteenth century in America, a more modern view predominated of childhood and adolescence as periods of life during which adults protected, nur-

17

tured, and prepared young people for the future (Kett 1977; Hawes and Hiner 1985). By the turn of the century, people created a variety of social, cultural, and legal institutions—schools, juvenile courts, child labor and welfare laws— to differentiate and separate children from adults. These cultural attitudes and legal agencies constitute the distinct status of adolescence we take for granted today. Because the ideas of childhood and adolescence as distinct and separate statuses lie embedded in our consciousness, shape our views of social reality, and constrain our vision of alternative possibilities, this study of the juvenile court begins by exploring those ideas about children and their implications for a separate juvenile justice system.

This chapter analyzes the relationship between social structural changes and shifts in the conception of youth that led to the creation of the juvenile court. Social structural changes associated with the transition from an agricultural to a modern, industrial society fostered a movement from informal systems to formal organizations of social control and altered the social construction of childhood and adolescence. In traditional agrarian society, the family household constituted the basic social and economic unit. Adults valued the labor that young people performed and integrated them quickly into the domestic economy. Youths became adults by working with, acquiring the skills of, and ultimately simply by functioning as adults. Family network, household economy, local community, and religious and cultural homogeneity provided cohesion and maintained informal social control.

In nineteenth-century America, industrialization rapidly displaced the household economy and separated work from the home. Industrial modernization encouraged migration from the rural countryside and immigration from foreign countries to urban manufacturing centers. These population changes weakened the informal systems of social control based in extended families, communities, and churches. In the larger cities, growing socioeconomic inequality fostered social class differences, and ethnic heterogeneity superseded the social, religious, and cultural homogeneity of life in farming villages and small towns. Class, religious, and ethnic differences produced cultural conflict and threatened traditional value systems.

The social and economic changes that separated work from the home also fostered a newer conception within the urban middle classes of the family as a "domestic haven," of the woman's proper role within her domestic "separate sphere," and of childhood as a period of dependency, vulnerability, and postponement of adult roles. The new vision of childhood led parents and others to differentiate and isolate children from adults. As the traditional networks of families, churches, and communities weakened, formal organizations played increasing roles in maintaining social control, social welfare, and fostering the new vision of children. Progressive reformers passed laws and created institutions, for example, schools and compulsory attendance laws and child labor and welfare laws, that reflected and advanced the changing imagery of childhood. Increased urbanization and immigration and the concentration of poor and ethnic minorities in crowded urban ghettos posed particular threats to social stability, cohesion, and integration. Fear of crime and disorder increased, and people worried that "alien" youths would contaminate and corrupt their children. Many Progressive programs bore a special responsibility to supervise, control, "Americanize," and assimilate immigrant youth into the dominant culture.

The Lives of Young People before the Invention of Adolescence

Before the Renaissance, people did not share common age-graded experiences or differentiate among themselves especially on the basis of age (Aries 1962; deMause 1974). Many infants born did not survive beyond their first birthdays, and adults treated young children with relative indifference. People perceived the young who managed to survive as small adults who did not require any special social or legal status. Lloyd deMause (1974:1) describes the early history of childhood as a "nightmare," a chronicle in which adults "killed, abandoned, beat, terrorized, and sexually abused" young people. Child-rearing practices, such as wet nursing, swaddling, physical restraint, immobilization, beating, and inattention, in the Middle Ages contributed to high rates of infant mortality (deMause 1974; Shorter 1975). The early and frequent deaths of infants and children from neglect, abuse, and disease discouraged intense parental emotional attachments, which further increased the risks of mortality for the young.

At an early age, young people typically interacted, worked, and played with people across the entire age spectrum. In *Centuries of Childhood*, Philippe Aries asserts, "In medieval society, the idea of *childhood* did not exist. . . . [The] awareness of the particular nature of *childhood*. . . . which distinguishes the child from the adult was lacking" (1962:128). The *idea* of *childhood* differs from that of *children*; the former implies a cultural abstraction while the latter connotes a physical or developmental status (Archard 1993). According to Aries (1962), the Middle Ages lacked a *modern* concept of childhood, one marked by a degree of age segregation between the worlds of children and adults. As evidence of the relative absence of social age grading, for example, historians note that premodern people neither knew their ages nor celebrated their birthdays (Kett 1977; Postman 1994).

Once children emerged from infancy and physical dependency, around the age of seven, adults quickly integrated them into an intergenerational peer group of work, recreation, sexuality, and communality. Before the invention of the printing press and the advent of literacy, most adults could not read and received minimal formal schooling. By about the age of seven, young people had mastered language and readily could participate as equals in the oral culture without need for prolonged formal education (Postman 1994). Preparation for life consisted of participatory "on the job training." Younger children hauled water, split wood, and performed other useful household tasks. By ages seven to ten, they often left their own homes to work as servants or apprentices in the homes of others (Illick 1974; Shorter 1975). Adults placed out older youths to work as apprentices, learn trades, augment the labor pool, and prepare for and engage in adult economic roles. Young people participated in most activities—playing games and amusements, drinking and gambling in taverns, witnessing or engaging in sexual behavior—without any special efforts to protect their "innocence" from adult realities (Aries 1962).

In a traditional, agrarian economy, the family constituted the basic social and economic unit. Premodern families lived more communally and less exclusively than today. Larger households included parents, their own children or those of other people, servants, apprentices, and relatives, who shared common living and sleeping quarters. Congregate living conditions, minimal physical privacy, and intense intergenerational interaction exposed young people to all aspects of adult activities. Young people at an early age witnessed, understood, and participated in adult work, play, and life and, de facto, functioned as adults.

When the European colonists migrated to America, they organized life around familiar kinship networks that integrated several generations and branches within a living and working unit (Rothman 1971; Hawes and Hiner 1985). Colonial America consisted of geographically isolated agricultural communities linked to the more commercialized societies of western Europe by a few port cities. Premodern colonial society interwove family and community, labor and leisure, and religion and public life into an integrated whole (Rothman 1971). Social ties and mutual interdependence bound residents to each other; people worshiped in the same churches and shared similar values. Neighbors intermarried, and kinship networks provided social cohesion and social control. Because of the integration of social and domestic life, the colonists viewed child rearing as a communal endeavor in which public and private responsibilities overlapped. Church leaders and other community members actively oversaw child rearing, and "town fathers and other public officials could enter homes to observe and correct family life" (Grubb and Lazerson 1982:45). The Puritans of New England often used the law to strengthen the linkages between the public and private spheres, to reinforce the responsibilities of families, and to enlist parents as agents of the commonwealth (Sutton 1988).

Childhood in colonial America entailed an ongoing process of becoming an adult rather than a discrete sequence of sharing common experiences or a distinctive legal status. Burton Bledstein summarized the continuous and fluid developments:

> Between the ages of seven and fifteen, he became the object of adult expectations which required that he curb idleness and mischievous passion, enter a calling or vocation usually that of his father, and master the habits of industry, frugality, and temperance. Patterns were informal and differed considerably from one person to another, from one community and region to another. There was no predetermined age at which a child would leave home, become apprenticed, or enter and leave school. . . . Always facing toward manhood, the colonial child matured quickly, with little time for self-indulgence, few memorable ceremonies

to distinguish his childhood, and the absence of an adolescent or pre-adult stage of life fraught with anxiety and emotional indecision. (1976:210–211)

In *Rites of Passage*, Joseph Kett (1977) characterized young people's stages of life as an uneven progression from dependence to semidependence to independence, rather than as common age-graded experiences. Youth juxtaposed a mixture of freedom and subordination; they fluctuated between the autonomy and mobility of semidependence when they left home to seek work and experience, and their obligations to work as apprentices or for their families.

Colonists treated children too young physically to work as total dependents until they could perform compensatory labor, farm chores, and household tasks. As children emerged from infancy and dependency, they vacillated between periods of semiautonomous independence and familial dependency, leaving home and returning until they eventually established their own homes (Kett 1977). Parents "placed out" their young children to live and work in the homes of other people as servants, woodchoppers, and water carriers as had their European predecessors (Hawes 1991). Between about the age of seven and puberty, young people left home to work as servants, to become apprentices, and to assume increasingly adult roles (Sutton 1988). Under contracts of apprenticeship, a master trained and educated his apprentices and acted with the authority of the natural parent. Older female children prepared for their future roles as wives, mothers, and workers by caring for younger siblings, acquiring domestic skills, and performing household chores. Placing-out and apprenticeship provide indicators of the communal, rather than exclusively nuclear familial, character of child rearing.

Colonial America experienced chronic labor shortages, and families and masters valued young people as sources of labor and services. Social, educational, and economic institutions quickly integrated youths into the workforce and hastened their transition to adulthood. Full economic integration of young people probably occurred by early puberty, when young people began to perform adult work. Apprenticeship trained and educated younger workers, added to the skilled workforce, and functioned as a system of social welfare and social control. Colonists placed out orphaned, wayward, destitute, or dependent children and integrated them into the family economy of their masters. Thus, even when young people left their own parental home, they lived in their master's home or in some other family's household, which maintained accountability and provided stability.

The coterminous location of home and workplace and the limited range of occupations enabled young people to learn most of their required economic skills either from their parents or from surrounding adults and quickly to achieve adult productivity. Parents also had a personal stake in their children's supervision, placement, apprenticeship, and acquisition of economic skills. Parents supported their children during infancy, and, in turn, when their offspring matured, parents expected and depended on their children to support them during their old age, a form of intergenerational social security based on mutual reciprocity (Kett 1977).

Peer groups and social institutions encompassed a broad range of ages and did not distinguish particularly between children, youths, and adults (Coleman et al. 1974). The age heterogeneity of the group reflected the diversity and absence of age differentiation in other social gatherings. Indeed, Kett (1977) attributes the imprecision of the term *youth* to the diversity of ages in peer groups and the lack of age-graded life experiences.

In an agrarian economy, age-graded formal education in schools virtually did not exist, for example, that all six-year-olds begin first grade. In *The Disappearance of Childhood*, Neil Postman (1994) argues persuasively that the acquisition of literacy constitutes one basis by which a culture differentiates children from adults. "The printing press created a new definition of adulthood *based on reading competence* and correspondingly a new conception of childhood *based on reading incompetence*. Prior to the coming of that new environment, infancy ended at seven and adulthood began at once" (Postman 1994:18). Only in a literate culture do adults possess intellectual skills that children must master as a prerequisite of adulthood, and thus age-graded schools constitute one of the principle institutions of a modern conception of childhood.

With the advent of printing and more general literacy, the process of schooling began to separate young people from adults. Most parents in colonial America either taught their children the rudiments of reading and writing if they were able or placed them with a neighbor for early instruction. In the early nineteenth century, most students attended school sporadically during periods when they did not work and learned little more than the rudimentary "3 R's." Teachers did not base school or curricula on age; the broad age range of students in the class reflected their erratic and seasonal attendance (Kett 1977). The early colonial efforts to establish universal, compulsory public education in larger New England communities failed. However, within a century after the War for Independence, formal education supplanted apprenticeship as the means of economic socialization, segregated young people in schools, dramatically impinged on families, and fostered the social construction of modern childhood and adolescence (Katz 1968, 1971).

Modern Social Construction of Childhood

An *idea* of *childhood* specifies the social, cultural, and physical characteristics that distinguish children from adults (Archard 1993). Because cultures initially define childhood and its mirror opposite, adulthood, by age, some boundary demarcates the two. An idea of childhood may consist of several dimensions or attributes, and people may engage in different forms of adult behavior at different ages. People may further subdivide the developmental period between infancy and adulthood into ever more refined gradations according to ages or attributes. Adolescence, for example, constitutes a crucial subdivision within the modern conception of childhood.

Within the past couple of centuries, western societies began to differentiate the period between infancy and adulthood and to evidence greater concern for the welfare and rearing of children. Aries (1962) traced the modernizing of the family and childhood to the upper bourgeois and nobility in the sixteenth and seventeenth centuries, when their indifference to their offspring began to diminish. Edward Shorter (1975) associated maternal willingness among the upper classes in the 1700s to care for their own children with a decline in mercenary extramural wet nursing and a reduction in infant morality rates. Postman (1994) noted that churchmen and moralists in the seventeenth and eighteenth centuries advocated greater responsibility for parents to raise their own children, to oversee their education, to restrict their indiscriminate contact with nonfamily members, and to protect their innocence. These changing views of children and parental responsibility gradually diffused downward through the social class structure over time.

In the early nineteenth century, a newer view of childhood began to alter child-rearing practices in America. By the end of the century, urban upper- and middle-class parents invested far greater efforts to prepare their children for adult roles and to restrict their autonomous departures from home. In *At Odds*, Carl Degler (1980) called the nineteenth century the "century of childhood," and attributed change in child-rearing methods to the emerging perception of children. "Children began to be seen as different from adults; among other things they were considered now more innocent; childhood itself was perceived as it is today, as a period of life not only worth recognizing and cherishing but extending. Moreover, simply because children were being seen for the first time as special, the family's reason for being, its justification as it were, was increasingly related to the proper rearing of children" (Degler 1980:66). Analyses of nineteenth-century children's books and parents' child-rearing manuals corroborate the emergence of new ideas of childhood during this period (Wishy 1968). Social historians concur that adults increasingly viewed children as vulnerable, innocent, and dependent beings whom parents needed to protect and prepare for life (Kett 1977; Platt 1977; Hawes and Hiner 1985). This vision of childhood supported the passage of many child-protective laws by the turn of the century.

The changing conception of childhood accompanied America's structural modernization and the transformation from a rural agricultural into an urban industrial society. During the first third of the nineteenth century, entrepreneurial capitalism, immigration, and urban growth fostered the processes of social change (Demos 1970; Grubb and Lazerson 1982). Factory production and wage labor began to displace self-sufficient family farming and craft work, to separate work from the home, and to change the vision of childhood and youths' economic socialization. Manufacturers coupled the steam engine and hydropower with other machinery, and economic activity began to shift from cottages, family farms, and small shops to factories. Mills and plants along the rivers of New England and the mid-Atlantic states began to erode the family economy, increased demands for unskilled and semiskilled machine tenders, devalued the skills of craftsmen, and undermined apprenticeship as a system of training and control (Cochran 1972; Brown 1976; Finestone 1976). Work in cotton and woolen textile mills provided young women with nonagricultural economic opportunities (Boylan 1985). As commercial exports to Europe expanded, the banking, warehousing, shipping, and insurance industries provided employment opportunities for young men.

Several features of early nineteenth-century America contributed to youths' autonomy and independence and rendered their social control and integration problematic. Mobile young people faced relatively few legal, institutional, or structural barriers. Youths previously dependent on parents for placement and economic advancement migrated from countryside to towns to enter commercial society (Kett 1977). Few and weak formal barriers—certification procedures, licensures, educational requirements—impeded youths' economic mobility (Coleman et al. 1974). Most activities did not require a high level of education or technical skills, and eighteen-year-old youths could perform most tasks as well as their elders. Moreover, fewer adults sat atop the pyramid-shaped age social structure and blocked the entrance of youths into the workforce. The rapid growth in economic opportunities in cities and the absence of occupational entry barriers contributed to youths' ability to make their way in the world.

The early transition to commercial and urban life also loosened informal social controls and contributed to youth crime. Mobility, disease, and social changes disrupted families and left many homeless children and adolescents on the streets (Hawes and Hiner 1985). Some young people lacked other realistic opportunities and engaged in crime to support themselves (Bernard 1992). As we will see in chapter 2, rising rates of youth crime in the East Coast cities during early modernization prompted public officials to create institutions such as the House of Refuge in 1825 to provide formal social control to supplement the informal controls previously provided by integrating youths into cohesive communities (Rothman 1971; Ferdinand 1991).

Modernization and Industrialization

In the first half of the nineteenth century, America encountered demographic, social, and economic changes that threatened cohesion and stability and began to alter the social construction of youth. However, even at the end of the Civil War, most Americans still lived in rural settings or small towns, and agriculture and small-scale factory production dominated economic life. Other than the larger eastern coastal cities, most communities remained small and homogeneous, and most people shared values of Protestantism, sobriety, respectability, and entrepreneurship (Wiebe 1967).

By the end of the nineteenth century and in little more than a generation, structural changes transformed America from a rural, agricultural society into an urban, industrial society (Hays 1957; Hofstadter 1955; Kolko 1963; Wiebe 1967). Before to industrialization, the family farm or home shop functioned as the locus of production. With the early rise of manufacturing, small firms typically produced a single product for a local or regional market. By the end of the nineteenth century, large factories employed hundreds of workers, and manufacturers clustered individual plants in industrial districts that used thousands of workers (Massey and Denton 1993). Although these structural changes occurred at different rates and times in different regions of the country, industrialization and bureaucratic rationalization transformed the economy, society, and the social construction of youth.

Between 1870 and World War I, railroads altered manufacturing and commerce, lay the foundation for an industrial economy, and ushered in a period of rapid economic growth (Hofstadter 1955; Hays 1957; Kolko 1963; Wiebe 1967; Cochran 1972). Railroads integrated the economy, tied local communities into regional and national markets, opened new commercial opportunities, and generated enormous demands for coal and steel. Rail access to national and international markets transformed agriculture from self-sufficient family farming into a mechanized commercial endeavor (Hofstadter 1955; Wiebe 1967). Gas, coal, and oil powered the engines of the industrial economy. New industries based on science, technology, chemicals, engineering, and manufacturing emerged (Chandler 1977; Noble 1977). Companies consolidated and integrated vertically and horizontally to take advantage of economies of scale. New office machinery such as the typewriter, adding machine, and cash register expanded the scope and control of business activity and increased economic rationality (Thorelli 1954).

Railroads linked the growth of population centers with large-scale manufacturing facilities. Freed from dependence on water for power and transportation, manufacturers located plants in cities connected by railroads. Lower transportation costs reduced barriers to competition and enabled national and regional firms to intrude increasingly on local markets. Mail-order companies like Sears and Roebuck and chain stores united wholesalers and retailers to provide standard merchandise, and advertisers communicated directly with consumers to sustain their demand for products (Cochran 1972).

Mass production for a mass society transformed the processes of making things as well. Scientific management and "time-and-motion" specialists reduced work to its simplest elements and harnessed workers to repetitive tasks. Standardized parts, components, and processes enabled interchangeable laborers to make uniform products. Specialization, standardization, and systematization transformed an earlier generation of craftsmen and artisans who made an entire item into an era of machine tenders, each of whom performed a discrete task on an assembly line. Manufacturers employed unskilled women and children to assemble interchangeable parts, and child labor superseded apprenticeship as the mode of economic socialization (Kett 1977).

As enterprises increased in size, managers required an administrative tool to coordinate capital, resources, technology, and labor. First railroads and then other types of firms adapted the hierarchical table of organization from the military command structure, applied it to large-scale economic activities, and synthesized bureaucracy with corporate organization. Corporation began to supplant individual ownership and partnership as the principal form of business organization. By the beginning of the twentieth century, about one thousand companies attained sufficient size, complexity, and diversity to employ a bureaucratic structure to standardize procedures, coordinate operations, and simplify transactions (Wiebe 1967).

During the transition from small private businesses to large public corporations, a new managerial class of professionals, engineers, technocrats, functional and technical specialists, experts, and corporate executives emerged and displaced individual owners (Cochran 1972; Chandler 1977; Herman 1981). Larger corporations required more highly educated people who could work cooperatively and interact impersonally to implement rational economic policies (Cohen 1985). People required a different type of preparation successfully to enter these newer business, commercial, and organizational environments.

Immigration

Industries' demand for labor attracted immigrants from Europe and rural Americans to the burgeoning cities to take advantage of new economic opportunities. Beginning in the 1880s, changes in immigrants' countries of origins accompanied dramatic increases in their numbers. In the first century of America's nationhood, most new settlers came from northern and western Europe and maintained the country's Anglo- and Protestant character. By the end of the nineteenth century, the new immigrants came increasingly from southern and eastern Europe. Before 1890, these "different" immigrants accounted for less than 20 percent of total migration. In 1900, they accounted for more than half, and, by 1910, they represented nearly three quarters of all immigrants (Ralph and Rubinson 1980). Moreover, the numbers of immigrants that fluctuated about a third of a million people per year during the last third of the nineteenth century suddenly swelled to about 1 million per year in the first decade of the twentieth century. The overall population nearly doubled from 57 million in 1885 to more than 100 million in 1915. Between 1890 and 1920, 18 million immigrants entered the United States (Grubb and Lazerson 1982). By 1920, immigrants or their sons and daughters made up half the total residents of the larger cities.

The dramatic changes in the numbers and ethnic origins of immigrants increased the difficulty of integrating and acculturating them. The newer eastern European immigrants differed in language, religion, political heritage, and culture from the Anglo-Protestant Americans who had preceded them (Hofstadter 1955; Higham 1981). Their cultural and linguistic differences and sheer volume hindered their assimilation. Although peasants in their former lands, the newer immigrants often arrived too poor to buy agricultural machinery, livestock, or farms; lacked other occupational skills; and settled in cities as unskilled laborers (Trattner 1984). These "alien hordes" concentrated disproportionately in the industrial cities of the Northeast and Midwest, swelled the large urban slums, and lived in desperate conditions of poverty. To the nativist mind, they personified the "dangerous classes." "It was easy to blame the immigrants for poverty and crime because they lived in the cheapest housing in the worst parts of the city. They crowded into ghettos which took on some of the characteristics of their residents' native countries" (Hawes 1971:140). These changing population patterns threatened irreversibly to alter the relative linguistic, cultural, and ethnic homogeneity that previously prevailed in predominantly rural, Anglo-Protestant America (Hofstadter 1955).

Urbanization

Fueled by migration from the rural countryside and the massive immigration from Europe, cities grew on an unprecedented scale. In the last third of the nineteenth century, the rural population doubled but the urban population increased nearly sevenfold (Hofstadter 1955; Platt 1977). Between 1860 and 1890, the urban population nearly quadrupled from about 6 million to 22 million; the number of cities with populations exceeding 50,000 residents increased from sixteen to fifty-eight (Clement 1985).

The social organization of cities changed with the massive infusions of new inhabitants from the countryside and abroad. Before the advent of structural steel, electricity, and public transportation, residential areas remained socially and economically heterogenous, and population density stayed low and evenly distributed. Until the last third of the nineteenth century, most people lived within walking distance of the places where they worked, and social, economic, and ethnic residential segregation did not separate the well-to-do people from the poor ones (Clement 1985; Massey and Denton 1993).

Industrial growth spurred population increases and altered the urban landscape. The immigrant poor crowded into the urban center surrounding the industrial core, the middle class and wealthier dispersed to the suburban periphery, and cities became segregated by socioeconomic class and ethnicity (Warner 1978). Cities expanded vertically and horizontally to accommodate people who no longer lived where they worked. Structural steel and elevators allowed builders to construct taller buildings into which landlords then could stack people more densely (Massey and Denton 1993). Streetcars and urban railroads fostered the growth of suburbs where the wealthier and middle classes resided (Warner 1978). As upper-and middle-class urban dwellers used new transportation to leave the crowded urban core, landlords converted their vacated single-family residences into multiple-family structures into which they crowded the new immigrants. Economic necessity forced the European immigrants who needed to live near their factory jobs into slums and ethnic enclaves.

Crowded ethnic ghettos, poverty, disease, disorder, and crime became conspicuous and threatening features of modern urban industrial life. For Anglo-

Protestant Americans, "raised in respectable quietude and the high-toned moral imperatives of evangelical Protestantism, the city seemed not merely a new social form or way of life, but a strange threat to civilization itself" (Hofstadter 1955:176). Anti-urban sentiments mingled with nativists' ethnic prejudices against foreign immigrants whom they regarded as sources of crime, juvenile delinquency, moral decline, and political corruption (Wiebe 1967).

Many immigrants from rural agrarian backgrounds also brought traditional conceptions of childhood with them. As a matter of economic necessity, they encouraged their children to work and allowed them to participate in adult activities. Editorial writers of the late nineteenth century often decried especially the adverse impacts of ghetto slums on young people. "Enter one of those human hives on a summer's evening. There is no sign of privacy. The most anxious mother cannot preserve [her children] from the contaminating influence of the most vicious adults. At an age when children should be innocent as lambs, they are too often steeped in the knowledge of every sort of vice and crime" (Hawes 1971:130). Thus, the changing cultural construction of childhood innocence held by many in the middle classes collided with the social realities of life of many poor and immigrant urban parents who did not subscribe to or could not afford fastidious concern about the vulnerability of young people.

Modern Family and Childhood

American social history encompasses the emergence of the modern nuclear family and the contemporary social construction of childhood. The shift from an agrarian family economy to corporate industrial production separated work from the home, contracted domestic arrangements from an extended kinship group into a more isolated nuclear family, and altered child-rearing practices. Spanning most of the nineteenth century and extending into the twentieth, through a gradual process of downward diffusion across social classes, families erected a shield of privacy against the outside world, relegated women to the "domestic sphere," and prolonged the dependent status of children (Lasch 1977; S. Rothman 1978). Especially within the upper and middle classes of merchants, entrepreneurs, and professionals, women assumed a larger role to maintain a proper moral environment and to supervise their children's development.

The structural transition from an agricultural to an urban industrial society dramatically altered young people's economic roles and their social and legal status. Modernization extended the period of childhood and supplanted apprenticeship, placing-out, and entry into the workforce with prolonged economic dependency. The separation between life in the home and work in the marketplace affected both children and their mothers who became primary caretakers. The prolongation of childhood consigned women to a life of greater domesticity as work environments no longer tolerated the presence of children. The "doctrine of separate spheres"—men as workers in the marketplace and women as wives, mothers, and caretakers in the home—provided cultural and ideological support for Victorian-era gender segregation (S. Rothman 1978).

Changes in family structure and functions accompanied the shift of economic functions from the family to other work environments (Kett 1977; Lasch 1977; Demos and Boocock 1978; Degler 1980). Culminating a trend that began centuries earlier, upper-and middle-class parents especially embraced the view of children as corruptible innocents who required special attention, solicitude, and instruction. The new vision of childhood altered child-rearing practices and imposed on parents the responsibility both to protect the child from the world and simultaneously to mold, shape, and prepare the child to realize her potential in it. "The child had become a hothouse plant, and the parent a careful horticulturist" (Sutton 1988:61).

The rise of domesticity sealed off the family from penetration by the surrounding world. The nuclear family erected barriers between the family and larger society and created a "new conception of the family as a refuge from the highly competitive and often brutal world of commerce and industry" (Lasch 1977:5). Middle-class families increasingly withdrew from indiscriminate community contact, established meaningful ties within the family, and sought relaxation and tranquility at the domestic hearth. Industrialization raised the standard of living and provided middle-class families with the ability to create attractive, tastefully furnished homes that became the center of social life (Berger and Berger 1984).

Within the increasingly privatized nuclear family, parents devoted greater energy to raising their children. Demographic changes in the numbers and spacing of children facilitated greater attention to each child. Especially among the urban middle classes, parents had somewhat fewer children and spaced them more closely together (Kett 1977; Demos and Boocock 1978). These demographic changes enabled middle-class women more systematically to nurture their children and to supervise their moral and social development. "The ideal of Christian nurture was a symbol of the desire of middle-class Americans to seal their lives off from the howling storm outside and to create in family and church the kind of environment that would guarantee the right moral development of children and youth" (Kett 1977:116).

As family life became increasingly child centered, parents socialized their children in a more structured and systematic fashion (Empey 1979). The more strenuous domestic regime of supervision, discipline, and moral and social inculcation stood in marked contrast to the parental indifference and autonomy children experienced only a few centuries earlier. Adults now perceived children as corruptible and innocent. Child-rearing literature used images of plasticity, softness, and malleability and described children as objects for adults to manipulate (Boylan 1985). As we will see in chapter 2, these assumptions of malleability informed Progressive reformers' commitment to the "rehabilitative ideal" in the juvenile court. Belief in children's plasticity led to greater stress on and attention to structuring the child's physical, social, and moral environment. Deferral of adult responsibilities rather than early assumption of adult roles became the child-rearing norm. Parents supervised their children closely to inculcate moral character, economic diligence, appropriate manners, sexual modesty, obedience and respect for adult authority, and self-control. By the turn of the century, the idealized conception of childhood provided a benchmark by which to measure parental success and a standard against which to evaluate children's deviance.

The concept of adolescence did not exist until the end of the nineteenth century. The "child-study" movement provided the intellectual framework for the social construction of childhood and adolescence.

> To speak of the "invention of the adolescent" rather than the discovery of adolescence underscores a related point: adolescence was essentially a conception of behavior imposed on youth, rather than an empirical assessment of the way in which young people actually behaved. The architects of adolescence used biology and psychology (specifically, the "storm and stress" thought to be inherent in youth), to justify the promotion among young people of norms of behavior that were freighted with middle-class values. (Kett 1977:243)

Studies by psychologist and educator G. Stanley Hall and others in the last third of the nineteenth century greatly influenced child-rearing practices and shaped Progressives' attitudes toward children later embodied in juvenile court, child labor, and compulsory school attendance laws. Hall and other child-study researchers asserted that childhood consisted of a series of developmental stages and sharply differentiated between children and adults. Hall's theory of recapitulation analogized child development with human evolutionary history—"ontogeny recapitulates phylogeny"—and compared childhood with primitive violent savagery and adulthood with mature developed society (Kett 1977:218). Recapitulation fit neatly with contemporaneous Darwinian evolutionary theory, and child-study proponents believed that their scientific discipline would provide insights into human culture, social development, and more effective socialization of the young. Professional specialties in many disciplines—for example, the medical specialty of pediatrics and the founding of children's hospitals, the systematization of education and age-graded curricula, and the psychological study of child development—all reflected the centrality of and cultural emphasis on children.

Several interrelated assumptions underlay the child-study movement and the modern construction of childhood: children progress through a developmental sequence of stages; during these developmental stages, children differ qualitatively from adults; efforts prematurely to hasten the unfolding of the developmental process would prove self-defeating; children should be excluded from adult activities and responsibilities until they complete their developmental tasks and attain full physical, psychological, and moral maturity, typically in their early twenties (Empey 1979). Child-study research used the concept of adolescence to justify the prolonged social and economic dependency of youths until they achieved psychological and emotional maturity. Hall's formulation of adolescence had many collateral applications: instruction manuals for parents on how to raise their children and for educators on how to administer the high schools in which they cloistered the young and in efforts to organize youths' leisure time in adult-sponsored activities. By the turn of the century, youth workers attempted to structure various activities for youths, for example, through Boy Scouts and recreation, and to restrict youths' opportunities to socialize without adult supervision (Coleman et al. 1974). Adult regulation of children's spare time gradually encompassed virtually all young people's pursuits. The "playground movement" organized children's games around the maxim that "a playground is not a playground without supervision" (Kett 1977:226). In short, child study in its various guises provided the rationale and justification to differentiate, separate, and segregate young people from adults.

Women, Children, and Child Saving

The separation of work from the home altered the social roles and economic value of children and their mothers. The modern social construction of childhood simultaneously excluded children from the world of work, reduced their economic contributions, prolonged their dependence, and imposed greater responsibilities on their parents. The separation of work from the home also contributed to the segregation of the sexes and the relegation of women primarily to the domestic sphere. The family became a unit of consumption rather than of production; urban middle-class fathers worked outside the home, and women remained at home and assumed priority in child rearing. The "cult of domesticity" and the "doctrine of separate spheres" redefined the roles of women and children and the social institutions they encountered. The conception of childhood as a developmental process placed a greater responsibility on mothers, especially in the middle and upper classes, to provide a proper family environment and to supervise their children's moral and social development and natural unfolding into adults.

The "cult of true womanhood" provided an idealized version of women's roles and defined them primarily in terms of domestic functions (Berger and Berger 1984). With the separation of work from the home, "the doctrine of separate spheres" viewed men's and women's domains as separate, intrinsically different, and hostile. The chaotic "outside world"—brutal, competitive, and immoral, contrasted with the "domestic" haven—stable, moral, and secure. While men engaged in the "dirty work" of commerce and industry, women remained at home with their children, free from contamination. Women cultivated the virtues of love, kindliness, morality, and altruism and succored their husbands upon their retreat from the forbidding outside world into the domestic family fortress (Lasch 1977; S. Rothman 1978).

Writers of child-rearing literature also contrasted the outside world with the domestic sphere and concluded that women only could raise children effectively in a home insulated from spiritual corruption. But proper child

rearing became more complicated as the same forces that rationalized commercial life also elevated and professionalized the domestic sphere (Boylan
1985). The child-study movement redefined the child "as a person with distinctive attributes—impressionability, vulnerability, innocence—which required a warm, protected, and prolonged period of nurture. . . . Educators and
moralists began to stress the child's need for play, for love and understanding,
and for the gradual, gentle unfolding of his nature. Child rearing became more
demanding as a result and emotional ties between parents and children grew
more intense at the same time that ties to relatives outside the immediate
family weakened" (Lasch 1977:5–6). Emphasizing the special nature of children elevated the child to a central position in middle-class households,
rendered the process of raising a child more complicated, and required mothers to devote considerable time and energy to children's welfare and development.

Middle-class women's educational opportunities expanded to equip them
better to maintain a home and to raise children. By the mid-nineteenth century, an influx of poor immigrant girls obviated middle-class girls' earlier roles
as babysitters and domestics, and continued education provided a suitable
outlet for them. "[T]he education of girls beyond puberty was more than just
a necessity created by their superfluous position in households. The same
revolution which upgraded motherhood virtually to the level of a professional
also sanctioned the appropriation by women of control over cultural life"
(Kett 1977:138). As the modern idea of childhood gathered momentum, co-
teries of experts and helping professionals provided mothers with guidance,
and further education enabled women better to fulfill their responsibilities
(Lasch 1977; Berger and Berger 1984).

In the cultural idealization of motherhood and wifely perfection, the family
provided the center of civic virtue, and women served as guardians of morality
against the dangers of the street and the competition of the marketplace.

> The woman of the bourgeois family has, above all, a "civilizational" mission,
> both within and beyond the household. Within the household, the woman is
> the "homemaker"—a companion and helper to her husband, a supervisor and
> "facilitator" of her children's development and education, arbiter of taste, cul-
> ture, and all the "finer things of life." But this civilizing mission also extends
> beyond the home, into social and cultural activities of an "edifying" nature, and
> (especially in America) into reformist politics. (Berger and Berger 1984:102)

Women's responsibilities as custodians of their children's moral development also provided an impetus to make the world in which their children
lived a better place. Although cultural stereotypes limited many economic,
political, and social opportunities, women's clubs and organizations for social
and civic improvement provided outlets and extensions of their domestic work
outside the home. Concern for social and moral welfare allowed women to
participate in certain public causes and thereby to expand the domestic sphere

into other arenas of social policy, such as temperance, anti saloon and anti prostitution movements (Degler 1980). For example, gambling, drinking and prostitution occurred in saloons and posed a severe threat to the sanctity of the home and the purity of the nation. Bourgeois women carried the new moral sensibility and often served as "the shock troops of the various movements that sought to evangelize other classes with the blessings of the middle-class family ethos" (Berger and Berger 1984:7).

"Child-saving" activities provided another venue into which to expand the domestic sphere. Child saving extended women's domestic roles as child rearers, caretakers, and carriers of moral virtues into the public realm. Decreased fertility, increased life expectancy, and enhanced education enabled many middle-class women to engage in a variety of child-saving activities (Platt 1977). They provided a primary impetus for the juvenile court, child welfare, child labor, and other social and legal reforms affecting children.

Middle- and upper-class women possessed the social and economic abilities to realize the newer child-rearing ideals themselves and actively to promote the *idea* of childhood to others (Kett 1977). However, all social classes and ethnic and religious groups did not subscribe equally to their newer conception of childhood. The newly arrived immigrants, for example, still adhered to a more traditional, premodern view of young people. Many legislative "reforms" during the past century reflect cultural conflicts over the construction of childhood, appropriate ways to socialize children, and the balance between private and public responsibilities for youth. As Joseph Kett observed, what most of the prominent reformers of the period "viewed as a Manichaean struggle between respectability and virtue on one side and a subculture of crime and depravity on the other might have been simply a conflict between a Protestant middle-class life-style which emphasized sobriety and self-restraint and an emerging urban lower-class life-style which valued spontaneity, gang loyalty, and physical prowess" (1977:90).

Middle-class reformers wielded the imagery of childhood as a potent cultural symbol, and the legal doctrine of *parens patriae*, the state as parent-surrogate, provided a powerful weapon in the cultural conflicts. The rise of family privacy and domesticity affirmed child rearing primarily as a private responsibility. The privatization of parental child-rearing responsibilities limited public authority to meddle in domestic arrangements and defined public intervention in the family as an abnormal intrusion. As a result, *parens patriae* intercession acquired negative connotations and occurred only in instances of indisputable parental failure. Thus, *parens patriae* and the state's public welfare role rest on an inherently limiting and self-defeating logic. "[I]f the state can intervene only in situations that are construed as abnormal or pathological, then by definition governmental programs can be extended only to the minority of families who are considered the poorest, the most disorganized, and the least effective in socializing their children" (Grubb and Lazerson 1982: 49).

Progressive Movement, Social Change, and State Authority

Around the end of the nineteenth century, social structural changes associated with modernization sparked the Progressive movement (Hofstadter 1955; Wiebe 1967). Progressivism encompassed a host of ideologies and addressed a broad spectrum of issues: economic regulation, criminal justice, social welfare, and political reform. Progressives sponsored laws to regulate railroads, to restrict corporate trusts and economic abuses, and to reform business practices (Thorelli 1954; Kolko 1965; Wiebe 1965; Bringhurst 1979). They legislated for urban public health and welfare reform and to improve child welfare (Wilensky and Lebeaux 1958; Tiffin 1982; Trattner 1984). They introduced civil service and "good government" reforms to limit the power of corrupt urban ethnic political bosses (Hays 1964; Sutton 1988). For our purposes, Progressive reformers embraced many child-saving programs to respond to myriad threats to child development: inadequate and broken families, dependency and neglect, poverty and welfare, education and work, crime and delinquency, recreation and play.

Historians debate the social origins and policy goals of the Progressives. By the beginning of the Progressive Era, roughly 1890–1914, the industrial transformation undermined traditional rural agrarian life and threatened Anglo-Protestant cultural hegemony. Historians attribute Progressive policies and innovation to a variety of motives, for example, humanitarian impulses, anti-immigrant hostility, a desire to control the changing social and economic environment, and a technocratic quest for administrative efficiency. In *The Age of Reform*, Richard Hofstadter (1955) ascribed elements of Progressivism to downwardly mobile members of the "old middle class" of small-town entrepreneurs whom the new urban and corporate elites eclipsed. Another theme of Progressivism involved attempts by the traditional, rural Protestant middle class to reassert its social values, primacy, and cultural dominance in conflict with foreign immigrants crowded into the urban centers (Hofstadter 1955). Progressivism appeared as a struggle by the "old" middle class concerned with respectability, orderliness, and self-discipline to "preserve and further its moral and social values against threats from above and below" (Ryerson 1978: 13).

Other historians describe Progressive reformers as members of the "new" urban industrial middle class. The Progressive movement included many members from the new managerial and technocratic class, graduates of colleges and universities, those with professional training, and the elites of business and corporate life. These reformers emerged in the urban industrial centers around the turn of the century, identified with each other on the basis of occupation and professional training, and cross-fertilized parallel reform movements (Wiebe 1967). The decline of the older social order provided them with an opportunity to develop rational, scientific, and managerial solutions to the problems created by social structural change (Hays 1957; Wiebe 1965;

Bledstein 1976). Others attribute many Progressive economic programs at the national level to the actions of corporate businessmen to enlist the state as an ally to stabilize and rationalize the economy (Kolko 1963, 1965; Weinstein 1968), and to accommodate working-class people to the inequalities of the new industrial order (Katz, Doucet, and Stern 1982; Platt 1977).

Modernization connotes a process of rationalization, an effort to control the world by rational calculation (Berger and Berger 1984). Progressive reformers shared a commitment to *rationality*, believed that professionals and experts could develop scientific solutions to social problems, and trusted the state to administer their programs objectively (Sutton 1988). Reflecting the interrelated processes of social structural change, modernity, and rationality, capitalism rationalized the economy, science and technology rationalized the physical world, and law and bureaucracy rationalized the political and social realm.

During the last third of the nineteenth century, many intellectual disciplines and professions proliferated. In *The Culture of Professionalism*, Burton Bledstein analyzed the emergence of the *idea* of professional expertise—"technical competence, superior skill, and a higher quality of performance"—as one aspect of rationalization, and the crucial role that expertise played in Progressive reform policies (1976:87). Many Progressives shared similar training and education, and their reform strategies reflected their professional socialization and organizational experiences. Most Progressive programs emphasized scientific rationality and expertise, technical and managerial solutions, and the role of the detached, objective authority.

Progressives invoked scientific rationality and claimed special expertise to legitimate their programs and to expand their professional authority (Bledstein 1976). Progressives often worked in a corporate and organizational context and frequently devised bureaucratic solutions to the problems posed by urban industrial life (Wiebe 1967). "[A] characteristic feature of Progressive movements was their tendency to see social control not as a moral or political problem, but primarily as an administrative problem. Progressives sought to depoliticize the growing demands for the protections of a welfare state by promoting reforms that emphasized administrative efficiency and professional expertise rather than substantive changes in the allocation of rights and economic resources" (Sutton 1988:124). Progressives believed that they could solve contentious social problems with rational and scientific methods and attempted to transform political and moral conflicts into technical managerial decisions made by experts in administrative agencies insulated from partisan strife.

Progressives believed that neutral, detached experts could apply knowledge rationally to formulate public policy without political distraction (Hofstadter 1955). They created governmental agencies to implement their economic and social reforms and enlarged and expanded the power of the state. They felt that benevolent public governmental action could ameliorate the dislocations of social change and provide a necessary counterbalance to the power of private corporations.

They also sought to use the state to inculcate their values in others (Allen 1964). "The most distinguishing characteristic of Progressivism was its fundamental trust in the power of the state to do good. The state was not the enemy of liberty, but the friend of equality—and to expand its domain and increase its power was to be in harmony with the spirit of the age. . . . The state was not a behemoth to be chained and fettered, but an agent capable of fulfilling an ambitious program" (Rothman 1980:60). They viewed individual and social welfare as coextensive and saw no need to interpose procedural safeguards to protect individuals from state benevolence.

Although Progressives used modern managerial techniques and organizational strategies, they derived their vision for social reforms from an earlier, more homogenous and traditional society. A shared moral consensus and supreme confidence in their own values sustained them. They used a variety of governmental agencies, for example, schools and juvenile courts, to "Americanize," assimilate, and acculturate immigrants and the poor to become sober, virtuous, middle-class Americans like themselves (Platt 1977; D. Rothman 1978, 1980).

> There was no crisis of values that had to be debated, no agonizing considerations of the comparative worth of different life-styles. To Progressives, all Americans were to enter the ranks of the middle class. The melting-pot metaphor implied not only an amalgam of immigrants into a common mold, but an amalgam of classes into a common mold. Everyone was to respect private property, send their children to school, and give up whatever vices—particularly intemperance—that they might have brought with them from the old world, in order to become hard-working and law-abiding. (D. Rothman 1978:75)

Progressives believed in the virtues of their social order and sought to enable those less fortunate to become upwardly mobile participants in it.

Progressives and the Child

Progressive reformers implemented a variety of child-saving strategies based on the changing cultural conception of childhood—child labor and welfare laws, compulsory school attendance laws, playground supervision, kindergarten, and juvenile court (Cremin 1961; Trattner 1965; Tiffin 1982; Rothman 1980). Reflecting the generic processes of professionalization and rationalization, the child-study movement systematized observation and analyses of children and expanded academic and scientific knowledge about child development and human growth. The scientific understanding of childhood provided Progressive reformers with the intellectual foundation to improve children's lives, to transform society, and to ensure a better future (Hawes 1991).

Many Progressive programs shared a unifying child-centered theme, and they both reflected and advanced the changing imagery of childhood (Wiebe

1967; Kett 1977). Efforts to simultaneously protect and supervise children structured child development and increased children's dependency. Progressives' child-saving reforms also reflected their antipathy to the immigrant hordes and their desire to save the second generation from perpetuating the Old World ways (Rothman 1980; Empey 1979).

Progressive child-saving strategies embodied two contradictory premises. The idealized conception of childhood provided a standard against which reformers measured parents' success and children's deviance. They assigned primary responsibility to private families to raise their children *and* expanded the role of the state and its public institutions to oversee families and to socialize children. The dominant culture privatized family life, created a domestic "haven," erected barriers to insulate parents and children, *and* simultaneously increased the power of the state to intervene as *parens patriae* when families failed to fulfill their responsibilities. In *Broken Promises*, W. Norton Grubb and Marvin Lazerson contend that the resolution of these contradictory and competing "private" and "public" responsibilities toward children often "took class-biased and racially motivated forms, with the surveillance powers of the juvenile court and the reforming impulses of the schools aimed at lower-class families whose childrearing 'failures' threatened" the social order (1982: 27). Distinctions between "our children" and "other people's children" recur in the formulation of child welfare and juvenile justice policies throughout the twentieth century.

Progressives enacted laws and created institutions to structure child development, to control and mold children, to protect them from exploitation, and to oversee their parents (Rothman 1980). Under their aegis, for example, child labor laws protected children from economic abuse and prolonged the financial dependency of childhood. As formal education increasingly became a prerequisite of future success, compulsory school attendance laws provided adults "with unprecedented control over the symbolic environment of the young" and enabled them to define the "conditions by which a child was to become an adult" (Postman 1994:45). Progressives created specialized agencies to enforce child labor, school attendance, and child welfare laws. Juvenile courts provided a means by which to define and control youthful deviance and to buttress other child-saving endeavors.

States adopted compulsory school attendance laws, child labor restrictions, and juvenile court laws at different times in different parts of the country in responses to the social structural changes in their regions (Coleman et al. 1974; Empey 1979). These three reforms—school, work, and delinquency—constitute the trinity of the legal and social construction of childhood. They reflect the central Progressive assumptions that strengthening the nuclear family, shielding the child from adult roles, postponing economic integration, formally educating him or her for upward mobility, and allowing the state to intervene in the event of parental or youthful deviance constituted the ideal way to prepare children for life.

Expanding Compulsory School Attendance for Children

Tax-supported public education and compulsory school attendance laws antedated the Progressive Era by more than half a century (Katz 1968). As early as the 1830s and 1840s, industrialization in New England and an influx of Irish immigrants aroused fears of social disorder. Among the first professional "educationists," Horace Mann in Massachusetts sought national unity through a system of public "common schools" that would assimilate foreigners, provide cohesion and stability for an unruly populace, and inculcate a common character among all citizens (Button and Provenzo 1981; Hawes 1991). A public school system attended by children of both well-to-do and poor families constituted an important institutional component of social integration and nation building. Proponents of compulsory school attendance enlisted business allies when educators claimed that operating steam- and power-driven machinery required literate workers and asserted that education made them more orderly, energetic, and productive.

The changing cultural conception of childhood also influenced early school reformers. Responding to the then prevailing pattern of seasonal and sporadic school attendance, reformers increasingly viewed "the ideal school as a controlled environment for the child. The school, ideally was not merely to be a casual, unstructured institution which the child encountered from time to time; it was to be as coextensive with childhood as conditions would permit. ... [T]he proper 'culture' of childhood demanded a segregation of children from adults in asylum-like institutions called schools" (Coleman et al. 1974: 18). Advocates of compulsory attendance viewed schools, quite apart from their educational value, as agencies of social control to keep youths off the streets, insulate them from adverse moral and social influences, and prevent their involvement in crime.

Common schools endorsed a shared set of social and political values, a collective culture for children of all classes and religions. Proponents viewed "common" schools as a moral crusade to reform society, to instill democratic values and patriotism, to "Christianize" immigrants and "Protestantize" Irish Catholics, and to transform young people into productive citizens imbued with virtues of industry, temperance, and frugality. As with Progressivism, historians differ over the motives and meanings of these early educational reforms. In *The Irony of Early School Reform*, Michael Katz (1968) characterized common school reforms as attempts to socialize a docile labor force, to inculcate dominant cultural values, and to foster support for the emerging industrial order. Others ascribe humanitarian and benevolent motives to school reforms as strategies to facilitate individual mobility or as a complex process of institution building linking the idea of childhood with social structural change (Finkelstein 1985).

Over the next century, schools and childhood became coextensive as "the one best system" of education—formalized, centralized, bureaucratized, standardized, and age-graded—spread from New England to the West and South after the Civil War (Tyack 1974). Postman posits a straightforward and causal relationship between literacy and schools, on the one hand, and the *idea* of childhood, on the other: "Where literacy was valued highly and persistently, there were schools, and where there were schools, the concept of childhood developed rapidly" (1994:39). This relationship prevailed in Progressive America as well, as school reformers lengthened the school year from weeks to months for the better part of the year, defined nonattendance as deviant, and coerced children's presence by compulsory attendance laws. By the turn of the century, formal education in school became most young people's primary developmental task. Schools provided reformers with the means to protect, supervise, and control children; to segregate youths by age; and to limit their experiences and interactions with the world outside their families (Finkelstein 1985).

Systematic age grading represented the most crucial Progressive educational reform for the social construction of *childhood*. Although common school advocates proposed age classification a half century earlier, as urban population density increased, age grading became more feasible. By the turn of the century, age grading spread upward from the lower elementary grades to secondary schools and into colleges. Age grading occurred in conjunction with industrialization. In an agricultural economy, young people interspersed seasonal labor with occasional school attendance and the ages of students in the classroom varied. In an industrial economy, in which people worked throughout the year and formal education preceded entry into the labor force, school administrators institutionalized the idea that students should attain a certain grade level at a certain age (Coleman et al. 1974).

Progressive reformers reconfigured schools as the salience of education for success in the corporate economy increased. The quest for bureaucratic rationality and administrative efficiency that pervaded American society altered schools' organization and expanded their role as agencies of social change and social control. School administrators replicated the bureaucratic structure of corporations and instituted hierarchical centralized controls (Tyack 1974). Schools borrowed the concept of efficiency from factories and applied "scientific management" theory to education and school administration (Button and Provenzo 1981).

The principles of scientific management that enabled manufacturers to combine standardized components on the assembly line also encouraged age grading of students in schools. School reformers readily applied the central features of mass production—standardized parts and production processes—to the learning environment. Teachers in age-graded schools could specialize in one grade, efficiently teach a whole class, move developmentally similar youngsters along a curricular conveyor belt, and achieve economies of scale. Further bureaucratic rationalization of education led to standardized curricula, norms for evaluating student performance, and tracking students on the basis of ability (Button and Provenzo 1981). School administrators regarded age-graded and standardized curricula as important elements of structure and order and as significant counterweights to the chaos and disorder in the lives of children from ethnically diverse, densely populated urban tenements. Cognitive tests and aptitude assessments allowed educators efficiently to classify, label, and separate young people. The cultural homogeneity of the psychologists, schoolmen, and reformers blinded them to any racial or ethnic biases inherent in their measurement tools.

The processes of education involved more than the acquisition of cognitive skills and information. Schools also attempted to instill a set of attitudes, values, discipline, and "time thrift" in students. The new industrial order required people who possessed the abilities to report for work punctually, concentrate on repetitive tasks, perform diligently and efficiently, adhere to schedules, and function within segmented and hierarchical organizations. School bureaucracies reproduced the corporate order and socialized children for their future roles in complex organizations. Postman contends that because "[q]uietness, immobility, contemplation, [and] precise regulation of bodily functions" are "unnatural" for energetic young people, "[t]he capacity to control and overcome one's nature became one of the defining characteristics of adulthood and therefore one of the essential purposes of education" (Postman 1994:46). Similarly, Barbara Finkelstein argues that learning to read and write detached the written word from face-to-face communication and that when students began school, "they entered an isolating world in which teachers used the printed word to effect a psychological transformation in their students" (1985:121).

As the corporate economy expanded at the turn of the century, formal education became a functional prerequisite of entry into many white-collar, middle-class careers and occupations. Office work, technical roles, and a complex machine technology required more extensive preparation than previously. During the last quarter of the nineteenth century, the number of professional schools increased dramatically and formal education provided access into various professions, for example, law, medicine, dentistry, and engineering (Bledstein 1976). Educational certification and professional licensure replaced family connections as the basis for personnel recruitment. A diploma served as a testament to discipline, manners, and decorum as well as to literacy or technical skills. Virtually for the first time, formal education correlated with attractive job opportunities and membership in the middle class (Kett 1977).

The waves of southern and eastern European immigrants arrived as unskilled laborers at about the same time that educational certification assumed greater significance for entry into professional, corporate, and managerial positions. Business and professional elites bureaucratized public schools in response to structural changes associated with immigration and urbanization (Katz 1968; Clement 1985). Public schools assumed primary responsibility to assimilate and Americanize immigrant children and to provide them with the linguistic ability, vocational skills, and personal discipline to function effectively in an industrial society. Schools also provided a comprehensive environment for social control of urban youths. "School reformers and officials alike increasingly complained about the polyglot and disorderly character of American society and defended the school as an agency which would at once bring the children of immigrants under social control and improve their chances for survival in the competitive economic life of America" (Coleman et al. 1974:20). By the turn of the century, most states adopted compulsory school attendance laws and increasingly enforced them (Kett 1977). The number of high school graduates rose steadily during the twentieth century, from only 2 percent of the seventeen-year-old population in 1870, to 16 percent in 1920, and 49 percent by 1940 (Carnoy and Levin 1985).

The primacy and prolongation of school attendance affected families and children. The now common pattern of adolescents remaining at home at least until they completed high school only emerged at the end of the nineteenth century as more structured, systematic, and age-graded education replaced part-time, random, and seasonal school attendance. As young people remained at home longer, their families sacrificed their economic contributions and young people imposed a drain on family resources. Until the end of the nineteenth century, urban teenagers worked in factories or as unskilled laborers and contributed significantly to family income. In the latter third of the nineteenth century, for example, children aged ten to nineteen earned about a quarter of the household income; in families of unskilled laborers, children contributed nearly one-third (Kett 1977). Over the course of the twentieth century, increasing numbers of adolescents graduated from high school rather than worked, and their delayed economic entry increased their financial dependency on their parents. Before World War I, only about 10 percent of youths graduated from high school, whereas by World War II, nearly half did. The number of gainfully employed children under sixteen declined during this period with the biggest drop occurring between 1910 and 1920 (Stern, Smith, and Doolittle 1975).

Middle-class parents recognized the changing patterns of occupational mobility, more easily relinquished their children's economic contributions, and invested in additional years of education to qualify them for more desirable jobs. Working- and lower-class families could not absorb as readily the costs of prolonged secondary education. Poorer parents depended more on their children's earnings and could not as readily afford the lost income and additional costs of supporting nonearning adolescents in the household (Kett 1977). Immigrant parents did not necessarily share the modern conception of childhood or did not appreciate that their children's leaving school early in order to work consigned them to dead-end jobs as common laborers (Rothman 1980). As a result, extended education and social mobility correlated with class and ethnic differences. Affluent parents absorbed the costs of prolonged education, and their children attended school well into their teen years, whereas the children of urban working-class families seldom remained in school beyond the sixth grade.

Progressive reformers regarded education as crucial to later success and enacted compulsory school attendance laws to ensure that parents did not deprive their children of their educational opportunities. Although a few northeastern states adopted compulsory school attendance about the time of the Civil War, public officials typically ignored or did not enforce them. While only six states had compulsory attendance laws in 1871, by 1900 virtually all the states in the North and Midwest had adopted them (Wiebe 1967).

As formal education became coextensive with childhood, truants posed a special problem. While their absence from school posed a danger to themselves and a waste of public money, their coerced presence could prove disruptive. In 1862, Massachusetts adopted a state law to incarcerate chronic truants in reform schools. By the end of the century, the juvenile court provided a primary mechanism to enforce truancy laws. In *Stubborn Children*, John Sutton (1988) suggests the close historical linkages between juvenile justice and educational reforms. Both rested on the social construction of childhood and employed similar bureaucratic strategies. Both systems functioned as mechanisms of socialization, social control, and social integration of young people. The Common School and House of Refuge movements in the first third of the nineteenth century reflected similar institutional responses to incipient industrialization and urbanization on the East Coast. By the end of the century, mass schooling provided a means to acculturate normal children while juvenile courts provided a means to control those who deviated.

Child Labor Laws

Child labor laws provided the second strategic element in the Progressives' formal construction of childhood. Although young people have worked throughout history, industrialization and power machinery increased the hazards to and dangers of economic exploitation of children. In the impersonal world of unskilled factory labor, children could tend machines as well as adults, and their labor depressed the wages of adult workers (Kett 1977). The mechanization of industry and the floods of immigration swept many children onto the factory floors. The impoverished foreigners came from cultures in which children traditionally worked and their families needed the additional income children provided to survive. The 1880 census officially recorded as working more than 1 million children between the ages of ten and fifteen, nearly one out of six youngsters (Clement 1985). By 1900 the census reported 1,750,000 children between the ages of ten and fifteen at work, and these estimates did not count the many child workers below the age of ten. By 1910 the number of child workers between the ages of ten and fifteen rose to about 2 million, 18 percent of all children in that age group. Only in the decades following World War I and as a result of child labor laws did the number of young child workers begin to decline.

Children in premodern economies typically worked alongside their parents or masters on the farm or in the shop, and both experienced similar working conditions. The rise of corporate manufacturing, the use of power machinery, and the physical and social separation between owners, managers, and workers exposed child and adult laborers to much more hazardous conditions. Walter

Trattner's history of the child labor movement, *Crusade for the Children* (1970), described the horrendous working conditions of children.

> Many descended into the dark and dangerous coal mines each day, or worked above ground in the coal breakers where harmful clouds of dust were so thick the light could scarcely penetrate even on the brightest days. Others were forced to crouch for hours at a time and face the blinding glare and stifling heat of glass factory furnace rooms. Many children spent their days or nights in the dull, monotonous, noisy spinning rooms of cotton mills, where humid, lint-filled air made it difficult to breathe, and where they were kept awake by cold water thrown in their faces. Others, perhaps only five or six-years old, shucked oysters and picked shrimp. Some worked in fruit and vegetable canneries sixteen hours a day, seven days a week, in sheds exposed to the weather. (41–42)

Children working under these conditions incurred staggering human, physical, and developmental costs. Young people suffered work-related diseases, injuries, disabilities, and death. Long hours of labor precluded education and trapped young workers in monotonous, dead-end unskilled drudgery.

Progressive reformers mobilized a crusade against child labor that coincided with the movement for compulsory school attendance. States passed child labor laws, established the minimum ages of workers, and limited the types of employment and numbers of hours that children could work. Labor unions joined the Progressives' efforts, motivated in part to protect the jobs and wages of working men from competing with young children and to preserve the father's authority within the family (Stern, Smith, and Doolittle 1975).

Child labor laws shared many of the same assumptions about childhood that underlay compulsory school attendance and juvenile court laws. These laws sought to preserve the family, to alleviate the impact of urban industrialism on vulnerable children, to defer the assumption of adult responsibilities, and to allow time for developmental unfolding and adequate preparation for adult roles. Child labor laws prevented children's economic exploitation, removed them from the workplace, returned them to their homes and schools, and reinforced a moratorium for adolescence during which they could prepare for success later in life (Marks 1975). Although protectionist in intent, child labor laws also excluded youth from productive economic activity, denied them economic roles or self-sufficiency, isolated them from adult work role models, and prolonged their financial dependency.

By the beginning of the twentieth century, twenty-eight states had passed laws that restricted child labor and required children to attend school (Empey 1979). Between 1910 and 1930, the number of children between ten and fifteen years of age gainfully employed declined nearly 75 percent, from 18 percent to about 5 percent (Stern, Smith, and Doolittle 1975; Ainsworth 1991). Although as late as 1930, two million youths under the age of eighteen worked, one-third of them under sixteen, the Great Depression of the 1930s completed the displacement of child workers from the marketplace. As the depression deepened, passage and enforcement of the federal Fair Labor Standards Act and state laws barred child labor and protected the jobs of adults from displacement by young workers (Coleman et al. 1974).

Conclusion

During the nineteenth century, social structural changes transformed the United States from rural, agrarian communities into an urban, industrial nation. Industrial modernization altered the nature of work, the prerequisites of economic participation, and the structure and function of families. American culture constructed a new social and legal status of childhood. At the beginning of the processes of change, most young people lived in small, homogenous agricultural communities and the value of their labor assured them a modicum of equality, autonomy, and social integration. The community participated in child rearing through an informal web of relationships: church, kinship, apprenticeship and work, and a broad-aged peer group.

The modern social construction of childhood promoted a newer conception of children, differentiated young people from adults, isolated youths from indiscriminate social contacts, and encapsulated them within their families and in organizations of formal social control. The modern conception affected the relationships between children, their parents, and the larger society. The newer image redefined childhood as a period of innocence, vulnerability, and dependency. With the separation of work from the home, mothers assumed greater responsibilities to raise children, to establish a suitable developmental environment, and to provide moral guidance.

Progressive reformers institutionalized childhood as a period of dependency and exclusion from the adult world, enacted a host of "child-saving" laws, and created formal organizations to enforce their new conception of childhood. Compulsory school attendance laws increased the amount of time per day and the number of days per year that youths spend in school. Education and literacy became children's primary developmental task, and schools assumed an expanding role to supervise and control young people. With the encapsulation of youths in schools, adults identified other characteristics and dimensions that further distinguished children and adults. Child labor laws excluded young people from meaningful economic roles, consigned them to part-time, ultimately dead-end jobs, and substantially increased their economic dependence. Compulsory school attendance and child labor laws isolated children from adults, deprived them of satisfying economic or social roles, and confined them in school with age-graded peers.

Both compulsory school attendance and child labor laws reflected Progressives' special concerns about poor and immigrant children. On the one hand, these laws acknowledged the disadvantaged circumstances under which they lived and provided institutional support to prolong and structure their childhood as a prerequisite of a more fulfilling and responsible adulthood. On the other hand, schools provided a powerful agency of acculturation and socialization, expanded states' control over other people's children, and protected the public from unsocialized youth.

The Progressives' solicitude for children resulted in unparalleled age segregation. By the end of World War I, virtually all states had enacted legal measures to enforce the new conceptions of childhood and adolescence. Over the next half century, they increasingly refined and elaborated on them. Today, successive generations of rigorously age-graded, lock-stepping cohorts of young people move through specialized child-serving institutions. Adolescence constitutes a period of almost complete economic superfluity during which time young people interact almost exclusively with same-aged peers, cut off from nonparental adult influences except in formal settings, and subject to the powerful socializing forces of their youth network. The cultural conception of young people as irresponsible and "different" from adults also supports the oppositional character of the youth culture—rebellious, hedonistic, present-oriented, and conformist—that contributes to youth crime, gang activity, alienation and self-medication through drugs and alcohol. In short, perhaps the contemporary problem for adolescents is *adolescence*. The socially constructed adolescent moratorium prolongs young people's dependence and irrelevance, inadequately structures their transition to adulthood, and leaves many young people disengaged and disconnected.

Progressive legal reforms institutionalized a binary cultural dichotomy between children and adults. Progressives redefined young people, whom earlier generations did not distinguish from older adults, as fragile, innocent, vulnerable, and malleable beings who required prolonged guidance, control, and supervision. The legal order embodies this conception of young people as incompetent, imposes restrictions on them to safeguard them from their own immaturity, and denies them full personhood and responsibility. In chapter 8, I review current developmental psychological research that questions many of Progressivism's premises about adolescents' social and legal incompetence. But childhood constitutes a social construct rather than a scientific fact, and the normative idea of an adolescent moratorium to prepare young people for adult autonomy remains a cultural fixture. In chapter 2, I analyze how the juvenile court emerged as one of the principle institutions to define and enforce the new social construction of childhood irresponsibility.

| | | | | TWO

The Juvenile Court and the "Rehabilitative Ideal"

Changes in *ideas* about *childhood* and *social control* during the nineteenth century led Progressive reformers to create the juvenile court in 1899. The social construction of *childhood* and *adolescence* provided a conceptual rationale for a separate system of social control for young people. Social structural and cultural changes also encouraged reformers to reformulate their ideology of crime causation and penal strategies of social control. The classical criminal law attributed criminal behavior to actors' "free will" and punished offenders for making blameworthy choices. During the nineteenth century, positivist criminology attributed criminality to antecedent forces that determined offenders' behavior and penologists proposed to reform and treat them rather than to blame and punish them. At the dawn of the twentieth century, Progressive reformers combined these new positive theories about crime causation and social control with the new ideas about childhood and created a social welfare alternative to criminal courts to regulate criminal and noncriminal misconduct by youth.

The modernizing social structural forces analyzed in chapter 1 provided the impetus to reformulate the ideology and practice of criminal justice. This chapter examines the impact of those social changes initially for the construction of separate correctional institutions for young people—houses of refuge and reformatories—and subsequently for the creation of a separate juvenile court and justice system for youth. At the beginning of the nineteenth century, initial industrialization, immigration, and urbanization weakened the forces of informal social control in small cohesive communities and motivated reformers to construct formal organizations of social control to provide an institutional alternative (Rothman 1971). Changes in correctional practices during the nineteenth century reflected changes in the ideology of crime causation. By the end of the nineteenth century, positivism provided a rational, scientific, and "empirical" alternative explanation to traditional criminal law's jurisprudential understanding of crime and penal policy. The positivists' "understanding" of criminals' motivations implied the correlative ability to cure them, and Progressive reformers embraced the "rehabilitative ideal" as the animating principle of their criminal and juvenile justice reforms. The Progressives' emphasis on "rehabilitation" placed the juvenile court on a number of cultural and criminological fault lines: determinism versus free will, treatment versus punishment, social welfare versus social control, intervening to alter social structural features versus changing individuals and the like. Throughout this chapter, I contend that the policy choices embedded in the early juvenile institutions and later juvenile courts reflected nineteenth-century reformers' fear of other people's children, especially the poor and immigrants, and their efforts to devise flexible state agencies for their formal social control.

Crime Control before the Invention of Adolescence

Until the early nineteenth century, the Anglo-American legal system treated young people who violated the criminal law, for better and worse, much as it did other offenders. Communities relied upon self-policing, social integration, and noninstitutional mechanisms to maintain informal social control. Family relationships, frequent interaction, and the good opinion of others induced most community members to conform. Colonists fined, flogged, and "shamed" in the pillory and stocks their local, minor deviants and whipped and then expelled outside "rogues and vagabonds" (Rothman 1971). Colonists executed recidivist and serious criminals, and young people suffered the same fate as did their elders (Rothman 1971; Streib 1987).

Before the Progressives created the juvenile court, the common law's infancy *mens rea* defense provided the only formal legal doctrine to protect young offenders charged with crimes (Fox 1970b; McCarthy 1977a; Weissman 1983; Walkover 1984). The classical criminal law recognized that sanctions could not deter persons who did not know "right from wrong," for example, those who are mentally ill and the very young, and excused them from criminal liability. The insanity and infancy defenses attempted to identify those offenders who lacked criminal responsibility and could not be blamed for their acts. The common-law infancy gradations reflected the intuitions of ancient Hebrews, Moslems, and Romans that infants—children incapable of speech—enjoyed immunity from criminal punishment because they lacked the understanding of "right from wrong" necessary for criminal responsibility (Ludwig 1950). The age at which a boy could begin to do a man's work at about seven years of age marked the necessary mastery of language and the stage at which he also might commit a man's crime. The common-law infancy doctrine conclusively presumed that children younger than seven years of age lacked criminal capacity, treated those fourteen years of age and older as fully responsible adults, and created a rebuttable presumption that those between seven and fourteen years of age lacked criminal capacity. In almost every culture, puberty marked the upper limit at which a society excused criminal conduct by young people (Ludwig 1950). Early Puritan statutes incorporated these common-law distinctions and sanctioned younger children's misdeeds, such as lying or profaning the Sabbath, differently from those of youths over fourteen years of age (Hawes 1971).

Institutions for Youths: Houses of Refuge and Reformatories

During the early nineteenth century, the social construction of adolescence as a developmental stage distinct from adulthood and new sensibilities about children began to pose problems for the criminal justice system. Judges sometimes dismissed charges, and juries occasionally refused to criminally convict young offenders in order to avoid imposing excessively harsh sentences. Dismissal or nullification excused from formal social control some youths, especially those charged with minor offenses (Fox 1970a; Platt 1977). Nineteenth-century reformers began to create special institutions for youths to avoid exempting them from criminal liability and social control (Sutton 1988; Bernard 1992). In the early-to mid-nineteenth century, the first age-segregated youth institutions, the houses of refuge, appeared in the East Coast cities (Hawes 1971; Mennel 1973). By midcentury, reformatories and youth institutions spread to the rural and midwestern regions of the country (Schlossman 1977; Sutton 1988). By the end of the century, the juvenile court appeared in Chicago, spread to other major urban centers, and completed the process of separating the system of social control of youths from adults (Platt 1977; Ryerson 1978; Rothman 1980). The temporal and geographic emergence of these various institutions corresponds with the processes of modernization, urbanization, and the social construction of childhood analyzed in chapter 1.

Houses of Refuge

Historians trace many features of the Progressive juvenile court to the earlier houses of refuge—"the formal beginning of the modern juvenile justice system"—that emerged in eastern cities during the middle third of the nineteenth century (Sutton 1988:43). The organizational differentiation and the creation of separate penal institutions for youths preceded the emergence of the juvenile court. "[I]n almost every state the legal and ideological innovations typically associated with the juvenile court (e.g., the extension of legal control over noncriminal children, the denial of due process, and the legalization of the rehabilitative ideal) had occurred before the advent of children's courts, as a result of earlier legislation establishing juvenile reformatories" (Sutton 1983:917). Correctional segregation of the young antedated their judicial separation.

The houses of refuge constituted the first specialized institutions for the formal social control of youth. Refuges appeared in the larger, eastern urban centers, first in New York and Boston in 1825, and in Philadelphia in 1828, in conjunction with the first burst of industrialization, immigration, and urbanization in Jacksonian-era America (Finestone 1976; Hawes 1971; Mennel 1973; Pickett 1969). The increased reliance on formal social control occurred during the transition from a rural agrarian society, in which community and family provided cohesion and informal social control, to a more heterogeneous, urban industrial society that required state-administered institutional controls (Rothman 1971). The migration of people from the countryside to work in factories and an increase in immigration to the cities weakened traditional social control. The development of a market economy and growth of commerce in cities widened social class differences and aroused fear of the poor. Early-nineteenth-century Americans attributed rising juvenile crime rates to "environmental corruption" caused by immigration, urbanization, poverty, and the disintegration of the earlier, stable social order (Katz 1968; Rothman 1971).

During the first third of the nineteenth century, Jacksonian-era reformers constructed a variety of institutions to isolate, insulate, and control deviants—prisons and penitentiaries for criminals, mental asylums for mentally ill persons, houses of refuge for delinquents, orphanages for dependent youths, and poorhouses for "paupers" or the able-bodied impoverished (Katz 1986). They created refuges and other asylums to respond to the specific problems and disorganization caused by social change and to provide examples of proper discipline to guide the community (Rothman 1971; Sutton 1988). Refuges shared many institution-building elements with the early "common schools" of the same era that also sought to bring young people under the formal control of public authority. Common schools provided a means by which to exhort middle- and upper-class urban families to provide moral discipline for their children; refuges provided an organizational tool with which to remove the children of the urban immigrants and lower classes whose families did not provide adequate moral direction (Finkelstein 1985). Both types of institutions reflected the process of nation building and the creation of a strong centralized state government with the legal authority and organizational ability to address social problems previously resolved informally and locally.

The reformers who built the refuges and other asylums attributed crime and deviance to "environmental corruption" associated with social change. In the aftermath of the American War of Independence, Enlightenment political doctrines influenced American penal reformers who assumed that rational criminal laws would deter most offenders and obviate the need for other forms of punishment (Hawes 1971; Sutton 1988). Enlightenment thinkers such as John Locke, Thomas Hobbes, and Jean-Jacques Rousseau posited that rational human beings possessed free will and made choices for which they bore responsibility. Jeremy Bentham used the "pleasure-pain" principle—people seek happiness and avoid pain—to devise a "utilitarian calculus" of penalties. Reformers assumed that graded sanctions would deter crimes if offenders derived more unhappiness from punishment than they gained pleasure from committing an offense (Cullen and Gilbert 1982). Because they assumed that rational actors would not choose to commit crimes and thereby suffer the consequences, penal reformers devoted less energy to devising correctional programs for those who miscalculated than they did to finely calibrating the scale of offenses and penalties (Rothman 1971).

Not surprisingly, rational criminal law reforms failed to eliminate crime, and Jacksonian reformers then studied the life histories of criminals, paupers, and dependents and traced the roots of deviance to their early childhood (Sutton 1988). Enlightenment doctrines viewed children as born innocent, rather than depraved, and attributed deviance to external corruption rather than to innate evil human nature. Locke's theories of youth and education characterized children as blank slates, tabula rasa, "as white paper, or wax to be molded or fashioned as one pleases (Pickett 1969:108)." Jacksonian-era reformers observed in the fluid urban life of early modernizing America ample sources of environmental corruption. They discerned a recurring relationship between a corrupting environment, pauperism, and subsequent criminality. Children who failed to receive appropriate family discipline fell victim to the vice and disorder rampant in the community and developed into criminals. Children failed to receive proper familial guidance for a variety of reasons: parental character flaws or neglect; family disruption by death, divorce, or desertion; and youths who left their homes and parental control.

Reformers believed that they could change deviants by removing them from evil influences, placing them in a properly constructed environment, and imposing a restorative discipline. Prisons and reformatories for adults and refuges for children reflected this shift from informal to formal institutional mechanisms of control. If adverse environmental influences caused deviance, then a facility that removed temptation and required them to work could undo it (Rothman 1971). Prisons, asylums, and refuges separated their inmates from the community and isolated them from each other. Because the reformers who managed the refuges often attributed crimes of youths to their parents' inadequacies, they removed children from their families to the greatest extent possible.

Early sponsors of the refuge and asylum movement included religiously motivated crusaders striving for moral and social uplift and conservative business elites frightened by social disorder and instability (Pickett 1969; Fox 1970a). In the early 1800s, juvenile delinquency consisted primarily of urban property crime committed by lower-class males against middle-and upper-class adults (Bernard 1992). Many of the reform efforts of the period reflected "self conscious efforts of moralists of the propertied classes to demarcate the life-style of middle class youths from that of children of the laboring poor," to reestablish social order, and to preserve existing property and status relationships (Kett 1977:87).

Refuge sponsors intended the houses of refuge literally as sanctuaries and havens that sheltered and reformed. The emerging ideology of *childhood* vulnerability and the social construction of *adolescent* malleability added an imperative to intervene to control youths' deviance and to separate adolescents from adult offenders (Schlossman 1977; Sutton 1988). Vagrant youths who lacked the ability to read or write, skills, or a trade would mature into a dangerous or dependent class of criminals or paupers—able-bodied men unwilling to work—who threatened the middle classes (Hawes 1971). Charles Dickens's description of young Oliver Twist's initiation into a life of crime under the tutelage of "the Artful Dodger" provided a vivid portrayal of life among the "dangerous classes" and influenced American's perceptions of their own social problems.

Many legal features incorporated into the juvenile court first appeared in the laws creating the houses of refuge. Refuge legislation embodied three legal innovations: a formal age-based distinction between juvenile and adults offenders and their institutional separation, the use of indeterminate commitments, and a broadened legal authority that encompassed both criminal offenders and neglected and incorrigible children. Reform groups used the ideology of childhood to create a "preventive model of control that focuses particular attention on noncriminal forms of juvenile misbehavior, a treatment regime that revolves around confining and classifying offenders, and a practical operating agenda characterized by coercion and repression" (Sutton 1988:68).

Refuges maintained flexible admission policies and received their young charges from judicial commitments, by referrals from overseers of the poor, from local constables who apprehended homeless waifs, and from parents who sought to control a disobedient child (Rothman 1971). They exercised jurisdiction over a vast range of "proper objects" under sixteen years of age—criminal offenders; disobedient children; orphaned, dependent, neglected, or unsupervised children; and other novices in antisocial behavior (Pickett 1969). Massachusetts legislation, for example, authorized refuge managers to receive "all such children who shall be convicted of criminal offenses, or.... [who violate laws] for suppressing and punishing of rogues, vagabonds, common beggars, and other idle, disorderly and lewd persons," as well as "all children who live an idle or dissolute life, whose parents are dead, or if living, from drunkenness or other vices, neglect to provide any suitable employment, or exercise any salutary control over said children" (Hawes 1971:52). Reformers intervened proactively to remove young people from the streets and to prevent them from becoming paupers or committing offenses. Refuges' emphasis on minor offenders or protocriminal behavior provided a precursor to the juvenile court's "status" jurisdiction. Reformers regarded minor offenders, unsupervised children, and children of immigrant parents as social victims and appropriate objects of benevolence. Refuges combined the discretionary authority of the family with the coercive power of the state.

Because most refuge inmates had not committed criminal offenses, the institution functioned as a juvenile poorhouse to combat incipient pauperism rather than simply as a penal facility to control criminality. In *The Cycle of Juvenile Justice*, Thomas Bernard emphasizes the close linkage between "pauperism" and "delinquency": "The literal meaning of the term 'delinquency' refers to a neglect or failure to perform tasks required by law or duty. . . . That meaning is quite similar to the meaning of the term 'pauper,' which refers to a poor person who neglects or fails to perform the tasks required by law or duty in society: hard, honest work" (Bernard 1992:67). By this analogy, the institutional response to delinquency coincided with responses to other forms of deviance such as poorhouses for paupers (Katz 1986). Refuge advocates exercised state authority to alleviate the adverse impact of social and economic changes on young people. They created private, charitable organizations chartered by the state but supported and run by philanthropic citizens. They characterized their reformatories as "schools" in the broadest educational sense to train "children in industry, morality, [and] the means to earn a living" (Schlossman 1977:10).

The legal doctrine of *parens patriae*—the right and responsibility of the state to substitute its own control over children for that of the natural parents when the latter appeared unable or unwilling to meet their responsibilities or when the child posed a problem for the community—provided the formal justification to intervene (Cogan 1970; Curtis 1976; Pisciotta 1982). The doctrine of *parens patriae* originated in the English chancery courts to protect the Crown's interests in feudal succession and to ensure the orderly transfer of property interests and feudal duties from one generation to the next and established royal authority to administer the estates of orphaned minors with property (Cogan 1970; Rendelman 1971). In the American colonies, local poor laws authorized the state to act in loco parentis to separate children from their destitute or neglectful parents (Rendelman 1971; Katz 1986).

In 1838, *parens patriae* formally entered American jurisprudence to justify the commitment of a juvenile to a refuge. In the leading case of the period, *Ex parte Crouse* (4 Whart. 9 [Pa. 1838]; Fox 1970a; Rothman 1980a), the Pennsylvania Supreme Court rejected legal challenges to peremptory incarceration of troublesome youths and uncritically accepted the refuge managers' humanitarian claims. A justice of the peace summarily committed Mary Ann Crouse to the Philadelphia House of Refuge upon her mother's petition that she could not manage her daughter. When Mary Ann's father objected to her confinement without the right to a jury trial, the Pennsylvania court dismissed his complaint noting that

> [t]he error on which the objection is founded is twofold. First in supposing that the mere commission of crimes is the reason for admission to the house; and secondly in imputing to the consequences of that admission the character and name of punishment. . . .

The object of the charity is reformation, by training its inmates to industry; by imbuing their minds with principles of morality and religion; by furnishing them with the means to earn a living; and above all, by separating them from the corrupting influences of improper associates. To this end, may not the natural parents, when unequal to the task of education, or unworthy of it, be superseded by the *parens patriae*, or common guardian of the community? It is to be remembered that the public has a paramount interest in the virtue and knowledge of its members, and that, of strict right, the business of education belongs to it. . . . The infant has been snatched from a course which must have ended in confirmed depravity; and not only is the restraint of her person lawful, but it would be an act of extreme cruelty to release her from it. (4 Whart. at 11 [Pa. 1838])

The courts adopted the refuge managers' rationale that it functioned as "a residential school for underprivileged children," an extension of the fledgling common-school movement (Schlossman 1977:10). Opinions like *Crouse* also reflected broader American legal and cultural views that "universal education was a social panacea; that children, especially children of the poor, had few legal rights; that impoverished parents lacked moral character and were incapable of providing healthy conditions for child rearing; and that anything which the government could to do instill their children with proper values was for the better" (Schlossman 1977:17).

The *Crouse* opinion reflected the ideology of environmentalism and preventive intervention, the breadth of the *parens patriae* doctrine, and the futility of legal challenges to state intervention. In *Crouse* the Court took the concept of *parens patriae* originally developed by chancery courts as an equitable concept applied to property rights among private parties and "transplanted it into a branch of the poor law where it was used to justify the state statutory schemes to part poor or incompetent parents from their children" (Rendelman 1971: 219). The *parens patriae* ideology assumed that public institutions could compensate for the failures and deficiencies of private families.

Refuge managers did not differentiate among criminal, dependent, orphaned, and troublesome youths and exercised the same legal authority regardless of the underlying basis of their commitment. Because cases such as *Crouse* did not distinguish between criminal and noncriminal conduct, Progressive reformers later adopted the refuges' strategy of undifferentiated commitments to bolster their claims that juvenile court delinquency proceedings were civil rather than criminal cases (Fox 1970a). Characterizing commitment proceedings as civil actions allowed both the refuges and the later juvenile courts to deny to youths criminal procedural safeguards such as the right to a jury trial.

Houses of refuge removed offenders from the community, isolated them from contaminating influences, and imposed a strict discipline to inculcate obedience and respect for authority (Pickett 1969; Rothman 1971; Mennel 1983). Refuge statutes abrogated parental authority, transferred legal custody to the refuge managers, and authorized them to minimize a child's contacts with relatives or prior associates. Managers imposed a routine of labor to teach work discipline and inculcate obedience to authority and provided education and religious training to reform deviants. Historians characterize a refuges as a "juvenile penitentiary," a scaled-down prison that reflected the managers' ambivalence about uplifting poor children and caretaking potentially dangerous young criminals (Schlossman 1977). Although refuge managers technically exercised jurisdiction over a youth for the duration of minority, typically children spent only one or two years in an institution before managers bound them as apprentices or placed them out with a rural farm family (Pickett 1969).

Reform Schools

In the mid-nineteenth century, penologists constructed a second type of youth institution—the reformatory—to shelter and reform young deviants (Kett 1977; Platt 1977; Schlossman 1977). Unlike urban houses of refuge, sponsors of family reform schools located them in rural pastoral settings to provide a wholesome agrarian environment. Several factors influenced their decisions to locate reform schools in rural settings: anti-urban sentiments and a desire to insulate children from corrupting city influences; the practices of refuge managers to place out urban youths with rural families; the work of Charles Loring Brace and the Children's Aid Society, which systematically placed urban orphan and dependent youths with midwestern farm families; and European "rustification" experiments that used a "cottage plan" to replicate a family environment to treat vagrant and criminal urban youths (Hawes 1971).

Charles Loring Brace, an influential American child welfare reformer, founded the Children's Aid Society and placed orphaned and abandoned urban children with rural families (Hawes 1971). Placing out homeless children in "a clean wholesome environment far removed from the deleterious influences of the urban squalor" provided an attractive alternative to housing them in institutions and orphanages (Lindsey 1994:14). Placing-out constituted a precursor of contemporary child welfare and foster-care policies and established that acting in a child's "best interests" took precedence over the interests of the child's family.

Massachusetts created the first state reform schools: the Lyman School for Boys in 1847 and the Lancaster School for Girls in 1855 (Schlossman 1977; Brenzel 1980). These and subsequent family reform schools used the "cottage plan" model, a setting in which a virtuous couple presided over a cottage of youths, provided a stable family environment, and supervised a program of labor and vocational training (Platt 1977; Mennel 1983). Reformatory managers adopted the cottage plan to replicate Brace's idealized rural farm families and used agricultural labor as a source of reform. Family reform schools expected daily personal contacts and expanded relationships to strengthen inmates' emotional bonding to their surrogate parents and to spur their moral regeneration. This correctional strategy also reflected the ideological changes in childhood that occurred during this period and that emphasized affectional discipline rather than physical coercion to persuade the child to good citizenship (Schlossman 1977).

The institutional responses coincided with nascent urbanism, early immigration, and the loss of local informal cohesion. Beginning in the 1840s, increased immigration by the Irish and then by successive waves of other ethnic groups posed a growing threat to social stability. For American society, acutely apprehensive about the disruptive influences of "different" people, incarceration provided an attractive strategy to control the poor and immigrants. Environmental explanations of deviance rationalized policies of confinement and supported programs of rigorous discipline. Despite refuge and reformatory managers' initial optimism about the corrective influences of well-constructed environments, by the end of the Civil War, both types of institutions became increasingly custodial and repressive (Rothman 1971, 1980). By the 1850s and 1860s, prisons, asylums, refuges, and reformatories had become little more than custodial warehouses, the special preserves of the poor and foreign born and their children. "Those who sought to reform juvenile delinquents in mid-19th century America spoke the lofty language of nurture and environmentalism. Reform schools, they claimed, were not prisons but home-like institutions, veritable founts of generous sentiment. In fact, they were prisons, often brutal and disorderly ones" (Kett 1977:132). As children of immigrants and the poor increasingly populated refuges and reformatories, the conditions deteriorated further. In an early version of "blaming the victims," institutional managers contended that "the aliens had only themselves to blame for the decline of the asylum, for they were untreatable or unmanageable" (Rothman 1980:24).

The Juvenile Court

Ideological changes in the cultural conception of children and in strategies of social control at the end of the nineteenth century culminated in the creation of a separate juvenile court in Cook County, Illinois, in 1899. Although the juvenile court contained some new features, such as a separate judiciary, earlier generations of refuge and reformatory innovators formulated most of the elements of a separate juvenile justice system: specialized penal institutions to segregate youths from adults, expansive legal authority over noncriminal youths, and a denial of the criminal procedural safeguards provided adults offenders. Establishing separate correctional institutions for youths constituted a condition precedent to the extension of jurisdiction over noncriminal offenders and the creation of a separate juvenile court. "[T]he reform school served as the vehicle and prerequisite for the formal, legal creation of delinquency as a deviant role for children. The institution not only required application of the delinquent label to juveniles who would under any circumstances have been considered criminal, but also implied inclusion of misbehaving and mistreated children and exempted them from the rule of law"

(Sutton 1988:119). Thus, the juvenile court emerged primarily as a "cere-monial" institution that enhanced and ideologically legitimated the ideology of childhood and ratified the institutional system of child social control that emerged during the nineteenth century.

The juvenile court culminated the century-long process of reconfiguring and differentiating youths from adults. The *idea* of adolescence as a distinctive stage of development provided the impetus legally to separate young offenders from criminals and to create a social welfare alternative to respond to criminal and noncriminal misconduct by youths. Historical accounts of the juvenile court movement vary from progressive-liberal to critical-revisionist. The for-mer view juvenile courts as benevolent humanitarian efforts to save children from social disorder and to protect them from their own flawed development and the adult criminal justice system (Hawes 1971). Revisionists characterize juvenile courts as expansive agencies of coercive social control that used their discretionary powers primarily to impose sanctions on poor and immigrant children (Fox 1970a; Platt 1977; Schlossman 1977; Rothman 1980; Sutton 1988).

Criminal justice and social control policies reflect underlying ideological assumptions—unstated presuppositions, values, and beliefs—about causes of crime and appropriate tactics and strategies to reduce it (Cullen and Gilbert 1982). Just as childhood represents a social construct, the particular forms of punishment also constitute a type of cultural artifact. "These cultural patterns structure the ways in which we think about criminals, providing the intellec-tual frameworks (whether scientific or religious or commonsensical) through which we see these individuals, understand their motivations, and dispose of their cases. Cultural patterns also structure the ways in which we feel about offenders" (Garland 1990:195). Classical criminal law assumed rational, free-willed moral actors made voluntary choices to commit crimes, and they de-served prescribed consequences for their acts. The criminal law reflected a retributive jurisprudence, blamed and punished offenders for the quality of their choices, the mens rea, and reacted to people as moral ends, not as objects or means to manipulate according to social utility.

In the late nineteenth and early twentieth centuries, Progressives refor-mulated their ideology of crime, modified criminal justice administration, and based social control practices on new theories about human behavior and social deviance. The ideological reconfiguration placed Progressive criminal justice programs on several cultural, jurisprudential, and criminological fault lines. Positive criminology asserted that antecedent forces—biological, psy-chological, social, or environmental—"determined" or caused criminal be-havior. Reflecting the modern rationalizing tendencies, they sought scientifi-cally to identify the causes of crime and delinquency in order to prescribe an appropriate remedy (Allen 1964; Matza 1964). "[T]he new scientific crimi-nologies put forward a conception of the criminal as an abnormal human type, shaped by genetic, psychological, or social factors and, to some extent, unable to resist an inherent tendency toward criminal conduct. Once again, these new conceptions helped bring about a restructuring of penal practices, so that a formal process of character assessment. . . . and specialist institutions and regimes were developed to deal with character types such as 'habituals,', 'inebriates', 'psychopaths', and 'delinquents' " (Garland 1990:208).

Positivism attributed criminal behavior to deterministic forces that compelled the offender to act as he did, rather than to a deliberate exercise of "malicious" free will. Determinism reduced offenders' moral responsibility for their crimes, and penologists attempted to reform them rather than to punish them for their offenses (Allen 1964, 1981; Matza 1964). "The positivist model demanded consideration of each criminal's background and personal traits as part of an intelligent disposition. It demanded a system of individualized justice in which punishment and deterrence were of limited relevance" (Ryerson 1978:22). Progressives shaped sanctions to fit the criminal rather than simply the crime.

Scientific Rationality and Positive Criminology

Progressives' ideological reinterpretation of crime and social control strategies drew support from several contemporaneous intellectual developments. Positivism constituted one manifestation of intellectual modernization and the cultural emphasis on scientific rationality, professionalism, and expertise. The Progressives' emphasis on scientific explanations reflected their continuing quest to subject all social problems to rational technical solutions from "scientific" management to the cure of crime. Some social scientists linked Charles Darwin's theory of evolution in *Origin of the Species* (1859) to changes in thinking about social organization and criminal behavior that influenced the directions of positive criminology. Louis Pasteur and Robert Koch's research on "germ theory" in the 1870s and 1880s provided a scientific basis for the practice of medicine and represented another intellectual development that inspired Progressives' reforms of social control practices.

Darwin's theory of evolution appealed to conservative businessmen and intellectuals, who asserted that in social and economic matters, as in biology, the competitive "struggle for existence" and the "survival of the fittest" would produce the best and strongest. Herbert Spencer popularized social Darwinism in his *Social Statistics*, decried public efforts to aid the diseased or the poor through welfare, public education, urban hygiene, or economic regulation and objected that social engineering interfered with processes of "natural selection" that weeded out the poor and unfit (Hofstadter 1955). Although Spencer's social Darwinism and similar theoretical formulations by his American counterparts, William Graham Sumner and Edward L. Youmans, achieved great popularity, a "kinder and gentler" version of social Darwinian thought asserted that people could control and modify the environment and thereby shape the course of evolution. Lester Frank Ward criticized the antireform implications of Spencer's social Darwinism and asserted in *Dynamic Sociology* that sociology provided an intellectual tool for individual and societal improvement (Wiebe 1967).

Positivist criminology built on Darwin's evolutionary ideas. Caesar Lombroso developed a theory of biological determinism that applied the scientific method to modern criminology. He gathered empirical data, made objective observations, and formulated a causal theory that criminals were born, not made; that crime was in their nature rather than their nurture; and that human action was determined rather than chosen. He identified criminals on the basis of certain physical "stigmata"—slopping foreheads, jutting jaws, absence of earlobes, irregularities of the skull, brain, face, and the like (Hawes 1971; Platt 1977). He observed a relationship between these physical characteristics and behavioral problems—irritability, vanity, vengefulness, and lack of moral awareness or character development. Lombroso found a disproportionately larger number of physical anomalies among criminals he studied than among the normal populations. He concluded that habitual criminals differed from normal people and represented atavistic throwbacks to earlier, more primitive stages of human evolution, a physically and psychologically distinct biological type (Hawes 1971). Social Darwinism, biological determinism, and scientific criminology also confirmed popular prejudices about the characteristics of the "criminal class," whose features and physiognomy corresponded closely to those of the waves of southern and eastern European immigrants pouring into America around the turn of the century.

Criminology's attribution of deviance to antecedent factors, such as biological determinism, redirected research efforts to identify the causes of crime by scientifically studying offenders (Ryerson 1978). Richard Dugdale's examination of the Jukes family in 1875, *A Study in Crime, Pauperism, Disease, and Heredity* represented one of the first applications of the scientific method to the study of crime in America. Dugdale attempted to explain the relative contributions of heredity and environment—nature and nurture—to the high levels of insanity, criminality, and vice among several generations of Jukes (Hawes 1971).

Although early positivistic criminology attributed criminal behavior to inherited or biological factors, social "pathologists" increasingly emphasized environmental explanations that attributed crime and deviance to social and economic conditions associated with industrialization, urbanization, and structural modernization. Progressive reformers appreciated the vulnerability of the urban immigrant poor to economic forces, ghetto slums, and social conditions beyond their control, although they often condemned those who succumbed to these deleterious influences with a touch of moralism (Platt 1977; Trattner 1984).

> The industrial city had many evils: its pace of life made parents too busy and too insensitive to supervise their children properly; its lavishness excited cupidity; in its crowds, the activities of criminals went unnoticed and potential criminals were emboldened by seeing that crime could pay; its economy drew children too early into the labor force, where they met adults of questionable character and where they found too much freedom. The city intensified the struggle for existence: the weakest were left by the wayside to grow bitter and

antisocial, and others developed a mood of suspicion and distrust. (Ryerson 1978:24)

The beneficial influences of the American social order could not penetrate those alien enclaves.

During the Progressive Era, the social science disciplines burst on the intellectual scene and entered university curricula (Hawes 1971; Bledstein 1976). Many college graduates studied the new disciplines of psychology, sociology, criminology, and social work and took courses on topics like "social pathology," "punishment of criminality," and "public and private charities" (Rothman 1980:46). As the processes of social reform became more scientific and professional, Progressives believed that the social sciences provided them with the tools to solve the problems caused by social dislocations. Social service personnel had a professional stake in environmental explanations of crime because those factors provided variables that they could manipulate and greater opportunities to intervene than did deterministic biological models (Lubove 1967; Hawes 1971). They could ameliorate social problems by altering the physical or social conditions that caused them through slum clearance, urban renewal, improved sanitation, education, and similar programs. Although professional practitioners purported to apply scientific principles, the rudimentary state of social science knowledge often left them free to impose their own personal prejudices about the causes and cures of deviance (Ryerson 1978).

Germ Theory and the Medical Model

Louis Pasteur and Robert Koch's discovery of "germs" represented another intellectual development that strongly influenced Progressives' reformulation of social control strategies. Before the mid-nineteenth century, most medical practitioners lacked basic scientific knowledge about the causal role of "germs"—bacteria, bacilli, and viruses—in disease or the genetic or functional causes of most illnesses. Medical practice consisted primarily of symptomatic treatment, folk remedies, and supportive comfort or leeching and bloodletting to relieve evil "humours." Germ theory provided physicians with a scientific foundation for their treatments. Once physicians established a causal relationship between particular microbes and diseases, they could develop appropriate treatment strategies and even preventive vaccines. The development of scientific knowledge about diseases, the elaboration and testing of causal models, and surgical and technological innovations to treat or prevent diseases transformed the practice of medicine from "bleeding" in a barbershop into a respected intellectual profession (Starr 1982).

At the turn of the century, Progressive criminal justice reformers aspired to scientific status and sought to strengthen the similarities between the causal determinism of the natural sciences and those of the social sciences. In its quest for scientific legitimacy, criminology borrowed both its methodology and vocabulary from the increasingly scientific medical profession. Just as germs caused diseases, deterministic assumptions redirected criminological research scientifically to study offenders in order to identify the causes of crime. The ability to identify the causes of crime implied the correlative ability to "cure" it through appropriate interventions. Medical metaphors—pathology, infection, diagnosis, and treatment—provided popular analogues for criminal justice professionals. The medical model of criminality emphasized diagnosis, prescription, and intervention to cure the problems of each offender.

Rehabilitative Ideal

The conjunction of positivist criminology, medical analogies to "treat" criminals, and the burgeoning social pathology professions provided the undergirding of the rehabilitative ideal, a prominent feature of all Progressive criminal justice reforms. Positivist ideology encouraged an activist strategy, and Progressives introduced a number of criminal justice reforms at the turn of the century—probation, parole, indeterminate sentences, and the juvenile court. All of these reforms emphasized "open-ended, informal, and highly flexible policies" to allow an individualized, case-by-case approach to the delinquent or criminal (Rothman 1980:43). Criminal justice professionals required unstructured, flexible discretion to diagnose, rehabilitate, and regulate each offender. They insisted that the ability to identify the causes and prescribe the cures for delinquency required an individualized approach, precluded uniform treatment or standardized criteria, and fostered maximum deference to professional expertise.

Probably not coincidentally, the increased variability, indeterminacy, and discretion associated with rehabilitative social control practices corresponded with the increasing volume and changing characteristics of offenders during this period. Just as the earlier houses of refuge appeared in the larger cities of the East Coast during their initial processes of urbanization, the juvenile court first made its appearance in Chicago under similar circumstances. The population of Chicago more than doubled between 1880 and 1890, and three-quarters of its adult population was born outside the United States. The influx of foreign immigrants evoked a more repressive nativist reaction to reassert their cultural influence (Finestone 1976).

Francis Allen has described elegantly the central assumptions of the rehabilitative ideal:

> [It] assumed, first, that human behavior is the product of antecedent causes. These causes can be identified. . . . Knowledge of the antecedents of human behavior makes possible an approach to the scientific control of human behavior. Finally, . . . it is assumed that measures employed to treat the convicted offender should serve a therapeutic function; that such measures should be designed to effect changes in the behavior of the convicted person in the interest of his own happiness, health, and satisfaction and in the interest of social defense. (Allen 1964:26)

A flourishing rehabilitative ideal requires both a belief in the malleability of human behavior, and a basic moral consensus about the appropriate directions of human change (Allen 1981). It requires a cultural consensus about means and ends and agreement about the goals of change and the strategies necessary to achieve them. Progressives believed that the new human behavioral sciences provided them with the necessary "technology," the tools with which to systematically change people. They also believed in the virtues of their social order and the propriety of imposing their middle-class values on immigrants and the poor. "Progressives were equally convinced of the viability of cultural uplift and of the supreme desirability of middle class life in cultural as well as material terms. . . . The model was clear: all Americans were to become middle class Americans" (Rothman 1980:49). No one could accuse the Progressives of "political correctness" or a hypersensitivity to diversity or multiculturalism.

Industrialization produced unprecedented prosperity that disinclined Progressives to seek radical alterations of the American political, economic, and social order. Rather, they pursued ameliorative reforms to restore social stability and maintain preexisting allocations of wealth and power. Modifying certain social conditions would allow immigrants and the poor to experience upward mobility and to share the Progressives' cultural values and high standard of living.

While positivism influenced Progressive policies to reform offenders rather than to punish them for their offense, it also diverted their attention from the broader, social structural policy implications of the reformers' analyses. The medical-clinical "rehabilitative" paradigm located the problems of poverty, crime, and delinquency in individuals rather than in their social context. "Reforms such as the juvenile court are ideologically significant because they preserved the notion that social problems (in this case delinquency, dependency, and neglect) could be dealt with on a case-by-case basis, rather than through broad-based efforts to redistribute wealth and power throughout society" (Krisberg and Austin 1993:32). Although Progressives recognized that environmental and social factors "caused" delinquency, their cultural self confidence induced them to design their programs to minister to deviant individuals rather than to alter criminogenic social structural features. Progressivism blended a liberal humanitarian desire to use governmental power to aid the less fortunate with a conservative impulse to control and repress those who differed from them and posed a threat to the social order. It rejected a more encompassing critique of political economy, the social structural sources of inequality or the policy implications of such analyses.

The Progressive reformers who created the juvenile court embraced positivist theory and attempted to implement the rehabilitative ideal more completely than did any other criminal justice innovators. In part, Progressives' greater enthusiasm reflected the social construction of childhood and the apparent prospects it promised of greater success. The ideology of *adolescence* emphasized the plasticity and malleability of young people. Child-study theory posited a process of developmental unfolding and implied that a properly structured moral and social environment could direct it. Because children represented the future, Progressives invested their greatest hope and optimism in saving children rather than in salvaging their poor and immigrant parents. "The child was the carrier of tomorrow's hope whose innocence and freedom make him singularly receptive to education in rational, humane behavior. Protect him, nurture him and in his manhood he would create the bright new world of the Progressive's vision" (Wiebe 1967:169).

Progressive reformers conceived of the juvenile court as a specialized agency, staffed by experts and designed to serve the needs of the "child at risk," whether an offender or a dependent or neglected child. Juvenile court professionals made discretionary, individualized treatment decisions to achieve benevolent goals and social uplift and substituted a scientific and preventive approach for the traditional punitive goals of the criminal law. The juvenile court's treatment ideology attributed young people's misdeeds to their environment or flawed developmental process rather than to a vicious free will. The social construction of childhood characterized children as innocent and free from vice, responsible neither for acting out their innate biological imperatives nor for failing to develop into responsible adults. Reformers responded to children's misconduct or social circumstances with a constructive nonpunitive strategy that "concentrated on providing a healthy, respectable family environment that would not interfere with and might guide the natural unfolding of a moral adult" (Ryerson 1978:30). If misbehavior represented a normal part of biological and social development, then moral education and social intervention would enable young people to internalize self-discipline and develop character (Kett 1977). The juvenile court intervened to ensure the *future welfare* of youths rather than to *punish* them for their past *offenses*. The medical model of delinquency rejected notions of *deserved punishment* because no child bore responsibility for her social or developmental circumstances and therefore her conduct. Thus, the treatment model rejected the idea of individual responsibility embodied in criminal law.

The juvenile court used the same legal justification, *parens patriae*, that houses of refuge employed previously to substitute state control over children for that of inadequate natural parents. Characterizing delinquency proceedings as civil fulfilled reformers' desire to remove children from the adult criminal system and allowed them to supervise and treat children more flexibly. By repudiating punishment, reformers could regulate adolescents' "lifestyle" behaviors—smoking, sexual activity, truancy, immorality, stubbornness, vagrancy, or living a wayward, idle, and dissolute life—that the criminal law typically ignored but that Progressives regarded as evidence of premature adulthood.

The juvenile court movement sought to remove youths completely from the criminal justice system as part of the broader social and cultural differentiation of children from adults. The criminal law's treatment of youths and adults as moral and psychological equals appalled the Progressives. In Chicago, at the end of the nineteenth century, adult criminal courts dealt with any offender over the age of ten and provided no specialized institutions or procedures for such young law violators (Hawes 1971; Colomy and Kretzmann

1995). Progressive "child savers" found the conviction and imprisonment of young people as adults "deeply shocking because it flew in the face of cultural conceptions of childhood which they and others held. It represented a scandal, a blatant contradiction between law and culture which became the object of reforming campaigns and was eventually resolved by legislation setting up special reformatories, juvenile courts, and a more welfare-oriented approach to young offenders" (Garland 1990:201–2). Although the ideal of institutionally separating juveniles from adults motivated the earlier House of Refuge movement, the continued commingling of juvenile with adult offenders led Progressives to advocate a completely separate judicial system for youths, a juvenile justice system.

The Progressive model of the juvenile court attempted to uncouple social welfare from penal social control. It distinguished the functions of juvenile courts from those performed by criminal courts by emphasizing assistance to children as a means of controlling their misbehavior. Progressives regarded the interests of young people and society as congruent; intervention to aid the child served the "best interests" of both the youth and the community. As a result, juvenile courts' architects envisioned the juvenile court as a welfare system rather than just a children's criminal court. Moreover, a desire for greater supervision and control, rather than for leniency, animated many reformers (Platt 1977). They sought a system to intervene affirmatively in the lives of many young people rather than one that simply punished younger offenders more leniently for their misdeeds. The rehabilitative juvenile court provided the middle ground between punishing youths in criminal court and overlooking minor misbehavior and allowing a youth's criminal career to escalate.

Status Jurisdiction

Conceived as a system of social welfare rather than of punishment, juvenile courts brought within their ambit of control young people's behavior that criminal courts previously ignored or handled informally. In addition to children who committed crimes or violated local ordinances, juvenile courts' jurisdiction also encompassed young people who engaged in behavior that would not be criminal if engaged in by adults: truancy, sexual immorality, "stubbornness," living a "wayward, idle, and dissolute life," and other manifestations of adult autonomy that conflicted with the ideology childhood (Sutton 1988). This broader jurisdictional definition included not only a child's criminal acts but her *status* or condition of being, indeed, her entire lifestyle. Even without empirically establishing a causal connection between, for example, profanity and robbery, Progressives used the status jurisdiction to legislate and regulate "their preferences in the realm of manners and morals. By allowing noncriminal behavior on the part of children to trigger the intervention of a probation officer into family life, the juvenile court reformers were placing their movement among a number of others which were, in the progressive period, sending numerous missionaries from the dominant culture to the lower classes to acculturate immigrants, to teach mothers household management and to supervise the recipients of charity" (Ryerson 1978:47). Thus, the status jurisdiction embodied the newer cultural conception of childhood, further legally separated youths from adults, and expanded state authority over child-rearing and family functions.

The Cook County Juvenile Court's original delinquency jurisdiction included only violations of state or local laws or ordinances. Reformers realized that restricting the new court's definition of delinquency only to crimes could cause it to function like a criminal court (Sutton 1988). Amendments in 1901 broadened the definition of delinquency also to include a youth "who is *incorrigible*; or who knowingly associates with thieves, vicious or immoral persons; or who is growing up in idleness and crime; or who knowingly frequents a house of ill-fame; or who knowingly patronizes any policy shop or place where any gaming device is, or shall be operated" (Hawes 1971:186, emphasis added). This expanded definition, like the earlier houses of refuge's jurisdiction over "proper objects," included the undefined term *incorrigible* and introduced a major element of vagueness, imprecision, and subjectivity into the court's inquiry into a youth's "condition of delinquency."

The juvenile court's status jurisdiction reflected the cultural construction of childhood and adolescence and authorized judicial intervention to enforce the dependent conditions of youth and to supervise children's moral upbringing. The status jurisdiction assumed that certain conditions adversely affected child development, constituted precursors of adult criminality, and allowed the court to forestall those precriminal tendencies. It extended juvenile courts' jurisdictional reach well beyond that of criminal courts (Garlock 1979). Critics note that the protoadult behavior that child savers selected to control, such as "drinking, begging, roaming the streets, frequenting dance halls, and movies, fighting, sexuality, staying out late at night, and incorrigibility—was primarily attributable to the children of lower class migrant and immigrant families" (Platt 1977:139). Designed to protect youths from the "sturm and drang" of adolescence, the status jurisdiction combined "a romantic view of childhood with particular fears of modern life, cities, overpressure, and overcivilization. ... The concept of adolescence was the creation of a distinctive mind set, an expression of a mélange of nostalgia and anxiety, and in its crudest mold an embodiment of Victorian prejudices about females and sexuality" (Kett 1977: 143).

Girls appeared in juvenile courts almost exclusively for the status "offense" of "sexual precocity," and they often received more severe dispositions than did boys involved in criminal misconduct. Sexually active young women exercised the ultimate adult prerogative and posed a fundamental challenge to Victorians' sexual sensibilities and Progressives' construction of childhood innocence. Juvenile court judges systematically discriminated against girls for "immorality" or sexual experimentation. Girls appeared in juvenile court far more often than did boys for noncriminal "sexual offenses," and judges incarcerated proportionally more girls than boys in reformatories (Schlossman and Wallach 1978). Cultural stereotypes about women's proper roles reinforced judicial efforts to isolate sexually active females, to safeguard them from exploitation, to preserve their long-term "marriageability," and to prevent them from reproducing.

Influenced by social Darwinian theories, eugenicists in the Progressive Era sought to discourage the "genetically inferior" from propagating. Many of the characteristics that Progressives associated with genetic inferiority also corresponded with features of the recent immigrants whose children disproportionately populated the juvenile courts. Thus, the juvenile court's status jurisdiction provided an opportunity for paternalistic intervention with "female youngsters of poor immigrant families [who] were particularly vulnerable. They grew up in slums, came from inferior racial stock, and were scarred by cultural norms that sanctioned the open display of male sexual interests" (Schlossman and Wallach 1978:82). Barbara Brenzel's (1980) study of the first training school for girls in Massachusetts in the 1850s found that the Lancaster institution housed primarily the daughters of Irish Catholic parents.

The juvenile court simultaneously affirmed the primacy of the nuclear family and expanded the power of the state to intervene in instances of parental inadequacy. The social construction of childhood depicted child rearing as too complex to relegate exclusively to the private sector or to unsupervised family prerogatives. Progressives did not expect lower-class or immigrant families caught in the conflict of cultures adequately to socialize and Americanize their children. The juvenile court provided one agency through which Anglo-Protestant Americans defined the norms of family life, enforced the standards of childhood to which the outsiders must adhere, and supervised the poor to ensure that the next generation adopted an acceptable middle-class way of life (Rothman 1980; Ryerson 1978). In *Love and the American Delinquent*, Steven Schlossman's (1977:58) class-based interpretation of the Milwaukee juvenile court contends: "In practice the juvenile court functioned as a public arena where the dependent status of children was verified and reinforced and where the incapacities of lower-class immigrant parents were, in a sense, certified. The juvenile court flunked parents just as the public school flunked children; in both instances the lower-class immigrant was the principal victim. While offering assistance and guidance, the court also gave its imprimatur to failure, societal and individual." The juvenile courts' professionals asserted their claims to expertise and prevailed most easily over lower-class, immigrant youths and their parents.

Juvenile Court Organization

The juvenile court constituted a typical Progressive innovation, a specialized public agency staffed by professionals and designed to respond to specific social problems. The courts' founders envisioned that social service personnel, clinicians, and probation officers would assist an expert judge to administer a social welfare agency for youths. Ideally, judges would make individualized dispositions in the "best interests" of the child guided by their empathic qualities, clinical insights, and training in social sciences and child development

(Rothman 1980). The analogy between the practice of medicine and the treatment of delinquency provided a powerful rationale for individualized judicial discretion, because no physician could prescribe a remedy without conducting a thorough, unrestricted examination. Because court reformers expressed benevolent intentions, individualized their solicitude, and guided their intervention by social science, they expanded judges' discretionary power to maximize diagnostic and treatment flexibility.

From their inception, juvenile courts varied markedly from each other. Statutory definitions varied among states, and courts varied within states (Sutton 1988). Reformers focused more energy on the legal symbolism of the court and the separation of children from adults than they did on its formal organization. "The reformers' aim was to protect children from the law, not to bring more law to bear on them. They had little inclination to specify what the court should look like as a legal institution. Thus they emphasized the personal and professional qualities of court personnel and largely ignored the formal properties of court decisionmaking" (Sutton 1988:160–61). The ideology of rehabilitation fostered diversity. In a system of discretionary justice, neither procedural rules nor legal formalities constrained the judge; her personality, preferences, and prejudices primarily determined the character of the court. Early evaluations of juvenile court operations devoted primary attention to the presiding judges' personalities and philosophies (Rothman 1980). Historical studies of the more familiar Chicago juvenile court (Platt 1977), the one founded by Judge Ben Lindsey in Denver (Colomy and Kretzmann 1995), and that inaugurated in Milwaukee (Schlossman 1977) reveal the decisive effect of the judge and the administrative diversity among juvenile courts. As will be seen in chapter 4, despite juvenile courts' constitutional domestication, a century later judicial diversity and organizational variability persist.

Reformers avoided legal details because they contemplated a welfare system rather than a judicial system. They assumed that rational, scientific analysis of the social facts and a "full understanding" of a youth's character and lifestyle would reveal the proper diagnosis and prescribe the cure. The juvenile court's methodology encouraged it to collect as much information as possible about the child, the surrounding circumstances, and the causes of delinquency. The factual inquiry about the "whole child" accorded minor significance to the details of the specific criminal offense. Rather, offenses functioned as "symptomatic" indicators of the need for a full-blown social inquiry but in themselves revealed little about a child's "real needs." Court personnel dispensed with formal rules and legal procedures and relied instead on principles of psychology, social work case evaluation, and their own professionalism.

A system of making decisions in the child's best interests that deems everything as relevant necessarily depends heavily on sound judgment and professional expertise. Progressives imagined that well-trained probation staff and social workers, mental hygiene clinics, and psychological diagnostic services would ensure the scientific expertise necessary to make appropriate dispositions. Despite the Progressive's hopes, however, most juvenile courts lacked either adequate clinical resources with which to make individualized therapeutic diagnoses and dispositions or welfare services and treatment resources with which to implement them. "Many courts did not have clinical services available and, further, judges often proved unwilling to defer to the experts in ways that Progressives had hoped" (Rothman 1980:243). From the juvenile court's inception, the reality of these courts as social service agencies never matched their rehabilitative rhetoric (Platt 1977; Schlossman 1977; Ryerson 1978; Rothman 1980; Sutton 1988).

Juvenile court judges directed their attention first and foremost to the "whole" child rather than to the specific crime. The juvenile court responded to the youth's "character and life-style, his psychological strengths and weaknesses. It was not his act but . . . his soul that was at issue" (Rothman 1980: 215). As the first judge of the Illinois juvenile court, Richard S. Tuthill, described his administrative practices:

> "I have always felt and endeavored to act in each case," he said, "as I would were it my own son who was before me in my library at home, charged with some misconduct." First the judge talked briefly with the child and tried to convince him that the court's purpose was not "to punish but rather to befriend and help." The court represented "the good people of the state" who were interested in his future. . . . "The point of the inquiry," the judge continued, was "not to find out whether . . . [the child] has done an act which in an adult, would be a crime and to punish him for that." Instead the judge tried to determine from the facts surrounding a supposed offense whether or not the child before him was "in a condition of delinquency." If he was, then the state could "enter upon the exercise of its parental care over the child." (Hawes 1971:159)

Treating the young offender rather than punishing him for his offense constituted the crucial element in the juvenile court's original conception. Progressives sited the juvenile court squarely on several criminological fault lines—treatment versus punishment, determinism versus free will, and offender versus offense—and endeavored to orient it in the direction of a diagnostic clinic and hospital, rather than a court and a prison. In chapter 3, I contend that when the United States Supreme Court in *In re Gault* (387 U.S. 1 [1967]) mandated some criminal procedural safeguards in delinquency proceeding, it focused judicial attention initially on deciding a youth's legal guilt or innocence, fundamentally altered the objective of the juvenile court's inquiry from needs to deeds, and upset the Progressives' precarious equilibrium.

In separating children from adult offenders, juvenile courts also rejected the jurisprudence and procedures of criminal prosecutions. The juvenile courts' underlying *ideas* of *positivism* and *childhood* rejected notions of blame and punishment for criminal acts. The juvenile court did not blame children but helped them, and criminal responsibility principles like insanity or infancy defenses that operated to excuse the morally blameless from penal consequences had no relevance in delinquency proceedings. Because *parens patriae* theory rested on the idea that the court helped the child rather than tried and punished the youth for a crime, no reasons even existed to determine a child's criminal responsibility.

Reformers proposed a physically separate court building to demonstrate the state's commitment to providing youths with their own form and forum of justice (Rothman 1980). To avoid the stigma of criminal proceedings, juvenile courts conducted confidential, private hearings and limited public access to court records. One unintended consequence of juvenile courts' confidentiality may have been to reduce public sympathy for juveniles. Segregated and confidential proceedings excluded public contact with young offenders, limited public knowledge and awareness of their circumstances, and eroded public identification with and sympathy for them (Garland 1990). In short, confidentiality further marginalized the alienated.

Juvenile court reformers introduced a euphemistic vocabulary further to avoid stigma and to eliminate any implications of a criminal prosecution (Schlossman 1977; Ryerson 1978). For example, court workers filed a petition "in the welfare of the child" to formally initiate a delinquency proceeding, rather than have prosecutors charge youths with a criminal complaint or indictment. Courts found youths to be "delinquent" rather than guilty of an offense, and youths received "dispositions" rather than sentences. Of course, euphemisms provide a cultural language by which "the aggression and hostility implicit in punishment are concealed and denied by the administrative routines of dispassionate professionals, who see themselves as 'running institutions' rather than delivering pain and suffering" (Garland 1990:235). Euphemisms transform the language of punishment and obscure its unpleasant reality, perhaps nowhere more completely than in juvenile courts.

Juvenile courts modified courtroom procedures to eliminate any implication of a criminal proceeding. Because the important issues involved the child's background and welfare rather than the commission of a specific crime, juvenile courts dispensed with juries, lawyers, rules of evidence, and formal procedures (Rothman 1980). Juvenile court judges discarded their judicial robes and elevated bench, conducted informal hearings in their chambers to make proceedings more personal and private, and tried to convince youths of the court's desire to solve youths' problems rather than to punish them for their offenses (Schlossman 1977). States' juvenile court laws classified delinquency proceedings as civil, rather than criminal, and most denied to juveniles a statutory or constitutional right either to a public trial or to a jury trial available to adults. A century later, the right to a jury trial represents the legal fulcrum on which turns the current symbolic and practical debate about the roles of treatment and punishment in juvenile courts.

Court personnel investigated a child's background *before* the hearing in order to identify the sources of misconduct and to develop an appropriate remedy. They systematically gathered information about the circumstances of a child's life rather than marshal evidence to prove the commission of a specific criminal act (Ryerson 1978). At a delinquency hearing, the judge sat with the child while court personnel presented a treatment plan to meet the child's real needs.

From the inception of juvenile courts, their judges evinced active hostility to the participation of lawyers in delinquency proceedings. "Although judges could not banish a lawyer from the courtroom altogether, they did not consider his presence either appropriate or necessary. Minnesota juvenile court judge Grier Orr boasted that in his courtroom 'the lawyers do not do very much . . . and I do not believe I can recall any instance where the same attorney came back a second time; he found that it was useless for him to appear . . . for an attorney has not very much standing when it comes to the disposition of children in juvenile court' " (Rothman 1980:216). Judges regarded the presence of lawyers and other criminal procedural safeguards as both irrelevant in a welfare setting and impediments to their child-saving mission. Conversely, practicing lawyers did not view the juvenile court as a "real" court. "Probably the feeling with a good many lawyers is that it is not a court of law as we understand the term" (Colomy and Kretzmann 1995:203). While attorneys in the early juvenile courts could assist their clients up to a point, "when the court wanted to intervene in intrafamilial affairs in order to 'prevent' future delinquency, there was virtually nothing anyone, even a lawyer could do about it except to delay the inevitable" (Schlossman 1977:167). In chapters 3 and 4, I report that at the time of the Court's *Gault* decision and subsequently, juvenile court judges continued to discourage the retention or appointment of counsel, limited their role as defenders, and sentenced more severely those youths who appeared with counsel.

Juvenile Court Dispositions

The juvenile court functioned as a coercive treatment agency, equipoised between the social casework treatment model, on the one hand, and criminal courts' punishment paradigm, on the other. Because juvenile courts could not rely solely on juveniles' voluntary compliance with their treatment program, they required the power to impose restraints. And youths' criminal violations provided the most common basis for the courts' coercive intervention. Despite their efforts to "decriminalize" delinquency proceedings, early juvenile court reformers acknowledged that "while we have greatly softened the proceeding, it is, nevertheless, difficult to get away wholly from the idea that it is a proceeding involving a charge against the child, and while we have, likewise, softened the character of the judgement, it still remains a judgment against the child" (Colomy and Kretzmann 1995:203). This unresolvable tension between coercion and treatment represented one of the fundamental criminological fault lines underlying the court.

Although Progressive reformers subscribed to deterministic theories of delinquency, they lacked either a scientific model of crime causation or an effective technology with which to intervene and change behavior. They anticipated that a process of atheoretical data collection would reveal the appropriate individual diagnoses and prescribe the proper treatments (Rothman 1980). Court workers compiled elaborate social histories and case studies but did not evaluate empirically the effectiveness of their rehabilitation programs. Instead, anecdotal examples and impressionistic reports provided "evidence" of their successes.

Juvenile courts judges' substantive authority matched their procedural latitude. Progressives blurred legal distinctions between dependent, neglected, noncriminal, and criminal children, deemphasized issues of criminal guilt or innocence, and enhanced judges' dispositional authority. Judges possessed broad power to leave youths in their homes, place them under the supervision of a probation officer, or transfer them to a suitable family home, institution, or reformatory (Hawes 1971). The ideology of rehabilitation encouraged juvenile court judges to intervene more extensively than their criminal court counterparts. The subjectivity of their assessments added a powerful element of unpredictability to the process (Rothman 1980).

Juvenile court judges imposed indeterminate and nonproportional dispositions that could continue for the duration of minority. Indeterminate meant that the judge set no specific limit to the length of sentence; it could continue indefinitely until adulthood. Nonproportional meant that no relationship existed between what the child allegedly did and the length of disposition; the trivial or serious nature of the offense imposed no limits in advance. The particular reason or offense that brought a child before the court affected neither the degree, the duration, nor the intensity of intervention. Each child's circumstances differed, and judges responded to "needs" rather than "deeds." Although penal reformers proposed indeterminate sentences as early as the 1870s, indeterminacy and nonproportionality achieved their fullest expression in the juvenile court (Cullen and Gilbert 1982). In theory, every youth held the key to his or her own release from confinement or supervision simply by reforming.

Juvenile court jurisprudence rejected blameworthiness and deserved punishment for *past offenses* in favor of a utilitarian strategy of *future-oriented* social welfare dispositions. In theory, judges decided why the child appeared in court and what the court could do to change the character, attitude, and behavior of the youth to prevent a reappearance (Ryerson 1978). "It was a social welfare agency, the central processing unit of the entire child welfare system. Children who had needs of any kind could be brought into the juvenile court, where their troubles would be diagnosed and the services they needed provided by court workers or obtained from other agencies" (Bernard 1992: 83). Courts decided each case on the basis of unspecified "clinical" considerations that did not necessarily apply to the next.

Juvenile courts resolved many cases informally and used probation as the disposition of first resort for the vast majority of delinquents (Schlossman 1977). Historians credit John Augustus Hall, a kindly Boston shoemaker, with originating the idea of probation in the 1840s when he began to supervise adult offenders released to him by the criminal courts. However, juvenile court legislation and practice systematized and expanded the use of probation as an alternative to institutions for younger offenders (Mennel 1973). Probation officers functioned as intermediaries to provide the court with information about the child and to supervise those youths whom the court returned to the community. Reformers envisioned probation as an alternative to dismissal rather than to confinement and used it to expand the scope of formal control over youths. Probation allowed courts to regulate the wide range of noncriminal status offenders and minor misdemeanants and provided an inexpensive alternative to home removal (Ryerson 1978).

The roles of probation officers evolved with the juvenile court. Probation officers succeeded an earlier generation of "friendly visitors," private citizens engaged in public charitable works, and served as "cultural missionaries" to uplift the child, transform the family, change the community, and reform the milieu of the lower-class ghetto (Lubove 1967; Schlossman 1977). Probation linked social welfare with the court, and enlisted the methods of scientific charity to further the aims of the justice system by identifying the sources of a child's delinquency.

After the turn of the century, psychology and Freudian psychiatry emerged as intellectual disciplines and further professionalized the practices of probation, social work, and juvenile courts. Increasingly, probation staff focused on the child's interior world, rather than on external structural forces, to resolve inner conflict and facilitate adjustment (Cravens 1985). In 1909, Dr. William A. Healy established the Juvenile Psychopathic Institute in conjunction with the Chicago juvenile court, attempted to locate the sources of delinquency within the psyche of each "troubled" youth, and fostered the national diffusion of the Child Guidance movement (Krisberg and Austin 1993). Probation adopted the techniques of mental testing, introduced more intensive therapeutic relationships between delinquents and caseworkers, and expanded the role of the juvenile court as a social services agency (Ryerson 1978). With the shift of social work practice from understanding the child's environment to unraveling her interior psychodynamics, the process of treatment became more complex, the prospects of reformation more elusive, and the universe of potential delinquents wider (Kett 1977). Psychological treatment models provided juvenile courts with a powerful therapeutic ideological rationale, legitimated their discretionary processes, and further insulated them behind a veneer of professionalism and expertise.

While probation constituted the disposition of first resort, Progressive reformers relied on institutional confinement as a disposition of last resort as well. Their feelings of tenderness did not cause them to shrink from toughness when required. The indeterminate and discretionary powers they exercised quickly to release some "rehabilitated" offenders also could result in the prolonged incarceration of other "incorrigible" youths. Progressives' willingness to incarcerate some delinquents reflected their elevation of the power of the court over the family and their determination to save poor and immigrant children (Rothman 1980). They expanded the cottage-plan model in youth reformatories, used surrogate cottage parents to create a "normal" family environment within the institution, and attempted to promote a child's adjustment and development. They relabeled reformatories as "vocational schools" or "industrial training schools" to emphasize their nonpenal character and added academic and vocational education to their "rehabilitative" program (Rothman 1980). In the 1920s and 1930s the rising influences of psychology and psychiatry prompted institutional administrators to engraft a hospital therapy regime onto the family and school models. Social workers, psychologists, and psychiatrists regarded the hospital–child guidance clinic models as especially appropriate for juvenile institutions where staff diagnosed and cured delinquency (Rothman 1980).

Psychologisms and rehabilitative rhetoric lent symbolic legitimacy to incarceration without significantly altering daily institutional routines. Practical programs and clinical personnel never approached juvenile justice reformers' therapeutic aspirations or claims; official rhetoric and cultural symbolism seldom match institutional reality. Efforts to present penal practices in quasi-scientific terms "promote a particular image of the state and of its authority, and of its relationship to offenders and other citizens. . . . [O]fficial adoption of scientific languages and rehabilitative forms in modern penal institutions has sometimes had more to do with the cultural symbolism involved than with the desire fully to implement the practices that they imply. As anyone who has compared official rhetoric to the actualities of institutions will know, many 'policies' exist more at the level of public representation than of operational practice" (Garland 1990:257). Progressives' rehabilitative rhetoric functioned to assert the incompetence of children, to define a relationship of dependency between juveniles and the state, to legitimate institutional practices to an uncritical public audience, and to obscure the reality of correctional practices.

Schlossman (1977) provides a compelling portrayal of the punitive workings of the Milwaukee juvenile court and Wisconsin institutions. In *The Best-Laid Plans*, Ellen Ryerson (1978) concludes that with only a few notable exceptions, such as Denver's Ben Lindsey, most juvenile court judges and probation personnel were mediocre and their programs ineffective. David Rothman's study, *Conscience and Convenience*, provides persuasive evidence that probation staff rarely possessed the resources, services, or expertise necessary to assist young people and that institutions seldom provided conditions conducive to rehabilitation: "The closer the scrutiny of juvenile confinement, the more inadequate and, indeed, punitive the programs turned out to be" (1980:268). Although claims of clinical expertise and treatment resources justified the juvenile court's programs, these essential features remained conspicuously absent. A study of the Lancaster School for Girls concludes that its program quickly transformed "a place of loving familial guidance . . . [into] more a place of punishment and incarceration" (Brenzel 1980:205). Another historical study of juvenile institutions describes them as little more than a last resort before prisons and contends that their punitive, exclusionary programs accentuated and amplified inmates' antisocial tendencies (Ferdinand 1991). Despite rehabilitative rhetoric and clinical euphemisms, incarcerated delinquents' institutional experiences remained essentially custodial and punitive.

The punitive character of Progressive juvenile institutions suggest the incompatibility between simultaneously maintaining custody and pursuing rehabilitation. The needs of institutional staff to secure order and control to protect themselves and to forestall external criticism necessarily take precedence over more ephemeral and amorphous goals like treatment. Institutional requirements of discipline and order, virtually at any cost, dictate the use of threats, backup sanctions, and escalating punishments. As Ryerson cautions, the "fusion of social control with greater humaneness is a tenuous one which typically dissolves, leaving the machinery for social control firmly entrenched—even if it is ineffective—after the spirit of humanitarianism has departed" (1978:33). When Progressives coupled inadequate budgets and ill-trained staff with the primitive state of psychology, psychiatry, and social work, the repressive character of juvenile institutions became almost inescapable. As chapter 7 demonstrates, a century later, conditions of juvenile incarceration have changed depressingly little.

From the inception of juvenile courts their judges could deny some young offenders the court's protective jurisdiction and transfer their cases to adult criminal courts. Judges typically used this authority to transfer older youths charged with more-serious offenses. Judges waived jurisdiction over perhaps 1 percent of youths per year (Rothman 1980). The ability to transfer highly visible or serious cases provided a safety valve to preserve the court's jurisdiction over the remaining youths and to protect it from political criticism for "coddling" young criminals. In chapter 6, I analyze recent increases in youth violence, the enormous pressures these trends place on juvenile courts to repress crime, and the legislation that transfers more young offenders to criminal court and thereby erodes the jurisdiction of the juvenile court.

Historians argue persuasively that Progressive reformers intended and designed juvenile courts to discriminate between middle-class children like their own and those of poor and immigrant parents, "other people's children" (Schlossman 1977; Platt 1977; Rothman 1980; Sutton 1988). "[F]rom the early nineteenth century to the present, the juvenile justice system, has systematically singled out lower-class children for punishment and ignored middle- and upper-class youth" (Schlossman and Wallach 1978:66). Rothman (1980) characterized as *"conscience and convenience"* the process by which judges decided which youths to assign to probation and which to dispatch to institutions. Modernization and social change threatened Anglo-Protestant Americans' cultural hegemony. The judges responded to children like their own with "tenderness"—supervising them on probation—and reacted to the "foreign" and "alien" youths with "toughness"—routing them to the institutions. "The exercise of judicial discretion helped to effect a dual system of criminal justice: one brand for the poor, another for the middle and upper classes. Judicial discretion may well have promoted judicial discrimination" (Rothman 1980: 71). Reformers intended juvenile courts from their inception, to exercise their broad powers more extensively over lower-class and immigrant populations than over the middle class and native born (Rothman 1980). Poor and immigrant children made up nearly three-quarters of the boys and girls who appeared in the Chicago and Milwaukee juvenile courts (Hawes 1971; Schlossman 1977).

The juvenile court *idea* of "individualized" justice almost inevitably entailed social, economic, cultural, and class discrimination. Because of their adverse position in the social structure, some people simply "needed" more help than did others. Poor youths came into contact more readily with agencies of control—police, welfare, and schools—than did the children of the middle class, and they presented more deeply rooted and intractable problems. They possessed fewer resources with which to defend themselves against state imposition. They appeared less likely to respond to the inadequate and ineffective services available and quickly filtered through the discretionary "benevolent" system into the more punitive one. Progressives' attempts to individualize justice necessarily implicated every other social inequality that affects people's long-term life chances. If judges sought to return offenders to society, "to transform 'them' into 'us,' " then those who already resembled "us" more closely would necessarily benefit from judicial discretion. "Once consideration shifted from the crime to the criminal, class distinctions came almost inevitably to assume new significance when punishments were meted out" (Rothman 1980:105–106).

From the beginning, juvenile court sentencing practices constituted a form of criminological triage based on social circumstances. Early court practitioners unabashedly

> classified delinquent children into three groups on the basis of social status, "which best indicates the dispositions to be made." Discharge or a warning was most applicable to children whose homes and social influences were "thoroughly good." Probation was suitable for those whose homes and social influences were "ineffective." Lastly, the "mentally or morally defective" children of low social status required institutional or foster home placement. "Probation is rarely a satisfactory disposition in such cases—and a discharge is worse." The often explicit assumption that "other people's children"—particularly those of the "dangerous classes"—were the true delinquents. (Colomy and Kretzmann 1995: 199)

The discretion Progressive reformers afforded to judges to dispose of youths on the basis of who they were, rather than what they had done, provided a powerful and legitimating rationale to respond differentially to youths.

Within a decade of the creation of the Illinois juvenile court system, ten states had established juvenile courts. Within a quarter of a century, all but two states had adopted juvenile court legislation (Krisberg and Austin 1993; Empey 1979). The rapidity with which the juvenile court idea spread reflected the diversity of its supporters, a spectrum that ranged from philanthropic child-saving women's organizations to criminal justice professionals. The women's clubs viewed the juvenile court as a tool with which to advance elements of their child-saving and child welfare agenda (Rothman 1980). Private charities and children's benevolent organizations viewed the court as necessary to counter the legal authority that parents, including "un-Americanized immigrant parents," otherwise exercised over their children (Sutton 1988). Criminal justice practitioners appreciated that juvenile courts' informality and flexibility enabled them to administer their growing caseloads more efficiently and provided greater supervision of problematic youths than available through the criminal process (Rothman 1980).

Conclusion

Industrialization, urbanization, and immigration threatened the culture and character of Anglo-Protestant America. The juvenile court represents a specific example of Progressive reformers' generic solutions to four interrelated problems of modernization: how to impose the "traditional values of the native elite" on the larger society, how to separate politics from administration; how to distribute authority among various levels of government, and how to integrate the work of charity and government (Sutton 1988). Characteristically, Progressives delegated discretion to professionals to solve individual problems within a bureaucratic setting. The occupational status of judges and the invocation of science and medicine in the guise of the rehabilitative ideal legitimated coercive intervention. However, the juvenile court's primary goal "was not a new technology of rehabilitation, but a comprehensive administrative apparatus that coordinated and formalized routine practices of the past" (Sutton 1988:148). The juvenile court provided legal authority for administrative discretion and provided continuity with earlier strategies to regulate the children of immigrants and the poor (Bernard 1992).

The juvenile court culminated a century-long evolution in the control of young offenders and their differentiation from adults. Although the earlier houses of refuge and reformatories provided specialized institutions for youths, the juvenile court completed the process and created a separate agency more extensively to regulate children. Juvenile court ideology postulated that children were immature, irresponsible, and needed care and guidance. The courts' jurisdiction affirmed the dependent status of children. Its dispositional authority enabled it to exercise control over children and to supervise their families.

Juvenile courts' authority to oversee children and their families embodied a conceptual contradiction. On the one hand, family life became increasingly privatized, it erected barriers between the domestic and outside worlds, and parents assumed greater responsibility to raise their own children. On the other hand, Progressives expanded the role of the state, assumed greater authority to intrude into private arrangements, and intervened when families failed in their obligations to their children (Grubb and Lazerson 1982). Progressives resolved the conflict between private autonomy and public authority by predicating *parens patriae* intervention on the failures of families, particularly those of the lower classes and immigrants. Although Progressives affirmed family privacy, the state provided the necessary counterweight to lower-class socialization gone awry. These contradictions inevitably skew the balance between social welfare and social control. "[C]hildren's institutions have been premised on class-biased conceptions of family deficiency, and they have embodied a class-differentiated conception of their goals. . . . The juvenile justice programs and the welfare system have consistently emphasized the need to watch over lower-class families and prevent their excesses. . . . [T]he fear of lower-class children has converted the promise to 'save the child' into the goal of protecting the community from their disruptive potential" (Grubb and Lazerson 1982:38).

Progressives' belief in their own benevolence and in the superiority of their vision of childhood and society blinded them to the possibility of cultural conflict in defining and controlling youthful deviance. Notwithstanding their child-saving motivations, juvenile court reformers created a powerful instrument of coercive social control. When juvenile court reformers espoused a commitment to uplift the downtrodden, they also preserved the power and privilege of the status quo. The juvenile court embodied both reformers' compassion for the child and their class and ethnic antagonisms. The ideology of *parens patriae* stipulated personal inadequacy or moral deficiency as preconditions for social welfare intervention. Either the child must commit an offense or violate the undefined norms of childhood or her parents must fail to meet middle-class child-rearing standards before Progressives would provide public support. Thus, a negative connotation inevitably attached to all public intervention.

Progressives ignored the social structural implications of their own theories of delinquency and instead addressed deviance in terms of personal shortcomings. "The focus on social reform implied that the 'blame' for poverty and dependency lay in the social conditions created and maintained by these powerful people, rather than in poor and dependent individuals themselves" (Bernard 1992:93). Social structure and political economy create the material inequalities that place the poor and marginalized at greater risk of crime, delinquency, and justice system intervention. Moreover, Progressives institutionalized childhood as a dependent social and legal status, and children least of all bore responsibility for their adverse circumstances. According to positivist theory, youths' detrimental family situations and injurious environmental conditions *caused* them to become delinquents. Despite the social structural implications of positivism, Progressive reformers chose to mend damaged individuals rather than to alter the social conditions that injured them or caused their misbehavior. Rather than proposing structural reforms to alleviate the conditions that they knew caused crime, they opted to "stand on the sidelines and administer first aid to the children who were the battle's victims" (Ryerson 1978:126). Saving children appealed to Progressives humanitarian impulses without engendering a more radical critique and the more fundamental social changes it entailed. By minimizing social structural explanations and maximizing children's and parents' inadequacies and responsibilities for their own plights, Progressives simultaneously undermined support for programs for children. Labeling children and their parents as deficient creates a self-fulfilling prophecy and reduces public responsibility to alleviate those personal deficits.

In their reformative zeal, Progressives did not consider the depersonalizing consequences of defining children as dependent and objects for them to mold. They naively assumed that they could combine social welfare and social control and failed to recognize the potential conflicts between protecting children and protecting society. They did not appreciate the inherent contradictions of providing social welfare services in a coercive institution. Rather, they delegated to the subjective discretion of each judge and court worker the authority to resolve the fundamental antagonisms between voluntarism and coercion and between welfare and control without any formal guidance.

Progressive reformers failed to perceive the operational contradictions between treating and punishing, between *parens patriae* and coercion, or the rapidity with which juvenile justice operatives could subordinate rehabilitative considerations to custodial concerns. Although the juvenile court hoped to rehabilitate errant youths, protecting the community from dangerous youths constituted its primary responsibility. They did not fully appreciate the organizational tensions inherent in a multipurpose court that coerced a "voluntary" therapeutic relationship and subordinated the rule of law to discretionary professional expertise. The juvenile court combined features of a social service agency, welfare system, and mental health clinic with the coercive power of a court of law. Nor did they recognize that juvenile court intervention, or indeed any measure of social control, may aggravate and intensify the behaviors it seeks to reduce. In short, Progressives embedded a number of cultural contradictions in the juvenile court without attempting to reconcile them. They subsumed the clash between individualized sentences and equality and the rule of law in "sound discretion" and "scientific expertise." They evaded the contradictions between the offender and the offense, between the social worker's desire to help and the judge's inclination to punish by conceptualizing the judge as a social worker.

Although Progressive ideology recognized that social structural and environmental conditions "caused" delinquency, they defined juvenile courts' delinquency jurisdiction on the basis of children's offenses rather than their real needs. Instead of pursuing a social welfare agenda and reducing the adverse conditions that caused delinquency, they combined social welfare and penal social control in the juvenile court. They espoused deterministic causal explanations of delinquent behavior but then individualized their sanctions. But if state coercion for criminal offenses constitutes "punishment," then punishing people for behavior that "society" caused supports charges of hypocrisy. On the other hand, if deterministic explanations reduce offenders' personal responsibility for their behavior, then "treatment" erodes the expressive functions that the criminal law serves by blaming and condemning people's choices.

Finally, juvenile jurisprudence embodies the inherent administrative conflicts between individualized discretion and the rule of law. Through most of juvenile courts' history, appellate courts uncritically rejected children's legal contentions that juvenile courts punished them without due process of law, echoed the expansive language of *Crouse*, and upheld the state's *parens patriae* authority to "rescue" and "rehabilitate" young people. Indeed, juvenile courts represent such a universal fixture of childhood that questioning the promise of the "noble experiment" challenges the legitimacy of the social construction of childhood itself. Until *Gault*, appellate courts assumed compatibility between juvenile courts' twin goals of promoting the best interests of the child and the welfare of the state and rejected requests for procedural safeguards.

The United States Supreme Court's decisions in the 1960s and 1970s extended some constitutional procedural safeguards to juveniles. The decisions imposed some legal formality and a modicum of equality on a system designed to ignore legal considerations in favor of individual considerations and personal circumstances. Chapter 3 examines the social and legal changes that led the Supreme Court to examine Progressive ideology and provided the impetus for the transformation of the juvenile court.

| | | | THREE

The Constitutional Domestication
of the Juvenile Court

The Progressive juvenile court embodied the idea of childhood vulnerability and affirmed the responsibility of families to raise their children. It simultaneously expanded the state's prerogative to act as *parens patriae* and to exercise flexible social control over young people's lives in their "best interests." Despite its enormous powers, few people questioned the *idea* of the juvenile court as a judicialized welfare system or as a therapeutic agency of social control for the first two-thirds of the twentieth century.

Systematic and critical reexamination of juvenile courts' cultural and legal premises emerged only in the 1960s and culminated in the Supreme Court's *In re Gault* decision in 1967 (Paulsen 1957, 1967). Several social, cultural, and political forces coalesced to erode support for coercive socialization by means of the juvenile, criminal justice, or social welfare systems. These groups questioned the legitimacy of state benevolence, the goal of rehabilitation, and the efficacy of coerced treatment and revealed the distance American society had moved from the earlier Progressive consensus that underlay the "rehabilitative ideal." Chapter 2 noted that a flourishing rehabilitative ideal requires basic societal agreement about the means and ends of rehabilitation. The public and political authorities must believe in the malleability of people and the availability of effective techniques to change their behavior, the means. They also must share a general accord about what it means to be rehabilitated and concur about the nature of the "finished product," the ends. In *The Decline of the Rehabilitature Ideal*, Francis Allen asserts that a flourishing rehabilitative

79

ideal requires "a society in which the dominant groups possess high confidence in their definitions of character and their standards of good behavior, in which resort to the public force to advance and defend those values is seen not only as appropriate, but as very nearly inevitable" (1981:11). Progressives optimistically believed that positivism, the new social sciences, and their medicalized methodology provided them with the tools with which to reform deviants. They uncritically endorsed the use of state power to socialize and acculturate the children of the poor and immigrants to become middle-class Americans like themselves.

By the time of *Gault* and the Warren Court's "due process revolution," the Progressives' consensus about state benevolence, the legitimacy of imposing certain values on others, and what rehabilitation entailed or how and when it occurred had all become matters of intense dispute (D. Rothman 1978; Cullen and Gilbert 1982). Pluralism, racial diversity, and cultural conflicts challenged Progressives' unanimity about the goals of rehabilitation. Empirical evaluations of rehabilitation programs undermined Progressives' assumptions that correctional personnel possessed the technical ability to treat inmates effectively and challenged the clinical expertise of therapists. Civil rights advocates questioned the benevolence of criminal justice officials and objected to the invidious and discriminatory consequences of discretionary decision making. As social and political deference to professionals' claims of expertise declined, the Supreme Court increasingly emphasized procedural formality and the rule of law to regulate administrative decision making. In the ensuing decades, the Court's decisions provided the impetus to transform the juvenile court from a nominally rehabilitative social welfare agency into a formal legal institution and fostered a convergence between the juvenile and criminal justice systems.

This chapter examines the social and legal context of the Warren Court's due process revolution in the 1960s and the impact of its decisions on juvenile courts. The Supreme Court critically reassessed criminal and juvenile justice practices in response to social structural changes that began several decades earlier. Those decisions also reflected a broader shift in constitutional jurisprudence to protect individual and civil rights. Two crucial demographic forces combined in the 1960s to provide the constitutional impetus for the due process revolution and the constitutional restructuring of penal practices. First, the generation born after World War II, the "baby boomers," created a demographic bulge; rates of crime and juvenile delinquency began to escalate in the 1960s as they moved through the age structure. This upsurge in youth crime created political pressures to "get tough" and repress, rather than rehabilitate, young offenders and led the Court, in turn, to provide greater procedural protections for criminal defendants. Second, the migration of African Americans from the rural South to the industrial North and West in the decades before and during World War II increased the urbanization of blacks and placed the issues of racial equality and civil rights on the national political agenda. Criminal justice reforms constituted part of the broader constitutional program to protect the rights of racial minorities. The synergy of campus youth rebellions, baby-boom crime rates, and urban racial disorders in the

1960s precipitated a crisis of "law and order" and brought issues of criminal justice administration and civil rights to the legal forefront. Finally, the legal recognition of racial divisions eroded the social consensus about means and ends that sustained the Progressives' rehabilitative ideal. In this chapter, I argue that, on the one hand, race provided the impetus for the Supreme Court to focus on procedural rights in states' juvenile and criminal justice systems to protect minorities' liberty interests. On the other hand, the Court's insistence on greater procedural safeguards transformed the juvenile court from a social welfare agency into a wholly owned subsidiary of the criminal justice system. And, as I argue in later chapters, *Gault*'s insistence on procedural safeguards legitimated the imposition of punitive sentences that now fall disproportionately heavily on minority offenders.

Baby Boom, Youth Culture, and Crime in the 1960s

Structural and demographic factors in the preceding decades shaped the political, legal and, constitutional changes of the 1960s: the end of the depression and increased affluence, the end of World War II, and the onset of the cold war, and population shifts from country to town, from city to suburb, and from south to north (Hodgson 1976). In particular, the migration of African Americans from the rural South to industrial cities of the North and West before and after the war transformed urban America, as whites simultaneously moved from cities to suburbs and isolated blacks in blighted inner-city ghettos (Lemann 1992; Massey and Denton 1993). The increased visibility and awareness of the "American dilemma" moved matters of race to the center of the nation's and the Warren Court's concerns about legal rights, crime policy, social welfare, and social justice.

In the 1930s, President Franklin Roosevelt responded to the Great Depression with New Deal programs that expanded the scope of the Progressive welfare state, further bureaucratized government, and shifted formal legal authority to state and national levels (Brown 1976). The United States emerged from World War II with its industrial base intact and as the strongest economic and military power in the world. With the end of the depression and World War II, affluence on an unprecedented scale engendered social optimism and consensus, an "end of ideology" ideology. Mass production and mass consumption produced a more homogeneous lifestyle (Mowry and Brownell 1981). Regionalism and class consciousness declined as national corporations and labor unions unified people and interests across the country. Educational opportunities expanded, geographic mobility increased, an interstate highway system linked the nation, and a portrait of national uniformity emerged. The mass media, especially television networks, promoted a mass culture and a standardized lifestyle.

In the flush of prosperity following World War II, couples who had postponed marriage and childbearing during the depression and the disruptions of war began to marry and have babies. The baby boom represented more than simply "pent-up demand"; more couples married, the interval between marriage and the birth of the first child declined, and fewer couples remained childless or had only one child (Strickland and Ambrose 1985). Postwar optimism and security made the economic costs of raising children appear less daunting and popular culture glorified motherhood and valued children. Dr. Benjamin Spock's *The Common Sense Book of Baby and Child Care* provided guidance for a generation of families that placed children's welfare at the center of domestic life.

In the halcyon days of the 1950s, a societal consensus supported the moral authority of leaders, as a grandfatherly Dwight Eisenhower presided over a prosperous nation, and fathers presided over their families. People generally respected community and familial norms, and young people committed relatively few or violent crimes. Of course, racial segregation and injustice, gender inequality within the family, the exclusion of women from many areas of employment and public life, and the marginalization of Catholics and Jews marred this otherwise idyllic vision, but those blemishes remained generally hidden from public view.

The demographic bulge created by the children of the baby boom moved through the age-social structure like the pig swallowed by the python. "Between 1960 and 1970 the proportion of the population between 14 and 24 jumped from 15% to 20% after declining for over 50 years. In absolute numbers the youth population grew by 50% in the sixties from 27 million in 1960 to 42 million in 1971" (Coleman et al. 1974:73). Even as the youth population exploded, child labor and compulsory school attendance laws excluded young people from the workforce, segregated them in schools, and fostered the development of a youth culture. Young people spent more time in schools than previous generations and interacted almost exclusively with same-aged peers. As young people's economic roles declined, social institutions for adolescents, such as schools and extracurricular activities, created a series of artificial roles and contrived organizations not tightly integrated into larger community structures (Coleman et al. 1974). Building on the Progressives' vision, the social construction of adolescence segregated youths from adult roles and responsibilities, cut them off from meaningful intergenerational interactions, and subordinated youths in settings dominated by adults. Although child labor and compulsory attendance laws provided the legal framework socially to isolate youth, the enormous increase in the youth population overwhelmed institutions to socialize and control young people. By the end of the 1960s, the Vietnam War further alienated youths and undermined the moral capacity of all the institutions created by their parents to provide social direction (Allen 1981).

Young people's exclusion from participation in the marketplace and their passive encapsulation in schools and on college campuses fostered the emergence of a youth culture within which young people exercised a degree of autonomy. Linked by mass-media advertising, television, and popular music, many young people in the postwar generation drifted from the adult-dominated culture into a counterculture of their own. "Sex, drugs, and rock-and-roll" described a youth lifestyle anathema to everything in which their parents believed. Young people's affluence sustained a separate "youth-oriented" market, the mass media linked them, and entrepreneurs catered to their "differentness" to exploit it (Coleman et al. 1974). Whereas in 1950, 3.9 million households owned a television set, a decade later, more than 50 million households did, about 90 percent of all homes (Strickland and Ambrose 1985). The pervasiveness of television fostered a debate over the effect of the mass media on youth, crime, and culture that persists to the present. Over subsequent decades, critics contended that television provided young people with access to "adult secrets," eroded childhood innocence, fostered premature adulthood and autonomy, and glorified and commercialized violence and desensitized people to its consequences (Winn 1983; Elkind 1988; Postman 1994).

Youth crime increased dramatically in the 1960s as the children of the baby boom reached adolescence and, by their sheer numbers, overwhelmed many agencies of social control. The number of young males aged fifteen to seventeen years—peak ages for many forms of criminality—doubled during this period (Allen 1981). As the children of the baby boom reached their crime-prone teenage years beginning in the mid-1960s, the rates of serious violent and property crimes increased more than 75 percent; the simple changes in the composition of the age structure of the population accounted for most of that rise (Wilson 1975; Cullen and Gilbert 1982). "Perceptions of increasing crime in the late 1960s brought with them a heightened sense of insecurity and fears of a collapse of public order. These perceptions were based in part on demographic realities" (Allen 1981:30). Social turmoil escalated and provided impetus to reevaluate juvenile and criminal justice systems' social control strategies. The crisis of law and order and the Nixon administration's "war on crime" in the late 1960s reflected popular perceptions of social and political collapse in the face of civil disorder and widespread criminality.

Black Urban Migration, Race Riots, and Civil Rights

In the 1960s the issue of race in American society provided the crucial link between distrust of governmental benevolence, concern about social service personnel's discretionary decision making, the crisis of law and order, and the Supreme Court's due process jurisprudence (Graham 1970; Debele 1987). Race emerged as a visible national issue because the injustice of racial segregation and discrimination no longer remained isolated, a rural southern phenomenon (Lemann 1992). In 1870, 80 percent of black Americans lived in the rural South; by 1970, 80 percent of black Americans resided in urban locales, half in the North and West (Massey and Denton 1993).

The roots of the great migration and the urbanization of blacks began half a century earlier. The outbreak of World War I in 1914 simultaneously in-

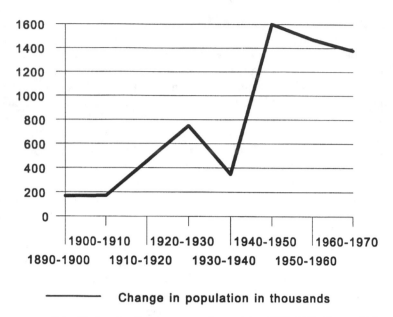

FIGURE 3.1. Black migration to nonsouthern states, 1890–1970. *Source*: U.S. Department of Commerce, Bureau of Census (1980) *The Social and Economic Status of the Black Population in the United States: An Historical View, 1790–1978* (Washington, D.C.: U.S. Government Printing Office), 15.

creased the demand for U.S. industrial production and reduced the availability of European immigrants to work in northern factories. Northern labor recruiters importuned rural southern blacks to migrate at the same time that the Mexican boll weevil invaded the South and devastated cotton production, and the mechanical cotton picker decreased the demand for black tenant and sharecropping farmers (Lemann 1992; Massey and Denton 1993). As Nicholas Lemann (1992) explains in *The Promised Land*, because of the historical relationship between blacks and cotton picking both during slavery and subsequently, the mechanization of the cotton industry constitutes one of the epochal events in American social history. "Between 1910 and 1920, some 525,000 African Americans left their traditional homes in the south and took up life in the north and during the 1920s, the outflow reached 877,000" (Massey and Denton 1993:29). Worsening economic conditions during the Great Depression impelled an additional 400,000 blacks to leave the South for northern cities. "Push" factors, as well as "pull" factors, motivated the black exodus. Southern racial hostility, Jim Crow laws, Ku Klux Klan violence, lynchings, poor segregated schools, and job discrimination provided additional incentives to migrate. Figure 3.1 graphically illustrates these migratory trends. Although the Great Depression temporarily depressed the net migration of blacks from southern states, the opportunities to work in industries associated with war production during the 1940s induced more than a million and a half blacks to leave their rural southern homes.

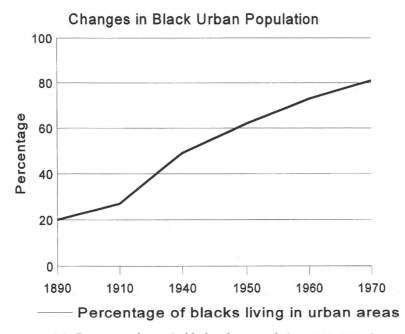

Changes in Black Urban Population

FIGURE 3.2. Percentage change in black urban population, 1890–1970. *Source*: U.S. Department of Commerce, Bureau of Census (1980) *The Social and Economic Status of the Black Population in the United States: An Historical View, 1790–1978* (Washington, D.C.: U.S. Government Printing Office), 14.

When blacks left the rural South, they moved primarily to cities. In the span of half a century, blacks shifted from about three-quarters living in rural environments to three-quarters residing in urban settings. During this massive migration, southern blacks poured into New York, Chicago, Los Angeles, Philadelphia, and other northern, midwestern, and western urban centers. Figure 3.2 graphically depicts the process of black urbanization. By World War II, the majority of blacks lived in urban America. During the war, twelve million men and women entered the armed forces, and fifteen million civilians relocated for new defense jobs. From 1940 to 1944, wartime defense contractors integrated their workforces, and the black population in urban areas increased dramatically.

As racial diversity increased outside the South, racial tensions escalated. Northern whites reacted to the flood of rural southern black migrants with alarm and hostility. Threats, bombings, and violence reinforced racial discrimination and segregation in housing, education, and employment. Enforced residential segregation laid the foundation for the urban black ghettos that now exist in virtually every major city. The black urban residential experience differed from that of preceding generations of ethnic immigrants for whom ghettos provided way stations, places to adapt and adjust before moving into mainstream society. The black ghetto remained more racially homogeneous, concentrated, and impermeable (Massey and Denton 1993). During the war years, blacks began to contest in courts racial barriers and discrimination in housing, transportation, education, and employment.

During the 1930s and 1940s, social anthropological research undermined nineteenth-century theories of racial and cultural inferiority. Franz Boas and Otto Lineberg challenged Herbert Spencer's social Darwinian ideas of western European racial superiority, and Margaret Mead brought their ideas to a broader public audience. Support for pluralism and cultural and racial diversity gained momentum during a war fought against a German regime espousing extremist racist theories. The internment of Japanese Americans during World War II and the persistence of Jim Crow laws in the South afterward nevertheless testified to the persistence of racial discrimination in the United States.

Racial divisions persisted after the war. In the period after 1945, suburbs surrounding major cities grew rapidly. Federal housing and mortgage policies subsidized privately owned single-family homes. Housing contractors introduced mass production in residential construction and spawned "Levittowns," suburban tract housing projects, and struggled to satisfy pent-up housing demand deferred during the depression and World War II (Katz 1989; Massey and Denton 1993). While the prosperity that fostered the baby boom also sustained suburban growth, "[g]overnment-guaranteed mortgages and tax deductions for mortgage interest payments made new homes available to millions with little or nothing down and low monthly payments. . . . Prosperity, easy credit, and a massive road-building program also increased the number of automobiles," without which the suburban lifestyle would not have been possible (Strickland and Ambrose 1985:541). Federal housing and highway policies contributed to and favored the development of predominantly white suburbs around the major cities and encircled urban poor and minority residents (Massey and Denton 1993). The federal government cut mortgage subsidies for the construction of rental units and the Federal Housing Administration "redlined" sections of cities threatened by the "Negro invasion" and reduced the availability of mortgage and home improvement loans there. Even as federal highway policy subsidized white dispersal, the location of interstate highways disrupted many black communities and created physical barriers to contain their expansion (Katz 1989).

The combinations of black in-migration to cities and white out-migration to the suburbs transformed the larger, older cities of the Northeast and Midwest. Although the overall population of these cities actually declined somewhat with the larger white exodus, black immigrants partially offset those losses, increased the overall racial concentrations, and many cities became increasingly nonwhite (Katz 1989). Industry and employment opportunities began to move with the whites on the highways and expressways to the readily accessible suburbs.

Despite the affluence and prosperity of postwar America, the plight of inner-city blacks demonstrated the need for social and legal reforms. Although Presidents Harry Truman and Dwight Eisenhower took some tentative steps to address racial issues, Congress resisted antidiscrimination laws, open housing laws, federal aid to education, and national health insurance. Even as the nation became increasingly urbanized, racist and conservative rural southern Democrats in Congress occupied key chairmanships of pivotal committees and blocked legislative initiatives for racial equality, social justice, and urban programs. During the cold war and McCarthy era, conservative congressmen placed advocates for civil rights and racial reform on the defensive.

Daniel Patrick Moynihan's (1965) prescient report on *The Negro Family: The Case for National Action* argued that urban male unemployment threatened the social fabric of the black community. The rapid transition from a rural agrarian to an urban industrial life disrupted black family life; many unskilled or semiskilled black males experienced unemployment or underemployment (Lemann 1992; Katz 1989). Without the economic ability to occupy the role of "breadwinner," fathers deserted their families, illegitimacy and welfare dependency increased, and youth crime surged. "At the heart of the deterioration of the fabric of Negro society is the deterioration of the Negro family. It is the fundamental source of weakness of the Negro community at the present time.... Unless this damage is repaired, all the efforts to end discrimination and poverty and injustice will come to little" (Moynihan 1965: 5). At the time, both black and liberal critics attacked the Moynihan report for "blaming the victims," but three decades later the structural and economic problems he identified remain among the foremost issues of criminal justice and urban public policy (Katz 1989; Wilson 1996).

Chapter 6 examines further the continuing structural transformation of cities and the emergence of the "urban underclass." A number of social structural forces coalesced to place an entire generation of young people, and especially minority youths, at tremendous developmental risk. Some of the structural and policy factors include continuing economic racial discrimination; racial segregation and concentrated poverty in deteriorated urban cores; the deindustrialization of cities and movement of manufacturing and service jobs to suburbs; inadequate public transportation systems to enable poor urban residents to reach suburban jobs; the growth of female-headed households, welfare dependency, and minority children in poverty; the deterioration of urban public education; and the destructive impact of crime and violence in these communities on their residents (Katz 1989; Wilson 1987, 1996; Jencks 1992; National Research Council 1993). Chapter 6 analyzes how those structural forces contributed to escalating rates of drug, gun, and violent youth crime in the 1980s and how, in turn, those crime trends and political perceptions of youth crime as black crime fostered "get-tough" juvenile justice policies.

During the 1960s, urban riots rocked American cities as black Americans reacted violently to decades of segregation, deprivation, social isolation, and alienation (Massey and Denton 1993; National Advisory Commission on Civil Disorders 1968). In the first nine months of 1967 alone, 164 urban race riots occurred and augured the possibility of a national race war (Lemann 1992). The National Advisory Commission on Civil Disorders (1968), popularly known as the Kerner Commission, attributed the riots to a legacy of racial discrimination in employment, education, social services, and housing. Established in the aftermath of the mid-1960s urban race riots, the Kerner Commission warned that the United States "was moving toward two societies, one black, one white—separate and unequal" (1968:1). Despite the historical prevalence and persistence of black segregation and poverty, the commission cautioned that continuing current policies would "make permanent the division of our country into two societies; one, largely Negro and poor, located in the central cities; the other predominantly white and affluent, located in the suburbs" (1968:22). The commission rejected a strategy of "ghetto enrichment" as a policy of "separate but equal" that would institutionalize and make permanent racial divisions in American society. It proposed instead "a policy which combined ghetto enrichment with programs designed to encourage integration of substantial numbers of Negroes into the society outside the ghetto" (Kerner Commission 1968:22). In *American Apartheid*, Douglas Massey and Nancy Denton (1993:9) contend that public policies create and foster persisting residential racial segregation, perpetuate high levels of black poverty, exacerbate the social and economic harms associated with racial isolation and concentrated poverty, and maintain the urban underclass. In many respects, contemporary urban poverty and youth crime and violence represent the culmination of social structural processes predicted by the Kerner Commission.

Despite the sympathetic findings of the Kerner Commission, Andrew Hacker argues *Two Nations* that the riots changed many whites' perceptions of the legitimacy of blacks' grievances and provided the context of subsequent racism in public policies:

> Whites ceased to identify black protests with a civil rights movement led by students and ministers. Rather, they saw a resentful and rebellious multitude, intent on imposing its presence on the rest of the society.... As the 1970s started, so came a rise in crime, all too many of them with black perpetrators. By that point, many white Americans felt they had been misused or betrayed. Worsening relations between the races were seen as largely due to the behavior of blacks, who had abused the invitations to equal citizenship white American had been tendering. (1992:22)

In chapters 6 and 7, I argue that the increased punitiveness of juvenile courts and the disproportionate minority overrepresentation in the juvenile justice system constitute one manifestation of these processes. The public and politicians support harsh get-tough policies because they perceive young, urban black males as *the* juvenile crime problem.

Decline of the Rehabilitative Ideal: Loss of Social Consensus and the "Crisis of Legitimacy"

Some analysts attribute the turbulence of the 1960s—campus riots, youth crime, urban racial disorders, and the apparent unraveling of the social fabric—to *synergism*, an interaction of demographic and social forces that produced an overall social effect greater than the sum of its various parts (Wilson 1975). The baby-boom demographic increase in the numbers of socially disconnected youths attained a "critical mass" sufficient to amplify increases in crime. Similarly, as a result of the black migration, "urban" became a euphemism for "black" in the minds of many white people. And the black migration did not result in a harmonious racially integrated society. "It was disruptive; it engendered hostility. The fabric of city life in the United States changed forever. . . . Street crime became an obsessive concern for the first time in decades. The beginning of the modern rise of conservatism coincides exactly with the country's beginning to realize the true magnitude and consequences of the black migration and the government's responses to the migration provided the conservative movement with many of its issues" (Lemann 1992: 200). Indeed, the demographic and social structural changes provided the impetus for the Warren Court's civil rights decisions as well as for the constitutional transformation of the juvenile court.

During the 1960s a number of political and cultural forces combined to undermine the Progressives' consensus about state benevolence, to erode support for imposing middle-class values on others, and to question the desirability of rehabilitation as a criminal justice goal and policy (Allen 1981; Cullen and Gilbert 1982). In turn, the popular and political unraveling of support for rehabilitation and conservative support for a "crackdown" on crime and racial minorities encouraged the Supreme Court to impose due process safeguards in juvenile and criminal justice to protect people from the state (Ryerson 1978).

Critics on the Left characterized rehabilitation programs as coercive instruments of social control through which the state oppressed the poor and minorities (Platt 1977). Radical critics emphasized that no criminal justice programs or reforms could ameliorate or avoid the inevitable consequences that flowed from racial inequality and economic and social injustice in the larger society (Cullen and Gilbert 1982). Liberal disenchantment with the rehabilitative ideal reflected a broader disillusionment with the ability of the state to "do good." David Rothman (1978) emphasizes the "limits of benevolence" and the failure of a paternalistic state to deal justly with its most vulnerable citizens. Liberals criticized correctional personnel's exercise of clinical discretion, emphasized the unequal consequences received by similarly situated offenders, and questioned the scientific foundations of "penal treatment" (American Friends Service Committee 1971).

Conservative critics advocated law and order, supported a "war on crime," and favored repression over rehabilitation (Graham 1970). They perceived a fundamental breakdown of the moral and legal order in rising crime rates, civil rights marches and civil disobedience for racial justice, students' protests against the Vietnam war, and urban and campus turmoil. In the broader political context, the civil rights movement created divisions within the Democratic Party between racial and social policy liberals and conservatives. Republicans seized upon crime control, affirmative action, and public welfare as wedge issues with which to distinguish themselves from Democrats in order to woo southern whites, and crime policies for the first time became a central issue in partisan politics (Beckett 1997). As a result of "sound-bite" politics, symbols and rhetoric have come to shape penal policies more than knowledge, social science research, or substance. Since the 1960s, politicians' fear of being labeled "soft-on-crime" has led to a constant ratcheting-up of punitiveness. Conservatives attributed crime and social disorder to a "permissive" society and advocated firm discipline for the young, restoration of patriarchy in the family, respect for authority, and an end to "coddling" criminals (Cullen and Gilbert 1982). Their efforts to get tough supported a succession of "wars" on crime and, later, on drugs, longer criminal sentences, increased prison populations, and disproportionate incarceration of racial minority offenders (Tonry 1995). I argue in chapters 6 and 7 that efforts to get tough on youth crime provide the impetus to transform the juvenile court into an explicitly punitive extension of criminal justice policies.

Although these various critics' perspectives, underlying assumptions and analyses, and policy prescriptions differed, their confluence substantially eroded the societal consensus about means and ends, and undermined public commitment to the rehabilitative ideal as a goal of penal policy. The decline of support for rehabilitation mirrored a broader decline in the legitimacy of public authority (Allen 1981). Whereas a Progressive's claim of compassion legitimated a program, by the 1960s a bureaucrat's claim to act benevolently on behalf of a client elicited primarily skepticism and closer scrutiny for self-serving interests. "To announce that you are prepared to intervene for the best interest of some other person or party is guaranteed to provoke the quick, even knee-jerk, response that you are masking your true, self-interested motives" (D. Rothman 1978:82).

Several features contributed to the modern malaise of distrust, suspicion, and alienation from government. The New Deal legislation during the depression strengthened the federal government's authority and influence over "local" social and economic problems. The centralization of government in Washington paralleled continuing economic concentration and the increasingly dominant role that national and multinational corporations played in local economic affairs. Industrialization spurred corporate concentration during the Progressive Era, but corporations consolidated their economic positions and social and political influence during the New Deal and post–World War II years.

As corporations and government agencies increased in scale and impact, they pursued their own bureaucratic imperatives. People, whom they theoretically served, viewed them increasingly as remote and distant entities impersonally manipulating the populace for their own organizational purposes (Brown 1976). During the earlier Progressive Era of modernizing growth, a collective sense of moral purpose sustained corporate and state bureaucracies' efforts to control and influence the processes and directions of social change. By the 1960s, popular disillusionment with the impact of change and "bigness" undermined that faith (Ryerson 1978).

A series of political and social shocks—the assassinations of President John Kennedy, Robert Kennedy, Martin Luther King, Jr., and Malcolm X and the escalating war in Vietnam—contributed further to public alienation, loss of faith in governmental benevolence, and the precipitous decline in the legitimacy of the state. "Vietnam" and "Watergate" provide shorthand descriptions of the widespread decline in governmental legitimacy, pervasive distrust of authority, and breakdown of social institutions (Cullen and Gilbert 1982; Douvan 1985).

By the end of the 1960s, the Civil Rights movement's insistence on equality, pluralism, and diversity, as well as broader cultural critiques of long-held beliefs and ideals, eroded the moral foundation of many public and private institutions (Hodgson 1976). The 1960's "cultural" challenge undermined the harmony and consensus that sustained public and social institutions only a decade earlier. In *The Twilight of Authority*, Robert Nisbet identified many social indicators of the "crisis of legitimacy": increased public hostility toward government, the decline of political parties and public participation in the political process, the erosion of patriotism, and increased criminality and lawlessness. "I know of no major poll that has not shown, over the past two decades, almost continuous decline in popular trust of government and its leaders, in expressed confidence in the political process, and in desire or willingness to participate directly in this political process" (Nisbet 1975:14). Although a decline in a sense of public purpose pervaded many political and legal institutions, criminal and juvenile justice systems experienced a precipitous loss of public confidence and self-confidence because Progressives had such high aspirations for them (Allen 1981).

The rise of an egalitarian spirit accompanied the erosion of social consensus in the United States in the 1960s. Beginning with the Supreme Court's decision in *Brown v. Board of Education* in 1954 and culminating in the Civil Rights movement in the late 1960s, equality became the watchword of law reform. Claims to equality by "different" people challenged the Progressives' desire to impose a middle-class lifestyle on everyone. The feminist, gay and lesbian, and antiwar political movements drew ideological support from the blacks' struggle for justice, adopted similar strategies and rhetoric, and shared a common critique of dominant cultural values and power arrangements. Judging social reality against the cultural ideals of equality embodied in the constitution further delegitimated the state (Douvan 1985).

Advocates of the "liberation" of children adopted the egalitarian rhetoric of the Civil Rights movement, and argued that young people, too, should enjoy liberty and freedom from legal oppression by the state and their parents. Richard Farson's *Birthrights* (1974) and John Holt's *Escape from Childhood* (1974) grounded the quest for children's rights in the broader social and cultural movements. Holt and Farson challenged the social construction of childhood dependence and vulnerability and advocated children's legal equality and political parity with adults. By contrast, other child advocates used similar language of "rights" to argue that children should receive greater protection and care rather than more legal equality, than adults (Hawes 1991).

In the 1960s and 1970s, Supreme Court decisions adjudicated the constitutional claims of youths and reflected the ambivalence between the competing "liberationist" and "protectionist" positions. On the one hand, the Court extended to young people some of the legal rights of adults. On the other, the Court subordinated children's claims to autonomy, equality, and rights to the interests of other authorities, institutions, and relationships. In *Making All the Difference*, Martha Minow (1990) explains that in the context of children's "rights," a commitment to equality reflects a judgment about young people's "political status," about how the law should treat them, rather than an empirical assessment of their cognitive abilities or capacity to exercise autonomy. When legislatures or courts draw legal lines between childhood and adulthood, those demarcations reflect social judgments about children's competence, needs, risks that autonomy poses to themselves and others, and young people's relationships with their parents, the community, and the state. The Supreme Court's juvenile court and children's rights decisions and subsequent legislative changes in juvenile justice administration reflect the collective cultural ambivalence about adolescents and the uneasy balance of dependency and autonomy, vulnerability and responsibility, and lack of capacity and presumed competency.

Questioning "What Works" and Loss of Consensus about the Scientific Means to Achieve "Rehabilitation"

A loss of faith in the technical ability of penal therapists to "treat" offenders accompanied the perceived decline in the legitimacy, benevolence, and compassion of state agencies. The Progressives' assumed human malleability and therapists' ability to change them by involuntary clinical intervention. Evaluation research raised considerable doubts about the utility of the social sciences, the efficacy of coerced therapy, and the inherent subjectivity of treatment. In *Struggle for Justice*, the American Friends Service Committee presented a devastating critique of the entire panoply of Progressive criminal justice reforms: rehabilitation, individualization, indeterminate sentences, and parole. They denounced most of the postulates of positivist penology as "pseudo-scientific" efforts to transform offenders into "patients," and insisted that "[m]ost if not all of the assumptions that underpin the treatment model are unsubstantiated or in conflict with basic humanitarian values" 1971:83).

David Garland's magisterial analysis of *Punishment and Modern Society* notes the erosion of support for rehabilitation: "Following a sustained critique, the notion of rehabilitation has come to seem problematic at best, dangerous and unworkable at worst" (Garland 1990:6). Critics of the "rehabilitative" enterprise insisted that treatment failed to reduce recidivism; debased offenders by treating them as "abnormal," "sick," or irresponsible; produced invidious and discriminatory decisions about similarly situated offenders; and introduced a cruel uncertainty into the process. They decried overly intrusive intervention, excessive and inappropriate confinement, disparate and unequal dispositions, and disregard of procedural fairness (American Friends Service Committee 1971; Cullen and Gilbert 1982). The discretion that penal authorities exercised to "rehabilitate" offenders often resulted in harsher sanctions than if courts punished them explicitly, posed "a threat to the political values of free societies," and lent itself to "debasement and the service of unintended and unexpressed social ends" (Allen 1981:34).

Empirical evaluations of treatment effectiveness raised substantial doubts about clinicians' ability to coerce behavioral changes and highlighted the subjectivity inherent in therapeutic justice (Martinson 1974; Allen 1981). Systematic evaluations critically analyzed treatment programs' efficacy, questioned their theoretical and scientific validity, and disputed whether their positive outcomes outweighed their coercive subjectivity. The evidence of "what works" led to the rather sobering conclusion that involuntary penal intervention rarely produced consistent, systematic, or long lasting changes in their clients (Lipton, Martinson, and Wilks 1975). Robert Martinson's widely disseminated and pessimistic review of the efficacy of penal treatment, "What Works?", concluded that "with few and isolated exceptions, the rehabilitative efforts that have been reported so far have had no appreciable effects on recidivism" (1974:25). Similarly, Francis Allen's seminal analysis concluded: "Either because of scientific ignorance or institutional incapacities, a rehabilitative technique is lacking; we do not know how to prevent criminal recidivism by changing the characters and behavior of the offenders" (1981:34). Chapter 7 reviews more extensively subsequent treatment evaluation research and concludes that the case for penal rehabilitation remains unproved, at best.

Critics who questioned the efficacy of rehabilitation also challenged clinicians' therapeutic expertise. In the absence of a proven scientific basis, clinical discretion amounted to standardless subjectivity that resulted in discriminatory decisions (American Friends Service Committee 1971; Allen 1981). In the juvenile courts, critics argued that scientific knowledge about child development reflected the child-rearing preferences of white middle-class and professional parents and that social workers' decisions simply revealed their class and racial biases (Grubb and Lazerson 1982). The Progressives' justice system reforms delegated discretionary authority to social service personnel and clinical experts, rather than to judges or elected public officials, to make critical social control decisions. Claims of professional expertise provided the rationale for them to exercise discretion. Evaluation research that challenged their scientific foundations also called into question the processes by which they made their decisions. An intimate association exists between standardless discretion and discrimination in the juvenile and criminal justice systems. As recalled from chapter 2, Progressives did not regard systematic discrimination against ethnic or racial minorities as an aberration of the treatment ideology but, rather, one of its major and deliberate assimilationist strategies, an effort to make "them" like "us." In the 1960s the discovery of pluralism and diversity, the validity of being "them," and an emphasis on equality rendered defense of a discriminatory regime more difficult.

Increasing youth crime, dissatisfaction with the treatment model, and a reduction in public resources to fund rehabilitative programs prompted calls for a return to classical principles of criminal law. During the 1970s, critics of rehabilitation, individualization, and indeterminate sentencing swung the penal policy pendulum toward determinate sentences and just-deserts to protect individual liberty and autonomy (Von Hirsch 1976). The "just deserts" critique of rehabilitation produced a strange amalgam of philosophical and political bedfellows: liberals concerned about unwarranted state intrusions, excessive discretion, and discriminatory decisions by criminal justice personnel and conservatives who denounced treatment as "soft on crime" and advocated a return to law and order and a reduced state welfare role (Cullen and Gilbert 1982). Although most criminological research analyzes the impact of just-deserts jurisprudence on criminal court sentencing practices (Tonry 1996), chapters 6 and 7 examine how the just-deserts critique affected juvenile courts' waiver and sentencing practices as well.

The Warren Court and the "Due Process Revolution"

The framers of the U.S. Constitution adopted the Bill of Rights and enumerated criminal procedural safeguards to protect citizens against the excesses of governmental power. The Progressives disregarded the possibility of conflict between governmental power and citizens' liberty interests, redefined some forms of state coercion as benevolent social services, and insulated them from formal legal limitations (D. Rothman 1978). Progressives' solicitude for the disadvantaged focused far more on responding to their "needs" than restricting the state's role. Under the guise of *parens patriae*, Progressives placed the poor and immigrants at a further disadvantage by casting them in a dependent, childlike role—as people to be "done to" or "done for" rather than "done with." "They did not require protection against the well-meaning parents, rights to be exercised against the paternalistic state" (D. Rothman 1978:70). Social welfare professionals' paternalistic ideology ignored the possibility that their clients might experience their benevolently motivated coercion as a punitive intrusion. "In their eagerness to play parents to the child, they did not pause to ask whether the dependent had to be protected against their own well-meaning interventions" (D. Rothman 1978:72). Throughout most of the twentieth century, uncritical faith in therapists' expertise and professionalism muted concerns about procedural safeguards to limit abuses. Moreover, the penal focus on individual pathology diverted public and political attention from a broader, social structural critique of the causes of crime, inequalities in the administration of juvenile and criminal courts, or issues of racial and social justice.

The need for procedural safeguards surfaced as critics questioned the benevolence of state coercion and the expertise of criminal justice and social service personnel. "It no longer seems appropriate to endow public or private officials with a wide latitude for the exercise of their authority. Since neither the motives, which are assumed to be social control, nor their decisions, which might well involve commitment to an institution, now seem acceptable, their prerogatives and powers must be carefully defined, bound in and circumscribed through detailed and precise laws and regulations" (D. Rothman 1978: 84). The antagonistic interests of the servers and served emerged with the erosion of the Progressives' assumptions about societal consensus. Once the Supreme Court recognized the punitive potential and conflicts of interests of benevolent coercion, it endorsed the familiar adversarial model, rather than a paternalistic one, to resolve disputes.

The Supreme Court resorted to adversarial procedural safeguards and other judicial rules to limit the state, to constrain discretion, and to protect people's freedom and liberties. Several threads weave through the fabric of the Supreme Court's "due process" jurisprudence: an increased emphasis on individual liberty and equality, a distrust of state power, an unwillingness to rely solely on good intentions and benevolent motives, and criticisms of discretion in the treatment of deviants. And the question of race tied together all these separate strands. Black migration during and after World War II increased nonsouthern minority populations, concentrated them in urban ghettoes, and eventually prompted the Supreme Court's civil rights decisions. Black migration and urbanization made issues of race a national, rather than regional, question. And the population shifts altered the balance of political power and thereby affected the characteristics of the justices whom Presidents Dwight Eisenhower, John Kennedy, and Lyndon Johnson appointed to the Court.

The Warren Court emerged to fill a public policy void created by southern congressional opposition to civil rights legislation. In the 1950s and 1960s, racial justice and urban social problems presented volatile political issues that the legislative branch failed or refused to address. By the 1960s the Court embarked on a course of judicial activism to protect individual rights, civil liberties, and minorities' interests from governmental and majoritarian impositions. The disadvantaged status of racial minorities in a society formally committed to legal equality posed a constitutional dilemma with international ramifications. In the cold war global competition with Communism for dominance in the decolonizing countries of the Third World, America's domestic racial relations belied the values of liberty, equality, and democracy it promoted so vigorously abroad (Hodgson 1976).

Beginning with the struggle for racial justice to desegregate schools in *Brown vs. Board of Education* (347 U.S. 483 [1954]), during the 1960s the Warren Court interpreted the Fourteenth Amendment of the Constitution and the Bill of Rights to restrict governmental intervention in citizens' lives, to extend equality to minorities and the disenfranchised, and to regularize administrative and criminal justice decision making (Graham 1970). The

Court's criminal procedure decisions followed closely upon its civil rights opinions because criminal accuseds consisted disproportionately of the poor, minorities, and the young. The Warren Court's due process revolution reformed the criminal and juvenile justice systems and the administration of social services. It represented a judicial effort to expand civil rights, to protect minorities from state officials, to impose the rule of law and procedural restraints on official discretion, and to infuse governmental services with greater equality (Graham 1970; D. Rothman 1978). It culminated a judicial shift from using the Constitution's commerce, contracts, and due process clauses to protect private property and economic interests from state and federal regulations to using the Bill of Rights, due process and equal protection clauses to protect civil rights and civil liberties against governmental encroachment and to provide criminal suspects with procedural protections. The Court's decisions redefined the relationship between individuals and the state and reflected the crucial linkage between race, civil rights, and criminal justice policies. Both the coercive sides of governmental benevolence and the explicitly punitive criminal justice systems affect the poor and minorities disproportionately; discretionary decision making places them at a disadvantage relative to white people. The erosion of social cohesion in the 1960s threatened the legitimacy of criminal and juvenile justice agencies. State and local law enforcement agents explicitly politicized criminal justice administration and used the criminal law to suppress rising racial militancy and the Civil Rights movement and to prosecute middle-class youths for antiwar and antidraft protest activities (Beckett 1997). For many young people in the counterculture, smoking marijuana symbolized an innocuous element of an "alternative lifestyle," and their criminal prosecution to suppress its use reflected another form of cultural imperialism. The decline of public authority deprived the criminal sanction of moral legitimacy and promoted a view of law as an instrument of oppression and social control wielded by those with power and influence.

The Supreme Court used three interrelated constitutional strategies to decide criminal procedure cases: incorporation, reinterpretation, and equal protection. First it "incorporated" many of the provisions of the Bill of Rights into the Fourteenth Amendment's due process clause and applied those provisions to the states. Second, it "reinterpreted" those provisions, redefined and expanded the meanings of those constitutional rights, and exercised greater judicial oversight over local law enforcement officials. Finally, it expanded greatly the principles of equal protection of law and extended constitutional safeguards to administrative officials previously immune from judicial scrutiny (Graham 1970). The Court used equal protection to redress imbalances between white and nonwhite and rich and poor defendants in states' criminal justice administration. Promoting equality and protecting minorities from arbitrary governmental action provided a central theme in the Court's decisions. In *The Due Process Revolution*, Fred Graham draws the direct connections between *Brown v. Board of Education*, racial equality, and criminal justice reforms:

As if it were not unfortunate enough to have a revolution in defendant's rights coincide with a crime scare, both developments are complicated further by their subtle connection with the problem of the Negro. The Supreme Court was drawn into reforming the criminal law when it set out to give Negroes equal rights before the civil laws and was faced with the absurdity of leaving them with no effective rights before the criminal law. Having outlawed Jim Crow, the Court had to humble John Law. (Graham 1970:12)

The Constitutional Context of Juvenile Cases

The Supreme Court used its constitutional due process strategy to reform states' social welfare and social control agencies as well as their criminal justice system procedures. The Court imposed more stringent restrictions and procedural requirements and required public officials to provide a "due process" hearing to people adversely affected by their decisions. In a series of decisions, the Court required states to provide citizens with due process, for example, when they attempted to civilly commit involuntarily mentally ill persons, to change prison inmates' custody classifications, to expel college students from a public universities, and to terminate the benefits of welfare recipients. Increasingly, whenever state action affected individuals, whether to punish, to classify for benefits, or even to assist them, the Court required the states to provide the people affected by those actions with an opportunity to participate in the process and be heard.

President's Commission on Law Enforcement and Administration of Justice

The President's Commission on Law Enforcement and Administration of Justice (Crime Commission) provided additional impetus for the Supreme Court's reform of criminal and juvenile justice (1967a, 1967b). The Crime Commission critically examined many aspects of juvenile justice administration, acknowledged that "the great hopes originally held for the juvenile court have not been fulfilled," and made a number of recommendations that Supreme Court decisions later endorsed and state legislatures adopted (1967a: 80). The Crime Commission (1967b) suggested, for example, that the juvenile court ultimately might evolve into a two-track system with separate criminal social control and social welfare functions. In such a system, public officials would divert and handle informally most minor delinquents and status offenders. "In place of the formal system, dispositional alternatives to adjudication must be developed for dealing with juveniles. . . . The range of conduct for which court intervention is authorized should be narrowed with greater emphasis upon consensual and informal means of meeting the problems of difficult children" (Crime Commission 1967b:2). Most juveniles commit trivial offenses, outgrow their delinquencies normally, and do not require formal intervention. The commission and other analysts recommended policies of "judicious non-intervention" (1967b:91) or even "radical nonintervention"

(Schur 1973) to avoid stigmatizing such juveniles. Chapter 5 directly links legislative policies in the 1970s to divert and decarcerate status offenders to these commission recommendations.

The commission also acknowledged that juvenile courts intervened to control crime rather than simply to treat youths and recommended that public officials refer more serious offenders for formal adjudication:

> The cases that fall within the narrowed jurisdiction of the court and filter through the screen of pre-judicial, informal disposition methods would largely involve offenders for whom more vigorous measures seem necessary. Court adjudication and disposition of those offenders should no longer be viewed solely as a diagnosis and prescription for cure, but should be frankly recognized as an authoritative court judgment expressing society's claim to protection. While rehabilitative efforts should be vigorously pursued in deference to the youth of the offenders and in keeping with a general commitment to individualized treatment of all offenders, the incapacitative, deterrent, and condemnatory aspects of the judgment should not be disguised. (Crime Commission 1967b:2)

The Crime Commission endorsed the punitive and condemnatory functions of the criminal law and noted:

> The juvenile court is a court of law, charged like other agencies of criminal justice with protecting the community against threatening conduct. Rehabilitation of offenders through individualized handling is one way of providing protection, and appropriately the primary way of dealing with children. But the guiding considerations for a court of law that deals with the threatening conduct is nevertheless protection of the community. The juvenile court, like other courts, is therefore obliged to employ all the means at hand, not excluding incapacitation, for achieving that protection. *What should distinguish the juvenile from the criminal courts is their greater emphasis on rehabilitation, not their exclusive preoccupation with it.* (1967a:81, emphasis added)

Because the second prong of the two-track juvenile justice system emphasized criminal law enforcement and the possibility of punishment, the Crime Commission (1967a) also recommended that juvenile courts provide criminal procedural safeguards to juvenile offenders. Benevolent motives and good intentions provided inadequate protections of young peoples' self-determination and freedom. The commission endorsed constitutional protections whenever the state supervised, controlled, or placed a child in an institution. "[I]n point of fact, the welfare and the needs of the child offender are not the sole preoccupation of the juvenile court, which has the same purposes that mark the criminal law. To the extent that this is so, the justification for abandoning the protective procedural guarantees associated with due process of law disappears" (Crime Commission 1967a:85).

In 1967, *In re Gault* (387 U.S. 1) inaugurated the due process revolution of the juvenile court and substantially transformed it from a social welfare agency into a legal institution. The "constitutional domestication" marked the first step in the procedural and substantive convergence of the juvenile and the adult criminal justice systems (Paulsen 1957, 1967; Feld 1984). Several years before *Gault*, Chief Justice Earl Warren addressed the National Council of Juvenile Court Judges and signaled the probable directions the Court would take. While Chief Justice Warren acknowledged that juvenile courts differed from criminal courts, he insisted that they "must function within the framework of law and that in the attainment of its objectives it cannot act with unbridled caprice" (1964:14). Although the Supreme Court only decides the specific legal issues that a case presents to it, Warren identified several "hypothetical" procedural issues that juvenile courts raised:

> I think lawyers can be most useful and helpful to the court. . . . I can suggest that a reasonable adherence to orderly presentation of the facts in a particular case will prevent miscalculations and minimize the possibilities of miscarriages of justice. . . . There is also a growing awareness on the part of the courts and the public of the right of each individual, whether child or adult, to a full and fair hearing. . . . [W]hat we are striving for is not merely "equal" justice for juveniles. They deserve much more than being afforded only the privileges and protections that are applied to their elders. (1964:15–16).

Soon after Warren's address to the juvenile court judges' association, the "hypothetical" case he described arrived on the Court's docket.

In re Gault involved the delinquency adjudication and institutional confinement of a youth who allegedly made a lewd telephone call of the "irritatingly offensive, adolescent, sex variety" to a neighbor woman (387 U.S. at 4). Police took fifteen-year-old Gerald Gault into custody, detained him overnight without notification to his parents, and required him to appear at a juvenile court hearing the following day. A probation officer filed a pro forma petition that alleged simply that Gault was a delinquent minor in need of the care and custody of the court. No complaining witnesses appeared, and the juvenile court neither took sworn testimony nor prepared a transcript or written memorandum of the proceedings. At the hearing, the juvenile court judge interrogated Gault about the alleged telephone call and he apparently made some incriminating responses. The judge did not advise Gault of the right to remain silent or the right to counsel or provide him with the assistance of an attorney. Following his hearing, the judge returned Gault to a detention cell for several more days. At his dispositional hearing the following week, the judge committed Gault as a juvenile delinquent to the State Industrial School "for the period of his minority [that is, until twenty-one], unless sooner discharged by due process of law." If a criminal court judge had convicted Gault as an adult, it could have sentenced him to only a $50 fine or two months' imprisonment for his offense. Because a juvenile court adjudicated Gault as a delinquent, however, he faced the possibility of incarceration for up to six years, the duration of his minority.

Rather than accepting uncritically the rehabilitative rhetoric of Progressive juvenile jurisprudence, the *Gault* Court examined the punitive realities of juvenile justice administration. The stark contrast between reformers' optimistic, idealistic expectations and juvenile courts' actual practical accomplishments provided the impetus for constitutional change. The Supreme Court reviewed the history of the juvenile court and the traditional rationales to deny procedural safeguards to juveniles. Progressives characterized delinquency proceedings as informal and civil, rather than as adversarial or criminal, and asserted that when the state acted as *parens patriae*, children should receive custody rather than liberty. The Court rejected these assertions and noted that denial of procedures frequently resulted in judicial arbitrariness rather than "careful, compassionate, individualized treatment" (387 U.S at 18). Although the Court hoped to retain the potential benefits of the juvenile process, it candidly appraised the claims of the juvenile court in the light of the realities of recidivism, the failures of rehabilitation, the stigma of a delinquency label, the breaches of confidentiality, and the arbitrariness of the process. A juvenile justice process free of constitutional safeguards neither abated recidivism nor lowered high crime rates among juvenile offenders. The Supreme Court described the realities of juvenile institutional incarceration and mandated elementary procedural safeguards as a prerequisite of confinement. These safeguards included advance notice of charges, a fair and impartial hearing, assistance of counsel, an opportunity to confront and cross-examine witnesses, and a privilege against self-incrimination.

Although the Court discussed the realities of the juvenile system and mandated procedural safeguards, it narrowly limited its holding to the adjudicatory hearing—the trial—at which a juvenile court decides whether a child has committed a criminal act (Rosenberg 1980; McCarthy 1981). The *Gault* Court held that juvenile proceedings required some adversarial procedural safeguards both to determine the truth of allegations *and* to limit the power of the state and preserve individual freedom. *Gault* did not limit juvenile courts' substantive jurisdiction or dispositional authority, and the Court insisted that providing procedural safeguards would not adversely affect their unique ability to process or treat juveniles. The Court specifically held that "[w]e do not in this opinion consider the impact of these constitutional provisions upon the totality of the relationship of the juvenile and the state. We do not even consider the entire process relating to juvenile 'delinquents' " (387 U.S. at 13).

By limiting its ruling to delinquency cases in which states charge a youth with a criminal offense and threaten to confine him in an institution, the Court implicitly endorsed the Crime Commission's recommendations and encouraged states to develop alternative strategies for noncriminal status offenders. In chapter 5, I argue that states accepted this invitation; created new nondelinquency labels, such as Persons in Need of Supervision (PINS) and Children in Need of Protection and Services (CHIPS); devised alternative, noninstitutional dispositions for noncriminal offenders; and continued to treat status offenders as if the Court never had decided *Gault* (Sutton 1988; Chesney-Lind and Sheldon 1992). And, as chapter 7 demonstrates, after a trial that provides the rudimentary protections required by *Gault*, in most states a juvenile court judge may impose any sentence that her "sound discretion" dictates. Indeed, after a fair trial, in most states today, a juvenile court judge still could sentence a youth to a training school for a term of years or the duration of her minority for a "lewd" telephone call.

In contrast to its narrow holding, Justice Abe Fortas, for the majority, based the Court's ruling on the Fourteenth Amendment's broad and general guarantees of "due process" and "fundamental fairness," rather than on the specific requirements of the Bill of Rights. The Court required notice of charges, assistance of counsel, and an opportunity to confront and cross-examine witnesses in delinquency hearings as a matter of "due process" rather than because the Sixth Amendment explicitly enumerated those procedural rights (387 U.S. 1, at 30). On the other hand, the Court relied on the specific provisions of the Fifth Amendment to guarantee juveniles the privilege against self-incrimination in delinquency proceedings:

> It would be entirely unrealistic to carve out of the Fifth Amendment all statements by juveniles on the ground that these cannot lead to "criminal" involvement. In the first place, juvenile proceedings to determine "delinquency," which may lead to commitment to a state institution, must be regarded as "criminal" for purposes of the privilege against self-incrimination. . . . [C]ommitment is a deprivation of liberty. It is incarceration against one's will, whether it is called civil or criminal. (*In re Gault*, 387 U.S. 1, at 49–50 [1967])

Once *Gault* applied the constitutional privilege against self-incrimination to delinquency proceedings, proponents of a treatment model no longer could characterize juvenile courts either as "noncriminal" or as "nonadversarial." The Fifth Amendment's privilege against self-incrimination, more than any other provision of the Bill of Rights, serves as the fundamental guarantor of an adversarial process and the primary mechanism to maintain a balance between the state and the individual. In other decisions, the Court described the policies of the Fifth Amendment as reflecting "our preference for an accusatorial rather than an inquisitorial system of criminal justice. . . . [and] our sense of fair play which dictates a 'fair state-individual balance by requiring the government to leave the individual alone until good cause is shown for disturbing him and by requiring the government in its contest with the individual to shoulder the entire load' " (*Murphy v. Waterfront Commission*, 378 U.S. 52, at 55 [1964]).

The Court's extension of the self-incrimination protection provides the clearest example of the *dual functions* that procedural safeguards serve in juvenile court adjudications: to ensure accurate fact-finding *and* to protect against governmental oppression. If reliable juvenile confessions and accurate fact-finding had been *Gault*'s sole concerns, then safeguards other than the Fifth Amendment privilege, for example, requirements that juveniles confess voluntarily, would have sufficed. As I explain further in chapter 4, in both *Gallegos v. Colorado* (370 U.S. 49 [1962]) and *Haley v. Ohio* (332 U.S. 596 [1948]), the Supreme Court already employed the Fourteenth Amendment's "voluntariness" test to determine the admissibility of juveniles' confessions and concluded that youthfulness constituted a special circumstance that required close judicial scrutiny. Although the Fifth Amendment functions, in part, to ensure accurate fact-finding and reliable confessions, *Gault* recognized it functioned also to limit governmental overreaching and to maintain a proper balance between the individual and the state:

> The privilege against self-incrimination is, of course, related to the question of the safeguards necessary to assure that admissions or confessions are reasonably trustworthy, that they are not mere fruits of fear or coercion, but are reliable expressions of the truth. The roots of the privilege are, however, far deeper. They tap the basic stream of religious and political principle because the privilege reflects the limits of the individual's attornment to the state and—in a philosophical sense—insists upon the equality of the individual and the state. In other words, the privilege has a broader and deeper thrust than the rule which prevents the use of confessions which are the product of coercion because coercion is thought to carry with it the danger of unreliability. One of its purposes is to prevent the state, whether by force or by psychological domination, from overcoming the mind and will of the person under investigation and depriving him of the freedom to decide whether to assist the state in securing his conviction. (387 U.S. at 47)

In this respect, *Gault* represents a premier example of the Warren Court's belief that expanding constitutional rights and adversarial procedures would restrict the coercive powers of the state, ensure the regularity of law enforcement, and thereby reduce the need for continual judicial scrutiny.

> Surely one of the most distinctive tendencies of the Warren Court was its allegiance to the adversary theory of criminal justice. Thus, a large part of the Court's work in the criminal area consisted of its efforts to revitalize the adversary process in those areas of the system in which it was always supposed to flourish. . . . Even more striking, however, are the cases in which the Court extended the adversary process into areas of the system in which, theretofore, adversary proceedings were unknown or rarely employed. (Allen 1975:530–531)

Although Justice Hugo Black concurred with the majority opinion in *Gault*, he argued that delinquents should receive the exact same criminal procedural safeguards that the Bill of Rights guaranteed for adults, rather than some "watered-down" judicial version of "fairness" embodied in the concept of "due process":

> Where a person, infant or adult, can be seized by the State, charged, and convicted for violating a state criminal law, and then ordered by the State to be confined for six years, I think the Constitution requires that he be tried in accordance with the guarantees of all the provisions of the Bill of Rights. . . . Undoubtedly this would be true of an adult defendant, and it would be a plain denial of equal protection of the laws—an invidious discrimination—to hold that others subject to heavier punishments could, because they are children, be denied these same constitutional safeguards. (387 U.S. at 61)

Justice Black recognized that criminal procedural parity might strike "a well-nigh fatal blow to much that is unique about the juvenile courts" (387 U.S.

at 60) but regarded a delinquency proceeding as the functional equivalent of a criminal prosecution.

In its subsequent juvenile court decisions, the Supreme Court further elaborated on the criminal nature of delinquency proceedings. In *In re Winship* (397 U.S. 358 [1970]), the Court decided that the prosecution must establish delinquency by the criminal standard of proof "beyond a reasonable doubt" rather than by a lower civil standard of proof, such as the "preponderance of the evidence." Because no provision of the Bill of Rights specifically defined the standard of proof in criminal cases, *Winship* first held that constitutional due process required prosecutors to prove an adult criminal defendant's guilt "beyond a reasonable doubt." The Court then required the same highest standard of proof in delinquency proceedings because it played an equally vital role there (397 U.S. at 365–367). Although *parens patriae* intervention may be a desirable method to deal with wayward youths, the *Winship* majority concluded that "intervention cannot take the form of subjecting the child to the stigma of a finding that he violated a criminal law and to the possibility of institutional confinement on proof insufficient to convict him were he an adult" (397 U.S. at 367). Rather, the Court required the highest standard of proof to protect juveniles against unwarranted convictions, to guard against abuses of governmental power, and to ensure public confidence in the administration of the criminal law. These considerations sufficiently outweighed the *Winship* dissenters' concerns that the higher standard might thwart juvenile courts' unique therapeutic functions and erode further "differences between juvenile courts and traditional criminal courts" (397 U.S. at 376–377).

Comparing the standard of proof used in delinquency cases with that required for involuntary civil commitment of mentally ill persons further demonstrates the Court's jurisprudential equation between criminal trials and delinquency proceedings. In *Addington v. Texas* (441 U.S. 418, 433 [1979]), the Court required only "clear and convincing" evidence for involuntary civil commitment proceedings and distinguished the loss of liberty there from that in delinquency hearings: "The Court [in *Winship*] saw no controlling difference in loss of liberty and stigma between a conviction for an adult and a delinquency adjudication for a juvenile. *Winship* recognized that the basic issue—whether the individual in fact committed a criminal act—was the same in both proceedings. There being no meaningful distinctions between the two proceedings, we required the state to prove the juvenile's act and intent beyond a reasonable doubt" (441 U.S. at 427–428). The *Addington* Court also noted that proof "beyond a reasonable doubt" in criminal cases functions to preserve the " 'moral force of the criminal law,'. . . . and we should hesitate to apply it too broadly or casually in noncriminal cases" (441 U.S. at 426).

Five years after *Winship*, the Court in *Breed v. Jones* (421 U.S. 519 [1975]), held that the double jeopardy clause of the Fifth Amendment prohibits a state from criminally reprosecuting a youth as an adult after previously convicting him for the same offense in a juvenile delinquency proceeding. Although the Court framed the issue in terms of the applicability of an explicit provision of the Bill of Rights to state proceedings, it again resolved the question by recognizing the functional equivalence and identical interests of defendants in delinquency proceedings and adult criminal trials. The Court reiterated:

> Although the juvenile-court system had its genesis in the desire to provide a distinctive procedure and setting to deal with the problems of youth, including those manifested by antisocial conduct, our decisions in recent years have recognized that there is a gap between the originally benign conception of the system and its realities. . . . [I]t is simply too late in the day to conclude . . . that a juvenile is not put in jeopardy at a proceeding whose object is to determine whether he has committed acts that violate a criminal law and whose potential consequences include both the stigma inherent in such a determination and the deprivation of liberty for many years. (421 U.S. at 528–529)

With respect to the risks and burdens associated with double jeopardy, the Court concluded that "we can find no persuasive distinction in that regard between the [juvenile] proceeding. . . . and a criminal prosecution, each of which is designed to 'vindicate [the] very vital interest in enforcement of criminal laws' " (421 U.S. at 531).

Despite their functional equivalency and similar purposes, the juvenile and criminal justice systems do not use identical, or even comparable, procedural safeguards. In *McKeiver v. Pennsylvania* (403 U.S. 528 [1971]), the Court declined to extend to juvenile courts all the procedural safeguards associated with adult criminal prosecutions. The Court in *McKeiver* held that the Constitution does not guarantee a right to a jury trial in a juvenile delinquency proceeding, because "due process" and "fundamental fairness" require only "accurate fact finding," a requirement that judges can satisfy as well as juries. Significantly, between the *Gault* and *McKeiver* decisions, the Supreme Court decided *Duncan v. Louisiana* (391 U.S. 145 [1968]), which held that the Fourteenth Amendment's due process clause applied the Sixth Amendment's right to a jury trial to state criminal prosecutions of adults because the jury was "fundamental to the American scheme of justice" (391 U.S. at 149). However, the Supreme Court decided *McKeiver* solely on the basis of Fourteenth Amendment due process and "fundamental fairness," without reference to the Sixth Amendment or its *Duncan* rationale. The Court noted that "the juvenile court proceeding has not yet been held to be a 'criminal prosecution,' within the meaning and reach of the Sixth Amendment, and also has not yet been regarded as devoid of criminal aspects merely because it usually has been given the civil label" (*McKeiver*, 403 U.S. at 541). The Court cautioned that "[t]here is a possibility, at least, that the jury trial, if required as a matter of constitutional precept, will remake the juvenile proceeding into a fully adversary process and will put an effective end to what has been the idealistic prospect of an intimate, informal protective proceeding" (403 U.S. at 545).

In suggesting that due process in the juvenile context required nothing more than accurate fact-finding, however, the *McKeiver* Court departed significantly from its own prior analyses in *Gault* and *Winship*. Those decisions emphasized the *dual* functions of constitutional criminal procedures to ensure accurate fact-finding *and* to protect against governmental oppression. For example, *Gault* granted juveniles the Fifth Amendment's privilege against self-incrimination in order to protect against governmental oppression even though juveniles' exercise of the right actually might impede accurate fact-finding. Indeed, at several places in the *McKeiver* opinion, the Court conspicuously omitted the privilege against self-incrimination from the list of rights—notice, counsel, hearing, confrontation, and cross-examination—it attributed to *Gault* (*McKeiver*, 403 U.S. at 532, 543). The *McKeiver* plurality no doubt recognized that *Gault*'s Fifth Amendment rationale "criminalized" delinquency proceedings. If juvenile courts may be characterized as criminal for purposes of the Fifth Amendment, then why not for purposes of the Sixth Amendment's right to a jury?

The *McKeiver* Court plurality denied that juveniles required protection against governmental oppression, rejected the argument that the inbred, closed nature of the juvenile court could prejudice the accuracy of fact-finding, and invoked the mythology of the sympathetic, paternalistic juvenile court judge:

> Concern about the inapplicability of exclusionary and other rules of evidence, about the juvenile court judge's possible awareness of the juvenile's prior record and of the contents of the social file; about repeated appearances of the same familiar witnesses in the persons of juvenile and probation officers and social workers—all to the effect that this will create the likelihood of prejudgment—chooses to ignore, it seems to us, every aspect of fairness, of concern, of sympathy, and of paternal attention that the juvenile court system contemplates. (403 U.S. at 550)

Rather than identifying the affirmative protections that procedural safeguards provide, the Court in *McKeiver* emphasized the adverse impact that a constitutional right to a jury trial would have on the flexibility and confidentiality of juvenile court proceedings. The Court feared that the right to a jury trial would disrupt juvenile courts, substantially alter their informal practices, and bring "the traditional delay, the formality, and the clamor of the adversary system and, possibly, the public trial" (403 U.S. at 550). Ultimately, the Court realized that the right to a jury trial would render juvenile courts procedurally indistinguishable from criminal courts and raise the question whether any reasons remained for a separate juvenile court.

While the Court feared that a constitutional right to a jury trial would adversely affect the juvenile court, it also doubted that the right would affirmatively aid or strengthen the functioning of the juvenile justice system. Although the *McKeiver* Court found faults with the juvenile process, it asserted that imposing jury trials would not correct those deficiencies and would make the juvenile process unduly formal and adversarial. Chapter 4 examines whether juveniles might benefit from increased formality in delinquency proceedings and whether the Court's earlier decision in *Gault* had effectively foreclosed its renewed concern with flexibility and informality in delinquency trials. *McKeiver* did not indicate how a more formal hearing might preclude subsequently imposing a therapeutic disposition. Although the Court decried the possibility of public trials, it neither analyzed why confidential proceedings constituted an indispensable element of juvenile justice nor addressed whether juveniles or the public might derive any advantages from the increased visibility and accountability of juvenile courts.

Ultimately, the *McKeiver* Court denied young offenders the right to a jury trial in juvenile court because it adhered to the ideal of *treatment of children* in a separate justice system. While the Court acknowledged the deficiencies and disappointments of the rehabilitative ideal, it did not want to express its "ultimate disillusionment," abandon those concepts, and return young offenders to the criminal justice system (403 U.S. at 546). Critically, however, the *McKeiver* Court did not analyze either the constitutional differences between *treatment* and *punishment* or between youths and adults that justified a different form of procedural justice for delinquents. Chapter 7 analyzes juvenile justice sentencing policies and practices and argues that treating juveniles closely resembles punishing adults and thereby undermines *McKeiver*'s rationale for different procedures in the two justice systems.

Conclusion

The migration of African Americans from the rural South to the urban industrial North during the first half of the twentieth century brought the issue of race to the political and legal foreground. The Supreme Court's civil rights decisions began to dismantle the legacy of de jure segregation and racial discrimination and to establish legal equality. The Supreme Court's due process strategy attempted to control states' criminal justice administration and foster the rule of law. In a similar fashion, *Gault* and its progeny began the "constitutional domestication" of the juvenile court and the recognition of young people's legal rights. Ironically, the demographic bulge of the baby boom and its escalating crime rates occurred simultaneously with the Court's attempts to reform states' criminal procedures. Despite the underlying structural and demographic complexities of the 1960s, many critics of the Warren Court's "liberal" decisions simplistically associated them with turmoil on campus, the anarchy of the youth culture, rising youth crime rates, and urban racial disorder. Subsequent decades have witnessed a more "conservative" legal era and a retrenchment in the Court's role to advance racial justice, civil rights, criminal procedural safeguards, and, for our purposes, the legal rights of young people.

Gault precipitated a procedural revolution that unintentionally but inevitably transformed the juvenile court. Progressive reformers focused on a child's social circumstances, environment, and "real needs"; intervened to rehabilitate rather than punish; and regarded proof of a specific offense as secondary. Although *McKeiver* declined to extend a constitutional right to a jury trial to juveniles, *Gault* and *Winship* endorsed the adversarial model, the right to counsel, the privilege against self-incrimination, the criminal standard of proof beyond a reasonable doubt, and the primacy of factual and legal guilt as a constitutional prerequisite of state intervention. As a consequence, the Court redefined delinquents as a subgroup of criminal defendants, rather than as a category of dependent children in need of services. By emphasizing criminal procedural regularity, the Court shifted juvenile courts' focus from "real needs" to "criminal deeds" and effectively altered delinquency proceedings from an inquiry about social welfare into a criminal prosecution. By imposing procedural limitations on coerced treatment, the Court acknowledged that young offenders required some protections even when the state purports to act in their best interests. By limiting *parens patriae* theory, the Court provided the impetus to reexamine the underlying premises of juvenile courts, and to shift them toward more traditional criminal law principles, such as punishment and personal accountability. By formalizing the connections between criminal behavior and sanctions, the Court made explicit the criminal law foundations of juvenile courts that Progressives deliberately tried to obscure. By providing juveniles with most, but not all, criminal procedural safeguards, the Court ironically legitimated the imposition of more punitive sentences.

The differences between the Court's rationale in *Gault* and in *McKeiver* reveal a more fundamental dilemma in the legal construction and social control of adolescents. The Supreme Court's constitutional jurisprudence of *youth* reflects a cultural ambivalence about "children's rights," vacillates between imagery of dependency and vulnerability and of responsibility and autonomy, and oscillates between seemingly "liberationist" and "protectionist" outcomes. While children enjoy some limited freedom of expression (*Tinker v. Des Moines School District*, 393 U.S. 503 [1969]) and protection against arbitrary suspension from school (*Goss v. Lopez*, 419 U.S. 565 [1975]), the Court subsequently subordinated juveniles' free speech rights to adults' interests in maintaining decorum and orthodoxy in schools (*Bethel School District v. Fraser*, 478 U.S. 675 [1986]; *Hazelwood School District v. Kuhlmeier*, 108 S. Ct. 562 [1988]). While the Court acknowledges young people's Fourth Amendment freedom from "unreasonable searches and seizures," it subordinates their privacy interests to a much greater extent than adults' in order to maintain school discipline (*New Jersey v. T.L.O.*, 469 U.S. 325 [1985]; *Vernonia School District v. Acton*, 515 U.S. 646 [1995]). While parents cannot absolutely veto their daughter's decision to obtain an abortion (*Bellotti v. Baird*, 443 U.S. 622 [1979]), the Court allows them to confine her involuntarily for "treatment" in a mental hospital without any judicial review because "parents know best" (*Parham v. J.R.*, 442 U.S. 584 [1979]).

These decisions waver between two competing visions of children and reflect legal and cultural ambivalence about adolescents. In some intances, the legal order regards young people as autonomous, responsible, and self-determining and, in other cases, views them as immature, incompetent, and subject to adult controls. "The Court's ambivalence swings between two starkly contrasting alternatives. One would extend adult rights to children; the other would treat children in important ways as subject to different authorities, institutions, and relationships than adults" (Minow 1995:277). The legal ambivalence reveals a simultaneous commitment to inconsistent positions. Recognition of young people as autonomous decision makers and possessed of legal rights conflicts with the cultural conception and social construction of adolescents as immature, irresponsible, and dependent on other adults.

Recent efforts to advance the legal rights of young people typically founder when they challenge traditional authority. Since the high-water mark of the Warren Court's due process revolution, most of the Supreme Court's decisions preserve the authority of adult institutions—parents, teachers, doctors, and juvenile courts—against either "liberationist" claims by youths for autonomy and equality or "protectionist" pleas for special consideration (Minow 1995). The Supreme Court's contradictory characterizations of young people as immature or as responsible provide it with a convenient rationale with which to minimize either claims for legal parity or special protections (Dale 1992). The Court decides the result that will maximize the legal and social control of young people and then selects from its alternative formulations the rationale to justify that predetermined outcome. The Court employs protectionist rhetoric to subordinate the legal rights of young people and uses autonomy rhetoric when self-determination facilitates adult social control (Geimer 1988; Minow 1995). An authoritarian vision of *parens patriae* that emphasizes discipline and control, rather than protection, explains most recent constitutional decisions affecting the rights of young people.

Since the *Gault, Winship*, and *McKeiver* decisions, legislative, judicial, and administrative responses have transformed the juvenile court and fostered a procedural and substantive convergence with adult criminal courts. Chapter 4 examines the formal procedural safeguards of the juvenile court. While, theoretically, delinquency proceedings increasingly resemble those of the adult criminal process, in reality, the quality of procedural justice for young people remains far less than the minimum insisted on for adult offenders. Courts and legislatures choose between competing characterizations of young people as autonomous and self-determining or as immature and incompetent in order to maximize their social control. Thus, the exercise of procedural rights in juvenile courts illustrates the more general social and legal construction of youth.

I I I I FOUR

Procedural Justice in Juvenile Courts

Law on the Books and Law in Action

Procedure and substance intertwine inextricably in juvenile courts. Progressives envisioned an informal court that made decisions in the child's "best interests." The Supreme Court in *Gault* emphasized the disjunctions between rehabilitative rhetoric and punitive reality and required greater procedural safeguards in juvenile courts (*In re Gault*, 387 U.S. 1 [1967]). Although *Gault* provided impetus for the procedural convergence between juvenile and criminal courts, a substantial gulf remains between theory and reality, between the "law on the books" and the "law in action." Theoretically, the Constitution and state laws entitle delinquents to formal trials and assistance of counsel. In reality, juvenile courts try youths using procedures to which few adults would consent. More than three decades ago, the Supreme Court in *Kent v. United States* observed that "the child receives the *worst of both worlds*: he gets neither the protections accorded to adults nor the solicitous care and regenerative treatment postulated for children" (383 U.S. 541, 556 [1966], emphasis added). In the "worst of both worlds" of contemporary juvenile justice youths continue to receive neither therapy nor justice, but instead experience punishment without the criminal procedural safeguards provided to adults.

Despite the criminalizing of juvenile courts, most states provide neither special procedures to protect juveniles from their own immaturity nor the full panoply of adult procedural rights. In some instances, states treat delinquents just like adult criminal defendants when formal equality redounds to their disadvantage. In other cases, they use less-adequate juvenile court safeguards when those deficient procedures provide a comparative advantage to the state. Legislators and judges manipulate the competing legal views concerning young people as autonomous and responsible or as immature and incompetent to maximize social control, to reinforce legal paternalism, and to enhance adult authority. By using the fluid concepts of childhood or rehabilitation, as in *McKeiver*, for example, the Supreme Court readily subordinates young people's legal claims to procedural parity. Similarly, the Court in *Parham v. J.R.* (442 U.S. 584, 603 [1979]) asserted that adolescents lacked the ability to make sound, self-regarding medical judgments; indulged an idealized view of family life; and delegated to parents the authority "voluntarily" to confine young people in mental institutions. By contrast, during the same term the Court in *Fare v. Michael C.* (442 U.S. 707 [1979]) asserted that minors possess the capacity to invoke or "voluntarily" waive Fifth Amendment *Miranda* rights without any assistance from parents or consultation with lawyers and insisted that they do so with adultlike technical precision.

Despite the theoretical and formal procedural convergence between juvenile and criminal courts, youths continue to receive the "worst of both worlds." This chapter analyzes juveniles' waivers of their Fifth Amendment privilege against self-incrimination and their relinquishment of the right to counsel as instances in which the legal system formally treats youths and adults as equals and thereby places delinquents at a disadvantage. Most states use the adult legal standard of "knowing, intelligent, and voluntary" under the "totality of the circumstances" to assess the validity of juveniles' waivers of constitutional rights (*Fare*, 442 U.S. 707). These legal policies characterize young people as autonomous and responsible even though youths may not possess the capacity of adults to exercise or relinquish their constitutional rights in a knowing and intelligent manner (Grisso 1980, 1981). On the other hand, pretrial preventive detention (*Schall v. Martin*, 467 U.S. 253 [1984]) and denial of jury trials and public trials (*McKeiver v. Pennsylvania*, 403 U.S. 528 [1971]) provide examples of states' use of special "juvenile procedures" for which no direct adult analogues exist to provide a comparative advantage to the state. Courts and legislatures invoke either notions of rehabilitation or a conception of young people as vulnerable, immature, or entitled to "custody rather than liberty" to justify these procedural differences.

The legal construction of adolescence in the juvenile justice process contains an inherent, internal contradiction. As a matter of logic and consistency, either young offenders possess the competence of adults or they do not. If they do, then they deserve the same legal rights as adults, for better or worse. If they do not, then they require special procedural protections that recognize their immaturity and limitations and that protect them. In the "worst of both worlds" of juvenile justice, however, courts and legislators pick and choose between competing "liberationist" and "protectionist" policies in order to maximize the social control of young offenders. In some instances, they treat youths like adults when juveniles manifestly cannot function on a par. In other cases, they invoke the imagery of childhood to deny to youths the rights that adults enjoy. Before analyzing these legal manipulations of the competing formulations of adolescence, however, I will describe the context of juvenile justice administration within which youths exercise their procedural rights.

Social Welfare versus Due Process and Just Deserts: Varieties of Juvenile Courts

Analytical models help to illuminate for examination the substantive ends, procedural means, and ideological assumptions and values that underlie a justice system. Juvenile courts' operational policies and organizational practices reflect the cultural ambivalence embedded in the conflicting legal constructions of youths. Herbert Packer's (1968) seminal *Limits of the Criminal Sanction* describes competing models of the criminal process—"due process" and "crime control"—and analyzes the value choices embedded in their details. His framework helps to illustrate the values and policy preferences submerged in the minutiae of juvenile justice administration as well.

The "due process" model attempts to restrict the coercive powers of the state and to ensure the reliability of the process (Packer 1968). Because of the adverse consequences of an erroneous conviction, it places primary emphasis on the justice system's accuracy rather than on its efficiency. Formal procedures enhance reliability, provide a check against the inherent fallibility of any justice system, limit official powers, and ensure respect for individual liberty and autonomy. The *Gault* and *Winship* decisions reflect "due process" values and the primacy of the rule of law.

The "crime control" model emphasizes the efficient repression of crime to ensure the liberty of law-abiding persons (Packer 1968). To suppress crime efficiently, an administrative process that relies heavily on professional discretion and expertise rather than formal procedures separates the probably guilty from the marginally innocent. In a context of heavy caseloads and limited resources, crime control requires informal administrative processes to apprehend, convict, and dispose of cases quickly with minimal adversarial challenge. Progressive reformers' conception of the juvenile court exemplifies many features of a crime control model: discretionary decision making, heavy reliance on professional expertise, trust in state officials, an informal administrative process rather than a formal adjudicative one, and an absence of legal counsel. The Court in *McKeiver* denied juveniles a right to a jury trial to preserve an informal, flexible juvenile court.

Due process and crime control models provide analogues for juvenile courts. Efforts to construct empirical or ideal-typical paradigms of juvenile courts typically contrast between a "social welfare" or "treatment" model and a "just deserts" or "due process" model (e.g. Stapleton, Aday, and Ito 1982; Corrado and Turnbull 1992). In a welfare model, youths bear little responsibility for their misdeeds and officials decide informally and without extensive public scrutiny whether a youth requires intervention and what form it should take. Professionals respond to a youth's "needs" rather than "deeds" and provide indeterminate, nonproportional rehabilitative dispositions to promote his future welfare. By contrast, the juvenile just-deserts model reflects neoclassical assumptions of criminal law and characterizes youths as substantially responsible and accountable for their behavior (American Bar Association and Institute of Judicial Administration 1980d). However, young people are not the moral equals of adults and deserve mitigated sanctions for reduced culpability. Questions of guilt, innocence, blame, and punishment occupy the central focus; the court uses formal criminal procedures to determine legal guilt. Determinate and proportional sanctions emphasize personal responsibility, foster equality among similarly situated youthful offenders, and sentence for past offenses rather than for future welfare.

The substantial variability of juvenile courts both within and between states vastly complicates analyses of the "law on the books" and the "law in action." Progressives fostered procedural informality and judicial discretion, and evaluations of court operations focused primarily on the personal predilections of the presiding judges (Mack 1909; Rothman 1980). Analyses of contemporary juvenile courts continue to emphasize organizational diversity and variable judicial interpretation and application of laws (Rubin 1985). Since *Gault* imposed some formal procedures and states increasingly pursue punitive as well as therapeutic purposes, juvenile courts no longer conform either to the traditional rehabilitative model or even to one another. Ethnographic and qualitative studies of a single juvenile court seldom generalize to other courts in other locales (Cicourel 1968; Emerson 1969; Bortner 1982; Humes 1996). Comparative organizational studies of juvenile courts reveal their variability (Sari 1976; Cohen and Kluegel 1978, 1979; Hasenfeld and Cheung 1985).

Juvenile courts vary on several structural, philosophical, and procedural dimensions. A national study of 150 metropolitan juvenile courts identified clusters of factors—status offender orientation, centralization of authority, procedural formality, and intake screening discretion—and developed an empirical typology of metropolitan juvenile courts (Stapleton, Aday, and Ito 1982). The typology confirmed "the existence of the two major types of juvenile courts ('traditional' and 'due process') suggested in the literature" (Stapleton, Aday, and Ito 1982:559). In addition, however, "transitional courts" occupied an intermediate point in the transformation from informal traditional courts to formal due process–oriented courts. Traditional courts intervene on an informal, discretionary basis, whereas legalistic courts emphasize more formal, rule-oriented decision making and greater recognition of juveniles' legal rights. The presence of defense counsel provides one important indicator of procedural, substantive, and structural variations among juvenile courts (Handler 1965; Stapleton and Teitelbaum 1972; Cohen and Kluegel 1978; Feld 1991). Formal, due process courts and informal traditional courts differ in their rates of pretrial detention and appointment of counsel, as well as in their sentencing and case-processing practices (Feld 1993b; Kempf, Decker, and Bing 1990).

While juvenile courts vary substantially among the states, they vary considerably within a single state as well. Statutes and court rules of procedure typically apply to all juvenile courts within a state, but juvenile justice administration varies substantially with social structure and geographic locale (Mahoney 1987; Kempf, Decker, and Bing 1990; Feld 1991). Whether youths live in metropolitan areas with full-time juvenile courts or in rural areas with part-time juvenile judges, for example, affects how the justice system screens, detains, processes, and sanctions their cases. In urban counties, marked by heterogeneous, racially diverse, and residentially mobile populations, juvenile courts typically adhere to a more formal, due process model (Feld 1991). By contrast, in more homogenous and stable rural counties, juvenile courts tend to subscribe to a more traditional, informal model. More formal, urban courts placed larger proportions of juveniles in pretrial detention and sentenced similarly charged youths more severely than did suburban or rural courts (Feld 1991; Snyder and Sickmund 1995). "Rural courts seem to adhere to traditional, pre-*Gault*, juvenile court *parens patriae* criteria in their handling of youths. Urban courts appear more legalistic in orientation and process cases more according to offense criteria" (Kempf, Decker, and Bing 1990:118). On the other hand, juvenile court judges in rural areas may commit youths to institutions for minor offenses for which prosecutors in urban counties would not even file a petition (Schneider and Schram 1983b). As a result of regional differences in juvenile justice administration and sentencing practices, a social structural pattern of "justice by geography" prevails in which where a youth lived, rather than what she did, significantly affected case processing, sentencing, and the probability of incarceration.

Even within urban settings, structural inequality may affect juvenile court sentencing policies and practices. In cities characterized by greater racial inequality, segregation, and concentrated poverty, politicians and the public may perceive young black males as especially threatening and use the juvenile justice system to impose more punitive sanctions to control these ominous "underclass" youths (Sampson and Laub 1993). These findings have special relevance to the disproportionate overrepresentation of minority youths in the juvenile justice systems because of the structural, demographic, and racial transformation of American cities. Urban juvenile courts appear to process youths more formally and sentence them more severely than do their rural counterparts. Because proportionally more black youths now reside in urban areas, they experience greater risk of exposure to these harsher juvenile court sanctions.

Although theoretical and empirical relationships exist between variations in social structure and in juvenile justice administration, findings of justice by geography and by judicial diversity vastly complicates the tasks of criminologists. The extensive inter-and intrastate variation in procedural formality, access to attorneys, and detention and sentencing practices confound our understanding of juvenile courts. Because juvenile courts constitute a variable, rather than a uniform, justice system, analyzing and interpreting aggregated statewide data without accounting for procedural, contextual, and structural characteristics or intrastate variations may systematically mislead and obscure rather than clarify our knowledge about the institution.

Juvenile Justice Process

Despite states' diversity, certain common features mark the organizational structure, sequence, flow, and winnowing of delinquency cases through juvenile courts around the country. States define juvenile court jurisdiction on the basis of age and subject matter. About three-quarters of states set the maximum age of jurisdiction at seventeen years, although a few place the ceiling at sixteen or even fifteen years; still others transfer some younger offenders to adult criminal court as well (Snyder and Sickmund 1995). Juvenile courts' subject-matter jurisdiction encompasses youths below the jurisdictional age who violate state or local criminal laws or ordinances; who commit status offenses, such as truancy, "runaway," curfew, or liquor violations; or who engage in other misbehavior that would not be a crime if committed by an adult and abused, neglected, or dependent children who need protection or social services.

Police refer about 85 percent of all delinquents to juvenile court for criminal offenses (Butts et al. 1995). Despite public concern about violent youth crime, juvenile courts charge the majority of delinquents with crimes against property, rather than with crimes against the person, and police refer most delinquents to the juvenile courts for misdemeanors, rather than for felonies (Snyder 1997; Sickmund et al. 1998). Table 4.1 reports national estimates constructed by the National Center for Juvenile Justice based on data from referrals to more than 1,500 juvenile courts in thirty states. The Federal Bureau of Investigation (FBI) Crime Index includes homicide, rape, robbery, and aggravated assault in the Violent Crime Index, and burglary, larceny, motor vehicle theft, and arson in its Property Crime Index (FBI 1996). Even when police arrest and refer youths to juvenile courts for felony-level Crime Index offenses, they allege primarily crimes against property, such as burglary, larceny, and auto theft, rather than crimes against the person, such as murder, rape, or robbery (Snyder 1997). About one-third (36%) of the cases of delinquents processed by juvenile courts allege crimes in the Property Crime Index, and fewer than one-tenth (8%) involve crimes in the Violent Crime Index. The bulk of juvenile courts' caseloads involves misdemeanor and nonindex offenses (58%). Despite the public fear of youth violence, juveniles courts handled more than three-quarters (78%) of juveniles for nonviolent crimes. Aggravated assaults accounted for about two-thirds (66%) of the referrals for even the most serious violent crimes.

The overall volume of juvenile courts' delinquency cases increased by almost one-half (45%) in the decade between 1986 and 1995 and by more than one-fifth (21%) between 1991 and 1995. Moreover, the decade witnessed an almost doubling of the total volume of all violent crime referrals (98%) and

TABLE 4.1. Delinquency Cases by Most Serious Offenses, 1995

Offense	Number of Cases	Percentage of Cases	Percent Change		
			1986–1995	1991–1995	1994–1995
Total	1,714,300	100%	45%	21%	7%
Personal Offense	377,300	22	98	36	8
Criminal Homicide	2,800	<1	84	20	−6
Forcible Rape	6,800	<1	47	19	4
Robbery	39,600	2	53	27	6
Aggravated Assault	93,200	5	137	33	6
Simple Assault	205,500	12	103	47	12
Other Violent Sex Offense	9,300	<1	50	9	−3
Other Personal Offense	20,100	1	72	−2	−4
Property Offense	871,700	51	23	3	3
Burglary	139,900	8	−2	−9	−2
Larceny-Theft	418,800	24	28	10	10
Motor Vehicle Theft	53,400	3	23	−26	−13
Arson	10,400	<1	78	42	10
Vandalism	121,700	7	40	9	−2
Trespassing	64,400	4	18	9	1
Stolen Property Offense	33,100	2	10	9	2
Other Property Offense	29,900	2	46	−5	6
Drug Law Violation	159,100	9	120	145	28
Public Order Offense	306,300	18	48	37	6
Obstruction of Justice	110,100	6	53	45	8
Disorderly Conduct	85,100	5	82	46	9
Weapons Offense	47,000	3	132	38	−9
Liquor Law Violation	12,200	<1	−39	−1	2
Nonviolent Sex Offense	10,500	<1	−21	−8	−4
Other Public Order Offense	41,300	2	19	31	17
Violent Crime Index*	142,400	8	99	30	5
Property Crime Index**	622,500	36	20	1	5

Source: Sickmund et al. 1998:1

Note: Detail may not add to totals because of rounding. Percent change calculations are based on unrounded numbers.

* Violent Crime Index includes criminal homicide, forcible rape, robbery, and aggravated assault.

** Property Crime Index includes burglary, larceny-theft, motor vehicle theft, and arson.

the most serious offenses in the Violent Crime Index (99%). Between 1991 and 1995, about a one-third increase occurred in the volume of juvenile court processing of all violent crimes (36%) and in the Violent Crime Index (30%). In chapters 6 and 7, I argue that the recent increases in serious youth violence drives many of the public policies to "get tough" and transfer young offenders to criminal courts and to sentence delinquents more harshly.

Typically, police, schools, parents, or probation officers refer cases either to the local prosecuting authority or to the juvenile court's intake unit. Prosecutors or intake probation staff divert or close almost half of these referrals with some type of *informal* disposition: dismissal, counseling, warning, referral to another agency, or informal probation. Theoretically, informal sanctions are voluntary; the offender must agree to the community service, restitution, or supervision disposition. Even in those cases in which prosecutors or the court do not file a formal petition, some type of informal court action or sanction may still occur. Court services personnel typically handle informally larger proportions of cases involving white, female, and younger juveniles, as well as those referred in rural jurisdictions (Snyder and Sickmund 1995). In somewhat more than half of the cases referred to juvenile courts, probation intake staff or the prosecuting authority file a delinquency petition to formally initiate the juvenile justice process. A petition constitutes a charging document comparable to a criminal complaint or grand jury indictment in the criminal process. Prosecutors file delinquency petitions in about half of the cases referred, although filing rates vary over time, among states, within states, and with the seriousness of the offense (Nimick et al. 1985; Snyder and Sickmund 1995). In different locales, the intake screening by juvenile courts and the charging policies of prosecuting attorneys vary substantially and affect the characteristics of the "official" delinquent populations (Rubin 1979; Feld 1989).

Police may attempt to question youths about their criminal involvement at various stages in the process. If police interrogate a youth in custody, then they typically provide a *Miranda* warning to ensure the admissibility in court of any statements obtained. Police deliver many youths to pretrial detention pending intake screening and the filing of a delinquency petition. Juvenile courts hold between one-fifth and one-quarter of youths in secure detention facilities for some period between the referral of their cases to court intake and the courts' disposition (Butts et al. 1995). Although local practices vary widely, court intake and detention staff hold many more juveniles briefly pending the arrival of a parent or release them within a day but before a formal detention hearing.

At the first court appearance, juvenile courts arraign a youth on the petition. Youths held in pretrial detention also receive a detention hearing at their first court appearance. Because the constitutional right to counsel attaches only after the state files a delinquency petition formally charging a youth, juvenile courts typically appoint counsel at this stage, if at all, to represent a juvenile (Feld 1993b). At the arraignment, the juvenile may admit or deny the allegations in the petition. In many cases, juveniles admit the charges at the arraignment and the court enters a disposition without appointing a defense attorney (Feld 1988a, 1993b). In other cases, a public defender, appointed at the arraignment, confers briefly with the juvenile before the youth admits or denies the charges. In rare instances, a child's family may retain a private attorney to represent the juvenile. As in the adult criminal process, juvenile courts resolve the vast majority of cases with a guilty plea rather than via a trial (Snyder and Sickmund 1995). In part, trials seldom occur, because most young offenders respond to police encouragement to "tell the truth" and incriminate themselves, and factual guilt often constitutes a foregone conclusion (Grisso 1981). Prosecutors, probation staff, and the juvenile court judge informally decide the outcomes of the vast majority of delinquency cases at pretrial stages or in negotiation with defense counsel, rather than at a formal hearing in court. The court's authority to impose dispositions ranges from outright dismissal to conditions of probation to institutional confinement. Juvenile court judges transfer about 2 percent of formally charged youths to adult criminal courts, although states prosecute many more young offenders as adults via other jurisdictional transfer strategies (Snyder and Sickmund 1995). Juvenile courts formally adjudicated as delinquents somewhat more than half of all youths against whom prosecutors filed petitions. Judges sentenced most adjudicated youths to probation (53%) and removed more than one-quarter (29%) from their homes for placement in foster or group homes or juvenile correctional institutions (Butts et al. 1995:9).

Formal Equality and Practical Inequality: Waiver of the Privilege Against Self-Incrimination

Among other procedural safeguards, the Supreme Court in *Gault* guaranteed juveniles the privilege against self-incrimination. The Fifth Amendment privilege embodies the guarantees of an adversarial process, places the defendant "off limits" as a potential source of evidence, and thereby establishes equality between the individual and the state. If a child admits her criminal behavior, then the other trial procedures *Gault* granted retain little practical significance. Although *Gault* involved the privilege against self-incrimination at a delinquency hearing, police give juveniles *Miranda* warnings before initiating custodial interrogation (*Miranda v. Arizona*, 384 U.S. 436 [1966]). Courts evaluate juveniles' waivers of their Fifth Amendment rights; other constitutional rights, such as the right to counsel; and the admissibility of confessions by assessing whether they made them "knowingly, intelligently, and voluntarily" under the "totality of the circumstances" (*Fare v. Michael C.*, 442 U.S. 707 [1979]).

Even before *Gault*, the Supreme Court cautioned trial judges about the effects of youthfulness and inexperience on the validity of waivers of rights and the voluntariness of confessions. In *Haley v. Ohio* (332 U.S. 596 [1948]), the Supreme Court reversed a fifteen-year-old youth's conviction based on his confession and ruled that "when, as here, a mere child—an easy victim of the law—is before us, special care in scrutinizing the record must be used. . . . He cannot be judged by the more exacting standards of maturity. . . . [W]e cannot believe that a lad of tender years is a match for the police in such a contest" (332 U.S. at 599–601). In *Gallegos v. Colorado* (370 U.S. 49 [1962]), the Court repeated its concern about the vulnerability of youth and the voluntariness of their confessions: "[A] 14-year-old boy, no matter how sophisticated,. . . . is not equal to the police in knowledge and understanding. . . . A lawyer or an adult relative or friend could have given the petitioner the protection which his own immaturity could not. . . . Without some adult protection against this inequality, a 14-year-old boy would not be able to know, let alone assert, such constitutional rights as he had" (370 U.S. at 54). Thus, the Court long has recognized that youths are not the equals of adults or police in the interrogation room and that they require greater procedural safeguards than adults require, such as the presence of counsel, to compensate for their vulnerability and susceptibility to coercive influences.

More recently, in *Fare* (442 U.S. 707), however, the Court retreated from its earlier solicitude for youths, at least for a sixteen-year-old offender with several prior arrests who had "served time" in a youth camp. *Fare* reaffirmed the adult "totality of the circumstances" test as the appropriate standard by which to gauge the validity of juveniles' waivers of rights and the admissibility of their confessions. *Fare* held that a youth's request to speak with his probation officer when police interrogated him constituted neither a per se invocation of his *Miranda* privilege against self-incrimination nor the functional equivalent of a request for counsel, which would have required further questioning to cease. The Court used the discretionary "totality" approach to provide trial judges with the flexibility necessary to protect juveniles who lacked sufficient capacity or who succumbed to coercive police practices more readily than did adults without unduly interfering with the ability of police to interrogate more-sophisticated juveniles.

Fare held that a child's request to speak with someone other than an attorney was simply one of many factors affecting the validity of a *Miranda* waiver, and the Court expressly declined to give children greater protection than it gave to adults (Rosenberg 1980). Rather, the Court insisted that children must invoke their legal rights with adultlike technical precision and denied that young people lacked the capacity validly to waive constitutional rights. By endorsing the adult waiver standard, the Court rejected the view that developmental or psychological differences between juveniles and adults justified or required different rules or special procedural protections.

Most states allow juveniles to waive *Miranda* rights and other constitutional rights using the adult totality-of-the-circumstances test. Judges typically focus on characteristics of the juvenile, such as age, education, and I.Q., and on circumstances surrounding the interrogation, such as the methods used and length of questioning when they evaluate the validity of any waiver or the admissibility of any statement. While appellate courts have identified many relevant factors, they do not assign controlling weight to any particular element and instead remit the weighing of different elements to the unfettered discretion of trial judges. The multitude of factors included in the totality approach, the lack of guidelines on how to weight each one, and the myriad combinations of factual situations make every case unique. Without clear-cut rules to protect children who lack the maturity or knowledge of adults, the totality approach leaves judicial discretion virtually unlimited and unreviewable. When judges actually apply the totality test, they exclude only the most egregiously obtained confessions and then only haphazardly (Feld 1984). *Fare*'s approval of judicial discretion parallels Packer's (1968) "crime control" model, accepts police interrogation as a legitimate law enforcement tool, posits coerciveness as a fact question in each case, and provides great latitude for police to exploit the vulnerability of youths.

Despite *Fare*'s adherence to the totality approach, reasons exist to question whether the typical juvenile can make a "knowing, intelligent, and voluntary" decision to waive her rights. Empirical studies of juveniles' comprehension of *Miranda* rights indicate that most youths who received the warnings did not understand them well enough to waive them in a "knowing and intelligent" manner. Thomas Grisso (1980, 1981, 1983) conducted tests to determine whether juveniles could paraphrase the words in the *Miranda* warning; whether they could define six critical words in the *Miranda* warning, such as "attorney," "consult," and "appoint"; and whether they could give correct true-false answers to twelve rewordings of the *Miranda* warning. He administered structured interviews designed by a panel of psychologists and lawyers to three samples of juvenile subjects and two samples of adult subjects and compared the juveniles' performances with the adult norms. Most juveniles who received the warnings did not understand them well enough to waive their rights "knowingly and intelligently." Only 20.9 percent of juveniles, as compared with 42.3 percent of adults, demonstrated adequate understanding of the four components of a *Miranda* warning, while 55.3 percent of juveniles, as contrasted with 23.1 percent of adults, exhibited no comprehension of at least one of the four components (Grisso 1980). Younger juveniles exhibited even greater difficulties understanding their rights. "As a class, juveniles younger than fifteen years of age failed to meet both the absolute and relative (adult norm) standards for comprehension. . . . The vast majority of these juveniles misunderstood at least one of the four standard *Miranda* statements, and compared with adults, demonstrated significantly poorer comprehension of the nature and significance of the *Miranda* rights" (Grisso 1980:1160). An earlier study found that more than 90 percent of the juveniles whom police interrogated waived their rights, that an equal number did not understand the rights they waived, and that even a simplified version of the language in the *Miranda* warning failed to cure these defects (Ferguson and Douglas 1970). A replication of Grisso's study in Canada reported that very few juveniles fully understood the warning and that the youths who lacked comprehension waived their rights more readily (Abramovitch, Higgins-Biss, and Biss 1993). In sum, juveniles simply lack the competence of adults to understand and therefore to waive constitutional rights in a "knowing and intelligent" manner.

Moreover, Grisso (1983) cautions that research conducted under "ideal" laboratory conditions may fail to capture sufficiently the individual characteristics, social context, and stressful coercive conditions associated with actual police interrogation. Children's responses to hypothetical questions in a relaxed atmosphere do not replicate adequately the conditions created by police who "can be gentle or tough, can explain the rights well or poorly, and in many ways can exert varying amounts of pressure to comply" (Abramovitch, Higgins-Biss, and Biss 1993:319). Typically, delinquents come from lower-income households and may possess less verbal skills or capacity to understand legal abstractions than those in these studies (Grisso 1980, 1981). Children from poorer and ethnic-minority backgrounds often express doubt that law enforcement officials will not punish them for exercising legal rights (Melton 1989). Immaturity, inexperience, and lower verbal competence than adults make youths especially vulnerable to police interrogation tactics.

Youths' social status relative to authority figures and police also renders them more susceptible than adults to the coercive pressures of interrogation. Most people believe that answering the police in a respectful and cooperative manner will benefit them, at least in the short run. Inexperienced youths may waive their rights and talk in the short-sighted and unrealistic belief that their interrogation will end more quickly and secure their release. Many people from traditionally disempowered communities, such as females, African Americans, and youths, pragmatically use indirect patterns of speech in order to avoid conflict in their dealings with authority figures (Ainsworth 1993). People with lower social status than their interrogators typically respond more passively, "talk" more readily, acquiesce to police suggestions more easily, and speak less assertively or aggressively (Driver 1968; Ainsworth 1993). Thus, *Fare*'s requirement that youths invoke *Miranda* rights forthrightly and with adultlike precision runs contrary to the normal and predictable social reactions and verbal styles of most delinquents.

Minors' lack of comprehension and vulnerability to coercive pressures raise questions about the adequacy of the *Miranda* warning as a procedural safeguard at interrogation. The Supreme Court intended the *Miranda* warning to inform and educate defendants, to enable them to assert their rights, and to ensure that they made waivers knowingly and intelligently. If most juveniles lack the cognitive capacity to understand the warnings or the psychosocial ability to exercise the rights, then ritual recitation of the *Miranda* litany hardly accomplishes those purposes.

States' laws recognize that younger people have different social and psychological competencies from those of adults and paternalistically impose a host of legal disabilities on children to protect them from their own limitations in contexts other than criminal law enforcement. For example, states limit youths' ability to enter contracts, convey property, marry, drink, drive, file a lawsuit, or even donate a pint of blood. While a few states recognize this developmental reality and apply similar restrictions on youths' ability to waive their legal rights, most states allow juveniles to waive their *Miranda* rights and right to counsel without restriction or assistance and to confront the power of the state alone and unaided. Thus, *Fare* employs a "liberationist" rather than "protectionist" construction of adolescence, affirms adolescents' ability to make autonomous legal decisions without additional special procedures, and enables police interrrogators to take advantage of their manifest social-psychological limitations relative to adults.

A few states have experimented with alternative strategies to compensate for youths' inherent vulnerabilities when police interrogate them. These jurisdictions use legal guidelines or per se rules to ensure the validity of a juvenile's waiver or confession and require the presence of an "interested" adult, such as a parent, or consultation with an attorney. The per se approach excludes any waiver or confession that a juvenile makes if police fail to adhere to the required procedural safeguards. The totality and per se approaches reflect the tensions between discretion and rules in Packer's (1968) crime control and due process models. The totality approach gives courts discretion to consider a youth's maturity but imposes minimal restrictions on police investigative work. The per se approach presumes that most juveniles lack maturity and requires special safeguards to protect them from their own limitations. Although a per se strategy provides additional safeguards to protect the vast majority of unsophisticated juveniles who need them, it may afford unnecessary protection for an occasional sophisticated youth who does not.

A few states require the presence of a parent at interrogation or an opportunity for a youth to consult with an "interested" adult as a prerequisite of the admissibility of any confession. These jurisdictions conclude that a parent's presence will mitigate the dangers of untrustworthiness, reduce coercive influences, provide an independent witness who can testify about any coercion police used, ensure the accuracy of any statements obtained, and relieve police of the burden of making judgments about a youth's competency (Feld 1984). States that require a parent's presence at interrogation recognize that most juveniles lack the maturity to understand their rights or the competence to exercise or waive them without consulting with a knowledgeable adult. Proponents believe that parental presence reduces a youth's isolation and fear and provides access to legal advice.

Courts that require parental presence as a prerequisite of a juvenile's waiver of rights assume that parent and child share an identity of interests and that parents adequately understand the legal situation and can function as effective advisers. However, the presence of parents during interrogation may not provide the envisioned benefit for the child and may increase, rather than decrease, the coercive pressures on a youth. Parents' potential conflict of interest with their child, emotional reactions to their child's arrest, or their own intellectual or social limitations may prevent them from playing the supportive role anticipated. Court cases report many instances in which parents coerce their children to confess to police (Feld 1984). Research indicates that most parents did not directly advise their children about the waiver decision and that those who did almost always urged the child to waive rights and confess (Grisso 1980). Parents appear predisposed to aggravate rather than to mitigate coercive police pressures at interrogation and to urge their child to waive the right to silence. Moreover, research on adults' ability to understand and intelligently exercise their own *Miranda* rights casts doubt on even well-intentioned parents' competence to assist their children. Parents seldom have legal training and may not understand or appreciate the legal problems that their child faces.

Instead of relying on judges to review the totality of the circumstances or parents to assist a youth at interrogation, states could require the presence of an attorney and consultation with counsel before to any juvenile's waiver of *Miranda* rights or the right to counsel. Waivers of *Miranda* rights and the right to counsel involve tactical and strategic considerations and an appreciation of legal consequences as well as an abstract awareness of the existence of the rights themselves. A per se requirement of consultation with counsel before any waiver of rights recognizes youths' immaturity and lack of experience with law enforcement and provides the only effective means to protect their interests. Only attorneys, rather than parents, possess the skills and training necessary to assist a child in the adversarial process.

Many professional groups have endorsed the appointment of and consultation with counsel as a prerequisite of any waiver of rights. The President's Commission on Law Enforcement and Administration of Justice (Crime Commission) (1967a) recommended appointment of counsel for juveniles whenever the possibility of coercive state action existed. The National Advisory Committee Task Force on Juvenile Justice Standards and Goals recommended that during police interrogation, states prohibit juveniles from "waiv[ing] the right against self-incrimination without the advice of counsel (1976:212)." The American Bar Association (ABA) and Institute of Judicial Administration proposed that juveniles should enjoy a mandatory and nonwaivable right to counsel that attaches "as soon as the juvenile is taken into custody . . . , when a petition is filed . . . , or when the juvenile appears personally at an intake conference, whichever occurs first" (1980e:89) These various proposals recognize that "the lawyer occupies a critical position in our legal system because of his unique ability to protect the Fifth Amendment rights of a client undergoing custodial interrogation. . . . Whether it is a minor or an adult who stands accused, the lawyer is the one person to whom society as a whole looks as the protector of the legal rights of that person in his dealings with the police and the courts" (*Fare*, 442 U.S. at 719).

Mandatory, nonwaivable appointment of counsel protects the rights of the juvenile and helps the courts efficiently to handle cases and to ensure that any decisions juveniles make truly are "knowing" and "intelligent." Clearly, a rule requiring courts to appoint counsel for juveniles before interrogation, as well as throughout the process, would substantially affect juvenile justice administration. The ability of police to obtain waivers from and interrogate youths likely would decrease. Indeed, courts decry the adverse effects that such procedural safeguards and per se rules would have on police interrogation and the efficient repression of crime. "It is apparent most courts, required to deal pragmatically with an ever-mounting crime wave in which minors play a disproportionate role, have considered society's self-preservation interest in rejecting a blanket exclusion for juvenile confessions" (*In re Thompson*, 241 N.W.2d 2, 5 [Iowa 1976]). Thus, states categorically reject the only recognized and effective safeguard to protect youths from their own vulnerability.

Despite the adverse impact that the presence of counsel would have on police's ability to interrogate youths, however, *Gault* and *Miranda* already ensure juveniles' access to counsel during interrogation and throughout the juvenile justice process if they know and are capable enough to request one. Only an ill-informed, inexperienced, or overwhelmed young person will cooperate with the police to her own detriment. Only an attorney can redress the imbalance between a vulnerable youth and the state. The issue is not one of legal entitlement but, rather, the ease or difficulty with which courts find that juveniles waive their *Miranda* and counsel rights, which, in turn, affects every other aspect of juvenile justice administration.

According to *Fare*, the Constitution does not require mandatory counsel for juveniles, prohibit them from waiving their Fifth Amendment rights without consulting with an attorney, or prevent them from confronting the coercive power of the state without assistance of counsel. *Fare* spurned the "protectionist" policy option to safeguard youths from the consequences of their own immaturity. As a result, most states reject the only truly effective protection for juveniles—assistance of counsel—in favor of the totality approach exactly because the latter enables police to take advantage of youths' susceptibility. The decision to put young offenders on the same procedural footing as adult criminal defendants results in practical inequality and a distinct disadvantage because of their inexperience and greater vulnerability to adult coercion. A "liberationist" policy that denies youths special safeguards to protect them from the adverse consequences of their own immaturity makes perfect sense as a "crime control" strategy that maximizes their social control.

Formal Equality and Practical Inequality: Waiver of Counsel in Juvenile Court

Procedural justice hinges on access to and effective assistance of counsel. *Gault* observed that juvenile courts' informality often resulted in arbitrary or erroneous decisions and that benevolent discretion provided an inadequate substitute for fair procedures (387 U.S. at 18). *Gault* based juveniles' right to counsel on the Fourteenth Amendment's due process clause rather than on the Sixth Amendment's explicit provision of counsel in criminal proceedings. The Court asserted that as a matter of due process "the assistance of counsel is. . . . essential for the determination of delinquency, carrying with it the awesome prospect of incarceration in a state institution" (*Gault*, 387 U.S. at 36–37). While *Gault* recognized that lawyers would make juvenile court proceedings more formal and adversarial, the Court asserted that their presence would impart "a healthy atmosphere of accountability" (387 U.S. at 38). *Gault* did not require judges automatically to appoint counsel whenever delinquents appeared in juvenile court but held only that "the child and his parents must be notified of the child's right to be represented by counsel retained by them, or if they are unable to afford counsel, that counsel will be appointed to represent the child" (387 U.S. at 41).

When *Gault* granted juveniles the right to counsel, it reflected the Warren Court's beliefs that adversarial procedures protected constitutional rights, limited the coercive powers of the state, ensured the regularity of law enforcement, and preserved individual liberty and autonomy. Several years earlier, in *Gideon v. Wainwright* (372 U.S. 335 [1963]), the Court incorporated the Sixth Amendment's guarantee of counsel and required state judges to appoint counsel for indigent adult defendants in felony proceedings. "[I]n our adversary system of criminal justice, any person haled into court, who is too poor to hire a lawyer, cannot be assured a fair trial unless counsel is provided for him" (*Gideon*, 372 U.S. at 344). Because *Gault* based its decision on the Fourteenth Amendment, rather than on the Sixth Amendment and *Gideon*, some ambiguity remained about the scope of appointed counsel in delinquency proceedings.

In *Argersinger v. Hamlin* (407 U.S. 25 [1972]), the Court considered whether the Sixth Amendment required states to appoint counsel for indigent adult defendants charged with and imprisoned for a minor offense and held that "absent a knowing and intelligent waiver, no person may be imprisoned for any offense, whether classified as petty, misdemeanor or felony unless he was represented by counsel" (407 U.S. at 37). In *Scott v. Illinois* (440 U.S. 367 [1979]), the Court clarified *Argersinger* and limited adult misdemeanants' constitutional right to court-appointed counsel to cases in which the judge actually sentenced the defendant to some form of incarceration. Prosecutors do not charge most delinquents with felony-level offenses (see table 4.1), and *Scott* limited misdemeanants' right to lawyers to cases of actual imprisonment. However, as a matter of due process, the "special circumstances" of youthfulness may require juvenile courts to appoint counsel even in less-serious and nonincarceration cases if a child appears unable to prepare an adequate defense because of the inherent disabilities of youth, substandard intelligence, or the complexities of the case (e.g., *Betts v. Brady*, 316 U.S. 455 [1942]). Most states' juvenile codes provide delinquents with a statutory right to court-appointed counsel even in misdemeanor cases that potentially may lead to confinement (Feld 1993b; U.S. General Accounting Office 1995b).

Implementation of *Gault*

At the time that the Supreme Court decided *Gault*, attorneys rarely appeared at delinquency hearings, by some estimates in fewer than 5 percent of cases (Note 1966). Historically, juvenile court judges declined to appoint lawyers for indigent juveniles, often attempted to discourage parents from retaining counsel, and hindered and obstructed those lawyers who did appear in their courts (Schlossman 1977; Rothman 1980). *Gault* did little initially to alter that judicial antipathy. Even in the 1960s. "[A] number of attorneys who had appeared in juvenile court cases discovered that the right to engage counsel could be an empty one under the procedures they encountered. Furthermore, as many as half the judges in the state [of California] were ill-disposed to the appearance of attorneys in juvenile court" (Lemert 1970:99).

Despite *Gault*'s formal ruling, the actual delivery of legal services to juveniles continued to lag behind. In the immediate aftermath of *Gault*, observers in two metropolitan juvenile courts monitored judicial compliance and reported that the judges neither adequately advised juveniles of their right to counsel nor appointed lawyers for them (Lefstein, Stapleton, and Teitelbaum 1969; Stapleton and Teitelbaum 1972). A 1968 study of juvenile court records found that lawyers represented only 27 percent of delinquents, that lawyers appeared in only 37.5 percent of the hearings observed, and that attorneys did not actively participate in two-thirds (66.7%) of those cases in which they appeared (Ferster and Courtless 1972). A post-*Gault* nationwide survey of 234 juvenile courts "revealed an astonishing disregard for due process by judges and very little activity by attorneys" (Creekmore 1976:136). Only 17 percent of courts employed lawyers full time, another 11 percent employed them part time, and in most instances lawyers had minimal influence on the trial process (Creekmore 1976).

In the three decades since *Gault*, the promise of representation and effective assistance of counsel still remains unrealized. In many states, half, or fewer than half, of all juveniles receive the assistance of counsel to which the law entitles them (Feld 1988a; ABA 1995). The juvenile defender project represented only 22.3 percent of juveniles in Winston-Salem, North Carolina, and only 45.8 percent in Charlotte, North Carolina, in 1978 (Clarke and Koch 1980). Other studies in the 1980s reported rates of representation of 26.2 percent and 38.7 percent in two southeastern jurisdictions (Aday 1986), of 32 percent in a large north-central city (Walter and Ostrander 1982), and 41.8 percent in a large midwestern county (Bortner 1982). In Minnesota throughout the 1980s and early 1990s, a majority of all juveniles appeared without counsel (Feld 1984, 1989, 1995). Rates of representation varied from county to county in Minnesota, ranging from nearly 100 percent in a few counties to less than 5 percent in several others (Feld 1989, 1991). A substantial minority of youths removed from their homes (30.7%) or confined in state correctional institutions (26.5%) lacked representation at their trials and sentencing (Feld 1989, 1993a). A virtually identical pattern prevailed in Missouri: lawyers represented only 39.6 percent of urban youths and 5.3 percent of rural juveniles; rates of representation differed substantially among judicial circuits; and judges removed from their homes a significant proportion of youths who appeared without counsel (Kempf, Decker, and Bing 1990).

Table 4.2 reports data from the only study that includes both complete statewide information from several states and makes interstate comparisons of the delivery of legal services (Feld 1988a). In three of the six states surveyed in the mid-1980s, lawyers represented only 37.5 percent, 47.7 percent, and 52.7 percent of juveniles charged with delinquency and status offenses. Public defenders or court-appointed lawyers represented the vast majority of all youths who had counsel. Finally, as one might expect, rates of representation varied with the seriousness of the offense; judges appointed lawyers more often for youths charged with felonies than for those charged with misdemeanor or status offenses.

Although lawyers appear more frequently with juveniles charged with serious offenses, the rates of representation also vary with geographic locale (Feld 1993b; U.S. General Accounting Office 1995b). Whereas lawyers more often represent serious offenders, young felons constitute a minority of juvenile court dockets in most states (table 4.1). Juveniles charged with minor property offenses, like vandalism or shoplifting, make up the largest group of youths

TABLE 4.2. Representation by Counsel (Private, Public Defender/Court Appointed)

	California	Minnesota	Nebraska	New York	North Dakota	Pennsylvania	Philadelphia
Number of Referrals	147,422	—	6,091	—	7,741	18,926	—
Number of Petitions	68,227	15,304	3,830	21,383	831	10,168	6,812
% Referrals/Petitions	46.3%	—	62.8%	—	10.7%	53.7%	—
% Counsel	84.9	47.7	52.7	95.9	37.5	86.4	95.2
Private	7.6	5.3	13.3	5.1	10.5	14.5	22.0
CA/PD*	77.3	42.3	39.4	90.8	27.1	71.9	73.2
Felony Offense v. Person	88.7	66.1	58.8	98.5	100.0	91.4	96.3
Private	11.2	9.9	14.7	4.3	—	22.0	29.9
CA/PD	77.5	56.3	44.1	94.2	100.0	69.4	66.4
Felony Offense v. Property	86.8	60.6	59.9	98.1	38.9	87.1	95.0
Private	9.0	6.2	14.4	8.3	12.2	15.1	20.5
CA/PD	77.8	54.4	45.5	89.7	26.7	72.0	74.5
Minor Offense v. Person	86.7	73.5	41.3	99.0	47.8	89.3	96.1
Private	8.6	7.3	14.9	9.5	17.4	16.4	22.4
CA/PD	78.1	66.1	26.4	89.5	30.4	72.9	73.7
Minor Offense v. Property	83.8	46.8	49.6	96.2	38.3	85.5	94.7
Private	6.1	5.3	14.1	6.5	12.5	11.9	16.1
CA/PD	77.7	41.4	35.5	89.7	25.8	73.6	78.7
Other Delinquency	83.4	55.5	48.9	96.8	33.1	82.1	93.2
Private	6.4	5.9	16.0	8.0	10.8	10.8	12.3
CA/PD	77.0	49.6	32.8	88.7	22.3	71.4	80.9
Status Offense	74.1	30.7	56.1	93.8	37.2	N/A	N/A
Private	3.3	3.9	10.3	2.3	7.3		
CA/PD	70.8	26.9	46.3	91.6	29.9		

Source: Feld 1988a:401

who appear without counsel and whom judges incarcerate without representation (Feld 1988a, 1989). In 1995 the U.S. General Accounting Office (GAO) (1995b) analyzed rates of representation in certain counties in three states and found that rates of representation varied among the states, within each state, and across offense and offense histories within each state. In 1990 and 1991, attorneys represented more than 90 percent of all youths in the "high representation" states of California and Pennsylvania but fewer than two-thirds (64.9%) of those in Nebraska (GAO 1995b), patterns similar to those reported half a decade earlier (Feld 1988a). In Minnesota, lawyers in rural counties represented only half of the delinquents charged with felony offenses (Feld 1991).

The ABA published two reports on the legal needs of young people. In *America's Children at Risk*, the ABA reported: "Many children go through the juvenile justice system without the benefit of legal counsel. Among those who do have counsel, some are represented by counsel who are untrained in the complexities of representing juveniles and fail to provide 'competent' representation" (1993:60). The ABA concluded that providing competent counsel for every youth charged with a crime would alleviate some of the endemic problems of juvenile justice, overcrowded conditions of confinement, racial disparities in processing, and inappropriate adjudication or transfer of youths to adult courts. In a second study, *A Call for Justice*, the ABA (1995) focused on the quality of lawyers in juvenile courts; surveyed public defender offices, court-appointed attorneys, law school clinics, and children's law centers; and observed attorney-client interviews and delinquency proceedings in urban, suburban, and rural settings in ten jurisdictions. Although the ABA commended those defense attorneys who represented their young clients vigorously and enthusiastically, it emphasized that they constituted the rare exception rather than the rule. The caseloads of public attorneys often detracted from the quality of representation (ABA 1995). Juvenile defenders reported that the conditions under which lawyers worked in juvenile courts often significantly compromised youths' interests and left many of them literally defenseless (ABA 1995). Defense lawyer–respondents also reported that many youths waived counsel and appeared in juvenile courts without representation.

Juveniles' Waivers of Right to Counsel

Several reasons explain why so many youths in so many jurisdictions remain unrepresented. Parents may refrain from retaining an attorney or accepting appointment of a public defender for their child. If a judge appoints counsel for a juvenile at public expense, the state may obtain reimbursement from her parents for attorney's fees and expenses if they can afford it (Feld 1989). Some parents may not appreciate the legal consequences of a delinquency adjudication. Others may feel that if their child "did it," she should admit rather than contest the matter. Public defender legal services often may be inadequate or nonexistent in nonurban areas (ABA 1995).

Some judges encourage and readily find waivers of counsel in order to ease their administrative burdens or because they remain committed to a traditional, rehabilitative role. Judges often give cursory and misleading advisories that inadequately convey the importance of the right to counsel and suggest that the waiver litany constitutes a meaningless technicality. Despite *Gault*, a continuing judicial hostility to an advocacy role persists in traditional treatment-oriented courts. "An attorney in traditional courts will find himself within a legal system which still considers itself non-adversary and seeks to serve goals not usually associated with other branches of law. . . . [H]e will face formal and informal pressures to conform his manner of participation in delinquency hearings to the values of these courts—for example, to be less of an advocate for the child's best interests" (Stapleton and Teitelbaum 1972: 38). Many judges and probation officers believed that their informal and "extra-legal methods" performed satisfactorily and resented *Gault*'s implications that they trampled on juveniles' rights (Lemert 1970). Judges also may dispense with an attorney if they predetermine that they will not incarcerate a youth after finding him delinquent (Bortner 1982; ABA 1995). Whatever the reasons and despite *Gault*'s promise of counsel, many juveniles never see a lawyer, waive their right to counsel without consulting with an attorney, fail to appreciate the legal consequences of relinquishing counsel, and face the power of the state without professional assistance.

Waiver of counsel is the most common explanation why so many youths appear without a lawyer. As with waivers of *Miranda* rights, most jurisdictions use the adult legal standard to assess whether a juvenile validly made a "knowing, intelligent, and voluntary" waiver of counsel under the totality of the circumstances (*Johnson v. Zerbst*, 304 U.S. 458 [1938]; *Fare v. Michael C.*, 442 U.S. 707 [1979]). In *Faretta v. California* (422 U.S. 806 [1975]), the Supreme Court held that an adult defendant in a state criminal trial had a constitutional right to proceed without counsel if he or she voluntarily and intelligently elects to do so. *Faretta* emphasized that the right to counsel guarantees to a willing defendant the "assistance of counsel" and was not "an organ of the State interposed between an unwilling defendant and his right to defend himself personally" (422 U.S. at 820). By endorsing the adult totality test as the standard by which to evaluate juveniles' waivers of rights, *Fare* eroded Progressives' "protectionist" assumption that children differ from adults and that courts should treat them more solicitously. Rather, *Faretta* and *Fare* allow juveniles to "waive" counsel, presume that youths possess the same degree of autonomy and competence as adult defendants, and permit and encourage youths to make legal decisions that ultimately redound to their detriment.

The crucial issue for juveniles, as for adults, is whether they can voluntarily and intelligently waive counsel, especially if they do so without consulting with a lawyer. The problem becomes more acute if the judges who advise youths about their right to an attorney seek a predetermined result, a waiver of counsel, which influences both the information they convey and their interpretation of the juvenile's response. Although appellate courts emphasize that "*exceptional efforts* must be made in order to be certain that an uncounselled juvenile fully understands the nature and consequences of his admission of delinquency" (*In re John D.*, 479 A.2d 1173, at 1178 [R.I. 1984]), many judges do not exert "exceptional efforts" and engage in only cursory colloquies with youths before deciding that they waived counsel (ABA 1995).

Many analysts criticize extensively the totality approach to juveniles' waivers of counsel as another instance in which treating juveniles like adults places them at a practical procedural disadvantage (Rosenberg 1980; Grisso 1980; Melton 1989). The research on juveniles' waivers of *Miranda* rights provides compelling evidence that youths, especially younger juveniles, do not possess the competence of adults to waive constitutional rights knowingly and intelligently. Research on juveniles' understanding of legal language and the justice process raises additional questions about their ability either to relinquish counsel without consulting with an attorney or to participate meaningfully without the assistance of counsel. Interviews with delinquents shortly after they appeared at a hearing and their lawyers had explained to them what had occurred indicated that 80 percent did not understand at least some of the legal and technical words used in the proceedings (Smith 1985). Juveniles' lack of understanding can have serious legal consequences, increase their dependency on probation officers for explanations, erode protection of juveniles' rights, and deprive the court of any moralizing or educative influences. Interviews with delinquents in Colorado juvenile courts reported that many of them found court proceedings confusing and that many youths had difficulty understanding legal vocabulary, rules, and procedures (Huerter and Saltzman 1992). Age, class, or ethnic differences and linguistic or cognitive deficits render young people more vulnerable than adults in formal legal proceedings.

Even if juveniles understand the language, court processes, and role of an attorney, many do not expect their lawyers to help them (Grisso 1983). Many question the reality of attorney-client confidentiality, particularly if their parents retain or the court appoints their lawyers. Others express doubt that lawyers will provide a vigorous adversarial defense (Grisso 1983). Lawyers frequently lack the training or skill to develop rapport with juveniles, to explain their roles in ways that youths can understand, or to listen and perceive situations as youths experience them (ABA 1995). Youths' skepticism may simply reflect lawyers' self-presentation. It may also reflect juveniles' experience with the performance of lawyers, many of whom often share the juvenile court's "benevolent" perspective and act as agents on its behalf. In one study, only one-third (34%) of the delinquents interviewed spoke positively of their attorneys, and most complained that "their attorneys gave up, would not explain what was happening, would not tell the judge what the youth wanted and was not on the youths' side. These youths had never met their attorneys before their court appearances" (Huerter and Saltzman 1992:354).

Attorneys often represent juvenile clients ineffectively when attorneys appear on their clients' behalf. Organizational pressures to cooperate, judicial hostility toward adversarial litigants, role ambiguity created by the dual goals of rehabilitation and punishment, reluctance to help juveniles "beat a case," or internalization of the court's treatment philosophy compromise the adversarial role that counsel play in juvenile court (Stapleton and Teitelbaum 1972; Bortner 1982; Feld 1989). Professional people desire to maintain stable co-operative working relations with other personnel in the system; this preference may conflict with effective advocacy in an adversarial process. Lawyers who internalize the juvenile court's "best interests" ideology may be reluctant to contest a disposition recommended by the "expert." Several studies question whether lawyers can actually perform effectively as advocates in a system rooted in *parens patriae* and benevolent rehabilitation and report that they actually may put their clients at a disadvantage at trial or sentencing (Stapleton and Teitelbaum 1972; Clarke and Koch 1980; Feld 1989). If judicial distaste for adversary methods may prejudice a client's case, a lawyer may adopt a more cooperative stance in order to obtain a more desirable disposition (Kay and Segal 1973).

Juvenile court judges' ideology and practice may place juveniles who appear with lawyers at a disadvantage when compared with similarly situated unrepresented youths. Procedural formality and the presence of an attorney aggravate the sentence a youth receives (Stapleton and Teitelbaum 1972; Clarke and Koch 1980; Bortner 1982; Feld 1988a, 1989, 1991). While similar factors may affect judges' decisions both to appoint counsel initially and later to impose a harsher disposition, the presence of an attorney apparently exerts an independent effect on the severity of the sentences. Judges incarcerated more juveniles represented by lawyers than juveniles without counsel even after controlling for the effects of other variables (Clarke and Koch 1980; Feld 1988a, 1989). "[R]egardless of the types of offenses with which they were charged, juveniles represented by attorneys receive more severe dispositions [35.8% vs. 9.6%]" (Bortner 1982:139–40). Another study reported that judges removed from the juveniles' homes 28.1 percent of all juvenile offenders appearing with lawyers as contrasted with 10.3 percent of juveniles appearing without counsel (Feld 1989, 1993a). Multiple regression analyses that simultaneously controlled for other legal variables indicate that the presence of an attorney constituted a significant aggravating factor in home removal and in secure confinement sentences (Feld 1989). A comparison of the disposition rates for juveniles in different categories of offense seriousness concluded that "there was a significant and consistence difference in the commitment rates of uncounseled and counseled cases: children without counsel were less likely to be committed, especially if they were in the intermediate risk groups" (Clarke and Koch 1980:301). Evaluation of the impact of counsel in six states' delinquency proceedings reported that "in virtually every jurisdiction, representation by counsel is an aggravating factor in a juvenile's disposition. . . . [W]hile the legal variables [of seriousness of present offense, prior record, and pretrial detention status] enhance the probabilities of representation, the fact of representation appears to exert an independent effect on the severity of dispositions" (Feld 1988a:393). Similar research in Canadian juvenile courts also reports a relationship between the presence of counsel and the severity of juveniles' sentences (Carrington and Moyer 1988a, 1988b, 1990).

Quality of Defense Counsel

Several reasons explain the apparent relationship between procedural formality and the judicial tendency to impose more severe sentences on represented juveniles. First, the lawyers who appear in juvenile court simply may be incompetent and prejudice their clients' cases. Second, juvenile court judges may determine early in a proceeding the probable disposition that they will impose and appoint counsel to provide a veneer of legitimacy if they anticipate a more severe sentence. Or, third, judges may sentence more severely juveniles who appear with counsel than those without because they invoke formal protections.

Although few studies systematically evaluate qualitatively the performance of defense counsel, their incompetence certainly provides one plausible explanation for the anomalous finding that the presence of lawyers aggravates delinquents' sentences. According to the ABA, diligent, zealous, and effective juvenile defense "representation was not widespread, or even very common" (1995:41). A study of defense counsel performance in New York, where judges routinely appointed lawyers for juveniles, reported many disturbing findings about the quality of representation.

> Using the most basic criteria of effectiveness—that the law guardian meet the client, be minimally prepared, have some knowledge of the law and of possible dispositions, and be active on behalf of his or her client—serious and widespread problems are evident.
> —Overall, 45% of the courtroom observations reflected either seriously inadequate or marginally adequate representation; 27% reflected acceptable representation, and 4% effective representation. . . .
> Specific problems center around lack of preparation and lack of contact with the children.
> —In 47% of the observations it appeared that the law guardian had done no or minimal preparation. In 5% it was clear that the law guardian had not met with the client at all. . . . Further, in 35% of the cases, the law guardians did not talk to, or made only minimal contact with their clients during the court proceedings. . . . In addition, ineffective representation is characterized by violations of statutory or due process rights; almost 50% of the transcripts included appealable errors made either by law guardians or made by judges and left unchallenged by the law guardians. (Knitzer and Sobie 1984:8–9)

Other observers of lawyers' performances in juvenile trials have characterized them as " 'only marginally contested,' and marked by 'lackadaisical defense efforts.' Defense counsel generally make few objections, and seldom move to exclude evidence on constitutional grounds. Defense witnesses rarely are called, and the cross-examination of prosecution witnesses is 'frequently perfunctory and reveals no design or rationale on the part of the defense attorney.' Closing arguments are sketchy when they are made at all" (Ainsworth 1991: 1127–28).

Organizational and institutional barriers exist to providing quality defense representation. The ABA summarized some of the systemic obstacles to quality defense representation: "[M]any juvenile public defender systems suffer from underfunding, low morale, high turnover, lack of training, low status in 'career ladders,' political pressure, low salaries and huge caseloads. Effective representation in court-appointed counsel programs was impeded by other factors, such as the appointment of unqualified, inexperienced attorneys; inadequate monitoring of performance; and problems of maintaining independence from the judiciary that appoints the lawyers" (1995:24). Private attorneys who appear in juvenile court often lack experience, fail to appreciate the seriousness of delinquency proceedings, or experience a conflict when they represent a young client whose parents pay her fee and expect to dictate the proceedings.

Juvenile defense attorneys often carry caseloads two, three, or four times higher than those recommended by professional standards. Although professional standards recommend a maximum caseload of no more than 200 delinquency cases annually per attorney, virtually every public defender office exceeds those standards (ABA 1995). A survey of public defenders in Washington State found many attorneys represented 500 delinquents or more; one rural defender represented more than 900 delinquents annually (Ainsworth 1991). In Minnesota, urban public defenders commonly carry caseloads of 600 to 800 delinquents (Feld 1995). Court workers in several juvenile courts reported that caseload pressures forced defense counsel into rushed appearances, inappropriate plea bargains, perfunctory trials, and ineffective representation (Sanborn 1994). The high volume of cases prevents attorneys from preparing adequately, filing motions, or even interviewing clients before they appear in court and poses the single greatest barrier to effective and quality representation (ABA 1995; Ainsworth 1991).

Overwork combines with inexperience to exacerbate the undistinguished performance of many defense attorneys. Public defender offices in many jurisdictions often assign either their least-capable or newest attorneys to juvenile courts to get trial experience. Many public defender offices regard juvenile court either as a training ground for neophytes or a place to assign senior attorneys to punish them or to minimize the damage they might do to adult defendants. "In some defender offices, assignment to 'kiddie court' is the bottom rung of the ladder, to be passed as quickly as possible on the way up to more visible and prestigious criminal court assignments" (Flicker 1983:2). In organizations that rotate their staff, public defenders may represent adult defendants, as well as delinquents, and may give their juvenile clients' interests short shrift in pursuit of the "real" work of their offices (Edwards 1993).

Court-appointed counsel may feel beholden to the judges who select them and restrain their advocacy. A desire to maintain an ongoing relationship with court personnel may outweigh a commitment to vigorously protect the interests of their often changing clients. Court-appointed lawyers may cooperate with judges to avoid alienating them regarding other clients or pending matters or to continue receiving appointments (Lemert 1970). Judicial commitment to a rehabilitative ideology may create a professional tension for lawyers tempted to adopt a more adversarial role. "The court officials' hostility to counsel's efforts has resulted in negative performance evaluations, slashed fees, and even pressure from the court to remove the offending attorneys from the panel" (Flicker 1983:4). As a result of organizational and professional constraints, many lawyers decline judicial appointments to defend delinquents.

Judges often share lawyers' reluctance to appear in juvenile courts and many avoid or resist assignment to juvenile court. In many states, juvenile courts are not courts of general jurisdiction but, rather, "inferior" probate or family courts with limited subject-matter jurisdiction (Edwards 1992; Snyder and Sickmund 1995). A juvenile court appointment constitutes either a stepping-stone to a more desirable judicial post or the end of the line of an undistinguished judicial career. "[T]he juvenile court is considered to be the lowest rung on the judicial ladder. Rarely does the court attract men [or women] of maturity or ability. The work is not regarded as desirable or appropriate for higher judgeships" (Handler 1965:17). From their inception, juvenile courts did not require judges to be law trained. At the time of *Gault*, most juvenile court judges were not even lawyers (President's Commission 1967a, 1967b). With only a few exceptions, juvenile court judges do not constitute the elite of the judicial profession.

Apart from the low social status of delinquents and the complex social and criminal problems these youths pose, juvenile court judges often assume greater administrative responsibilities than do judges in courts of general jurisdiction. Proportionally fewer juvenile court judges process a much larger volume of cases than do their criminal court counterparts because procedural informality facilitates expedited handling. In addition to handling larger numbers of cases, the more difficult and complex social, if not legal, issues exact a greater human toll on judges. In addition, juvenile court judges often oversee detention facilities, supervise probation staff, coordinate the delivery of social services, and advocate for the interests of children in the community (Edwards 1992; Humes 1996). Despite the breadth of their roles, however, juvenile court judges occupy low status in the legal and judicial community because of the social welfare rather than legal dimensions of their work. The historical quest for a physically separate juvenile court building led to judicial isolation. Juvenile courts housed in separate quarters, often qualitatively below the standards of adult courts, segregate judges from their judicial colleagues and the broader legal community (Edwards 1992:35).

Apart from the methods of delivering legal services, the conditions of employment in juvenile courts seldom contribute to quality representation. Long hours, low pay, inadequate support and social service resources, and a depressing sense of futility combine with heavy caseloads and difficult clients to discourage all but the most dedicated lawyers from devoting their professional careers to advocacy on behalf of children. These organizational impediments had a devastating impact on the quality of representation in juvenile court. "Children represented by overworked attorneys receive the clear impression that their attorneys do not care about them and are not going to make efforts on their behalf. In one jurisdiction where it was clear that many attorneys had no relationship with their clients and demonstrated little involvement in the proceedings, a youngster said that his hearing 'went like a conveyor belt' "

(ABA 1995:47). Thus, the negative effects that lawyers have on their clients' sentences truly may reflect the quality of legal personnel, the adverse working conditions created by the sheer volume of cases, or the organizational imperatives that managing a court docket fosters to subordinate the rule of law and limit due process advocacy ideals.

The negative association between defense representation and the more-severe sentences juveniles receive may be spurious rather than causal. Judges may decide to appoint a lawyer initially because of the eventual sentence they expect to impose, rather than because the presence of an attorney adversely affects the ultimate sentence. For example, a judge's prior familiarity with a juvenile may induce her to appoint counsel if more-severe consequences seem likely when she finds the child delinquent (Aday 1986). In most states, the same judge presides at a youth's arraignment or detention hearing and then later tries the case and imposes a sentence. A detention hearing may expose a judge to a youth's social history file or personal circumstances, prior record of police contacts, and previous delinquency adjudications that may affect later decisions (Feld 1984). Judges may read youths' presentence social report before the trial and "[i]n most cases the judge decides his plan of action before the hearing" (Lemert 1970:188). Thus, the relationship between procedural formality and sentencing severity phenomenon may result from judges' exposure to prejudicial evidence at earlier stages of the process, ex parte conversations with probation officers, or premature review of a presentence investigation that influences later dispositions (Emerson 1969). In short, judges may attempt to conform to the dictates of *Scott* and appoint counsel in cases in which they expect to impose more-severe sentences. Because *Scott* barred incarceration without representation, it created a dilemma of how to decide before trial whether a later sentence will result in confinement and therefore require appointment of counsel without simultaneously prejudging the case and prejudicing the defendant.

Finally, a direct and causal relationship may exist between procedural formality and sentencing severity. Juvenile court judges may treat more formally and sentence more severely juveniles who appear with counsel than those who appear without counsel. Within statutory limits, if a lawyer represents a youth, then a judge may feel less reluctant to impose a harsh sentence, because adherence to the forms of due process insulates any sentence from appellate reversal (Duffee and Siegel 1971). Juvenile court judges may exact a punitive price for the use of lawyers and formal procedures similar to that imposed on adult criminal defendants who insist on a jury trial rather than who plead guilty (Alschuler 1983). While not explicitly punishing represented juveniles *because* they appear with counsel, judges may sentence more leniently those youths who appear unaided and contritely throw themselves on the mercy of the court.

The apparent relationship between procedural formality and sentencing severity has special implications for minority delinquents. Urban courts tend to be much more "due process" oriented and procedurally formal *and* to sentence youths more severely. A larger proportion of minority youths reside in urban jurisdictions than do white juveniles. Even within urban settings, minority youths appear to have higher rates of representation than do their white counterparts (Feld 1993b). Thus, social structure and race may interact with process formality to place minority youths at a comparative disadvantage.

More than three decades after *Gault*, simply getting attorneys into juvenile courts remains problematic. The appropriate role for attorneys to play once they appear also poses difficulties. Analysts question whether attorneys can function as adversaries in juvenile courts grounded in *parens patriae* ideology and, yet, whether any reason exists for their presence in any other role (Platt and Friedman 1968; Guggenheim 1984). To a greater degree than their criminal court counterparts, juvenile court judges dominate the entire justice process. In closed, discretionary proceedings, they can mobilize a variety of pressures to induce defense attorneys' cooperation. "The defense lawyer who is seen as obstreperous in her advocacy will be reminded subtly, or overtly if necessary, that excessive zeal in representing her juvenile clients is inappropriate and counter-productive. . . . For most defense lawyers, withstanding the psychological debilitation attendant upon being the sustained focus of judicial and prosecutorial disapproval is hopeless" (Ainsworth 1991:1129).

Apart from institutional pressures to cooperate, some lawyers resist simply transplanting the adversarial role of criminal defense attorneys into delinquency proceedings. They perceive differences between adult and juvenile defendants or between "punitive" criminal court sentences and "therapeutic" juvenile court dispositions. The legacy of *parens patriae* encourages some lawyers to sacrifice their clients' legal rights to their perceived long-term "best interests." The ideology of childhood encumbers some attorneys with moral qualms that do not plague them with respect to somewhat older criminal defendants and limits their abilities to vindicate young people's legal rights. The "cultural baggage" of childhood and organizational co-optation incline lawyers to negotiate or mediate rather than to advocate as an adversary in a criminal proceeding.

Appellate Review of Juvenile Court Decisions

Organizational obstacles also limit juveniles' ability to appeal from adverse trial judge decisions or sentences. Appellate review corrects trial judges' factual errors and ensures that they interpret and apply the law correctly. At the time of *Gault*, juveniles rarely appealed because they lacked both trial counsel and the necessary transcripts (Comment 1968; President's Commission 1967b). Even now, court rules and procedures in some states do not provide delinquents with an automatic right to appeal, most states do not provide effective means with which to vindicate the right, and, as a result, juvenile court judges have scant incentive to comply with legal mandates or to fear reversal of their decisions (Krisberg and Austin 1993; Harris 1994).

Many juveniles still lack counsel at trial who can make a record and obtain a transcript, and even fewer have access to appellate counsel (Harris 1994). Juvenile public defenders' caseloads often preclude the luxury of filing appeals;

many defender offices neither authorize their staffs to handle appeals nor advise their clients of the possibility of appeal (ABA 1995). The only empirical study that compared rates of appeals by criminal defendants and juvenile delinquents in cases involving adult and juvenile institutional confinement reported that convicted adults appealed more than ten times as often as did juveniles (Harris 1994). The study controlled for differences in the types of potential procedural errors in adult and juvenile proceedings, such as those involving jury selection or instructions, and attributed the differences in rates of appeals to the persistence of a *parens patriae* rehabilitative culture even among lawyers in public defender offices (Harris 1994). Many juveniles' lawyers regarded "appeals as an obstacle to getting the child back on track. . . . [They] view the attorney's role as a combination of advocate and guardian, with a goal of salvaging the children" (Harris 1994:223). In short, juvenile courts' ideologies of treatment and childhood discourage trial representation, co-opt or exclude defense counsel, and sustain organizational pressures against trial advocacy and appellate challenges.

Appellate courts can only clarify points of law if juveniles present legal issues to them; the absence of appeals prevents the development of a comprehensive body of juvenile court case law. The tendency of higher courts to sustain the broad discretion exercised by trial courts subverts the incremental growth of a body of juvenile court case law. The relative paucity of appellate cases, in turn, detracts from lawyers' conception of juvenile courts as courts of law, deprives lawyers of the legal tools with which to represent their clients, and further discourages attorneys' presence.

Most juvenile courts hear delinquency cases informally, behind closed doors, and without a jury, visibility, or public accountability. The juvenile justice process places young people at a considerable disadvantage because they do not possess the linguistic abilities or legal capacities of adults. Judges, court personnel, and other authority figures easily overwhelm juveniles in an alien and intimidating judicial environment. Delinquents fail to understand legal terminology and passively acquiesce to judges' suggestions to waive counsel and expedite proceedings. Even when lawyers do represent youths, organizational co-optation and the low visibility of the proceedings allow attorneys working under the pressure of crushing caseloads to cut corners. Judges administering heavy court dockets may tacitly or overtly encourage defense lawyers to cooperate and avoid challenge. Most juvenile courts function with a small cadre of co-opted regular public defenders or court-appointed counsel. Very few "outsiders" penetrate the "closed system," and even fewer successfully challenge its bureaucratic imperatives.

A juvenile court that recognized that youths differ somewhat from adults would provide younger offenders with additional procedural safeguards, such as mandatory, nonwaivable assistance of counsel, in order to offset the disadvantages of immaturity and inexperience in the justice process. Implementing a true "protectionist" policy would provide juveniles more, rather than less, procedural protections than adults are provided. Instead, the crime control reality of informal, administrative discretion with minimal adversarial challenge, trumps *Gault*'s due process ideal to maximize the social control of adolescents.

Special Juvenile Court Procedures that Provide an Advantage for the State: Preventive Detention

While waivers of the privilege against self-incrimination and the right to counsel constitute instances in which formal procedural equality results in practical inequality, in other instances the juvenile justice system denies delinquents procedural equality with adult criminal defendants and instead uses special juvenile procedures such as preventive detention and denial of jury and public trials. These policies provide younger offenders with *less*-effective safeguards even than those adult criminal defendants receive and place them at a comparative disadvantage in the justice process. Again, these seemingly contradictory procedural policies reflect selective judicial and legislative manipulation of competing cultural and legal conceptions of young offenders as autonomous and responsible, on the one hand, or as dependent and vulnerable, on the other, to maximize their social control and subordinate them to adult authority.

Juvenile courts hold in secure detention facilities about 20 percent of all youths referred to them. In 1992, juvenile courts detained nearly one-third of a million (about 296,100) youths during the processing of their cases (Butts et al. 1995). Juvenile courts detained youths charged with crimes against the person at higher rates than they did those charged with crimes against property. However, police referred nearly three times as many youths for property offenses as for person offenses, and property offenders (47%), rather than violent offenders (24%), made up the largest plurality of detained youths. Drug offenders (9%) and public order offenders (20%) constituted the remainder of youths in detention. Studies of detention consistently report that prosecutors charge most detained delinquents with property or minor offenses, rather than with violent offenses (GAO 1983; Frazier and Bishop 1985; Feld 1991). Further reflecting the variability of state practices, on any given day, four states—California, Florida, Michigan, and Ohio—held nearly half of all youths confined in secure detention facilities (Snyder and Sickmund 1995).

In *Schall v. Martin* (467 U.S. 283 [1984]), the United States Supreme Court upheld the constitutional validity of juvenile preventive detention statutes. However, the statutes that most states use lack objective standards or administrative criteria and allow judges to exercise unbridled discretion to detain. Many juvenile justice analysts criticize the misuse, overuse, and abuse of pretrial detention statutes that provide no meaningful standards, use minimal procedures, and result in the detention of many juveniles who pose no threat to themselves or others (Sarri 1974; Schwartz 1989b; Schwartz and Barton 1994). Although preventive detention statutes enable juvenile courts to restrict children's liberty far more extensively than criminal courts preventively restrain adult defendants, empirical studies discern no apparent rationale for initial juvenile detention decisions (Frazier and Bishop 1985). Moreover, after controlling for offenses and criminal history, juvenile courts detain disproportionately more female and minority youths (Snyder and Sickmund 1995). Abysmal conditions of confinement in many overcrowded secure detention facilities belie any therapeutic purpose. Finally, pretrial detention negatively affects subsequent sentences that juveniles receive; detaining a youth before trial increases the likelihood of additional postadjudication sanctions as well. In short, juvenile preventive detention constitutes a highly arbitrary and capricious process of short-term confinement for which neither a tenable rationale, an empirical basis, a meaningful process, nor a comparable adult analogue exists. In operation, detention punishes some youths almost randomly or discriminatorily and then punishes them again because the court punished them before.

Juvenile pretrial detention practices contrast sharply with the limited circumstances under which criminal courts preventively detain adult defendants. The Supreme Court in *United States v. Salerno* (481 U.S. 739 [1987]), upheld the constitutionality of the federal Bail Reform Act of 1984 (18 U.S.C. §§ 3141–3156 [1984]) which authorized criminal courts to preventively detain some adult criminal defendants. The statute in *Salerno* used restrictive offense criteria and authorized courts to detain only those defendants charged with crimes of violence, crimes punishable by death or life imprisonment, and major drug offenses or a felony committed by a defendant with two prior convictions of those listed offenses (18 U.S.C. § 3142(f) [1984]). Moreover, in an adversarial hearing, the prosecutor must establish "by clear and convincing evidence" that the defendant will flee, obstruct justice, or injure or intimidate a witness or juror and that no release conditions "reasonably" ensure the safety of any other person and the community (18 U.S.C. § 1342(e) [1984]). The Court subordinated an adult's liberty interests to the interests of community safety only "when the Government musters convincing proof that the arrestee, already indicted or held to answer for a serious crime, presents a demonstrable danger to the community" (*Salerno*, 481 U.S. at 750). Although all preventive detention statutes suffer from the vice of restricting a person's liberty based on anticipated future behavior rather than on proof of past misconduct, the statutory regime authorized for young people provides an instructive comparison.

In *Schall v. Martin* (467 U.S. 253 [1984]), the Court authorized a juvenile court judge to preventively detain a juvenile if it found a *"serious risk"* that the child "may. . . . commit an act which if committed by an adult would constitute a *crime*" (467 U.S. 255, emphasis added). The statute, whose validity the Court reviewed in *Schall*, did not specify either the nature of the present offense, burden of proof, substantive criteria, type of future crime, the probability of occurrence, or the type of evidence that the juvenile court should consider when predicting that a youth posed a "serious risk" to commit any crime, however trivial, in the future. Instead, it allowed each judge subjectively to use the vague statute to detain virtually any youth.

The *Schall* majority reversed lower-court decisions that invalidated the statute because those courts found that judges lacked the technical ability to predict future criminal conduct and that detention constituted punishment before to trial. Rather, *Schall* concluded that the detention statute served a "legitimate state objective" of preventing crime, afforded adequate procedural protections, and comported with constitutional due process (467 U.S. at 263–264). Three justices dissented and argued that because the statute infringed youths' "fundamental" liberty interests, the state must demonstrate a "compelling" interest to justify restrictions and provide more adequate procedural safeguards. They also contended that because judges could not accurately predict dangerousness, the use of preventive detention could not significantly reduce crime.

The *Schall* Court began its constitutional analysis of pretrial detention by positing that juveniles do not enjoy the same liberty interests as adults. "[J]uveniles, unlike adults, are *always in some form of custody*. Children, by definition, are not *assumed* to have the capacity to take care of themselves. They are *assumed* to be subject to the control of their parents, and if parental control falters, the State must play its part as *parens patriae*. In this respect, the juvenile's liberty interest may, in appropriate circumstances, be subordinated to the State's *parens patriae* interest in preserving and promoting the *welfare* of the child" (*Schall*, 467 U.S. at 265, emphasis added). *Schall* resurrected "paternalistic" assumptions and *parens patriae* ideology with the conclusory assertion that children have minimal rights to liberty, autonomy, or self-determination and thereby allowed states to abridge juvenile's liberty interests more readily than those of adults.

Schall concluded that preventively detaining juveniles served several legitimate goals. The Court noted that crime prevention constituted "weighty social objective," found that juveniles committed a substantial amount of serious crimes, and emphasized that "the harm suffered by the victim of a crime is not dependent upon the age of the perpetrator" (*Schall*, 467 U.S. at 264–265). Of course, adults commit most of the serious and violent crimes, but states do not use procedures or criteria like those endorsed in *Schall* to detain them. Moreover, prosecutors do not charge most juveniles preventively confined with serious violent crimes (Schwartz and Barton 1994; Snyder and Sickmund 1995). *Schall* also invoked the imagery of childhood, asserted that detention "protect[ed] the juvenile from his own folly" by preventing any injury caused by victim resistance or police arrest, and halted the downward spiral into criminality to which their immaturity and lack of self-restraint otherwise might lead them (467 U.S. at 265). Because every state's juvenile code included similar preventive detention provisions (467 U.S. at 267 n. 16), the *Schall* Court recognized that a decision to invalidate such a common practice would have a substantial impact.

Schall characterized pretrial restraint as an incidental aspect of legitimate governmental regulation and "consistent with the regulatory and *parens pa-*

triae objectives relied upon by the State and . . . not used or intended as punishment" (467 U.S. at 269). The *Schall* majority also upheld the statutory criteria—"serious risk" of any future crime—as adequate to guide judges' preventive detention decisions. *Schall* rejected the lower courts' findings that judges lacked the ability accurately to predict future criminal conduct, simply by asserting that juvenile and criminal court judges could and did predict "dangerousness" regularly. "[F]rom a legal point of view there is nothing inherently unattainable about a prediction of future criminal conduct . . . and we have specifically rejected the contention, based on the same sort of sociological data relied upon by appellees and the district court, 'that it is impossible to predict future behavior and that the question is so vague as to be meaningless' " (*Schall*, 467 U.S. at 278 n. 30). While judges often make predictions, *Schall* ignored the crucial question whether they can do so with an acceptable degree of accuracy. The Court also declined to itemize the specific factors on which judges should base their decisions. In previous juvenile court decisions, however, the Supreme Court recognized that the absence of substantive criteria undermined the value of any procedural protections. In *Kent v. United States*, for example, the Court concluded that "unless statutory clarity exists, other guarantees of procedural due process cannot be meaningful. Typical procedural due process requirements . . . may be of little avail when the tribunal is free to apply its own standard of what constitutes reasonable conduct" (383 U.S. 541, 561 [1966]). In *Kent*, the Court recognized that low-visibility proceedings that affect people readily victimized by arbitrary official action especially require specific and objective standards to guide decisions.

Predicting Dangerousness

The Progressives sited the juvenile court on a number of criminological fault lines. One critical dimension involves predictions and the policy question whether to intervene or sanction based on offenders' *past* conduct or on a forecast about *future* welfare or behavior. A crucial difference between the majority and dissenting opinions in *Schall* hinged on the validity and reliability of predictions and the propriety of using them in criminal and juvenile justice decision making. Unlike the *Schall* majority, the dissent relied on legal analysts and psychological, criminological, and clinical studies that bolstered its conclusion that "no diagnostic tools have as yet been devised which enable even the most highly trained criminologists to predict reliably which juveniles will engage in violent crime" (467 U.S. at 293). The role of predictive judgments, in turn, affect the relative importance of procedural safeguards and the use of rules and objective indicators versus professional discretion to make decisions. Historically, juvenile courts' ideology and practices reflect a "future-welfare" orientation and rely heavily on experts to predict, for example, youths' future dangerousness, "amenability to treatment," and the probable efficacy of alternative treatment programs. *Schall*'s invocation of the "protectionist" rationale implicates submerged but critical assumptions about the role of predictions in juvenile justice.

Judges and clinicians implicitly or explicitly predict people's present or future dangerousness in a variety of criminal justice, juvenile justice, and mental health settings. Predictive judgments about dangerousness pervade juvenile court detention, sentencing, and waiver decisions; criminal court bail release, sentencing, probation and parole, and death penalty decisions; and decisions to involuntarily commit or release mentally ill persons (Morris and Miller 1985). In order to predict "dangerousness" accurately or to prevent future crimes, one must be able to identify the *type* and *magnitude* of behavior anticipated, the *probability* that a particular individual will engage in that behavior, and how that individual's probability differs from the *base expectancy rate* of that type of behavior in the general population. Equipped with this knowledge, someone then must make a social or legal valuation about acceptable levels of risk and harm and infringements of personal liberty. This process involves a moral and value judgment, rather than empirical data, about how to balance societal risk and individual liberty and who must bear the risks of harm and erroneous predictions.

Because predictive decisions pervade the legal systems, social scientists have conducted extensive research to identify characteristics that distinguish currently or potentially dangerous actors from the general population. Despite *Schall*'s confidence that judges can predict dangerousness "from a legal point of view," a substantial body of empirical research strongly contradicts their ability to do so validly, reliably, and accurately. A summary of that research literature concluded that judges' ability to identify dangerous offenders "presupposes a capacity to predict future criminal behavior quite beyond our present technical ability" (Morris 1974:62). Psychologists, psychiatrists, criminologists, and lawyers criticize the assumption that judges or mental health professionals can make valid and accurate predictions about future dangerousness (Monohan 1981). In an amicus brief, the American Psychiatric Association explicitly denied that clinicians possessed any special competence to predict violent behavior or to assist judges or juries attempting to predict the future dangerousness of a capital defendant (*Barefoot v. Estelle* (463 U.S. 880, 899–902 [1983]). A leading scholar on predicting dangerousness concluded that "the 'best' clinical research currently in existence indicates that psychiatrists and psychologists are accurate in no more than one out of three predictions of violent behavior over a several-year period among institutionalized populations that had both committed violence in the past . . . and who were diagnosed as mentally ill" (Monohan 1981:77). Other analysts corroborate the "one-in-three" rule of thumb for accurately predicting long-term violence (Morris and Miller 1985).

Several reasons account for the difficulty of predicting future dangerousness. The success of predictions depends, in part, on the *base rate frequency* with which the anticipated future event occurs. Once the base expectancy rate of occurrences falls below 50 percent, predictive accuracy declines precipitously (Gottfredson 1987). Comparing the odds of successfully predicting coin flips versus rolls of pairs of dice indicates that we can predict frequent recurrent events more readily and accurately than less-common and highly variable ones. Unless an individual belongs to a particular group that has a very high base rate of offending, decision makers will encounter great difficulty predicting either which offenders will commit a crime in the future or to reduce much crime through preventive detention. "When base rates are low—as they appear to be for pretrial juvenile crime—the capacity to make accurate individual predictions of short-term criminality is particularly questionable" (Fagan and Guggenheim 1996:426).

Moreover, when judicial prognosticators attempt to make predictions, inevitably they will make mistakes. The nature, balance, and consequences of those errors raise important moral and legal policy issues. We may distinguish between "positive" and "negative" predictions—whether a particular event will or will not occur—and between "true" and "false" predictions, whether or not the predicted outcome occurred. A "true positive" means that the predicted event subsequently occured, that is, an accurate prediction. In the context of preventive detention, a decision to detain a "true positive" would "prevent" a later crime. A "false positive" prediction identifies as potentially dangerous a person who, if subsequently released, would not engage in the predicted future behavior. In the context of preventive detention, judges deprive these youths of liberty because they share the characteristics of a larger group of "potentially dangerous" youths, some of whom will realize their criminal proclivities. If a judge erroneously predicts and detains a "false positive," the court imposes unwarranted incarceration on an innocent individual *and* obtains no incapacitative or crime prevention benefit because that person would *not* have offended if left at liberty.

Unfortunately, a very strong tendency exists for judges to overpredict. In addition to the inherent inaccuracy of predictions—easily two errors out of three—criminal justice predictions balance conservatively the risk to the community versus the loss of individual liberty. Biased feedback encourages judicial decision makers to become more cautious over time as "false negatives"—released offenders predicted to be "safe"—commit further crimes (Glaser 1987). Bureaucratically, the safe decision becomes one to detain and sacrifice individual liberty to obtain a hypothesized community benefit. Because the individual remains confined, no way exists to disprove the validity of the prediction. Adjusting the "true/false" ratio and "widening the net" to capture a few more "true positives" who will offend invariably preventively confines far more *innocent* "false positives" who would not offend.

The inevitable judicial tendency to overpredict dangerousness raises moral and policy question about the acceptable degree of *in*accuracy that impinges on liberty. How many false positives—people who would not reoffend if released—can a morally defensible legal system incarcerate for no benefit in order to confine those fewer but unidentifiable individuals who actually will reoffend? Should judges speculate about a "serious risk" of future crime when doing so means that they erroneously will preventively detain larger numbers of presumptively innocent false positives? How can a society balance predictive marginal crime reduction versus actual loss of individual liberty?

Despite the inaccuracy of predicting dangerousness, prognosticators use several different methodologies that create different risks of errors and abuse. *Clinical* and *actuarial* predictions constitute the two primary methods to forecast the probability of a future event occurring. With clinical prediction, a decision maker reviews whatever information she deems relevant and bases her prediction on professional training, diagnostic interviews, psychometric tests, and clinical intuition. Clinical prediction requires the prognosticator to integrate all available information about the individual and to develop "some psychological hypothesis regarding the structure and the dynamics of this particular individual. On the basis of this hypothesis and certain reasonable expectations as to the course of outer events, we arrive at a prediction of what is going to happen" (Meehl 1954:4). The accuracy of clinical prediction depends heavily on the experience, professional expertise, technical competence, and intuition of the person making the judgment.

Actuarial or statistical prediction, on the other hand, empirically measures the relationship between independent predictor variables, for example, age or prior offenses, and the dependent variable or behavior to be predicted, for example, crime or violence. The person making a statistical prediction examines the individual only to ascertain the presence of the independent predictor variables. "The combination of all of these data enables us to *classify* the subject; and once having made such a classification, we enter a statistical or actuarial table which gives the statistical frequencies of behaviors of various sorts for persons belonging to the class" (Meehl 1954:3, emphasis added). Actuarial prediction employs objective indicators and correlational statistics to yield a probability statement. Actuarial prediction entails a judgment about the risks of an aggregate group and imputes those probabilities to individuals who share the characteristics of that group.

Actuarial prediction demonstrates clear-cut superiority over clinical methods in the accuracy and reliability with which it predicts future behavior (Monohan 1981). "It would be difficult to mention any other domain of social science research in which the trend of the data is so uniformly in the same direction, so that any psychiatrist or psychologist who disfavors the objective, actuarial approach in a practical, decision-making context should be challenged to show his familiarity with this research literature and invited to rebut the theoretical argument and empirical evidence found therein" (Livermore, Malmquist, and Meehl 1968:76 n. 4). Many factors contribute to the relative superiority of actuarial over clinical predictions. When people make clinical predictions, they tend not to use information reliably, to disregard base rate variability, to assign inappropriate weight to predictive information, to consider factors that are not predictive, and to be misled by spurious correlations (Gottfredson 1987). The life insurance industry provides the strongest evidence of the relative efficacy of statistical over clinical prediction methodology to predict mortality. It "bets" billions of dollars a year on the relative predictive accuracy of the few variables—for example, age, sex, height/weight ratio, smoking habits, simple blood tests, blood pressure, and EKG—that it includes in typical actuarial life-expectancy tables rather than on more extensive clinical evaluations and a "full understanding" of the individual.

Although predictive judgments play a crucial role in juvenile justice administration, unfortunately *Schall* endorsed the less-reliable method by which to predict young people's future behavior. Psychometric tests, clinical insights about the "whole child," and judicial intuition contribute little to improve the accuracy of predictions. On the other hand, using social, behavioral, demographic, or other validated "risk" factors associated with probabilities of offending that exceed the base expectancy rates for that population can improve somewhat the validity and reliability of detention decisions. Although many juveniles with a prior violent offense will not commit another violent act, an extensive record of past violent behavior provides the best predictor of future violent behavior (e.g., Wolfgang, Figlio, and Sellin 1972). Risk-assessment instruments, a variant of actuarial tables, provide one method by which to rationalize and objectify detention decisions.

Factors other than a prior history of offenses also appear to correlate with the probability of future criminal misconduct. To varying degrees, age, sex, race, and socioeconomic class correlates with official criminality. Purely in terms of probabilities, we would predict that nonwhite lower-class adolescent males, as an aggregate, would have a greater likelihood of future criminal violence than would, for example, white middle-class women aged thirty and over. Despite individual variability, over the course of many predictions, we would make money consistently following such a betting strategy.

For obvious reasons, however, many independent variables with marginal predictive value cannot provide a legal basis for actuarial prediction or risk assessment. To detain, for example, a black offender but not a similarly situated white one would violate constitutional equal protection, even if validated statistical tables demonstrated that blacks youths, as a class, have a greater probability of subsequent criminal involvement than do whites ones. The juvenile justice system continues to rely almost exclusively on discretionary clinical prediction methods because they allow decision makers to obscure their use of these socially sensitive predictor variables. Explicit inclusion of a "suspect" factor in an actuarial prediction table, even if statistically valid, would violate the Constitution. However, individualized discretion allows judges to subsume these same factors into their clinical "insight" without constitutional affront. Clinical prediction "launders" marginally valid actuarial variables by submerging them in the depths of professional judgment.

Moreover, despite the empirical relationships that may exist between predictive factors, such as sex, age, race, family structure, socioeconomic status, and census track of residence, and a juvenile's probability of future offending, these factors remain beyond a youth's control. Because social status factors are not an individual's *fault*, sanctioning or confining her based on factors she neither can control nor change would punish her for a *status*. Basing predictions on status variables also biases decisions against lower-status and racial minority offenders (Tonry 1987). Present offenses and cumulative records represent the only variables with both predictive validity and over which offenders can exercise some control. Perhaps intuitively, juvenile court judges already rely on these offense factors to make detention, sentencing, and waiver decisions.

Courts could base preventive detention decisions on the seriousness of the present offense or an extensive prior record. Using such criteria, judges could decide cases more easily, decrease subjective speculation and invidious discrimination, and reduce inappropriate and excessive preventive detention (Schwartz and Barton 1994). But formal, objective guidelines also would restrict heavily their exercise of "sound judicial discretion." In essence, *Schall* affirms judicial discretion, elevates "crime control" over "due process" values and the rule of law, and delegates to each judge the authority to balance the risk to the community and an individual's liberty on an idiosyncratic and ad hoc basis.

The Procedural Context of Detention Decisions

The process that judges use also affect the accuracy of their predictions. The *Schall* dissent recommended more elaborate procedural safeguards, objective offense criteria, and an explicit standard of proof, such as the Court later approved for adults in *United States v. Salerno* (481 U.S. 739 [1987]). The *Schall* majority instead endorsed an informal discretionary process. Within three days after an initial appearance, the juvenile court conducted a detention hearing at which it typically received only police reports or a petition stating probable cause and perhaps a probation officer's summary of an intake interview. Courts rarely received clinical evaluations, psychiatric or psychological examinations, or verified information regarding school performance, family functioning, and the like. Even if youths had prior contacts with the juvenile court, it typically cannot obtain and verify current information within the time in which it must hold a detention hearing. Courts normally appoint defense counsel only shortly before the detention hearing, if at all; attorneys have minimal opportunity to gather or verify background information about the child or to determine the availability of other nonsecure placement alternatives. The lower court in *Schall* found that juvenile court judges appointed counsel "*only moments* before convincing reasons must be presented to the court for not ordering pretrial detention" and that judges made their detention decisions in proceedings that typically lasted five to fifteen minutes (*United States ex rel. Martin v. Strasburg*, 513 F. Supp. 691, 701–02 [S.D.N.Y. 1981], emphasis added). Unlike clinical predictions based on "full understanding" of the "whole child," juvenile court judges make preventive detention decisions in a matter of minutes, based on unverified and incomplete information with a formulaic recital that the juvenile satisfies the "serious risk" statutory standard (McCully 1994). Thus, even if judges accurately could predict future crime, juvenile detention hearings do not provide the forum, the information necessary, or the reflective opportunity to do so validly.

How well do judges exercise the discretionary authority that *Schall* granted them to predict future dangerousness? Whom do they confine? What consequences do juveniles held in pretrial detention experience? Ironically, *Schall* created a unique "natural experiment" and provided an opportunity to assess the accuracy of judicial predictions (Fagan and Guggenheim 1996). The original trial court judge in *Schall* ruled the statute unconstitutional and entered a restraining order that barred preventive confinement. However, the trial judge entered the order only against the commissioner who administered the detention facilities, rather than the family court judges. As a result, the ruling allowed judges to continue to predict youths' dangerousness but prohibited the facilities to which the judges committed the youths from detaining them. Juvenile judges and the commissioner continued to detain youths for reasons other than their "serious risk" of future crime, such as the danger they posed to themselves or their risk of flight. However, during the three years that the restraining order applied, judges predicted that seventy-four youths posed a "serious risk" of any crime and ordered them incarcerated, but the commissioner released them. Thus, the judges made their predictions *and* the youths remained at liberty to validate their predictions. The researchers constructed a matched sample of juveniles during this period whom judges predicted would not commit a crime and did not detain and compared both samples' subsequent offenses during their period of pretrial liberty to assess the validity and accuracy of judges' predictions of dangerousness (Fagan and Guggenheim 1996).

The detention prediction involves an impressionistic amalgam of actuarial and clinical components, what *Schall* described as the "experienced prediction based on a host of variable factors" (467 U.S. at 274). These elements include judicial experience, the cumulative knowledge gained from making detention decisions over time, the "normative consensus" of the court room "working group" about the dangers posed by particular "types" of individuals and cases (Glaser 1987), and inferences about potential threat drawn from "the defendant's demeanor, dress, and perceptions of the quality of supervision from parents or caretakers" (Fagan and Guggenheim 1996:423). Others, less charitably, might describe such predictions as subjective, idiosyncratic judgments based on unsystematic experience derived from biased samples, unarticulated hunches, and untested hypotheses (D. Gottfredson 1987). Differences in organizational culture and courtroom working groups' assessments of risks introduce further variability in predictions, undermine uniform justice administration, and institutionalize inaccurate predictive judgments (Glaser 1987).

Prosecutors charged only about one-third (36.9%) of the *Schall* youths with a violent felony, and fewer than half (47.8%) of the youths had any prior charges of violence (Fagan and Guggenheim 1996). Prosecutors charged most youths with property offenses or misdemeanors, and one-tenth (11.6%) appeared in juvenile court for the first time. Because the statute allowed judges to preventively detain youths whom they predicted would commit a crime between their arraignment and trial, the study analyzed juveniles' rearrest rates during the ninety-day maximum period within which they must be tried. Nearly two out of three (59.4%) juveniles whom judges predicted constituted a "serious risk" of any crime and ordered confined constituted false positives whom police did not rearrest during the pendency of their cases. Presumably, judges preventively detain "dangerous" youths to avoid future violence, but police subsequently arrested only 19.8 percent of the *Schall* youths for violent crimes. Judges would have confined four youths erroneously in order to prevent violence by one. "The high rate of false positives demonstrates that the ability to predict future crimes—and especially violent crimes—is so poor that such predictions will be wrong in the vast majority of cases" (Fagan and Guggenheim 1996:447).

Although *Schall* implied that juvenile court judges detained "dangerous" young offenders, few offender or offense characteristics distinguish detained juveniles from nondetained juveniles; the *majority* of preventively detained juveniles do not face charges for serious or violent offenses (Coates, Miller, and Ohlin 1978; Bailey 1981; Frazier and Bishop 1985; Butts et al. 1995). States vary enormously in rates of pretrial detention of juveniles, and five states account for half (51.5%) of all detention admissions. After controlling for variations in violent crime arrest rates, teenage unemployment, youth populations, offenses, and prior records, it appears that the availability of detention facility bed space exerts by far the strongest influence on juvenile detention rates (Krisberg and Schwartz 1983; Bookin-Weiner 1984; Frazier and Bishop 1985). Judges apparently apply juvenile detention statutes without any systematic rationale. Multivariate analyses can explain very little variance in detention decisions using conventional legal or sociodemographic variables and conclude that the broad, standardless statutes promote idiosyncratic judicial decisions (Frazier and Bishop 1985).

Racial Disparities in Detention

Without objective criteria or validated indicators, detention statutes remit speculative judgments about future behavior to each judge's discretion and foster seemingly random decisions. In addition to the dangers of erroneous predictions, unstructured discretion also fosters arbitrary, unequal, and discriminatory decisions. As the dissent emphasized in *Schall*, "government officials may not be accorded unfettered discretion in making decisions that impinge upon fundamental rights. . . . [E]xcessive discretion fosters inequality in the distribution of entitlements and harms, inequality which is especially troublesome when those benefits and burdens are great; and discretion can mask the use by officials of illegitimate criteria in allocating important goods and rights" (467 U.S. at 306–307).

Judges often apply vague and imprecise statutes in a discriminatory fashion. Juvenile justice entails a multistage decision-making process. Earlier discretionary rulings cumulate and affect later ones (McCarthy and Smith 1986; Fagan Slaughter, and Hartstone 1987). Although the relative effect of legal and sociodemographic factors on detention decisions varies, virtually every study reports that juvenile courts detain a disproportionately large number of mi-

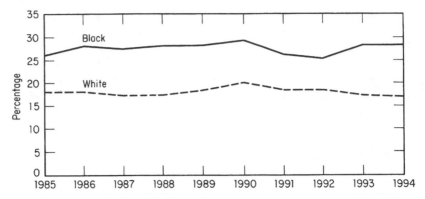

FIGURE 4.1. Detention for all offenses, by race, 1985–1994. *Source*: National Center for Juvenile Justice (1996) *Easy Access to Juvenile Court Statistics* (Pittsburgh, Pa.: National Center for Juvenile Justice).

nority offenders. After controlling for the present offense and prior records, a juvenile's race consistently exerts an independent effect on detention decisions (McCarthy and Smith 1986; Pawlak 1977; Schwartz et al. 1987; Pope and Feyerherm 1990a, 1990b). Between 1977 and 1982, the proportion of minority youths held in detention centers increased from 41 to 51 percent, a growth rate that did not reflect either racial demographic or arrest rate trends (Krisberg et al. 1986). Although juvenile courts detained about 20 percent of all referred youths, white juveniles experienced somewhat lower detention rates (18%) and black (25%) and other racial minority (22%) juveniles experienced somewhat higher rates (Butts et al. 1995). After controlling for offense seriousness, black youths had higher rates of detention than whites in every offense category; the greatest racial disproportionality occurred in detention rates for drug referrals (26% white versus 47% black) (Butts et al. 1995). Recent disproportionate increases in minority admissions reflect judicial disparities in detaining black youths charged with drug possession or sale (Snyder 1990). Analyses of changes in racial disproportionality in juvenile justice processing between 1985 and 1989 report that the proportion of white youths detained *decreased* 12.6 percent while that for nonwhite youths *increased* 41.5 percent (McGarrell 1993). For youths referred for drug offenses, the white detention rate *decreased* 17.2 percent while the nonwhite detention rate *increased* 235.8 percent (McGarrell 1993). A study of felony cases referred by police and detained by juvenile courts found that a youth's race affected both decisions, even after controlling for weapons use, victim injury, and socioeconomic and family structure (Wordes, Bynum, and Corley 1994).

The data reported in figure 4.1 provide another indicator of the effect of judicial discretion on the racial characteristics of youths held in pretrial detention. During the period from 1985 through 1994, judges detained about

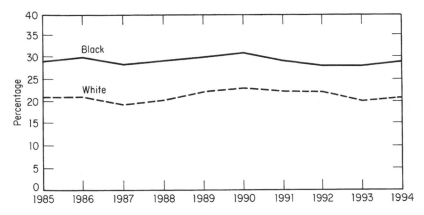

FIGURE 4.2. Detention for personal offenses, by race, 1985–1994. *Source*: National Center for Juvenile Justice (1996) *Easy Access to Juvenile Court Statistics* (Pittsburgh, Pa.: National Center for Juvenile Justice).

20 percent of all youths referred to juvenile courts. Of that 20 percent, however, in 1984, judges detained about 18 percent of white youths and 26 percent of black youths. By 1994, judges detained somewhat fewer white juveniles (17%) and proportionally more black juveniles (28%). While rates of detention vary with the types of offenses, within every offense category, judges detained proportionally more black juveniles than whites. For example, judges detained about one-quarter (25% in 1985 and 24% in 1994) of all youths charged with crimes against the person (see figure 4.2). However, in both years, they detained only 21 percent of white youths but 29 percent of black juveniles charged with crimes against the person. An even larger disparity occurred for youths charged with drug offenses, as shown in figure 4.3. Although judges detained 21 percent of all drug offenders in 1985 and 27 percent in 1994, black juveniles accounted for virtually all the increase in the rate of detention (Snyder 1990). Judges detained 18 percent of white juveniles for drug offenses in 1985 and the same percentage, 18 percent, a decade later. By contrast, judges detained 34 percent of all black juveniles in 1985, nearly twice the proportion of white youths; their rate of detention increased to 56 percent in 1989 and to 44 percent in 1994. Although black juveniles represented only about one-third of court referrals in 1994, they accounted for more than two out of five youths (43%) held in pretrial detention. Thus, discretionary detention decisions have a disproportionate impact on minority juveniles, and, over the past decade, these disparities increased (Snyder 1990).

Female juveniles also experience higher rates of pretrial detention than do male juveniles charged with similar offenses. Male delinquents commit more than three times as many offenses as females overall and an even larger proportion of the serious and violent crimes (Snyder and Sickmund 1995). De-

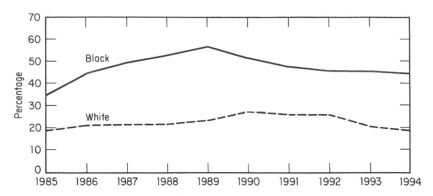

FIGURE 4.3. Detention for drug offenses, by race, 1985–1994. *Source*: National Center for Juvenile Justice (1996) *Easy Access to Juvenile Court Statistics* (Pittsburgh, Pa.: National Center for Juvenile Justice).

spite these differences in patterns of offending, however, juvenile court judges detain proportionately more female than male delinquents charged with minor and status offenses (Chesney-Lind 1977, 1988; Chesney-Lind and Shelden 1992; Feld 1993b). For example, juvenile courts detained 44 percent of males for serious FBI Crime Index offenses, compared with only 23 percent of females (Schwartz and Barton 1994). The disproportionate detention of females for minor offenses provided one impetus to deinstitutionalize status offenders.

Conditions of Confinement in Detention

The *Schall* Court denigrated juveniles' liberty interests and trivialized the institutional conditions under which most states detained juveniles. The majority of juveniles' confinements occur in pretrial detention centers, rather than in postadjudication commitments to training schools or other correctional facilities. Juvenile courts admit nine times as many youths to detention facilities and adult jails as they ultimately commit to juvenile correctional institutions (Sarri 1976; Schwartz and Barton 1994). Ironically, extensive litigation, judicial decisions, and critical reports documented the prisonlike character of the detention facility that housed the inmates in *Schall (Martarella v. Kelley*, 349 F. Supp. 575 [S.D.N.Y. 1972]; Feld 1984). Unfortunately, custodial, jail-like conditions prevail in juvenile detention facilities around the nation (Schwartz and Barton 1994). More than half (53%) of all detained youths resided in overcrowded facilities operated above their designed capacity (Snyder and Sickmund 1995). As a result of increased use of detention, the proportion of overcrowded facilities rose in the past decade, especially the largest urban facilities that house more than 220 residents. More than two-thirds (67%) of urban facilities that hold more than three-quarters (77%) of all detained youths operated above their rated capacity (Snyder and Sickmund 1995).

Several factors contribute to increased overcrowding in detention facilities. Increased procedural formality and more serious juvenile court penalties may lead to more contested cases that, in turn, extend the duration of juveniles' pretrial confinement. In addition, an increasing number of states use juvenile detention facilities as places for postadjudication confinement as a part of a probationary sentence (Schwartz 1989b; Schwartz and Barton 1994). Judges sentence juveniles convicted of minor offenses, probation violations, and contempt of court to short terms in detention facilities (Schwartz 1989b). As judges commingle pre-and postconviction juveniles in detention facilities, these institutions perform functions similar to those of adult jails.

Juvenile courts in many nonurban settings often lack detention facilities and may preventively detain juveniles in adult jails under conditions even worse than those endured by adult inmates (Schwartz, Harris, and Levi 1988). Courts provide graphic descriptions of the conditions of confinement for juveniles held in adult jails that lacked educational, treatment, or recreational programs and whose deliberate institutional policies "result[ed] in harsher treatment for pre-trial detainee children than for adult prisoners, many of whom have been convicted and sentenced" (D.B. v. Tewksbury, 545 F. Supp. 986, at 904 [D.C. Ore. 1982]). Juveniles confined in adult jails commit suicide at nearly five times the rate of youths in the general population (Flaherty 1980).

Referring to pretrial juvenile facilities as "detention centers" or "receiving homes" should not obscure the reality that they perform similar functions and closely resemble adult jails (Guggenheim 1977; Barton and Schwartz 1994). "Over half a million juveniles annually detained in 'junior jails,' another several hundred thousand held in adult jails, penned like cattle, demoralized by lack of activities and trained staff. Often brutalized. Over half the facilities in which juveniles are held have no psychiatric or social work staff. A fourth have no school program. The median age of detainees is fourteen; the novice may be sodomized within a matter of hours. Many have not been charged with a crime at all" (Wald 1976:119). One juvenile court judge candidly acknowledged that "[p]hysical conditions of detention are often abominable,. . . . outdated, overcrowded, and not amenable to humane, rehabilitative treatment models" (McCully 1994:165). By contrast, the Schall majority cynically invoked children's welfare and characterized these conditions as parens patriae equivalents of parental supervision.

Apart from the conditions inherent in confinement, pretrial imprisonment significantly affects detained juveniles and their families. Detention adversely affects current employment and future job prospects, disrupts educational continuity, and separates youths from their families (Fagan and Guggenheim 1996). Negative self-labeling and the prison experience impair juveniles' ability to prepare a legal defenses. Although judges apparently do not base their initial decisions systematically on offense criteria or any other rational factors, detention itself increases both a juvenile's probability of conviction and the like-lihood of institutional confinement following adjudication (Coates, Miller, and Ohlin 1978). "[B]eing detained before adjudication had an independent effect on the likelihood of commitment, entirely apart from the fact that both detention and commitment had some common causal antecedents" (Clarke and Koch 1980:294). A youth's pretrial detention status exerts a greater influ-ence on their subsequent dispositions than do other legal or sociodemographic variables (McCarthy 1987). After controlling for crime severity and prior rec-ords, juvenile courts processed more detained youths further into the system, adjudicated them delinquent more frequently, and sentenced them more se-verely than youths who remained at liberty. The independent effects of deten-tion on rates of adjudication and commitment stem from the fact that "[t]he child's ability to defend himself may have been impaired by detention, either because he was prejudged by the same court that later decided his case, or because it was harder for him to talk to his lawyer and otherwise prepare his defense" (Clarke and Koch 1980:295). Juvenile courts more often process youths held in pretrial detention formally rather than informally, and formally prosecuted youths typically receive more severe dispositions than do those whose cases courts dispose of informally (Frazier and Bishop 1985). Pretrial detention operates as a self-fulfilling prophecy (McCarthy 1987). Once a judge singles out youths, for whatever reasons, and predicts that they pose greater risks of future criminality, she constrains herself to sanction those youths more severely. Because judges disproportionately detain minority youths, these ad-verse short-term and long-term consequences affect them more.

Many policy analysts and professional organizations recommend that states use offense criteria, risk-assessment instruments, or other administrative guidelines to reduce excessive pretrial detention, to reserve detention for high risk youths, and to develop less-restrictive alternatives for youths who pose minimal threat to public safety. Some recommend that judges detain only those youths whom prosecutors charged with a serious crime of violence that, if proved, would likely result in commitment to a secure facility; who escaped from an institution; or who would not appear at subsequent proceedings based on a demonstrated history of prior failures to appear (ABA and Insti-tute of Judicial Administration–980b). Similarly, the National Advisory Committee on Criminal Justice Standards and Goals in its *Report of the Task Force on Juvenile Justice and Delinquency Prevention* recommended detention only "[t]o prevent the juvenile from inflicting bodily harm on others" (1976: 390).

State laws *could* specify, like *Salerno* requires for adults, explicit offense-based detention criteria or construct empirically validated risk-assessment in-struments to enumerate the categories of serious present offenses and prior records that provide compelling evidence of future "dangerousness." In ad-dition, state laws *could* create a presumption to release all nonfelony offenders and place a heavy burden on the prosecution to prove both a need for secure detention and exhaustion of all nonsecure alternative placements. States *could* provide additional procedural safeguards and specify a higher standard of proof before making preventive detention decisions. Although states *could* promulgate substantive standards, apply the rule of law to the confinement decision that directly affects most delinquents' lives, and reduce the disparate and unequal incarceration of young offenders, most states decline to do so. Instead, they use less-adequate procedures for juveniles than they require for adults, maximize judicial discretion, and place juveniles at a comparative disadvantage in the justice system. Moreover, judicial discretion often appears synonymous with racial disparities and disproportionate minority over-incarceration.

Special Juvenile Court Procedures that Provide an Advantage for the State: Denial of Jury Trial and Public Trial

The Supreme Court in *McKeiver v. Pennsylvania* denied to juveniles a constitutional right to a jury trial because it found that "due process" and "fundamental fairness" in delinquency proceedings required only "accurate fact finding," which a judge could provide as well as a jury (403 U.S. 528, at 543 [1971]). Without citing any empirical evidence, *McKeiver* simply posited parity between the factual accuracy of juvenile delinquency bench trials and adult criminal jury trials. *McKeiver* reflected both the Burger Court's general skepticism toward juries as fact-finders and its adherence to a *parens patriae* model of juvenile justice. Ultimately, *McKeiver* reflected the Court's perception that children differ fundamentally from adults, that juvenile courts' "treatment" differs from criminal courts' "punishment," and that youths' "rehabilitation" requires a more informal, nonadversarial system of justice.

About a dozen states grant juveniles the right to a jury trial or to a public trial (Feld 1995; Ainsworth 1991; Sanborn 1993b). However, the vast majority of states uncritically follow *McKeiver* and use special juvenile court procedures—closed, confidential, informal bench trials—that place delinquents at a procedural disadvantage in comparison with adult criminal defendants. While delinquency trials share most of the functional characteristics of criminal prosecutions, juvenile courts provide youths with a lower quality of procedural justice than the minimum insisted on for adults. Even though most adult defendants do not exercise their right to a jury trial, prosecutors and defense counsel practice criminal law in the shadow of that constitutional right. The possibility that a defendant *may demand* a jury trial affects prosecutors' charging decisions, evidentiary evaluations and suppression hearings, the visibility of the process, and plea-bargaining strategies. Jurors function as autonomous decision makers and provide the ultimate check on prosecutors and judges. By contrast, many of the other procedural deficiencies associated with juvenile courts result directly or indirectly from denying youths access to a jury, maintaining a closed, informal process and thereby preclude visibility and accountability of juvenile justice administration.

Accurate Fact-Finding

McKeiver's assertion that accurate fact-finding in delinquency proceedings does not require juries contradicts the Court's logic and rationale in *In re Winship* (397 U.S. 358 [1970]). *Winship* required "proof beyond a reasonable doubt" to convict both delinquents and criminals because of the seriousness of the proceedings and the potential consequences for both juvenile and adult defendants. The same rigorous standard of proof for both adults and juveniles ensures the highest possible accuracy, avoids convicting innocent people, sustains public confidence in decisions, and guarantees similar outcomes in juvenile and criminal proceedings. In everyday practice, juvenile court judges disregard the evidentiary burden of *Winship* with impunity (Bernard 1992).

Juries and judges "find" facts differently. Juries serve special protective functions to ensure factual accuracy, use a higher evidentiary threshold when they apply *Winship's* beyond reasonable-doubt standard of proof, and acquit more readily than do judges (Kalven and Zeisel 1966). Substantive criminal guilt represents a complex social assessment of moral culpability and "legal guilt" and not just an arid determination of "factual guilt" (Packer 1968; Arenella 1983). Because substantive criminal laws typically constitute general prohibitions, the jurors' familiarity with their case's factual details enables them to apply the community's values in their verdict. The power to nullify and acquit "factually guilty" defendants provides a crucial nexus between the original legislative decision to criminalize certain conduct and the community's felt sense of justice in the application of that law to the particulars of the case.

Researchers attribute the greater likelihood of juries than judges to acquit defendants to several factors, including differences in jury and judge evaluations of evidence, jury sentiments about the "law" (jury equity), and jury sympathy for the defendant. The classic study of *The American Jury* attributes the substantial differences between judges' and juries' verdicts to jurors' use of a higher evidentiary threshold of proof beyond a reasonable doubt (Kalven and Zeisel 1966). "If a society wishes to be serious about convicting only when the state has been put to proof beyond a reasonable doubt, it would be well advised to have a jury system" (Kalven and Zeisel 1966:189–90). Comparative analyses of criminal procedures also attribute jurors' higher evidentiary threshold to laypeople's greater desire than professional judges' for *more evidence* on which to convict, especially in cases of circumstantial proof (Damaska 1973).

A defendant's "youthfulness" provides another instance of jury-judge differences in decision making and elicited substantially more sympathy from jurors (Kalven and Zeisel 1966). *McKeiver's* denial of juries renders it easier to convict youths in juvenile court trials without a jury than in adult proceedings with one. Juvenile court judges may be more predisposed, than criminal court judges or juries to find jurisdiction despite deficiencies of proof in order to "help" an errant youth. "When judges do not intend to punish the juvenile but provide care and treatment, proof beyond a reasonable doubt can seem somewhat irrelevant" (Bernard 1992:143). A study of juvenile justice administration in California compared, among other things, the attrition rates of similar types of cases in juvenile and adult courts and concluded that "it is easier to win a conviction in the juvenile court than in the criminal court, with comparable types of cases" (Greenwood et al. 1983:30–31).

Many rules that govern the admissibility of evidence at trial differ when parties try a case before a jury or a judge alone (Damaska 1973; Feld 1984). Although practical administrative reasons support these evidentiary differences, the stated reason is that, unlike juries, judges' professional training, temperament, and experience enable them to separate and compartmentalize inadmissible from admissible evidence when they decide a case (Feld 1984). Appellate courts regularly presume that inadmissible evidence that clearly would prejudice a jury would not improperly influence a trial judge exposed to the same information even when the judge erred by admitting it originally (Feld 1984). Despite these assumptions, judges appear to convict defendants more readily than do juries because of judges' exposure to inadmissible evidence, such as evidence excluded at a suppression hearing, withdrawn guilty pleas, and knowledge of the defendant's criminal record from which the legal process insulates juries (Kalven and Zeisel 1966).

A variety of institutional and organizational reasons contribute to juvenile court judges' greater propensity than that of juries to convict young offenders. Fact-finding by judges and juries differs intrinsically because the former preside over hundreds of cases every year whereas the latter may hear only one or two cases in a lifetime. The experience of routinely hearing many cases dulls many judges' fact-finding sensibilities and causes them to consider evidence less meticulously, to evaluate facts more casually, and to apply less stringently than do jurors the concepts of reasonable doubt and presumption of innocence (Ainsworth 1991). Although judges occasionally agonize over decisions, as professionals who function in a bureaucracy they necessarily routinize their activities and develop rational detachment and self-confidence in their decision-making ability.

The social, economic, and educational characteristics of judges differ from those of the members of a typical jury pool and affect how judges decide a case. Through voir dire, litigants may question jurors about their backgrounds, attitudes, beliefs, and experiences to determine how those characteristics might influence their decisions in a case. No comparable opportunity exists to explore a judge's background to detect judicial biases or to determine how their personal characteristics might affect judgments. In addition to the novelty of deciding cases, juries and judges evaluate testimony differently. Juvenile court judges control their courtrooms and often question witnesses about their testimony, whereas jurors cannot obtain evidentiary clarification that in turn, may leave more residual "doubt." Juvenile court judges hear testimony from the same police and probation officers on a recurring basis and develop a settled opinion about their credibility, whereas jurors encounter every witness anew with fewer preconceptions. Similarly, as a result of hearing earlier charges against a juvenile or her siblings or presiding over a detention hearing or pretrial motion to suppress evidence, a judge may have a predetermined view of a youth's credibility, character, and guilt.

Fact-finding by a judge differs from that of a jury because an individual, professional fact-finder does not have to discuss either the law or the evidence with a group before reaching a verdict. A judge must instruct a jury explicitly about the law it applies to a case, and appellate courts review the accuracy of their statements of the law. The formal instruction on proof beyond a reasonable doubt reinforces the differences between the judge and jury's evidentiary threshold. In bench trials, by contrast, judges give no instructions, which makes it more difficult for appellate courts to determine whether the judge correctly understood, interpreted, and applied the law and renders their legal errors less visible or susceptible to reversal (Ainsworth 1991).

Defendants reasonably may question the impartiality and fairness of their trials whenever judges possess information that would not be admitted in a jury trial because of concern that it would prejudice fact-finders. The legal fiction that judges can successfully compartmentalize and disregard inadmissible evidence when they decide an offender's guilt becomes particularly troublesome in juvenile courts where the same judge typically handles a youth's case at several different stages of the process. Compared with the criminal process, the juvenile trial system may be inherently prejudicial.

> Where judges sit as the sole triers of fact, prejudice is assured. Not only are judges prejudiced in favor of their own system, but frequently the system itself prejudices juveniles who come before them. It is not uncommon for judges to hear more than one case involving the same child over a period of time. After the first case, the judge learns about the child, his family and environment. As "jurors," judges are extremely cynical. With their knowledge of the common alibis which children use, they would be disqualified automatically if they were on a jury panel. But when a child, perhaps an innocent one, comes before the judge and pleads the same defense the judge disbelieved in another case involving another juvenile a week before, the child will surely lose. (Guggenheim 1978:8)

The juvenile justice process presents many opportunities for evidentiary contamination. Both nonurban judges who preside over juvenile proceedings for years and urban specialist judges may become familiar with youths' or their siblings' prior involvement in the system and hold predispositions about problem children and families. In one interview study, virtually all (90%) court workers reported that judges remembered youths' previous crimes or court appearances, and nearly two-thirds concluded that these recollections adversely affected juveniles' ability to receive a fair trial (Sanborn 1994). In order to decide the appropriate pretrial placement of a juvenile, a detention hearing exposes a judge to a youth's "social history" file, prior record of police contacts, and delinquency adjudications (ABA and Institute of Judicial Administration 1980c). When the same judge then decides the admissibility of evidence in a suppression hearing and then the guilt of the juvenile in the same proceeding, the risks of prejudice become almost insuperable (Feld 1984). In some courts, judges routinely received and read probation officers' social history reports and dispositional recommendations before the youth's trial (Sanborn 1994). An analysis of European "inquisitorial" criminal procedures analogous to juvenile bench trials concludes that exposures to these types of "knowledge may tip the scales against the continental defendant in some close cases where the common law defendant would be acquitted" (Damaska 1973: 519). To whatever degree a judge cannot intellectually compartmentalize the inadmissible from the admissible evidence or exclude influences of which they may be unaware, the juvenile justice process denies juveniles a fair trial and deprives them of an impartial tribunal to determine their guilt based solely on admissible evidence. The juvenile court process aggravates the risk of prejudice even more significantly than do adult bench trials because criminal defendants can avoid the risk by *demanding* a jury trial if they fear prejudice. Because *McKeiver* rejected the constitutional right to a jury trial, it denied to juveniles the only procedural safeguard to avoid or reduce those risks of prejudice.

Preventing Governmental Oppression

The Supreme Court long has recognized that juries serve a special role in preventing governmental oppression. In *Baldwin v. New York*, the Supreme Court emphasized that "[t]he primary purpose of the jury is to prevent the possibility of oppression by the Government; the jury interposes between the accused and his accuser the judgment of laymen who are less tutored perhaps than a judge or panel of judges, but who at the same time are less likely to function or appear as but another arm of the Government that has proceeded against him" (399 U.S. 66, 72 [1969]). In *Duncan v. Louisiana* (391 U.S. 145 [968]), the Court held that fundamental fairness in *adult* criminal proceedings required access to a jury to ensure both factual accuracy *and* to prevent governmental oppression. *Duncan* emphasized that juries protect against a vindictive prosecutor or a weak or biased judge, inject the community's values into law, and increase the visibility and accountability of justice administration:

> Providing an accused with the right to be tried by a jury of his peers gave him an inestimable safeguard against the corrupt or overzealous prosecutor and against the compliant, biased, or eccentric judge. If the defendant preferred the common-sense judgment of a jury to the more tutored but perhaps less sympathetic reaction of the single judge, he was to have it. Beyond this, the jury trial provisions. . . . reflect a fundamental decision about the exercise of official power—a reluctance to entrust plenary powers over the life and liberty of the citizen to one judge or to a group of judges. Fear of unchecked power. . . . found expression in the criminal law in this insistence upon community participation in the determination of guilt or innocence. (391 U.S. at 156)

In liberal democratic theory, the lay-citizen jury represents the ultimate "separation of power" and "check and balance" on the other branches of government (Damaska 1975). In daily practice, the availability of a jury provides an important constraint on lower criminal courts' tendency to provide "rough justice." Observers report, for example, that after the Washington Supreme Court granted adult misdemeanants a state constitutional right to a jury trial, the quality of justice routinely afforded defendants improved dramatically (Ainsworth 1995).

McKeiver uncritically accepted the assertion that juvenile courts rehabilitate rather than punish delinquents, failed to inquire about a need for procedural protections against "benevolent" coercion, and ignored the role of constitutional procedures to prevent governmental oppression. Rather, the Court noted that delinquents' requests for procedural safeguards such as jury trials ignore "every aspect of fairness, of concern, of sympathy, and of paternal attention that the juvenile court system contemplates" (*McKeiver*, 403 U.S. 528, 550 [1971]). Justice Byron White concurred in *McKeiver* and observed that indeterminate juvenile sentences and the "eschewing [of] blameworthiness and punishment for evil choices" satisfied him that "there remained differences of substance between criminal and juvenile courts" (403 U.S. at 553). Because *McKeiver* hypothesized that juvenile courts provide only positive rehabilitative efforts, the Court never examined those substantive differences, the "reality" of treatment, or the need for additional procedural guarantees. Chapter 7 examines whether juvenile courts eschew punishment in favor of rehabilitation either in theory or practice, concludes that juvenile courts perform the same social control functions as do criminal courts, and argues that therefore youths require at least comparable procedural safeguards as adults receive.

The majority of states deny juveniles the right to a jury trial to preserve the "idealistic prospect of an intimate, informal protective proceeding" and to avoid "the traditional delay, the formality, and clamor of the adversary system and, possibly the public trial" (*McKeiver*, 403 U.S. at 545, 550). The dissent in *McKeiver* disputed the Court's concerns about the adverse impact of procedural safeguards in juveniles courts and insisted that "there is no meaningful evidence that granting the right to jury trials will impair the function of the court" (403 U.S. at 564). The experience of the few states that provide youths with criminal procedural parity do not justify the *McKeiver* plurality's fears of excessive delays. Research contemporaneous with *McKeiver* concluded that in states that provided delinquents with a jury trial, juveniles seldom used them; juries neither adversely affected courts' efficiency nor interfered with their rehabilitative efforts (Burch and Knaup 1970). Surveys of states report that juveniles exercise the right to a jury trial in only about 1 to 3 percent of cases (Shaughnessy 1979; Feld 1995). Although we lack data on the rates and outcomes of juvenile versus adult jury trials for comparable offenses, observers generally conclude that delinquents exercise the right even less frequently than do criminal defendants (Rosenberg 1993; Feld 1995).

Although most states deny delinquents the right to jury trials as a matter of law, some analysts questions whether, in practice, significant procedural differences actually exist between juvenile and criminal courts. In daily operation, criminal courts convict the vast majority of adult defendants on the basis of a guilty plea rather than a trial by jury. Some contend that the right to a jury trial is one valuable "chip" in the poker game of plea bargaining, and adult defendants may require more tokens because they play for higher stakes (Rosenberg 1993). However, the potential differences in consequences do not explain why younger offenders should play with fewer chips than do somewhat older players. Court workers and attorneys report that both charge and sentence plea bargains commonly occur in juvenile courts (Sanborn 1993a; ABA 1995). Defense counsel negotiate pleas to protect their clients' records and to conserve resources, whereas prosecutors bargain to overcome evidentiary deficiencies, reduce their caseloads, and minimize burdens on witnesses and the court (Sanborn 1993a).

Differences in the severity of sentences imposed in juvenile and criminal courts do not justify denying youths a right to a jury trial. Before *McKeiver*, the Supreme Court in *Baldwin v. New York* (399 U.S. 66 [1969]), rejected the argument that adults charged with "petty" offenses do not require a jury trial and granted a constitutional right to a jury trial for any prosecution that carried a *potential* term of six months or longer. *Baldwin* based the right to a jury on the statutorily *authorized* penalty that a court *might impose* rather than whether the judge actually imprisoned the defendant, such as would trigger the right to counsel under *Scott v. Illinois*. Because every state's juvenile sentencing statutes authorize dispositions that may continue for a term of years or for the duration of minority, *every* delinquency adjudication carries a potential sanction of six months or longer and none could be seemed "petty" under *Baldwin* (Feld 1988b; Snyder and Sickmund 1995).

McKeiver also feared that granting juveniles a right to a jury trial would result in a public trial as well (403 U.S. at 550). The majority of states exclude the general public from delinquency hearings. Courts and scholars justify confidential proceedings "to hide youthful errors from the full gaze of the public and bury them in the graveyard of the forgotten past" (*Gault* 387 U.S. 1, 24), to avoid labels that limit juveniles' life chances, and to minimize deviant self-concepts (Lemert 1967). Sealing or expunging juvenile court records further reinforces the goals of confidentiality and avoiding labels.

The *Gault* Court noted that juvenile courts regularly compromised confidentiality and provided information about a youth's court contacts to the FBI, military, government agencies, and private employers. Moreover, *McKeiver* did not analyze how abridging confidentiality might intensify negative self-labels beyond those inherent in the legal proceedings themselves (Mahoney 1974). Juvenile courts in most states allow students, social workers, lawyers, and social scientists who lack any particular interest in the child or case to observe proceedings. Their presence vitiates confidentiality without affording the real procedural protections of a public trial. Chapter 6 analyzes states' increased use of delinquency records to enhance the sentences that courts impose on both juveniles and young adult offenders as further erosion of confidentiality.

In other decisions, the Court subordinated juvenile courts' confidentiality to other important policy goals. In *Smith v. Daily Mail Publishing Co.* (443 U.S. 97 [1978]), the Court ruled that freedom of the press to publish lawfully obtained information about a crime committed by a juvenile prevailed over a state's desire to protect delinquents' privacy. In *Davis v. Alaska* (415 U.S. 308 [1974]), the Court ruled that a criminal defendant's right of access to a witness's confidential juvenile court record in order effectively to confront, cross-examine, and impeach her testimony took precedence over the juvenile's privacy interests. Thus, the Court implicitly acknowledges that confidentiality does not constitute an indispensable element of a juvenile justice system when litigants present other countervailing interests.

Currently about half a dozen states grant juveniles an unqualified right to a public trial, and another dozen open delinquency proceedings to the public or press depending on a youth's offense or age (Note 1983; Sanborn 1993b). These policies reflect the public's interest to learn the identity of a juvenile offender so as to protect themselves, to encourage parents to exercise greater control over their children, and to increase the visibility, accountability, and performance of the juvenile justice system. Confidentiality provisions often protect bureaucratic functionaries more effectively than they do delinquents. Opening proceedings may improve the quality of procedural justice and subject those who administer the court to public scrutiny. At the symbolic level, public trials provide another instance of the criminalizing of juvenile justice. Juvenile courts no longer constitute a closed confidential forum in which the state acts as *parens patriae* to resolve family problems but, rather, a public proceeding to determine criminal guilt.

Because juvenile courts decide whether a youth committed a crime, public trials prevent governmental oppression and constitute an inherently important reason to limit confidentiality. Justice William Brennan's concurring-dissenting opinion in *McKeiver* recognized that procedural safeguards ensured accurate fact-finding *and* prevented governmental oppression and that juveniles also required protection from the state. Moreover, he suggested that alternative procedural methods, such as a public trial, could make delinquency proceedings visible and accountable and provide the functionally equivalent protection of a jury trial. In *In re Oliver* (333 U.S. 257 [1948]), the Supreme Court held that a criminal defendant had a right to a public trial and condemned secret criminal proceedings: "Whatever other benefits the guarantee to an accused that his trial be conducted in public may confer upon our society, the guarantee has always been recognized as a safeguard against any attempt to employ our courts as instruments of persecution. The knowledge that every criminal trial is subject to contemporaneous review in the forum of public opinion is an effective restraint on possible abuse of judicial power" (*Oliver*, 330 U.S. at 270). *Oliver* noted that public trials bring cases to the attention of an unknown witness who can then voluntarily come forward to provide testimony, provide citizens with information about the administration of justice, and promote confidence in the judiciary.

Although jury trials and public trials conflict with juvenile courts' traditional informality and confidentiality, *Gault* rejected informality in favor of an adversarial process. Public trials provide a check on potential abuses of judicial power and may be even more critical in juvenile than in adult criminal court proceedings. Juvenile court judges exercise broader discretion than do criminal court judges, even though the former often are less qualified or competent. Youths lack the right to appeal judges' decisions either to the conscience of the community embodied in the jury or to the public or lack the practical ability even to appeal their cases to a higher court. Appellate courts acknowledge that the juvenile cases they review exhibit far more procedural errors than do comparable adult cases and suggest that secrecy may foster a judicial casualness toward the law that visibility might constrain. The Alaska Supreme Court, for example, observed that juvenile courts often commit "much more extensive and fundamental error than is generally found in adult criminal cases" (*R.L.R.*, 487 P.2d 27, 38 [Alaska 1971]). Although public access would reduce confidentiality, it would encourage juvenile courts to adhere more closely to the procedures that the law requires and provide the public with needed information about the quality and fairness of juvenile justice administration.

Confidential delinquency proceedings also erode the socializing, educative, or deterrent influence that imposing sanctions may have on other delinquents. By insisting that punishment constitutes treatment, by administering individualized sanctions in closed and confidential proceedings, and by obscuring any relationship between an act and its consequences, the juvenile justice system virtually eliminates the word *threat* from its vocabulary and precludes the communication of any moral message to other young offenders. Although the effectiveness of sanctions to deter criminal or delinquent behavior remains unproved (Blumstein, Cohen, and Nagin 1978), juvenile courts' confidential and individualized sanctions undermine any certainty or predictability.

For juvenile justice personnel, the cultural and constitutional symbolism of a jury and public trial far outweighs their practical significance. The denial of an open hearing or a jury trial affirms that juvenile courts differ somehow from their adult criminal counterparts. Conversely, to provide youths with jury trials would acknowledge that juvenile courts actually punish, as well as treat, young offenders or that youths require protection even from state benevolence. Moreover, providing delinquents with criminal procedural parity with adults would eliminate virtually all the procedural reasons to maintain a separate juvenile justice system. Criminal courts already exist to try offenders. Denying to youths charged with crimes and incarcerated the right to a jury trial that the Constitution guarantees any adult defendant undermines the fundamental legitimacy of the juvenile justice process itself.

Juvenile courts perform social control functions similar to those exercised by any criminal court. Claims that they intervene solely to provide rehabilitation and therapy when youths commit crimes are inaccurate and deceptive. Juveniles readily perceive the hypocrisy of courts' finding that they committed a crime, albeit obscured by euphemisms, and imposing a sanction, experienced as penal in all but name, without providing them the procedural rights afforded adults. Based on courtroom dramas and publicized criminal trials, young people share a cultural understanding of the components of a "real" trial. The contrast between depictions of a jury trial and a vigorous defense lawyer and the "actualized caricature" of a juvenile bench trial fosters a sense of injustice that delegitimates the legal process (Ainsworth 1991; Melton 1989). Despite the close formal and functional resemblance between delinquency and criminal proceedings, *McKeiver*'s denial of public and jury trials places juvenile offenders at a comparative disadvantage and exposes youths to the coercive power of the state under circumstances the law does not tolerate for adults.

Conclusion

The United States Supreme Court's jurisprudence of youth possesses two competing cultural constructions and legal conceptions of young people. On the one hand, it views them as innocent, vulnerable, fragile, and dependent *children*. When the Court characterizes youths as *children*, it invokes "paternalistic" rationales to enable their parents and the state to protect and nurture them and subordinates their autonomy to the longer-term interests of the adults they will become. On the other hand, the Court's jurisprudence sometimes characterizes young people as autonomous and responsible *adultlike* people. The Court adopts this "liberationist" posture when young people engage in adultlike activities, such as frightening criminal behavior, and treats them as the formal and legal equals of their elders. In this chapter, I argue that the Supreme Court chooses between these two competing legal constructions in order to subordinate youths to adult authority and to maximize their social control. States condone the procedural deficiencies of juvenile courts because they deal with young criminals, and, as a result, *young* offenders continue to receive the "worst of both worlds."

Gault and *Winship* assumed that young people needed formal and adversarial procedural safeguards to protect them from state coercion. But, if youths cannot effectively exercise their procedural rights, then a veneer of formal legal equality does not redress young people's practical disadvantages in the justice process. Young people may not believe that they can exercise their legal rights without suffering adverse consequences. Youths remain more vulnerable to police interrogation than do adults, waive their *Miranda* rights more readily, and provide evidence of guilt that negates the utility of any trial rights. Even though juveniles are less able than adults to vindicate their legal interests without effective assistance of counsel, juvenile court judges often rely on "waiver" of the right to deny delinquents access to lawyers. But without assistance of counsel, youths in low-visibility proceedings cannot assert their meager procedural and substantive rights either at trial or through an appeal.

Social psychological research on juveniles' waivers of *Miranda* rights and the right to counsel indicates that young people require more procedural protections than adults require, rather than the same or fewer safeguards, in order to achieve procedural equality and to enable them to exercise those rights they theoretically possess. A "protectionist" juvenile justice process would recognize the unique vulnerabilities of youths and provide additional safeguards to protect them from their own developmental disabilities, rather than to use formal equality to take advantage of their limitations. Instead of insisting that youths invoke the right to counsel with adultlike technical precision, as in *Fare*, a "protectionist" strategy would require mandatory appointment of counsel. Only such a policy could compensate for juveniles' vulnerability to adult coercion, lack of experience, and inability either to protect themselves, to contact a lawyer, or to obtain representation independently.

Juvenile courts invoke "protectionist" policies primarily when doing so enhances the social control of youths. *Schall* invoked child welfare and *parens patriae* rationale to posit a right to "custody not liberty" and to authorize juvenile courts to preventively detain youths more easily than adults. *McKeiver* denied youths charged with crimes and confined in institutions the right to a jury or a public trial that every adult defendant enjoys. Despite youths' theoretical procedural rights, juvenile courts find virtually all youths referred to them guilty of some offense and thereby acquire authority to impose a disposition and control their lives. The Court's rejection of juveniles' criminal procedural parity with adults enabled states to intervene more extensively in the lives of young offenders but did nothing to ensure the delivery of the *parens patriae* social welfare services that purportedly justify those differences.

Procedural justice provides a legal system with its legitimacy. People's perceptions of justice depend not simply on the outcomes of their case and whether they win or lose but on the nature of the process that determines the result. People's views of procedural justice rest on the process's equality and consistency, its respectful treatment of the parties, litigants' ability to participate in it and to affect outcomes, and the decision maker's basic fairness (Melton 1989; Ainsworth 1991). The rule of law promotes equality and the consistency of the process. Procedural rights, especially the right to counsel, enable parties to participate and exercise some control over the process that affects them and foster their respectful treatment. Ethical decision making presumes a fair, honest, and unbiased fact-finder who does not act arbitrarily. Judged by these simple measures of fairness, even the "constitutionally domesticated" juvenile court often fails to satisfy core elements of procedural justice. Individualized discretion subverts the rule of law. Subjective and standardless decision making fosters discriminatory practices. The denial to young offenders of the procedural rights, such as jury and public trials, deemed necessary for every other person charged with a crime offends norms of equality. The absence of counsel undermines youths' ability to participate in the process. Judicial exposure to a youth's social background and prior criminal record creates an appearance, if not actuality, of prejudgment that undermines confidence in a fair, unbiased, and ethical fact-finder. In short, juvenile courts employ a process to which few, if any, adults charged with a crime and facing the prospect of confinement would consent to have their guilt determined.

The procedural details of a justice system reflect a cultural conception of the relationship between the individual and the state. Our constitutional adversary system reflects an ideological commitment to sovereign individuals and their equality with the state. An adversary system assumes that "an irreconcilable conflict between the individual and the state exists in the administration of criminal law. Because state officials cannot be trusted and consummate deviltry on their part cannot be ruled out, the best procedural design is one in which the individual and the state engage as adversaries in a highly formalized battle" (Damaska 1975:530). Thus, the policy and value choices embedded in the "due process" and "crime control" models reflect competing perceptions of the balance between individual autonomy and state power.

The traditional juvenile court's inquisitorial design represented an effort to implement a paternalistic model of justice in a highly diverse and pluralistic culture. *Gault* exemplified the Warren Court's due process ideology, incorporated the privilege against self-incrimination in order to establish equality between delinquents and the state, and institutionalized the adversary process. *McKeiver* clearly recognized that extending to juveniles all the criminal procedural rights of adults quickly could lead to the elimination of a separate juvenile court. "If the formalities of the criminal adjudicative process are to be superimposed upon the juvenile court system, there is little need for its separate existence. Perhaps that ultimate disillusionment will come one day, but for the moment we are disinclined to give impetus to it" (*McKeiver*, 403 U.S. at 551).

In the decades since *Gault*, the Supreme Court has preserved the *idea* of a separate justice system by manipulating the competing legal conceptions of youths as autonomous and responsible or as dependent and vulnerable. As a result, states treat juveniles like adults when formal equality redounds to their disadvantage and use special juvenile court procedures when they provide an advantage to the state. All the procedural rights and constitutional decisions analyzed in this chapter reflect, in varying ways, a constitutional retrenchment from *Gault's* ideological premises of a trial as a battle between equals and of youths as rights-bearing individuals. They reflect instead a constitutional preference for a more paternalistic and authoritarian process that treats children as "subjects" and manipulates them as "means" to become the adults those in power feel they should become. To whatever extent young offenders differ from adults in their ability to deal with or participate in the legal process, they require more procedural safeguards, rather than fewer, to achieve functional equality. Despite juveniles' development limitations, however, juvenile courts provide youths with fewer and less-effective safeguards than those afforded adult criminal defendants in order to maximize the courts' social control.

In chapter 3, I placed the Warren Court's due process revolution in its broader social structural and civil rights context, as part of a constitutional strategy to protect the liberty interests of racial minorities. The Warren Court assumed that procedural rights would ensure administrative regularity and equal enforcement of substantive laws. In the context of juvenile courts, however, procedural reforms cannot compensate for the highly discretionary substantive standards—"best interests of the child" or a "serious risk" of future crime—that preclude evenhanded enforcement and lend themselves to discriminatory applications.

The *Gault* decision represents a constitutional procedural revolution that failed *and* that produced unintended negative consequences. Delinquents, then and now, continue to receive the "worst of both worlds," neither solicitous care and regenerative treatment nor the criminal procedural rights of adults. While *McKeiver* could deny procedural equality, the Court could not compel states to deliver social welfare services. As a result, delinquents experience punishment but without adult criminal procedural justice. Despite *McKeiver*'s endorsement of a "rehabilitative" juvenile court, *Gault*'s insistence on some criminal procedural regularity shifted the focus of delinquency hearings from paternalistic assessments of a youth's "real needs" to proof that she committed a crime. Thus, *Gault* formalized and made explicit the connection between criminal conduct and coercive intervention, "criminalized" juvenile courts, and fostered their procedural and substantive convergence with criminal courts. Although youths lack criminal procedural parity with adult defendants, *Gault*'s decision to provide them with any procedural safeguards at all served to legitimate more-punitive sanctions. Once states grant youths a semblance of procedural justice, however inadequate, it becomes easier for them to depart from a purely rehabilitative model of juvenile justice. Providing any procedural rights legitimates the imposition of punitive, as well as therapeutic, sanctions. In chapters 6 and 7, I argue that the ultimate irony of *Gault* is that those increasingly punitive juvenile sanctions fall disproportionately on minority delinquents, the very youths whom the Warren Court initially set out to protect.

| | | | FIVE

Social Control and Noncriminal Status Offenders

Triage and Privatization

Chapters 1 and 2 analyzed the emergence of the newer conception of childhood that accompanied modernization during the nineteenth century and the embodiment of that conception in the juvenile court's status jurisdiction. Progressive reformers legislatively enacted their imagery of childhood as a period of vulnerability and dependency. They regarded certain protoadult activities as inconsistent with their *idea* of children and inimical to their long-term development. They viewed adolescence as a period of preparation for adulthood and during which to defer adult roles. Families and schools bore primary responsibility to socialize, supervise, and control young people. Progressives envisioned young people as nested in these primary agencies, enforced children's dependency within these entities, and viewed children's autonomy from them as threatening to young people and the community. If a young person "escaped" from this overlapping network of supervision, then she was literally "out of control." Juvenile court provided an organizational mechanism to regulate children, to reinforce the authority of the other institutions that controlled children, and to oversee the adequacy of their families' supervision. The Progressives conceived of the juvenile court as a benign substitute for parental inadequacy, as *parens patriae*, and included status offenses in its definition of delinquency so that public authorities could respond to vulnerable children at risk and their deficient families (Teitelbaum and Harris 1977).

The juvenile court buttressed other child-rearing authorities, and part of its mission included enforcing other people's rules about childhood, for example, parents' discipline or schools' regulations. Virtually all the behaviors subsumed in the status jurisdiction represent efforts either to reinforce the authority of the primary socializing agencies, to reinstate controls over youths, or to enforce the norms of childhood. Within a framework of liberation or protectionism, an element of authoritarianism, as well as paternalism, animated status jurisdiction ideology. "Much of the adult reaction to youth seems to reflect a concern with obedience *per se*, a reflection that youth are still children who owe obedience to their parents and other adult authorities" (Grubb and Lazerson 1982:162). Because "incorrigible," "stubborn," or runaway children threatened parental control, juvenile courts intervened to reinforce parents authority. When truant children "escaped" from and threatened the control of schools, juvenile court intervened to reassert their influence. Youthful behaviors such as "waywardness," "immorality," alcohol consumption, and sexual experimentation posed a threat to a youth's long-term development, offended Progressives' sensibilities about the nature of children, and constituted adult activities forbidden to young people (Schlossman 1977). The essential characteristic of status offenses is behavior in which adults may engage but which the state prohibits for young people simply because of their age, that is, their status as children.

At earlier times in the juvenile courts' history, status offenders made up as much as half of their docket (Schlossman 1977; Rubin 1985). As a result of several reforms in the post-*Gault* era, however, the numbers of status offenders referred to and formally petitioned in juvenile courts have decreased substantially. Still, police, parents, probation officers, and schools referred nearly 100,000 youngsters to juvenile courts in 1992 for such juvenile misconduct as running away, truancy, ungovernability, curfew violations, sexual activity, and possession or consumption of liquor (Butts et al. 1995). Juvenile courts filed formal petitions against somewhat more than half (56%) of the status offenders referred to them. Courts charged more than twice as many girls as boys with running away from home (27% versus 12%), and charged the largest proportion of boys with liquor violations (38%) (Butts et al. 1995). Ultimately, judges removed about 10 percent of these noncriminal youths from their homes.

"Juvenile Nuisances" and Their Control

Systematic challenges to juvenile courts' extensive authority to intervene in the lives of noncriminal young people only emerged during the 1960s. While helping troubled children constitutes an inherently attractive notion, critics questioned extensively the definition and administration of status jurisdiction in the post-*Gault* decades (Teitelbaum and Gough 1977; Allinson 1983). Much of the policy debate about status jurisdiction centers on means rather than ends and especially on whether juvenile courts provide the most appropriate organizational mechanism to discourage young people from engaging in undesirable or self-injurious behavior or to deliver needed services (Rosenheim 1976). The President's Commission on Law Enforcement and Administration of Justice (Crime Commission) (1967a, 1967b) recommended that states narrow the range of conduct for which juvenile court could intervene. As stated in chapter 3, the Crime Commission suggested that juvenile courts develop a "two-track" system to separate their criminal and noncriminal jurisdictions. With respect to the status jurisdiction, the Crime Commission proposed that "[t]he range of conduct for which court intervention is authorized should be narrowed with greater emphasis upon consensual and informal means of meeting the problems of difficult children" (1967b:2). Its "two-track" approach appealed to conservatives who favored a more punitive response toward young criminal offenders and to liberal civil libertarians who favored a more legalistic approach that limited judicial discretion over non-criminal youths.

Many professional groups reexamined juvenile courts' status jurisdiction since the 1970s, and most recommended limitations on the grounds for and intensity of judicial intervention, administrative reforms, or elimination of status jurisdiction (Handler and Zatz 1982; National Council on Crime and Delinquency 1975; American Bar Association (ABA) and Institute of Judicial Administration 1982). The ABA and Institute of Judicial Administration's *Juvenile Justice Standards Relating to Noncriminal Misbehavior*, for example, proposed that "the present jurisdiction of the juvenile court over noncriminal behavior—the status offense jurisdiction—should be cut short and a system of voluntary referral to services provided outside the juvenile justice system adopted in its stead" (1982:2). Most reform proposals emphasized youths' voluntary participation in programs and provision of services by personnel who are not associated with the juvenile justice process.

Critics of status jurisdiction emphasize the negative effects of coercive intervention on noncriminal youths; the disabling effects that court involvement has on families, schools, and other agencies that refer status offenders to the court; and the legal and administrative problems that these laws pose for juvenile justice administration (Andrews and Cohn 1974; Katz and Teitelbaum 1978; Rosenberg 1983). Some criticize status intervention as a one-sided effort by parents and courts to impose a particular standard of behavior on young people, especially young women (Chesney-Lind and Shelden 1992; Rosenberg and Rosenberg 1976). Others characterize it as a chimera of assistance that promises impoverished parents' access to social and clinical resources but consigns their problem children to custodial institutions (Andrews and Cohn 1974). Defenders of juvenile courts' jurisdiction over noncriminal youths' misconduct emphasize that the state cannot remain indifferent to family dysfunction, truancy, or premature and self-injurious autonomy and that the community needs some mechanism to intervene authoritatively when a child is "out of control" (Edwards 1992).

The vigorous policy debate about the scope of status jurisdiction reflects the competing cultural and legal visions of young people as vulnerable and dependent or as autonomous and responsible. A protectionist stance emphasizes the dependent and vulnerable nature of children, their need for adult guidance, and the state's *parens patriae* and child welfare role in supervising their upbringing. A liberationist or noninterventionist stance emphasizes young people's autonomy and responsibility, the "normality" of low-level deviance and rebelliousness during youths' struggle to develop an independent identity and questions the effectiveness of coercive intervention to resolve intrafamily disputes. The competition between, and legal resolution of, these conflicting visions reflect the societal ambivalence about youthful autonomy and control. Although states have enacted many legal reforms of status jurisdiction since the 1970s, the juvenile justice and ancillary welfare and mental health systems resolve the underlying tensions between autonomy and dependency in ways that continue to maximize the social control of young people.

In the following sections, I review post-*Gault* criticisms of status jurisdiction and examine the reforms put forward in the 1970s and 1980s in response. In these analyses, I argue that juvenile justice system responses and court decisions have subverted policies nominally promulgated to enhance youths' autonomy and to limit state intervention and that they have, instead, widened the net of control over noncriminal youths. Moreover, these reforms provided the impetus to further "medicalize" adolescence as deviance in the 1980s, to respond to troublesome youths in a less-visible "hidden system" of private psychiatric and chemical dependency facilities with fewer procedural safeguards, and to create an industry with a fiscal stake in confining young people. Finally, these status jurisdictional reforms constitute one crucial component of the juvenile justice "triage" system that increasingly removes many middle-class, white, and female juveniles to private sector institutions and relegates young black male delinquents to public training schools and youth prisons.

The Criticisms of Status Jurisdiction

Adverse Impact of Judicial Intervention on Children

When the Supreme Court decided *Gault* in 1967, nearly all states' juvenile codes classified status offenses as a form of delinquency. Juvenile courts found a youth to be a generic "delinquent" whether she committed a serious crime or a misdemeanor, ran away from home, or truanted from school. Because the broad definition of delinquency assumed that youths need assistance, juvenile courts possessed the same dispositional authority over all youths, regardless of their underlying "symptomatic" misconduct. They detained and incarcerated noncriminal status offenders in the same institutions with youths convicted of criminal offenses (Rosenberg and Rosenberg 1976; Handler and

Zatz 1982). Some reports indicated that juvenile courts committed as many as half of all youths confined in training schools for noncriminal status misconduct (Sussman 1977b).

Status offenses like running away and incorrigibility often resulted from intrafamily conflicts, and juvenile courts often encountered greater difficulties returning these youths to their homes than they did youths charged with crimes. As a result, noncriminal status offenders often served longer periods in institutions than did those convicted of serious offenses. Because of the gendered nature of troublesome conduct and parents' responses to it, juvenile courts detained more often and confined for longer periods girls charged with status offenses than they did boys charged with status or criminal violations (Frazier and Cochran 1986; Chesney-Lind 1988). In 1983, for example, juvenile court detained 12 percent of girls charged with status offenses as compared with 9 percent of boys (Snyder and Finnegan 1987). A summary of the research reported that among status offenders, girls experienced a greater probability of juvenile court referrals than did boys and, following referral, experienced greater probabilities than did boys that court personnel would file formal petitions, place girls in pretrial detention, and subsequently incarcerate them (Bishop and Frazier 1992).

Feminist criminologists criticized juvenile courts' status jurisdiction as a crucial link in the "enforcement of girls' obedience to a special set of expectations about their deportment, their sexuality, and their obedience to familial demands" (Chesney-Lind and Shelden 1992:6). We recall from chapter 2, that juvenile courts, from their inception, reacted much more harshly to girls who "act like women" than to their male "partners in crime" and detained and incarcerated females at higher rates than they did boys (Schlossman and Wallach 1978; Brenzel 1980). In the 1970s, girls made up nearly two-thirds (62%) of youths charged with ungovernability, incorrigibility, or running away (Andrews and Cohn 1974). Status offenses accounted for about three-quarters of all the charges against girls in the juvenile justice system (Chesney-Lind 1977). Status offenses provided the vehicle through which the court enforced cultural norms about adolescent sexuality and parental authority, administered a de facto double standard of justice for boys and for girls, and "trained women to know their place" (Chesney-Lind 1977).

Adverse Impact of Status Jurisdiction on Sources of Referral

Because the status jurisdiction presumes that young people are nested in primary socializing agencies, juvenile courts functioned to reinforce those agencies' authority and thereby to enforce "other people's laws." The recourse of these primary agencies to coercive public authority, in turn, often disabled their internal ability to resolve conflict informally, voluntarily, and consensually. Social service agencies, schools, and families sometimes used the court's power to impose solutions on young people rather than to address the underlying sources of conflict. Effectively, the court became "a vehicle for parents to coerce their children into adopting rigid codes of behavior and a dumping ground for the children of neglectful or unstable parents who wish to divest themselves of custodial responsibilities" (Rosenberg and Rosenberg 1976: 1128).

Parental referrals overloaded juvenile courts with intractable family disputes and diverted scarce judicial resources from other tasks, and intervention often exacerbated rather than ameliorated family conflict (Andrews and Cohn 1974). In some cases, court personnel found it easier to proceed against a juvenile as a status offender rather than to maintain an action against the parents in a neglect proceeding, especially if the latter obtained counsel and vigorously defended against court intervention (Rosenberg and Rosenberg 1976). Some critics argue that juvenile courts sometimes charged as runaways and confined many girls who fled from sexual abuse at home rather than proceeding against their abusers (Chesney-Lind and Shelden 1992). In other cases, court personnel identified with parents struggling to control rebellious adolescents. Because parents refer their girls more readily than their boys for sexual experimentation, parents implicate the court in enforcing a sexual double standard of behavior (Chesney-Lind and Shelden 1992). Juvenile courts almost uncritically act to reinforce parental authority and uphold traditional sexual roles.

Adverse Impact of Status Jurisdiction on Juvenile Courts

The status jurisdiction posed difficult legal issues of "void for vagueness," equal protection, and procedural justice for juvenile courts (Katz and Teitelbaum 1978). Progressive reformers regarded status behavior both as undesirable in its own right and as a harbinger of future criminality if left unchecked. They assumed that noncriminal misconduct provided an accurate predictor of subsequent delinquency and gave judges broad authority to prevent unruliness or immorality from ripening into criminality. Typical legislative language gave courts jurisdiction over a minor who, among other shortcomings, "persistently or habitually refuses to obey the reasonable and proper orders or directions of his parents, . . . or who is beyond the control of such person, . . . or who is a habitual truant from school, . . . or who from any cause is in danger of leading an idle, dissolute, lewd or immoral life" (Cal. Welf. & Inst. Code § 601 [West 1960]). But not all such misconduct necessarily indicated serious disturbance or future criminality. The status jurisdiction threw a very wide net that encompassed virtually all youths and then allowed judges selectively to respond to those entangled in it.

Courts strike down on "void for vagueness" grounds criminal laws that prohibit adults from engaging in "indecent" or "immoral conduct" or "failing to give a reasonable account" (e.g., *Papachristou v. Jacksonville*, 405 U.S. 156 [1972]). The Supreme Court invalidates, for example, criminal loitering or vagrancy statutes on vagueness grounds both because they fail to provide "fair warning" or give sufficient notice to private citizens of what conduct the law prohibits or permits and because the ordinances lack adequate objective standards with which to gauge public officials' evenhanded application (LaFave and Scott 1986). Effectively, overly broad and imprecise legislation delegates to police and courts discretion to define crimes on ad hoc bases. Vague statutes lend themselves to arbitrary and discriminatory enforcement, and their application raises issues of equal protection (*Kolender v. Lawson*, 461 U.S. 352 [1983]).

In contrast with courts' invalidation of adult loitering or vagrancy statutes, state courts routinely uphold equally standardless status offense legislation when applied to young people (Rosenberg 1983; Rubin 1985). As a result, almost any misbehavior theoretically could bring a child within the ambit of vague status offense prohibitions. Status jurisdiction effectively delegates to parents or judges the power to define misconduct and to decide over which children juvenile courts should exercise their broad authority. The vague and overly broad definitions of status offenses provide neither young people nor the judges who enforce them with guidance on the behaviors they permit or prohibit. Like preventive detention based on a "serious risk," the absence of substantive standards undermines the utility of procedural safeguards. A lawyer can provide a child with very little practical assistance when a statute proscribes conduct such as habitually deporting herself so as to endanger her morals (*E.S.G. v. State*, 447 S.W.2d 225 [Tex. 1969]) or being in danger of falling into habits of vice or immorality (*S.S. and L.B. v. State*, 299 A.2d 560 [Me. 1973]) and when such prohibitions lack objective criteria against which to measure the exercise of judicial discretion.

The lack of statutory precision and the absence of standards to guide decision makers invite arbitrary and capricious enforcement. Critics of status intervention often complained that decisions reflected individual judges' personal values and prejudices rather than the rule of law. The exercise of standardless discretion to regulate noncriminal misconduct disproportionately affected poor, minority, and female juveniles (Teilmann and Landry 1981; Chesney-Lind 1988). When judges predict which youths will become criminals, they typically identify lower-class and non white juveniles as likely prospects for coercive intervention. Just as Progressive reformers used status jurisdiction to enforce a paternalistic sexual double standard (Schlossman and Wallach 1978), contemporary critics observe that administration of status jurisdiction continues to have a clearly gendered impact (Chesney-Lind and Shelden 1992). Parents and courts use status proceedings to "hold girls legally accountable for behavior—often sexual or in some way related to sex—that they would not consider serious if committed by boys" (Sussman 1977b:183).

The Supreme Court decision in *Gault* affected only the procedural rights of delinquent youths charged with crimes and facing the possibility of institutional confinement. As a matter of state laws, status offenders often receive less-extensive procedural safeguards even than constitutionally mandated for delinquents (Sussman 1977a; Smith 1992). Because the juvenile court, by definition, does not charge a status offender with a crime, some states used this as a rationale to deny youths the privilege against self-incrimination (*In re Spalding*, 273 Md. 690 [1975]), the right to counsel (*In re Walker*, 282 N.C.

28 [1972]; Feld 1988a, 1989), or to proof beyond a reasonable doubt (*In re Henderson*, 199 N.W.2d 111 [Iowa 1972]; Rosenberg and Rosenberg 1976). As a result, prosecutors and courts often found it easier to prove "incorrigibility" and establish jurisdiction than to prove the elements of a criminal offense or parental neglect (Rosenberg 1983; Rosenberg and Rosenberg 1976).

Reform of Status Jurisdiction

The reexamination of status offenses accompanied the decline of the rehabil-itative ideal and the increased procedural formality associated with delin-quency proceedings. "[I]t no longer appeared justifiable to include status of-fenders in the same process as those whose delinquent acts were also crimes for adults" (Farrington, Ohlin, and Wilson 1986:127). Judicial and legislative disillusionment with juvenile courts' treatment of noncriminal youths in the decades since *Gault* prompted three types of policy reforms: diversion, dein-stitutionalization, and decriminalization (Empey 1973; Hellum 1979). These legislative and administrative changes attempted to respond to the criticisms levied against status offenses both in theory and in practice, reflected a greater tolerance of youths' autonomy and independence, and indicated a recognition of the limits of law to solve social and family problems.

Congress passed the federal Juvenile Justice and Delinquency Prevention (JJDP) Act in 1974 (42 U.S.C. §§ 5601–5640 [1983]) to provide federal lead-ership in the reform of status offenses. The JJDP Act required states, as a condition of receiving federal formula grants, to initiate a process to remove noncriminal offenders from secure detention and correctional facilities. The JJDP Act required states to submit a plan designed to ensure that "within two years. . . . juveniles who are charged with or who have committed offenses that would not be criminal if committed by an adult . . . shall not be placed in juvenile detention or correctional facilities" (42 U.S.C. § 5633(a)(12)(A) [1988]). Concurrently with passage of the JJDP Act, several states prohibited confinement of noncriminal "children in need of supervision" in delinquency institutions, and others barred their confinement with delinquents in secure detention facilities as well. Legal restrictions on the institutional commingling of status with delinquent offenders in secure detention and correctional fa-cilities provided the impetus to divert some status offenders from juvenile courts and to decarcerate those who remained in the system (Handler and Zatz 1982).

Diversion

Gault's due process reforms increased the procedural formality and the ad-ministrative costs of processing all young offenders and provided an impetus to address the cases of many juvenile "nuisances" informally. Diversion pro-grams constitute one reform strategy to minimize formal intervention and to provide supervision or services on an informal basis (Lemert 1981). Just as the original juvenile court diverted youths from adult criminal courts, theoretically diversion programs shift away from juvenile court youths who otherwise would enter that system (Sutton 1988). Proponents of diversion contend that it provides an efficient gatekeeping mechanism, constitutes the first line of case sorting and routing, and avoids stigmatizing or labeling some minor offenders. Diversion conserves scarce judicial resources and provides an informal means to respond to misbehavior that a formal system might otherwise ignore. Diversion provides more efficient and flexible access to reintegrative community resources and rehabilitative services than via a formal process.

Despite the theoretical rationale for handling youths outside the juvenile justice system, substantial evidence exists that justice system personnel have co-opted diversion reforms and converted them into an additional and expanded tool of social control. Ironically, an innovation intended to enhance youths' autonomy and to reduce state intervention became a device to extend informal controls further into the normal population. Although voluntarism and nonjustice system implementation provided the original premises of status offense divestiture and diversion reform, analysts question whether juvenile justice personnel have implemented diversion programs coherently or consistently with those assumptions (Klein 1979; Polk 1984). Numerous practical obstacles exist to effective implementation of diversion reforms: inadequate program rationales, inappropriately selected youths, insufficiently developed treatment programs or services delivery, and juvenile justice bureaucratic resistance to reform (Klein 1979). The ideology of juvenile justice—early identification and treatment—expands inherently and readily lends itself to overreaching. Diversion programs seldom restrict themselves to youths who would otherwise enter the juvenile justice system, but they do encompass many young people whom police previously might counsel, reprimand, and release if they had any police contacts at all (Klein 1979). Moreover, police or juvenile court personnel operate many diversion programs themselves and thereby retain effective control over juvenile offenders. "The tendency is for police and probation officers to treat such programs as opportunities to expand their informal surveillance activities. Because most diverted juveniles continue to be under court jurisdiction, such extralegal criteria as program rules and client demeanor can be used to justify subsequent incarceration; in programs involving families, unindicted siblings can become vulnerable to legal controls as well" (Sutton 1988:206). If program personnel can coerce a youth to participate by threatening to file a petition and formally process a youth who fails to comply with their dictates, then participation in a diversion program cannot be regarded as truly "voluntary."

Although the Crime Commission's recommendations theoretically intended to reduce the court's client population, the actual practice of diversion has had the opposite effect and "widened the net of social control" (Klein 1979; Polk 1984; Sutton 1988). Following the JJDP Act's mandate, the arrest rate for status offenses decreased 21.1 percent between 1975 and 1979 (Krisberg and Schwartz 1983). But, despite a declining youth population and decreasing status arrests, the overall numbers of status offenders and delinquents referred to court remained relatively constant, and police subjected juveniles whom previously they would have released to other forms of informal intervention. Analyses of juvenile court referrals during a four-year period before and after the adoption of a status offender diversion program in St. Louis reported an increase both in the numbers of youths supervised in diversion *and* in the number of youths referred to juvenile court after controlling for the size of the youth population at risk (Decker 1985). Analyses of decarceration of status offenders in Illinois also reported a recategorization of some youths as delinquents and a simultaneous widening of the net of control (Spergel, Reamer, and Lynch 1981). The creation of community-based program resources provided police with a convenient way to dispose of minor cases. Although the numbers of youths in secure detention declined, the overall number of cases under supervision and known to the court increased substantially (Spergel, Reamer, and Lynch 1981).

Diversion provided a rationale to shift discretion from the core of the juvenile justice process to its periphery. While juvenile court decisions are subject to some review and oversight as a result of the greater procedural formality associated with *Gault*, by contrast, police and intake gatekeepers continue to make low-visibility discretionary decisions on an informal basis with neither written standards nor formal accountability. In his comprehensive study of the history of regulating *Stubborn Children*, John Sutton concludes that diversion "sanctified and encouraged a strategy for circumventing due process, assured that programs would stay in the discretionary hands of local officials, and encouraged the privatization of long-term social control" (1988:215). Similarly, Scott Decker's "net-widening" analysis concludes that "[b]ecause of the vagueness of the statutes defining status-offense conduct, the low visibility of police decisions in such situations, the low probability of judicial review of these decisions, these programs present an even greater opportunity for abuse" (1985:215). In short, diversion reforms re-created elements of the pre-*Gault* juvenile court and provided a mechanism to coercively supervise minor deviants in an informal, standardless process without any procedural safeguards.

Deinstitutionalization

Federal and state prohibitions on secure confinement of noncriminal youths with delinquents in pretrial detention and training schools spurred efforts to deinstitutionalize them. The JJDP Act provided federal funds to states to develop programs to remove noncriminal youths from delinquency facilities and created the federal Office of Juvenile Justice and Delinquency Prevention (OJJDP) to administer the formula grants (Schwartz 1989b). Although the original 1974 JJDP Act (§ 223(a)(12)) provided the impetus to deinstitutionalize status offenders (DSO) and to relocate them from secure to community-based facilities, a 1980 amendment to the JJDP statute allowed states to qualify for federal funds even if status offenders remained in institutions if there was "substantial compliance" with OJJDP guidelines, if the noncompliance was *de minimis*, or if juvenile court judges committed noncriminal youths to institutions for violating a "valid court order."

As a result of the DSO initiatives, the numbers of status offenders in secure detention facilities and institutions declined dramatically by the early 1980s (Handler and Zatz 1982; Krisberg and Schwartz 1983; Schneider 1984a). The total admission of status offenders to pretrial detention facilities declined substantially between 1974 and 1982, and the admissions of female decreased 45 percent (Krisberg et al. 1986). The proportion of boys confined in training schools for status offenses declined from 22.7 percent in 1971 to 1.1 percent in 1987, and the proportion of girls institutionalized for noncriminal misconduct decreased from 71.4 percent to 10.9 percent (Schwartz, Steketee, and Schneider 1990). An evaluation of the impact of the federal decarceration mandate concluded: "The placement of adjudicated status offenders in secure public institutional facilities has been virtually eliminated. . . . [S]tatus offenders [are] no longer be[ing] sent to the large red-brick institutions. . . . There has been a substantial reduction in the use of detention for preadjudicated status offenders" (Handler and Zatz 1982:88–89).

Juvenile courts committed a relatively small proportion of all status offenders to secure institutions. Even following the DSO mandate, most noncriminal offenders remain eligible for home removal and commitment to "forestry camps," other medium security facilities, or group homes (Sutton 1988). Although the numbers of noncriminal youths in detention and secure facilities declined dramatically, girls rather than boys accounted for most of those status offenders who remained (Chesney-Lind and Shelden 1992). In one study, girls accounted for 17.7 percent of youths charged with status offenses and detained compared with only 3.3 percent of boys (Schwartz, Steketee, and Schneider 1990).

Following the decarceration mandate, states differed over whether juvenile courts could use their inherent authority to hold status offenders who failed to obey a "valid court order" in criminal contempt and then confine them in delinquency institutions. Some state courts held that juvenile courts could not use their contempt power to "bootstrap" recalcitrant status offenders to delinquents if they refused to comply with judges' dispositional orders, while other state courts authorized judges to incarcerate a status offender as a "last resort" if other, less-restrictive alternatives proved ineffective (Federle 1990). Although state policies varied, amendments to the JJDP Act in 1980 weakened federal restrictions on secure confinement and thereby encouraged states to expand judges' contempt and incarceration authority. The amendments allowed judges to charge status offenders who ran away from nonsecure community placements or who violated court orders with criminal contempt of court, a delinquent act, and to incarcerate them in secure training schools (42 U.S.C. § 5633(a)(12)(A) (1983); Costello and Worthington 1981; Schwartz 1989b). The National Council of Juvenile and Family Court Judges lobbied Congress heavily for the "valid court order" exception in order to increase their discretion and strengthen their power to enforce judicial mandates (Schwartz 1989b). Their representatives contended that without the power to incarcerate noncriminal youths, deinstitutionalization allows "a child ultimately to decide for himself whether he will go to school, whether he will live at home, whether he will continue to run, run, run away from home, or whether he will even obey orders of youth court" (Chesney-Lind and Shelden 1992:117).

The "valid court order" exception enables juvenile court judges to convert a status offender into a delinquent by holding a youth who violates a court order in criminal contempt of court. Even if noncriminal conduct provides both the basis for finding the initial status jurisdiction and for the subsequent court order violation, a court that finds a youth delinquent for criminal contempt may then incarcerate her (Costello and Worthington 1981). Juvenile court judges' use of this power to bootstrap status offenders to delinquents remains an important continuing source of gender bias in juvenile justice. "[T]he typical female [status] offender not in contempt has a 1.8% probability of incarceration, which increased markedly to 63.2% if she is held in contempt. In short, females referred to juvenile court for contempt following an earlier adjudication for a status offense receive harsher judicial dispositions than their male counterparts" (Bishop and Frazier 1992:1183).

Even though subsequent probation violations may result in incarceration, juveniles initially charged with status offenses still enjoy fewer procedural rights than do youths charged with delinquency (Smith 1992). *Gault* addressed only the constitutional rights of youths charged with crimes and who faced possible institutional confinement. As long as states charge status offenders with noncriminal misconduct and prohibit their initial incarceration in delinquency institutions, they may use different, less-formal procedures for status adjudications (Chesney-Lind and Shelden 1992). Typically, status offenders received fewer procedural safeguards and less access to counsel at their initial adjudication, even though those proceedings provide the jurisdictional predicate for subsequent confinement (Feld 1988a, 1989).

The quandary over appropriate responses to status offenders who violate conditions of probation pose the fundamental dilemma of deinstitutionalization. If a court lacks authority to force a youth to comply with its order through the threat of and possible secure confinement, then effectively deinstitutionalization constitutes decriminalization. In that eventuality, some contend that a state should candidly repeal its status offense legislation (Bernard 1992). Because deinstitutionalization threatens juvenile court judges' hegemony over young people and challenges the normative conception of childhood, the National Council of Juvenile and Family Court Judges has been its most ardent opponent (Schwartz 1989b; Chesney-Lind 1988).

Decriminalization

Before to the 1974 federal impetus to decarcerate noncriminal offenders, status offenses constituted a form of delinquency. California began the process of redefining its status jurisdiction in 1961, as did New York in 1962, to more formally distinguish among types of young offenders. By the early 1980s, almost every state decriminalized, or more properly, "de-delinquentized," conduct that juvenile codes made illegal only for children, such as incorrigibility, running away, and truancy. States relabeled noncriminal misconduct with new legislative classifications, such as Persons, Children, or Minors in Need of Supervision (PINS, CHINS, MINS) or Children in Need of Protection and Services (CHIPS) (e.g. N.Y. Family Ct. Act § 712(b) [McKinney Supp. 1983]; Cal. Welf. & Inst. Code §§ 600–602 [West 1960]; Rubin 1985; Sutton 1988). The statutory reconfiguration of status offenses took several forms: repeal of jurisdiction over general "incorrigibility" or "stubbornness" while retaining jurisdiction over age-specific misconduct such as running away, violating curfew, and consuming alcohol and by relabeling nondelinquent status offenders as PINS, MINS, or CHINS. Another recent legislative strategy relabels and shifts these "juvenile nuisances" to the juvenile court's dependency or neglect jurisdiction further to emphasize their vulnerability rather than offensivity (Sutton 1988; Bishop and Frazier 1992). Such label changes simply shift youths from one jurisdictional category to another without significantly limiting courts' dispositional authority, other than the power to commit them to secure confinement in delinquency institutions.

By manipulating jurisdictional categories, juvenile court personnel may relabel former status offenders downward as dependent or neglected youths, upward as delinquent offenders, or laterally into the private mental health sector. The broad discretion available to juvenile court professionals allows them to classify many minor criminal offenders as status offenders or, conversely, status offenders as minor delinquents (Schneider 1984b). In some cases, court personnel previously used the "status" label to avoid the stigma or procedural formality associated with a delinquency proceeding. Following divestiture of status jurisdiction in Washington State, police categorized youths whom previously they would have charged with status offenses as delinquents. The cumulative effect of discretionary decisions continued "to bring status offenders under the jurisdiction of the court at a rate almost as great as had existed prior to the reform" (Schneider 1984b:367). Courtroom observers report that following decriminalization of status offenses, prosecutors charged many girls with criminal-type offenses for behavior that they previously would have charged as status offenses, for example, loitering instead of running away or burglary when girls broke into their parents' homes to obtain food or clothing to prolong their running away (Mahoney and Fenster 1982). Similarly, after Washington State decriminalized status offenses, some police and courts "redefined" them as minor criminal offenders so that juvenile courts could retain jurisdiction and dispositional authority over them. "[B]ecause many status offenders are not simply runaways or truants but also engage in delinquent activities, it is possible for many such youths to be 'relabeled' delinquents rather than remain classified as status offenders. This relabeling may then result in referrals to juvenile court ... [and] appears to have been the case for about 50 percent of the runaways contacted by police ... subsequent to the divestiture law" (Castellano 1986:496–497). Additional indirect evidence exists of relabeling as a strategy to reincarcerate noncriminal offenders. While the proportion of girls confined in training schools for status offenses declined from 71.4 percent in 1971 to 10.9 percent in 1987, the proportion of girls confined for minor delinquencies rose dramatically. In 1987, juvenile courts confined over half (55.8%) of girls for misdemeanor offenses, compared with only 42.8 percent of boys (Schwartz, Steketee, and Schneider 1990).

Only a few states attempted to fully decriminalize status offenses and divest juvenile courts of all authority to intervene in the lives of noncriminal youths. Maine repealed its status offense legislation in 1977 and enacted an "interim care" law, which authorized temporary state intervention for abandoned, runaway, or seriously endangered children (Me. Rev. Stat. Ann. tit. 15, §§ 3103, 3501 [West 1980]). In 1978 the state of Washington repealed its status offense legislation, gave juvenile courts limited jurisdiction over "families in conflict," and authorized police to hold runaway or endangered children in nonsecure custody for only short periods (Wash. Rev. Code Ann. § 13.32A.050 [West 1982]). An evaluation of status jurisdiction divestiture concluded that "Washington succeeded in eliminating runaway and other status offenses from the jurisdiction of the juvenile court; these incidents are no longer grounds for court referrals, detention, or any other type of formal sanction or required treatment" (Schneider 1984b:367). Although court personnel relabeled some of these divested youths as minor criminal offenders, many others remained beyond the reach of the juvenile justice system.

Opponents of status offense reforms sometimes may manipulate a sensational, highly visible case to demonstrate the need for and to reintroduce controls over noncriminal youths. Following the murder of a young runaway girl in 1993, the Washington Legislature reinstated police and court authority to hold noncriminal youths in secure facilities for up to five days (Wash. Rev. Code Ann. §13.40.050 [West 1995]). The "felt need" to "do something" often results in the confinement of noncriminal offenders despite the absence of evidence that incarceration policies contribute to their short-or long-term welfare. Efforts to deinstitutionalize and decriminalize status offenders ultimately fail because of state and local authorities' and parents' desires to remove disruptive and troublesome youths from the community or from their homes. As the JJDP Act's efforts to divert and deinstitutionalize status offenders reveal, as long as noncriminal youths remain involved with the juvenile justice system, the public will regard them as offenders and exert efforts to control them (Grubb and Lazerson 1982).

The "Hidden System" of Social Control: Mental Health, Chemical Dependency, and the "Medicalization" of Adolescent Deviance

The JJDP Act's mandate and state decarceration policies made it more difficult to confine noncriminal youths in traditional delinquency institutions. As a result, courts may divert or refer and parents may "voluntarily" commit many youths to psychiatric and chemical dependency facilities in the private sector. These private treatment facilities constitute a parallel, "hidden system" of social control for youths and a growth industry for service providers. Many troublesome youths—especially females and children of middle-class families with mental health or chemical dependency medical insurance benefits— whom juvenile courts previously dealt with as status offenders now enter private mental health or substance abuse treatment facilities, which can provide levels of security comparable to those in public institutions (Schwartz 1989a).

Coinciding with the deinstitutionalization of status offenders, between 1974 and 1979 admissions to private correctional facilities and programs increased 30 percent, and admissions of females increased 44 percent (Krisberg et al. 1986). Between 1979 and 1982, admissions to private correctional programs increased an additional 28 percent (Krisberg et al. 1986). Another study reports that the numbers of adolescents confined in private psychiatric facilities more than quadrupled between 1980 and 1984 (Weithorn 1988). Private long-term institutional and open facilities now hold larger proportions of status offenders and nonoffenders than do public facilities, and parents "voluntarily" admitted about 40 percent of these noncriminal youths to confinement (Snyder and Sickmund 1995).

Both racial and gender differences mark the distribution of youths in public correctional and private "treatment" institutions. As we will see in chapter 7, juvenile courts sentence a disproportionate and increasing numbers of minority offenders convicted of crimes to public delinquency institutions. By contrast, increasing numbers of white, middle-class, and female juveniles find their way into the private institutional "treatment" system (Chesney-Lind and Shelden 1992). As a result of "get-tough" policies that shift criminal young offenders to public institutions and decarceration policies that relegate noncriminal offenders to private facilities, the racial complexion of traditional juvenile training schools is becoming increasingly darker (Krisberg et al. 1986).

As federal and state laws limit the authority of juvenile courts to confine status offenders, in some jurisdictions a lucrative mental health and chemical dependency industry provides alternative services for families to incarcerate troublesome adolescents. Clinical professionals may relabel status offenses and diagnose noncriminal youths' "acting out" behavior as a form of mental illness or a symptom of chemical dependency. Significantly, parents may institutionalize their "sick" children in secure settings comparable to those in juvenile justice facilities but without the due process formalities the Court required in *Gault*.

The Supreme Court in *Parham v. J.R.* (442 U.S. 609 [1979]) ruled that the only due process rights to which the Constitution entitles juveniles when their parents "voluntarily" commit them to secure treatment facilities are a physician's determination that hospitalization is medically appropriate (Weithorn 1988). As a matter of due process, "a staff physician will suffice, so long as he or she is free to evaluate independently the child's mental and emotional condition and need for treatment" (*Parham*, 442 U.S. at 607). The Court noted that due process does not require a law-trained fact-finder and that physicians using medical diagnostic procedures can adequately assess a child's need for treatment. *Parham* presumed that children had minimal liberty interests and that parents acted in their children's "best interests" to protect them. As in *Schall*, the Court minimized young people's independent liberty interests by noting that "this interest is inextricably linked with the parents' interest in and obligation for the welfare and health of the child, [and] the private interest at stake is a combination of the child's and parents' concerns" (442 U.S. at 600 [1979]). The Court rejected the youths' request for any preadmission formal judicial review, such as a due process hearing, erected no procedural barriers to the parents' decision to commit youths even over their objections, required no substantive admission standards or postcommitment judicial review, and instead characterized placement as a "voluntary" treatment decision. The Court simply analogized between parental authority to consent to medically appropriate treatment of a physical ailment and a mental illness despite the differences in presenting symptoms, the validity of the diagnostic process, and the consequences for the youth. The Court invoked the state's *parens patriae* interest in helping parents to commit their children without creating an "admission process [that] is too onerous, too embarrassing, or too contentious" (442 U.S. at 605). The Court regarded an adversary preadmission process as inimical to parent-child relations and successful long-term treatment and endorsed a summary process. Thus, as a constitutional matter, parents may commit their child to a mental institution without any form of judicial review, provided only that the hospital will accept the child for treatment. The institutionalized child has no legal recourse to petition for release.

Parham assumed that parents' "natural affection" led them to act in their children's "best interests" and that "parents possess what a child lacks in maturity, experience, and capacity for judgment required for making life's difficult decisions" (442 U.S. at 602). Although the *Parham* majority assumed an idyllic family harmony, the dissenting justices pointed out that a parent's decision to confine her child may indicate sufficient domestic conflict and turmoil to invalidate that presumption. The *Parham* majority found as a "fact" that young people lacked competence to make or participate in commitment decisions. "Most children, even in adolescence, simply are not able to make sound judgments concerning many decisions, including their need for medical care or treatment. Parents can and must make those judgments" (442 U.S. at 603). The Court invoked the cultural and legal conception of children as vulnerable and immature, presumed the incompetence of all youths as a class, and denied them any recourse against parental impositions to which they might object.

States' juvenile chemical dependency and mental health commitment statutes vary as much as do their juvenile codes. As a matter of state law, a few jurisdictions provide older adolescents with a right to a precommitment hearing or to a postcommitment review and to the assistance of counsel comparable to that afforded to adult committees. The majority of states do not use the same procedural safeguards for juveniles that they employ in adult commitment proceedings and thereby facilitate parents' "voluntary" confinement of their children (Ellis 1974; Weithorn 1988; *Parham*, 442 U.S. at 612 n 20).

Clearly, some children's psychological dysfunctions or substance abuse require medical attention and even residential treatment. However, fewer than one-third of committed youths manifest severe or acute mental disorders, such as psychoses or depressions, maladies that account for about two-thirds of adult civil commitments (Weithorn 1988). Unfortunately, we lack epidemiological evidence with which to determine either the current prevalence of serious adolescent mental disorders, their rates among youths and adults, or whether they occur more frequently among young people today than a decade ago and might account for the dramatic increases in juvenile rates of psychiatric confinement (Weithorn 1988).

Equally clearly, many "voluntary" commitments result from status offense-like social or behavioral conflicts, self-serving parental motives, and medical entrepreneurs coping with underutilized hospitals. Compared with adults, juveniles admitted for inpatient mental health treatment suffer from less-serious disorders but stay longer once parents hospitalize them (Schwartz, Jackson-Beeck, and Anderson 1984; Jackson-Beeck, Schwartz, and Rutherford 1987). Clinicians diagnose and commit many juveniles for conduct disorders of the "aggressive" or "nonaggressive" variety (Weithorn 1988). The former diagnoses subsume behaviors such as violence, personal confrontations, and theft, and the latter include discipline problems at home or school with symptoms such as running away and truancy. These "behavioral disorders" manifest symptoms for which a judge could adjudicate a youth as a delinquent or a status offender. A second common diagnosis for inpatient adolescent confinement consists of preadult "personality disorders" or "oppositional disorders," which include "symptoms" such as stubbornness, rule violations, and arguments (Weithorn 1988). Although many professionals regard these manifestations as transitory behaviors typical of adolescents, in the hands of an accommodating clinician, they provide bases for parental commitment. "Whereas in prior years, the juvenile justice system institutionalized trouble-making youth as status offenders, recent legal reforms have closed the doors of juvenile justice institutions to a sizable population of difficult children. Families and community agencies seeking intensive intervention have turned increasingly to mental hospitals: the only institutional alternative that is available, provides easy access, and is adequately funded by third-party payment" (Weithorn 1988:799).

Although deinstitutionalization reforms provided the impetus to remove many status offenders from public delinquency institutions, they did not "liberate" youths outright. Analyses of long-term trends in public and private juvenile correctional facilities report that during the decade of the 1970s, the total rate of youths in residence remained very stable, but the proportion of youths in private residential facilities grew tremendously (Lerman 1982, 1984). In 1970, private residential facilities housed only 13 percent of youths, but by 1979, 48 percent of juveniles resided in private facilities. The growth in private sector confinement coincided directly with the decarceration of status offenders (Lerman 1984).

Coinciding with the deinstitutionalization of status offenders, the rate of juvenile psychiatric commitments in Minneapolis–St. Paul hospitals doubled between 1976 and 1983 from 91 to 184 youths per 100,000 (Schwartz, Jackson-Beeck, and Anderson 1984). Between 1978 and 1984 in Minnesota, juvenile psychiatric inpatients as a proportion of total inpatients increased from 16 to 26 percent, and juvenile chemical dependent inpatients in hospitals and treatment centers increased from 17 to 22 percent (Jackson-Beeck 1985). Between 1979 and 1985, the confinement of girls in private, for-profit institutions increased about 25 percent (Chesney-Lind and Shelden 1992).

Although *Parham* involved a public psychiatric facility, parents commit increasing numbers of youths to proprietary psychiatric hospitals that operate for profit. *Parham*'s due process analysis assumed a staff physician who is "*free to evaluate independently*" the child's mental condition and need for treatment (442 U.S. at 607). The Court's due process analysis relied heavily on the scientific validity of psychiatric and psychological diagnoses and the professional impartiality of hospital staff. Because admitting physicians may be stockholders or participate in incentive compensation plans to maximize profits or reduce costs, they may confront a conflict of interest when potential patients and empty beds converge.

Health care policy reforms have produced excess bed capacity in many hospitals as reduced medical and surgical lengths of stay have decreased utilization and forced hospital administrators to seek alternative ways to maintain occupancy rates (Schwartz 1989b). Simultaneously, state insurance regulations increasingly require insurers to reimburse for mental health treatment, as well as for physical medical care. Most insurance policies and Medicaid plans include a structural bias toward inpatient, rather than outpatient, therapy and spend the bulk of mental health payments on residential care (Weithorn 1988). Because outpatient treatment providers may receive lower or no reimbursement, some well-intentioned parents may opt for inpatient treatment, not because it is the most appropriate, but simply because third-party insurance makes it affordable.

The combination of psychiatric hospitals' seeking profits, insurance and Medicaid coverage for inpatient mental health care, and malleable diagnostic categories enables entrepreneurs to "medicalize" adolescent deviance and parents to incarcerate troublesome children without any meaningful judicial supervision. This amalgamation of factors provides an attractive alternative to the public juvenile justice system to respond to "youthful nuisances." "The psychiatric hospital is a special target of health care corporations. Its profit margins are large, investment costs are low, inpatient psychiatric care is now widely insured, and the complexity (and perhaps ambiguity) of psychiatric diagnosis and treatment makes cost control efforts by insurers and the government difficult" (Weithorn 1988:816). These trends also reflect mental hospitals' use of slick and misleading advertising techniques to seduce parents to commit their children (Schwartz 1989a). Many advertisements pander to parental anxieties about the "normal" turbulence of youths. Advertising that targets parents experiencing difficulty controlling their children carries the potential to further expand the net of controls and introduce more inappropriate youths into the inpatient mental health system (Weithorn 1988). Psychiatric and chemical dependency facilities now provide a significant form of institutional control for many middle-class and upper-middle-class youths whose confinement insurance premiums subsidize but whose "behavior problems . . . do not require hospitalization and for which there is little evidence that psychiatric intervention is appropriate or effective" (Schwartz 1989b:143).

The Progressives conceived of "delinquency" as symptomatic of an underlying disturbance and proposed to treat it. In a similar vein, the contemporary "medicalizing" of adolescence as deviance and treatment of troublesome children appeal to the modern sensibility. And, like the institutional reality of Progressive delinquency confinement, recent analysts question the reality of psychiatric and substance abuse hospitalization for treatment. Observers characterize many "treatment" programs as "degrading and abusive." "Many hospital programs consist of rigid and punitive 'behavior modification' regimens that rely heavily on the use of isolation and solitary confinement, often for minor or petty infractions of rules. In some programs children are required to wear hospital gowns until they earn enough points to wear their own clothes. Also, such practices as mail censorship, prohibitions against visitation (including no contact with parents), and the use of mechanical restraints are commonplace" (Schwartz 1991:195).

A substantial body of research exists evaluating the effectiveness and conditions of confinement in public juvenile correctional institutions. Unfortunately, no comparable body of systematic studies exists of the conditions of confinement or the effectiveness of private psychiatric or chemical dependency facilities' efforts to treat youths' mental disorders or substance abuse. "Available studies do not clearly show which components of hospital treatment contribute to successful outcomes. Neither do they allow conclusions about whether children treated as hospital inpatients would have better, worse, or similar outcomes with nonhospital treatment" (Schwartz 1989a:2–3). Private facilities' ability to limit research access and to invoke medical privilege to protect the confidentiality of their records precludes systematic external evaluation of their effectiveness. Their admission decisions create population selection biases that invalidate any internal evaluation studies they may conduct because they lack adequate control groups. Anecdotal "success" stories and individual testimonials do not provide the evidence of safety or efficacy required for other types of medical interventions. In short, parents and insurers may spend vast sums of money to confine many youths without any substantial evidence of benefit.

Parham provides the constitutional analogue to *Gault* for the civil commitment of adolescents. Unlike *Gault*'s commitment to due process for institutionalized youths, however, *Parham* adopted a hands-off position that provides no comparable protections when parents, rather than the state, seek their children's confinement. Thoughtful analyses of the hospitalization of trouble-some youth provide a series of legislative policy prescriptions to restrict in-appropriate confinement (Weithorn 1988). Private and governmental finan-cial sources could shift the system of incentives to encourage service providers to use community mental health and outpatient treatment rather than con-finement as the primary response to the mental health needs of many youths currently institutionalized. Legislatures could adopt a preadmission review procedure to evaluate the validity of commitment decisions that does not rely solely on the benevolence of parents or the professionalism of staff physicians. Legislation could provide more explicit and objective substantive criteria and diagnostic bases for the commitment process. Because financial considerations may conflict with childrens' liberty interests and skew the judgments of com-mitting physicians, advocacy programs and review procedures could monitor more extensively the for-profit segment of the private juvenile confinement industry. Despite the policy options, most states choose not to implement them.

In many respects, the mental health system represents a conceptual and administrative successor to the original idea of the juvenile justice system. The juvenile court adopted a "delinquency" label to encompass a broad spectrum of "troubled" children, emphasized "sickness" rather than "badness," and treated them in an informal process. As procedural formality and substantive criteria reassert the connection between delinquent and criminal behavior, a successor generation of "child savers" promotes a newer version of determin-ism to treat a new variety of "disturbed" child-client. Armed with the "dis-ease" models of mental health, alcoholism, and substance abuse, these pro-fessionals propose that they can treat, for example, the disruptive symptoms of "conduct disorder" manifest as "oppositional defiant disorder." And, un-like the Supreme Court's skepticism in *Gault* about the rehabilitative claims of juvenile justice professionals, *Parham* delegates to the mental health pro-fessionals unreviewed and unreviewable authority to make institutional com-mitment decisions. In most jurisdictions, legislators do not respond to chil-dren's claims of unwarranted commitment by promulgating substantive standards, increasing procedural safeguards, or mandating the same commit-ment process used for adults. Rather, they delegate to service providers the power to license personnel and increase their professionalism as a strategy to improve the quality of decisions.

The Problems of Children, or Children Are the Problem

Historically, the child welfare, juvenile justice, and mental health systems dealt with relatively fungible and interchangeable populations of youths. Bureau-crats shifted youths from one system to another depending on social attitudes, available funds, and imprecise legal definitions. Delinquents, status offenders, mentally ill children, and dependent children constituted a generic category of "youth in trouble." The imprecise and permeable boundaries of the over-lapping and interlocking child-care systems expand and contract to accommodate them. "The movement to deinstitutionalize status offenders fit well with the federal expansion of the child welfare boundaries and the movement for community-based alternatives. In the private sector, all three goals could be commingled under nonprofit or proprietary auspices without upsetting the statutes or funding guidelines. . . ." (Lerman 1984:26). Thus, the numbers of youths confined and treated in the "hidden system" of private psychiatric and chemical dependency treatment facilities increased as the confinement of status offenders declined.

The private sector mental health and chemical dependency industries constitute the institutional successor to the juvenile justice system for the care and control of problematic youths (Lerman 1980, 1982). The JJDP Act's mandate to deinstitutionalize status offenders instead resulted in transinstitutionalization and placement of youths in alternative private facilities. Troublesome and nuisance youths whom juvenile courts in the past would have committed to publicly funded institutions now "most likely receive 'community treatment' in a private facility" (Lerman 1984:12). Sutton (1988:209) attributes the phenomenon to an accommodation between informal surveillance and fiscal constraints. As the expenses of institutional confinement increased, nondelinquency treatment systems provide cost-effective social control alternatives because federal or private insurance funds underwrote many of the costs.

Whether the state or parents incarcerate juveniles in their "best interests," for adjustment reactions symptomatic of adolescence, or for chemical dependency, these trends revive the imagery of diagnosis and treatment on a discretionary basis without regard to formal due process considerations. The appropriate social and legal responses to minor, nuisance, and noncriminal youngsters go to the heart of the juvenile court's mission and the normative concept of childhood on which it is based. The debate polarizes advocates of authority and control of youth (Arthur 1977) and those who view intervention too often as discriminatory, ineffective, and a denial of rights (Murray 1983; Rubin 1985).

The existence of status jurisdiction also implicates the relationships between children, their parents, and the state. While parents possess broad constitutional latitude within which to raise their children as they see fit, to what extent may or should parents be allowed to invoke the *parens patriae* power of the state to enforce their rules against their unruly children. The broad scope of parental authority and the exclusion of the state from the details of child rearing serves to protect family autonomy and promote individuality. It is unclear, then, by what rationale parents enlist the state to enforce their child-rearing decisions (Guggenheim 1985). For example, if public policies preclude parents from vetoing their daughter's decision to obtain an abortion—"a decision that has potentially traumatic and permanent consequences" (*H.L. v. Matheson*, 450 U.S. 398, 412 [1981])—on what basis can they invoke the state to resolve more mundane parent-child disputes?

Although a few states have experimented with or eliminated status juris-diction entirely and allow noncriminal intervention only in cases of depend-ency or neglect, juvenile court judges strongly resist removal of status juris-diction, because any contraction of their authority over children leads to further convergence with criminal courts. Historical analyses of legislative re-sponses to status offenders conclude that much of the policy debate is sym-bolic, that many of the adaptations are cosmetic, and that the differentiation of status offenders from delinquents serves to perpetuate the traditional ju-venile court by reserving the former for informal treatment while consigning the latter to formal punishment and by extending the net of controls more deeply into the "normal" adolescent population (Sutton 1988). Clearly, the juvenile justice system may successfully co-opt reform efforts nominally de-signed to enhance youths' autonomy to enforce their dependency. Similarly, the Supreme Court in *Parham* invoked the imagery of childhood vulnerability to maximize the social control of youths by their parents and the state without requiring any evidence that youths benefit from coercive intervention. And, finally, the ideology of childhood and a child's right to "custody rather than liberty" reinforces a cultural propensity to use confinement as a primary strat-egy to deal with troublesome young people.

Whether a court system should intervene coercively in the lives of noncri-minal young people involves both empirical and value judgments. Unfortu-nately, we simply lack the empirical data with which to conduct an informed cost-benefit calculus about the relative efficacy of coercive intervention, pro-vision of social welfare services on a voluntary basis, or doing nothing through the justice system about the problems in young people's lives. How effectively do juvenile justice programs meet the needs of noncriminal youths? Is a court system the most appropriate means to deliver social services to youths? How many noncriminal youths respond to coercive judicial intervention who would not have accepted voluntarily an offer of adequate and useful social services? Do we rely on coercion because the recipients of proffered services recognize that many programs lack quality or substance? If courts really intervene to exercise control rather than to provide services, is the simple fact that their subjects are young sufficient justification? How many youths who would have outgrown transitory domestic conflict if left alone does judicial coercion harm? Do we use coercive intervention to control other people's children when their parents' child-rearing practices fail our middle-class standards of adequacy or when their children threaten to disrupt our control of our own children?

Without adequate data to answer some of these questions, public officials formulate status offense policy based on their cultural conception of children and their own value judgments about youths' autonomy and dependency. If one believes that many youths' noncriminal misbehavior involves transitional adolescent rebelliousness that they will outgrow in time, then court interven-tion uses limited judicial and service resources ultimately to no purpose and perhaps to some harm. Even if one believes that adults should exercise exten-sive controls over youths, the question remains whether a justice system reinforced with mechanisms of institutional confinement constitutes the most appropriate and least-destructive way to regulate youths.

The efforts to reform and eliminate the status jurisdiction represent an effort to distinguish between adolescent behaviors that have long-term negative effects on their lives and those behaviors that are more ambiguous in their consequences but to which adults react with hostility. We formulate markedly different policies if we regard status offenses and petty crimes, such as vandalism, really as "normal" aspects of adolescence, rather than if we view them as precursors and extensions of crime or grievous affronts to adult authority. Margaret Rosenheim emphasizes the dangers of "problemization" and the tendency of service professionals to organize to cure and to classify the "normal" as "pathological." She proposes instead that we think of "juvenile nuisances as essentially normal . . . [and] assume that much juvenile misconduct is minor, although annoying or troubling, and rarely persistent or deeply alarming. . . . [T]he task of public policy is to ease for all (and certainly not to augment) the pain of growing up, and to ease for some the special pain of growing up poor or disadvantaged" (1976:56–57). If status offenses reflect *mere* rebelliousness or transitory behaviors, then institutional mechanisms to provide appropriate social services on a voluntary basis and to smooth the transition to adulthood seem preferable to policies of incarceration and coercive control.

Recent efforts to decarcerate and decriminalize status offenders represent a form of criminological triage. As the juvenile court strategically withdraws from enforcement of a normative conception of childhood, it sheds the "soft end" of its jurisdiction. Contrary to the Progressives' generic conception of delinquency, the reforms recognize that not all forms of misconduct are equal and limit dispositions on the basis of the seriousness of the offense. According to any theory of justice and proportionality, noncriminal misbehavior and affronts to adult norms are not serious enough to result in institutional confinement. But classifying misbehavior based on its seriousness and limiting the intensity of dispositions accordingly violate the juvenile court's principles of indeterminacy and individualized justice in the child's best interests. It represents instead a schema of proportionality and graduated sanctions.

The attempts to remove status offenders and some delinquents from detention facilities and institutions coincided with another countervailing trend in the states to "get tough" and increase the punitiveness of juvenile justice toward youths charged with crimes and to transfer the most serious and chronic offenders to criminal courts for prosecution as adults. These patterns reflect a further convergence between juvenile and criminal courts, a gradation of sanctions, and an elaboration of principles of proportionality across the entire juvenile justice continuum.

I I I I SIX

Delinquent or Criminal?

Juvenile Courts' Shrinking Jurisdiction over Serious Young Offenders

Public frustration with crime, fear of recent increases in youth violence, homicide and offenses involving guns, and the racial characteristics of many violent young offenders fuel a popular desire to "get tough." Widespread misgivings about the ability of juvenile courts either to rehabilitate chronic and violent young offenders or simultaneously to protect public safety bolster policies to "crack down" on youth crime and provide the impetus to prosecute larger numbers of youths as adults. These initiatives either simplify the transfer of young offenders to criminal courts and expose waived youths to substantial sentences as adults or require juvenile court judges to impose determinate or mandatory minimum sentences on those youths who remain in the juvenile system. Both strategies de-emphasize rehabilitation and individualized consideration of the offender, stress personal and justice system accountability and punishment, and base transfer and sentencing decisions on the seriousness of the present offense and prior record. Sentencing young offenders as adults increases the number of chronological juveniles (i.e., below age 18) confined in prisons and poses substantial challenges for adult correctional officials. Juvenile institutional administrators confront similar difficulties as judges confine more-serious young delinquents for longer periods.

Increasingly, people and politicians view juvenile courts' traditional commitment to rehabilitation as a bias toward leniency often to the detriment of protecting the public or satisfying the victim. For more than three decades, conservatives have denounced juvenile courts for "coddling" young criminals, and, more recently, state legislators have adopted more-punitive policies toward young offenders in both the juvenile and criminal justice systems. This chapter examines the boundary of criminal "adulthood" and responsibility and the processes by which states determine whether to prosecute youths in juvenile or criminal courts. Distilled to its essence, how and why does the legal system decide which young offenders to prosecute as criminals or as delinquents, and what difference does it make for youths, for public safety, and for juvenile and criminal justice administration?

Every state uses one or more statutory devices to prosecute some youths below the maximum age of juvenile court jurisdiction as adults. The principal legal devices include judicial waiver, legislative offense exclusion, and prosecutors' choices among concurrent jurisdictions. Each of these strategies allocates to a different branch of government—judicial, legislative, and executive—the decision whether to prosecute a youth as a criminal or a delinquent. They reflect different ways of asking and answering similar questions: who are serious offenders; by what criteria should the state identify them; what characteristics of offenders and offenses should determine the outcome of the process; which branch of government can best make these decisions; and how should the juvenile or adult systems respond to them? All waiver strategies attempt to reconcile the rhetorical and cultural conceptions of children as naive innocents with the frightening reality that some youths commit heinous, vicious, "adult"-type crimes. Violent or chronic youth crime highlights the cultural contradiction between competing conceptions of children as dependent and vulnerable and as autonomous and responsible. Waiver mechanisms choose between these conflicting constructions of young people, define the boundaries of criminal adulthood, and retrospectively ascribe criminal responsibility to some youths.

Because the Progressive creators of the juvenile court situated it on a number of cultural and criminological fault lines, the "simple" question whether a young offender should be tried and sentenced as a juvenile or as an adult poses many difficult theoretical and practical dilemmas. For example, typical judicial waiver legislation requires a judge to decide whether a youth is "amenable to treatment" or poses a threat to the public. Such laws presume that juvenile courts can rehabilitate at least some youths, that judges possess diagnostic tools that enable them to classify for treatment, and that they can predict offenders' future dangerousness. Considered at another level, recent changes in waiver legislation provide an indicator of the jurisprudential shift in emphasis from rehabilitation to retribution, as statutes increasingly emphasize characteristics of the offense rather than of the offender. Jurisdictional waiver policies that define the boundary of adulthood also implicate the relationship between juvenile and criminal court sentencing practices and highlight the need for a coherent sentencing policy to rationalize social control of career offenders on both sides of the juvenile-adult divide. Finally, trying and sentencing youths as adults reflect fundamental changes in cultural assumptions about their criminal responsibility because waiver renders at least some chronological juveniles eligible for the death penalty.

I organize this chapter into three sections and trace relationships between social and legal changes. The first section continues the social history from chapters 1, 2, and 3 and analyzes the social structural and racial transformation of America during the past three decades. During this period, the racial segregation of blacks in urban America, the migration of whites to the suburbs, and the macrostructural transition from an industrial to an information economy coalesced and influenced patterns of youth crime. The second section analyzes changes in serious youth crime and, especially, the escalation in gun violence and homicide among young urban black males in the late 1980s and early 1990s. I locate this narrow band of criminal activity within the broader structural changes occurring in urban America. These age-and race-specific crime patterns, in turn, provided the recent political impetus to "criminalize" more youths, to punish them as adults, and to adopt more-punitive policies in the juvenile justice system. The third section analyzes changes in waiver laws adopted in response to escalating urban youth violence. These statutory modifications reveal the changing jurisprudence of juvenile courts and their shift in emphases from treatment to punishment and from the offender to the offense.

All the current transfer policy innovations—reducing the maximum age of juvenile court jurisdiction, lowering the age of eligibility for criminal prosecution, removing some serious crimes from juvenile court jurisdiction regardless of the offender's age, and making it easier to transfer more juveniles to criminal courts—are premised on retaining a two-systems approach. The preservation of two justice systems, one for juveniles and another for adults, raises a number of perplexing criminal policy issues: arbitrary and idiosyncratic patterns of discretionary decisions by judges and prosecutors that result in inconsistent waiver and retention decisions; perpetuation of two information systems that often prevent criminal court judges from learning about prior juvenile offenses; anomalous punishment patterns in which violent young offenders sentenced as adults receive much harsher sentences than do violent youths retained in juvenile courts, while transferred property offenders often receive less-severe sentences as adults than do those sentenced in juvenile court; stark racial disparities in sentencing in the juvenile justice system that new transfer policies exacerbate; and the failure of criminal courts to recognize the diminished responsibility and immaturity of many juvenile offenders convicted as adults. In the third section, I analyze the costs and benefits of various waiver sentencing policies and the consequences of jurisdictional bifurcation for the social control of career criminal offenders.

The Structural Transformation of Postindustrial America

As we recall from chapter 2, a little over a century ago, the industrial revolution transformed America from a rural agrarian to an urban industrial society.

People moved from farms to cities to work in the factories that grew around transportation junctions. Immigrants poured into urban centers in the Northeast and Midwest to take advantage of increased economic opportunities. Cities grew rapidly in size, structural complexity, and social diversity to accommodate these massive population infusions. Assembly-line labor fostered mass production and mass consumption as relatively unskilled workers manufactured more things more cheaply and enjoyed a material lifestyle undreamed of by previous generations. And Progressive reformers created the juvenile court to enable them to integrate, acculturate, and control young people.

As mentioned in chapter 3, the United States emerged from World War II with its factories undamaged and as the major economic power in the world. From the 1950s to 1970s, a single wage earner, almost always a man, could support a family comfortably. Men with only a high school degree could get relatively high-paying, secure jobs with benefits in the manufacturing, automobile, steel, and construction industries. Rates of family formation soared in the post–World War II era as couples married and began to raise the children who became the baby-boom generation. Aided by governmental highway, housing, and mortgage policies, suburbs expanded rapidly around the major urban centers. Because a working man alone could support a family in a middle-class lifestyle, most women did not work outside the home. A two-parent household in which a father worked and a mother remained at home to raise their children constituted the cultural norm (Lasch 1977; Berger and Berger 1984). Until the mid-1960s, youth crime rates remained relatively low, and issues of racial segregation and social and gender inequality remained relatively submerged.

Beginning in the 1970s and accelerating in the 1980s, a number of macrostructural economic, family, demographic, and social changes dramatically altered this landscape. These structural and criminogenic forces contributed to escalating urban youth violence in the late 1980s and provided a powerful impetus for the transformation of the juvenile court. The postindustrial transition from a manufacturing to a service and information economy adversely affected the ability of semiskilled high school graduates economically to sustain "the American Dream." Full-time employment in manufacturing decreased from 26 percent in 1969 to 19 percent in 1984, while the service sectors—finance, insurance, real estate—increased from 13 to 28 percent and surpassed manufacturing employment (Katz 1989). The emphasis on knowledge and information produced a widening earnings gap between high school and college graduates as the better educated got richer and the less well educated got poorer. In less than twenty years, as a result of structural economic changes, the gap between high school and college graduates' earnings widened both because the educated earn more and because the uneducated earn less. As recently as 1975, college graduates earned only about 25 percent more than did high school graduates. Two decades later, the average earning difference was almost 100 percent, both because college graduates' earning capacity increased and because high school graduates' real earning capacity decreased about 25 percent (Jencks 1992; National Research Council 1993).

With the downward spiral of manufacturing employment and family incomes, more women entered the paid labor force. For some women, entry into the workforce reflected expanding economic and educational opportunities and changes in culturally defined gender roles. But the decline of high-paying jobs for less-skilled workers in manufacturing also meant that many men no longer could support their families on a single wage. Many women entered the workforce out of economic necessity to supplement declining family incomes and to try to maintain a middle-class lifestyle. The number of women with children under the age of six who worked outside the home increased from 10 percent in 1950 to 20 percent in 1960, more than 30 percent in 1970, and to nearly 60 percent by 1990 (Lindsey 1994). About three-quarters of women with school-age children now work full time outside the home (National Commission on Children 1991). Moreover, the number of hours that women work increased by one-third during the 1980s (National Research Council 1993). Correspondingly, the time available to guide and supervise their children declined as more parents worked outside the home. Residential mobility further weakened ties to community and reduced access to familial networks at the same time that the economic resources available to many families declined (Melton 1993).

As women's integration into the economy increased, rates of divorce, out-of-wedlock births, and the numbers of children raised in single-parent households rose. Within the past three decades, the number of marriages that ended in divorce quadrupled, and the number of children in families divided by divorce tripled. Between 1970 and 1990, the proportion of children living with two parents decreased from 85 to 73 percent of all households, and the number of children living in households headed by a single mother increased 53 percent (National Research Council 1993). Since 1960 the proportion of children born to an unmarried woman increased from 5 percent (22% among blacks) to nearly one birth in four (60% among blacks) (Snyder and Sickmund 1995). Teenage mothers recorded even higher proportions of out-of-wedlock childbearing, about 40 percent of white babies and approximately 90 percent of black infants (National Commission on Children 1991). As a result of divorce and out-of-wedlock births, the proportion of single-parent families raising children under age eighteen has doubled in the past two decades to nearly one in four children. The increase in single-parent female-headed households with dependent children has resulted in larger numbers of young people living in or near poverty (National Research Council 1993).

As noted in chapter 3, the black migration from the rural South to the urban North in the 1920s and 1930s demographically began to transform the larger older cities. Black Americans became increasingly urban, and whites simultaneously began to move from the cities to the suburbs. Between the end of World War II and 1960, about one-third of all African Americans who remained in the South migrated to other parts of the country and the majority of all blacks lived in central cities. The processes of suburbanization that accelerated in the post–World War II decades spatially transformed many cities. Federal housing policies, bank mortgage and real estate sales practices, and construction of interstate highways contributed to the growth of predominantly white suburbs surrounding increasingly poor and minority urban cores. In the 1950s and 1960s, urban renewal and highway construction disrupted and destroyed many urban black communities.

Macrostructural economic changes within the past two decades have resulted in the deindustrialization of the urban centers in which minorities live disproportionately. The shifts from manufacturing to service industries, the bifurcation of the labor market into low-and high-wage sectors, and the relocation of growth industries outside the central cities have had a cumulative, deleterious effect, especially on urban minority residents (Sampson 1987; Wilson 1996). Although some industrial cities revitalized their downtown centers with office towers, many of the newer service, knowledge and information technology industries located in the suburban periphery where residential development expanded (Massey and Denton 1993). In the postindustrial economy, the largest domestic economic growth occurred in the service and information sectors and in suburban, rather than urban, locales. As a result, job losses have occurred primarily in those higher paying, lower skilled manufacturing industries to which urban minorities previously had greater access, and job growth has occurred in the suburbs and in sectors of the economy that required levels of education beyond that possessed by many urban minority workers (Wilson 1987). Moreover, without adequate public transportation systems, many of the better paying, higher skilled jobs remain inaccessible even to inner-city residents who possess the requisite ability and training.

As a result of the macrostructural economic transformation and the demographic, spatial, and racial reorganization of cities, the past several decades have witnessed the emergence of an urban "underclass" living in concentrated poverty and in racial, social, and cultural isolation (Sampson 1987; Jencks and Peterson 1991; Katz 1993; Wilson 1987, 1996). Three decades ago, then Assistant Secretary of Labor Daniel Patrick Moynihan (1965) warned, in *The Negro Family: The Case for National Action*, that male unemployment in the urban African American community contributed to the increase of fatherless families and widespread child poverty and proposed economic and training policies to address the problem of black male joblessness. Since Moynihan issued his prophetic warnings, many of those dire predictions have come to pass. Black male unemployment, out-of-wedlock childbirth, racial isolation, concentrated poverty, and urban violent crime have increased (Wilson 1987; Massey and Denton 1993). These negative social indicators appear most conspicuously among the structural underclass and account for the disproportionate overinvolvement of young, urban black men in violent and lethal crime.

William Julius Wilson (1987, 1996) attributes the decline of two-parent black families to the structural transformation of inner cities that reduced young black males' employment prospects and increased rates of out-of-wedlock childbirths among poor black women. Since the mid-1960s, the passage of civil rights legislation enabled many middle-class blacks to take advantage of increased economic opportunities and to leave the ghettoes. Their mobility deprived the urban minority communities of the human resources necessary for social stability and amplified the effects of concentrated poverty and racial isolation among the "truly disadvantaged" who remained. Simultaneously, structural changes decreased the demands for unskilled and semi-skilled labor in the manufacturing sectors that previously had provided black men who had little formal education with access to higher wage jobs. The deindustrialization of the inner urban core reduced the pool of "marriageable" black men who could support a family. Because more than one-third of all black men in urban centers and more than one-half of young black males aged eighteen to twenty-nine are unemployed, underemployed, or have withdrawn from the labor market, many inner-city women rationally conclude that such men do not make promising life partners (Wilson 1987, 1996). As marriage to unemployed or unemployable black males became less attractive, unwed child-bearing and female-headed families proliferated among poor black women. The decisions by young black women not to marry the fathers of their children account for virtually all the increase in the number of children in female-headed households and in poverty (Edelman 1987).

Douglas Massey and Nancy Denton (1993) argue in *American Apartheid* that public policies and private institutional arrangements—federal highway, mortgage and housing policies, real estate sales practices, bank mortgage loan practices, and insurance industry decisions—created and sustain racial segregation, amplify and exacerbate the harmful consequences of concentrated poverty, and adversely affect the economic and social welfare of black Americans.

> [R]esidential segregation has been instrumental in creating a structural niche within which a deleterious set of attitudes and behavior—a culture of segregation—has arisen and flourished. Segregation created the structural conditions for the emergence of an oppositional culture that devalues work, schooling, and marriage and that stresses attitudes and behaviors that are antithetical and often hostile to success in the larger economy. . . . Residential segregation is the institutional apparatus that supports other racially discriminatory processes and binds them together into a coherent and uniquely effective system of racial subordination. (Massey and Denton 1993:8).

Similarly, Robert Sampson and Janet Lauritsen attribute the negative effects of concentrated poverty to deliberate public policies to "contain" and isolate minorities:

> Opposition from organized community groups to the building of public housing in "their" neighborhoods, de facto federal policy to tolerate extensive segregation against blacks in urban housing markets, and the decision by local governments to neglect the rehabilitation of existing residential units . . . have led to massive segregated housing projects which have become ghettos for minorities and the disadvantaged. The cumulative result is that even given the same objective so-

cioeconomic status, blacks and whites face vastly different environments in which to live, work, and raise their children. (1997:338)

Thus, racial segregation, cultural isolation, and concentration of poverty constitute the cumulative community structural consequences of a host of disparate public policy decisions.

Despite urban population growth in the past forty years, as a result of "white flight" American society remains effectively segregated with many African Americans contained in inner-city ghettoes. More than one-third of all blacks live intensely segregated from whites, confined in spatially isolated, geographically concentrated, densely inhabited, and contiguous areas tightly clustered within the urban core. Residents of the urban ghettoes seldom encounter white people within their own or adjacent neighborhoods, have few social contacts with people from other groups, and have little direct experience with the culture, norms, and behaviors of the dominant culture. The linguistic divergence between Standard American English and Black English Vernacular provides one powerful anthropological indicator of the extreme degree of cultural isolation (Massey and Denton 1993). Wilson argues that for youths who grow up in the ghetto culture, "joblessness, as a way of life, takes on a different social meaning; the relationship between schooling and post-school employment takes on a different meaning. The development of cognitive, linguistic, and other educational and job-related skills necessary for the world of work in the mainstream economy is thereby adversely affected" (1987:57).

Racial segregation amplifies the effects of poverty by concentrating it and thereby exacerbating other social ills. For example, nearly three-quarters of all poor urban blacks live in poverty areas, whereas nearly three-quarters of all poor whites live in nonpoverty areas (Sampson and Wilson 1995). "By building physical decay, crime, and social disorder into the residential structure of black communities, . . . segregation also concentrates conditions such as drug use, joblessness, welfare dependency, teenage childbearing, and unwed parenthood, producing a social context where these conditions are not only common but the norm" (Massey and Denton 1993:13). Urban youths' limited residential mobility restrict their potential for social mobility as well. Children's places of residence typically determine the quality of the schools they attend, the public services they receive, the social and personal characteristics of those with whom they grow up, their risks of exposure to and victimization by crime and violence, their access to job networks, and their opportunities to develop good work patterns. The qualitative decline of urban public schools and high dropout rates further diminish the opportunities and prospects of many minority youths. Poor urban schools and low educational expectations undermine black youths' social and economic potentials and make it more difficult to escape the effects of concentrated ghetto poverty (Kozol 1991). The structural shift to the knowledge and information sectors requires more and better education at the same time that quality of educational opportunities available to many urban minority and poor children declines.

Social structural, economic, and family organizational features of cities and communities account for substantial variations in rates of violent crime (Sampson and Wilson 1995). Crime does not result simply from individual choices, and young people do not just wake up one day and decide to be criminals. Criminologists long have recognized the relationships between community structural characteristics, such as economic status, residential mobility and population turnover, informal social organization, family disruption, and rates of crime and delinquency. Rates of violence and crime vary among racial and social groups over time and reflect the social conditions to which they are exposed. In this formulation, the social structural conditions of communities constitute independent variables, and rates of crime and violence constitute the dependent variables (Zimring and Hawkins 1997). However, contemporary social arrangements do not expose all ethnic and racial groups equally to criminogenic structural conditions. To the contrary, "the most important determinant of the relationship between race and crime is the differential distribution of blacks in communities characterized by 1) *structural social disorganization* and 2) *cultural social isolation*, both of which stem from the concentration of poverty, family disruption, and residential instability" (Sampson and Wilson 1995:44, emphasis added).

"High crime neighborhood" provides a racially neutral euphemism for an urban, inner-city minority environ characterized by concentrated poverty, social disorganization, and cultural isolation. For many urban black youths, employment in the illegal economy provides an alternative to joblessness and poverty (Anderson 1990). The urban structural transformation, deindustrialization, and rise in concentrated poverty contributed to the rise in youth gangs, drug dealing, and violence (Klein 1995; Hagedorn 1998). "Crime has become an attractive alternative to working for many poor, less educated young men. Among this group, particularly black high school dropouts, criminal involvement has become so common that it must be considered a major determinant in evaluating their rates of participation in legal labor markets" (National Research Council 1993:33). Beginning in the mid-1980s, the "crack" cocaine epidemic and the dramatic rise in urban inner-city violence exacerbated all these features (Blumstein 1995). Young black urban men entered the violent drug economy in droves as the remaining good-paying, legitimate jobs shifted from central cities (Hagedorn 1998). Thus, social and demographic changes that began during the 1970s provided the macrostructural conditions for escalating youth violence in the 1980s and for the legal responses to youth crime in the 1990s.

Youth Crime and Violence: Persistence and Change

Rates of crime, youth crime, and violence fluctuate markedly over time; change represents the only constant. Any description or interpretation of crime trends is especially sensitive to the baseline selected for comparison. If we compare current serious crime rates with those reported in 1980, we observe only modest overall changes, whereas if we contrast them with the lower rates recorded in the mid-1980s, we might ascribe more substantial increases. And if we disaggregate overall crime rates and focus on specific offenses, such as homicide, even starker patterns emerge over the course of the past decade.

The Federal Bureau of Investigation (FBI) annually publishes national data on crimes known or reported to police and arrests made by law enforcement in its *Crime in the United States: Uniform Crime Reports*. Local law enforcement agencies transmit data to state agencies and the FBI, based on reports from victims of crimes or investigations. If authorities apprehend perpetrators, then reports of their ages allow us to compare juvenile and adult arrest rates and to assess changes in crime rates over time. The FBI Crime Index, in section II of the *Uniform Crime Reports*, includes both violent and serious property crimes and provides the most widely cited measure of trends in offenses (FBI 1996). The Crime Index records four *violent crimes*—murder and nonnegligent manslaughter, forcible rape, robbery, and aggravated assault—and four serious *property crimes*—burglary, larceny-theft, motor vehicle theft, and arson. Typically, we analyze crimes and arrests either as absolute numbers or as rates per 100,000 population to control for changes in population composition and express comparisons between years as percentages of change. Unfortunately, we cannot directly compare FBI juvenile arrest rates with juvenile court workloads. While FBI data report arrests of offenders under eighteen years of age, juvenile court jurisdiction ends at age fifteen, sixteen, or seventeen in different states, and many states exclude some serious crimes by younger juveniles. Thus, states already prosecute many chronological minors as adults because of the states' definitions of juvenile court jurisdiction (Snyder and Sickmund 1995).

Figure 6.1 depicts the overall rates of crime in the FBI Crime Index and the separate rates for violent and property crimes for all offenders—juveniles and adults—spanning two decades from 1974 to 1995. In 1974, police reported to the FBI about 4,850 crimes per 100,000 population, of which 461, or 9.5 percent, constituted violent crimes. By 1980 the Crime Index rate per 100,000 had climbed to 5,950, of which 597 constituted violent offenses, slightly more than 10 percent of the total. Serious crime rates declined during the middle 1980s and rebounded by the early 1990s to overall rates still somewhat lower than those recorded in 1980. For example, in 1991, at the peak of the rebound, the serious Crime Index rate was 5,898, of which 758 constituted violent offenses, or 12.9 percent (FBI 1996:58). By 1995 the serious crime rate had subsided to the levels previously recorded in the mid-1970s. Thus, during these two decades the overall serious crime rate oscillated within a plus or minus 10 percent range at around 5,500 offenses per year.

Although the aggregate rate of all serious Index offenses in the early 1990s remained somewhat below the peak rate recorded in 1980, this total obscures the substantial increase in violent offending that occurred during the same period. Between 1974 and 1995, the rate of property crime increased from 4,389 to 4,593, or about 4.6 percent (FBI 1996:58). Measured between the

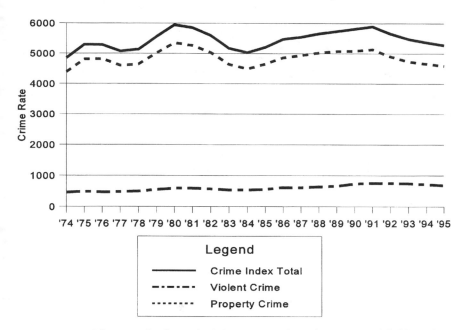

FIGURE 6.1. Crime rate in the United States, 1974–1995 (per 100,000 inhabitants). *Source*: Federal Bureau of Investigation (1996) *Crime in the Unites States, 1995: Uniform Crime Reports* (Washington, D.C.: U.S. Government Printing Office), 58.

recent peak in 1991 and 1995, the property crime rate actually decreased 10.5 percent. As these comparisons indicate, descriptions of crime trends are highly sensitive to the bases we select. The same current crime rate may be "better" or "worse," depending on the comparison reference point we choose. By any measure, however, in recent years the overall serious property crime rates, to which juveniles contribute disproportionately, appear either relatively stable or even modestly decreasing.

By contrast, the overall rate of violent crime increased dramatically. Between 1974 and 1991, the recent peak year, the rate of violence rose from 461 to 758 per 100,000, or 64.4 percent. Between 1986 and 1995, the rate of violence increased 10.8 percent. Beginning in 1986, the rate of violent crime surpassed the previous high recorded in 1980 and escalated rapidly thereafter. In the five-year period between 1989 and 1993, the already high rate of violent crime increased an additional 12.5 percent, while the serious property crime rate *decreased* 6.7 percent. Thus, the overall rates of violent crime and property crime by all offenders followed somewhat different trajectories within the past decade.

It is virtually a criminological truism that young people commit a disproportionate amount of crime and the age-crime curve represents a universal fixture of criminology. Age-specific arrest rates rise sharply and peak in the mid- to late-teen years, decline quickly by the midtwenties, and then subside more

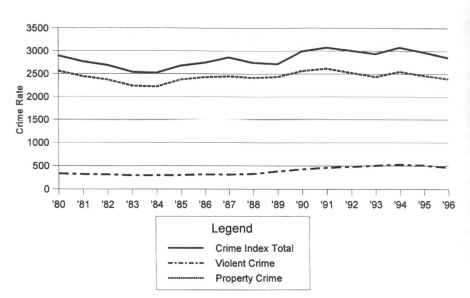

FIGURE 6.2. Juvenile arrest rate for Index crimes, 1980–1996 (per 100,000 juveniles aged 10–17). *Source*: Howard N. Snyder (1997) *Juvenile Arrests, 1996* (Washington, D.C.: U.S. Department of Justice, Office of Juvenile Justice and Delinquency Prevention), 4.

gradually (Blumstein 1995; Farrington 1986). Analysts postulate an almost invariant relationship between age and crime that persists across cultures and over time (Hirschi and Gottfredson 1983). While aggregate crime rates peak during late adolescence and early adulthood, the rates for different types of property and violent offenses and individuals vary more extensively. The age-crime curve reflects adolescents' increased autonomy, freedom from parental supervision, lack of social and economic integration, and susceptibility to peer group processes (Farrington 1986).

The patterns of serious crimes committed by juveniles generally mirrored the overall national pattern of serious crimes. As figure 6.2 indicates, the arrest rates of juveniles aged ten to seventeen for offenses in the FBI Crime Index declined in middecade from the peak rates recorded in 1980 and then gradually rebounded to rates that approached the earlier peak. In 1990, police arrested juveniles for property crimes at a rate virtually unchanged from that recorded a decade earlier. Between 1980 and 1996, the juvenile arrest rate for property crimes declined 7.1 percent. By contrast, between 1980 and 1994, the most recent peak, the juvenile arrest rate for violent crime increased 58 percent. And, as measured from the nadir recorded in 1983, the arrest rates of juveniles for all violent crimes increased 78.3 percent.

As figures 6.1 and 6.2 indicate, the bulk of arrests for all crimes in the FBI Crime Index involves property offenses rather than violent crimes. During the 1980s the juvenile arrest rate for property crimes remained basically stable, decreased slightly, and then increased slowly. In 1995, juveniles accounted for

30.2 percent of all crime arrests and for 34.7 percent of all arrests for property crimes. By contrast, juveniles accounted for only 18.7 percent of arrests for all violent crimes, compared with 81.3 percent of arrests for adults (FBI 1996).

Although violent crimes constitute a smaller component of the overall serious Crime Index and juveniles constitute a smaller proportion of all arrests for violence, the rates of juvenile violence, especially homicide, have surged dramatically since the mid-1980s. Nationally, arrests of juveniles for property crimes increased only 2.2 percent between 1986 and 1995 and decreased 0.4 percent between 1991 and 1995. By contrast, the juvenile arrest rate for all violent crimes increased 67.3 percent in the decade between 1986 and 1995 and 12 percent just between 1991 and 1995. Although adults commit most of the violent offenses and their rates increased as well, the proportional changes for adults were not nearly as great. For example, the adult arrest rate for violent crimes increased 31.4 percent between 1986 and 1995, and only 0.5 percent between 1991 and 1995 (FBI 1996).

Chronological juveniles account for only about one homicide arrest in seven. For example, in 1995, police arrested juveniles for about 15 percent of all homicides; police arrested 2,560 juveniles for murders while they arrested 14,141 adults over eighteen years of age (FBI 1996). However, over the past decade, the rate of increase for juvenile homicide arrests was the greatest for any offense category. Between 1986 and 1995, homicide arrests of juveniles increased 89.9 percent while the corresponding arrest rate for adults actually declined 0.3%. In short, within the past decade, the juvenile component of all violent crimes expanded, the rate of growth far outstripped the corresponding increases for adults, and juveniles murdered people at unprecedented rates.

Figure 6.3 provides a graphic illustration of the changing patterns of youth violence over the past three decades. It depicts the arrest rates per 100,000 juveniles aged ten to seventeen for all violent offenses and for homicide. I multiplied the homicide rate by a factor of ten (10) to place it on the same scale with overall violent arrests. Between 1965 and the previous peak in 1980, the overall juvenile violent crime arrest rate more than doubled from about 154 to 338 arrests of youths per 100,000. Similarly, the juvenile homicide arrest rate nearly doubled during the same period from 3.3 to 6.4 arrests per 100,000 youths aged ten to seventeen. Between 1980 and 1996, the overall juvenile violent arrest rate increased an additional 39.2 percent, from about 338 to 465 arrests per 100,000. By contrast, the juvenile homicide arrest rate over the same period increased 54.4 percent, from 6.4 to 9.9 arrests per 100,000. Figure 6.3 indicates a sudden and sharp increase in juvenile arrests for violence in the narrow period between about 1986 and 1994. Aggravated assaults constitute the largest component of violent crimes and account for about half or more of all the arrests of juveniles for violence (FBI 1996). Apparently, changes in the mid-1980s in the way that police classified simple and aggravated assaults and an upgrading of some marginal assaults from the former to the latter explains a substantial proportion of the overall increase in reported arrests for aggravated assaults and thus for violent crimes in the Crime Index. (Zimring 1998). However, homicide reports are less susceptible to data arti-

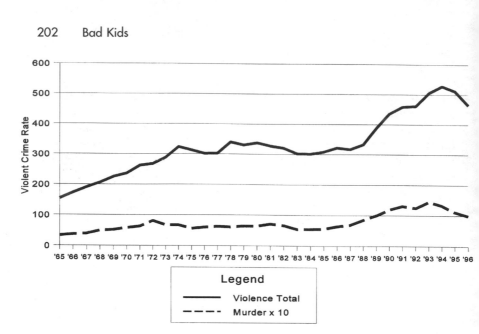

FIGURE 6.3. Juvenile violence and homicide rate, 1965–1996 (per 100,000 juveniles aged 10–17). *Sources*: Howard N. Snyder (1997) *Juvenile Arrests, 1996* (Washington, D.C.: U.S. Department of Justice, Office of Juvenile Justice and Deliquency Prevention), 4; National Center for Juvenile Justice (1996) *Easy Access to Juvenile Court Statistics* (Pittsburgh, Pa.: National Center for Juvenile Justice).

facts or to changes in police reporting practices. And in the span of a decade, between 1984 and 1993, the juvenile homicide arrest rate increased 269 percent, from a rate of about 5.4 to 14.5 arrests per 100,000 juveniles, with the fastest run-up occurring in the three years before and after 1990.

Even as the juvenile violence and homicide rates increased at a faster pace than those of adults, the age of juvenile arrestees declined. In 1995, police arrested juveniles under age fifteen for about 5.6 percent of all violent offenses. These youngest offenders also accounted for about 13.5 percent of all juvenile homicide arrestees (FBI 1996). Moreover, the increase in homicide arrests of the youngest juveniles rose most rapidly. In the period between 1985 and 1993, arrests of juveniles aged thirteen and fourteen increased 162 percent and those of juveniles aged fifteen increased 207 percent (Maguire and Pastore 1994). The rapid escalation in juvenile violence in the mid-1980s, arrests of increasingly younger juveniles for violence, and especially the dramatic rise in homicide arrests provide the backdrop for public concerns about youth crime.

Two additional aspects of youth crime and violence in the period beginning in the mid-1980s have special relevance for understanding subsequent changes in juvenile court waiver and sentencing legislation in the early 1990s. Differences in arrest rates for violent crimes by juveniles of different races and the unique role of guns in the dramatic surge in homicides in the late 1980s account for most of the changes in patterns of youth crime and violence in the past decade. The intersection of race, guns, and homicide fanned the public

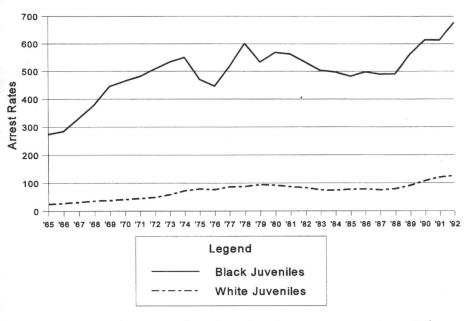

FIGURE 6.4. Juvenile arrest rate for violent crimes, by race, 1965–1992. *Source*: Kathleen Maguire and Ann L. Pastore, eds. (1994) *Sourcebook of Criminal Justice Statistics—1993* (Washington, D.C.: U.S. Department of Justice, Bureau of Justice Statistics), 447.

and political "panic" that, in turn, led to the recent get-tough reformulation of juvenile justice waiver and sentencing policies.

Police arrest black youths for a disproportionate amount of all violent offenses. As Figure 6.4 indicates, in recent years police arrested black juveniles under the age of eighteen years for all violent offenses at a rate about five times greater than that of white youths. And police arrested black youths for homicide at a rate more than seven times that of white youths. In a special section on "Juveniles and Violence" in *Crime in the United States: 1991*, the FBI reported that between 1980 and 1990, the homicide arrest rate for black juveniles increased about three times as quickly as that for white juveniles (145% versus 48%) and police arrested blacks for murder at a rate 7.5 times greater than they did whites (FBI 1992). Research that does not rely on official statistics also documents the disproportionate minority youth over-involvement in violent crime (Wolfgang, Figlio, and Sellin 1972; Tracy, Wolfgang, and Figlio 1990; Hindelang 1978; Cook and Laub 1998). Because most crime and violent crime are intraracial, black youths experience a far greater likelihood of violent victimization than do their white counterparts. For example, in 1991, black males aged fourteen to seventeen years experienced a homicide victimization rate eight times higher than that inflicted on white males (Snyder and Sickmund 1995). For young males aged fifteen to nineteen, the black:white homicide victimization ratio was more than eleven to one (Reiss and Roth 1993).

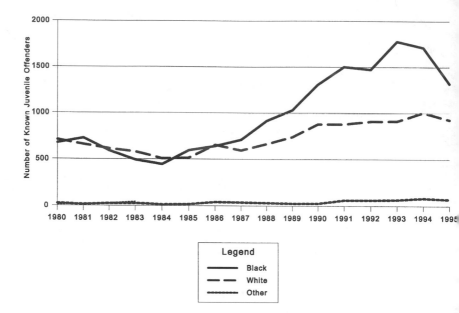

FIGURE 6.5. Juvenile arrests for homicide, by race, 1980–1995. *Source*: Melissa Sickmund, Howard N. Snyder, and Eileen Poe-Yamagata (1997) *Juvenile Offenders and Victims: 1997 Update on Violence* (Washington, D.C.: Office of Juvenile Justice and Delinquency Prevention), 13.

Figure 6.5 shows the actual numbers, rather than rates, of juveniles arrested for homicide by race. For example, in 1995, the FBI estimated that 21,600 people were murdered; law enforcement agencies "cleared" about two-thirds (62%) of those cases with arrests of one or more offenders. Police identified a juvenile as an offender in about 14 percent (1,900) of all homicides and implicated about 2,300 juveniles for those deaths (Sickmund, Snyder, and Poe-Yamagata 1997). And, in 1995, police arrested black juveniles for more than half of all those murders. As figure 6.5 illustrates, during the early to mid-1980s, police arrested roughly equal numbers of black and white juveniles for homicide. Beginning in 1986, when the youth homicide rates began to escalate sharply, arrests of black and white juveniles also began to diverge abruptly. Between 1986 and 1993, arrests of white juveniles for homicide increased about 40 percent while those of black youths jumped 278 percent.

Finally, figure 6.6 identifies the role of guns as the proximate cause of the sharp escalation of youth homicide that began in the mid-1980s. Figure 6.6 reflects the number of juvenile offenders implicated in homicides over the sixteen-year time span and the causes of their victims' deaths. The number of deaths that juveniles caused by means other than firearms averaged about 570 per year and fluctuated stably within a range of about a plus or minus 10 percent. In short, juveniles continued to kill people with knives, blunt objects, and hands and feet just as they always did. By contrast, between 1984 and

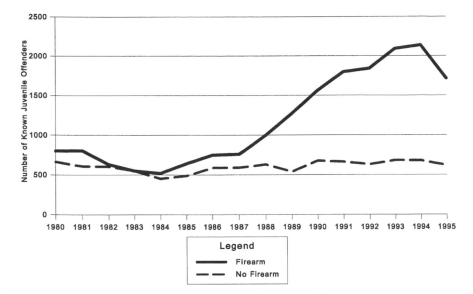

FIGURE 6.6. Juvenile homicides, by gun and non-gun, 1980–1995. *Source*: Melissa Sickmund, Howard N. Snyder, and Eileen Poe-Yamagata (1997) *Juvenile Offenders and Victims: 1997 Update on Violence* (Washington, D.C.: Office of Juvenile Justice and Deliquency Prevention), 14.

1994, the number of deaths caused by firearms increased 412 percent. Thus, in the span of the decade, arrests of adolescents for killings nearly tripled *and* the availability and use of firearms by juveniles account for almost the *entire* increase in youth homicides. Because of the relative stability of the number of nongun homicides, virtually all the variance in homicides reflects changes in the gun component of murders. Thus, "fluctuations in the proportion of youth homicide committed with guns might explain eighty percent of the variation in total homicide rates" (Zimring 1996:29). And because of the disproportionate involvement of black youths in violence and homicide, both as perpetrators and as victims, almost all these "excess homicides" involving guns occurred within the urban young black male population (Blumstein 1995; Blumstein and Cork 1996; Cook and Laub 1998). "Violence is not just a black problem, but it is an American problem that has the largest proportional impact by far among African-Americans" (Zimring and Hawkins 1997:87).

For the public, the increase in murder rates accompanying the proliferation of guns among youths constituted the most specific and frightening change in juvenile crime within the past decade. Figure 6.3 shows both a sharp increase in overall youth violence rates beginning in the mid-1980s and an escalation in youth homicide rates. Figures 6.4 and 6.5 suggest the racial composition of those changes in youth violence. Figure 6.6 demonstrates the unique contribution of guns to the carnage. Alfred Blumstein (1995; Blumstein and Cork 1996) analyzed these changing patterns of age- and race-specific homicide rates and attributed the dramatic increase in youth homicides to the crack cocaine drug industry that emerged in large cities during the mid-to late 1980s. The low price and addictive properties of "crack" increased the number of buyers and the number of weekly transactions and thereby increased the number of sellers to accommodate the demand. Drug distribution attracted youths because juveniles faced lower risks of severe penalties than adults faced, and especially attracted young urban African American males who lacked alternative economic opportunities (Blumstein and Cork 1996). Youths in the drug industry take more risks than do adults and arm themselves for self-protection and to resolve disputes. The ready availability of guns abets the prevalence of lethal violence because those involved in illegal markets cannot resolve their disputes through formal mechanisms (Reiss and Roth 1993). Although guns constitute a "tool of the trade" in the drug industry, their proliferation and diffusion within the wider youth population for self-defense and status also have contributed to the escalation of homicides (Blumstein and Cork 1996). As more young men become increasingly fearful of each other and arm themselves defensively, both the killings and the fear expand (Cook and Laub 1998). As figure 6.6 reveals, the increased use of guns to commit murders accounted for virtually all the increase in the homicide rate for older youths in the past decade. It suggests the importance of the "instrumentality" effect, the deadliness of the weapon as a determinant of fatal results (Cook 1991; Zimring and Hawkins 1997). The lucrative and violent drug industry, in turn, further accelerated the deterioration of urban neighborhoods, hastened the exodus of stable families, undermined the authority of community leaders, weakened inhibitions against violence, and provided illicit role models to attract children and adolescents into crime (National Research Council 1993). Thus, most of the differences in rates of lethal violence follow directly from public policies that allow the greater availability of handguns in the United States than, for example, in any European or other developed countries (Zimring and Hawkins 1997). Moreover, because laws prohibit juveniles from purchasing handguns, youths acquired most of their weapons via burglary, illegal purchases, or barter (Cook, Molliconi, and Cole 1995).

The social structural changes analyzed in the beginning of this chapter provide a theoretical explanation for the levels and concentrations of youth violence within the urban black male population. Homicide is heavily concentrated in big cities, and in 1992 the twenty largest cities with 11.5 percent of the total population recorded 34 percent of the total homicides and a median rate more than three times the national average (Zimring and Hawkins 1997). And, within cities, homicide rates are the highest in the slum neighborhoods in which poor blacks live exclusively. High levels of racial segregation and high rates of concentrated black poverty combine to create "an ecological niche within which rates of crimes, levels of violence, and risks of victimization are high" (Massey 1995:1203). In these dangerous environments, youths develop both individual and collective defenses for self-protection by arming themselves and joining gangs that exacerbate and foster a vicious cycle of violence. Young people adapt to an impoverished and violent culture by developing aggressive and intimidating strategies to deter violence and forestall their victimization. The "code of the streets" places a premium on securing and maintaining "respect" from and deference by others, which promote and encourage violence (Anderson 1990; Fagan and Wilkinson 1998). The ready availability of guns increases the lethality of the ensuing altercations. Because of the strong relationship between poverty, crime, and violence, racial hyper-segregation concentrates victimization risks within the black community. These patterns provide whites with additional incentives to maintain segregation, which sustains the conditions for the cycle of violence, reinforces whites' prejudices, and fosters further segregation (Massey 1995).

Several observations and policy implications emerge from the foregoing data and analyses. First, contrary to popular, media, and political impressions, the overall rate of *all* serious crime and youth crime *did not* increase substantially during the past decade but oscillated within a "normal" plus or minus 10 percent range that has prevailed since the late 1970s. Second, violent crimes constitute a small component of the overall FBI Crime Index offenses, about 10 to 15 percent, and juveniles account for a minority of all offenders arrested for violent crimes. Within this subset, the rate at which police arrested youths for *violent* crimes did increase significantly and far more sharply than it did for adults. Although homicide constitutes the smallest component of the Violent Crime Index, fluctuating between 1 and 2 percent of all arrests for violence, and juveniles account for only about 15 percent of homicide arrests, their rate of arrests for murder experienced the fastest growth. Despite juveniles' disproprotionate contribution to the increased rate of arrests for violence, however, juveniles accounted for only 30 percent of the overall increase in all violence between 1988 and 1992 and for only about one-quarter (26%) of the increase in murders (Snyder and Sickmund 1995). Serious crime, violence, and homicide are not a uniquely "juvenile" phenomenon but a "young man" problem. Young men between the ages of fourteen and twenty-four commit most of the serious and violent crimes. For example, these young men make up about 8 percent of the population but commit nearly half (48%) of all murders (Fox 1996). While juvenile crime and violence pose serious public policy issues, young adult offenders still commit most of the crime and violence. Third, police arrest African American youths at much higher rates than they do white juveniles for all crimes of violence and especially homicide (Zimring and Hawkins 1997). Thus, juvenile or criminal justice policies that "crack down" on violent offenders inevitably and predictably will have a disproportionate impact on minority youth. Similarly, social welfare or crime prevention programs to reduce levels of violence also will benefit black youths disproportionately. Finally, we can attribute virtually the entire increase in the lethality of youth violence to the proliferation of guns among the young within the past decade (FBI 1992; Blumstein 1995; Fox 1996). Thus, any public policies seriously designed to reduce youth violence and homicide rates necessarily require efforts to decrease substantially the availability of handguns held by youth. As we look at these patterns over the past decade, murders with guns committed by young black men constitute the most significant change in youth crime. Although homicide and lethal violence are very serious criminal policy problems, this very narrow segment of the overall youth crime phenomenon has driven the entire public and political debate to "get tough."

Changes in Waiver Legislation: The Shrinking Jurisdiction of Juvenile Courts

Within the past decade, the prevalence of guns in the hands of children, the apparent randomness of gang violence and drive-by shootings, the disproportionate racial minority role in homicides, and media depictions of callous youths' gratuitous violence have inflamed public fear. Politicians have exploited those fears, decried a coming generation of "superpredator" suffering from "moral poverty," and demonized young people in order to muster support for policies under which youths can be transferred to criminal court and incarcerated. Some analysts predict a demographic "time bomb" of youth crime in the near future to which minority juveniles will contribute disproportionately (Fox 1996; Zimring 1998). Thus, the increase in gun homicide by young black males in the late 1980s provided a much broader political impetus to crack down on all young offenders in general and violent minority offenders in particular.

Recent changes in youth crime and violence and the get-tough legislative responses they have engendered raise a host of complex juvenile and criminal policy issues. Can the current juvenile justice system adequately control chronic and violent young offenders? What alternative measures might better ensure public safety? Do legislative changes in waiver statutes, youth sentencing policies, or rates of confinement have an appreciable impact on youth crime or public safety? How much more money should a state spend to increase rates or lengths of incarceration? What other social service, educational, or training programs that could prevent or reduce youth crime will receive less support as a result of expenditures on incarceration? Perversely, if states spend more money to confine juveniles and reduce funds for crime prevention programs, will they exacerbate rather than ameliorate youth crime in the future? Legislators often allocate scarce resources and make value judgments about the impact or effectiveness of social and criminal justice policies based on their subjective perceptions, ideological preconceptions, political calculus, or wishful hopes, rather than on objective data and informed policy analyses (Blumstein 1993). Political slogans, rather than empirical evidence or evaluation research, often guide efforts to formulate youth crime, juvenile court waiver, and sentencing policies (Farrington, Ohlin, and Wilson 1986).

Transfer of juvenile offenders for adult prosecution provides the conceptual and administrative nexus between the more deterministic and rehabilitative predicates of the juvenile justice process and the freewill and punishment assumption of the adult criminal justice system. Although juvenile courts theoretically attempt to rehabilitate all young offenders, a small but significant proportion of miscreant youths resist the courts' benevolent efforts. These youths are typically either older delinquents nearing the maximum age of juvenile court jurisdiction, chronic recidivists who have not responded to prior intervention and for whom successful treatment may not be feasible during the time remaining to the juvenile court, or youths charged with a very serious violent crime like rape or murder (Podkopacz and Feld 1995, 1996; U.S. General Accounting Office 1995a). Politicians and the public perceive these youths as mature and sophisticated criminal offenders. Moreover, these career offenders may account for a disproportionate amount of all juvenile crime. Highly visible, serious, or chronic offenses evoke community outrage or fear, which politicians believe only punitive adult sanctions can mollify. Mechanisms to prosecute some youths as adults provide an important safety valve, permit the expiatory sacrifice of some youths to quiet political and public clamor, and enable legislators to avoid otherwise irresistible pressures to lower the maximum age of juvenile court jurisdiction (Feld 1978).

Jurisdictional waiver represents a type of *sentencing* decision. In response to the escalation of youth violence in the late 1980s, politicians, members of the public, juvenile justice personnel, and criminologists debated extensively the relative merits of different strategies to transfer some serious young offenders to criminal courts. Juvenile courts traditionally assigned primary importance to rehabilitation and attempted to individualize treatment. Criminal courts accorded greater significance to the seriousness of the offense committed and attempted to proportion punishment accordingly. All the theoretical differences between juvenile and criminal courts' sentencing philosophies become visible in transfer proceedings and in legislative policy debates.

Transfer laws simultaneously attempt to resolve both fundamental crime control issues and the ambivalence embedded in our cultural construction of youth. The jurisprudential conflicts reflect many current sentencing policy debates: tensions between rehabilitation or incapacitation and retribution, between focusing on characteristics of the offender and the seriousness of the offense, between discretion and rules, and between indeterminacy and determinacy. Waiver laws attempt to reconcile the contradictory impulses engendered when the child is a criminal and the criminal is a child. What processes best enable us to choose between competing conceptions of youths as responsible and culpable offenders and as immature and salvageable children? In the early stages of a criminal career and prospectively, what criteria best differentiate between adolescent-only offenders and life-course persistent offenders?

Although the technical and administrative details of states' transfer legislation vary considerably, judicial waiver, legislative offense exclusion, and prosecutorial choice of forum represent the three generic approaches employed (Feld 1987; Fritsch and Hemmens 1995; Snyder and Sickmund 1995; U.S. General Accounting Office 1995a). They emphasize a different balance of sentencing policy values, rely on different organizational actors and administrative processes, and elicit different information to determine whether to try and sentence a particular young offender as an adult or as a child.

Judicial waiver represents the most common transfer policy in virtually all states (Snyder and Sickmund 1995; U.S. General Accounting Office 1995a). A juvenile court judge may waive juvenile court jurisdiction on a discretionary basis after conducting a hearing to determine whether a youth is amenable to treatment or poses a danger to public safety. These case-by-case clinical assessments reflect the traditional individualized sentencing discretion characteristic of juvenile courts.

Legislative offense exclusion frequently supplements judicial waiver provisions. This approach emphasizes the seriousness of the offense committed and reflects the retributive values of the criminal law (Feld 1987; Snyder and Sickmund 1995). Because legislatures create juvenile courts, they possess considerable latitude to define their jurisdiction and to exclude youths from juvenile court based on their age and the seriousness of their offenses. A number of states, for example, exclude youths sixteen or older and charged with murder from juvenile court jurisdiction (Sanborn 1996). Legislative line drawing that sets the maximum age of juvenile court jurisdiction at fifteen or sixteen, below the general eighteen-year-old age of majority, results in the criminal prosecution of the largest numbers of chronological juveniles, for example, about 176,000 chronological juveniles in 1991 (Snyder and Sickmund 1995). Recently, Wisconsin and New Hampshire lowered their juvenile court jurisdictional age from seventeen to sixteen, thereby criminalizing large numbers of youths on a wholesale, rather than retail, basis.

Prosecutorial waiver, the third method, is used in about a dozen states to remove some young offenders from the juvenile justice system. With this strategy, juvenile and criminal courts share concurrent jurisdiction over certain ages and offenses, typically older youths and serious crimes. Prosecutors may, for example, exercise their discretion to select either juvenile or adult processing for youths sixteen or older and charged with murder (McCarthy 1994; Snyder and Sickmund 1995). Because of the constitutional doctrine of separation of powers, courts ordinarily do not review discretionary executive decisions, and most judicial opinions characterize prosecutorial transfer as an ordinary charging decision (Feld 1978). To the extent that a prosecutor's decision to charge a case in criminal court divests the juvenile court of jurisdiction, prosecutorial waiver constitutes a form of offense-based decision making like legislative offense exclusion (Thomas and Bilchik 1985).

Each type of waiver strategy has supporters and critics. Proponents of judicial waiver endorse juvenile courts' rehabilitative philosophy and argue that individualized decisions provide an appropriate balance of flexibility and severity (Zimring 1991; Fagan 1990). Critics object that judges lack accurate clinical tools with which to assess amenability to treatment or to predict dangerousness and that their exercise of standardless discretion results in abuses and inequalities (Feld 1990a; Fagan and Deschenes 1990). Proponents of offense exclusion favor "just-deserts" sentencing policies; advocate sanctions based on relatively objective factors, such as offense seriousness, culpability, and criminal history; and value consistent, uniform, and equal handling of similarly situated offenders (Feld 1981b, 1983). Critics question whether legislators can remove discretion without making the process excessively rigid and overinclusive (Zimring 1981b, 1991). Proponents of prosecutorial waiver claim that prosecutors can act as more neutral, balanced, and objective gate-keepers than either "soft" judges or get-tough legislators (McCarthy 1994). Critics observe that prosecutors succumb to political pressures and symbolically posture on crime issues, exercise their discretion just as subjectively and idiosyncratically as judges, and introduce extensive geographic variability into the justice administration process (Bishop and Frazier 1991).

Selecting a waiver strategy from among these competing and contradictory claims implicates many fundamental issues of sentencing policy. Defining the boundary between juvenile and criminal court depends, for example, on whether policymakers adopt a juvenile or criminal court's jurisprudential "point of view" and focus primarily on treatment and characteristics of the offender or on punishment and the seriousness of the offense. If policymakers endorse criminal laws' retributive values, then the present offense or prior record dominates and transfer decisions lend themselves to relatively mechanical rules, excluded offenses, or presumptive guidelines. If waiver policies reflect a commitment to offenders' rehabilitation, then judges must use more indeterminate and discretionary processes to make individualized assessments of youths' "amenability to treatment" or "dangerousness." Selecting between juvenile and criminal courts, treatment and punishment, and offender or offense creates a binary forced choice when deciding whether to try and sentence a young offender as a criminal or as a child.

For analytical purposes, I juxtapose punishment and treatment as mutually exclusive penal goals, although in daily practice both juvenile and criminal courts often commingle the two. Punishment focuses retrospectively on the nature of the offense, whereas therapy orients prospectively on the needs of the offender. When a state *punishes*, it imposes unpleasant consequences for *past offenses*; the offender violated a legal prohibition and *deserves* the prescribed consequences (Hart 1968; von Hirsch 1976). By contrast, rehabilitation assumes that certain antecedent factors caused undesirable behavior, focuses on the person's psychodynamic or social circumstances, and prescribes remedial intervention to alleviate those conditions and thereby improve the offender's *future welfare* (Allen 1981; Packer 1968). These deterministic assumptions constitute the central tenets of positive criminology and the juvenile court's rehabilitative ideal.

In this chapter and the next, I analyze whether juvenile court waiver and sentencing laws and practices emphasize characteristics of the *offender* or the seriousness of the *offense, future welfare* or *past behavior*, to decide cases. If legislators or judges focus on the past offense when they impose sentences, then they typically employ mandatory minimum or determinate and proportional sanctions to punish, incapacitate, or deter. In the context of waiver to criminal courts, *offense-based* criteria dominate and the present offense or prior record control prosecutors' or judges' transfer decisions. If judges focus on characteristics of the offender when they sentence, then they typically impose indeterminate and nonproportional dispositions that provide wide latitude to rehabilitate (Morris 1974; von Hirsch 1986). In the context of waiver decisions, judicial assessments of a youth's amenability to treatment or dangerousness reflect this flexible, discretionary sentencing policy (Feld 1987). Judges' decisions reflect a *prediction* about an offender's likely *future* course of conduct and development.

David Matza's classic study of juvenile courts, *Delinquency and Drift* (1964), analyzed the competing policies, factual bases, and value premises embedded in sentencing and waiver decisions. The "principle of offense" embodies a policy of equality and treats similar cases similarly based on a narrowly defined frame of relevance. "The principle of equality refers to a specific set of substantive criteria that are awarded central relevance and, historically, to a set of considerations that were specifically and momentously precluded. Its meaning . . . has been to give a central and unrivaled position in the framework of relevance to considerations of *offense* and conditions closely related to offense like *prior record*, and to more or less preclude considerations of status and circumstance" (Matza 1964:113–14, emphasis added). By contrast, the "principle of individualized justice" differs from the principle of offense in two fundamental ways. First, the principle of individualized justice entails a much more inclusive framework of relevance in which everything may become significant. "The principle of individualized justice suggests that disposition is to be guided by a *full understanding* of the client's personal and social character and by his 'individual needs' " (Matza 1964:114–15, emphasis added). Rather than focusing narrowly on the specific offense, a system of individualized justice considers the offender's entire condition and circumstances, deems all personal and social factors relevant, and does not assign controlling significance to any one element. Second, because "the kinds of criteria it includes are more diffuse than those commended in the principle of offense, . . . [t]he consequence of the principle of individualized justice has been mystification" (Matza 1964:116). Because every decision depends on multiple factors that may not control results in other cases, predicting outcomes becomes difficult. Juvenile courts' traditional system of individualized justice reflects aspects of Herbert Packer's (1968) "crime control" model with its heavy reliance on professional expertise and administrative discretion.

Within the past two decades, determinate, offense-based sentencing systems increasingly have superseded indeterminate, offender-oriented sentencing regimes both for adults and for juveniles (Twentieth Century Fund Task Force 1976; Cullen and Gilbert 1982; Tonry 1996). Proponents of just deserts oppose indeterminate sentences because such a system vests standardless discretion in judges and correctional administrators who can neither justify empirically their differential treatment of similarly situated offenders nor demonstrate effective rehabilitation techniques nor defend the inequalities and disparities that individualized sanctions produce (American Friends Service Committee 1971; Greenberg 1977; Fogel 1979; von Hirsch 1976). Because of its retributive foundation, a just-deserts framework imposes determinate and proportional sentences based primarily on the seriousness of the offense, culpability, or past criminal conduct, rather than on personal characteristics. The just-deserts challenge to individualized sentencing practices encompasses juvenile court waiver and sentencing policies as well (Feld 1987, 1988b). Critics of judicial waiver and individualized sentencing question whether judges are able to make valid diagnoses or predictions and object to delegating those decisions to social service personnel. Because judges lack reliable clinical tools with which to assess amenability to treatment or to predict dangerousness, their exercise of standardless discretion results in inconsistent and discriminatory outcomes.

Analyzing waiver as a sentencing decision addresses two interrelated policy issues: the bases for sentencing and waiver practices within juvenile courts and the relationship between juvenile and criminal court sentencing practices. The first implicates individualized sentencing decisions and the tension between discretion and the rule of law. The second implicates the contradictory criteria that juvenile and criminal court judges use when the former waive and the latter sentence offenders. Formulating rational and consistent social control responses to *serious* and *chronic* young offenders requires coordinated responses to youths who make the transition between the two systems. I emphasize *serious* and *chronic* young offenders because waiver laws and policies affect two, somewhat different, albeit overlapping populations—violent offenders and persistent offenders. Waiver decisions affect both types of juveniles, but criminal court judges sentence differently violent youths and chronic offenders currently charged with property crimes.

It is unfortunate that neither arbitrary legislative age-and-offense lines nor idiosyncratic judicial or prosecutorial waiver decisions have any criminological relevance other than their legal consequences. Waiver statutes increasingly use offense criteria in a vain effort to constrain judicial sentencing discretion and to improve the fit between transfer decisions and criminal court sentencing practices. Ultimately, however, legislative amendments fail because they build upon and embody the binary dichotomies—either treatment or punishment, either offender or offense, either child or adult—that purportedly distinguish juvenile from criminal courts.

Judicial Waiver and Individualized Sentencing Decisions

From the juvenile court's inception, judges could deny some young offenders its protective jurisdiction and send them to criminal court (Rothman 1980). Judicial waiver practices reflect juvenile courts' traditional approach to individualized sentencing and focus on attributes of the offender to decide whether to treat a youth as a juvenile or to punish him as an adult (Zimring 1981b, 1991). In *Kent v. United States* (383 U.S. 541 [1966]), the United States Supreme Court formalized the judicial waiver process and required juvenile courts to provide youths with some procedural protections, such as assistance of counsel, access to social service investigations and other records, and written findings and conclusions that an appellate court could review (383 U.S. at 554–557 [1966]). Because a juvenile could lose the benefits of juvenile court— private proceedings, confidential records, and protection from the stigma of a criminal conviction—*Kent* concluded that "there is no place in our system of law for reaching a result of such tremendous consequences without cere-mony" (383 U.S. at 554).

Subsequently, in *Breed v. Jones* (421 U.S. 519 [1975]), the Court applied the double jeopardy clause of the Fifth Amendment to delinquency convic-tions and required states to decide whether to try and sentence a youth as a juvenile or as an adult before proceeding to a trial on the merits of the charge. The Court posited a functional equivalency between an adult criminal trial and a delinquency proceeding and described virtually identical interests im-plicated by prosecution in either system—"anxiety and insecurity," a "heavy personal strain," and the burdens of defending a case (421 U.S. at 528–529).

Kent and *Breed* provide the formal procedural framework within which judges make waiver decisions. But the substantive bases of waiver decisions pose the principal difficulty. Until recent amendments, most states' waiver statutes allowed juvenile court judges to transfer jurisdiction based on their discretionary assessment of subjective factors, such as youths' "amenability to treatment" or "dangerousness" (Feld 1995; Snyder and Sickmund 1995). For example, the Supreme Court in *Kent* appended to its opinion a list of sub-stantive criteria that juvenile court judges might consider:

> An offense falling within the statutory limitations . . . will be waived if it has prosecutive merit and if it is heinous or of an aggravated character, or . . . if it represents a pattern of repeated offenses which indicate that the juvenile may be beyond rehabilitation under Juvenile Court procedures, or if the public needs the protection afforded by such action.
>
> The determinative factors which will be considered by the Judge in deciding whether the Juvenile Court's jurisdiction over such offenses will be waived are the following:
> 1. The seriousness of the alleged offense . . .
> 2. Whether the alleged offense was committed in an aggressive, violent, pre-meditated or willful manner.
> 3. Whether the alleged offense was against persons or against property . . .
> 4. The prosecutive merit of the complaint . . .
> 5. The desirability of trial and disposition of the entire offense in one court when the juvenile's associates in the alleged offense are adults. . . .
> 6. The sophistication and maturity of the juvenile as determined by consid-eration of his home, environmental situation, emotional attitude and pattern of living.
> 7. The record and previous history of the juvenile . . .
> 8. The prospects for adequate protection of the public and the likelihood of reasonable rehabilitation of the juvenile . . . (383 U.S. 541 app. at 566–567)

Legislatures specify amenability criteria with varying degrees of precision and often adopt the general, contradictory list of *Kent* factors. Although some states limit waiver to felony offenses and establish some minimum age for adult prosecutions, typically sixteen, fifteen, or fourteen, others provide neither of-fense nor minimum age restrictions (Snyder and Sickmund 1995).

In practice, judges apparently operationalize "amenability" and "danger-ousness" by considering three sets of variables. The first consists of a youth's age and the length of time remaining within juvenile court jurisdiction. Juvenile court judges waive older youths more readily than younger offenders (Fagan and Deschenes 1990; Podkopacz and Feld 1995, 1996; U.S. General Accounting Office 1995a). A youth's age in relation to the maximum dispositional jurisdiction restricts judges' sanctioning powers and provides an impetus to waive older juveniles or those whose offenses deserve a longer sentence than available in juvenile court. A youth's age may serve as a proxy for prior delinquency, because older juveniles have had a longer opportunity to acquire a prior record. Conversely, judges may view younger offenders as less blameworthy or responsible than their older and more culpable peers. Judges in states whose juvenile court dispositions can continue until age twenty-one waive youths at about half the rate as do judges in states whose jurisdiction ends at age eighteen or nineteen (Snyder and Hutzler 1981; Vereb and Hutzler 1981; Nimick, Szymanski, and Snyder 1986).

A second constellation of "amenability" factors include a youth's treatment prognosis as revealed in clinical evaluations and by prior correctional interventions. Once a juvenile exhausts the available treatment services and correctional resources, transfer becomes increasingly more likely (Podkopacz and Feld 1995, 1996).

Finally, judges pragmatically assess "dangerousness" and the threat a youth poses to others based on the present offense and prior record. Dangerousness variables include the seriousness of the offense, whether the youth used a weapon, and the length of the prior record (Podkopacz and Feld 1995, 1996; Howell 1996). Balancing "dangerousness" factors involves a trade-off between offense seriousness and offender persistence.

Asking judges to decide youths' "amenability to treatment" or "dangerousness" implicates some of the most fundamental and difficult issues of penal policy and juvenile jurisprudence. A law mandating an "amenability" inquiry assumes that effective treatment programs exist for at least some serious or chronic young offenders, presumes that classification systems exist with which to differentiate among youths' treatment potentials or dangerousness, and presumes that clinicians or judges possess diagnostic tools with which to make an appropriate disposition for a particular youth. Evaluation research challenges these legislative presuppositions, raising questions whether interventions systematically improve the social adjustment or reduce recidivism among chronic or violent young offenders and whether judges or clinicians possess the ability to identify those who will or will not respond to treatment (Feld 1983, 1987). I will defer until chapter 7 a thorough assessment of "what works" in juvenile treatment programs. However, a cogent analysis and summary of the "treatment" literature conclude that "either because of scientific ignorance or institutional incapacities, a rehabilitative technique is lacking; we do not know how to prevent criminal recidivism by changing the characters and behavior of offenders" (Allen 1981:34). Without theoretically grounded and consistently effective treatment programs, judges can scarcely classify offenders for different types of intervention (Sechrest 1987). Statutes that authorize judges to waive jurisdiction if a youth poses a threat to public safety require judges to predict future dangerousness even though clinicians or jurists lack the technical capacity reliably to predict low base-rate serious criminal behavior (Monohan 1981; Morris and Miller 1985). In chapter 4, I analyzed the extensive research evidence that strongly questioned whether judges can validly or reliably predict future criminal behavior. Again, a summary of that research literature concludes that the "capacity to predict future criminal behavior [is] quite beyond our present technical ability" (Morris 1974:62).

Judicial waiver criteria, such as "amenability to treatment" and "dangerousness," give judges broad, standardless discretion. Adding long lists of factors, such as those appended in *Kent*, do not provide objective guidance to structure discretion (Twentieth Century Fund Task Force 1978). "[T]he substantive standards are highly subjective, and the large number of factors that may be taken into consideration provides ample opportunity for selection and emphasis in discretionary decisions that shape the outcome of individual cases" (Zimring 1981b:195). Amorphous lists of contradictory factors reinforce judges' discretion and allow them selectively to emphasize one element or another to justify any decision. Judicial waiver statutes and decisions share certain features with the standardless capital punishment statutes condemned by the Supreme Court in *Furman v. Georgia* (408 U.S. 238 [1972]). Both "[c]apital punishment in criminal justice and waiver in juvenile justice share four related characteristics: (1) low incidence, (2) prosecutorial and judicial discretion, (3) ultimacy, and (4) inconsistency with the premises that underlie the system's other interventions" (Zimring 1981b:195). In addition, waiver also exposes some transferred juveniles to the possibility of capital punishment.

The subjective nature of waiver decisions, the absence of effective guidelines to structure outcomes, and the lack of objective indicators or scientific tools with which to classify youths allow judges to make unequal and disparate rulings without any effective procedural or appellate limitations. Empirical studies provide compelling evidence that judges apply waiver statutes in an arbitrary, capricious, and discriminatory manner. Several nationwide, state-by-state and intrastate analyses report enormous variations in both rates of waiver and the types of cases transferred (Hamparian et al. 1982; U.S. General Accounting Office 1995a). A study of waiver decisions involving a sample of violent youths in four different jurisdictions, controlled for both offense and offender variables and concluded that no uniform criteria guided transfer decisions. "[W]e found . . . a rash of inconsistent judicial waiver decisions, both within and across sites. . . . [F]or youths who may be tried and convicted in criminal court and subjected to years of imprisonment in a secure institution, such subjective decision-making is no longer justified" (Fagan and Deschenes 1990:347). Even within a single jurisdiction, judges cannot administer, interpret, or apply discretionary waiver statutes consistently from county to county or court to court (Hamparian et al. 1982; Feld 1987, 1990a). Research in several states reports a contextual pattern of "justice by geography" in which where youths lived, rather than what they did, determined their juvenile or adult status (Edwards 1977; Hamparian et al. 1982; Heuser 1985; Feld 1990a, 1995). In some states, for example, rural judges waive youths more readily than do urban judges (Hamparian et al. 1982; Feld 1990a; Poulous and Orchowsky 1994). A study of waiver decisions in Pennsylvania reported that Philadelphia juvenile courts typically transferred black robbers, whereas judges in the rest of the state most often waived white property offenders (Lemmon, Sontheimer, and Saylor 1991). A study of decisions by different judges in one juvenile court reported that "the various judges within the same urban county and court applied the same law and *decided cases* of similarly-situated offenders *significantly differently*. These judicial differences influenced both the characteristics of youths waived or retained and the subsequent sentences imposed upon them as juveniles or adults" (Podkopacz and Feld 1995:172, emphasis added).

In addition to justice by geography and by judicial idiosyncrasy, a youth's race also appears to affect waiver decisions (Hamparian et al. 1982; Fagan, Forst, and Vivona 1987). A study of transfer decisions in Philadelphia reported an interracial effect; judges waived more readily black youths with white victims than youths exhibiting any other offender-victim racial patterns (Eigen 1981a, 1981b). A study of waiver of violent youths also found disparities in the rates of transfers of minority and white offenders. Although the research found no direct evidence of sentencing discrimination, "it appears that the effects of race are indirect, but visible nonetheless" (Fagan, Forst, and Vivona 1987:276). An analysis in four states that examined the effects of race on judicial waiver decisions found that

> blacks were more likely than whites to have their cases waived for violent, property, and drug offenses. For violent offenses, the differential rates are fairly consistent across states, with black juveniles having waiver rates from 1.8 times to 3.1 times higher than whites. The differences varied more widely for drug offenses. . . . Pennsylvania black juveniles were more than twice as likely to have their cases waived than whites . . . Arizona's waiver rates for whites were twice those of California; while for blacks, Arizona's rates were 55 times those of California. (U.S. General Accounting Office 1995a:59)

One methodologically sophisticated study that analyzed judicial waiver practices in an urban setting controlled for offender, offense, and court process variables and found no significant racial disparities: "[T]he apparent racial disparities in judicial waiver administration stem from significant differences in the types of offenses with which prosecutors charge minority and white youths, rather than from discriminatory decision-making once they are charged. Prosecutors charge most minority juveniles with violent crimes and more white offenders with property offenses; most differences in waiver administration result from the way the juvenile court processes violent and property offenses, regardless of race" (Podkopacz and Feld 1995:177). Because waiver constitutes the final stage of a cumulative process, selection bias may obscure discriminatory screening and charging decisions made at early stages such as by prosecutors.

Waiver serves latent as well as manifest functions. Juvenile court judges may transfer some youths to safeguard the jurisdiction of their courts, and organizational or political concerns may explain as much about waiver decisions as the dangerousness or treatability of a youth. By relinquishing authority over a small fraction of offenders and "portraying these juveniles as the most intractable and the greatest threat to public safety, the juvenile justice system not only creates an effective symbolic gesture regarding protection of the public but it also advances its territorial interest in maintaining jurisdiction over the vast majority of juveniles and deflecting more encompassing criticisms of the entire system" (Bortner 1986:69–70). Thus, idiosyncratic differences in judicial philosophies, a youth's race, the locale of a waiver hearing, or organizational politics explain transfer decisions as much as a youth's offense or personal characteristics.

Legislative Exclusion and Prosecutors' Choice of Forum

Legislative waiver provides the principal conceptual alternative to judicial waiver. Some states exclude from juvenile court jurisdiction youths of certain ages charged with specified offenses or with particular prior records. Concurrent jurisdiction legislation gives to prosecutors the power to choose in which forum to try a case based on the offense charged and without justifying that decision in a judicial hearing.

Youths have challenged statutes that exclude them from juvenile court on the basis of their age and offense or that delegate to prosecutors the power to do so. Youths argue that "automatic adulthood" denies them the procedural safeguards required by *Kent* and constitutes an arbitrary legislative classification that violates equal protection (Feld 1978). They claim that charging decisions that remove them from juvenile court without a judicial hearing violate due process. They argue that arbitrary legislative classifications that require youths charged with certain offenses to be prosecuted as adults violate equal protection. However, appellate courts consistently reject both these due process and equal protection challenges and uphold offense exclusion or prosecutorial waiver statutes (*United States v. Bland*, 472 F.2d 1329 [D.C. Cir. 1972]; Feld 1978). Invoking the doctrine of separation of powers, the judiciary generally declines to review prosecutors' charging decisions. "Within the limits set by the legislature's constitutionally valid definition of chargeable offenses, 'the conscious exercise of some selectivity in enforcement is not in itself a federal constitutional violation' so long as 'the selection was [not] deliberately based upon an unjustifiable standard such as race, religion, or other arbitrary classification' " (*Bordenkircher v. Hayes*, 434 U.S. 357 [1978]). Moreover, legislatures regularly create classifications based on serious and minor offenses. As long as appellate court judges can attribute to the legislature a "rational basis" to treat serious offenders differently from minor offenders—for example, a belief that serious offenders pose a greater threat to the public, exhibit greater culpability, respond less readily to rehabilitative efforts, or interfere with the treatment of less-serious offenders—these judges affirm the constitutional validity of the classification (Feld 1987).

Youths have no constitutional right to a juvenile court; it exists only as a matter of legislative grace. Legislatures create juvenile courts by statute and define their jurisdiction, powers, and purposes. What they create, they may also modify or take away. States freely set juvenile courts' maximum jurisdiction at seventeen, sixteen, or fifteen years of age as a matter of state policy and without constitutional infirmity. If they define juvenile court jurisdiction to include only those persons below a jurisdictional age and whom prosecutors charge with a nonexcluded offense, then, *by statutory definition,* all others are adults for purposes of the criminal law. Despite their constitutional validity, these statutes conflict with the individualized rehabilitative philosophy of juvenile courts.

Critics of offense exclusion question whether legislators can exclude offenses and remove discretion without making the process excessively rigid and overinclusive (Zimring 1981b, 1991). In a get-tough climate, politicians experience considerable difficulty resisting their own impulses to adopt expansive lists of excluded "crimes de jour." Once a legislature adopts an excluded offense or presumptive waiver statute, the list of offenses often lengthens quickly and results in the trials of far more youths as adults than would occur under a more flexible, discretionary system. For example, California amended the offense criteria in its presumptive waiver seven times between 1977 and 1993 and doubled the initial list of eleven serious violent crimes to include twenty-three offenses, including drug crimes, carjacking, and escape from a correctional facility (Feld 1995). Critics of prosecutorial waiver strategies contend that locally elected prosecutors often succumb to the same get-tough pressures that influence legislators. Prosecutors often lack the experience or maturity that judges possess, exercise their discretion just as subjectively and idiosyncratically as do judges, and introduce additional geographic variability (Bishop, Frazier, and Henretta 1989; Bishop and Frazier 1991).

In short, excluded offense or prosecutorial waiver legislation may suffer from the rigidity, inflexibility, and overinclusiveness characteristic of mandatory sentencing statutes (Tonry 1995, 1996). In practice, offense exclusion shifts discretion from judges, who determine a youth's delinquent or criminal status in a waiver hearing, to prosecutors, who do so by manipulating the charges filed against a youth. States that use a concurrent-jurisdiction prosecutor-choice strategy simply make the allocation of power and sentencing authority explicit. While a rule-of-law approach can improve on unstructured judicial discretion, offense exclusion and prosecutors' choice laws do not provide either a jurisprudentially satisfactory or politically practical solution.

Toward an Integrated Sentencing System for
Young Career Offenders

Judicial or prosecutorial waiver and offense exclusion laws determine the ultimate dispositions of serious young offenders. States base the distinctions between treatment as a juvenile and punishment as an adult on waiver decisions or legislative lines that have no criminological significance other than their legal consequences. These jurisprudential antinomies may frustrate attempts to rationalize social control of serious and persistent young offenders. By adopting these policies, legislatures create false dichotomies and fail to acknowledge that young people mature constantly and criminal careers evolve over time. Adolescence constitutes a developmental continuum; young people do not graduate from irresponsible childhood one day to responsible adulthood the next, except as a matter of law.

Moreover, the strong correlation between age and criminal activity makes the current jurisdictional bifurcation especially problematic. The rates of many kinds of criminality peak in mid-to late adolescence, exactly at the juncture between the juvenile and criminal justice systems (Blumstein et al. 1986; Farrington 1998). Research on criminal careers indicates that young offenders do not specialize in particular types of crime, that serious crime occurs within an essentially random pattern of persistent delinquent behavior, and that a small number of chronic delinquents commit many of the offenses and most of the violent crimes perpetrated by juveniles. Serious offenders are persistent offenders who simply add violent crimes to their diverse repertoire of active lawbreaking. Although the seriousness of a youth's initial or current offense provides little basis by which to distinguish those who will or will not reoffend, a prior record of offending provides the best indicator of future criminal behavior.

Research on the development of delinquent and criminal careers indicates that many youths engage simultaneously in both trivial and serious law violations. Police arrest and process youths primarily as a function of the frequency, rather than the seriousness, of their delinquent behavior (Wolfgang, Figlio, and Sellin 1972; Hamparian et al. 1978; Strasburg 1978). Young career offenders do not specialize in particular types of crime, and their serious crime occurs within an essentially random pattern of delinquent behavior. "[O]ffenders do not specialize even at the later stages of their careers. Offenders continue to engage in a variety of crime types throughout their careers" (Petersilia 1980:352). However, the small proportion of chronic delinquents commit many of the offenses and most of the violent crimes perpetrated by juveniles.

Marvin Wolfgang, Robert Figlio, and Thorsten Sellin's pathbreaking *Delinquency in a Birth Cohort* (1972) analyzed the official delinquent careers of all males born in 1945 and residing in Philadelphia from their tenth until their eighteenth birthdays. For virtually all purposes most of the significant differences in frequency and seriousness of delinquency occur between those juveniles with one or two delinquencies and those with five or more offenses (Wolfgang, Figlio, and Sellin 1972). While one-third (34.9%) of all the boys recorded at least one delinquency, nearly half (46.4%) desisted after their initial experience and had no further contact with the police. Of those offenders who committed a second delinquency, an additional one-third (34.9%) desisted from further offending. Offenders inflicting personal injury desisted after one offense (43%) at about the same rate as did other types of offenders. The most significant differences occurred between those juveniles with one or two delinquencies and those whom police arrested five or more times. The probabilities of subsequent criminal activity remained quite high and continued into adulthood for these chronic offenders. Although the likelihood that they would commit a serious or violent offense remained low for any given delinquent event, this relatively small group of chronic offenders accounted for a disproportionately large amount of the total volume of serious crime. The chronic offenders constituted only 6 percent of their birth cohort and 18 percent of the delinquents but committed more than half (52%) of the total delinquencies, two-thirds or more of all the violent offenses, and all the homicides. Moreover, the pattern of offending continued into adulthood; as they aged, chronic offenders accounted for an increasingly larger proportion of the total and violent crimes committed by their cohort.

A number of subsequent longitudinal cohort studies confirm the relationships between chronic, serious, and life-course persistent career offending (Petersilia 1980; Blumstein et al. 1986). A study of the delinquent careers of a second Philadelphia cohort born in 1958 again reported that about one-third of youths had only one delinquent contact, and youths with one or two offenses exhibited similar patterns of desistance as in the earlier cohort (Tracy, Wolfgang, and Figlio 1990). However, a somewhat larger proportion of youths became chronic offenders (7% of all boys and 23% of all delinquents), and these youths accounted for an even larger proportion of all the delinquencies committed by their cohort (61%), including more than two-thirds of all violent offenses. A study of violent juvenile offenders in Columbus, Ohio, reported that of those juveniles with at least one arrest for a violent crime, police rearrested about one-third (36%) by age twenty-five, compared with 62 percent of those with two to four juvenile arrests and more than three-quarters (78%) of those with five or more juvenile arrests (Hamparian et al. 1978).

Other research on delinquent and criminal careers reports that while most youths desist after one or two contacts, chronic offenders who become life-course persistent offenders exhibit a substantial probability (70–80%) of continuing to commit crimes through adulthood (Petersilia 1980; Hamparian et al 1985; Blumstein et al. 1986). These studies suggest that we can best identify serious offenders by their cumulative persistence rather than by the nature of their initial or current offense. The number of contacts a young offender has with police and the juvenile justice system provides the most reliable indicator of future criminality.

Age of onset of delinquency provides another important indicator of career criminality and a strong predictor of recidivism (Farrington 1986, 1998; Greenwood 1986). Youths whose delinquency careers begin early and who become chronic offenders as juveniles are more likely to continue serious and violent offending into adulthood. "[T]hose individuals who are arrested as juveniles are three to four times more likely to be arrested as adults than are those who are not arrested as juveniles" (Greenwood 1986:163). Regardless of the nature of their original offense, youths first convicted of delinquency between ages ten and thirteen became chronic offenders at significantly higher rates than did those convicted later (Blumstein, Farrington, and Moitra 1985). An analytical review of criminal career research reports that the age at which youths recorded their initial police contact provided a powerful predictor of the length and seriousness of their criminal careers (Petersilia 1980).

Waiver statutes and youth sentencing policies unsystematically attempt to differentiate between adolescent-only offenders and life-course persistent offenders but confront an immediate and frustrating trade-off between serious and chronic offenders. For virtually all purposes, most of the significant differences among delinquents occur between adolescent-only offenders, those juveniles who desist after one or two delinquencies, and chronic offenders, those with five or more justice system involvements. Rational sentencing policy requires integrated, consistent, and coordinated penal responses to young career offenders on both sides of the current juvenile-adult line, especially when they make the transition between the two systems (Twentieth Century Fund Task Force 1978). Unfortunately, the recent escalation in youth violence and homicide has focused legislative attention primarily on serious offenses, rather than on chronic offending, thereby fostering an over- and underinclusive response to the problems posed by young career criminals. Waiver policies may punish severely one youth's isolated act of violence while sanctioning nominally a chronic offender's current property crime.

Despite the research on criminal careers, juvenile and criminal courts' sentencing practices often may work at cross-purposes and frustrate rather than harmonize responses as serious and chronic young offenders move between the two systems. Until the recent amendments of waiver laws, criminal courts typically imposed longer sentences on older offenders because of their cumulative adult prior records but whose current rate of criminal activity was on the wane and sentenced more leniently chronic younger offenders whose rate of criminal activity was increasing or at its peak (Boland and Wilson 1978; Boland 1980; Greenwood, Petersilia, and Zimring 1980).

The lenient responses to many young career offenders when they first appear in criminal courts occur because the criteria for removal from juvenile court and sentencing practices in adult criminal court often lack congruence. A number of studies examine the sentences that criminal courts imposed on judicially waived juveniles and report a "lack of fit" between waiver decisions and criminal court sentences (Feld 1987, 1995). The "punishment gap" allows chronic and active young criminal offenders to fall between the cracks of the juvenile and criminal justice systems (Greenwood, Petersilia, and Zimring 1980; Hamparian et al. 1982; Podkopacz and Feld 1995, 1996).

The punishment gap occurs because judicial waiver decisions involve two, somewhat different but overlapping populations of young offenders, older chronic offenders currently charged with property crimes, *and* violent youths, some of whom may be persistent as well. Criminal courts respond differently to these two types of offender clusters because of the differences in the nature of their present offenses. About a decade ago, prosecutors filed waiver motions against fewer than 2 percent of all delinquents and juvenile court judges transferred only about one-third (34.3%) of youths for violent offenses and waived the largest proportion of juveniles for property crimes, such as burglary (40.3%) (Nimick, Szymanski, and Snyder 1986). Even though the number of waiver motions increased 68 percent between 1988 and 1992, they still make up fewer than 2 percent of all delinquency petitions. Although prosecutors sought waivers for a larger proportion of youths charged with violent crimes (2.4%) than with property offenses (1.3%), because of their numerical predominance, the largest number and proportion of waived juveniles were property offenders (5,200 and 45% of all waivers), rather than person offenders (4,000 and 34% of all waivers) (Snyder and Sickmund 1995). Thus, despite the recent rise in violent youth crime, juvenile court judges continued to transfer the largest plurality of youths for property offenses (45%), rather than for crimes against the person (34%) (Snyder and Sickmund 1995). Only in 1993 did the proportion of waived violent offenders (42%) first exceed that of property offenders (38%) (Snyder, Sickmund, and Poe-Yamagata 1996).

The nature of the offenses for which juvenile courts transferred juveniles and their relative youthfulness affected their first criminal court sentences. Although analyses of dispositions of youths tried as adults in several jurisdictions report substantial variation in sentencing practices, a policy of leniency often prevails. Earlier studies reported that urban criminal courts incarcerated younger offenders at a lower rate than they did older offenders, youthful violent offenders received lighter sentences than did older violent offenders, and for about two years after becoming adults, youths benefited from informal lenient sentencing policies in adult courts (Greenwood, Abrahanse, and Zimring 1984). Although the seriousness of a youth's present offense primarily influenced the severity of the adult sentence imposed, "youth, at least through the first two years of criminal court jurisdiction, is a perceptible mitigating factor" (Twentieth Century Fund Task Force 1978:63). A nationwide study of judicial waived youths sentenced as adults found that criminal courts subsequently fined or placed the majority (54%) of transferred juveniles on probation. Even among those confined, 40 percent received maximum sentences of one year or less and only about one-quarter (28%) received sentences of five years or more (Hamparian et al. 1982).

More recent research reported that juvenile court judges continue to waive primarily older chronic offenders charged with a property crime like burglary, rather than with a violent crime, and criminal courts subsequently fined or placed on probation most juveniles judicially transferred (Gillespie and Norman 1984; Heuser 1985; Feld 1995). Studies in several states consistently reported that criminal court judges typically imposed more lenient sentences on chronic property offenders as adult first-time offenders than on comparable adults. An evaluation of the adult sentences received by juvenile felony defendants in Oregon reported that juvenile court judges waived a majority of youths for property rather than violent offenses and that criminal courts incarcerated only 55 percent of the youths convicted of felonies and sentenced the rest to probation (Heuser 1985). Moreover, nearly two-thirds of the youths confined as adults received jail terms of one year or less and served an average of eight months, about the same sentences that juvenile courts would impose on juveniles with prior records or convicted of felonies. A study of youths waived in Utah reported that prosecutors charged the majority of transferred juveniles with property crimes, rather than with violent offenses, and courts did not imprison a majority of those convicted as adults (Gillespie and Norman 1984). Adult criminal courts sentenced to prison less than one-third (30.8%) of the transferred juveniles convicted in a western metropolitan county (Bortner 1986). The judges returned most of the juveniles to the community shortly after conviction because of "their first-time offender status in the adult system, the relatively minor nature of their offenses, and the brevity of their offense histories *compared to adult offenders*" (Bortner 1986:57, emphasis added). Another study compared the sentences received by youths tried as adults and those retained in juvenile court in an urban county and found that "the juvenile court sentenced youths found delinquent for non-presumptive, property offenses for terms longer than their adult counterparts" (Podkopacz and Feld 1995:164). Research in Minnesota reported that criminal courts imprisoned property offenders, the majority of juveniles waived and sentenced as adults, at lower rates than they did adults convicted of comparable offenses (Feld 1995). In short, most of the research reported that criminal court judges imprisoned judicially transferred youths at lower rates than they did adults convicted of comparable offenses and that many incarcerated juveniles received sentences of one year or less, often shorter than the sentences juvenile court judges could impose on "deep-end" delinquents.

Several other factors also contribute to the justice systems' failure to sentence persistent young offenders consistently when they make the transition to criminal court. Qualitative differences between juveniles' and adults' offenses and youths' group participation may contribute to the anomalous breach in social control. Juveniles' crimes may differ qualitatively from those committed by adults even within serious offense categories. Younger offenders may be less likely to be armed with guns, to inflict as much injury, or to steal as much property as adults charged with comparable offenses, and these age-related differences may affect the eventual sentences criminal courts impose (Greenwood, Petersilia, and Zimring 1980; McDermott and Hindelang 1981; Greenwood 1986). Similarly, juveniles commit their crimes in groups to a much greater extent than do adult offenders, and criminal court judges typically sentence accessories more leniently than principals (Zimring 1981a; 1998; Greenwood 1986). Because police arrest juveniles as multiple perpetrators of a single crime more frequently than they arrest adults, arrest statistics tend to overstate youths' contribution to the overall amount of violent crime. For example, juvenile robberies involve two or more actors about twice as often as do adult robberies (Greenwood, Petersilia, and Zimring 1980). About half of all juveniles arrested for homicide were involved in crimes with more than one criminal actor (Snyder, Sickmund, and Poe-Yamagata 1996). Thus qualitative differences in youths' offenses or their degree of participation may affect their eventual criminal sentences.

Recent Changes in Waiver Statutes

Within the past two decades, state legislatures have extensively modified their transfer laws. These changes occurred initially in the late 1970s in response to the initial upsurge in youth crime and violence (figure 6.3) and even more so within the past decade in response to the escalation of youth homicide (figures 6.3–6.6; Feld 1987, 1995). Legislatures use offense criteria either as a form of sentencing guidelines to limit judicial discretion, to guide prosecutorial charging decisions, or automatically to exclude certain youths from juvenile court jurisdiction. These amendments use offense criteria to integrate juvenile transfer and adult sentencing practices and to reduce the punishment gap. Waiver laws that focus on offense seriousness and criminal history, whether obtained as a juvenile or an adult, rather than amorphous clinical considerations, better enable adult courts to respond more consistently to chronic and violent young offenders and to maximize social control of young career offenders. I cannot overemphasize either the amount and scope of legislative activity or the rapidity with which these changes spread (Snyder and Sickmund 1995; U.S. General Accounting Office 1995a). Since 1992, forty-eight of the fifty-one states and the District of Columbia have amended provisions of their juvenile codes, sentencing statutes, and transfer laws to target youths who commit chronic, serious, or violent crimes (Torbet et al. 1996). These amendments constitute a tidal wave of law reform responding to the rise of violence and homicide. The overarching legislative theme is a shift from the principle of individualized justice to the principle of offense, from rehabilitation to retribution.

Judicial Waiver

Although judicial waiver remains the predominant method of transfer, about three dozen states recently have amended waiver statutes to reduce their inconsistent application, to lessen intrajurisdictional disparities, and to improve the fit between waiver decisions and criminal sentencing practices (Fritsch and Hemmens 1995; Snyder and Sickmund 1995). Lawmakers use offense criteria as a type of sentencing guidelines to control judicial discretion, to focus on serious offenders, and to increase the numbers of youths waived. Reflecting these statutory changes, the numbers of youths judicially waived in the United States increased 68 percent between 1988 and 1992, from about 7,000 cases to about 11,700 (Snyder and Sickmund 1995). During this same period, the numbers of youths judicially transferred for violent crimes increased 100 percent, from about 2,000 to 4,000 cases. In 1993, judges transferred about 11,800 juveniles, of whom prosecutors charged 5,000 with violent crimes (Snyder, Sickmund, and Poe-Yamagata 1996).

Legislative amendments that focus on serious crimes, often in combination with prior records, restrict judicial discretion and increase the probabilities that criminal courts will impose significant sentences following waiver. These amendments use offense criteria to limit judicial waiver only to certain serious offenses, to identify certain offenses alone or in combination with prior record for special procedural handling, or to prescribe the dispositional consequences that follow from proof of serious offenses or prior records. Some states use offense criteria to make transfer hearings mandatory for certain categories of offenses or to create a presumption for transfer and shift to the youth the burden of proof to demonstrate why the juvenile court should retain jurisdiction (Feld 1987, 1995). Other states have enacted "once waived, always waived" provisions so that criminal courts decide all subsequent cases involving transferred chronological juveniles (Torbet et al. 1996). About twenty states have lowered from sixteen to fourteen or even twelve the ages of youth at which judges may transfer those charged with serious offenses to criminal courts (Fritsch and Hemmens 1995; Torbet et al. 1996). Recent changes also shift the jurisprudential focus of waiver hearings from the offender to the offense. States have rejected "amenability to treatment" as the primary waiver criterion in favor of "public safety," defined by the present offense, prior record, and youth's culpability (Feld 1995).

Offense Exclusion

Nearly two-thirds of the states now exclude some serious offenses from juvenile court jurisdiction (Snyder and Sickmund 1995; U.S. General Accounting Office 1995a). These exclusion statutes typically supplement judicial waiver statutes. While some states exclude only youths charged with capital crimes, murder, or offenses punishable by life imprisonment, others exclude longer lists of offenses or youths charged with repeat offenses. Because most excluded offense legislation targets serious violent offenses—murder, rape, kidnapping, or armed robbery—youths identified by such provisions face the prospects of substantial sentences if convicted as adults. Since 1992, nearly half the states have expanded the lists of excluded offenses, lowered the ages of eligibility for exclusion from sixteen to fourteen or thirteen years of age, or granted prosecutors authority to "direct-file" more cases in criminal court (Fritsch and Hemmens 1995; U.S. General Accounting Office 1995a; Torbet et al. 1996). As a result, increasing numbers of younger offenders charged with very serious crimes find themselves "automatically" in criminal court. However, as legislators zealously expand lists of excluded offenses to encompass less-serious crimes or lesser included offenses and lower the ages of youths at which prosecutors may charge youths as adults, they also reduce the certainty that criminal court judges will impose significant adult sentences. Moreover, legislation in several excluded offense jurisdictions allows criminal court judges to "transfer back" some youths for disposition in juvenile court (Snyder and Sickmund 1995). Because chronological juveniles charged with excluded offenses begin in adult courts, we have virtually no data on either the numbers of youths in criminal courts below the general jurisdictional age, the subsequent sentences they receive, or the numbers or dispositions of those youths whom criminal court judges "transfer back" to juvenile courts.

Under concurrent-jurisdiction statutes, legislators also grant prosecutors more authority to charge youths directly in criminal courts. Again, the number of states that authorize this direct-file strategy has more than doubled within the past decade (Feld 1987; Fritsch and Hemmens 1995; Snyder and Sickmund 1995). A few states provide charging guidelines based on the *Kent* criteria or other offense factors to structure prosecutorial direct-file decisions, although most leave the decision to individual prosecutors. As with excluded offense legislation, we lack extensive data on the numbers of youths against whom prosecutors directly filed in criminal court. However, prosecutors in some jurisdictions may charge as many as 10 percent of chronological juveniles in adult court (U.S. General Accounting office 1995a). Indeed, by some calculations, prosecutors in Florida alone may direct-file as many juveniles into criminal courts in that state as judges waive judicially nationwide (Bishop, Frazier, and Henretta 1989; Bishop and Frazier 1991).

Criminal Court Careers of "Targeted" Juvenile Offenders

Judicial waiver statutes that use offense criteria explicitly to target serious violent offenders and laws that grant prosecutors discretion to choose the forum or that exclude violent offenses from juvenile court jurisdiction increase the likelihood that young offenders will receive significant sentences as adults. As mentioned earlier in this chapter, until the recent spate of statutory amendments, prosecutors typically charged most judicially waived juveniles with property offenses, not violent crimes, and criminal courts neither imprisoned most of these adult first-time offenders nor imposed sentences longer than those available in juvenile courts. The research on the adult sentences received by violent youths produces different results (Snyder and Sickmund 1995).

Restricting waiver to serious offenses and specifying special procedures apparently increase the likelihood that juvenile courts will waive and that criminal courts will impose significant adult sentences. Several studies examined the sentences that waived or excluded youths receive when tried as adults in jurisdictions that target them as serious offenders and found that their probabilities of significant adult sanctions increased. In 1976, California amended its judicial waiver statute, created a presumption that juvenile courts should waive youths charged with certain serious crimes, and shifted the burden of proof to the juvenile (Cal. Welf. & Inst. Code § 707(b) [West 1976]; Feld 1981b). Initial evaluations indicated that the changes increased the number of youths tried, convicted, and sentenced as adults after being charged with one of the enumerated violent offenses (Teilmann and Klein n.d.). Criminal court judges in Los Angeles did not sentence juveniles tried as adults more leniently than they did other offenders, the gravity or violence of the crime rather than the age or record of the offender determined the sentence for more serious crimes, and the prior juvenile record influenced the severity of the first adult sentence for marginal crimes like burglary (Greenwood, Petersilia, and Zimring 1980). A study in a northern California county reported that prosecutors filed waiver motions for presumptive-transfer violent offenses four times more often than for property offenses, and judges waived about half the youths. Youths transferred and convicted as adults for violent crimes received substantially greater punishments based solely on the seriousness of the present offense than did youths retained in juvenile court or transferred as chronic property offenders (Barnes and Franz 1989). As a result of the changes in the law, by the early 1990s California juvenile courts waived the vast majority of youths to adult courts for violent offenses (85.1%) (U.S. General Accounting Office 1995a).

A number of studies have analyzed prosecutorial waiver practices in Florida. The majority of youths whom prosecutors direct-filed in Dade County (Miami), Florida, consisted of older males with multiple felony charges, primarily property crimes (55% burglary) and prior delinquency convictions, and criminal courts imprisoned approximately two-thirds of them (Thomas and Bilchik 1985). An examination of a broader sample of Florida direct-file cases reported that between 1979 and 1987, the percentage of youths transferred increased from 1.29 to 7.35 percent of all delinquency petitions, and the proportion of transfers directly filed by prosecutors increased from 48 to 88 percent of all waivers (Bishop, Frazier, and Henretta 1989; Bishop and Frazier 1991). Prosecutors charged a majority (55%) of direct-file youths with property felonies and fewer than one-third of youths with crimes against the person. Moreover, as legislative amendments expanded prosecutors' authority to directly file, the proportion of violent offenders transferred actually *declined* from 30 percent in 1981 to 20 percent in 1984 (Bishop, Frazier, and Henretta 1989). Prosecutors apparently transferred many youths simply because they neared the age-jurisdictional limits of juvenile courts. A comparison of the characteristics of youths against whom prosecutors directly filed with those retained and confined in the "deep end" of the juvenile system found that the latter youths appeared to be more serious offenders than the transferred youths as measured by their present offenses, number and quality of prior records, and prior correctional dispositions (Frazier 1991). A comparison of the post-conviction recidivism of youths whom prosecutors directly filed in 1987 for noncapital or life offenses with a matched sample of retained juveniles found that by all measures, the youths whom prosecutors tried as adults did *worse*— they committed additional and more-serious offenses more quickly than did those youths retained in juvenile jurisdiction. "Overall, the results suggest that transfer in Florida has had little deterrent value. Nor has it produced any incapacitative benefits that enhance public safety" (Bishop et al. 1996:183).

The transfer decision has profound consequences for waived violent youths even though the decision itself often lacks any apparent or consistent rationale. A study of the dispositions received by waived and retained youths in four urban sites whom prosecutors charged with a violent offense and who had a prior felony conviction reported that criminal courts incarcerated more than 90 percent and imposed sentences five times longer than those given to youths with similar offense characteristics but who remained in juvenile court (Rudman et al. 1986). "[B]ecause the criminal justice system is not limited by the jurisdictional age considerations of the juvenile justice system, violent youths convicted and sentenced in criminal court receive considerably longer sentences, in adult secure facilities, than their counterparts retained by the juvenile court" (Rudman et al. 1986:89). However, the analysts could not identify the factors that juvenile court judges used initially to distinguish between the juveniles whom they waived or retained within this sample of violent youths (Fagan and Deschenes 1990).

A natural quasi-experiment compared young robbery and burglary offenders in New York whose excluded offenses placed them in criminal court with a similar sample of fifteen-and sixteen-year-old youths in matched counties in New Jersey whose age and offenses placed them in juvenile courts (Fagan 1995, 1996). The New York criminal courts convicted and incarcerated a somewhat larger proportion of youths, but both justice systems imposed sentences of comparable length. Although burglary offenders in both jurisdictions reoffended at about the same rate, adult robbery offenders in New York reoffended more quickly and at a higher rate than did the juveniles in New Jersey. "Rather than affording greater community protection, the higher recidivism rates for the criminal court cohort suggest that public safety was, in fact, compromised by adjudication in the criminal court" (Fagan 1995:254). Criminalizing adolescent crimes provides only symbolic benefits but allows youths to acquire criminal records earlier and thereby receive more-severe sentences for subsequent adult offenses.

Several studies consistently indicate that criminal courts imprison more often and impose longer sentences on violent youths tried as adults than do juvenile courts. Although violent offenders constituted a small subset of all juveniles judicially waived in Oregon, criminal courts incarcerated 75 percent of the violent juveniles and imposed prison sentences in excess of six years (Heuser 1985). In Hennepin County (Minneapolis), Minnesota, criminal courts convicted and incarcerated transferred youths at higher rates than juvenile courts did the retained juveniles (Podkopacz and Feld 1995, 1996). Although juvenile courts imposed longer sentences on young property offenders than did criminal courts, the latter sentenced the violent young adults to terms about five times longer than those received by violent delinquents (Podkopacz and Feld 1996). In Arizona, criminal court judges incarcerated only 43 percent of all transferred juveniles but imprisoned youths convicted of violent crimes almost three times as often as they did youths convicted of other types of offenses (McNulty 1996).

The use of offense criteria to structure discretion or to exclude offenses theoretically increases the certainty and predictability of justice system responses. Several investigations analyze whether laws that mandate adult prosecution deter youths from committing serious crimes. New York has no judicial waiver provisions, and juvenile court jurisdiction ends at age fifteen. New York adopted legislation in 1978 to exclude juveniles thirteen years or older charged with murder and fourteen years or older charged with kidnaping, arson, and rape (N.Y. Penal Law § 30.00(2) [McKinney 1978]); Singer 1996). The legislature intended to increase the certainty of adult prosecution, impose more-severe sentences on juvenile offenders, and deter youth crime (Singer and McDowall 1988; Butterfield 1995; Singer 1996). Many New York youths spontaneously reported in interviews that they consciously would reduce or cease their delinquent involvements in midadolescence, "based on their perceptions of differences in the criminal justice system's treatment of juvenile and adult criminals" (Glassner, Glassner, Ksander, and Berg 1983: 221). However, evaluations of the effect of the legislation did not find any systematic decline in juvenile arrests for the excluded offenses. "An organizational change and an increase in the severity of punishment does not necessarily lead to reductions in violent juvenile crime" (Singer and McDowall 1988:20). An analysis of the genesis and administration of New York's excluded offense legislation concludes that contextual and organizational variations and individualized decision making erode the certainty of law enforcement and undermine the law's deterrent effect. "[S]ystems of legislative waiver, like judicial waiver, maintain individualized sources of legal discretion" (Singer 1996:150).

Other attempts to measure the deterrent effects of the threat of adult sanctions compared rates of offending between juveniles and young adults in states with different maximum ages of juvenile court jurisdiction. One study reported lower official and self-reported rates of offending for youths in states that defined seventeen-year-olds as "adults" rather than as juveniles, but the report also found that police reluctance to process these younger "adults" as formally as somewhat older youths may have neutralized the prospect of criminal prosecution. In part, then, informal system responses may vitiate the effect of offense exclusion legislation and "attempts to use the greater severity of punishment inherent in adult status to deter juvenile crime could backfire if the minimum age for adult status is set too low" (Ruhland, Gold, and Hekman 1982:374).

Another quasi-experiment measured the deterrent effect of excluded offense legislation in Idaho by comparing juvenile arrest rates in Idaho with those in Montana and Wyoming (Jensen and Metsger 1994). A comparison of juvenile arrest data before and after Idaho excluded youths fourteen years or older and charged with murder, rape, and robbery from juvenile court jurisdiction found that violent juvenile crimes actually *increased* in Idaho and *decreased* in the comparison states following the changes. The study concluded that "the movement away from the traditional juvenile court model to the more punitive criminal justice system did not deter youth from committing violent crimes" (Jensen and Metsger 1994:102).

Persistent and Violent Young Offenders

Waiver laws, in all their guises, confront two somewhat different but overlapping populations of offenders—persistent and violent youths. One group consists of chronic offenders currently charged with property crimes, but their extensive delinquency histories, prior correctional exposures, and advancing age in relation to juvenile courts' maximum jurisdiction render them eligible for adult prosecution (Podkopacz and Feld 1995; U.S. General Accounting Office 1995a). A second group consists of violent offenders. While some violent youths also are chronic offenders, others have less-extensive prior records or exposure to juvenile correctional treatment. Judges appear likely to waive violent offenders at younger ages than they do property offenders (Podkopacz and Feld 1995; McNulty 1996). For example, whereas 71.9 percent of all youths whom Arizona juvenile court judges waived were seventeen years of age, prosecutors charged 75 percent of the youths transferred at age fourteen with violent crimes but only 43.7 percent of the oldest waived juveniles (McNulty 1996).

Because of differences in rates and types of offending by race (e.g., figures 6.4 and 6.5), laws that target violent offenses for presumptive judicial waiver or for automatic exclusion indirectly have the effect of identifying larger proportions of black juveniles than white youths and exposing black juveniles to more severe adult penal consequences. As the number of judicially waived cases increased from 1988 onward and the proportion of violent offenses among waived cases increased, the percentage of black juveniles judicially waived to criminal court increased from 43 to 50 percent for all transferred youths. Although juvenile court judges waived an equal proportion of black and white youths (49%) in 1989, by 1993 the proportion of waived white youths decreased to 45 percent while black youths made up 52 percent of all waived juveniles (Snyder, Sickmund, and Poe-Yamagata 1996).

The inconsistencies in criminal court sentencing practices—shorter adult sentences for waived property offenders than for those tried as juveniles and dramatically longer sentences for violent youths tried as adults—reflect jurisdictional bifurcation and the interplay between the differing characteristics of these two types of waived youths. States continue to amend their waiver statutes to find the "right" mechanism to separate children from criminals and to reconcile the sentencing disparities between the two systems. Since 1978, for example, at least forty-four states have amended their waiver laws to ease the transfer of youths to criminal courts (U.S. General Accounting Office 1995a). During this period, nearly two dozen states have excluded certain offenses from juvenile court jurisdiction (Fritsch and Hemmens 1995; Snyder and Sickmund 1995). Despite these legislative revisions, the "correct" solution eludes states because each statutory strategy suffers from inherent and irremediable flaws. Discretionary and idiosyncratic prosecutorial and judicial waiver decisions exacerbate the "lack of fit" between transfer and criminal court sentencing practices and undermine the rationality of social control. Legislative offense exclusion suffers from rigidity and inflexibility and fails to respond to young career offenders whose present offense is nonviolent. All these deficiencies stem from categorical classifications—child or adult, treatment or punishment, juvenile or criminal court—and jurisdictional bifurcation. Finally, as a result of binary thinking, once a youth reaches criminal court, any semblance of childhood ends—old enough to do the crime, old enough to do the time.

Criminal Court Processing and Sentencing
of Waived Juvenile Offenders

The recent changes in waiver laws increase the numbers of chronological juveniles charged, tried, detained, and sentenced in criminal courts. Because
many states amended their waiver statutes without analyzing their effects on
various components of the justice systems, the influx of young offenders in
criminal courts often imposes greater demands on prosecutorial and judicial
resources without corresponding increases in personnel. In many states,
waived juveniles' pretrial detention status remains ambiguous and may result
in lengthy confinement pending an appeal by the youth or by a prosecutor if
a judge denied a waiver motion (Torbet et al. 1996). An evaluation of conditions of confinement found "a growing percentage of the detainees were
juveniles waiting transfers. These juveniles were often detained for many
months, straining the capacity of the [detention] centers, which were designed
for short-term confinement, to provide effective programming" (Parent et al.
1997:3). Similarly, as criminal courts impose more-severe sentences on young
offenders, prison populations rise without any corresponding increases in bed
space or age-appropriate programs.

Despite legislative efforts to transfer more youths to criminal courts, surprisingly few studies compare the rates of conviction or sentences of waived
or excluded youths with those of retained juveniles or similar adult defendants.
The few studies of waived juveniles' experiences in criminal courts suggest
that criminal courts convict them at higher rates than do juvenile courts and
perhaps more readily than they do other adult defendants (U.S. General Accounting Office 1995a; Fagan 1995, 1996). One analysis of conviction rates in
seven states found that rates varied from state to state and by type of offense
but that criminal courts convicted waived juveniles at about the same rate as,
or at higher rates than, courts convicted other young adult offenders (U.S.
General Accounting Office 1995a). Another study reported higher rates of
conviction and some type of incarceration for waived youths in criminal courts
than for those retained in juvenile courts (Podkopacz and Feld 1995, 1996).
Of course, these higher conviction rates may reflect prior prosecutorial and
judicial screening decisions and the sample selection bias of youths waived to
criminal court.

Adult criminal courts sentence waived young offenders primarily on the
basis of the seriousness of their present offense. The emphasis on the present
offense reflects ordinary criminal sentencing practices, as well as the failure to
include juvenile convictions systematically in young adults' criminal histories.
As a result, criminal courts often sentence violent and persistent young offenders significantly differently. The former may receive substantial sentences
of imprisonment including "life without parole" or the death penalty. As
noted above, many studies report that waived violent youths receive sentences
four or more times longer than do their retained juvenile counterparts. Moreover, violent youths often receive these disparate consequences simply because
judges or prosecutors idiosyncratically or legislators arbitrarily decided to try

them as adults rather than as juveniles. Persistent offenders, by contrast, often receive more lenient sentences as adult "first-time offenders" than do their retained juvenile counterparts. Young property offenders sentenced in criminal court benefit from the comparative leniency accorded to property offenders generally, to younger offenders specifically, and to those without substantial adult prior criminal histories. As a result, chronic property offenders sentenced as juveniles often receive longer sentences than do youths whom judges waived because they were not "amenable to treatment" or posed a threat to the community.

Use of Juvenile Records to Enhance Youths' Criminal Sentences

One important source of the punishment gap and the failure to sentence chronic offenders appropriately stems from the failure to integrate juvenile and criminal offense records. The two justice systems' inability to maintain centralized repositories of offenders' prior records of arrests and convictions or to integrate them across both justice systems frustrates sentencing of persistent career offenders when they make the transition between the two systems. Although extensive juvenile criminality and early onset provides the most reliable indicators of a criminal career, the failure to combine criminal histories across both systems creates a disjunction that "serious offenders can exploit to escape the control and punishment their chronic or violent offenses properly deserve" (Farrington, Ohlin, and Wilson 1986:126).

Criminal courts often lack access to the juvenile component of offenders' criminal histories because of the confidentiality of juvenile court records, the functional and physical separation of juvenile and criminal court staff who must collate and combine these records, sheer bureaucratic ineptitude, and the difficulty of maintaining an integrated system to track offenders and compile complete criminal histories across both systems (Petersilia 1981; Greenwood 1986). Juvenile courts' practices of sealing or expunging records to avoid stigmatizing offenders impedes the use of juvenile court records to identify young career offenders and to enhance their subsequent sentences. "The prohibitions against merged juvenile and adult records, the failure to routinely include juvenile court data in police record systems, and the sealing and purging of juvenile records create a situation in most jurisdictions in which criminal justice authorities frequently make their decisions with no information about police contacts with juveniles" (Blumstein et al. 1986:193). Because of difficulties in obtaining access to juvenile court records, criminal sentencing practices often disregard significant juvenile offense histories (Greenwood, Abrahamse, and Zimring 1984).

Policies on access to juvenile records pose a conflict between the rehabilitative goals of the juvenile court and the public safety interests in identifying career criminals. Although juvenile courts restrict access to records in order to avoid stigmatizing youths for minor offenses or who desist, "the bifurcation does not seem reasonable for juveniles whose delinquency careers are serious and who persist into serious adult offending. Thus, while juvenile records should continue to be protected from general public access, the adult criminal justice system should have access to juvenile records of at least those offenders arrested as adults on a felony charge" (Blumstein et al. 1986:197). Access to juvenile records provides an important mechanism to coordinate juvenile and criminal court sentencing of career offenders. Including the juvenile record in a waived youth's adult criminal history score could reduce the punishment gap when criminal courts sentence chronic but nonviolent young offenders (Petersilia 1981).

Despite the traditional confidentiality of and restricted access to juvenile courts records, states increasingly use prior juvenile convictions to enhance adult sentences (Miller 1995; Torbet et al. 1996). Research on the development of criminal careers supports inclusion of juvenile prior convictions for sentence enhancements because the small subset of chronic delinquents commits a disproportionately large number of the total violent and serious property crimes. A record of persistent offending, whether as a juvenile or as an adult, provides the "best evidence" of career criminality. The traditional role of confidentiality in juvenile court proceedings to avoid stigmatizing delinquents hinders criminal courts' access to juvenile conviction records and bureaucratic separation of the two systems hampers record sharing even where allowed.

Several states' sentencing guidelines and the U.S. Sentencing Commission's guidelines include some juvenile prior convictions in an adult defendant's criminal history score (Feld 1995; U.S. Sentencing Commission 1995: § 4A1.2). Under California's "three-strikes" sentencing law, a juvenile adjudication can constitute a prior felony conviction for purposes of sentence enhancements (Cal. Penal Code § 667(d)(3) [West 1994]). A survey of state statutes reports that about half of states systematically consider juvenile records in setting adult sentences (Miller 1995). Sentencing judges assert the importance of access to defendants' prior records of juvenile convictions (e.g., *United States v. Davis*, 48 F.3d 277, 280 [7th Cir. 1995]).

Some states include the juvenile record as a discretionary "factor" to consider when available, whereas others formally include some component of a juvenile record in calculating a youth's criminal history score (Miller 1995). Most states' sentencing guidelines weight juvenile prior offenses less heavily than comparable adult convictions and include, for example, only juvenile felonies committed after age sixteen (Feld 1981b, 1995). However, other states do not distinguish qualitatively between juvenile and adult prior convictions and count both equally in an offender's criminal history score (e.g., Kan. Stat. Ann. § 21–4170(a) [1995]).

States' expanded uses of juveniles' prior records to enhance the sentences of young adult offenders raise troubling issues because of the inferior quality of the procedural justice by which juvenile courts obtained those convictions. As we recall from chapter 4, many juvenile courts adjudicate youths delinquent without the assistance of counsel and most states deny juveniles access to a jury trial. The Supreme Court has ruled that a state may not use a felony conviction obtained without a lawyer or a *valid waiver* of counsel to enhance subsequent criminal sentences (*United States v. Tucker*, 404 U.S. 443 [1972]). The social psychological research reviewed in chapter 4 seriously questioned juveniles' competency to waive counsel and suggested that youths required greater procedural protections than did adults to offset their relative disadvantage in the justice process. The denial of a right to a jury trial in juvenile courts also should limit the use of juvenile convictions to enhance adult sentences. *McKeiver* asserted that juveniles received treatment rather than punishment. "Supervision or confinement is aimed at rehabilitation, not at convincing the juvenile of his error simply by imposing pains and penalties" (*McKeiver v. Pennsylvania*, 403 U.S. 528, at 552 [1971]). Unfortunately, states use those convictions obtained with less-stringent procedures to *treat* youths as juveniles in order subsequently to *punish* them more severely as adults. Appellate courts uphold this practice and reason that if a conviction was valid at the time it was obtained, then judges may use those juvenile adjudications obtained without a jury trial or counsel in order to enhance a subsequent adult sentence (e.g. *United States v. Williams*, 891 F.2d 212 [9th Cir. 1989]). A few judges dissent from the federal sentencing guidelines' "policy of treating adult sentences and periods of incarceration like juvenile sentences and periods of confinement for purposes of calculating a defendant's criminal history score" (*United States v. Johnson*, 28 F.2d 151, 157 [D.C. Cir 1994].) It does seem contradictory to provide youths with fewer procedural safeguards in the name of rehabilitation and then to use those convictions to punish them more severely. Although rational sentencing policy supports systematic use of juvenile records of convictions, justice and fairness require adult criminal procedural safeguards to ensure their quality and legitimate their use.

The increased use of juvenile court records to enhance criminal sentences reflects a more widespread erosion of confidentiality in juvenile court proceedings. Recent juvenile code amendments increase public access to juvenile court proceedings, expand centralized repositories of juveniles' fingerprints and arrest records, and broaden the dissemination of information about juvenile delinquency adjudications (Torbet et al. 1996). Between 1992 and 1995, ten states expanded public access to delinquency proceedings; now nearly half of all states permit or require public access to juvenile proceedings involving youths charged with violent, serious, or repeat offenses. About half the states maintain a central repository to hold juvenile arrest and disposition records (Miller 1995). Forty-six states and the District of Columbia allow police to fingerprint juveniles for at least some types of offenses (Miller 1995; Torbet et al. 1996). States increasingly authorize information sharing among juvenile courts, law enforcement, schools, and youth-serving agencies to coordinate services and social control.

Waiver, Proportionality, and Capital Punishment

Waiver of youths to criminal courts for sentencing as adults implicates legal and cultural understandings of juveniles' criminal responsibility. While juvenile court dispositions may continue for the duration of minority, criminal sentences imposed on youths convicted of a serious felony may be substantially longer. Waiver legislation that excludes capital offenses from juvenile court jurisdiction exposes some youths to the possibility of execution for crimes they committed as juveniles (Streib 1987). By refining the procedures by which states individualized culpability assessments and exposed juveniles to adult sanctions, the Supreme Court in *Kent v. United States* (383 U.S. 541 [1966]) legitimated the execution of juveniles. "[T]he question of whether a 16-year old accused of murder will stay in juvenile court, or be tried in criminal court for a capital crime, will depend on an individual judge assessing whether that 16-year-old is 'mature' and 'sophisticated.' If he is found to be 'sophisticated,' his reward can be eligibility for the electric chair" (Zimring 1982:xii). Imposing sentences of "life without parole" on waived youths for crimes they committed at thirteen or fourteen years of age and executing them for crimes they committed at sixteen or seventeen years of age challenges the social construction of adolescence and the idea that juveniles are less criminally responsible than adults.

Questions about young people's criminal responsibility arise in the broader context of culpability and deserved punishments, the tension between retributive and utilitarian sentencing policies, and the social and legal construction of childhood. Laws that expose children to mandatory life terms or to the death penalty constitute a political and cultural judgment that young people may be just as blameworthy and culpable as their somewhat older counterparts. Some assert, for example, that "[t]here is little reason left for not holding juveniles responsible under the same laws that apply to adults. The victim of a fifteen-year-old mugger is just as much mugged as the victim of a twenty-year-old mugger, the victim of a fourteen-year-old murderer or rapist is just as dead or as raped as the victim of an older one" (van den Haag 1975:174). The trend to waive more juveniles to criminal courts coincides with the increased willingness of criminal courts and juries to sentence more adult offenders to death and to impose mandatory terms of life imprisonment. In chapter 8, I analyze whether young offenders deserve the same punishment as adults and propose a sentencing policy that formally recognizes youthfulness as a mitigating factor. In the absence of such a policy, the law in most states simply treats young people in the criminal justice system as the equals of adults, for example, "adult crime, adult time."

The Death Penalty for Juveniles

Both historically and presently, some states execute people for crimes they committed as children. States have executed nearly three hundred youths for crimes committed before they were eighteen years of age, and courts currently impose about 2 percent of death penalties on minors (Streib 1987). Since the reinitiation of capital punishment in 1973 after *Furman v. Georgia* (408 U.S. 238 [1972]), states have executed eleven offenders for crimes they committed as juveniles, eight since 1990 (Streib 1998). During this period, judges have pronounced death sentences on 173 offenders for crimes committed as juveniles, or 2.7 percent of all capital sentences (Streib 1998).

The Supreme Court considered the culpability of young offenders on several occasions in the 1980s in the context of juvenile death penalty litigation. In *Thompson v. Oklahoma* (486 U.S. 815 [1988]), the Court pondered whether a state violated the Eighth Amendment prohibition on "cruel and unusual punishments" by executing a youth for a heinous murder he committed when he was fifteen years old. Both the plurality and dissenting *Thompson* opinions attempted to discern whether a national consensus supported or opposed executing juveniles. The Court conducted a proportionality analysis to determine whether the penalty exceeded the youth's blameworthiness, and a plurality concluded that "a young person is not capable of acting with the degree of culpability [as an adult] that can justify the ultimate penalty" (*Thompson*, 486 U.S. at 823) and overturned the capital sentence.

Thompson considered whether the culpability of juveniles equaled that of adults and whether they deserved the same sentence. Several earlier death penalty decisions also emphasized the youthfulness of an offender as a mitigating factor. In *Lockett v. Ohio* (438 U.S. 586, 604 [1978]), the Supreme Court ruled that a sentencing court must consider a youth's age as a mitigating factor. In *Eddings v. Oklahoma*, the Supreme Court noted that "just as the chronological age of a minor is itself a relevant mitigating factor of great weight, so must the background and mental and emotional development of a youthful defendant be duly considered in sentencing" (455 U.S. 104 at 116 [1982]). *Eddings* emphasized that despite the seriousness of crimes committed by youths, they "deserve less punishment because adolescents may have less capacity to control their conduct and to think in long-range terms than adults" (455 U.S. at 115 n 11).

The *Thompson* Court emphasized that deserved punishment must reflect individual culpability and concluded that "[t]here is also broad agreement on the proposition that adolescents as a class are less mature and responsible than adults" (487 U.S. at 834). Even though the Court found Thompson responsible for his crime and deserving of punishment, it concluded that he should not be punished as severely as an adult, simply because of his age. "[Y]outh is more than a chronological fact. . . . Our history is replete with laws and judicial recognition that minors, especially in their earlier years, generally are less mature and responsible than adults. Particularly 'during the formative years of childhood and adolescence, minors often lack the experience, perspective, and judgement' expected of adults. . . . [L]ess culpability should attach to a crime committed by a juvenile than to a comparable crime committed by an adult" (487 U.S. at 834). Even when youths caused blameworthy injuries, their choices reflected less culpability than that of adults. The Court noted: "Inexperience, less education, and less intelligence make the teenager less able to evaluate the consequences of his or her conduct while at the same time he or she is much more apt to be motivated by mere emotion or peer pressure than is an adult. The reasons why juveniles are not trusted with the privileges and responsibilities of an adult also explain why their irresponsible conduct is not as morally reprehensible as that of an adult" (*Thompson*, 487 U.S. at 835). States often act paternalistically, impose restrictions, and treat young people differently from adults—for example, serving on a jury, voting, marrying, driving, and drinking—because of their lack of experience, maturity, and judgment. The Court noted the irony of suddenly finding juveniles as culpable as adults for purposes of capital punishment: "[T]he very assumptions we make about our children when we legislate on their behalf tells us that it is likely cruel, and certainly unusual, to impose on a child a punishment that takes as its predicate the existence of a fully rational, choosing agent. . . ." (*Thompson*, 487 U.S. at 825, n. 23).

The following year in *Stanford v. Kentucky* (492 U.S. 361 [1989]), a different plurality of the Court upheld the death penalty for juveniles who committed murders at sixteen or seventeen years of age. Of the thirty-eight states and the federal government that authorize the death penalty, twenty-one states allow the execution of offenders for crimes committed at age sixteen, and an additional four permit their executions for crimes committed at age seventeen (Streib 1987; Snyder and Sickmund 1995). At the doctrinal level, the *Stanford* plurality simply disagreed with the justices in *Thompson* who found that a societal consensus existed against executing people for crimes committed as juveniles. The *Stanford* justices also rejected *Thompson's* culpability analysis and the "socioscientific evidence concerning the psychological and emotional development of 16-and 17-year-olds. . . . [A]s the adjective 'socioscientific' suggests (and insofar as evaluation of moral responsibility is concerned perhaps the adjective 'ethico-scientific' would be more apt), it is not demonstratable that no 16-year-old is 'adequately responsible' or significantly deterred" (492 U.S. at 378 [1989]). Thus *Stanford* remitted to state legislatures the task of formulating a death penalty sentencing policy for older juveniles.

As cultural and legal artifacts, *Thompson* and *Stanford* differed in their conceptions of young people. *Thompson* reflected an altruistic paternalism and proffered protective reasons to reject the death penalty for children. It reflected a view articulated in other legal contexts that "the peculiar vulnerability of children [and] their inability to make critical decisions in an informed, mature manner" entitled them to special protection under the Constitution (*Belotti v. Baird*, 442 U.S. 622, at 634 [1979]). *Stanford*, by contrast, rejected the imagery of vulnerability, invoked the language of responsibility, endorsed an authoritarian view that young people deserved the same punishments as adults, and signaled that youthfulness carried no special legal dispensation unless a state affirmatively chose to provide it.

Proportionality and Youthfulness

The Supreme Court gives states even greater constitutional deference to formulate sentencing policies outside the context of capital punishment, upholds mandatory life sentences even for drug crimes, and eschews proportionality analyses (*Harmelin v. Michigan*, 111 S. Ct. 2680 [1991]). Earlier, in *Solem v.*

Helms (463 U.S. 277 [1983]), the Supreme Court employed proportionality analyses in a nondeath penalty case and used a three-part test to assess whether a particular sentence was disproportional: the severity of the penalty in relation to the gravity of the offense, a comparison with the sentences imposed for other types of crimes within the same jurisdiction, and a comparison with the sentences imposed in other states for the same type of crime. In *Harmelin v. Michigan*, however, the Supreme Court upheld a *mandatory* sentence of life imprisonment without possibility of parole for possession of cocaine and rejected the defendant's claim that the mandatory penalty precluded judicial consideration of any personal mitigating circumstances, as required by the death penalty cases. *Harmelin* rejected the idea that the Eight Amendment grants criminal defendants any right to proportionality between the seriousness of the crime and the severity of the sentences (111 S. Ct. at 2686).

The Court's deference to states' criminal policy judgments grants state legislators virtually unreviewable authority to prescribe penalties for crimes. The Court's rejection of proportionality as a constitutional limit on states' criminal sentences has special significance for juveniles tried as adults. Sound bites of contemporary politics—"adult crime, adult time" or "old enough to do the crime, old enough to do the time"—convey current youth sentencing policy. Many of the most serious crimes for which juvenile courts waive and criminal courts convict youths carry substantial sentences, mandatory minima, or even "life without parole." Exclusion statutes with no minimum age restrictions expose even very young offenders to such harsh penalties.

Although the federal sentencing guidelines explicitly reject "youthfulness" as a reason to mitigate sentences outside the guidelines range, several states' laws recognize "youthfulness" as a mitigating factor. These statutes typically enumerate discretionary mitigating factors that include some recognition of "youthfulness," for example, "the defendant's age [or] immaturity" (N.C. Gen. Stat. § 15A-1340.16[e][4] [1996]) or simply "the youth of the offender" (La. Stat. § 905.5[f] [West 1997]). Under aggravating-mitigating sentencing laws, trial court judges regularly consider youthfulness both de jure and de facto; appellate courts remand them for resentencing if they do not (e.g., *State v. Strunk*, 846 P.2d 1297 [Utah 1993]). However, states that recognize youthfulness as a mitigating factor simply treat it as one element to weigh with other factors when sentencing youths (*State v. Adams*, 864 S.W.2d 31 [Tenn. 1993]).

In most jurisdictions, whether a trial judge treats youthfulness as a mitigating factor rests within his or her judgment, and failure to exercise leniency does not constitute reversible error or an abuse of discretion. Appellate courts regularly affirm mandatory sentences of life without parole for thirteen-year-old juveniles convicted as adults and reject any special consideration of the youth's age (e.g., *State v. Massey*, 803 P.2d 340 [Wa. Ct. App. 1990]; *State v. Furman*, 858 P.2d 1092 [Wa. Sup. Ct. 1993]). In a singular exception, the Nevada Supreme Court ruled that a mandatory term of "life without parole" imposed on a fourteen-year-old convicted of murder constituted "cruel and unusual punishment" under the state constitution (*Naovarath v. State*, 779 P.2d 944 [Nev. 1989]). Because the waiver statute excluded murder from ju-

venile court jurisdiction with no minimum age restriction (Nev. Rev. Stat. §
62.040 [1979]), the court held that there must be some very young age at
which a criminal sentence of life without parole would constitute a "cruel and
unusual" punishment (*Naovarath*, 779 P.2d 944). The court concluded that
even for the most serious crimes, a sentence of life without parole constituted
a disproportionately "cruel and unusual" penalty because of "the undeniably
lesser culpability of children for their bad actions, their capacity for growth
and society's special obligation to children" (*Naovarath*, 779 P.2d at 948).
Although *Naovarath* affirmed proportionality analyses and juveniles' reduced
culpability, it provided virtually no practical protections or limitation on the
legislature's power to prescribe severe penalties for youths. By a three-to-two
vote, the court held only that, in order to pass constitutional muster, a youth
must receive a parole hearing at some time in the distant future.

Correctional Consequences for Youths Sentenced as Adults

As a result of recent changes in waiver laws, criminal courts sentence increasing numbers of youths to adult correctional facilities. We know remarkably
little about the number of juveniles in prison because most states do not
classify inmates on the basis of the court processes that brought them there.
Many youths who committed their crimes as chronological juveniles may be
adults by the time courts have waived, convicted, and sentenced them to
prison. Because of the recency of many changes in waiver statutes, the correctional population or programming consequences of these policy changes
have not yet been fully realized. However, several recent surveys of state correctional administrators estimate that offenders younger than eighteen years
of age accounted for about 2 percent of new court commitments to prisons
(U.S. General Accounting Office 1995a; Snyder and Sickmund 1995; Parent
et al. 1997).

As mentioned earlier, criminal courts sentenced juveniles waived for property and for violent crimes differently as adults, and recent waiver legislative
amendments increasingly target violent youths. As a result, among persons
sentenced to prison, criminal courts commit a substantially larger proportion
of younger offenders for violent crimes than they do adults. For example, of
youths under age eighteen sentenced to prison, 50 percent had been convicted
of violent crimes, compared with 29 percent of all adults admitted to prison.
The percentages of youths committed to prison who had been convicted of
serious violent crimes exceeded the proportions for sentenced adults for murder (7% versus 3%), for robbery (22% versus 10%), and for assault (13%
versus 8%). Moreover, because of the disparities in rates of violent offending
by race, criminal courts sentenced a majority of black youths (54%) to prison
for violent offenses and a majority of white youths (57%) for property crimes.
Because of the differences in lengths of sentences imposed for violent and
property offenses, racial disparities in prison inmate populations will continue
to grow over time.

The infusion of juvenile offenders poses a challenge to correctional officials to develop more programming and age-appropriate conditions of confinement for young or more vulnerable inmates. Subject to variations in state laws and available facilities, correctional options for handling juveniles include straight adult incarceration with minimal differentiation between juveniles and adults other than routine classification of inmates by age, offense, size, or vulnerability; graduated incarceration in which youths begin their sentences in a juvenile or separate adult facility and then serve the remainder of their sentences in the adult facility; or age-segregated incarceration either in separate facilities within the prison or in separate youth facilities for younger adults (LIS 1995; Torbet et al. 1996).

Recent surveys report that nearly all states confine juveniles-sentenced-as-adults in adult correctional facilities either with younger adult offenders or in the general population if the juvenile is of a certain age, for example, sixteen (Torbet et al. 1996). "In 1994, thirty-six states dispersed young inmates in housing with adult inmates (half as a general practice and half only in certain circumstances). Nine states housed young inmates with those aged eighteen to twenty-one, but not with older inmates. Only six states never housed young inmates with people eighteen and older; they either have transferred young inmates to their state juvenile training schools until they reached the age of majority or have housed them in segregated living units within an adult prison" (Parent et al. 1997:5). Prison officials regard juveniles convicted in criminal courts as adults and employ the same policies, programs, and conditions of confinement for waived youths as for other adult inmates (U.S. General Accounting Office 1995a).

The influx of younger offenders poses management, programming, and control challenges for correctional administrators (Parent et al. 1997). Younger inmates may engage in more institutional misconduct. Techniques appropriate to manage adults may be less effective when applied to juveniles. Evaluations of young offenders' prison adjustment are mixed. A few states report that youths pose special management problems or commit more disciplinary infractions than do older inmates, while other states report few differences (LIS 1995). One systematic study of the prison adjustment of young offenders in Texas compared a sample of waived youths convicted of violent crimes committed before the age of seventeen with a matched sample of incarcerated inmates aged seventeen to twenty-one at the time of their offenses. The waived violent youths adapted less well, experienced more difficulty adjusting to institutional life, accumulated more extensive disciplinary histories, earned less good time, and received higher custody classifications (McShane and Williams 1989).

Policy Implications

Three decades of economic and demographic change have altered urban social structure and racially transformed America. During this period, the macrostructural transition from an industrial to an information and service economy, white migration to the suburbs, and racial segregation and concentration of poverty among some blacks have generated an urban structural underclass. In the mid-to late 1980s, serious youth crime and, especially, gun violence and homicide escalated at unprecedented rates among young urban black males. Analysts attribute the unique age-and race-specific crime pattern to the confluence of broader structural changes including the deindustrialization of cities, the racial concentration of poverty and single-parent households, and the inner-city crack cocaine epidemic. In turn, media depictions of gang and gun violence by minorities—"if it bleeds, it leads"—fanned public fears and provided political impetus to "criminalize" more youths and punish them as criminals and to adopt more-punitive juvenile justice policies. In the span of half a decade, nearly every state amended its waiver laws in response to the real or perceived escalation of urban minority youth violence. These statutory modifications shifted juvenile courts' foci from treatment to punishment, from offender to offense, and fostered convergence between the jurisprudence of the juvenile and criminal justice systems.

The sentencing policies advocated by get-tough politicians, for example, "adult crime, adult time" or "old enough to do the crime, old enough to do the time," provide popular and successful sound bites to reassure the public and demonstrate their "toughness." As a result of demagogic appeals, no candidate dares to run on a platform that her opponent can characterize as "soft on crime," and politicians avoid thoughtful discussions of complex crime policy in an era of 30-second commercials (Beckett 1997). Sound-bite politics also provide an important indicator of the changing cultural and legal conception of young people. Originally, juvenile courts characterized young people as vulnerable and morally incapable of committing a crime. By contrast, the current formulations often depict even very young offenders as depraved "superpredators" and the moral and criminally responsible equals of adults. But both formulations rest on artificial dichotomies—either child or adult, either treatment or punishment, either juvenile or criminal court—and as a result neither can address adequately developmental continuities, gradations of criminal responsibility, or the social control of young career offenders.

As a result of *Stanford* and *Harmelin*, formulating a youth sentencing policy properly lies in the hands of legislators rather than courts. Unfortunately, because legislators perceive political advantage in "cracking down" on youth crime, especially black youth crime, they transfer more juveniles to criminal court for prosecution as adults and ignore all differences between adolescents' and adults' criminal responsibility and culpability. Once waived, states' criminal sentencing laws and practices punish juveniles as if they possessed the criminal capacity of adults, and the legal system treats them just like other offenders. The constitutional ban on "cruel and unusual punishments" only prohibits states from executing youths fifteen years of age or younger but does not provide youths with either proportionality or culpability analyses or any other protection from draconian sentences. By punishing youths as adults, the legislators reject juvenile courts' deterministic premises that youths' crimes are not youths' fault and the assumptions of immaturity and irresponsibility that underlie every other disability that the law imposes on youths, for example, restrictions on drinking, driving, contracting, and voting. Because a legislature can and should formulate a developmentally appropriate youth sentencing policy, in chapter 8 I will present a sentencing framework that builds on the differences between young people and adults. Because responsibility and culpability provide the bases for deserved punishments, a formal recognition of youthfulness as a "mitigating" factor can properly reflect differences between juveniles and adults in maturity and judgment.

This chapter identifies several sentencing policy conundrums that stem from maintaining two separate criminal justice systems—one for juveniles and another for adults—that pursue contradictory policies. The various efforts to formulate waiver strategies unsuccessfully attempt to reconcile the irreconcilable. Judicial waiver statutes give judges broad discretion to decide which children are criminals but do not meaningfully define the bases or criteria by which to make the determination. Idiosyncratic decisions produce invidious and unjustifiable disparities among similarly situated offenders and a lack of fit between judicial waiver and criminal court sentences. Prosecutorial direct-file provisions suffer from all the vagaries and subjectivity of individualized judicial discretion and, in addition, lack the virtues of objctives criteria, written reasons, an evidentiary record, or appellate review. Legislative offense exclusion suffers from rigidity, overinclusiveness, and the demagogic tendency of get-tough politicians to adopt ever-expansive lists.

Recently, amendments to some states' waiver statutes use offense criteria to control judicial discretion and to coordinate juvenile and criminal court sentencing practices. Others excise offenses from juvenile court jurisdiction. The various approaches represent a significant challenge to juvenile courts' rehabilitative philosophy and indicate a shift to a more retributive policy. Statutes that use offense criteria to define "public safety," to create a presumption for waiver, or to shift the burden of proof to juveniles reduce judicial discretion. Laws that exclude youths from juvenile court jurisdiction eliminate discretion, repudiate rehabilitation, and deny judges the opportunity to treat some youths. Amendments that base youths' "adult" status on the offense charged narrow juvenile court jurisdiction and reduce its client population.

Legislators, prosecutors, and judges transfer youths to criminal court so that they may receive longer sentences as adults than they could have received in the juvenile justice system. However, a number of studies consistently report a punishment gap and question whether criminal court judges actually impose more-severe sanctions than juvenile courts would if they had retained jurisdiction. Older chronic property offenders constitute the bulk of juveniles judicially waived in most states. These youths apparently receive shorter sentences as adults than do similar property offenders disposed of in juvenile court. By contrast, youths convicted of violent offenses in criminal courts receive substantially longer sentences than do their violent juvenile counterparts. Because waiver decisions occur around the peak of youths' criminal careers, jurisdictional bifurcation undermines the ability of the criminal justice system to respond adequately to either persistent or violent offenders. Without an integrated criminal record system, chronic offenders may slip through the cracks and receive inappropriately lenient adult sentences.

All the current transfer policy changes—lowering the maximum age of jurisdiction or the minimum age of eligibility for criminal prosecution, excising additional offenses from juvenile court jurisdiction, and making it more certain and easier to transfer youths to criminal courts—assume the continued existence of two justice systems, one for juveniles and another for adults. But preserving two systems engenders many complex criminal policy issues: arbitrary and idiosyncratic waiver and retention decisions by judges and prosecutors, separate information systems that restrict criminal court judges' access to juveniles' records of prior offenses, anomalous patterns in which waived violent offenders receive much harsher sentences and transferred property offenders receive more lenient sentences as adults than either would if sentenced as a juvenile, and racial disparities in processing that transfer policies targeting violent youths exacerbate. For juveniles and adults convicted of comparable crimes, dramatic sentencing disparities raise issues of justice and fairness. No coherent sentencing policy rationales justify either type of disparity. Rather, some youths experience significantly different consequences than do others simply because of the disjunction between two separate criminal justice systems.

The issue of race recurs throughout this chapter. Social structural changes and the criminogenic characteristics of communities place minority youths disproportionately at risk of criminality *and* victimization. And the sharp increase in gun homicide by young black urban males a decade ago constituted the proximate cause of all the subsequent legislative policies to "get tough" and "crack down" on youth crime and violence. While no society can or should tolerate lethal violence, is it simply a historical fortuity that the sudden repudiation of juvenile courts' rehabilitative mission coincides with the punitive response to "other people's children," the poor and the black? On the one hand, public policies create social structures and community conditions that place black youths disproportionately at risk to engage in crime and, especially, violence (Zimring and Hawkins 1997). On the other hand, facially neutral juvenile justice policies that respond to youth violence inevitably have a disparate racial impact. These analyses indicate that juvenile justice policies that target violence predictably increase the number of minority youths transferred to criminal courts, expose black youths to more-severe sentences as adults, and result in greater numbers of black youths confined in adult prisons for longer periods.

| | | | SEVEN

Punishment, Treatment, and the Juvenile Court

Sentencing Delinquents

The Progressives envisioned a more encompassing justice system for youths than a criminal process that simply punished them. Juvenile courts' *parens patriae* ideology attempted to combine social welfare with penal social control. As we recall from chapter 2, the "rehabilitative ideal" envisioned a specialized judge who decided each case in that child's "best interests." Because reformers pursued benevolent goals and individualized their solicitude, they did not circumscribe narrowly judges' power. Rather, they maximized discretion to diagnose and treat and minimized procedural safeguards and rules that might pose obstacles to intervention. They subordinated legal proof of criminal guilt to a youth's social circumstances (Schlossman 1977).

Despite juvenile courts' historic discourse of "compassionate care" and "individualized treatment," the Supreme Court in *Gault* acknowledged the disjunctions between rehabilitative rhetoric and punitive reality when it mandated procedural safeguards (Feld 1990b). "So wide a gulf between the State's treatment of the adult and of the child requires a bridge sturdier than mere verbiage, and reasons more persuasive than cliché can provide. . . . 'The rhetoric of the juvenile court movement has developed without any necessarily close correspondence to the realities of court and institutional routines' " (*In re Gault*, 387 U.S. 1, at 30 [1967]). The reality more closely resembles an assembly line of overburdened and underfunded courts quickly disposing of crushing caseloads of disproportionately minority offenders with limited options or successful outcomes (Krisberg and Austin 1993; Humes 1996). This chapter explores the disjunctions between juvenile justice rhetoric and reality. Despite reformers' initial optimism, the sentences that juvenile court judges impose and the facilities and programs to which they commit delinquents convicted of crimes differ little either in theory or in practice from those imposed on adult offenders.

Within the past two decades and in response to the same structural forces and changes in youth crime analyzed in chapter 6, states' juvenile court jurisprudence, sentencing laws, policies, and practices have become increasingly more punitive. The "triage" policies that divert status offenders away from the juvenile system and waive serious offenders to criminal courts enable juvenile courts to "get tough" and punish the remaining criminal delinquents. More formal and restrictive law enforcement practices accompany this trend toward punishment (Krisberg et al. 1986). *Gault's* extension of some legal rights to delinquents provided a veneer of due process that legitimated the imposition of more-severe sanctions.

For the Supreme Court in *McKeiver*, the differences between juvenile treatment and criminal punishment provided the primary rationale to deny delinquents jury trials and to maintain a juvenile system separate from the adult criminal system (Gardner 1982; Feld 1988b). Although most people readily understand that punishment involves an involuntary and coerced loss of personal liberty or autonomy because a person committed a crime (Hart 1968), those elementary features eluded the Supreme Court in *McKeiver*. Justice White's concurring opinion highlighted the distinctions between "treatment" in juvenile courts and "punishment" in criminal proceedings.

> [T]he juvenile justice system rests on more deterministic assumptions. . . . Reprehensible acts by juveniles are not deemed the consequence of mature and malevolent choice but of environmental pressures (or lack of them) or of other forces beyond their control. . . . [H]is conduct is not deemed so blameworthy that punishment is required to deter him or others. Coercive measures, where employed, are considered neither retribution nor punishment. Supervision or confinement is aimed at rehabilitation, not at . . . imposing pains and penalties. Nor is the purpose to make the juvenile delinquent an object lesson for others, whatever his own merits or demerits may be. A typical disposition in the juvenile court . . . may authorize confinement until age 21, but it will last no longer and within that period will last only so long as his behavior demonstrates that he remains an unacceptable risk if returned to his family. Nor is the authorization for custody until 21 any measure of the seriousness of the particular act that the juvenile has performed. (*McKeiver v. Pennsylvania*, 403 U.S. 528, at 552 [1971], White, J., concurring)

The indeterminate and nonproportional length of juvenile dispositions and the "eschewing [of] blameworthiness and punishment for evil choices" satisfied the justices that "there remained differences of substance between criminal and juvenile courts" (*McKeiver*, 403 U.S. at 551–552). Justice Stewart's dissent in *Gault* emphasized a similar distinction between juvenile and criminal sentencing practices, observing that "a juvenile proceeding's whole purpose and mission is the very opposite of the mission and purpose of a prosecution in a criminal court. The object of the one is *correction of a condition*. The object of the other is conviction and *punishment for a criminal act*" (*Gault*, 387 U.S. at 79, Stewart, J., dissenting, emphasis added).

The justices in *McKeiver* who uncritically accepted the rhetoric of *parens patriae* described juvenile justice theory rather than reality, defined punishment narrowly, and then failed to analyze either the differences between punishment and treatment or whether juvenile courts actually provided the latter. The differences between treatment as a child and punishment as an adult have both procedural and substantive implications. *McKeiver* assumed that the juvenile system afforded only positive rehabilitative treatment and denied youths procedural protections against state coercion. By contrast, the Supreme Court in *Duncan v. Louisianna* (391 U.S. 145 [1968] recognized that punishment required procedural safeguards, such as a jury, to protect against governmental oppression. In chapter 4, I analyzed many of the procedural deficiencies of juvenile courts that follow from *McKeiver*'s conclusion that youths required fewer procedural protections. Similarly, in this chapter, I examine juvenile courts' sentencing laws and practices, all of which assume that real substantive differences exist between treatment as a delinquent and punishment as a criminal. Despite the fundamental importance of the distinction, *McKeiver* did not examine the "treatment" that delinquents receive in the juvenile justice system.

Perhaps the Court's failure to distinguish between treatment and punishment stemmed from its own constitutional uncertainty about the conceptual differences between the two. Although *McKeiver* posited the theoretical premises of rehabilitation, it provides few indicators of whether juvenile courts achieve their aspirations. Maybe the Court refrained from systematically analyzing the differences between punishment and treatment because it realized that, practically, none might exist for youths convicted of crimes and confined in institutions. If the Court could not distinguish between the two, then the Constitution would require it to invalidate a staple of states' systems of social control. Perhaps more charitably, the Court possessed less information about the reality of juvenile justice than we do today. Courts adjudicate constitutional claims primarily in the realm of legal abstractions. Lawyers may not present complex social science data or daily experiences in ways that make those abstractions real. The President's Commission on Law Enforcement and Administration of Justice (1967a, 1967b) had only begun to reveal the bankruptcy of juvenile courts' treatment ideology when the Supreme Court decided its landmark juvenile court cases. And twenty-five years of judicial, legislative, and administrative changes have dramatically transformed the institution that *McKeiver* appraised. Regardless of the purposes and practices of juvenile courts then, the subsequent decades have witnessed their accelerating convergence with criminal courts.

In chapter 6, I contrasted the principle of offense with the principle of individualized justice to analyze waiver processes and distinguished between punitive frameworks that focused on past offenses and rehabilitative systems that emphasized offenders' future welfare. Although most juvenile and criminal justice sentencing systems have hybrid purposes and pursue multiple goals, within the past decades states increasingly use determinate and mandatory minimum sentences (Cullen and Gilbert 1982; Tonry 1996). Critical questions about the effectiveness of coerced treatment, the discretionary powers exercised by penal experts, and the invidious impact of indeterminate sentences contributed to the shift in penal policies. Proponents of "just deserts" endorse equality for similarly situated offenders and favor presumptive or determinate sentences based on relatively objective characteristics like present offense and criminal history rather than subjective predictions of future welfare or danger.

Juvenile courts exhibit a similar change in sentencing philosophy as political pressures to "get tough" on youth crime and to control "lenient" judicial discretion increase the punitiveness of juvenile sanctions. Again, for analytical clarity I will examine the tensions between just deserts and rehabilitation—determinacy and indeterminacy, offense and offender, past and future—in the routine sentencing of delinquents. This chapter analyzes juvenile court sentencing laws and policies, judicial administration, and correctional practices. Statutes and practices that base a youth's sentence on past conduct—the present offense or prior record—typically impose determinate and proportional, or mandatory minimum, sanctions for purposes of retribution or deterrence. Statutes and practices that sentence offenders to improve their future welfare—diagnoses or predictions about the effects of intervention on a person's future course of conduct—typically employ indeterminate and nonproportional dispositions for purposes of rehabilitation or incapacitation. Recently, many states have enacted determinate and mandatory minimum juvenile sentencing statutes to regulate judicial discretion, to enhance the certainty and predictability of sanctions, and to displace rehabilitative, indeterminate sentences with more punitive ones (Feld 1988b; Sheffer 1995; Torbet et al. 1996). In practice, a youth's present offense and prior record dominate juvenile court sentencing decisions. A youth's past deeds rather than future needs strongly affect the sanctions imposed. Evaluations of sentencing practices, treatment effectiveness, and conditions of confinement reveal increasingly punitive juvenile justice and corrections systems. These indicators strongly suggest that despite juvenile courts' persisting rehabilitative rhetoric, *treating* juvenile delinquents closely resembles *punishing* adult offenders.

This jurisprudential and administrative convergence erodes *McKeiver*'s constitutional foundation and the rationale for a separate criminal justice system for young offenders. If juvenile courts effectively punish delinquents, then the theoretical justification to deny young offenders all criminal procedural safeguards disappears. The loss of a "treatment" rationale calls into question other juvenile court sentencing practices as well. For example, states often invoke the treatment rationale to impose longer sentences on juveniles than they could inflict on adults convicted of the same offense. In *People v. Olivas* (17 Cal. 3d 236, 551 P.2d 375, 131 Cal. Rptr. 55 [1976]), the California Supreme Court limited the sentence that a criminal court could impose on a young adult committed to the California Youth Authority to the maximum term that it could impose on an adult sentenced for the same offense. By contrast, in *People v. Eric J.* (25 Cal. 3d 522, 601 P.2d 549, 159 Cal. Rptr. 317 [1979]), the court refused to apply the *Olivas* adult sentence limits to juvenile courts' commitments of delinquents to the same California Youth Authority facilities. Instead, *Eric J.* allowed juvenile courts to sentence delinquents for longer terms than adults convicted of the same offense could receive because "[j]uvenile commitment proceedings are designed for the purposes of rehabilitation and treatment, not punishment" (601 P.2d at 554). If juvenile courts punish without criminal procedural safeguards and sentence minor offenders more severely than they do adults, then what reasons exist to maintain a separate inferior justice system for youths charged with crimes?

Punishment and Treatment: The Constitutional Framework that *McKeiver* Ignored

Although *McKeiver* uncritically subscribed to a benevolent, therapeutic vision of juvenile courts, in other decisions the Supreme Court has developed criteria to assess whether states' coercive actions constitute punishment or are simply incidental aspects of a regulatory system. Some indicators to which the Court looks to determine whether state intervention constitutes punishment or treatment include

> [w]hether the sanction involves an affirmative disability or restraint, whether it has historically been regarded as punishment, whether it comes into play only on a finding of *scienter*, whether its operation will promote the traditional aims of punishment—retribution and deterrence, whether the behavior to which it applies is already a crime, whether an *alternative purpose* to which it may rationally be connected is assignable for it, and whether it appears excessive in relation to the *alternative purposes* assigned are all relevant to the inquiry, and may *often point in different directions.* (*Kennedy v. Mendoza-Martinez*, 372 U.S. 144, at 168–169 [1963], emphasis added)

Even when a state confines a person for criminal conduct, the Court still must determine whether the incarceration is to punish her or to achieve some "alternative purpose." For example, in order to decide whether a person can invoke the Fifth Amendment privilege against self-incrimination in a "sexually dangerous persons" commitment process, the Court had to determine whether the purpose of confinement was to punish or treat (*Allen v. Illinois*, 478 U.S. 364 [1986]). Although the state initiated the "commitment" proceeding by filing criminal charges and used many criminal procedures, a five-to-four majority of the *Allen* Court allowed the state to compel Allen to submit to a psychiatric interview because the commitment was "essentially civil in nature" and its aim was to provide "treatment, not punishment" (478 U.S. at 367). The Court noted that the *statutory purpose* was to provide "care and treatment," commitment was *indeterminate,* and "the State has *disavowed any interest in punishment*, provided for the *treatment* of those it commits, and established a system under which committed persons may be *released* after the briefest time in confinement" (478 U.S. at 369–370, emphasis added). Because the state did not commit Allen to punish him, he could not invoke the privilege against self-incrimination.

The Court in *Allen* distinguished its holding in *Gault* that granted delinquents the protections of the Fifth Amendment by noting that "[t]he Court in *Gault* was obviously persuaded that the State intended to *punish* its juvenile offenders. . . . Here, the State serves its purpose of *treating* rather than *punishing* sexually dangerous persons by committing them to an institution expressly designed to provide psychiatric care and treatment" (478 U.S. at 373, emphasis added). Despite *Allen*'s reformulation, however, *Gault* granted delinquents the privilege against self-incrimination because "commitment is a deprivation of liberty. It is incarceration against one's will, whether it is called 'criminal' or 'civil' " (*Gault*, 387 U.S at 50). Finally, *Allen* concluded that the "patient" failed to disprove the state's claim of "treatment" by showing that his confinement was "essentially identical to that imposed upon felons with no need for psychiatric care" (*Allen*, 478 U.S. at 373). The *Allen* Court acknowledged that "*conditions of . . . confinement* [could] amount to 'punishment' and thus render 'criminal' the proceedings which led to confinement" (478 U.S. at 374, emphasis added).

Despite *Allen*'s reluctance to recognize involuntary confinement for criminal violations as punishment per se, thoughtful analysts of juvenile justice recognize that

> when, in an authoritative setting, we attempt to do something *for* a child "because of what he is and needs," we are also doing something *to* him. The semantics of "socialized justice" are a trap for the unwary. Whatever one's motivations, however elevated one's objectives, if the measures taken result in the compulsory loss of the child's liberty, the involuntary separation of a child from his family, or even the supervision of a child's activities by a probation worker, the impact on the affected individuals is essentially a punitive one. Good intentions and a flexible vocabulary do not alter this reality. This is particularly so when, as is often the case, the institution to which the child is committed is, in fact, a peno-custodial establishment. (Allen 1964:18)

Mendoza-Martinez and *Allen* suggest some criteria by which to evaluate whether juvenile courts punish or treat delinquents when they convict them of crimes and confine them in training schools—statutory purpose, indeterminate commitment and prompt release, treatment services rather than incarceration, and appropriate conditions of confinement. Even though a judge must find that a delinquent committed a crime "beyond a reasonable doubt" before institutional confinement, criminal conviction and incarceration do not constitute punishment if the state does so for some other *alternative purpose* such as "crime prevention," as in *Schall v. Martin* (467 U.S. 283 [1984]), or "treatment," as in *Allen*. Unfortunately for *McKeiver*'s constitutional conclusion, a critical examination of legislative purpose clauses, court opinions, juvenile court sentencing laws, judicial sentencing practices, conditions of institutional confinement, and evaluations of treatment effectiveness does not "point in different directions." Rather, these various indicators consistently reveal that juvenile courts increasingly and explicitly punish delinquents for crimes.

Formal Legal Purpose of Juvenile Courts

Most states' juvenile court statutes contain a purpose clause or legislative preamble. Legislatures enact these statements of the law's rationale to aid courts in interpreting the statute. The Supreme Court's "punishment" decisions often review the stated purpose of the sanction and are "focused upon the intent of the alleged punisher as an essential element to determine the presence or absence of punishment" (Gardner 1982:816–817). For example, *Allen* invoked the statutory preamble to bolster its conclusion that the state committed him in order to provide "treatment."

When the Progressives created the Cook County juvenile court in 1899, they announced a benevolent purpose

> to secure for each minor . . . such care and guidance, preferably in his own home, as will serve the moral, emotional, mental, and physical welfare of the minor and the best interests of the community; to preserve and strengthen the minor's family ties whenever possible, removing him from the custody of his parents only when his welfare or safety or the protection of the public cannot be adequately safeguarded without removal; and, when the minor is removed from his own family, to secure for him custody, care, and discipline as nearly as possible equivalent to that which should be given by his parents. (Ill. Ann. Stat. ch. 37, ¶ 701-2 [West 1972]).

Other preambles declare the additional purpose of "remov[ing] from a minor . . . the taint of criminality and the penal consequences of criminal behavior, by substituting therefore an individual program of counseling, supervision, treatment, and rehabilitation" (N.H. Rev. Stat. Ann. § 169-B:1 II [1979]).

In the decades since *Gault* and *McKeiver*, many states have revised their juvenile codes' statement of legislative purpose, de-emphasized rehabilitation and the child's "best interests," and asserted the importance of public safety, punishment, and accountability in the juvenile justice system (Feld 1988b; Sheffer 1995). States' redefined purposes of juvenile courts include penal objectives such as "the protection and safety of the public" (Cal. Welf. & Inst. Code § 202 [West Supp. 1988]), "the application of sanctions which are consistent with the seriousness of the offense" (Fla. Stat. Ann. § 39.001(2)(a) [West Supp. 1988]), to "render appropriate punishment to offenders" (Haw. Rev. Stat. § 571-1 [1985]), to "enforc[e] the legal obligations children have to society" (Ind. Code Ann. § 31-6-1-1 [Michie 1980]), "to promote the concept of punishment for criminal acts" [Tex. Fam. Code Ann. § 51.01(2)(A) [Vernon 1995]), and to "promote public safety [and] hold juvenile offenders accountable for such juvenile's behavior" (Kan. Stat. Ann. § 38-1601 [1997]).

A distinctive feature of many recent juvenile purpose clause amendments is the explicit emphases that they place on accountability and punishment (Walkover 1984; Giardino 1997).

Some courts recognize that these amended preambles signal basic changes in philosophical direction, "a recognition that child welfare cannot be completely 'child centered' " (*State ex rel. D.D.H. v. Dostert*, 269 S.E.2d 401, 409 n. 8 [W. Va. 1980]). Courts, as well as legislatures, increasingly acknowledge that punishment constitutes an acceptable purpose of juvenile courts' dispositions. The Washington Supreme Court reasoned that "sometimes punishment is treatment" and upheld the legislature's conclusion that "accountability for criminal behavior, the prior criminal activity and punishment commensurate with age, crime and criminal history does as much to rehabilitate, correct and direct an errant youth as does the prior philosophy of focusing upon the particular characteristics of the individual juvenile" (*State v. Lawley*, 91 Wash. 2d 654, at 656–657, 591 P.2d 772, at 773 [1979]). In a similar fashion, the Nevada Supreme Court endorsed punishment as an appropriate purpose of its juvenile courts. "By formally recognizing the legitimacy of punitive and deterrent sanctions for criminal offenses, juvenile courts will be properly and somewhat belatedly expressing society's firm disapproval of juvenile crime and will be clearly issuing a threat of punishment for criminal acts to the juvenile population (*In re Seven Minors*, 99 Nev. 427, at 432, 664 P.2d 947, at 950 [1983]).

The West Virginia Supreme Court thoughtfully examined the tensions between punishment and treatment and noted that "caring for the juvenile and controlling the juvenile are often quite contradictory processes. Much of our juvenile law at the moment is predicated upon a healthy skepticism about the capacity of the State and its agents to help children when they are incarcerated in one of the juvenile detention facilities. Thus, the control of juveniles and the treatment of juveniles (if that expression can be used without conjuring Kafkaesque images) are frequently irreconcilable goals" (*State ex rel. D.D.H. v. Dostert*, 269 S.E.2d 401, at 408–409 [W. Va. Sup. Ct. 1980]). The *D.D.H.* court summarized the inherent conflicts and limits of the juvenile court treatment model:

> In reaching the conclusion that rehabilitation alone does not exhaust the goals of a juvenile disposition, and that responsibility and deterrence are also important elements in our juvenile philosophy, we have not simply embraced a conservative theory that juvenile delinquents need to be punished. Liberals and conservatives alike may find solace in this opinion because we acknowledge what has been an unspoken conclusion: *our treatment looks a lot like punishment.* . . . [B]oth share the conclusion that *treatment is often disguised punishment.* . . . Once the rehabilitative model is accepted, the next fight is always to show that "treatment" is often a caricature—something worthy of a story of Kafka or a Soviet mental hospital. Therefore, while the conservatives throw up their hands because they believe punishment works better than treatment, the juvenile advocates return increasingly to punishment on the grounds that punishment is much less punishing than "treatment." (*D.D.H.*, 269 S.E.2d at 415–416)

Unlike *D.D.H.*, most legislators and judges fail to consider adequately whether a juvenile justice system can punish youths without providing them with criminal procedural safeguards, such as a jury trial. Any ancillary social benefits or individual reforms that may result from punishment do not obviate the need for procedural safeguards even if a state incarcerates a youth who committed a crime for a shorter term than an adult or calls the place of confinement a "reform school."

Juvenile Court Sentencing Statutes and Judicial Practices

Sentencing statutes and judicial practices provide other indicators of the purpose of juvenile court sentences. Originally, juvenile court judges imposed indeterminate and nonproportional sentences to meet a child's "real needs" (Mack 1909; Rothman 1980). In principal, an offense constituted only a diagnostic symptom, and treatment personnel released the offender once they determined that rehabilitation had occurred. By contrast, when courts punish offenders, they typically impose determinate or mandatory minimum sentences based on the gravity of the past offense. "The distinction between indeterminate and determinate sentencing is not semantic, but indicates fundamentally different public policies. Indeterminate sentencing is based upon notions of rehabilitation, while determinate sentencing is based upon a desire for retribution or punishment" (*In re Felder*, 93 Misc. 2d 369, at 377, 402 N.Y.S.2d 528, at 533 [N.Y. Fam. Ct. 1978]). Contrasting indeterminate, nonproportional, and offender-oriented dispositions with determinate, proportional, and offense-based sentences provides another indicator of juvenile courts' increasing reliance on punishment as a response to delinquency.

Indeterminate and Determinate Sentencing Statutes

Juvenile courts historically intervened to achieve the offender's "best interests." One early juvenile court advocate observed: "The problem for determination by the judge is not, Has this boy or girl committed a specific wrong, but What is he, how has he become what he is, and what had best be done in his interest and in the interests of the state to save him from a downward career. It is apparent at once that the ordinary legal evidence in a criminal court is not the sort of evidence to be heard in such a proceeding" (Mack 1909:119–120). Theoretically, judges responded to the conditions that caused a youth's delinquency, rather than punished him for past misconduct. The "treatment model" of delinquency disposition involved diagnoses, classification, prescription, intervention, and prognoses.

Most states' juvenile codes authorized juvenile courts to impose indeterminate sentences because penal therapists cannot predict in advance the course or duration of treatment necessary to attain success. While some statutes instruct judges to consider the "least restrictive alternative," most allow the court to confine a delinquent within a range for a period of years or until the of-fender reaches the age of majority or some other statutory limit. In *Gault*, for example, the judge committed the fifteen-year-old boy to the State Industrial School "for the period of his minority [that is, until age twenty-one], unless sooner discharged by due process of law" (387 U.S. at 7–8), although a judge could have sentenced an adult convicted of making a similar "lewd phone call of the adolescent sexual variety" to a maximum fine of fifty dollars or im-prisonment for up to two months. Traditionally, juvenile court judges exer-cised unrestricted discretion to dismiss, place on probation, remove from home, or institutionalize a youth.

In many states, once a judge commits a youth to the state's juvenile cor-rectional agency, the judge loses control over the youth, and the correctional authority or parole board decides when to release the juvenile from custody (Krisberg and Austin 1993). Indeterminate sentencing statutes typically pro-vide for an unspecified period of confinement and a wide range between the minimum and maximum terms available. Corrections officials base their re-lease decisions, in part, on youths' behavior during confinement and progress toward rehabilitative goals, rather than on formal standards or the offense. By contrast, when judges sentence juveniles under a determinate or presumptive sentencing framework, they typically impose proportional sanctions within a relatively narrow dispositional range based on the seriousness of the offense, offense history, and age. In several states, courts impose mandatory sentences based on the offense for which they convicted the youth. In other states, correctional administrators determine youths' presumptive length of institu-tional stay or eligibility for parole shortly after their commitment based on formal standards that prescribe terms proportional to the seriousness of the offense or prior record (Coates, Forst, and Fisher 1985).

For the first two-thirds of this century, utilitarian, preventive, and rehabil-itative ideologies dominated sentencing practices (Cullen and Gilbert 1982). Penal policy reflected the view that the state should treat rather than punish offenders, that the duration of confinement should relate to rehabilitative needs and treatment progress, and that therapists possessed the scientific ex-pertise and technical means to reform offenders. In chapter 3, I analyzed the precipitous decline of support for the rehabilitative ideal in the 1970s. The retreat from rehabilitation reawakened the quest for penal justice and provided the impetus to sentence similarly situated offenders equally based on more objective factors, such as the offense rather than personal characteristics. In a system in which successful reform of offenders continues to elude correctional administrators, the quest for consistent sentences acquires greater allure.

Currently, about half of the states use some type of determinate or man-datory minimum offense-based sentencing provisions to regulate aspects of juvenile dispositions, institutional commitment, or release (Feld 1988b; Shef-fer 1995; Torbet et al. 1996). As with legislative changes in waiver statutes, amendments to juvenile court sentencing statutes allocate to the judicial, leg-islative, and executive branches the power to make commitment and release decisions. Determinate sentencing provisions restrict judicial sentencing discretion, mandatory minimum statutes reflect legislative sentencing discretion, and correctional or parole release guidelines enable the executive branch to determine the length of confinement (Feld 1988b; Guarino-Ghezzi and Loughran 1996). And, as with waiver, these provisions use offense criteria to rationalize sentencing decisions, to increase the penal bite of juvenile court sanctions, and to enable legislators symbolically to demonstrate their "toughness" (Altschuler 1994). These strategies exemplify politicians' "felt need" to respond to serious and persistent offenders and provide additional indicators of juvenile courts' shift from treatment to punishment.

Controlling Judicial Discretion—Determinate Sentences in Juvenile Courts

In 1977 the state of Washington departed dramatically from the traditional rehabilitative model, revised its juvenile code to emphasize just deserts, and became the first state to enact a determinate sentencing statute for delinquents (Schneider and Schram 1983a, 1983b; Castellano 1986). Among other goals, the purposes of the new law were to "[p]rotect the citizenry from criminal behavior," to "[m]ake the juvenile offender accountable for . . . criminal behavior," and to "[p]rovide for *punishment commensurate with the age, crime, and criminal history of the juvenile offender*" (Wash Rev. Code Ann. § 13.40.010(2) [West Supp. 1996] emphasis added). The law used determinate, presumptive sentencing guidelines to achieve individual and systemic accountability and based youths' sentences on the seriousness and persistence of their offending, rather than their "real needs." According to the law's legislative sponsor, the code revisions reflect a movement "away from the *parens patriae* doctrine of benevolent coercion, and closer to a more classical emphasis on justice" (Becker 1979:307).

The Washington guidelines created three categories of offenders—serious, middle, and minor—with presumptive and proportional sentences for each based on a youth's age, offense seriousness, and prior record (Wash. Rev. Code Ann. § 13.40.020 [West Supp. 1996]; Fisher, Fraser, and Forst 1985). The statute provided standard dispositional ranges that included both upper and lower limits, specified aggravating and mitigating factors for sentencing within the range, and allowed a judge to depart from the standard range only if imposing the presumptive sentence would result in a "manifest injustice." A sentencing commission developed dispositional ("in/out") and length of stay guidelines based on the present offense, age, and prior record; prohibited confinement of a first or minor offender; and provided that serious offenders serve sentences ranging from 125 weeks to three years. Institutional staff make security level assignments, facility placements, program recommendations, and set a release date by the time a youth has served 60 percent of the minimum sentence imposed (Fisher, Fraser, and Forst 1985).

The Washington code revisions embodied a philosophical shift from treatment to punishment and significantly increased the proportionality and consistency of juvenile court sentencing practices (Ainsworth 1991). "Sentences in the post-reform era were considerably more uniform, more consistent, and more proportionate to the seriousness of the offense and the prior criminal record of the youth than were the sentences in the rehabilitation system which existed before 1978" (Schneider and Schram 1983b: 76). Analysts noted that "dispositions are carefully tailored to hold juveniles accountable in proportion to the culpability of their acts and their criminal history" (Walkover 1984:531) and reported a stronger relationship between the seriousness of offenses and youths' lengths of institutional stay than prevailed under the indeterminate regime (Fisher, Fraser, and Forst 1985). Despite greater equality and uniformity in sentencing, social structural and geographic variations in juvenile justice administration continued to produce higher rates of referral and confinement for minority than for white delinquents (Bridges et al. 1995).

Because *McKeiver* relied on the purported distinctions between punishment and treatment to deny delinquents a right to a jury trial, juveniles typically frame their constitutional challenges to penal sentencing provisions by requesting a jury trial to protect them from "punishment." After Washington adopted its just-deserts juvenile code, a youth argued that the amended purpose clause and determinate sentencing provisions rendered the proceedings criminal and entitled him to a jury trial (*State v. Lawley*, 91 Wash. 2d 654, 591 P.2d 772 [Wash. 1979]). As *McKeiver* and *Allen* illustrate, however, courts can manipulate the fluid concepts of "punishment" and "treatment" as flexibly as they maneuver between competing constructions of youths as vulnerable and dependent or as autonomous and responsible to achieve the courts' desired legal results. The Washington Supreme Court acknowledged that determinate sentences might seem to convert a delinquency proceeding into a criminal prosecution but reasoned in Orwellian fashion that "sometimes punishment is treatment" and concluded that proportional punishment could be as "rehabilitative" as individualized treatment (*Lawley*, 91 Wash. 2d at 656–657, 591 P.2d at 773–774). The dissent in *Lawley* analyzed the purpose clause and sentencing laws and argued that because juvenile courts first decide whether a youth committed a crime and then punish proportionally to the offense, the juvenile court must provide a jury trial. "[I]t is no longer the primary aim of the juvenile justice system to attend to the welfare of the offending child, but rather to render him accountable for his acts, to punish him, and to serve society's demand for retribution. While the punishment prescribed may well be less than that imposed upon offending adults for the same offense, it nevertheless involves . . . a loss of liberty" (*Lawley*, 91 Wash. 2d at 662, 591 P.2d at 775–776. The dissent concluded that once the state decided to punish juvenile offenders, then it must provide criminal procedural safeguards.

A decade later, the Washington Supreme Court reaffirmed its denial of a state constitutional right to a jury trial, primarily because it feared the adverse impact of jury trials on juvenile justice administration (*State v. Schaaf*, 109 Wash. 2d 1, 743 P.2d 240 [Wash. 1987]). Even though juvenile courts impose determinate sentences for criminal behavior, *Schaaf* asserted that youths differed in their degree of accountability and therefore their need for procedural safeguards. "The penalty, rather than the criminal act committed, is the factor that distinguishes the juvenile code from the adult criminal justice system. . . . [T]he purpose of the juvenile system is to provide an alternative to incarceration in adult correctional facilities" (109 Wash. 2d at 7, 743 P.2d at 243). However, any offense that carries a *potential* penalty of six months of confinement entitles an adult a right to a jury trial (*Baldwin v. New York*, 399 U.S. 6 [1969]), and the right does not hinge on whether a judge sentences the defendant to a minimum or maximum security facility. Again, a dissenting justice argued that Washington's juvenile courts "have so far departed from a 'rehabilitative' model of juvenile justice as to render any differences from adult criminal justice too minor to justify the withholding of the right to a jury trial" (*Schaaf*, 109 Wash. 2d at 23, 109 P.2d at 250–251). The dissent emphasized the many real similarities rather than the nominal differences between the juvenile and adult criminal justice systems and concluded that "rehabilitation no longer remains a substantial goal of the juvenile criminal justice system" (*Schaaf*, 109 Wash. 2d at 27, 743 P.2d at 253).

A number of other jurisdictions also employ offense-based sentencing principles in their juvenile courts (Sheffer 1995; Torbet et al. 1996). In New Jersey, juvenile court judges consider offense, criminal history, and statutory "aggravating and mitigating" factors to sentence juveniles determinately (N.J. Stat. Ann. §§ 2A:4A-43(a),-44(a), (d) [West 1987]). The New Jersey code revisions reflected a desire to promote greater proportionality and equality and to reduce "justice by geography" in sentencing (New Jersey Juvenile Delinquency Disposition Commission 1986). Oklahoma adopted a "serious and habitual juvenile offender" law that targets violent youths and persistent offenders with three separate felony adjudications and creates a mechanism to develop determinate sentencing guidelines (10 Okla. Stat. Ann. tit. 10 § 7303.5.3 [West 1995]). In 1994 the Arizona Legislature mandated the Arizona Supreme Court to promulgate dispositional guidelines that focused on the seriousness of a youth's present offense and prior record to regularize judges' institutional commitment decisions (McNulty and Russell 1995). In 1996, Texas adopted "Progressive Sanctions Guidelines" to "ensure . . . uniform and consistent consequences and punishments that correspond to the seriousness of each offender's current offense, prior delinquent history . . . [and] balance public protection and rehabilitation while holding juvenile offenders accountable" (Tex. Fam. Code Ann. § 59.001 [Vernon 1996]). The Texas guidelines assign a youth to one of seven "sanction levels" based on the seriousness of the offense and attach different dispositional consequences to each severity level. Some proponents of rehabilitative juvenile courts attempt to reconceptualize punitive principles like determinacy and proportionality—"progressive sanctions" and "graduated sanctions"—to serve treatment goals (Wilson and Howell 1995).

Legislative Sentencing Decisions—Mandatory Minimum
Terms of Confinement

Nearly half (twenty-two) of the states use some type of offense-based guidelines to regulate judicial sentencing discretion. These statutes typically include
age-and-offense criteria to define serious or persistent offenders and to prescribe their sentences. Juvenile codes in many states allow or require judges
to impose mandatory minimum sentences for certain serious crimes or "designated felonies" (Feld 1988b; Sheffer 1995). Under some laws, judges retain
discretion whether or not to impose the mandated sanctions, whereas others
require a judge to commit youths convicted of a defined offense for the mandatory minimum period (Torbet et al. 1996). In Delaware, for example, the
judges "shall" sentence any youth convicted of any second felony within one
year to a minimum term of six months' confinement (Del. Code Ann. tit. 10,
§ 1009 [Supp. 1996]).

While states' nomenclatures vary, these mandatory minimum sentencing
laws typically apply to "violent and repeat offenders," "mandatory sentence
offenders," "aggravated juvenile offenders," "habitual offenders," "serious juvenile offenders," or "designated felons" (e.g., Ala. Code § 12-15-71.1 [1990];
Colo. Rev. Stat. § 19-1-103 [1993]; Feld 1988b). The statutory criteria target
those violent and persistent juvenile offenders over whom juvenile courts do
not waive jurisdiction either because of their youthfulness or lesser culpability.
Youths charged with violent crimes like murder, rape, robbery, and aggravated
assault or those who have prior felony convictions constitute the primary
legislative concerns. Recent amendments add to the lists of "serious offenders"
youths charged with crimes involving firearms or who commit violent or drug
crimes on school grounds (e.g., Ark. Ann. Stat § 9-27-330(c) [1989]). And, as
with changes in waiver laws, the rate of legislative change accelerates. "Since
1992, fifteen states and the District of Columbia have added or modified statutes that provide for a mandatory minimum period of incarceration of juveniles committing certain violent or other serious crimes" (Torbet et al. 1996:
14).

Most of these mandatory minimum sentencing statutes target youths similar to or somewhat less serious or younger than those eligible for waiver or
automatic exclusion to criminal court. If juvenile courts retain jurisdiction
over serious offenders, then legislators use mandatory minimum sentences to
ensure that judges and corrections officials confine these youths for significant
terms. For youths convicted of these serious offenses, the statutes prescribe
mandatory minimum terms of confinement that range from twelve to eighteen
months, to age twenty-one, or to the adult limit for the same offense (Feld
1988b). For example, in Georgia, juvenile court judges may sentence a youth
convicted of a "designated felony" (Ga. Code § 15-11-37(2) [1994]) to the
Department of Youth Services for a term of five years with a minimum period
of confinement of twelve months or eighteen months, depending on the offense, in a "youth development center." If a youth commits a second "designated felony" or seriously injures a person sixty-two years of age or older,

then a judge has no discretion and must impose a mandatory eighteen-month minimum sentence. In 1990, Alabama enacted a "serious juvenile offender" law that provided mandatory minimum sentences—"shall be committed"—for youths convicted of a class A felony or felonies involving physical injury or the use of a firearm (Ala. Code § 12-15-71.1(a), (b) [1990]). In 1993, Louisiana enacted a mandatory sentencing statute that targeted youths convicted of violent felonies, for example, rape, kidnapping, and armed robbery, that provided that the juvenile "court *shall commit* the child . . . [to] *a secure detention facility* until the child attains the age of twenty-one years *without benefit* of parole, probation, suspension of imposition or execution of sentence" (La. Children's Code art. 897.1 [1993], emphasis added). Regardless of the statutory details, mandatory minimum sentences based on youths' serious or persistent offending preclude individualized consideration of their "real needs." *Allen* emphasized the possibility of "release after the briefest time in confinement" as one indicator of a therapeutic rather than punitive sanction. Moreover, mandating extended minimum terms of confinement for serious offenders increases the average length of stay and institutional populations and exacerbates overcrowding (Krisberg and Austin 1993).

Executive Sentencing Decisions—Correctional or Parole Release Guidelines

A number of states' departments of corrections have adopted administrative security classification and release guidelines that use offense criteria to specify proportional or mandatory minimum terms of institutional confinement (Forst, Friedman, and Coates 1985; Feld 1988b). These administrative guidelines constitute still another form of offense-based sentencing. Unlike presumptive or mandatory sentencing statutes that attempt to regulate judicial sentencing discretion, parole guidelines affect only those youths whom judges commit to states' correctional agencies. Except when constrained by presumptive or mandatory minimum sentencing statutes, judges in most states retain discretion over the "in-out" decision whether or not to commit a youth.

The Arizona Legislature required its Department of Corrections to adopt guidelines for juveniles' length of confinement to promote the sentencing goals of deterrence, public protection, and proportionality. The agency created five categories based on the seriousness of the offense and specified mandatory minimum terms that range in length from three to eighteen months to govern release decisions (Ariz. Rev. Stat. Ann. § 8-241 [West 1987]; Arizona Department of Corrections 1986). Minnesota's Department of Corrections adopted determinate "length of stay" guidelines based on the present offense and other "risk" factors, such as prior record and probation or parole status (Minnesota Department of Corrections 1980; Feld 1981b, 1995). Georgia's Division of Youth Services employs a "uniform juvenile classification system" that classifies committed delinquents into one of five categories of "public risk" with corresponding correctional consequences based primarily on the seriousness of the present offense (Forst, Friedman, and Coates 1985). The Massachusetts

Department of Youth Services uses an offense-based classification system to determine committed youths' minimum length of stay and level of security (Guarino-Ghezzi and Loughran 1996). The California Youthful Offender Parole Board decides the release eligibility of juveniles committed to the California Youth Authority based on a seven-category scale of offense seriousness (Forst and Blomquist 1991). Other states use similar offense-based classification systems to determine institutional lengths of stay and security levels of committed youths (Guarino-Ghezzi and Loughran 1996).

All of these de jure sentencing provisions—determinate and mandatory minimum laws, and correctional and parole release guidelines—share the common feature of offense-based dispositions that explicitly link the length of time delinquents serve to the seriousness of the crime they committed, rather than to their real needs. They represent different methods to regulate judicial discretion, to relate the duration and intensity of a youth's sentence to the offense and prior record, and to incorporate elements of penal proportionality. These offense-based statutory strategies reject basic assumptions of juvenile justice, for example, that juvenile sentences and youth corrections operate in the child's best interests, that individualized treatment requires an open-ended indeterminate process, and that the crime committed does not predict or determine the length of time required for reform. Moreover, these changes strongly contradict *McKeiver*'s rationale that juvenile courts sentence delinquents for the "alternative purpose" of rehabilitation.

"Blended Jurisdiction"—Enhanced Juvenile Sentencing Statutes

Although states' adoption of determinate and mandatory juvenile sentencing laws reflect the influence of just-deserts jurisprudence and punitive politics, delinquency sentences invariably differ from criminal sentences because juvenile courts' maximum age jurisdiction limits their potential duration. Because juvenile courts lose authority over offenders when they attain the age of majority or some other statutory termination date, they cannot fully achieve proportionality when sentencing either older chronic juveniles or those youths convicted of very serious crimes. The jurisdictional limits heighten public and political perceptions that juvenile courts inadequately punish or control some youths and provide impetus either to increase juvenile courts' sanctioning powers further or to transfer more youths to criminal courts.

Statutes that increase juvenile courts' punitive capacity or give criminal courts a juvenile or youthful offender sentencing option represent another offense-based sentencing strategy to respond to violent and persistent young offenders. These "blended" jurisdiction laws attempt to meld the sentencing authority of juvenile courts with that of criminal courts, to provide longer sentences for serious crimes than juvenile courts otherwise could impose, or to increase the "rehabilitative" sentencing options available to criminal courts (Feld 1995; Torbet et al. 1996). These blended sentences provide juvenile courts with the option to punish, as well as to treat, and criminal courts with alternatives to imprisonment for some youths charged with serious or repeated offenses. Several variants of "youthful offender," "blended," or "extended jurisdiction" sentences exist. The type of sanctions depend on whether the prosecutors try the youth initially in juvenile or in criminal court.

Convicted in Criminal Court and Sentenced as "Youthful Offender"

For decades, states and the federal government have used a "youthful offender" status to preserve "therapeutic" sentencing options in criminal courts following the trial of young offenders as adults. A youthful offender status constitutes an intermediate category of chronological juveniles sentenced as adults as well as young adult offenders, typically sixteen to twenty-one years of age at the time of sentencing. Youthful offender laws separate this group by age, either in separate facilities or in age-segregated sections within adult facilities, limit the maximum penalty that criminal courts may impose to a period shorter than that authorized for adults, and provide for some relief from disabilities of conviction following successful completion of the sentence. Under the federal Youth Corrections Act, subsequently repealed when Congress adopted the federal sentencing guidelines, federal judges had discretion to commit convicted offenders between the ages of sixteen and twenty-two to special facilities as youth offenders if they determined that the youth would "benefit" from treatment (18 U.S.C. §§ 5005–5026 [1976]). The California Youth Authority Act provides criminal court judges with the option of sentencing young adults and waived youths convicted as adults to the Youth Authority for housing and programs, rather than to prison, and the authority's jurisdiction continues until age twenty-five (Cal. Welf. & Inst. Code § 1731.5 [West 1995]). Because Florida prosecutors direct-file many chronological juveniles into criminal court (Bishop, Frazier, and Henretta 1989; Bishop and Frazier 1991), the state's Youthful Offender Act provides criminal court judges with an alternative to sentencing them all as adults (Fla. Stat. § 958 [1995]). Based on a presentence investigation report and applying statutory *Kent*-like criteria, a criminal court judge may sentence a youth either as a youthful offender or to prison. In New York, criminal court jurisdiction begins at age sixteen, but youths as young as thirteen years of age charged with murder or youths fourteen or fifteen years old charged with other violent crimes may be prosecuted as "juvenile offenders" (JOs). Criminal courts may give youths sixteen to nineteen years old a "youthful offender" (YO) status. Youths sentenced as JOs/YOs may receive a closed hearing, sealed record, or shorter sentence in a separate facility operated by the Division for Youth, rather than a straight sentence to the Department of Corrections (Singer 1996). Laws in several states give judges the option to sentence youths convicted as adults to some type of youthful status in lieu of prison commitment (Torbet et al. 1996).

Convicted in Juvenile Court but Sentence Increased

A second variant of "blended" sentencing begins with a youth's trial in juvenile court and then authorizes the judge to impose enhanced sentences beyond those used for ordinary delinquents (Feld 1995; Torbet et al. 1996). New Mexico, Minnesota, and Texas provide three different versions of these enhanced sanctions for youths whom judges have not transferred to criminal court for prosecution as adults.

In 1993, New Mexico created a three-tier classification of "delinquent offender," "youthful offender," and "serious youthful offender" (N.M. Stat. Ann. § 32A-2-3(C), (H), (I) [Michie 1993]; Mays and Gregware 1996). The prosecutor selects the category into which to charge a young offender based on age and offense. A youth sixteen or seventeen years of age and charged with first-degree murder constitutes a "serious youthful offender," and the court *must sentence* the youth as an adult. "Youthful offenders" consist of juveniles fifteen to eighteen years of age charged with legislatively designated aggravated or violent crimes, such as second-degree murder, assault, rape, or robbery, or youths charged with any felony who have had three prior felony adjudications within the previous two-year period. All "delinquents" and "youthful offenders" in New Mexico enjoy a statutory right to a jury trial in juvenile court; the same judge presides over a case whether it is tried as a juvenile or criminal proceeding (Mays and Gregware 1996). Following conviction as a "youthful offender," the juvenile court judge conducts a quasi-waiver sentencing hearing to decide whether to sentence the juvenile as an adult or as a youthful offender. Depending on the judge's assessment of a youth's "amenability to treatment or rehabilitation," the court may impose either an adult criminal sentence or a juvenile disposition with jurisdiction extended until age twenty-one (N.M. Stat. Ann. § 32A-2-20 [Michie 1993]). Essentially, New Mexico tries and convicts youths in juvenile court with adult criminal procedural safeguards, and then the judge decides whether to impose an extended juvenile sentence or an adult sentence.

In 1995, Minnesota created an intermediate category for serious young offenders called "extended jurisdiction juvenile" (EJJ) prosecutions (Minn. Stat. Ann. § 260.126 [West 1995]; Feld 1995). The statutes restrict eligibility for EJJ prosecutions to youths sixteen years of age or older and charged with presumptive commitment to prison offenses like murder, rape, aggravated robbery, and assault, to youths whom judges decline to waive to criminal courts and sentence instead as EJJs, and to younger juveniles whom judges determine in an EJJ hearing meet offense-based "public safety" criteria (Feld 1995). Juvenile courts try these EJJ youths in juvenile courts but provide them with all adult criminal procedural safeguards, including the right to a jury trial. The right to a trial by jury constitutes an essential component of this quasi-adult status, because the judge imposes both a delinquency disposition and an adult criminal sentence, the execution of which is stayed, pending compliance with the juvenile sentence (Minn. Stat. Ann. § 260.126 [West 1995]; Feld 1995). The EJJ law extends juvenile court dispositional jurisdiction until age twenty-one rather than ending at age nineteen as it does for ordinary delinquents. If an EJJ youth violates the conditions of the juvenile sentence, then the court may revoke the probation and execute the adult criminal sentence (Feld 1995). Trying youths in juvenile courts with adult criminal procedural safeguards preserves access to juvenile correctional resources, provides longer periods of correctional supervision and control, and retains the possibility of adult incarceration if youths fail on probation or reoffend. Several other states recently have emulated this blended sentencing strategy (Torbet et al. 1996).

In 1987, Texas adopted a determinate sentencing law for juveniles convicted of certain violent crimes or as habitual offenders to provide an alternative to sentencing them either as ordinary delinquents or waiving them for adult prosecution (Tex. Fam. Code Ann. §§ 53.045, 54.04(d)(3) [Vernon 1996 & Supp. 1998]; Dawson 1988, 1990b; Fritsch, Hemmens, and Caeti 1996). To invoke the determinate sentencing law, the prosecutor must allege one of the enumerated violent or habitual crimes in a petition submitted to a grand jury. If a youth is indicted and convicted, "the court or jury may sentence the child to commitment to the Texas Youth Commission with a possible transfer to the institutional division or the pardons and paroles division of the Texas Department of Criminal Justice for a term of not more than" forty years for a capital or first-degree felony, twenty years for a second-degree felony, or ten years for a third-degree felony (Tex. Fam. Code Ann. § 54.04(d)(3) [Vernon Supp. 1998]). Juveniles receive the same procedural rights as do adult criminal defendants, including the right to a jury trial. Juveniles begin their determinate sentences in juvenile facilities, and at age eighteen, a court conducts a sentencing review hearing using *Kent*-like statutory criteria to decide whether to retain them within the juvenile correctional system for the duration of their minority, until age twenty-one, or to complete their determinate sentence in the adult correction system. The Texas law greatly increases the power of juvenile courts to impose substantial sentences on youths under fifteen years of age, the minimum age for transfer to criminal court, as well as on older juveniles, and gives prosecutors a powerful plea-bargaining tool and alternative to adult prosecution (Dawson 1988, 1990b; Fritsch, Hemmens, and Caeti 1996). In 1995 the Texas Legislature increased from the original list of six to fourteen the number of offenses for which youths could receive determinate sentences and increased the maximum length of determinate sentences from thirty to forty years (Tex. Fam. Code Ann. §§ 53.045, 54.04(d)(3) [Vernon 1996 & Supp. 1998]). Determinately sentenced youths served actual terms considerably longer than those served by youths convicted as ordinary delinquents (Fritch, Hemmens, and Caeti 1996). A few other states, for example, Colorado and Massachusetts, have enacted provisions like Texas's that enable a juvenile court judge to impose a sentence on a youth convicted of a serious crime that extends beyond the maximum age of the juvenile court dispositional jurisdiction with completion of the sentence in adult correctional facilities (Torbet et al. 1996).

Although the New Mexico, Minnesota, and Texas statutes differ in many details, the blended jurisdiction strategies share several common features. Because these laws provide intermediate offenders with adult criminal procedural safeguards, they can openly acknowledge the reality of juvenile punishment. Once a state gives a juvenile the right to a jury trial and other criminal procedural safeguards, then it retains the option to punish without apology and thereby gains greater flexibility to treat a youth as well. These various enhanced sentencing strategies recognize that age-jurisdictional limits of juvenile courts create binary forced choices, either juvenile or adult, either treatment or punishment. By trying a juvenile with criminal procedural rights, these states preserve the option to extend jurisdiction for a period of several years or more beyond that available for ordinary delinquents. Finally, these statutes recognize the futility of trying to rationalize social control in two separate systems. These blended provisions embody the procedural and substantive convergence between juvenile and criminal courts, provide a conceptual alternative to binary waiver statutes, and recognize that adolescence constitutes a developmental continuum that requires an increasing array of graduated sanctions. Some proponents of juvenile courts criticize blended jurisdiction provisions because they erode the conceptual and legal foundations for an entirely separate juvenile justice system (Zimring 1998).

Juvenile Court Sentencing Practices—Principle of Offense and Racial Disparities

A number of actors in the juvenile justice process—police, intake social workers, detention personnel, prosecutors, and judges—make dispositional decisions; their decisions cumulate and affect the judgments that others make subsequently (McCarthy and Smith 1986; Bishop and Frazier 1988). Juveniles' prior records reflect discretionary decisions that people in the justice process make over time, and previous dispositions affect later sentences (Henretta, Frazier, and Bishop 1986). Despite recent changes in sentencing laws, however, juvenile court judges continue to exercise greater discretion than do criminal court judges because juvenile courts' *parens patriae* ideology still presumes a need to look beyond the offense to the child's best interests.

Within this flexible dispositional process, minority youths are disproportionately overrepresented at every stage of the juvenile justice process (Krisberg et al. 1987; Pope and Feyerherm 1990a, 1990b). An analytic review of juvenile court sentencing research concluded that "there are race effects in operation within the juvenile justice system, both direct and indirect in nature" (Pope and Feyerherm 1992:41). Studies consistently report that racial disparities exist in case processing after controls for offense variables, that inequalities occur at various stages of the process in different jurisdictions, and that discriminatory decisions increase minority overrepresentation as youths proceed further through the system. For example, a recent study of juvenile justice decision making in Florida reported that black youths make up 15 percent of the youth population at risk for delinquency, 28 percent of those arrested and larger proportions of those arrested for drug and violent crimes, but over half of the youths confined in short-term detention facilities (62%) and long-term correctional institutions (60%) (Bishop and Frazier 1996).

The discretion inherent in a *parens patriae* system raises concerns that the cumulative impact of individualized decisions contributes to the substantial overrepresentation of minority youths. What methodologists might call "sample selection bias," others may view as racial discrimination. Quite apart from overt discrimination, juvenile justice personnel may perceive black youths as more threatening or likely to reoffend than white youths and may process them differently (Sampson and Laub 1993; Singer 1996). More benignly, if juvenile courts sentence youths on the basis of social circumstances that indirectly mirror socioeconomic status or race-related characteristics, then minority youths may receive more severe dispositions than do white youths because of their personal conditions or real needs.

In chapter 2, I argued that Progressives deliberately designed and intended juvenile courts to discriminate between white middle-class children like their own and the children of poor and immigrant parents, those "other people's children" (Platt 1977; Rothman 1980). If young people's real needs differ because of social circumstances, such as poverty or a single-parent household that correlate strongly with race, then the ideology of "individualized treatment" necessarily will have a racially disparate impact. Racial disproportionality in a system designed to differentiate on the basis of social structural, economic, or personal circumstances should come as no surprise. But in a society formally committed to racial equality, punitive sentences based on social and personal attributes that produce a disparate racial impact implicate the legitimacy, fairness, and justice of the process.

Minority overrepresentation may also reflect racial group differences in involvement in criminal activity. As we recall from chapter 6, for example, police arrested black youths for violent offenses at rates about five times higher than they did white youths; differences in the seriousness of minority youths' offenses may account for apparent sentencing disparities. If court personnel and judges base their screening decisions and youths' sentences on juveniles' offenses and criminal history, then minority overrepresentation may result from real differences in the incidence and prevalence of offending by race (Wolfgang, Figlio, and Sellin 1972; Hindelang 1978).

The structural context of juvenile justice decision making also may redound to the detriment of minority juveniles. For example, urban courts tend to be more formal and to sentence all juveniles more severely (Kempf, Decker, and Bing 1990; Feld 1991, 1993b). Urban courts also have greater access to detention facilities, and youths held in pretrial detention typically receive more-severe sentences than do those who remain at liberty (Feld 1993b; Bishop and Frazier 1996). Proportionally, more minority youths live in urban environs and police disproportionately arrest and detain them for violent and drug crimes (Snyder and Sickmund 1995). Thus, the geographic and structural context of juvenile justice administration, crime patterns, urbanism, "underclass threat," and race may interact to produce minority overrepresentation in detention facilities and correctional institutions.

The Principle of Offense

Despite sometimes discrepant findings, two general conclusions emerge clearly from the research evaluating juvenile court sentencing practices. First, the principle of offense—present offense and prior record—accounts for virtually all the variance in juvenile court sentences that can be explained. Every methodologically rigorous study of juvenile court sentencing practices reports that judges focus primarily on the seriousness of the present offense and prior record when they impose sentences; these legal and offense variables typically explain about 25 to 30 percent of the variance in sentencing (Clarke and Koch 1980; Horowitz and Wasserman 1980; McCarthy and Smith 1986; Fagan, Forst, and Vivona 1987; Bishop and Frazier 1996). In short, juvenile court judges attend to the same primary sentencing factors as do criminal court judges. Second, after controlling for legal and offense variables, the individualized justice of juvenile courts produces racial disparities in the sentencing of minority offenders. Other than the principle of offense and age, gender, and detention status, youths' race appears as a significant factor in most multivariate sentencing studies (Pope and Feyerherm 1992; Bishop and Frazier 1996).

While youths' chronic or serious offending may indicate greater "treatment needs," courts necessarily respond to their criminal behavior regardless of their ability to change it. As noted in chapter 3, the President's Commission on Law Enforcement and Administration of Justice (1967a; 1967b) explicitly recognized the punitive character of juvenile court intervention and the legitimacy of society's claim to protection from youth crime and tacitly endorsed offense-based sanctions. Subsequently, several juvenile justice policy groups recommended that states replace indeterminate sentencing laws with formal dispositional criteria and sentences proportional to the seriousness of the offense (American Bar Association and Institute of Judicial Administration 1980e; National Advisory Committee on Criminal Justice Standards and Goals 1980).

Practical administrative and bureaucratic considerations impel judges to give primacy to offense factors when they sentence juveniles. Organizational desire to avoid public exposure, unfavorable political and media attention, and "fear of scandal" constrain judges to impose more-restrictive sentences on youths who commit more-serious offenses (Matza 1964; Cicourel 1968; Emerson 1969). One ethnographic study observed that

> juvenile court decision-making comes to be pervaded by a sense of *vulnerability* to adverse public reaction for failing to control or restrain delinquent offenders. ... [Fear of scrutiny and criticism increases pressures] to impose maximum restraints on the offender—in most instances incarceration. Anything less risks immediate criticism. But more than this, it also exposes the court to the possibility of even stronger reaction in the future. For given any recurrence of serious

illegal activity, former decisions that can be interpreted as "lenient" become difficult to defend. (Emerson 1974:624)

Other court analysts emphasize that the juvenile court judge is ultimately responsible and responsive to the public. "He will have to explain . . . why the 17-year-old murderer of an innocent matron was allowed to roam the streets, on probation, when just last year he was booked for mugging. . . . Somehow, an invoking of the principle of individualized justice and a justification of mercy on the basis of accredited social-work theory hardly seems appropriate on these occasions" (Matza 1964:122). By sentencing serious juvenile offenders more formally and restrictively, judges can deflect unfavorable retrospective scrutiny and political criticism.

Several organizational features further encourage judges to assign priority to youths' offenses. Juvenile court judges must administer heavy caseloads, reconcile individualized assessments with bureaucratic efficiency, respond to occasional external demands for severity, and maintain stable working relationships with social service professionals who may advocate for leniency. The principle of offense provides an efficient organizational tool with which to classify the "risks" that youths pose to the public and, by way of "scandal," to the court. Because juvenile courts routinely collect information about present offense and prior records, these factors provide a simple rule of thumb by which to make, defend, and legitimate sentencing decisions. One study reported that, despite claims of individualization, juvenile court judges appeared to base their sentencing decisions primarily on youths' present offense and prior record. "[C]omparisons of juvenile and adult sentencing practices suggest that juvenile and criminal courts in California are *much more alike than statutory language would suggest*, in the degree to which they focus on aggravating circumstances of the charged offense and the defendant's prior record in determining the degree of confinement that will be imposed" (Greenwood et al. 1983:51, emphasis added). Every multivariate quantitative study reports that the seriousness of the present offense and prior record constitute the primary variables explaining sentencing decisions (e.g., McCarthy and Smith 1986; Fagan, Slaughter, and Hartstone 1987; Bishop and Frazier 1988, 1996).

Racial Disparities in Sentencing

The second consistent finding from juvenile court sentencing research is that, after controlling for the present offense and prior record, individualized sentencing discretion is often synonymous with racial discrimination (Dannefer and Schutt 1982; McCarthy and Smith 1986; Krisberg et al. 1987; Pope and Feyerherm 1990a, 1990b, 1992). A review of earlier juvenile court sentencing studies found "Clear and consistent evidence of a racial differential operating at each decision level. Moreover, the differentials operate continuously over various decision levels to produce a substantial accumulative racial differential which transforms a more or less heterogeneous racial arrest population into a homogeneous institutionalized black population" (Liska and Tausig 1979:

205). A review of juvenile justice sentencing two decades later reached the same conclusion. "[R]acial discrimination appears most widespread—minorities (and youth in predominantly minority jurisdictions) are more likely to be detained and receive out-of-home placements than whites regardless of 'legal' considerations. Because processing in the juvenile justice system is deeply implicated in the construction of a criminal (or 'prior') record, experiences as a juvenile serve as a major predictor of future processing" (Sampson and Lauritsen 1997:362).

As noted previously, some of the differences in minority youths' overrepresentation in the juvenile justice system reflects real differences in rates of offending by race (Wolfgang, Figlio, and Sellin 1972; Hindelang 1978; FBI 1996). However, multivariate research that controls for the effects of the seriousness of the present offense, prior record, and other legal variables would account for those differentials. Concerns about racial disparities focus on the residual effects of a youth's race after controlling for those other variables. In addition, analyses of self-reported delinquency by youths of different races concluded that "it does not appear that the differences in incarceration rates between racial groups can be explained by differences in the proportions of persons of each racial group that engage in delinquent behavior. Even if the slightly higher rates for more serious offenses among minorities were given more importance than is statistically indicated, the relative proportions of whites and minorities involved in delinquent behavior could not account for the observed differences in incarceration rates" (Huizinga and Elliot 1987: 212). While the principle of offense accounts for some degree of racial disparities, it does not account for the remaining differences in rates of incarceration by race (Krisberg et al. 1987).

In 1988, Congress amended the Juvenile Justice and Delinquency Prevention (JJDP) Act to require states receiving federal funds to ensure equitable treatment on the basis, inter alia, of race and to assess the sources of minority overrepresentation in juvenile detention facilities and institutions (42 U.S.C. § 5633(a)(16) [Supp. 1993]). In response to this JJDP Act mandate, a number of states examined and found racial disparities in their juvenile justice systems (e.g., Bishop and Frazier 1988, 1996; Pope and Feyerherm 1992; Krisberg and Austin 1993; Bridges et al. 1995; Kempf-Leonard, Pope, and Feyerherm 1995). A review of these evaluation studies reported that, after controlling for offense variables, minority youths were overrepresented in secure detention facilities in forty-one of forty-two states and in all thirteen of thirteen states that analyzed other phases of juvenile justice decision making and institutionalization (Pope 1994).

Discretionary decisions at various stages of the justice process amplify racial disparities as minority youths proceed through the system and result in more-severe dispositions than for comparable white youths. The research emphasizes the importance of analyzing juvenile justice decision making as a multistage process, rather than focusing solely on the final dispositional decision. For example, dramatic increases in referral rates of minority youths to juvenile courts in seventeen states resulted in corresponding increases in detention and institutional placement (McGarrell 1993). Juvenile courts detain black youths at higher rates than they do white youths charged with similar offenses, and detained youths typically receive more-severe sentences (Bortner and Reed 1985; Frazier and Cochran 1986; Krisberg and Austin 1993).

Most recent studies confirm that minority youths receive more-severe dispositions than do white youths even after controlling for relevant legal variables. While offense criteria affect initial screening, detention, and charging decisions, as cases progress through the adjudicatory process, youths' race affects their dispositions and minority youths receive more-severe sentences. Research in Florida controlled for legal and process variables and found that a juvenile's race directly affected decisions at several stages. While black youths made up 28.4 percent of the initial referrals, court intake recommended formal processing of 59.1 percent of the cases involving black youths, compared with 45.6 percent of the white youths. Youths formally petitioned to juvenile court included 47.3 percent of black youths, compared with 37.8 percent of the white youths, thereby increasing the minority composition of the cohort from 28.4 percent black to 32.4 percent black (Bishop and Frazier 1988). Of the youths adjudicated delinquent, the courts incarcerated 29.6 percent of black youths, compared with 19.5 percent of white youths. "The probability of an initial referral resulting in movement through the system to a disposition of incarceration/transfer is nearly twice as great for blacks (10.2%) as for whites (5.4%)" (Bishop and Frazier 1988:251). While the principle of offense primarily governs juvenile justice responses to serious offenders, when offense factors do not dictate dispositions, justice personnel's exercise of discretion places minority youths at even greater disadvantage. "Black youths charged with minor offenses are considerably more likely to be adjudicated delinquent than white youths referred for identical offenses" (Bishop and Frazier 1988: 257). Analyses of more-recent Florida data reinforce these findings. "While the magnitude of the race effect varies from stage to stage, there is a consistent pattern of unequal treatment. Nonwhite youths referred for delinquent acts are more likely than comparable white youths to be recommended for petition to court, to be held in pre-adjudicatory detention, to be formally processed in juvenile court, and to receive the most formal or the most restrictive judicial dispositions" (Bishop and Frazier 1996:405–406).

A similar cumulative process of racial amplification appears in sentencing in California's juvenile justice system, where African American juveniles constitute 8.7 percent of the youth population but 37 percent of youths in confinement. Although police arrest black youths at rates 2.2 times greater than their share of the population, judges institutionalize them at rates 4.6 times greater than those of white youths (Krisberg and Austin 1993). Even among youths referred for violent felonies, California juvenile courts detained almost two-thirds of African Americans, compared with fewer than half of white juveniles, and sentenced to the California Youth Authority 11.4 percent of black youths compared with only 3.4 percent of white youths. "[R]ace does play at least an indirect role in juvenile court decision making. . . . African-American males are being overrepresented at extremely high rates from the

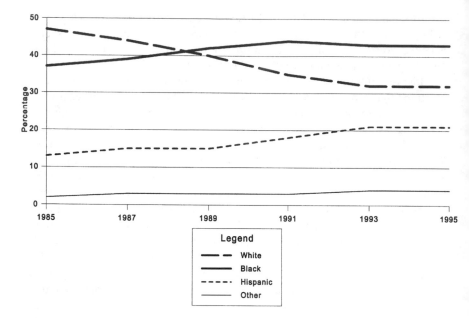

FIGURE 7.1. Juveniles in custody, by race/ethnicity (one day counts for public facilities). *Source*: Office of Juvenile Justice and Deliquency Prevention (1996) *Census of Public and Private Detention, Correctional and Shelter Facilities, 1985–1995* (Washington, D.C.: Office of Juvenile Justice and Deliquency Prevention), 1

point of detention through commitments to the state training school system ... [and] continue to receive more severe dispositions than their counterparts" (Krisberg and Austin 1993:133).

A comprehensive review of the juvenile sentencing literature concluded that most studies found racial disparities in juvenile justice administration and that cumulative decisions by court personnel heightened these disparities as youths moved through the system (Pope and Feyerherm 1990a, 1990b). Two-thirds of the studies reviewed showed either direct or indirect evidence of discrimination against minority youths. A national study of incarceration trends reported incarcerations rates for minority youths three to four times greater than those of white juveniles (Krisberg et al. 1987). Moreover, judges sentenced most minority youths to public secure facilities and committed more white youths to private facilities. By 1991, juvenile courts confined fewer than one-third (31%) of non-Hispanic white juveniles in public long-term facilities; minority youths made up more than two-thirds (69%) of confined youths (Snyder and Sickmund 1995). Juvenile courts committed black juveniles at a rate nearly five times higher than that of white youths, and blacks constituted 49 percent of all youths in institutions (Snyder and Sickmund 1995).

Figure 7.1 depicts one-day counts of youths confined in public detention and correctional facilities. It provides one indicator of the proportional changes in the racial composition of institutional populations for the 1985–

1995 period. During the decade, the overall numbers of youths in custody on a given day increased almost 40 percent, from 49,322 to 68,983. Despite the overall increase in daily custody populations, the percentage of white juveniles confined in public facilities actually *declined* 7 percent, while the percentage of confined black juveniles *increased* almost 63 percent. Thus, the overall increases and percentage changes reflect the sharp growth in minority youth in confinement. Because of these changes in the numerical composition of confined delinquents, the proportion of white juveniles in custody declined from 47 to 32 percent of all youths, while the proportion of blacks increased from 37 to 43 percent and that of Hispanics increased from 13 to 21 percent of all confined youths.

Although the principle of offense accounts for most of the racial differences in youths' sentences, two features associated with the principle of individualized justice also explain the impact of race on dispositions. In a system of individualized justice, "parental sponsorship" and "residential space availability" may qualify or modify traditional criminal sentencing principles (Matza 1964). To the extent that juvenile court sentencing decisions reflect a desire to "avoid scandals," the ability of parents to provide "outpatient" supervision and community controls may shape youths' dispositions. The number of parents in a household provides juvenile justice personnel with a shorthand tool to assess the levels of supervision available, influences case processing decisions, and adversely affects black youths (Singer 1996). Juvenile court personnel whom researchers questioned about racial disparities in case processing responded that "delinquent youths from single-parent families and those from families incapable of (or perceived to be incapable of) providing good parental supervision are more likely to be referred to court and placed under state control" (Bishop and Frazier 1996:409). Juvenile court personnel felt that even though black youths' social circumstances placed them at a systematic disadvantage because larger proportions came from single-parent households, courts properly considered these factors when they screened and sentenced youths. If one subscribes to a utilitarian or treatment ideology, then these kinds of variations in youths' personal backgrounds and their real needs *should affect* case outcomes.

The availability of public bed space and parents' ability to purchase private treatment also may affect case processing and dispositional outcomes. As we recall from chapter 5, parents may "voluntarily" commit their children to private mental hospitals and chemical dependency facilities. This option provides middle-class families who have medical insurance with a dispositional alternative to processing minor and status offenders in the juvenile court. "Youths from affluent families may take advantage of these [private] treatment options and avoid formal processing. Minority youths who are less affluent can only obtain comparable services by being adjudicated delinquent and then committed to residential facilities" (Bishop and Frazier 1996:408). Moreover, disparities in the case processing of black youths occurred most conspicuously for those charged with less-serious offenses (Bishop and Frazier 1988, 1996). In a justice process attuned to "treatment needs," parents who can purchase private services may "buy" their children's way out of the system, while children of less-affluent parents proceed by default through the public sector. And if providing appropriate service to meet the child's real needs constitutes a primary concern of a system of individualized justice, then allowing affluent parents to purchase treatment simultaenously serves the child's best interests and reduces the state's fiscal burdens.

Juvenile courts, as extensions of criminal courts, give primacy to offense factors when they sentence youths. To the extent that *parens patriae* ideology legitimates individualization and differential processing, it also exposes "disadvantaged" youths to the prospects of more extensive state intervention. Of course, if states provided exclusively benign and effective treatment services to youths in institutions, then this might mute some of the concerns about racial disparities or socioeconomic inequalities.

Conditions of Confinement and Evaluations of Effectiveness

Examining juvenile correctional facilities and evaluating their effectiveness provide another indicator of the shift from treatment to punishment in juvenile justice. Juvenile courts intervene extensively in the lives of many young offenders. Juvenile court judges removed from their homes more than one-quarter (28%) of youths petitioned and adjudicated delinquent and placed them in group homes, privately operated facilities, ranches, camps, "boot camps," or training schools (Snyder and Sickmund 1995). Courts and correctional administrators confined about three-quarters of youths placed in public long-term facilities in training schools (Snyder and Sickmund 1995). Between 1979 and 1989 the rate of juvenile confinement increased 45 percent and the absolute numbers of youths in confinement increased 30 percent, despite an 11 percent decline in the number of eligible youths in the population during the decade (Altschuler 1994). Another study reported that the rate of confinement of juveniles increased from 241 per 100,000 juveniles in 1975 to 353 per 100,000 in 1987, or about 45 percent, and the number of children confined in public facilities increased 19 percent (National Research Council 1993). Reflecting the racial disparities in juvenile court sentencing practices, minority youths now constitute the majority of all offenders confined in training schools (Snyder and Sickmund 1995).

The Supreme Court in *Gault* correctly perceived incarceration as a severe penalty, a substantial deprivation of autonomy, and a continual reminder of one's delinquent status, all of which constitute elements of punishment (387 U.S. at 26–27). The contradictions between the rhetoric of rehabilitation and the reality of conditions of confinement motivated the *Gault* Court to grant juveniles some procedural safeguards.

> [H]owever euphemistic the title, a "receiving home" or an "industrial school"
> for juveniles is an institution of confinement in which the child is incarcerated

for a greater or lesser time. His world becomes "a building with whitewashed walls, regimented routine, and institutional hours...." Instead of mother and father and sisters and brothers and friends and classmates, his world is peopled by guards, custodians, state employees, and "delinquents" confined with him for anything from waywardness to rape and homicide. (*Gault*, 387 U.S. at 27)

Punitive delinquency institutions have characterized the juvenile justice system from its inception. Historical analyses of the early training schools described institutions that failed to rehabilitate and scarcely differed from their adult penal counterparts (Schlossman 1977; Rothman 1980). One account of juvenile correctional programs under the aegis of Progressivism concluded: "The descent from the rhetoric to the reality of juvenile institutions is precipitous. ... No matter how frequently juvenile court judges insisted that their sentences of confinement were for treatment and not punishment, no matter how vehemently superintendents declared that their institutions were rehabilitative and not correctional, conditions at training schools belied these claims" (Rothman 1980:268).

Conditions of Confinement

Evaluations of juvenile correctional facilities in the decades following *Gault* reveal a continuing gap between the rhetoric of rehabilitation and its punitive reality. The titles of some of the criminological and journalistic studies of juvenile correctional facilities reveal their content: *Juvenile Victimization: The Institutional Paradox* (Bartollas, Miller, Dinitz 1976), *Neutralizing Inmate Violence: Juvenile Offenders in Institutions* (Feld 1977), *Weeping in the Playtime of Others: America's Incarcerated Children* (Wooden 1976), and *Bodily Harm: The Pattern of Fear and Violence at the California Youth Authority* (Lerner 1986). Research in Massachusetts described violent and punitive facilities in which staff physically punished inmates and frequently failed to prevent inmates' physical abuse and homosexual rape by other inmates (Feld 1977, 1981a). Aggressive, dominant youths oppressed the lower-status inmates in the cottages. "The direct physical assaults and abuse were substantial and real. The attendant psychological trauma was equally apparent. These victims of terrorization were afraid of other inmates. Their fear emboldened others who, by their aggression, reinforced their fear" (Feld 1977:160). A contemporaneous study in Ohio revealed a similarly violent and oppressive institutional environment to "rehabilitate" young delinquents. Black inmates dominated the institutional subculture, and white juveniles experienced material, physical, and sexual exploitation. The study indicted the correctional system as "anti-therapeutic, anti-rehabilitative, and as exploitative and demeaning of keepers and kept alike" (Bartollas, Miller, and Dinitz 1976:259). A study of the Texas juvenile correctional system found extensive staff and inmate violence, degrading make-work tasks, beating and hazing of "fresh fish" by other boys and by staff, "picking" for hours at a time with heavy picks, and "grass pulling" by hand for six hours per day (Guggenheim 1978). The California Youth Authority (CYA) sought to implement the juvenile court's "rehabilitative ideal." In the 1960s, staff introduced into the CYA juvenile institutions a variety of psychologically oriented treatment programs, such as group therapy and guided-group interaction, experimented with and evaluated many models of diagnoses and treatment, and sought without success effective treatment modalities (Krisberg and Austin 1993). Despite these efforts, by the 1980s, youths committed to the CYA system clearly experienced punishment rather than treatment in overcrowded and dangerous youth prisons (Lerner 1986; Forst and Blomquist 1991). The CYA conducted an extensive review of its institutions and concluded that "a young man convicted of a crime cannot pay his debt to society safely. The hard truth is that the CYA staff cannot protect its inmates from being beaten or intimidated by other prisoners" (Lerner 1986:12). The research attributed the violence to inappropriately designed facilities, inadequate staffing, and substantial overcrowding, all of which "promote the formation and ascendancy of prison gangs" (Lerner 1986:14). An evaluation of Louisiana training schools described institutions populated predominantly by black juveniles, whom guards regularly physically abused, kept in isolation for long periods, restrained with handcuffs, and confined in "punitive" facilities surrounded by high chain-link fences topped with coiled razor wire (Human Rights Watch 1995). Observers described educational, vocational, and clinical programs as meager or nonexistent. "The physical surroundings of the four correctional facilities foster intimidation and punishment. The programming and counselling are inadequate to provide a full treatment program and . . . there was little evidence that the children were being treated with respect and dignity at most times" (Human Rights Watch 1995:40).

A study sponsored by the Office of Juvenile Justice and Delinquency Prevention (OJJDP), *Conditions of Confinement: Juvenile Detention and Corrections Facilities*, used nationally recognized professional standards to assess the quality of 984 juvenile detention centers and training schools that housed more than two-thirds (69%) of all the confined delinquents in the nation (Parent et al. 1994). It reported endemic institutional overcrowding. In 1991, almost half (44%) of all long-term public institutions operated above their design capacity, as did more than three-quarters (79%) of the largest facilities, those which housed more than 350 inmates (Snyder and Sickmund 1995). Nearly two-thirds (62%) of all delinquent inmates resided in overcrowded facilities operating well above their design capacity. As states sentenced more youths to juvenile institutions, they increased their prisonlike character, relied more extensively on fences and walls to maintain perimeter security, and used surveillance equipment to provide internal security (Snyder and Sickmund 1995). The OJJDP evaluation classified nearly half (46%) the training schools as medium or maximum security facilities with perimeter fences, locked internal security, or both (Parent et al. 1994).

Coinciding with these post-*Gault* evaluation studies, lawsuits challenged conditions of confinement in juvenile correctional facilities and alleged that they denied inmates' their Fourteenth Amendment due process "right to treatment" or violated the Eighth Amendment's prohibition on "cruel and unusual punishment." When a state incarcerates a person for purpose of treatment or rehabilitation, due process requires that conditions of confinement bear some reasonable relationship to the purpose for which the state commits the individual (*Youngberg v. Romeo*, 457 U.S. 307 [1982]). "Persons who have been involuntarily committed are entitled to more considerate treatment and conditions of confinement than criminals whose conditions of confinement are designed to punish" (Youngberg, 457 U.S. at 322). Since *McKeiver* and juvenile court theory reject punishment for crimes, delinquents have a "due process interest in freedom from unnecessary bodily restraint which entitled them to closer scrutiny of their conditions of confinement than that accorded convicted criminals" (*Santana v. Collazo*, 714 F.2d 1172 [1st Cir. 1983]). Juvenile institutions constitute peculiar hybrids that combine elements of both mental health and *parens patriae* ideology with the ordinary criminal justice system. But, if "treatment" differs from "punishment," then juvenile corrections must do something more than simply confine criminals.

These "right to treatment," "cruel and unusual punishment," and "conditions of confinement" cases also provide an impartial judicial view of the reality of juvenile corrections. Judicial opinions and investigative reports from around the country report routine staff beatings of inmates, the use of psychotropic drugs for social control purposes, extensive reliance on solitary confinement, and a virtual absence of meaningful rehabilitative programs. During the 1970s and 1980s, courts attempted to define the nature of juvenile "treatment" that justified fewer procedural safeguards. More recent litigation attempted to define constitutionally adequate minimum conditions of confinement without prescribing any affirmative obligations to provide treatment (e.g., *D.B. v. Tewksbury*, 545 F. Supp. 896 [D.C. Ore. 1982]. Quite apart from their legal theories, however, these cases provide an independent assessment of conditions in juvenile institutions. Courts report that staff routinely beat inmates with a "fraternity paddle," injected them with psychotropic drugs for social control purposes, and deprived them of minimally adequate care and individualized treatment (*Nelson v. Heyne*, 355 F. Supp. 451 [N.D. Ind. 1972], 491 F.2d 352 [7th Cir. 1974]*aff'd, cert. den., Heyne v. Nelson*, 417 U.S. 976 [1974]). Other judges found inmates confined in dark, cold, dungeonlike cells in their underwear, routinely locked in solitary confinement, and subjected to a variety of punitive practices (*Inmates of Boys' Training School v. Affleck*, 346 F. Supp. 1354 [D.R.I. 1972]). Decisions in Texas found numerous instances of physical brutality and abuse, including hazing by staff and inmates, staff-administered beatings and teargassing, homosexual assaults, excessive use of solitary confinement, repetitive and degrading make-work, and minimal clinical services (*Morales v. Turman*, 383 F. Supp. 53 [E.D. Tex. 1974], *rev'd on other grounds*, 535 F.2d 864 [5th Cir. 1976]). One juvenile correctional system confined youths in padded cells with no windows or furnishings and only flush holes for toilets and denied inmates access to all services, programs, and reading materials except a Bible (*Morgan v. Sproat*, 432 F. Supp. 1130 [S.D. Miss. 1977]). Another court found inmates locked in solitary confinement, beaten and sprayed with mace by staff, required to scrub floors with a toothbrush, and subjected to punitive practices, such as standing and sitting for prolonged periods without changing position (*State v. Werner*, 161 W. Va. 192, 242 S.E.2d 907 [1978]). One judge found that the conditions of juvenile pretrial detainees who were held in an adult jail were deliberately punitive and worse than those experienced by adult convicts (*Tewksbury*, 545 F. Supp. 896). Reports of abusive practices in the press and in other opinions describe youths shackled spread-eagled to their bed frames, locked in isolation for "mouthing off" or swearing and restrained with handcuffs, leather straps, or leg irons (Krisberg et al. 1986; *Alexander S. v. Boyd*, 876 F. Supp 773 [D.S.C. 1995]). A review of additional, unreported cases litigating conditions of confinement around the country concluded that there is "growing evidence that harsh conditions of confinement continue to plague juvenile detention centers and training schools" (Krisberg et al. 1986:32). Nearly two-thirds (65%) of all delinquents confined in training schools reside in facilities subject to a court order or consent decree governing conditions of confinement and the adequacy of the "treatment" programs (Parent et al. 1994). It is unfortunate, that these cases are not atypical, as the list of judicial opinions documenting institutional abuses demonstrates (e.g. Krisberg et al. 1986; Feld 1995; *Alexander S.*, 876 F. Supp 773).

Despite extensive judicial findings of deplorable conditions of confinement, juvenile correctional facilities probably remain less harsh or abusive than most adult prisons. Interviews with violent juvenile offenders confined in training schools and comparable waived youths placed in adult correctional facilities indicate that the juveniles rated their training schools' treatment and programs, services, and institutional personnel more positively than did the youths confined in prisons (Forst, Fagan, and Vivona 1989). Even large training schools do not typically house as many inmates locked in individual cells as do adult maximum security prisons. Moreover, youths incarcerated in the juvenile correctional system may exhibit lower recidivism rates than do comparable waived youths incarcerated in adult prisons. One study compared recidivism rates of fifteen-and sixteen-year-old robbery and burglary offenders processed as adult offenders in two southeastern counties in New York with comparable youths processed as juveniles in two contiguous counties in northern New Jersey (Fagan 1995, 1996). It found that the New York "adult" robbery offenders had higher rates and frequency of reoffending than did those processed in New Jersey as juveniles, although the outcomes for the burglary offenders did not differ between the two systems. Another study compared juveniles whom prosecutors waived to criminal court in Florida with a matched set of equivalent cases retained in the juvenile justice system and found that the transferred youths reoffended more often, more quickly, and more seriously than did those youths confined in the juvenile correctional system (Bishop et al. 1996). Despite these apparent comparative advantages, however, juvenile institutions certainly do not provide such benign and therapeutic facilities as to justify depriving those confined in them adequate procedural safeguards. Rehabilitative euphemisms, such as "provid[ing] a structured treatment environment," should not disguise the punitive reality of penal confinement (OJJDP 1993:21).

In addition to conditions of confinement, the lengths of sentences that juvenile court judges impose also bear on the question of "punishment" and the need to furnish criminal procedural safeguards. Several factors affect juveniles' average length of stay in institutions around the country: states' upper age limit and dispositional jurisdiction, the correctional mix between state and local and public and private facilities, and state sentencing policies. In California, for example, juveniles sentenced to the California Youth Authority remain in custody an average of 523 days, although youths in most other states typically serve average sentences of about one year or less (Forst and Blomquist 1991). Across the nation, juveniles charged with crimes against the person serve about one year, and property offenders, about seven months on the average (Snyder and Sickmund 1995). Although violent juveniles serve shorter sentences than those that convicted adults may serve, substantial terms of confinement of one to two years or more are not inconsequential. As we recall from chapter 4, adult criminal defendants have a constitutional right to a jury trial for any offense that carries a *potential* sentence of six months or more of confinement (*Baldwin v. New York*). Delinquents confined for person, property, drug, and weapons offenses *all actually serve* average sentences longer than six months and thus would be entitled to a jury if tried as adults (Snyder and Sickmund 1995).

Although incarcerating youths in the general population in adult facilities holds little appeal, the well-documented prevalence of staff violence, inmate aggression, and homosexual rape in juvenile prisons provides scant consolation (Bartollas, Miller, and Dinitz 1976; Feld 1977, 1981a). Evaluations of juvenile institutions consistently attribute violent inmate subcultures to staff security arrangements and organizational policies. Authoritarian efforts to impose control and maintain internal security tend to alienate inmates from staff and increase levels of covert inmate violence within the subculture (Bartollas, Miller, and Dinitz 1976; Feld 1977; Lerner 1986). As states confine more youths in overcrowded facilities, staff security policies to manage larger groups of youths aggravate the violent character of the inmate subculture. Thus, organizational imperatives may frustrate even well-intended corrections personnel.

The recent changes in juvenile court sentencing legislation exacerbate the deleterious side effects associated with institutional overcrowding (Krisberg et al. 1986). Youths confined under get-tough sentencing laws to long terms often constitute the most serious and chronic delinquent population. Yet the institutions that house them often suffer from overcrowding, limited physical mobility, and inadequate program resources. Overcrowding also contributes to higher rates of inmate violence and suicide (Parent et al. 1994). These juvenile correctional "warehouses" exhibit most of the negative features of adult prisons and function as little more than youth prisons in which inmates "do time" (Greenwood and Zimring 1985). The large custodial institutions enable politicians to demonstrate their toughness, provide the public with a false sense of security, afford employment for correctional personnel, and minimize the demands placed on custodial staff to maintain institutional order but do little to improve the life chances of troubled youths (Greenwood and Zimring 1985; Bernard 1992).

Evaluation research indicates that incarcerating young offenders in large, congregate juvenile institutions does not effectively rehabilitate and may affirmatively harm them (Bartollas, Miller, and Dinitz 1976; Feld 1977; Andrews et al. 1990; OJJDP 1993). By contrast, experiments with supervision and treatment in the community suggest that many confined youths do not require institutional restraints (Coates, Miller, and Ohlin 1978). "[R]ecidivism among the most violent delinquents can be reduced up to 70% in small, secure, treatment-oriented juvenile facilities. This same type of juvenile does poorly when punished in large custody-oriented juvenile institutions" (Bernard 1992: 163–164). A randomized design that followed cases of five hundred youths confined in institutions or placed at home in intensive supervision programs reported that recidivism rates of the two groups did not differ substantially but that community supervision cost only about one-third as much as institutional confinement (Barton and Butts 1991).

As early as the 1960s, states experimented with community-based corrections in group homes and halfway houses as an alternative to institutional confinement (Krisberg and Austin 1993). In the early 1970s, the Massachusetts Department of Youth Services (DYS) closed its training schools for delinquents, returned most committed youths to their families or placed them in community-based facilities, and purchased private treatment services (Bakal 1973; Coates, Miller, and Ohlin 1978; Miller 1991; Guarino-Ghezzi and Loughran 1996). The "deinstitutionalization" experiment represented a "radical" attempt to "treat" young offenders in the community rather than to confine them. Residential programs in Massachusetts typically house fewer than thirty delinquents, and community programs and supervisory staff maintained correspondingly low caseloads (Krisberg and Austin 1993). Although the Massachusetts DYS operates a few small secure facilities, it contracts with private service providers for most nonsecure residential placements. Evaluations conducted fifteen years after Massachusetts closed its training schools concluded that recidivism rates remained comparable to or lower than those of other states' institutional populations and provided supervision and services at lower costs (Krisberg, and Steele 1991).

The Massachusetts experience and other research suggest that small community-based intensive supervision programs may reduce or postpone some delinquents' likelihood or rate of reoffending (Greenwood and Zimring 1985; Steele, Austin, and Krisberg 1989; OJJDP 1993). Promising programs provide a continuum of services from early secure care in small nondebilitating settings with a maximum of fifteen to twenty residents, individualized treatment, accountability, and case management, followed by community reintegration with extensive aftercare supervision and intervention (Fagan 1990; Krisberg and Austin 1993; Altschuler 1994). A few states' sentencing laws attempt to integrate punishment with treatment for serious and habitual offenders by combining a period of confinement with a period of aftercare that uses multiagency case-management techniques to facilitate a youth's reentry into the community (e.g., Cal. Welf. & Inst. Code § 501(a) [West 1995]).

Despite the manifest failures of large institutions to rehabilitate young offenders or reduce recidivism, the apparent success in Massachusetts with closing training schools (Coates, Miller, and Ohlin 1978; Guarino-Ghezzi and Loughran 1996), the relative superiority or cost-effectiveness of small community-based facilities over congregate facilities as humane living environments, and the feasibility of dealing with many youths in their communities rather than in confinement (Fagan 1990; Krisberg and Austin 1993; Altschuler 1994), the correctional pendulum currently swings toward incarcerating more delinquents for longer periods in institutions. We possess considerable evaluation research and knowledge about the types of correctional environments conducive to adolescent growth and development. And a century of experience with training schools and youth prisons demonstrates that they constitute the one extensively evaluated and clearly *ineffective* method to "treat" delinquents (OJJDP 1993). Despite these consistent research findings, politicians and correctional administrators rely on institutional controls and penal confinement with ever greater vengeance. Longer terms of punitive confinement in overcrowded custodial warehouses increasingly populated by minority youths hardly constitutes the therapeutic "alternative purpose" envisioned in *McKeiver*.

Treatment Effectiveness

Progressive reformers expressed considerable optimism that delinquents' youthfulness and greater malleability would enable them to respond more readily to treatment. By contrast, a comprehensive assessment of rehabilitation research conducted by the National Academy of Sciences questioned both the efficacy of juvenile justice interventions and the assumption that youths manifest greater treatment responsiveness.

> It may be implicitly assumed by many that age is an important element in classification because it is, or should be, easier to rehabilitate youthful offenders. *That seems a dubious prospect at best.* By any measure currently available, rates of involvement in criminal activity subsequent to adjudication are at least as high for juveniles as for adults with similar offense histories. It could be argued that given the same circumstances it might be more difficult to rehabilitate juveniles than adults because their very youth is indicative that they have no prolonged periods of satisfactory behavior patterns to which they might be restored by proper treatment (Sechrest, White, and Brown 1979:50–51, emphasis added).

Evaluations of juvenile institutional programs provide little evidence that they effectively treat youths or reduce their recidivism rates (Lab and Whitehead 1988, 1990; Whitehead and Lab 1989). Robert Martinson's negative assessment of "What Works?" concluded with the observation that "[w]ith few and isolated exceptions, the rehabilitative efforts that have been reported so far have had no appreciable affect on recidivism" and challenged the fundamental premises of the juvenile court (1974:25). A later review of correctional evaluation research concluded that "[t]he blanket assertion that 'nothing works' is an exaggeration, but not by very much" (Greenberg 1977:141). More-recent evaluations counsel skepticism about the availability of correctional programs that consistently or systematically rehabilitate adult or serious juvenile offenders (Lab and Whitehead 1988, 1990). "The current research literature provides no basis for positive recommendations about techniques to rehabilitate criminal offenders. The literature does afford occasional hints of intervention that may have promise, but to recommend widespread implementation of those measures would be irresponsible. Many of them would probably be wasteful, and some would do more harm than good in the long run" (Sechrest, White, and Brown 1979:102).

Evaluations of training schools, the most common form of institutional "treatment" for the largest numbers of serious and chronic delinquents, report consistently negative findings. Most state training schools "fail to reform . . . [and] make no appreciable reductions in the very high recidivism rates, on the order of 70 to 80 percent, that are expected for chronic offenders" (Greenwood and Zimring 1985:40). A recent analysis in Minnesota of recidivism rates of youths released from state correctional and private facilities in 1985 and 1991 found that between 53 and 77 percent continued their criminal careers into adulthood (Feld 1995; Minnesota Legislative Auditor 1995). The study concluded that "Minnesota's most-used residential programs have shown a limited ability to change entrenched criminal values and behavior patterns among juveniles" (Minnesota Legislative Auditor 1995:75). Analyses of recidivism among 926 males released from Washington State's residential facilities in 1982 reported that over half (58.8%) reoffended within one year and more than two-thirds (67.9%) reoffended within two years (Steiger and Dizon 1991). A study of 527 males released from ten residential facilities in Pennsylvania in 1984 reported that police rearrested more than half (57%) and that courts recommitted to residential facilities or prisons about one-quarter (23%) within two years (Goodstein and Sontheimer 1987). Given the realities of institutional "treatment," such negative results hardly come as a surprise. If a decade of schooling and a lifetime of parenting failed to socialize a youth, then it seems improbable that six months or a year in an overcrowded youth prison will "cure" delinquents.

Several factors account for the inability to demonstrate consistent, effective, and positive juvenile correctional outcomes. Many evaluations of treatment effectiveness lack methodological rigor (Sechrest, White, and Brown 1979). Others may use insufficiently sensitive outcome measures. For example, evaluations that use more sensitive measures of behavioral changes such as reductions in rates or severity of crime, suppression effects, or time between crimes, rather than simply recidivism measures, might better ascertain incremental effects of intervention (Fagan 1990). Many treatment programs lack a theoretical rationale or consistent intervention strategies based on that rationale. Some evaluation studies fail to assess whether the program staff actually implemented the prescribed treatment with integrity (Gendreau and Ross 1987). Finally, even if viable rehabilitative strategies exist, clinicians may lack techniques with which to classify offenders for appropriate forms of intervention to maximize their "responsivity." "[S]ome form of classification for treatment is necessary . . . [and] efforts to date have been too little grounded in theory, too simplistic, and too much focused on individual, personal characteristics of offenders. . . . At the root of classification problems is the lack of any dependable means of treatment or intervention for offenders, again whether for juveniles or adults" (Sechrest 1987:317). Thus, the failure to show treatment effects may reflect either methodological flaws, poorly conceived or implemented programs, an inability accurately to match subjects with programs, or the absence of viable methods successfully to treat serious or chronic young offenders.

Despite these generally negative results, evaluation researchers continue the quest for the elusive "rehabilitative" grail. One methodological strategy to identify "what works" entails meta-analyses or studies of studies. By coding each evaluation study on a number of variables (e.g., characteristics of the research design, subjects studied, type of treatment applied, and outcome measures) and combining and reanalyzing the studies, meta-analyses attempt to separate treatment effects from differences due to uncontrolled characteristics of the subjects or other limitations of research design (Logan and Gaes 1993). One meta-analysis of juvenile correctional treatment evaluations appearing in the professional literature between 1975 and 1984 and meeting certain criteria of methodological rigor concluded that "[t]he results are far from encouraging for rehabilitation proponents" (Lab and Whitehead 1988:77).

Proponents of treatment reject the contention that "nothing works" and offer literature reviews, meta-analyses, or program descriptions that report that some interventions may produce positive effects on selected clients under certain conditions (Gendreau and Ross 1979, 1987; Greenwood and Zimring 1985; Fagan 1990). Some analysts describe both the deficiencies of evaluation research and the elements of successful programs and argue that "we consider the 'nothing works' conclusion to be simplistic overreaction to the empirical evidence" (Greenwood and Zimring 1985:70). Others contend that "it is downright ridiculous to say 'Nothing works' " and attribute negative findings to service providers' failure to implement and maintain successful experimental treatment programs (Gendreau and Ross 1987:395). Some contend that "the conclusion that 'nothing works' may be based more on the absence of empirical evidence that treatment is effective than on conclusive evidence that treatment does not work" (Fagan 1990:236).

Several meta-analyses of evaluation studies concluded that some residential treatment programs for delinquents produce positive results. A meta-analysis of 111 studies published between 1960 and 1983 concluded that "delinquents . . . respond[ed] positively to treatment on many criteria. The change was modest in some cases, substantial in others, but overwhelmingly in a positive direction" (Garrett 1985:306). A review of 46 studies published between 1980 and 1990 reported that one of the ten treatment modalities—family therapy—produced positive effects and observed that "research on juvenile offenders is in its early stage of development" (Roberts and Camasso 1991:437). Another meta-analysis of 46 studies reported that treatment strategies that developed juvenile offenders' cognitive skills appeared to show positive effects and observed that rehabilitation occurs in "some settings when applied by some practitioners and when measured by some criteria" (Izzo and Ross 1990:141). A comprehensive meta-analysis reported positive effects when offenders received clinically appropriate psychological treatments "according to the principles of risk, need, and responsivity" (Andrews et al. 1990:384). Because offenders' needs differed, successful programs employed comprehensive diagnostic procedures to match them with appropriate services and used several complementary interventions for those at greatest risk of reoffending. One extensive meta-analysis of juvenile treatment programs concluded that treating delinquents decreased recidivism rates about 5 percent, from 50 to 45 percent (Lipsey 1992). The most recent, comprehensive meta-analysis of 200 studies of interventions with serious juvenile offenders reported that "[t]he average intervention effect for these studies was positive, statistically significant, and equivalent to a recidivism reduction of about 6 percentage points, for example, from 50% to 44%" (Lipsey and Wilson 1998:330). Some types of programs, for example, interpersonal skills, family, training and behavioral programs, reduced recidivism rates of both institutionalized and noninstitutionalized youths 15 to 20 percent, although many of these treatment effects were based on findings from very small numbers (three to six) of studies. Even optimistic assessment of "rehabilitation" conclude only that "several methods seem promising, but none have been shown to usually produce major reductions [in recidivism] when applied broadly to typical composite samples of offenders" (Palmer 1991:340).

Typically, positive treatment effects occur in small experimental programs that provide an intensive and integrated response to the multiplicity of problems—educational deficits; family dysfunction; inadequate interpersonal, social, and vocational skills; and poverty—that delinquent youths present. Generally, the most positive treatment effects occur only under optimal conditions, such as high treatment integrity in an established program with services provided by mental health or other nonjuvenile justice correctional personnel (Lipsey and Wilson 1998). Research on the elements of effective correctional programs suggest some "promising directions" either to provide more humane short-term correctional experiences or to improve youths' long-term life chances.

My critique of juvenile justice *does not* rest on the premise that "nothing works." To the contrary, some model programs may work for some offenders under appropriate conditions. Research evidence indicates several elements of correctional programs that can ensure more humane conditions of confinement and contribute to youths' future well-being. But the theoretical possibility of effective treatment for some youths does not justify the punitive reality experienced by most delinquents. Unfortunately, most states do not elect to provide these programs or services to delinquents generally. Rather, they incarcerate most juveniles in euphemistically sanitized youth prisons. Even if model programs can reduce recidivism rates, public officials appear unwilling to provide such treatment services when they confront fiscal constraints, budget deficits, and competition from other, more politically potent interest groups. Organizational imperatives to achieve "economies of scale" mandate confining ever larger numbers of youths and thereby preclude the possibility of matching offenders with appropriate treatment programs. If either consistently favorable outcomes or universal access remain far from certain, then it seems difficult to justify confining most youths with fewer procedural safeguards than those provided to adults offenders. If correctional administrators do not provide effective services in responsive environment, then do any practical differences exist between treatment and punishment?

Conclusion

From the original Progressive reformers to the Supreme Court in *McKeiver*, proponents have rationalized juvenile courts' procedural deficiencies because they "treat" rather than "punish" young offenders. However, the contemporary juvenile justice system explicitly punishes youths for their crimes and renders such claims increasingly untenable. In recent decades, politicians and judges candidly acknowledge incapacitation and punishment as purposes of juvenile intervention, use offense criteria to achieve proportionality, and demand increasingly severe sanctions to repress youth crime. Proponents of get-tough policies contend that juvenile courts "coddle" young criminals, fail to punish them adequately for their initial depredations, and thereby encourage them to commit additional and more serious offenses.

These punitive policies repudiate the humanitarian impulses that underlay the original juvenile court. The rhetorical emphases on "accountability" and "culpability" reflect a shift in the ideology of childhood from vulnerability and dependency to autonomy and responsibility. A similar change in the assumptions of social control from determinism to freewill choice legitimates states' imposition of punishment and erodes the foundations of a separate juvenile justice system. In the juvenile court's current incarnation, children do not differ significantly from adults and treatment does not differ significantly from punishment.

The recent changes in sentencing laws and administrative practices reflect a philosophical ambivalence about the continued viability of "treatment" as a justification for a separate juvenile justice system. The statutory amendments and judicial and correctional practices have eliminated most of the significant differences between the juvenile and criminal processes. Sentencing laws that constrain judges to impose determinate sentences based on the present offense and prior record call into question any therapeutic "alternative purpose" of juvenile sanctions. Mandatory minimum statutes that base youths' sentences on the seriousness of their offenses avoid any reference to offenders' "real needs" or "best interests." Statutory revisions of juvenile code purpose clauses place greater emphasis on "accountability" and "protecting public safety" and reduce rhetorical support for traditional rehabilitative goals. A California court succinctly summarized these changes when it concluded that "the purposes of the juvenile process have become more punitive, its procedures formalistic, adversarial and public, and the consequences of conviction much more harsh" (*In re Javier A.*, 159 Cal. App. 3d 913, at 963–1964, 206 Cal. Rptr. 386, at 421 [1984]). Even the staunchest advocates of a "rehabilitative" juvenile court have responded to these trends, constructed philosophical and theoretical rationales to incorporate punishment as a valid component of a treatment disposition, and endorsed "graduated sanctions" that instill "accountability" (Wilson and Howell 1995).

The recent changes in juvenile court sentencing practices reveal the tensions between the principle of offense and the principle of individualized justice. On the one hand, juvenile court judges emphasize penal considerations and function as extensions of the criminal process when they sentence young offenders. Practical bureaucratic and administrative considerations place a premium on criminal justice decisional criteria like present offense and prior record. On the other hand, juvenile courts reflect their *parens patriae* foundation and judges purport to "individualize" their dispositions. Even the most powerful variables—present offense and prior record—explain only a modest amount (25 to 30%) of the outcomes of sentencing decisions. Thus, juvenile justice sentencing remains highly discretionary, and the relationship between criminal behavior and severity of sanctions remains highly attenuated. But juvenile courts' formal rejection of proportionality threatens the legitimacy of their decisions. "[A] scheme of punishment that does not generally reflect the principle of proportionality is inexplicable and therefore arbitrary and unjust. Calling a scheme 'treatment' which amounts to punishment does not alleviate the injustice; whatever treatment is actually received may moderate but does not erase the injustice" (Hazard 1976:12). In the absence of a principle of proportionality, minor offenders can and do receive much more severe dispositions than serious offenders receive. Younger offenders, adjudicated as delinquents, may receive longer sentences than adults convicted of identical offenses. Similarly situated offenders, defined as "similar" on the basis of their present offense or prior record, can receive markedly dissimilar dispositions because of their differing "needs." Because the individualized justice of the juvenile court classifies youths on the basis of their personal circumstances, then in a society marked by great social, economic, and racial inequality, minority youths consistently find themselves at a disadvantage. Recent changes in juvenile sentencing statutes reflect legislative disquiet with the underlying premises of individualized justice, the idiosyncratic exercises of judicial discretion, the lack of proportionality between youths' crimes and consequences, and the invidious inequalities that ensue.

Both the "treatment" and "punishment" strategies of social control locate the "causes" of delinquency in the individual offender, rather than in criminogenic social structures, communities, or political economy. The strategies prescribe alternative methods to induce offenders to change their behavior. Like the Progressives a century ago, the contemporary "punishment" approach ignores the broader social structural factors that "cause" delinquency and crime and thereby ensure their continued replication. From their inception, juvenile justice policies inexorably expanded the authority of the state to intervene in the lives of poor and minority youths, failed to address the economic and social circumstances that give rise to their disproportionate over-representation in the justice system, and thereby perpetuated injustice and inequality. Because Progressives created juvenile courts to discriminate, they readily lend themselves to contemporary policies to punish "other people's children." As long as larger proportions of minority, especially African American, youths grow up in single-parent households, live in greater poverty and social isolation, drop out of mediocre urban schools at higher rates, remain structurally unemployed and unemployable, and realistically have limited future prospects, they face greater risk of criminality and higher probabilities of incarceration when juvenile courts' individualized justice focuses on their personal circumstances and real needs (National Research Council 1993). While young people certainly can and do make "choices" about their behavior, social structural conditions and economic opportunities mediate the quality of their choices. Ultimately, juvenile and criminal justice policies can do very little to alter the social structural forces that impel some youths to "choose" crime and others to "choose" college.

The juvenile and criminal justice systems use the wrong indicators to evaluate the effectiveness of rehabilitation programs or sentencing policies. Criminal justice policies emphasize utilitarian considerations, use cost-benefit accounting procedures to measure effectiveness, and rely on easily obtained and objective indicators of program outcomes, for example, reductions in recidivism. But recidivism measures law enforcement activities or differential targeting of a "suspect pool," as well as changes in individuals' behaviors. In order for juvenile courts to rehabilitate young offenders, they must equip a youth with social and economic skills, cognitive abilities, and psychic resources; reintegrate him or her into a functioning community; and provide employment opportunities and economic stability. In short, any juvenile justice intervention must couple individual changes with structural opportunities. But high rates of concentrated poverty and structural unemployment, especially for urban and minority youths, pose substantial barriers to juvenile courts' successful reintegration of their delinquent clientele. Juvenile courts lack the resources necessary to prepare youths for a future, to provide educational and economic opportunities, to facilitate stability and self-sufficiency, or to expedite youths' successful transition to responsible adulthood. Despite juvenile courts' rhetoric of rehabilitation, from their inception they have lacked essential resources exactly because they direct their social control at other people's children (Rothman 1980). Providing for child welfare is a social responsibility, not a judicial one. Society collectively bears responsibility to provide for the welfare of children by supporting families, commuities, schools, and social institutions that nurture all young people. Because juvenile courts cannot and do not function as the social service agencies that the Progressives envisioned, then by default they function simply as extensions of the criminal justice system.

| | | | EIGHT

Abolish the Juvenile Court

Sentencing Policy When the Child Is a
Criminal and the Criminal Is a Child

In the three decades since *Gault*, judicial decisions, legislative amendments, and administrative changes have transformed the juvenile court from a nominally rehabilitative welfare agency into a scaled-down, second-class criminal court for young people. These revisions have converted the historical ideal of the juvenile court as a social welfare institution into a penal system that provides young offenders with neither therapy nor justice. Even as legal reforms foster increased punitiveness and convergence with criminal court, juvenile courts deflect, co-opt, ignore, or accommodate constitutional procedural mandates with minimal institutional change. They use courtroom procedures under which no adult would consent to be tried if she faced the prospect of confinement and then incarcerate youths in prisonlike settings for substantial terms.

Popular concerns about youth crime, especially drugs, guns and violence, bolster policies to repress rather than to rehabilitate young offenders. Instead of leading and educating the public about the structural complexity of crime and justice systems' limited ability to reduce it, politicians propose simplistic "get-tough" policies and pander to people's fears. While opinion polls indicate some public support for juvenile courts' rehabilitative mission and for lenient treatment of first-time and minor young offenders, they simultaneously affirm the popular view that the criminal justice system should punish chronic property and violent young offenders as adults (Schwartz 1992; Maguire and Pastore 1995). Chapters 6 and 7 document the legal consequences of these more punitive attitudes. In an era of governmental "downsizing" and get-tough crime policies, it seems unlikely that legislators will allocate scarce resources and expand treatment services for delinquents in the face of competition from other, more potent interest groups. Indeed, public unwillingness to provide for the welfare of all children, much less for those who commit crimes, forces us to question whether the juvenile court can or should be rehabilitated.

The recent procedural, jurisdictional, and sentencing policy changes reflect ambivalence about the purposes of juvenile courts and the social control of children. As noted in chapter 5, the diminution of status offense jurisdiction reflects juvenile courts' strategic withdrawal from preventing delinquency or enforcing normative conceptions of childhood. As observed in chapter 6, the transfer of more-serious offenders for criminal prosecution further reduces juvenile courts' clientele and indicates popular and political rejection of rehabilitative policies. And, as seen in chapter 7, the criminological "triage" at the "soft" and "hard" ends of their jurisdiction impel juvenile courts to function increasingly like criminal courts for those ordinary delinquents who remain. Despite the "criminalizing" of juvenile courts, youths whom judges remove from home or incarcerate in institutions for terms of months or years receive substantially fewer procedural safeguards than do adults convicted of comparable crimes. As a result, juvenile courts punish delinquents in the name of treatment but deny to them protections available to criminals. In view of this convergence with criminal courts, do we need a separate, procedurally deficient justice system simply to punish middle-level younger offenders?

Most juvenile justice scholars and practitioners recognize juvenile courts' functional convergence with criminal courts but recoil at the prospect of abolishing them and trying and sentencing all offenders in criminal court. They argue that significant developmental differences exist between young people and adults or that rehabilitation still differs from punishment and urge policymakers to maintain the distinctions between delinquents and criminals (Rubin 1979; Gardner 1987; Melton 1989; Dawson 1990a; Springer 1991; Rosenberg 1993; Scott and Grisso 1998). Some emphasize children's physical vulnerability or psychological immaturity. Others contend that juvenile courts protect young offenders from even more punitive criminal justice policies (Walkover 1984; Melton 1989). Still others assert that juvenile courts provide the only forum in which to consider all the legal matters—crime, neglect, dependency, and abuse—that affect children and their families (Edwards 1992). Ultimately, proponents of a separate juvenile justice system invoke the Progressives' fall-back position—despite juvenile courts' procedural deficiencies and substantive bankruptcy, criminal courts constitute even worse places to try and sentence younger offenders (Rosenberg 1993; Geraghty 1998).

The Progressives located the juvenile court on several cultural and criminological fault lines—childhood and social control. As a result, penal policy confronts a fundamental dilemma when the child is a criminal and the criminal is a child. Despite public fear of youth crime, do we really regard a fourteen-year-old and a twenty-four-year-old offender as moral and criminal equals who deserve exactly the same consequences for the same harms? If we really do, then how can states justify denying youths equality for all other legal purposes, for example, the right to vote, to drink, or to drive? We base all of these and myriad other legal disabilities on youths' inexperience and lack of mature judgment. Because we do not regard young people as the moral equals of adults, then why and how do we blame, punish, protect, or treat young offenders differently?

This chapter explores three possible resolutions to the dilemma posed when the child is a criminal and the criminal is a child: a "rehabilitative" juvenile court, a juvenile version of a criminal court, and an integrated criminal court. Proponents of a welfare-oriented juvenile court urge that we "reinvent juvenile justice" and restructure juvenile courts to pursue their original rehabilitative purposes (Krisberg and Austin 1993). Advocates of a juvenile version of a criminal court propose that we honestly acknowledge juvenile courts' criminal social control functions, incorporate punishment as a legitimate component of delinquency sanctions, and provide all criminal procedural safeguards but in judicially separate delinquency proceedings (American Bar Association and Institute of Judicial Administration 1980e; Melton 1989; Forst and Blomquist 1991). Advocates of an integrated criminal court recommend that we abolish juvenile court jurisdiction over criminal conduct, try all offenders in criminal courts, and introduce certain procedural and substantive modifications to accommodate the youthfulness of younger offenders (Feld 1988b, 1993a; Ainsworth 1991, 1995).

In this chapter, I endorse an integrated criminal court as a better solution to the conundrum posed when a child is a criminal. I will first explain why neither a rehabilitative juvenile court nor a juvenile version of criminal court can "work" as their proponents envision. I argue that traditional juvenile courts' deficiencies reflect a fundamental flaw in their conception rather than *simply* a century-long failure of implementation. Juvenile courts attempt to combine social welfare and criminal social control in one agency and inevitably do both badly because of the inherent contradiction in those two missions. On the other hand, a juvenile version of a criminal court is an institution without a rationale. Because we already have criminal courts, without some other social welfare rationale, a juvenile version of a criminal court simply would be redundant and a temporary way station on the road to full integration.

If we uncouple social welfare from criminal social control, then we can abolish juvenile courts and formally recognize youthfulness as a mitigating factor in criminal sentencing to accommodate the reduced culpability of younger offenders. Young people differ from adults in their breadth of experience, temporal perspective, willingness to take risks, maturity of judgment, and susceptibility to peer influences. These generic and developmental characteristics of adolescents affect their opportunity to learn to be responsible, to develop fully a capacity for self-control, and provide compelling policy rationale to mitigate their criminal sentences. I propose an age-based "youth discount" of sentences—a sliding scale of developmental and criminal responsibility—to implement the lesser culpability of young offenders in the legal system. Only an integrated justice system can avoid the legal dichotomies and contradictory policies inherent in all current binary formulations—either adult or child, either punishment or treatment. Finally, I explore the benefits that accrue from formally recognizing youthfulness as a mitigating factor when sentencing young offenders. These advantages include enhanced protection for the many young offenders whom criminal courts already sentence as adults; affirmation of individual responsibility; integration of criminal records for sentence enhancements; development of a coherent sentencing policy toward chronic offenders that avoids the "punishment gap"; elimination of the sentencing disparities associated with waiver decision making; rejection of the ideology of individualized justice that fosters racial, gender, and geographic disparities; and, ultimately, simple honesty about the reality of criminal social control in the juvenile court.

Rehabilitate the "Rehabilitative" Juvenile Court?

The *parens patriae* juvenile court rests on the dual ideas of "treatment" and "children." It provided a mechanism to protect, reform, and treat "innocent" children and rejected the criminal law's jurisprudence of guilt, blameworthiness, and punishment. It affirmed deterministic models of behavior and adopted paternalistic policies to treat the child as an object for adults to shape and manipulate in her "best interests," rather than as an autonomous and responsible person. As the preceding chapters demonstrate, however, ideological and jurisprudential changes have blurred both the "treatment-punishment" and "child-adult" dichotomies. Increasingly the juvenile court functions as a system of criminal social control to protect society from young offenders, rather than as a welfare agency to nurture and protect vulnerable children from a wrathful community. In this revised formulation of adolescence, the justice systems more often emphasize young people's "almost adult" status rather than their "childlike" qualities. When these agencies encounter "other people's children," especially poor and minority youths, the ambivalence and conflict experienced when the child is a criminal "[are] easily converted to hostility and take[] institutional form in social policies to control and incarcerate youth rather than to enhance their development" (Grubb and Lazerson 1982:156).

Inadequate Social Welfare

Despite the erosion of juvenile courts' sustaining rationale, some proponents contend that we cannot declare the experiment a failure, because public officials have never made a real attempt to implement juvenile courts' rehabilitative goals (Ferdinand 1991). State agencies, rather than juvenile courts, control the institutions and programs to which judges send delinquents. From their inception, these correctional facilities have had more in common with prisons than with hospitals or clinics (Schlossman 1977; Rothman 1980). By the time of *Gault*, the juvenile courts' failures of implementation were readily apparent (President's Crime Commission on Law Enforcement and Administration of Justice 1967a, 1967b).

Juvenile courts lack necessary resources because providing for child welfare is a societal responsibility, not simply a judicial one. Historically and currently, public officials deny juvenile courts adequate resources because of pervasive public antipathy to their clients, those who are poor, disadvantaged, and minority offenders (Grubb and Lazerson 1982; Krisberg and Austin 1993). Thus, any proposal to reinvigorate the juvenile court as a social welfare agency first must address why political leaders who have failed to provide minimally adequate resources and personnel for the past century now will do so. The ideological shift from treatment to punishment and the accompanying "criminalizing" of the juvenile court may portend a more fundamental shift from public responsibility for citizens' welfare to private individual responsibility.

Proponents of a rehabilitative juvenile court also must account for and avoid the failures of earlier generations of juvenile court reforms. Many reforms reflect organizational responses to crises of legitimacy and serve primarily to deflect or neutralize critics. For example, as chapter 6 illustrates, the escalation in youth homicide fostered extensive policy debate about only the relative merits of different ways to "crack down" and transfer more youths to criminal court and thereby to preserve the juvenile court for the "less bad" remaining delinquents. Juvenile justice specialists frame policy options within a "scientific paradigm" of expertise and professional competence to assert a veneer of legitimacy. The ensuing technical tinkering narrows the range of debate, produces symbolic rather than substantive reforms, and fails to address issues of discretion and penal social control or the relationships between social structure and crime, gun, or social welfare policies (Sutton 1988). "Successful reform policies were not efficient technical solutions to problems of crime and poverty as much as they were effective strategic responses to assaults on institutional autonomy. Juvenile justice legislation did not strengthen the application of the rule of law to children; on the contrary, reforms were designed to blur the fine line between public and private conduct and to strengthen the hand of discretionary authority" (Sutton 1988:240).

Others attribute the failures of child welfare policies to contradictions embedded in *parens patriae* ideology and divisions between public and private obligations toward young people (Grubb and Lazerson 1982). Because parents bear primary responsibility to raise their own children, public programs to assist other people's children stipulate that parents demonstrably must fail at the task as a prerequisite of receiving public assistance. But, stigmatizing the clients of social programs by making failure a requirement of eligibility undermines public support for those programs and ensures their inadequacy. "Public stinginess has itself hurt poor children, since they are the children most in need of public support. But the injuries go further: in a class society, . . . [f]ear of other people's children then compromise whatever public commitment to children exists by elevating social peace to a goal equal to that of supporting children suffering from structural inequalities" (Grubb and Lazerson 1982:93).

If we formulated a child social welfare policy ab initio, would we select a juvenile court as the most appropriate agency through which to deliver social services and make criminality a condition precedent to the receipt of services? If we would not create a court to deliver social services, then does the fact of a youth's criminality confer on it any special competency as a welfare agency? Many young people who do not commit crimes desperately need social services, and many youths who commit crimes do not require or will not respond to the meager services available. Because our society chooses to deny adequate social welfare services to meet the "real needs" of all young people, juvenile courts' treatment ideology serves primarily to legitimate the exercise of judicial coercion of some *because of their criminality*. In short, little commends the *idea* of a juvenile court as a social welfare delivery system except bureaucratic inertia.

Individualized Justice and the Rule of Law

Quite apart from its unsuitability as a social welfare agency, the individualized justice of a rehabilitative juvenile court fosters lawlessness and thus detracts from its role as a court of law. Despite statutes and procedural rules, juvenile court judges purport to decide each case to achieve a child's best interests. But a treatment ideology without a scientific foundation breeds lawlessness. Social control practices more often reflect political, cultural, or professional beliefs than valid theories about crime causation or proven intervention strategies. If judges evaluate each child's real needs, then every case is unique and decisional rules or objective criteria cannot constrain clinical intuitions. The *idea* of treatment entails individualization, indeterminacy, nonproportionality, and a disregard of normative valuations of offense seriousness (Morris 1974). Unlike punishment, which implies limits, treatment may continue "for the duration of minority." Thus, juvenile courts in theory and in practice sentence or treat minor offenders severely and sanction serious offenders mildly.

Some analysts thoughtfully defend the "inequality" of individualized justice. The criticism that "individualization entails inequality and unfairness implicitly chooses one of the possible criteria of equal treatment—usually kind or gravity of offense" (Teitelbaum 1991:395). Accordingly, one can only object to unequal treatment if one assumes that offenders are similarly situated based on their offense; if one adopts some other criterion for sanctions, then objections to inequality become incoherent. If one accepts juvenile courts' ideology of individualized justice, then disparate outcomes for youths charged with similar offenses or even co-offenders do not provide a valid basis for criticism. Judges decide cases within an extremely wide frame of relevance, freely evaluate them on the basis of professional or practical considerations, and have no obligation to use the same criteria to resolve subsequent cases (Matza 1964). Of course, if offenses do not provide an appropriate criterion by which to gauge inequality, then why do states define juvenile court jurisdiction on the basis of a youth's offenses rather than some other attribute of her real needs?

Rejecting proportionality and determinacy deprives juvenile courts' sanctions of any moralizing or educative role in pronouncing the "wrongfulness" of behavior. Some courts recognize the contradictions between treatment and justice and try to reinstate proportionality as a component of rehabilitation. One court observed, for example, that proportional sanctions "can significantly contribute to the rehabilitation of a delinquent by teaching him that conduct does have consequences and that, so far as the judge can make them so, the results of antisocial behavior are predictable . . . If you commit a little crime, you pay a little price. If you commit a greater crime, the pain is a little greater. A first offense can be treated leniently, but if you do it again, you are subjected to an escalating series of winces—and you had better believe it because the judge does not promise severe consequences and then just slap your wrist (*In re L.J.*, 546 A.2d 429, 436 [D.C. Ct. App. 1988]). Similarly, confidential juvenile proceedings to avoid stigmatizing youths prevent the court from communicating any possible deterrent threat to other "would be" offenders. Lenient treatment, no matter how well clinically justified, may undermine public confidence. Even proportional sanctions for which no public or offender audience exists may erode the legitimacy of the justice process.

If judges possess neither practical scientific bases by which to classify youths for treatment nor demonstrably effective programs to prescribe for them, then the exercise of "sound discretion" simply constitutes a euphemism for idiosyncratic subjectivity. Racial, gender, geographic, and socioeconomic disparities constitute almost inevitable corollaries of an individualized treatment ideology. At the least, judges will sentence youths differently based on extraneous personal characteristics for which they bear no responsibility. If juvenile courts provided exclusively benign and effective services, then perhaps differential processing of male and female, urban and rural, or black and white juveniles might be tolerable. At the worst, however, judges impose haphazard, unequal, and discriminatory punishment on similarly situated offenders without any effective procedural or appellate checks.

Is the discretion that judges exercise to classify for treatment warranted? Do the successes of rehabilitation justify its concomitant lawlessness? Do the incremental benefits of juvenile court intervention for some youths outweigh the inevitable inequalities and racial disparities that result from the exercise of individualized discretion for others? These questions require more sophisticated cost-and-benefit policy analyses than a Progressives child-saver's claim that "if we save even one child, then it is worth it." In chapter 7, I reviewed the evaluation research of "what works" and assessments of the impact of juvenile court intervention on recidivism rates. Again, my argument does not rest on the proposition that "nothing works." To the contrary, some demonstration and model programs do "work" for some delinquents under some conditions, although none do so consistently or systematically for all offenders (Lipsey and Wilson 1998). Although some treatment does "work" for some youths, states do not routinely provide these model demonstration services universally for ordinary, run-of-the-mill delinquents. It is exactly because we do know some of the elements of successful interventions that the consistent failure to provide them represents a deliberate policy choice. In any event, in the face of unproven efficacy and uncertain resources, the possibility that rehabilitation may occur does not justify incarcerating young offenders with fewer procedural safeguards than we provide to adults charged, convicted, and confined for crimes.

Procedural informality constitutes an essential adjunct of a "welfare" court's substantive discretion; juvenile courts predicate their informal process on the promise of benign and effective treatment. If substantive rules and principles like proportionality and determinacy do not constrain judicial decision making, then procedures cannot limit their authority either, because every case is unique. Lawyers manipulate legal rules for their clients' advantage, and a discretionary court without objective criteria or decisional rules constitutes unfamiliar and unfavorable legal terrain. "Most lawyers and legislators prefer legal rules whose application is predictable and whose correct application can be assessed on appeal. Otherwise it is nearly impossible to identify and correct bad decisions" (Tonry 1995:147). The continuing absence or co-optation of defense counsel in many jurisdictions reduces the likelihood that juvenile courts will adhere to existing legal mandates. The informal and confidential nature of delinquency proceedings reduces the visibility and accountability of the process and precludes external checks on coercive interventions. As long as the mythology prevails that juvenile court intervention constitutes only benign coercion and that, in any event, children should not expect more, youths will continue to receive the "worst of both worlds" (*Kent v. United States*, 383 U.S. 541, at 556 [1966]).

Failure of Implementation versus Conception

The fundamental shortcoming of the juvenile court's welfare *idea* reflects a failure of conception rather than *simply* a failure of implementation. The juvenile court's creators envisioned a social service agency in a judicial setting and attempted to fuse its social welfare mission with the power of state coercion. The juvenile court *idea* that judicial clinicians successfully can combine social welfare and penal social control in one agency represents an inherent conceptual flaw and an innate contradiction. Combining social welfare and penal social control functions only ensures that the court performs both functions badly. Providing for child welfare is a societal responsibility, not a judicial one, and the polity declines to provide those necessary resources because juvenile courts' clients are poor, disproportionately minorities, *and* criminal offenders. As a result, juvenile courts subordinate social welfare concerns to crime control considerations.

The conflicted impulses engendered between concern for child welfare and punitive responses to criminal violations form the root of the ambivalence embedded in the juvenile court. The hostile reactions that people experience toward other people's children whom they regard as a threat to themselves and their own children undermine benevolent aspirations and elevate concerns for their control. Juvenile justice personnel simultaneously profess child-saving aspirations but more often function as agents of criminal social control. Because they possess few resources besides the power to incarcerate for crimes, juvenile courts function as agencies of social control.

The juvenile court inevitably subordinates social welfare to criminal social control because of its built-in penal focus. State laws do not define juvenile courts' social welfare jurisdiction on the basis of those characteristics which children are not responsible for and which social services or intervention could improve. For example, juvenile court statutes do not define eligibility for services or create an enforceable right or entitlement based on young people's lack of access to decent education, lack of adequate housing or nutrition, unmet health needs, or impoverished families, *none of which are their fault*. In all these instances, children bear the social burdens of their parents' circumstances literally as innocent bystanders (Grubb and Lazerson 1982; National Research Council 1993). If states defined juvenile courts' jurisdiction on the basis of young people's real needs for social welfare, then they would declare a broad category of impoverished and at-risk children eligible for public assistance and services. Such a policy would require structural reforms to alleviate concentrated poverty, a substantial reallocation of social resources, and a strong public commitment to children's welfare.

Instead, states' juvenile codes define juvenile courts' jurisdiction on the basis of a youth's commission of a crime, a prerequisite that detracts from a compassionate response. Unlike the adverse social conditions for which young people bear no responsibility, criminal behavior represents the one characteristic for which adolescent offenders do shoulder at least some responsibility. As long as juvenile courts define eligibility for "services" on the basis of criminality, they highlight the aspect of youths that rationally elicits the least sympathy and ignore their personal circumstances or social conditions most likely to evoke a desire to help. "Of all the groups which make a claim upon public sympathy and fellow feeling, criminal offenders often seem to have the weakest claims and this is particularly the case if they are represented as a willful danger to the public, rather than as inadequate, or maladjusted, or as themselves victims of social injustice" (Garland 1990:237). Thus, juvenile courts' defining characteristic simply reinforces the public's antipathy to young people by emphasizing that they are criminals, first and foremost. Recent changes in juvenile court waiver and sentencing policies to emphasize punishment, "accountability," and personal responsibility further reinforce juvenile courts' penal foundations and reduce the legitimacy of young offenders' claims to compassion or humanitarian assistance.

Because juvenile courts operate in a societal context that does not provide adequate social services for children in general, juvenile justice intervenes in the lives of those who commit crimes for purposes of social control rather than of social welfare. This in-built contradiction places the juvenile court in an untenable position. "It is unable to deliver on the promise of rehabilitation, and yet it is stuck with the duty to control youth and must therefore incarcerate many of them. But since it can not give up on the hope of rehabilitation, incarceration is gentle—usually short-term, in minimum security facilities or community placements, or on probation—and fails to protect the community from those who are truly violent" (Grubb and Lazerson 1982:179). This conflict between rehabilitative and retributive impulses fuels the "cycles of juvenile justice," the historical oscillations between severity and leniency (Bernard 1992). And, unlike the proponents of a reinvigorated, rehabilitative juvenile court, young offenders recognize the fundamental inconsistency between a judge's initially deciding that delinquents committed a crime, condemning the behavior, and then offering to help and improve offenders' lives (Matza 1964; Fox 1970b).

A century ago Progressive reformers had to choose between initiating social structural reforms that would ameliorate inequality and criminogenic forces or ministering to the individuals damaged by those adverse social conditions. Driven by class and ethnic antagonisms, these reformers ignored the social structural and political economic implications of their own deterministic theories of delinquency and chose instead to "save children" and, incidentally, to preserve their own power and privilege. Child saving satisfied humanitarian impulses without engendering fundamental social change or threatening political economic relations (Platt 1977; Rothman 1980). As a result, the juvenile court welfare *idea* espoused social structural or deterministic explanations of delinquent behavior and then individualized its sanctions. On the one hand, to punish people for behavior that society "caused" may lead to charges of hypocrisy. On the other hand, to subscribe to deterministic explanations of behavior undermines individual responsibility and erodes the expressive, condemnatory function of criminal law.

A century later, we face similar choices between rehabilitating "damaged" individuals in a criminal justice system and initiating more fundamental social structural changes. In making these choices, the juvenile court welfare *idea* may constitute an obstacle to child welfare reform. The *existence* of a juvenile court provides an alibi to avoid fundamental improvement. Conservatives may deprecate the juvenile court as a welfare system that fails to "crack down" or "get tough" and thereby "coddles" young criminals. Liberals may bemoan its lack of resources and inadequate options, none of which address the underlying structural causes of crime. But either stance is akin to sticking fingers in the dike while the flood of adverse social indicators of youth pour over the top in a torrent. A society collectively provides for the welfare of its children by supporting families, communities, schools, and social institutions that nurture all young people and not by cynically incarcerating its most disadvantaged children "for their own good." "The resources of the criminal [and juvenile] justice system are few. The answers to poverty, underemployment, and racial bias must be sought elsewhere, in schools and social welfare programs and broad-based social policies. To look to the criminal [and juvenile] justice system to solve fundamental social problems would be foolish and doomed to fail" (Tonry 1995:163). Neither juvenile court judges nor any other criminal justice agencies realistically can ameliorate the social ills that afflict young people or significantly reduce youth crime.

A Juvenile Version of a Criminal Court: Due Process and Reduced Punishment

A separate juvenile justice system requires a more sophisticated rationale than simplistic treatment versus punishment formulas. As chapter 7 demonstrates, in reality few practical differences exist between those two purposes. But, if we acknowledge that juvenile courts punish young offenders, then we assume an obligation to provide them with all criminal procedural safeguards because "the condition of being a boy does not justify a kangaroo court" (*In re Gault*, 387 U.S. 1, at 28 [1967]). The *McKeiver* Court feared that requiring procedural parity with adults would end the juvenile court experiment but ignored that failing to do so perpetuated injustice. To treat similarly situated offenders dissimilarly, to punish juveniles in the name of treatment, and to deny them basic safeguards foster a sense of injustice that thwarts any reform efforts.

The current juvenile court provides neither therapy nor justice *and* cannot be rehabilitated. The alternative policy options are either to make juvenile courts more like criminal courts or to make criminal courts more like juvenile courts. Whether we try young offenders in a separate juvenile court or in a unified criminal court, we must reconsider basic premises and address issues of substance and procedure. Issues of substantive justice include developing and implementing a doctrinal rationale—diminished responsibility, reduced capacity, immaturity of judgment, or truncated self-control—to sentence young offenders differently, and more leniently, than older defendants. Issues of procedural justice include providing youths with *all* the procedural safeguards adults receive *and* additional protections that recognize their immaturity and vulnerability in the justice process.

Many analysts acknowledge that "the assumptions underlying the juvenile court show[] it to be a bankrupt legal institution" that functions as an extension of criminal courts and requires a new rationale to justify its continued existence (Melton 1989:166). Rather than abolishing the juvenile court, however, they propose to transform it into an explicitly penal juvenile justice system that provides enhanced procedural protections and imposes less-severe punishment than do criminal courts because of youths' reduced culpability (Rubin 1979; American Bar Association and Institute of Judicial Administration 1980d; Walkover 1984; Melton 1989; Gardner 1989; Forst and Blomquist 1991; Rosenberg 1993). They proffer a variety of rationales for a juvenile version of a criminal court. "No longer will the juvenile court be seen as a quasi-judicial court-clinic but, rather, as a real court, administering real justice in its traditional retributive and distributive meanings. . . . [J]uveniles should have to pay for their crimes; but . . . society has a duty to its young delinquents to help them to gain moral and civic equilibrium" (Springer 1991:398). This "substitute protection" model rejects full equivalency with criminal courts and emphasizes the vulnerability of young people. "By focusing on children's lesser capacity to be culpable, a sorely needed justification for the existence of a separate juvenile court is provided, limits on the state's power to intervene in the lives of its citizens are reaffirmed, and the role played by the infancy defense in legitimating juvenile court jurisdiction is highlighted . . . [T]he infancy defense reinforces both the authority of the juvenile court to assign blame and the intellectual and institutional integrity of our criminal law" (Walkover 1984:562). Melding punishment with reduced culpability provides a rationale for a two-track criminal justice system based on categorical differences between the criminal responsibility of youths and adults.

The American Bar Association (ABA) and Institute of Judicial Administration's *Juvenile Justice Standards* provide the paradigm of a juvenile version of a criminal court. The twenty-six volumes of *Juvenile Justice Standards* recommend the repeal of jurisdiction over status offenders, scaled-down proportional and determinate sentences to sanction delinquent offenders, restrictive offense criteria to regularize pretrial detention and judicial transfer decisions, and all criminal procedural safeguards including nonwaivable counsel and jury trials (McCarthy 1977a; Wizner and Keller 1977; Flicker 1982). Under the *Juvenile Justice Standards*, "the rehabilitative model of juvenile justice is rejected and the principles of criminal law and procedure become the cornerstones of a new relationship between the child and the state" (McCarthy 1977a: 1094). The *Juvenile Justice Standards Relating to Dispositions* provide: "The purpose of the juvenile correctional system is to reduce juvenile crime by maintaining the integrity of the substantive law proscribing certain behavior and by developing individual responsibility for lawful behavior. This purpose should be pursued through means that are fair and just, that recognize the unique characteristics and needs of juveniles, and that give juveniles access to opportunities for personal and social growth" (1980a:Standard 1.1). Although the standards on *Juvenile Delinquency and Sanctions* (1980d) recommend proportional and determinate sanctions scaled down from the adult lengths, the standards on *Dispositions* emphasize that juvenile court judges should individualize youths' sentences to maximize their developmental competencies. "The standards are intended to encourage the development of more meaningful ways of providing rehabilitative programs" (1980a:18). Although personal culpability provides the basis for delinquency conviction and remedial intervention, the different volumes of standards do not attempt to reconcile conflicts between determinate and proportional sentences on the one hand and individualized sanctions on the other. Rather, the standards employ a version of "limiting retributivism" (Morris 1974), wherein a youth's offense determines the appropriate sentence range and utilitarian considerations dictate the nature and intensity of disposition within that range. While culpability considerations affect the degree of guilt and sentence length, the *Juvenile Justice*

Standards attempt to retain a more forward-looking dispositional focus than does criminal punishment (Weissman 1983).

While proponents of a juvenile version of a criminal court advocate shorter sentences for reduced culpability and more procedural protections, they offer few reasons to implement these policies in a separate juvenile court rather than in an integrated criminal court. The *Juvenile Justice Standards* assert that "removal of the treatment rationale does not destroy the rationale for a separate system or for utilization of an ameliorative approach; it does, however, require a different rationale" (1980a:19 n 5). Even though the *Juvenile Justice Standards* propose virtually to replicate adult criminal procedure and sentencing, they bury in a footnote in one volume their sole attempt to justify a separate juvenile court system: "Juveniles may be viewed as incomplete adults, lacking in full moral and experiential development, extended unique jural status in other contexts, and deserving of the social moratorium extended by this and all other societies." (1980a:19 n5). I agree that young people differ from adults in ways that affect their degree of criminal responsibility and deserved punishment, (Feld 1997) but the standards fail to explain why youths require a separate juvenile court to convict them or to impose shorter sentences. Critics rightly contend that once the standards reject *parens patriae* and rehabilitation as bases for delinquency sanctions and substitute penal goals, they offer no justification for a separate juvenile court (Wizner and Keller 1977).

Other proponents of a separate, juvenile version of a criminal court offer additional rationales. Some contend that any justice that accommodates the unique aspects of younger offenders will require some distinctive procedures, judicial specialization, or dispositional facilities and that existing juvenile courts provide a practical and less-risky organization in which to make these adjustments (Rubin 1979). However, juvenile courts' ability to co-opt innovations and reforms and to preserve existing organizational relations suggest that only a clean break with the personnel and practices of the past would enable the justice system to provide criminal procedural safeguards and implement different sentencing policies (Sutton 1988).

Proponents of a juvenile version of a criminal court point to the manifold deficiencies of criminal courts—ineffective defense counsel, excessive caseloads, poor administration, inadequate sentencing options—to justify a separate justice system for young offenders (Rubin 1979; Rosenberg 1993; Geraghty 1998). Like their Progressive predecessors, contemporary defenders of a separate juvenile court deflect criticism back to criminal courts and point to the "[o]vercriminalization, ineffective defense representation, rehabilitation rhetoric, and severe punishments [that] have characterized criminal courts." (Rubin 1979:296). Because no social or political will exists to reform or provide resources for criminal courts, proponents expect critics to prove conclusively juvenile courts' irredeemable bankruptcy "before we surrender to the very system whose deficiencies inspired the first juvenile court" (Edwards 1992: 19). Others accuse advocates of juvenile court abolition of indulging "a somewhat idealized or romanticized vision of adult courts in which the criminal guarantees of the Bill of Rights are meaningfully enforced" (Rosenberg 1993: 173). They argue that children would not receive a fairer process in crowded criminal courts where overwhelmed prosecutors and ill-prepared defense counsel crank out guilty pleas with minimal incentives to act in a child's best interests (Rosenberg 1993; Geraghty 1998). In short, as bad as juvenile courts concededly are, their defenders contend that criminal courts remain far worse places for younger offenders. However, as chapters 4 and 7 demonstrate, charges of excessive caseloads, ineffective defense counsel, inadequate sentencing options, inattention to children's real needs, and assembly-line justice apply equally to juvenile courts (Dawson 1990a; American Bar Association 1995). An unsentimental comparison of the relative quality of juvenile and criminal "justice" leaves little basis on which to decide whether either system treats young people or adult defendants justly and fairly. If the state charged you with a crime, under which system of procedures would you rather be tried?

Still others argue that a punitive juvenile court provides an intermediate level of punishment more commensurate with the lower degree of juveniles' criminal responsibility (Gardner 1987; Melton 1989). Lesser punishment entails more than simply shorter sentences. Part of a criminal sanction includes public denunciation, a condemnation of behavior (von Hirsch 1993). Calling a younger offender a "delinquent" rather than a "criminal" may convey an intermediate level of stigma more in accord with the deserved degree of opprobrium (Gardner 1987). Although we may speculate about the relative amount of stigma associated with *delinquency* and *criminal* labels, only a separate justice system can assign that lesser denunciation and blame.

A juvenile version of a criminal court would impose shorter sentences than do criminal courts, which constitutes their primary substantive difference. As we recall from chapter 6, the length and harshness of punishment imposed in juvenile court remain substantially less than that inflicted in criminal courts on serious young offenders. A separate juvenile court may be the only way to achieve uniformly shorter sentences and to insulate youths from get-tough criminal sentencing policies (Gardner 1989). Although advocates of a juvenile version of criminal court assume that an integrated criminal court necessarily would equate children with adults and sentence them with indiscriminate harshness, this equation is a jurisprudentially false one (Wizner and Keller 1977; Walkover 1984). As I will suggest, criminal courts can readily—and should—recognize young people's reduced culpability and blameworthiness.

Because a juvenile version of a criminal court would punish delinquents, albeit with shorter sentences than adults receive, proponents advocate procedural safeguards on a par with criminal defendants, including the right to a jury trial. (ABA and Institute of Judicial Administration 1980c). Although the *Juvenile Justice Standards* recognize that the right to a jury trial would significantly change juvenile court practices, they recommend a jury to neutralize potential judicial bias, to enhance the visibility of the process, to require judges to give instructions about the law so that appellate courts can review legal issues, and to improve the quality of fact-finding and ensure that jurors decide cases based solely on evidence admitted at trial (1980c; Ainsworth 1991; Feld 1993a).

The American Bar Association formulated the *Juvenile Justice Standards* during the late 1970s and before research found a relationship between procedural formality and severity of sanctions in juvenile courts (Feld 1991, 1993b). Criminal defendants long have recognized that one price they pay for exercising the right to a jury trial rather than pleading guilty will be a longer sentence following conviction (Alschuler 1983). In theory, judges sentence criminal defendants convicted by juries more severely than defendants who plead guilty because those convicted failed to cooperate with prosecutors or to show remorse. In reality, courts enhance defendants' sentences to penalize them for burdening the justice system and to discourage them from exercising their formal rights (Alschuler 1986).

As discussed in chapter 4, the presence of an attorney constituted an aggravating factor when judges sentenced delinquents. Youths who appeared with lawyers in juvenile courts received more severe sentences than did those convicted without counsel. Similarly, research on geographic variability in juvenile justice administration also suggests a relationship between process formality and sentencing severity (Kempf, Decker, and Bing 1990; Feld 1991). If the Court in *McKeiver* had granted to juveniles the right to a jury trial, one predictable juvenile justice system response would have been "escalating penalty structures, plea bargaining, and extortion in juvenile justice" to ensure that as few delinquents exercised their right to a jury trial as did adult criminal defendants (Zimring 1982:82).

In view of the relationship between procedural formality and sentencing severity, one may question whether a juvenile version of a criminal court could continue to afford the more lenient sentences that its advocates assume. Rather, legal changes that push juvenile courts increasingly in the direction of greater process formality—lawyers insisting on the rule of law, jury trials, judicial openness, visibility, and accountability, proportional and determinate sentencing guidelines—would accelerate the convergence between juvenile and criminal courts, increase their repressiveness, and further erode proposed sentencing differentials. Perhaps, juvenile court judges only can be lenient, albeit idiosyncratically, because they exercise their discretion behind closed doors. Proponents of the juvenile version of a criminal court did not even recognize, much less answer, the question whether such a model simply would postpone rather than avoid the inevitable convergence between the two justice systems.

To further darken this already pessimistic analysis, thoughtful scholars question whether "real" reforms can occur within the existing juvenile justice system (Sutton 1988; Schwartz 1989b). Too many people have fiscal, professional, or ideological stakes in maintaining current institutional arrangements easily to modify the discretionary apparatus directed at young people. "[I]t would require a thoroughgoing reallocation of legal responsibility, a sharp reduction of official discretion, and a radical pruning of the dense web of patronage exchanges between public and private sectors. Moves of this sort would be catastrophic for the individuals and groups that have a stake in the existing system. They will not occur because we lack the political will" (Sutton 1988:257). The emergence of transinstitutionalization as a response to the deinstitutionalization of status offenders analyzed in chapter 5 reveals how fluidly the delinquency, welfare, and mental health systems and private-sector service providers adapt to even significant jurisdictional reforms.

Young Offenders in Criminal Court: Youthfulness as a Mitigating Factor

Many state-imposed restrictions on young people's freedom assume that "during the formative years of childhood and adolescence, minors often lack the *experience, perspective* and *judgment* to recognize and avoid *choices* that could be detrimental to them" (*Bellotti v. Baird*, 442 U.S. 622, 635 [1979], emphasis added). Juvenile courts' "treatment" ideology, for example, adopted a paternalistic stance because young people's immaturity and poor judgment caused them to make criminal choices that threatened their and others' well-being. Because the deterministic treatment model depicted delinquents as victims rather than perpetrators, it left little or no room for personal responsibility. But most of what juvenile courts characterize as treatment constitutes punishment because we do not really believe that youths fully lack responsibility and self-control. States punish youths because they do possess sufficient culpability to be held accountable for their behavior, albeit not necessarily to the same degree as adults.

If the child is a criminal and the "real" reason he appears in court is for formal social control, then states could abolish juvenile courts' delinquency jurisdiction and try youths in criminal courts alongside their adult counterparts. But if the criminal is a child, then states must modify their sentencing provisions to accommodate the youthfulness of some defendants. Politically popular sound bites—"old enough to do the crime, old enough to do the time" or "adult crime, adult time"—do not analyze adequately the complexities of a youth sentencing policy. My proposal to abolish the juvenile court constitutes neither a mindless endorsement of punishment nor a primitive throwback to earlier centuries' views of young people as miniature adults. Rather, it honestly acknowledges that juvenile courts currently exercise criminal social control, asserts that young offenders in a criminal justice system *deserve* less-severe consequences for their misdeeds than do more mature offenders simply because they are young, and addresses the many problems created by trying to maintain binary, dichotomous, and contradictory criminal justice systems based on an arbitrary age classification of a youth as a child or an adult.

Formulating a youth sentencing policy entails two tasks. First, I will develop a rationale to sentence young offenders differently, and *more leniently*, than older defendants. Explicitly punishing young offenders rests on the premise that adolescents possess sufficient cognitive capacity and volitional controls to be responsible for their behavior, albeit not to the same extent as adults. Developmental psychological research, jurisprudence, and criminal sentencing policy provide rationale why young offenders deserve less-severe consequences for their misdeeds than do older offenders and justify formal recognition of youthfulness as a mitigating factor. Second, I will propose a "youth discount" as a practical administrative mechanism to institutionalize the principle of youthfulness in sentencing. A sentencing policy that recognizes youthfulness as a mitigating factor and provides a youth discount fosters greater honesty about the role of the justice system and greater realism about young people's developmental capacity and criminal responsibility.

Differences in experience, perspective, and judgment affect adolescents' ability fully to appreciate the moral content of legal commands, to apply those rules to social situations, and to obey the law. Youths have not fully developed the capacity to control their impulses or to resist temptation. Young people develop self-control over time by gaining experience and exercising self-control. Youths confront many situations and circumstances during adolescence that sorely test their newly emerging capacity for self-control and mature judgment. During adolescence, young people begin to develop the capacity to resist peer pressure, although it takes them several years to refine this social skill. Young people's inexperience, limited judgment, and restricted opportunities to exercise self-control partially excuse their criminal behavior.

Juveniles' Criminal Responsibility

Questions about youths' accountability or responsibility arise at two different stages of the criminal process, either when deciding guilt or when imposing a sentence. In the former instance, questions about responsibility focus on the minimum age at which a state may find a person guilty of an offense. Can a child of five, nine, eleven, or thirteen years of age "commit" a crime, that is, act with the requisite criminal intent? In making judgments about criminal responsibility, the criminal law's mens rea construct focuses narrowly on cognitive ability and capacity to make choices and excludes from the definition of an offense the goals, values, emotions, and psychic factors that motivate a person's choices. In the absence of insanity, compulsion, or some other legal excuse, any actor who has the capacity to choose to act otherwise than the way she did possesses criminal responsibility.

For questions of criminal responsibility and guilt, the common law's insanity and infancy mens rea defenses provide most of the answers. Mens rea defines the legal state of mind required to commit a crime and overlaps with the concept of legal or criminal responsibility. These doctrines excuse from criminal liability only those who lack the requisite criminal intent, the mens rea, because of mental illness or immaturity (Morris 1982). "In requiring *mens rea* in the sense of legal responsibility, the law absolves a person precisely because his deficiencies of temperament, personality or maturity distinguish him so utterly from the rest of us to whom the law's threats are addressed that we do not expect him to comply" (Kadish 1968:275). Because these mens rea defenses excuse an offender when the state cannot prove a crucial element of the offense, that is, criminal intent, the common law employs a very low cognitive threshold—knowledge of "right from wrong"—to establish criminal guilt. Knowledge of "right from wrong" entails only minimally rational understanding and contact with reality. Because of this low cognitive threshold, the infancy mens rea defense does not provide an especially useful analytical prism through which to view youthfulness as a "special circumstance." Even very young children may act purposefully and with knowledge of the wrongfulness of their conduct.

Quite apart from decisions about guilt or innocence, individual capacity and criminal responsibility also affect appropriate sentences. Even if a court finds a youth criminally responsible for causing a particular harm, should the law treat a fourteen-year-old and a twenty-four-year-old as moral equals and impose an identical sentence, or should youthfulness mitigate the severity of the consequences? If political sound bites like "old enough to do the crime, old enough to do the time" do not adequately answer these complex normative, moral, and legal questions, then on what principled bases do we distinguish between the two in sentencing?

Contemporary juvenile courts typically impose shorter sentences on serious young offenders than adult offenders convicted of comparable crimes receive. Shorter sentences enable most young offenders to survive the mistakes of adolescence with a semblance of their life chances intact. The juvenile court reifies the idea that young people possess less criminal responsibility and deserve less punishment than do adults. Shorter sentences recognize that young people *do differ somewhat* from adults and that their immaturity affects the quality of their judgments and self-control. These differences stem from physical, psychological, or developmental characteristics of young people and are by-products of the legal and social construction of youth.

A formal mitigation of punishment based on youthfulness constitutes a necessary component of a criminal justice system in order to avoid the equally undesirable alternatives of either excessively harsh penalties disproportionate to culpability on the one hand or of nullification and excessive leniency on the other. Youthfulness provides a rationale to mitigate sentences to some degree without excusing criminal conduct.

Shorter sentences for young people do not require a separate justice system in which to try them. Both juvenile and criminal courts separate determinations of guilt or innocence from sentencing and restrict consideration of individual circumstances largely to the latter phase. Criminal courts may impose lenient sentences on young offenders when appropriate. Rather than relying on the vagaries of judicial discretion, however, formally recognizing youthfulness as a mitigating factor represents the better sentencing policy.

A variety of doctrinal and policy reasons justify sentencing young people less severely than their adult counterparts. The common law's infancy mens rea defense antedated positivism's deterministic assumptions and concluded several centuries earlier that some young people lacked criminal capacity. The classical criminal law assumed that rational actors make blameworthy choices and deserve to suffer the consequences of their freely chosen acts. The common law recognized and exempted from punishment categories of people who lacked the requisite moral and criminal responsibility, for example, mentally ill and young persons. It conclusively presumed that children less than seven years old lacked criminal capacity and treated those fourteen years of age and older as fully responsible. Between the ages of seven and fourteen years, the law rebuttably presumed criminal incapacity (Fox 1970b; McCarthy 1977b; Weissman 1983; Walkover 1984). The common-law infancy gradations reflect developmental differences that render youths less *culpable* or criminally responsible than their adult counterparts and provide a first approximation of a rationale for shorter sentences for youths than for adults. Juvenile court legislation simply extended upward by a few years the general presumption of youthful criminal incapacity.

The extent to which young offenders, like their adult counterparts, *deserve* punishment hinges on the meaning of *culpability*. Respect for the integrity of the individual provides the underlying rationale of *deserved punishment* (von Hirsch 1976; Hart 1968). "Just-deserts" theory treats a freewill moral agent as an "end," a sovereign person, rather than a "means" to be manipulated to serve some ulterior utilitarian social objective, including her own well-being. Blaming a culpable actor for her voluntary choice to do "wrong" and giving her the consequences that her choice deserves respect her integrity as a morally responsible individual. Deserved punishment emphasizes censure and condemnation for blameworthy choices (von Hirsch 1976, 1985). "[P]unishing someone conveys in dramatic fashion that his conduct was wrong and that he is blameworthy for having committed it" (von Hirsch 1976:79). As long as criminal law rests on a moral foundation, the idea of blameworthiness remains central to ascribing guilt and allocating punishment (Morris 1974, 1982; Morse 1985). Penalties proportionate to the seriousness of the crime reflect the connection between conduct, choice, and blameworthiness.

Because commensurate punishment proportions sanctions to the seriousness of the offense, it shifts the analytical focus to the meaning of seriousness. Two elements—*harm* and *culpability*—determine the seriousness of an offense (von Hirsch 1976). Evaluations of the act or the harm focus on the degree of injury inflicted, risk created, or value taken. A perpetrator's age has little bearing on assessments of harmfulness, because the victim of a crime is just as injured by a youth as by an adult and the need for social defense exists against both. "The victim of a fifteen-year-old mugger is as much mugged as the victim of a twenty-year-old mugger, the victim of a fourteen-year-old murderer or rapist is just as dead or as raped as the victim of an older one" (van den Haag 1975:174).

But evaluations of *seriousness* also include the quality of the actor's *choice* to engage in the criminal conduct that produced the harm. Just-deserts theory and criminal law grading principles base the degree of deserved punishment on an actor's culpability. For example, a person may cause the death of another individual with many different "states of mind"—with premeditation and deliberation, intentionally, "in the heat of passion," recklessly, negligently, or accidentally. The criminal law treats the same objective consequence or harm, for example, a dead person, very differently depending on the nature of the choices that the actor made.

Youthfulness acquires special salience when gauging the culpability of *choices*—the blameworthiness of acting in a particular harm-producing way. Persons' moral responsibility for their actions provides the precondition to legally deserved consequences. In a framework of deserved punishment, it would be fundamentally unjust to impose the same penalty on offenders who do not share equal culpability. If young people are neither fully responsible nor the moral equals of adults, then they do not *deserve* the same legal consequences even for their blameworthy misconduct.

Responsibility for criminal choices hinges on cognitive and volitional competence. Do young offenders make criminal choices that constitute the moral equivalents of those made by more mature actors? If we focus narrowly on only the rational capacity to make instrumental choices to do wrong, then we could view even very young actors as criminally responsible. For example, a six-year-old child can act purposively to "steal" the toy of a friend even though she "knows" and can articulate that such conduct is "wrong." When young children make voluntary and instrumental choices to engage in prohibited conduct, they possess some moral ability to understand its wrongfulness and require some sanction to hold them accountable and to teach them that violating rules has consequences. However, despite children's ability to make reasoned choices and to engage in goal-oriented behavior, we do not regard them as full moral agents. The criminal law views young actors differently exactly because they have not yet completely internalized moral and legal norms, developed sufficient empathic identification with others, or had sufficient opportunity to develop the ability to restrain their actions. They possess neither the rationality, cognitive capacity, nor the self-control, volitional capacity, to equate their criminal responsibility with that of adults.

Developmental Psychology

Developmental psychology posits that young people move through a series of psychological stages and that their operational processes, legal reasoning, internalization of social and legal expectations, and ethical decision making change as they pass through these stages (Piaget 1932; Kohlberg 1963, 1969; Tapp and Levine 1974; Tapp and Kohlberg 1977). Children's moral reasoning at different stages differs from that which they use at other stages and differs qualitatively from that which adults use (Skolnick 1975; Piaget 1932; Kohlberg 1963, 1964, 1969). The descriptions of the developmental sequence and

changes in cognitive processes parallel strikingly the imputations of responsibility associated with the common-law infancy defense and suggest that, by
midadolescence, youths acquire most of the legal and moral values and reasoning capacity that will guide their behavior through later life (Tapp 1976).
Somewhere between about eleven and fourteen years of age, children achieve
the highest stage of cognitive development, the "formal operational" stage, in
which they think abstractly and hypothetically, weigh and compare consequences, and consider alternative solutions to problems (Siegler 1986). Justice
William Douglas's dissent in *Wisconsin v. Yoder*, which exempted Amish children from compulsory school attendance laws at age fourteen, relied on research by Jean Piaget and Lawrence Kohlberg to bolster his opinion that "there
is substantial agreement among child psychologists and sociologists that the
moral and intellectual maturity of the 14 year-old approaches that of the
adult" (306 U.S. 205, 245 [1972]).

Developmental psychological research on the cognitive decision-making
ability of adolescents confirms that "for most purposes, adolescents cannot be
distinguished from adults on the grounds of competence." (Melton 1983b:
100). When youths solve problems or make informed-consent decisions for
psychotherapy or medical treatment, social psychologists find few bases on
which to distinguish the quality of decisions made by adolescents fifteen years
of age or older from those made by adults in terms of either their reasoning
processes, the information used, or the qualitative outcomes (Melton 1983a,
1983b; Cauffman and Steinberg 1995). Research on young people's ability to
make competent medical decisions generally supports the equation between
adolescents' and adults' cognitive abilities. A review of several psychological
studies of adolescents' reasoning processes, understanding, and use of information about medical conditions and treatment options found that adolescents and adults generally made qualitatively comparable decisions (Scott
1992; Scott and Grisso 1998). One study of adolescents' responses to medical
and psychological treatment hypotheticals reported that fourteen-year-olds
did not differ significantly from adults in their comprehension, understanding
of alternatives, reasoning, and decision-making processes (Weithorn and
Campbell 1982). A review of psychological research on minors' ability to
knowingly, competently, and voluntarily provide informed consent to medical
treatment found little evidence to distinguish the ability of adolescents fifteen
years of age or older from that of adults (Grisso and Vierling 1978).

The empirical support for adolescents' cognitive equality with that of adults
derives primarily from research on informed medical consent that emphasizes
subjective preferences rather than qualitative outcomes (Scott 1992). Because
informed-consent policies promote patients' autonomy to make medical decisions, cognitive psychological research focuses narrowly on youths' ability
to understand and appreciate information about risks and alternatives and to
use that information in a rational process. Many of the studies do not compare
directly the responses of adolescents with those of adults in similar situations
and can only impute equivalency (Gardner 1989). Moreover, most of the
decision-making studies occurred in a laboratory setting in which researchers

posed hypothetical treatment scenarios and provided respondents with complete information. "Controlled laboratory experiments can not hope to capture the decision-making process that occurs when an adolescent is deciding whether to have intercourse for the first time, whether to abort a pregnancy, or whether to grab a ride home from a party with a friend who has been drinking" (Steinberg and Cauffman 1996:250).

It remains unproved, however, whether the ability to make hypothetical medical decisions under structured laboratory conditions constitutes adult-equivalent competence, maturity, judgment, and responsibility in other contexts that focus on objective outcomes, rather than on subjective preferences or in real-life situations with actual consequences. "[T]he informed consent model is too narrow in scope to adequately illuminate differences between adolescents' and adults' decision-making because it overemphasizes cognitive functioning (e.g. capacity for thinking, reasoning, understanding) and minimizes the importance of noncognitive, psychosocial, variables that influence the decision-making process" (Steinberg and Cauffman 1996:250).

Claims of some developmental psychologists that adolescents' cognitive competency approximates that of adults proves too much for purposes of youth sentencing policy. Get-tough proponents then could argue that states should punish youths for crimes just as they punish adults. In the narrow mens-rea-as-capacity formula, if a person makes a blameworthy choice, then she deserves the same punishment as another actor who makes a comparable choice (Hall 1960). For purposes of guilt, mens rea is binary; an actor either possesses criminal capacity or does not. Virtually all youths over whom juvenile courts exercise jurisdiction can distinguish between right and wrong. If they cannot, then they properly litigate the issue in the context of an insanity defense. No special doctrinal protections exist for youths older than fourteen years of age tried in criminal courts absent some "diminished responsibility" doctrine that ameliorates punishment on the grounds of reduced culpability (Arenella 1977; Morse 1985).

Many developmental psychologists question the appropriateness of advocating for presumptive legal equality based on adolescents' cognitive parity with adults to make informed medical decisions (Gardner 1989; Scott, 1992; Scott, Repucci, and Woolard 1995; Cauffman and Steinberg 1995). Cognitive capacity alone does not constitute the only relevant dimension on which policymakers can distinguish between young people and adults. More recent research indicates that child development occurs more continuously and gradually, rather than as an all-or-nothing invariant stage and sequence, and that young people use different reasoning processes simultaneously in different task domains (Siegler 1986; Gardner, Scherer, and Tester 1989; Scott 1992). Youths' developmental skills and knowledge may accrue unevenly in different task areas, rather than as a uniform increase in overall capacity. Moreover, differences in language ability, knowledge, experience, and culture affect the ages at which different individuals' various competencies emerge. "Progress toward completion of cognitive and moral developmental stages can be detoured or delayed by cultural, intellectual, and social disadvantages" (Grisso

1996:233). Comprehensive analytical reviews of developmental psychological research conclude that while those findings undermine support for the treatment of adolescents as incompetent and categorically different from adults, they do not support the converse proposition that young people and adults therefore function equally and that no legally significant differences exist between them (Scott 1992; Scott and Grisso 1998).

As a matter of sentencing policy, even a youth fourteen years of age or older who abstractly knows right from wrong, who understands intentionality, and who possesses the requisite criminal mens rea for a finding of guilt still deserves neither the blame nor the comparable punishment of an adult offender. Juveniles possess less ability than adults possess to make sound judgments or moral distinctions or to act with the same culpability as adults. Because youths possess less ability than adults possess to make moral judgments, to control their impulses, or to appreciate the consequences of their acts, they *deserve* less punishment than does an adult even when they commit the same criminal harm (Silberman 1978).

Certain characteristic developmental differences distinguish the quality of judgments that young people make from those of adults and justify a somewhat more protective stance toward younger decision makers. "[T]he intuition behind paternalistic policies is that developmentally linked traits and responses systematically affect the decisionmaking of adolescents in a way that may incline them to make choices that threaten harm to their own and others' health, life, or welfare, to a greater extent than do adults" (Scott, Reppucci, and Woolard 1995:227). Attributions of responsibility involve volitional controls—the ability to exercise self-control, as well as cognitive capacity—knowledge of right from wrong. Concepts like "psychosocial maturity" or "temperance" provide bases for assessing qualities of judgment or the decision-making competencies of adolescents compared with adults (Steinberg and Cauffman 1996; Cauffman and Steinberg 1995). Mature judgments result from the interaction of cognitive and psychosocial factors, and deficiencies in either domain may undermine competent decisions. Crucially, for purposes of comparing the quality of judgment and self-control, adolescents and adults may differ in their breadth of experience, short-term versus long-term temporal perspectives, attitudes toward risk, impulsivity, and the importance they attach to peer influences (Scott 1992; Steinberg and Cauffman 1996). Developmentally unique attributes of youth—for example, temporal perspectives, attitudes toward and acceptance of risk, and susceptibility to peer influences—affect young people's qualities of judgment in ways that distinguish them from adults, bear on their degree of criminal responsibility, and the sentences that they deserve. "Protective legal policies directed toward minors, however, are based not only on the presumption that adolescents differ from adults in these capacities, but also that their choices and behavior are affected, in ways that distinguish them developmentally from adults, by other decision-making factors. . . . (Scott, Reppucci, and Woolard 1995:222).

A developmentally informed youth sentencing policy would emphasize quality of "judgment" rather than narrow cognitive capacity; ask whether young people characteristically make poorer quality choices than they would when they are somewhat older because of adolescent-specific emotional, psychosocial, or developmental differences; and reflect young people's lesser developmental capacities. If adolescents likely will make better, adult-quality decisions with maturity, "then the case for protecting the opportunities and prospects of that future adult from the costs of her immature youthful judgment and choices seems powerful" (Scott, Reppucci, and Woolard 1995:228). Sentencing policies can and should protect young people from the adverse consequences of their developmentally less competent decisions.

Adolescents and Risk Taking

Risk entails a chance of loss; risk-taking behavior entails conduct that exposes the actor to those potential adverse consequences (Furby and Beyth-Marom 1992). Young people are more impulsive, exercise less self-control, fail adequately to calculate the long-term consequences, and engage in more risky behaviors than do adults. Adolescents may estimate the magnitude or probability of risks, may use a shorter time frame, or may focus on opportunities for gains rather than possibilities of losses differently from adults. The greater prevalence of accidents, suicides, and homicides as the primary causes of deaths among youths reflect their greater "risk-taking" behavior (Gardner 1993). Teenagers' greater proclivity to engage in unprotected sex, to speed and drive recklessly, and to engage in criminal behavior reflect their taking risks with health and safety (Hirschi and Gottfredson 1983; Scott, Reppucci, and Woolard 1995).

Criminal behavior constitutes a specific form of highly risky behavior, and every theory of crime attempts to account for the age-specific nature of offending (e.g., Gottfredson and Hirschi 1990). The differences between adolescent and adult decision making with regard to risk are relevant in assessing criminal responsibility for the quality of their choices. An extensive review of the empirical literature on risk taking and cognitive development reports "mixed results regarding the degree to which adolescents may be taking more risks than other age level[s]," and cautions that "we know very little about either overall decision-making competence among adolescence or the development of specific skills that are necessary for or that facilitate effective decision-making" (Furby and Beyth-Marom 1992:38). A decision-making calculus requires the actor to identify possible outcomes, identify possible consequences that may follow from each option, evaluate the positive or negative desirability of those consequences, estimate the likelihood of each of those various consequences occurring, and develop a decisional rule to optimize outcomes (Furby and Beyth-Marom 1992).

Experimental and developmental psychological literature suggests that adolescents approach the various decision-making steps differently from adults. Youths may engage in riskier behavior than adults do because youths differ in both the extent of knowledge they possess and the amount of information they actually use when they make decisions. Unlike informed-consent cognitive tests performed under laboratory conditions with all relevant information, in less-structured, real-life conditions adolescents simply may possess or use less information about risks than do adults. Adolescents' estimation of risks, for example, may be linked with experience, and they may calculate probabilities of risks differently from adults (Furby and Beyth-Marom 1992). Even though young people may possess more cognitive competence than the law assumes, we cannot directly equate their "cognitive competence with things like knowledge, experience, and intelligence. . . . A child may simply not know as much or have experienced as much as an adult. That is not to say that, relative to what they have experienced and do know, each may not have the same ability to make rational decisions" (Archard 1993:66). Rather, young people's risky choices may reflect a more truncated frame of reference or more limited fund of knowledge.

Even when adolescents possess and use comparable information, they may assign different subjective values to the alternative consequences. Youths' developmentally influenced cost-benefit calculus may induce them to weigh benefits and consequences differently and to discount negative future consequences in ways that may systematically skew the quality of their choices. "[R]elative to adults, adolescents appear to view long-term consequences as less important than short-term consequences, and may thus see many risks . . . as inconsequential, since the importance of longer term consequences is reduced by uncertainty about the future" (Cauffman and Steinberg 1995: 1773). In some instances, youths may simply perceive risky behavior as posing lower probabilities of eventuating than do adults (Gardner and Herman 1990; Cauffman and Steinberg 1995). "[A]dolescents [may] judge some negative consequences in the distant future to be of lower probability than do adults or to be of less importance than adults do" (Furby and Beyth-Marom 1992: 19). In other cases, youths' subjective valuations of risks and consequences may cause them to make different choices from those of adults. Adolescents also may weigh the negative consequences of *not* engaging in risky behaviors differently from adults. For example, just saying "no" to drugs may not mean the same thing to a teenager seeking peer acceptance and good feelings as it does to an adult with greater appreciation of the risks of drugs and more to lose from involvement in the justice system. Similarly, an adolescent's decision to "joy-ride" with friends in a stolen car or to participate in a robbery may reflect a different risk calculus from an adult's in terms of a greater emphasis on short-term benefits versus long-term negative legal consequences (Scott, Reppucci, and Woolard 1995). Youths' impulsivity, unrealistic optimism, or feelings of "invulnerability" and "immortality" may contribute to risk taking (Furby and Beyth-Marom 1992). In addition to a sense of personal invulnerability, adolescents engage in health-threatening activities because they do not regard such behavior as extremely risky or unsafe (Cauffman and Steinberg 1995).

Rational choice theory also helps to explain adolescents' greater propensity for risk taking. People make utility-maximizing choices within a context of constraints, and people at different places in their life course will make different valuations of uncertain future events (Gardner 1993). Knowledge about one's self, environment, and life trajectory increase with age and affect a person's short-term versus long-term calculus. Because young people have much less clarity about their futures than do adults, "a focus on the immediate rather than the long-term consequences of a decision is a rational response to uncertainty about the future" (Gardner 1993:77). As a result, young people may discount negative future consequences because they have more difficulty than adults have with integrating a long-term future result into their more limited experiential baseline. Adolescents may discount the costs in the longer-term future and weigh more heavily shorter-term benefits (Gardner and Herman 1990).

Another developmental perspective for assessing adolescent risk taking emphasizes *temperance* or the ability to limit impulsivity and to evaluate a situation thoroughly (Steinberg and Cauffman 1996). Developmental psychological studies examine ways in which adolescents' judgments may differ from adults because of adolescents' disposition toward sensation seeking, impulsivity related to hormonal or physiological changes, and mood volatility. Sensation seeking refers to people's preferences for intense and novel experiences, and in middle to late adolescence, youths appear to place a higher priority on thrill seeking than do adults (Cauffman and Steinberg 1995). For example, hormonal and physiological changes, mood volatility, and predisposition toward sensation seeking affect the quality of decision making and maturity of judgments and cause adolescents to experience more difficulty controlling their impulses than adults do (Steinberg and Cauffman 1996). Because a predisposition to risk taking reflects generic developmental processes, rather than malevolent personal choices, it provides one sentencing policy rationale to protect the adult that a youth eventually will become from the detrimental consequences of immature decisions (Scott 1992).

Peer Group Influences

Adolescents respond to peer group influences more readily than do adults because of the crucial role of peer relationships in their identity formation (Erikson 1968). Youths' greater desire for acceptance and approval renders them more susceptible to peer influences as they adjust their behaviors and attitudes to conform to those of their contemporaries (Scott, Reppucci, and Woolard 1995). "[S]ocial status appear[s] to be an important factor to many adolescents, and this may contribute to risky decision-making" (Cauffman and Steinberg 1995:1773).

As Franklin Zimring observed, "Young people commit their crimes, as they live their lives, in groups" (1981a:867). Police arrest a larger proportion of two or more juveniles for involvement in a single criminal event than they do adults (Snyder and Sickmund 1995). Young people's greater susceptibility to peer group influences and group process dynamics than their older counterparts lessens, but does not excuse, their criminal responsibility. Group-offending places normally law-abiding youth at greater risk of involvement and reduces their ability publicly to withdraw. Because of the social context of adolescent crime, young people require time, experience, and opportunities to develop the capacity for autonomous judgments and to resist peer influences. "[B]etween the ages of 10 and 18, adolescents grow more able to make decisions on their own, and . . . sometime between the ages of 12 and 16, peer pressure begins to play a smaller role in adolescent decision-making" (Steinberg and Cauffman 1996:254). Because the group nature of youth crime renders all equally criminally liable, it poses a challenge to formulate a youth sentencing policy that recognizes differential participation and culpability of different adolescent members of a group.

Reduced Culpability

As recalled from chapter 6, in *Thompson v. Oklahoma* (487 U.S. 815 [1988]), the Supreme Court analyzed the criminal responsibility of young offenders and provided some additional support for shorter sentences for reduced culpability for youths older than the common-law infancy threshold of age fourteen. The *Thompson* plurality vacated Thompson's capital sentence because the Court concluded that a fifteen-year-old offender could not act "with the degree of culpability that can justify the ultimate penalty" (486 U.S. at 834). Although the Court provided several rationales for its decision, it explicitly decided that juveniles are less culpable for the same crimes than are their adult counterparts. Also, *Thompson* reaffirmed several earlier decisions that also emphasized that youthfulness constitutes an important mitigating factor when judges sentence young defendants (e.g., *Eddings v. Oklahoma*, 455 U.S. 104, at 116 [1982]).

Subjective Time

Quite apart from differences in culpability, because of differences in their "time perspective," juveniles deserve less-severe punishment than do adults for comparable criminal harms. Although we measure penalties in units of time—days, months, or years—youths and adults subjectively and objectively conceive of and experience similar lengths of time differently (Piaget 1969; Cottle 1976; Friedman 1982). The developmental progression in thinking about and experiencing time—future time perspective and present duration— follows a developmental sequence that affects the evolution of mature judgment and criminal responsibility. The ability to project events and consequences into the future evolves gradually during adolescence into early adulthood (Steinberg and Cauffman 1996). Without a mature appreciation of future time, juveniles may be less able to understand or fully realize the consequences of their acts, may give excessive weight to immediate goals, and, as a result, engage in riskier behavior. "[A]dolescents, particularly in the early and middle teen years, are more vulnerable, more impulsive, and less self-disciplined than adults. Crimes committed by youths . . . deserve less punishment because adolescents have less capacity to control their conduct and to *think in long-range terms* than adults" (Twentieth Century Fund Task Force 1978:7, emphasis added).

Because juveniles do not experience present time duration equivalently with adults, a policy of "adult crime, adult time" that imposes equal sentence lengths on adults and juveniles would be disproportionately more severe for the latter. Because of developmental differences, time *seems* to pass more slowly when we are younger. Developmental psychological research supports older people's common observation that time seems to speed up as they age. Consequently, young people experience objectively equivalent sentences subjectively as more severe and of longer duration. Analogously, if we think of a sentence as a fraction of our life and conceive of our age as the denominator, then the same numerator will make up a larger proportion of a young person's life than of an older individuals. While a three-month sentence may be lenient for an adult offender, for a child it represents the equivalent of an entire summer vacation—a very long time. One year in the life of a sixteen-year-old represents 6 percent of her total life span; the same period represents only 3 percent of a thirty-two-year-old offender's life. Because of these developmental differences in the ways that adults and juveniles subjectively experience the passage of time, it would be unjust to impose equal sentences on both even for similar offenses. Because juveniles depend on their families for support more than do adults, sentences of home removal or confinement are more developmentally disruptive than they would be for more completely formed and independent adults.

A Youth Sentencing Policy Rationale

Certain characteristic developmental differences between adolescents and adults distinguish their quality of judgment, psychosocial maturity, and self-control and justify a different criminal sentencing policy for younger offenders. Youths differ from adults in several dimensions that directly affect both their degree of criminal responsibility and deserved punishment: breadth of experience, short-term versus long-term temporal perspectives, attitudes toward and acceptance of risks, and susceptibility to peer influences. These developmentally unique attributes affect young people's capacity to comprehend fully the consequences of their actions and their empathic identification with others. Moreover, it takes time and experience to develop the capacity to exercise self-control. While young offenders possess sufficient understanding and culpability to hold them accountable for their acts, their choices deserve less blame than do those of adults because of their truncated self-control. Their crimes are less blameworthy, not simply because of reduced culpability and limited appreciation of consequences, but because their life situations have understandably limited their capacity to learn to make fully responsible choices.

When youths offend, the families, schools, and communities that socialize them bear some responsibility for failing to do so adequately. "[Y]outh crime as such is not exclusively the offender's fault; offenses by the young also represent a failure of family, school, and the social system which share responsibility for the development of youth" (Twentieth Century Fund Task Force 1978:7). Human beings depend on others for nurture, which includes the ability to develop and exercise the moral capacity for constructive behavior. The capacity for self-control and self-direction is not a matter of luck or good fortune but a socially constructed developmental process that provides young people with the opportunity to develop a moral character.

Community structures affect social conditions and the contexts within which adolescents grow and interact with peers. Unlike presumptively mobile adults, because of their dependency juveniles lack the means or ability to escape from their criminogenic environments. Franklin Zimring (1982) describes the "semi-autonomy" of adolescence as a "learner's permit" that gives youths the opportunity to make choices and to learn to be responsible but without suffering fully the long-term consequences of their mistakes. A youth sentencing policy minimizes the harm young persons do themselves, reduces to a minimum the harm sanctions inflict on them when they harm the community, and "preserves the life chances for those who make serious mistakes" (Zimring 1982:91). The ability to make responsible choices is learned behavior, and the dependent status of youth systematically deprives them of chances to learn to be responsible. Inevitably, when we grant young people autonomy in order to learn to make mature judgments, they will abuse that trust. Young people's socially constructed life situations understandably limit their capacity to develop self-control, restrict their opportunities to learn and exercise responsibility, and support a partial reduction of criminal responsibility. Adolescence itself limits opportunities fully to develop and internalize responsible adult-quality decision making. Youths' susceptibility to peer group influences reflects truncated development of their own capacity to make autonomous and independent judgments. Thus, a youth sentencing policy must recognize youths' reduced opportunities and abilities to learn and to make responsible choices. Such a policy would entail both shorter sentence durations and a higher offense-seriousness threshold before a state incarcerates youths than for older offenders.

Administering Youthfulness as a Mitigating Factor at Sentencing: The "Youth Discount"

Implementing a rational and developmentally informed youth sentencing policy entails legal, moral and social judgments. I propose what a reasonable, responsible, and humane legislature *should do* when it considers the criminal who is a child, rather than what the Constitution permits or requires of states. Because of developmental differences and the social construction of adolescence, younger offenders are less criminally responsible than more mature law violators. But they are not so fundamentally different and inherently incompetent as the current legal dichotomy between juvenile and criminal courts suggests. The binary distinction between child and adult that provides the bases for states' legal age of majority and the jurisprudential foundation of the juvenile court ignores the reality that adolescents develop along a continuum and creates an unfortunate either-or choice in sentencing. In view of the developmental psychological research that suggests several ways in which youths' culpability systematically differs from that of adults, should the criminal law adopt a "youth-blind" stance and treat fourteen-year-olds as the moral equivalents of adults for purposes of sentencing, or should it devise a youth sentencing policy that reflects more appropriately the developmental continuum? If criminal sentences reflect the *seriousness* of an offense, then the law should recognize developmentally specific qualitative differences in the culpability of choices that adolescents make. Thus, developmental research and sentencing policy clearly justify a policy of youthfulness as a mitigating factor.

Shorter sentences for reduced responsibility represents a more modest but attainable reason to treat young people differently from adults than the rehabilitative justifications advanced by Progressive child savers. In this context, adolescent criminal responsibility represents a global judgment about the degree of youths' deserved punishment, rather than a technical legal judgment about whether a youth possessed the requisite mens rea or mental state required by the criminal code. The criminal justice system can do nothing to alleviate the harm that youths already have caused to their victims. However, sentencing policies can reduce somewhat the long-term harm that adolescents cause to themselves as a result of their characteristically exercised poorer judgment. "[I]f the values that drive risky choices are associated with youth, and predictably will change with maturity, then our paternalistic inclination is to protect the young decision-maker . . . from his or her bad judgment" (Scott 1992:1656). Protecting young people from the full penal consequences of their poor decisions reflects a policy to preserve their life chances for the future when they presumably would make more mature and responsible choices. Such a policy simultaneously holds young offenders accountable for their acts because they possess sufficient culpability and yet mitigates the severity of consequences because their choices entail less blameworthiness than those of adults.

As recalled from my analyses of proportionality in sentencing waived juveniles in chapter 6, criminal courts in some states already consider "youthfulness" in the context of aggravating and mitigating factors and may impose shorter sentences on a discretionary basis. Although the federal sentencing guidelines reject "youthfulness" as a reason to depart from the guidelines range (U.S. Sentencing Commission 1995:§ 5H.1), several states' sentencing laws do recognize "youthfulness" as a mitigating factor. These statutes enumerate several mitigating factors that may include some elements of "youthfulness," for example, "the defendant's *age, immaturity,* or limited mental capacity" (N. Car. Gen. Stat. § 15A-1340.16(e)(4)[1996], emphasis added); "the defendant was *too young to appreciate the consequences* of the offense (Fla. Stat. § 921.0016(4)(k)[1996], emphasis added)"; or simply "the *youth of the offender* at the time of the offense (La. Rev. Stat. Ann. § 905.5(f)[West 1997], emphasis added). Under these aggravating-mitigating sentencing laws, trial court judges consider "youthfulness" when they sentence a young defendant. "[C]ourts should consider the concept of youth in context, i.e. the defendant's age, education, maturity, experience, mental capacity or development, and any other pertinent circumstance tending to demonstrate the defendant's ability or inability to appreciate the nature of his conduct" (*State v. Adams*, 864 S.W.2d 31, 33 [Tenn. 1993]). However, judges who consider youthfulness among other aggravating and mitigating factors do not assign controlling weight to it when they impose a sentence. Again, as recalled from chapter 6, whether a judge treats youthfulness as a mitigating factor rests within her "sound discretion." Failure to afford a young offender leniency does not constitute reversible error or an abuse of discretion.

A statutory sentencing policy that integrates youthfulness and limited opportunities to learn self-control with principles of proportionality and reduced culpability would provide younger offenders with categorical fractional reductions of adult sentences. Because youthfulness constitutes a universal form of "reduced responsibility" or "diminished capacity," states should treat it unequivocally and categorically as a mitigating factor without regard to nuances of individual developmental differences. Treating youthfulness as a formal mitigating sentencing factor represents a social, moral, and criminal legal policy judgment about degrees of responsibility, rather than a discretionary clinical or psychiatric evaluation of culpability. Such a categorical approach avoids the risks of subjectivity inherent in individualized culpability determinations such as "amenability to treatment."

This categorical approach would take the form of an explicit "youth discount" at sentencing. A fourteen-year-old offender might receive, for example, 25 to 33 percent of the adult penalty; a 16-year-old defendant, 50 to 66 percent; and an eighteen-year-old adult, the full penalty, as is presently the case. The "deeper discounts" for younger offenders correspond to the developmental continuum and their more limited opportunities to learn self-control and to exercise responsibility. A youth discount based on reduced culpability functions as a sliding scale of diminished responsibility. Just as adolescents possess less criminal responsibility than do adults, fourteen-year-old youths should enjoy a greater mitigation of blameworthiness than would seventeen-year-olds. Because the rationale for youthful mitigation rests on reduced culpability and limited opportunities to learn to make responsible choices, younger adolescents bear less responsibility and deserve proportionally shorter sentences than do older youths. The capacity to learn to be responsible improves with time and experience. With the passage of time, age, and opportunities to develop the capacity for self-control, social tolerance of criminal deviance and claims for mitigation based on youthfulness decline.

Several youth sentencing policy groups and scholars implicitly endorse the concept of a youth discount, or sliding scale of criminal responsibility for younger offenders. The ABA and Institute of Judicial Administration's *Juvenile*

Justice Standards Relating to Dispositions emphasize the relationship between age and sanctions: "The age of the juvenile is also relevant to the determination of the seriousness of his or her behavior. In most cases, the older the juvenile, the greater is his or her responsibility for breaking the law" (1980a:35). The Twentieth Century Fund Task Force on Sentencing Policy Toward Young Offenders, in *Confronting Youth Crime*, also concludes that most young offenders, by ages thirteen or fourteen, should be held accountable, at least to some degree, for the criminal harms they cause. Youths of that age "are aware of the severity of the criminal harms they inflict and that, much as they *fall short of maturity or self-control*, they are morally and should be legally responsible for intentionally destructive behavior. The older the adolescent, the greater the degree of responsibility the law should presume" (1978:6–7, emphasis added). The sentencing principles of frugality or parsimony of punishment (Morris 1974) and the "least restrictive alternative" also provide support for a youth discount. The *Juvenile Justice Standards* propose that "the court should employ the least restrictive category and duration of disposition that is appropriate to the seriousness of the offense, as modified by the *degree of culpability* indicated by the circumstances of the particular case, and by the *age* and prior record of the juvenile (1980a: 34, emphasis added). The National Advisory Committee for Criminal Justice Standards and Goals also endorses the idea of a youth discount: "In choosing among statutorily permissible dispositions, the court should employ the least coercive category and duration of disposition that are appropriate to the seriousness of the delinquent act, as modified by the degree of culpability indicated by the circumstances of the particular case, *age* and prior record" (1980:440, emphasis added).

Discounted sentences that preserve young offenders' life chances require that the maximum sentences they receive remain substantially below those imposed on adults. "The principle of diminished responsibility makes life imprisonment and death penalties inappropriate," for example, even in cases of intentional murder (Twentieth Century Fund Task Force 1978:17). Several of the "serious offender" and "designated felony" juvenile sentencing statutes reviewed in chapter 7 provide examples of sentence lengths for serious young offenders considerably shorter than the sentences their adult counterparts receive and suggest some "discount" rates. The *Juvenile Justice Standards Relating to Delinquency and Sanctions* (1980d) used adult sentence lengths to establish ordinal proportionality, classified all crimes into five categories based on the penalty attached to them, and then provided substantially shorter, scaled-down juvenile sanctions for the same offenses with a maximum period of secure confinement of thirty-six months for the most serious crimes. The American Law Institute's *Model Penal Code* recommended special sentencing provisions for "young adult offenders" with a maximum length of four years and noted that "the special sentence should relate to the *duration* of commitment . . . adapted to the age of the offender" (1957:25, emphasis added). For youths below the age of fourteen, the common-law infancy mens rea defense would acquire new vitality for proportionally shorter sentences or even noncriminal dispositions.

The rationale for a youth discount also supports requiring a higher in/out threshold of offense seriousness as a prerequisite of imprisonment. Because juveniles depend on their families more than do adults, removal from home constitutes a more severe punishment. Because of differences in "subjective time," youths experience the duration of imprisonment more acutely than do adults. Because of the rapidity of maturational changes during adolescence, sentences of incarceration are more developmentally disruptive for youths than for adults. Thus, states should require a higher threshold of offense seriousness and a greater need for social defense before confining a youth than might be warranted for an adult offender.

The specific discount value—the amount of fractional reduction and the raised in/out threshold—reflects several empirical and normative considerations. It requires an empirically informed sentencing policy judgment about adolescent development and criminal responsibility. To what extent do developmentally specific physical, social, and psychological characteristics of youth—depreciation of future consequences, risk taking, peer influences, lack of self-control, hormonal changes, and lack of opportunities to learn to make responsible choices—induce them to engage in criminal behavior simply because they are young and that reasonable adults have learned to avoid? How much developmental difference should a state require to produce what degree of moral and legal mitigation in its sentencing policy? To what extent will severe, unmitigated penalties so alter youths' life course that they will be unable to survive the mistakes of adolescence with their life chances intact? Developmental psychological research provides only suggestive directions rather than definitive answers to these sentencing policy questions (Scott and Grisso 1998). Indeed, contemplating a youth discount implicates the social construction of adolescence itself.

Only states whose criminal sentencing laws already impose realistic, humane, and determinate sentences that enable a judge actually to determine "real-time" adult sentences can readily implement a proposal for explicit fractional reductions of youths' sentences (Frase 1991; Tonry 1987, 1995). One can only know the value of a "youth discounted" sentence in a sentencing system in which courts know in advance the standard or "going rate" for adults. In many jurisdictions, implementing a youth discount system would require significant modification of the criminal sentencing statutes, including presumptive sentencing guidelines with strong upper limits on punishment severity, elimination of all mandatory minimum sentences, and some structured judicial discretion to mitigate penalties based on individual circumstances (Tonry 1995, 1996). In short, the criminal sentencing system must be defensible in terms of equality, equity, desert, and proportionality. Attempts to apply idiosyncratically youth discounts within the flawed indeterminate or draconian mandatory minimum sentencing regimes that many states use currently runs the risk simply of reproducing all their existing inequalities and inconsistencies.

Individualization versus Categorization

Youthful development is highly variable. Young people of the same age may differ dramatically in their criminal sophistication, appreciation of risks, or learned responsibility. Chronological age provides, at best, a crude and imprecise indicator of criminal maturity and the opportunity to develop a capacity for self-control. However, a categorical youth discount that uses age as a conclusive proxy for reduced culpability and a shorter sentence remains preferable to an individualized inquiry into the degree of criminal responsibility possessed by each young offender. The criminal law represents an objective standard. Attempts to integrate subjective psychological explanations of adolescent behavior and personal responsibility into a youth sentencing policy cannot be done in a way that can be administered fairly without undermining the objectivity of the law. Developmental psychology does not possess reliable clinical indicators of moral development or criminal sophistication that equate readily with criminal responsibility or individual accountability. For young criminal actors who possess at least some degree of criminal responsibility, relying on inherently inconclusive or contradictory psychiatric or clinical testimony to precisely tailor sanctions hardly seems worth the judicial burden and diversion of resources that the effort would entail. The administrative experiences with the insanity and diminished responsibility defenses in the criminal law and with judicial assessments of "amenability to treatment" in waiver proceedings teach that efforts to individualize culpability assessments founder on clinical subjectivity, differences among experts about symptomology and their effects on choices, the inability of juries and judges rationally and consistently to assess culpability, and uncertainty about the penal purposes being advanced by the inquiry (Goldstein 1967; Kadish 1968; Morse 1984, 1985). Thus, for ease of administration, age alone remains the most useful criterion on which to allocate mitigation.

Youthful mitigation of criminal responsibility represents a legal concept and a social policy judgment that does not correspond with any psychiatric diagnostic category or developmental psychological analogue about which a forensic expert could testify. Unlike the insanity defense, a youth discount does not attempt to assess whether antecedent forces, such as a mental illness, caused or determined the young offender's behavior or impaired her capacity to choose. Rather, it conclusively presumes that young people's criminal choices differ qualitatively per se from those of adults. Youthfulness constitutes a form of legal "partial responsibility" or diminished capacity without any need for specific clinical indicators other than a birth certificate.

A youth discount that bases fractional reductions of sentences on age as proxy for culpability also avoids the conceptual and administrative difficulties of a more encompassing inquiry into diminished responsibility (Arenella 1977), a "rotten social background" (Delgado 1982), or "social adversity" (Tonry 1995). Although the criminal law's "diminished responsibility" doctrine attempts to link a sane defendant's mental abnormality with some reduced degree of criminal responsibility, efforts to evaluate subjective culpability result in inconsistent, confusing and arbitrary applications. "[A] finding of diminished responsibility does not negate the defendant's criminal responsibility; it merely mitigates his punishment because his mental disability makes him less culpable than the normal defendant who committed the identical criminal act" (Arenella 1977:850). Diminished responsibility allows the defendant to introduce psychological evidence about why he was less responsible than an ordinary person as a formal mitigation of punishment, although it is unclear to what legal formulas that evidence corresponds (Arenella 1977). Similarly, a "rotten social background" defense posits that a person raised in a manifestly criminogenic environment—grinding deprivation and poverty, minimal parental or familial support, exposure to violence and abuse, tutelage in crime by older youths "on the street"—cannot make the same moral choices as those born in more advantageous circumstances and should not be held to the same degree of criminal responsibility (Delgado 1982). However, if the criminal law recognized a "rotten background" or "social adversity" defense, then it would denigrate its claimants by implying that "those people are not responsible adults whose moral choices matter. Since recognition of moral autonomy entails acknowledgment of people's responsibility for their willed actions, a social adversity defense cutting that link would deny the actor's autonomy" (Tonry 1995:141). Moreover, unlike age, which everyone outgrows with time, formal recognition of social determinism would stigmatize all members of the disadvantaged class and reduce their incentives to refrain from criminality (Tonry 1995). The difficulty of determining whether particular social conditions should mitigate or excuse criminal liability would undermine the objectivity and deterrent functions of criminal law. More fundamentally, defenses that recognize deficiencies of character as excuses for criminal liability undermine the value of responsibility and encourage deterministic claims of lack of culpability (Kadish 1987). Juvenile courts' treatment ideology mistakenly denies that young people are morally responsible actors whom the law may hold accountable for their behavior.

A youth sentencing policy requires formal mitigation to avoid the undesirable forced choice between either inflicting undeservedly harsh punishments on less-culpable actors or "doing nothing" about the manifestly guilty (Bernard 1992). Mitigation avoids the pressures judges and juries historically experienced to nullify and acquit the "somewhat guilty" or to punish excessively the "partially" responsible. A formal policy of youthful mitigation also provides a buffer against the inevitable political pressures to ratchet up sanctions every time youths sentenced leniently subsequently commit a serious offense. The *idea* of deserved punishment also limits the imposition of *too little* punishment as well as too much. Although the overall cardinal scale of penalties for juveniles should be considerably less than that for adults, a failure to sanction when appropriate, as juvenile court treatment ideology dictates in some instances, can deprecate the moral seriousness of offending. Indeed, juvenile court judges de facto reinstate the principle of offense and punish young offenders exactly because a treatment ideology cannot justify clinically, lenient or disparate, individualized sentences (Matza 1964).

Youthfulness and Group Criminality

As noted earlier, young offenders commit their crimes in groups to a much greater extent than do adults. Although the law treats all participants in a crime as equally responsible and may sentence them alike, young people's susceptibility to peer group influences requires a more nuanced assessment of their degree of participation, personal responsibility, and culpability. "The pervasive problem of the adolescent accessory aggravates the difficulty of determining appropriate sanctions for youth crime" (Zimring 1981a:883). The group nature of youth crime affects sentencing policy in several ways. Because of susceptibility to peer influences, the presence of a social audience may induce youths to participate in criminal behavior in which they would not engage if alone. Even though the criminal law treats all accomplices as equally guilty, they may not all bear equal responsibility for the actual harm inflicted and may *deserve* different sentences. To some extent, state criminal sentencing laws already recognize an offender's differential participation in a crime as a "mitigating" factor. Some states' juvenile court waiver laws and juvenile sentencing provisions also focus on "the *culpability* of the child in committing the alleged offense, including the level of the child's *participation in planning and carrying* out the offense" (Feld 1995, emphasis added). Thus, the group nature of adolescent criminality requires some formal mechanism to distinguish between active participants and passive accomplices with even greater "discounts" for the latter.

Virtue of Affirming Partial Responsibility for Youth

In the Broadway musical *West Side Story*, The Jets sing the song, "Gee, Officer Krupke," in which they invoke many of the popular deterministic explanations of their delinquency. One boy complains, "Our mothers all are junkies, Our fathers all are drunks," and the chorus responds, "We never had the love that every child ought a get." Another youth observes that he's "depraved on account I'm deprived," and others' self-diagnoses observe, "We are sick sick sick, Like we're sociologically sick." One boy prescribes "a analyst's care! It's just his neurosis that ought a be curbed—He's psychologically disturbed" (Sondheim 1956:114–116). In short, the delinquents readily understood cultural explanations of criminality, invoked exculpatory appeals to determinism, and employed "techniques of neutralization" to relieve themselves of responsibility for their behavior (Sykes and Matza 1957).

One of the principal virtues, Abraham Goldstein (1967) argues in his seminal defense of *The Insanity Defense*, is that it dramatically affirms the idea of individual responsibility. Because the criminal law emphasizes blame, the insanity defense attempts to distinguish between the "mad" and the "bad," between the "sick" and the "evil" in order to reinforce the concept of personal responsibility. The *idea* of personal responsibility and holding people accountable for their behavior provides an important counterweight to a popular culture that endorses the idea that everyone is a victim, that all behavior is determined and no one is responsible, and that therefore the state cannot blame wrongdoers (Sykes 1992). Similarly, in *The Limits of the Criminal Sanction*, Herbert Packer argues that regardless of how psychologists or philosophers ultimately resolve the "free will versus determinism" debate, it is desirable to act "as if" responsible people make voluntary choices.

> The idea of free will in relation to conduct is not, in the legal system, a statement of fact, but rather a value preference having very little to do with the metaphysics of determinism and free will. . . . Very simply, the law treats man's conduct as autonomous and willed, not because it is, but because it is desirable to proceed as if it were. It is desirable because the capacity of the individual human being to live his life in reasonable freedom from socially imposed external constraints . . . would be fatally impaired unless the law provided a *locus poenitentiae*, a point of no return beyond which external constraints may be imposed but before which the individual is free—not free of whatever compulsions determinists tell us he labors under but free of the very specific social compulsions of the law. (Packer 1968:74–75).

The Progressives located the juvenile court on several cultural and criminological fault lines. The juvenile court's rehabilitative ideal elevated determinism over free will, characterized delinquent offenders as victims rather than perpetrators, and envisioned a therapeutic institution that resembled more closely a preventive, forward-looking civil commitment process rather than a criminal court. By denying youths' personal responsibility, juvenile court's treatment ideology reduces offenders' duty to exercise self-control, erodes their obligation to change, and sustains a self-fulfilling prophecy that delinquency occurs inevitably for youths from certain backgrounds.

Affirming responsibility encourages people to learn the virtues of moderation, self-discipline, and personal accountability. Acknowledging that we *punish* young offenders for their misconduct "becomes part of a complex of cultural forces that keep alive the moral lessons, and the myths, which are essential to the continued order of society. In short, even if we have misgiving about blaming a particular individual, because he has been shaped long ago by forces he may no longer be able to resist, the concept of 'blame' may be necessary" (Goldstein 1967:224). Because a criminal conviction represents an official condemnation, the idea of "blame" reinforces for the public and provides for the defendant the incentive to develop individual responsibility. A culture that values autonomous individuals must emphasize both freedom and responsibility.

While the paternalistic stance of the traditional juvenile courts rests on the humane desire to protect young people from the adverse consequences of their bad decisions, protectionism disables young people from the opportunity to learn to make choices and to be responsible for their natural consequences. Even marginally competent adolescents can only learn self-control by exercising their capacity for autonomy. Accountability for criminal behavior may facilitate moral development and legal socialization in ways that the traditional rejection of youthful criminal responsibility cannot.

The Virtues of an Integrated Criminal Justice System

A graduated age-culpability sentencing scheme in an integrated criminal justice system avoids the inconsistencies and injustices associated with the binary either-juvenile-or-adult drama currently played out in judicial waiver proceedings and in prosecutorial charging decisions. It avoids the "punishment gap" between the two systems when youths make the transition from the one to the other. As we recall from chapter 6, depending on whether or not a judge or prosecutor transfers a case, the sentences that violent youths receive may differ by orders of magnitude. Moreover, appellate courts avoid proportionality analyses and allow criminal court judges to sentence waived youths to the same terms applied to adults without requiring judges to consider or recognize any differences in youths' degree of criminal responsibility. By contrast, waived chronic property offenders typically receive less-severe sanctions as adults than they could have obtained as persistent offenders in the juvenile system. As noted in chapter 7, the sentencing principles and practices of juvenile courts resemble more closely those of criminal courts. As a result, the disparities of consequences that follow from a waiver decision become even less defensible. Because of the "life and death" consequences at stake, transfer hearings consume an inordinate amount of juvenile court time and energy (Dawson 1990a).

An integrated criminal justice system eliminates the need for transfer hearings, saves the considerable resources that juvenile courts currently expend ultimately to no purpose, reduces the punishment gap that presently occurs when youths make the passage from the juvenile system, and ensures similar consequences for similar offenders. Adolescence and criminal careers develop along a continuum. But the radical bifurcation between the two justice systems confounds efforts to respond consistently and systematically to young career offenders.

A sliding scale of criminal sentences based on an offender's age as proxy for culpability accomplishes much more directly what the various "blended jurisdiction" statutes attempt to achieve indirectly. Also, in chapter 7, we saw that the variants of "intermediate" sanctions ultimately reflect the binary alternatives of either a sentence limited by juvenile court age jurisdiction or a dramatically longer criminal sentence imposed on a youth as an adult. While those statutes attempt to smooth the juncture between the two systems, the existence of two separate systems thwarts the fusion.

Integrated Record Keeping

The absence of an integrated record-keeping system that enables criminal court judges to identify and respond to career offenders on the basis of their cumulative prior record constitutes one of the more pernicious consequences of jurisdictional bifurcation. Currently, persistent young offenders may "fall between the cracks" of the juvenile and criminal systems, often at the age at which career offenders approach their peak rates of offending. An integrated criminal court with a single record-keeping system can maintain and retrieve more accurate criminal histories when courts sentence offenders. Although a youth discount provides appropriate leniency for first-or second-time offenders, integrated records allow courts to escalate the "discounted" sanctions for chronic and career offenders.

Decriminalize Kid's Stuff

Despite juvenile courts' overcrowded dockets and inadequate treatment resources, their procedural deficiencies and informality allow them to process delinquents too efficiently. Expedited procedures, fewer lawyers and legal challenges, and greater flexibility allows juvenile court judges to handle a much larger number of cases per judge than do criminal courts and at lower unit cost (Snyder and Sickmund 1995; Feld 1995). Merging the two systems would introduce an enormous volume of cases into an already overburdened criminal justice system that can barely cope with its current workload.

A youth sentencing policy should distinguish between "adolescent-only" and "life-course persistent" offenders. As recalled from chapter 6, extensive research indicates that criminal behavior is normative for most adolescents, and the majority of "adolescent-only" offenders spontaneously desist from criminality as a normal part of the maturational process. Only a small cadre of any birth cohort become chronic offenders and persist in a life of crime into adulthood. This small group of chronic career offenders constitutes the most appropriate target of any law enforcement strategy. Prosecutors forced to allocate scarce law enforcement resources would use the seriousness of the offense and the persistence of offending to rationalize charging decisions and to "divert" or "decriminalize" most of the "kid stuff" that currently provides the grist of the juvenile court mill. Unlike a rehabilitative system inclined to extend its benevolent reach, an explicitly punitive process would opt to introduce fewer and more criminally "deserving" youths into the system. The well-documented phenomenon of desistance indicates that *most* young offenders spontaneously abandon their tentative criminal involvements without justice system intervention and that maturation accounts for most of the success of diversion and informal probation.

Sentencing Expertise

Contemporary proponents of a specialized juvenile court contend that judges require substantial time and commitment to become familiar with youth development, family dynamics, and community resources and cite judges' dispositional expertise as one justification for a separate juvenile court (Edwards 1992). Whether juvenile court judges actually acquire such expertise or possess the resources with which to use it remains unclear. In many jurisdictions, nonspecialist judges handle juvenile matters as part of their general trial docket or rotate through juvenile court on short-term assignments without developing any special sophistication in sentencing juveniles (Rubin 1979; Edwards 1992). Even in specialized juvenile courts, the court services personnel, rather than the judge herself, typically possess the information necessary to recommend appropriate dispositions. Within the range of sentence lengths determined by the offense and reduced by the youth discount, courts still could provide young offenders with whatever social or welfare services they deem appropriate.

Age-Segregated Dispositional Facilities and "Room to Reform"

Questions about young offenders' criminal liability or their degree of accountability differ from issues about the appropriate place of confinement or the services or resources the state should provide to them. Even explicitly punitive sentences do not require judges or correctional authorities to confine young people with adults in jails and prisons, as is the current practice for waived youths, or to consign them to custodial warehouses or "punk prisons." States should maintain separate, age-segregated youth correctional facilities to protect both younger offenders and older inmates (Twentieth Century Fund Task Force 1978). Even though youths are somewhat responsible for their criminal conduct, they may not be the physical or psychological equals of adults in prison. While some youths may be vulnerable to victimization or exploitation by more physically developed adults, other youths may pose a threat to older inmates. As noted in chapter 6, younger offenders have not learned to "do easy time," pose more management problems for correctional administrators, and commit more disciplinary infractions while they serve their sentences. A study of prison rule violations reported that "[a]ge was the prisoner characteristic that related most directly to prison rule violations ... [and] the younger the age category, the larger the percentage of inmates charged with rule violations" (Stephan 1989:2). Thus, both program and control considerations dictate age classification of inmates. Existing juvenile detention facilities, training schools, and institutions provide the option to segregate inmates on the basis of age or other risk factors. Insisting on humane conditions of confinement can do as much to improve the lives of incarcerated youths as the "right to treatment" or the rehabilitative ideal (Feld 1977, 1981a). Some research indicates that youths sentenced to juvenile correctional facilities may reoffend somewhat less often, seriously, or rapidly than comparable youths sentenced to adult facilities (Fagan 1995, 1996; Bishop et al. 1996; Winner et al. 1997). If consistently replicated, these findings provide modest support for a separate youth correctional system, rather than for an entire separate juvenile justice system.

Virtually all young offenders will return to society at some point, and the state should provide them with the resources for self-improvement on a voluntary basis because of the state's basic responsibility to its citizens and its own self-interest. If a state fails to provide opportunities for growth and further debilitates already disadvantaged youths, it guarantees that it will incur greater long-term human, criminal, and correctional costs. A sentencing and correctional policy that offers young offenders "room to reform" does not covertly reinstate a treatment ideology but facilitates young offenders' constructive use of their time and the resources available. With maturity, most young offenders develop a capacity for self-control and desist from criminality. Providing them with opportunities to reform requires more than simple custodial confinement. Education, social services, and economic training contribute to personal growth and perhaps improve the life chances of adolescents at risk, even if they do not demonstrably reduce recidivism rates. Although the states bear an obligation to provide the means and incentives for personal change, a youth's sentence should not depend fundamentally on either clinically perceived "real needs" or apparent responsiveness to "coerced treatment." One can uncouple social welfare from criminal social control and divorce treatment from punishment only by providing the opportunity for change on a voluntary basis.

Eliminate Civil Disabilities

An arrest record and criminal justice system involvement adversely affect youths' employment prospects and further restrict their access to legitimate labor markets (National Research Council 1993; Freeman 1991; Sullivan 1989). Although criminal sentencing authorities require access to prior records to identify chronic and career offenders, young first-or second-time offenders need not suffer all the disabilities and losses of rights associated with a conviction. A legislature can provide young offenders with relief from collateral consequence, restore civil rights, or nullify the effects of felony convictions upon the conclusion of a sentence and supervision.

Conclusion

Law reforms that tinker with the boundaries of childhood or modify judicial procedures or social control practices do not appear appreciably to reduce the probabilities of offenders' recidivism or increase public safety. Even far-reaching justice system changes can have only a modest effect on social problems as complex as crime and violence. But our justice systems reflect our deepest values and highest aspirations, and better and worse ways exist to organize them. The "due process" and "crime control" models, for example, reflect different values about relationships between the individual and the state and between democratic and authoritarian tendencies in the justice systems (Packer 1968).

A proposal to abolish the juvenile court and to try all young offenders in an integrated justice system makes no utilitarian claims but represents a commitment to honesty about state coercion. States bring young offenders who break the law to juvenile court for social control and to punish them. Juvenile courts' rehabilitative claims fly in the face of their penal reality, undermine their legitimacy, and impair their ability to function as judicial agencies. Because punishment is an unpleasant topic, public officials and juvenile justice personnel attempt to evade those disagreeable qualities by obscuring their reality with rehabilitative euphemisms, psychobabble, and judicial double-speak like "sometimes punishment is treatment."

Even though the juvenile and criminal justice systems perform similar social control functions, the juvenile court constitutes a powerful symbol that people relinquish reluctantly. Some contend that structuring the juvenile court as a "social welfare agency rather than a criminal court . . . operates as a symbol that shapes the thinking and behavior of the people who work in the court. In a world full of symbols that push people toward punishment of juveniles, the language of treatment in juvenile justice seems worth retaining, even if reality does not always live up to the intentions" (Bernard 1992:160). Others argue that a rehabilitative ideology provides a counterweight to punitive practices and requires the state to take seriously its responsibility to provide for the welfare of offenders (Cullen and Gilbert 1982).

While the rehabilitative ideal of the juvenile court may provide a symbolic buffer against more punitive policies, characterizing penal coercion as "social welfare" seems both dangerous and dishonest. The *idea* of rehabilitation inherently and seductively expands, widens nets of social control, and promotes abuse through self-delusion (Allen 1964, 1981; Cohen 1978). While the ideas that "something works" or "we ought to help" may sustain juvenile justice practitioners, the paternalism of a treatment ideology subordinates youths' exercise of rights. Judges who regard themselves as decent and caring people acting in the child's best interests believe that they can protect youths more effectively than any procedural rights. And, ultimately, youths incarcerated in the name of treatment recognize that the justice system has deceived them.

The shortcomings of the rehabilitative juvenile court run far deeper than inadequate resources or unproven treatment techniques. Rather, the flaw lies in the very *idea* that the juvenile court can combine successfully criminal social control and social welfare in one system. Similarly, a separate juvenile version of a criminal court cannot succeed or long survive because it lacks a coherent rational to distinguish it from the "real" criminal court. A scaled-down separate criminal court for youths simply represents a temporary way station on the road to substantive and procedural convergence with the criminal court. Only an integrated criminal justice system that formally recognizes adolescence as a developmental continuum may more effectively address many of the problems created by our binary conceptions of youth and social control.

Enhanced procedural protections, a youth discount for sentences, and age-segregated dispositional facilities recognize and respond to the "real" developmental differences between young people and adult offenders in the criminal justice system. Because these policy proposals require state legislators courageous enough to adopt them, several thoughtful commentators question whether elected public officials in a get-tough political environment would make explicit the leniency implicit in the contemporary juvenile court. While the public unknowingly may tolerate nominal sanctions administered to young offenders in low-visibility juvenile proceedings, politicians may balk at openly acknowledging such a policy of moderation. A policy of leniency— youthfulness as a mitigating factor in sentencing—may be a difficult crime control strategy to sell to "law-and-order" politicians (Bernard 1992). Many elected officials prefer to demagogue about crime and posture politically to "crack down" on youth crime than responsibly to educate the public about the realistic limits of the justice system to control it (Beckett 1997). Some would rather fan the flames of fear for political advantage even though escalating rates of imprisonment ultimately lead only to fiscal and moral bankruptcy.

The same developmental psychological and policy rationales that support a youth discount also reveal that youths require more procedural protections than adults, rather than fewer, in order to cope with the complexities of the justice system. As discussed in chapter 4, youths' vulnerability, immaturity, susceptibility to coercion, and inability to deal effectively with trained law enforcement and legal and judicial personnel require enhanced procedural protections to place them on an equal footing with adult defendants. Again, thoughtful scholars question whether get-tough politicians would provide vulnerable youths with additional procedural safeguards if, for example, doing so made it more difficult for police to interrogate youths, to take advantage of their vulnerability, and to obtain confessions to aid in their convictions. Why would legislators who fail to provide juveniles with procedural parity in the current "benevolent" juvenile justice system provide youths with even greater procedural safeguards after they merged them into an integrated criminal justice system (Rosenberg 1993)?

I propose to abolish the juvenile court with considerable trepidation. On the one hand, combining enhanced procedural safeguards with a youth discount in an integrated criminal court provides young offenders with greater protections and justice than they currently receive in the rehabilitative juvenile system and more proportional and humane consequences than judges presently inflict on them as adults in the criminal justice system. Integration may foster a more consistent crime control response than the current dual system permits to violent and chronic young offenders at various stages of the developmental and criminal career continuum. On the other hand, politicians may ignore the significance of youthfulness as a mitigating factor and instead use these proposals to escalate the punishment of young people. Although abolition of the juvenile court, enhanced procedural protections, and a youth discount constitute essential components of a youth sentencing policy package, nothing can prevent get-tough legislators from selectively choosing only those elements that serve their punitive agenda, even though doing so unravels the threads that make coherent a proposal for an integrated court.

In either event, the ensuing debate about a youth sentencing policy would require public officials to consider whether to focus primarily on the fact that young offenders are *young* or *offenders*. A public policy debate when the child is a criminal and the criminal is a child forces a long overdue and critical reassessment of the entire social construction of "childhood." To what extent do adolescents really differ from adults? To what extent do their differences in competency and judgment result from physical or psychological developmental processes or from social arrangements and institutions that systematically disable young people and deprive them of opportunities to learn to be responsible? To what extent can politicians invoke the imagery of youth as responsible and autonomous in order to punish them without undermining the competing cultural conceptions of children as vulnerable and dependent and who need nurturance and protection? If politicians ultimately insist on treating young people primarily as offenders and the equals of adults, then can they simultaneously maintain other age-graded legal distinctions, such as denial of the right to vote or to exercise self-determination?

The political and legal culture easily justifies an inferior justice system for young people because it presumes that they differ fundamentally from adults. Young people will continue to receive "the worst of both worlds," a quality of justice we would deem as intolerable for adults and harsh punishment disproportionate to their culpability, as long as public officials can rationalize that children deserve only custody and not liberty (*Schall v. Martin*, 467 U.S. 253 [1984]) or adhere to the mythology that juvenile courts exercise only "benign" coercion (*McKeiver v. Pennsylvania*, 404 U.S. 528 [1970]). Politicians embrace the ideology of therapeutic justice because the state directs its flexible apparatus of social control at children. Most people tolerate an intolerable juvenile justice because they believe that it will affect only other people's children—children of other colors, classes, and cultures—and not their own. Juvenile courts tap a resonant legitimating theme because they invoke *parens patriae* and child welfare ideals even as they impose penal controls on young offenders.

Epilogue

A century ago, the transition from an agrarian to an industrial society changed our cultural *ideas* about childhood and strategies of penal social control and led to the creation of the juvenile court. More recent structural changes have eroded support for strategies of social control based on positivism and the "rehabilitative ideal" and modified the social construction of childhood. The shift from an industrial to an information and service economy, the migration of rural southern blacks to cities and whites to suburbs, the deindustrialization of the urban core, and the concentration of poverty among urban blacks have changed the patterns and public perceptions of youth crime and the justice systems' responses to it. States' juvenile justice systems now emphasize personal accountability and punish young offenders rather than treat them. The emergence of punitive social control policies has eroded one of the two foundational ideas of the juvenile court.

To justify prosecuting children as criminals or punishing them as delinquents, legislators, prosecutors, and judges invoke images of young offenders as responsible and autonomous people, rather than as dependent and vulnerable children, and as deliberate rather than determined, offenders. The political demonization of young black males as morally impoverished "superpredators" and the depiction of delinquents as responsible offenders have eroded the Progressives' social construction of "childhood" innocence and vulnerability. Consequently, very little distinguishes juvenile and criminal justice systems' ideologies or practices. Most of the differences that do remain between the two justice systems redound to the disadvantage of young people. States provide an inferior justice system for younger offenders to maximize their social control because cultural conceptions of youths do not envision them as "real" people entitled to the same legal protections or to exercise the same rights as other citizens.

The Progressives' *idea* and *ideal* that they successfully could combine criminal social control and social welfare in one agency constitute both the essential premise and the fundamental flaw of the juvenile court. By contrast, if crime and public policies uncouple social welfare from social control, then they can better pursue child welfare directly. Analysts of other Progressive child welfare policies identify inherent contradictions and failed strategies similar to those that I attribute to juvenile courts (e.g., Grubb and Lazerson 1982; Katz 1989; Lindsey 1994). For example, in *The Welfare of Children*, Duncan Lindsey argues that the traditional "residual" approach to child welfare provided minimal, time-limited services for those who fell through the social safety net "as inexpensively and conveniently as possible, enough to satisfy the social conscience but no more" (1994:16). The discovery of the "battered child syndrome" and the enactment of mandatory abuse reporting requirements shifted child welfare agencies' focus from providing care and social services to investigating reports of abuse and produced a child protection system that provides neither safety nor services. The transformation of the child welfare system into a child protection system has neither reduced the numbers of child abuse fatalities nor enhanced children's safety but has "reduced the number of children receiving services, while increasing the number of families being investigated for abuse" (Lindsey 1994:125). In *Broken Promises*, Norton Grubb and Marvin Lazerson's (1982) analyses of child welfare policies contend that *parens patriae* ideology strikes the balance between public and private responsibility for children by defining eligibility for public assistance on the basis of parental failure. Because parental inadequacy and family pathology constitute prerequisites of public support, *parens patriae* ideology stigmatizes parents and reduces political support for child welfare programs. "Indeed, that is a fundamental characteristic of the American approach to poverty: the young are punished for what are considered the transgressions of their parents and the failure of private responsibility" (Grubb and Lazerson 1982:186–187). In a variety of guises, child welfare policies fail because they define eligibility for services negatively (Katz 1989). Juvenile courts require youths to commit crimes, child welfare and protection agencies requires children to be abused, and public welfare require parents to be abject failures to receive services.

My proposal to abolish the juvenile court represents an effort to uncouple social welfare and social control policies. On the one hand, such an endeavor would provoke a reexamination of criminal justice strategies toward younger offenders. On the other hand, such a strategy would enable public policies to address directly the "real needs" of all children regardless of their criminality. Social structural forces, political economic arrangements, and legal policies affect the social conditions of young people. Social institutions produce many of the untoward features that policymakers ascribe to adolescents. The social order significantly determines young people's access to opportunities and the lives they may fashion for themselves as adults. If public policies perpetuate and do not alleviate the substantial inequalities that limit many young people's life chances, then they inevitably diminish their life prospects. A society committed to equality of opportunity must adopt policies to ensure that all children, regardless of their parents' socioeconomic circumstances, have at least a fair start and a meaningful chance to succeed. Current public policies contribute to the social isolation of many youths, the desperate poverty of one child in five, and the high rates of criminality that prevail among young people in general and urban black males in particular. Public policies can modify the social order, improve the present circumstances of young people, and better facilitate their successful transition to responsible and competent adulthood.

If states frame child welfare policies in terms of child welfare rather than of crime control, then the possibilities for positive interventions for young people expand dramatically. For example, a public health approach to youth crime and violence that identified youths' social, environmental, community structural, and ecological correlates, such as concentrated poverty, school test scores, availability of handguns or shots fired, or the commercialization of violence would suggest wholly different intervention strategies than simply incarcerating minority youths. Youth violence occurs as part of a social ecological structure in areas of concentrated poverty, high teenage pregnancy, and welfare dependency. Such social indicators could identify census tracts or even zip codes for community organizing, economic development, and preventive and remedial intervention.

Poverty constitutes the biggest single risk factor for the welfare of young people. "[T]he diverse ways in which poverty harms children and adolescents, inflicts lasting damage, and limits their future potential points to the reduction of poverty as a key step toward improving the conditions of many of the nation's youths" (National Research Council 1993:236). Family income directly affects the quality of children's lives and their social opportunities in myriad ways. It determines, for example, the quality of their housing, neighborhoods, schools, health care, nutrition, and personal safety. Children in poverty experience malnutrition, inadequate clothing, substandard housing, lack of access to health care, deficient schools, and dangerous, crime-ridden streets and neighborhoods (National Commission on Children 1991). Every other adverse social indicator of the circumstances of youth—illness, suicide, drug abuse, teenage pregnancy, school dropout, crime, and violent victimization—correlates strongly with living in poverty (Hamburg 1992). Children in an affluent society consigned to live in prolonged poverty suffer from a form of chronic abuse. Eliminating this pervasive, undifferentiated child abuse requires far more extensive social resources and political economic reforms than any juvenile justice or child welfare system possibly can muster.

More children live in poverty in the United States, one in five, than in any other western industrialized nation. Recent comparisons reveal that the rate of child poverty in the United States (20.4%) is more than double that of Canada (9.3%) and Australia (9%), and four to eight times greater than that of western European industrial democracies such as France (4.6%), Germany (2.8%), and Sweden (1.6%) (Lindsey 1994). According to the National Commission on Children, "children are the poorest Americans. One in five lives in a family with an income below the federal poverty level. One in four infants and toddlers under the age of three is poor. Nearly 13 million children live in poverty, more than 2 million more than a decade ago. Many of these children are desperately poor; nearly five million live in families with incomes less than half the federal poverty level" (1991:24). Using a definition of "low income" as families with incomes less than 185 percent of the poverty line, the National Research Council (1993) estimated that in 1990 more than four children in every ten lived in poor or near-poor settings.

Children make up the largest age group in poverty, and, as a result of macrostructural economic changes and family demographic forces since the 1970s, their situation has worsened (Katz 1989). While 15 percent of children lived below the poverty line in 1974, by 1986, 21 percent did, a 40 percent increase. Among the impoverished young, minority children disproportionately experience the most dire penury and personal circumstances.

As the international comparisons indicate, in an affluent society like the United States, the political economy, rather than natural scarcity, allocates resources; public policies produce social and economic inequalities and concentrated poverty. The growth in child poverty over the past two decades reflects deliberate policies to prefer certain interest groups and classes, for example, the elderly and wealthy, over other groups, such as the young, the poor, or families raising children. The structure of the income tax code and health care, antidiscrimination, housing, minimum wage, child-care, employment, and macroeconomic policies all are components of a child welfare and family policy and affect parents' abilities to raise their children (National Commission on Children 1991).

The social and community structural determinants of youth crime and violence also suggest several future directions for a child welfare policy freed from the constraints of a juvenile court. Because poverty constitutes the biggest single risk factor for youth development, public policies must address directly child poverty to facilitate youths' transition to adulthood. Because minority children disproportionately bear the brunt of economic inequality, universal child welfare policies will especially enhance their life chances (Wilson 1987; Edelman 1987). Because the sharp increase in homicides caused by firearms provided most of the political impetus to transform the juvenile court into a scaled-down criminal court and to "crack down" on youth crime, public policies must address directly the prevalence of guns among the young. Three child welfare policy directions include providing a hopeful future for all young people, pursuing racial and social justice, and eliminating access to and use of handguns by the young.

A Hopeful Future for All Young People

As a result of structural and economic changes since the 1980s, the ability of families to support and raise children, to prepare them for their transition to adulthood, and to provide them with a more promising future has declined (National Commission on Children 1991; National Research Council 1993). Many social indicators of the status of young people—for example, poverty, homelessness, violent victimization, and crime—are negative, and some of those adverse trends are accelerating. "[T]he evidence is clear and compelling that persistent poverty exacts a significant price on children's health, development, educational attainment, and socioeconomic potential. . . . These effects become more pronounced by adolescence" (National Research Council 1993:20). Without realistic hope for their future, young people fall into despair, nihilism, and violence. "Numerous studies describe the sense of 'futurelessness' and fatalism that is experienced by adolescents whose dependent status does not allow them to escape neighborhoods in which violent death is a daily occurrence, and they consider that many urban youths who murder believe that there is no future to consider" (Grisso 1996:234). Teenage pregnancy and youth crime rates provide social indicators of youths who envision no futures for themselves, have nothing to lose in the present, and who impose the costs of their alienation and hopelessness on others.

Poverty constitutes the biggest risk factor for child development, and public policies must enhance the economic status of families with children (National Commission on Children 1991). In addition to a developmental infrastructure for all children—for example, universal health care, affordable decent child care, and quality public education—public policies must ensure an economic safety net for families with children. Many income policies common to other western industrial democracies—family and children's allowance, child tax credits and deductions, and direct transfer payments—ensure that parents possess sufficient minimum economic resources with which to care for their children (Lindsey 1994). Among the advanced economies, the United States alone does not provide a children's allowance. Unless a family commands at least most of the resources that an "average family" does, it cannot participate in or meaningfully prepare its children to enter the cultural mainstream (Katz 1989). Thus, income transfer, tax deduction, earned income tax credit, minimum wage, and other economic policies should make children's economic well-being a priority.

A generation ago, the elderly represented the largest segment of the population in poverty, and income transfer programs have virtually eliminated their penury. Since the 1970s, federal expenditures on Social Security, Supplemental Security Income (SSI), and Medicare have reduced the proportion of people aged sixty-five or older living below the poverty line from 40 percent in 1966 to 9 percent in 1989 (Lindsey 1994). By contrast, children now make up the largest group of poor people. As the economic circumstances of the elderly improved, those of children declined. Between 1969 and 1987, the percentage of children living in poverty increased one-third, while public policies cut the poverty rate of the elderly in half (Lindsey 1994). In 1990 the federal government spent about *ten times as much* on programs for seniors as it did on those for children under eighteen years of age.

In response to the desperate plight of young people, policy analysts have identified many elements of public programs and economic policies to provide for children's welfare. In *Today's Children*, David Hamburg (1992) provides a social developmental prescription for children at each stage of life to enable them to become successful adults. In *Families in Peril*, Marian Wright Edelman (1987) describes social policies and political strategies to implement them that would improve the life chances of children and, especially, minority children in poverty. In *Losing Generations*, the National Research Council (1993) analyzes the social structural contexts within which adolescents engage in risky behavior and prescribes remedial strategies to reduce their risk-taking activities. In *Beyond Rhetoric*, the National Commission on Children (1991) prescribes many public policy strategies—health care, education, jobs and income, and moral climate—to improve the social infrastructure and better enable families to raise their children. In *The Welfare of Children*, Duncan Lindsey (1994) draws on the example of Social Security and proposes a "Children's Future Security Account" to provide young people with resources to invest in their human capital, to make the transition to adulthood, and to offer them realistic hope for the future. Under Lindsey's proposal, at the time of each child's birth, the government would create an account in her name, make periodic deposits into it, and invest and administer the funds like an Individual Retirement Account. When children reach age eighteen, the accumulated funds would provide them, and especially poor children, with resources to acquire additional education or technical training and to invest in their human capital and would provide hope and a realistic opportunity for upward social mobility regardless of their parents' economic circumstances. Significantly, none of these analysts' proposals assign any role to the juvenile court as a component of a child welfare policy.

Racial and Social Justice

The disproportionate overrepresentation of minority youths in the juvenile justice system, as well as in concentrated poverty, makes imperative the pursuit of racial and social justice. Politicians and the public view youth crime, violence, and child poverty through a prism of race and social class (Hacker 1992; Gans 1995). They characterize both crime and poverty as the *private* problems of minority families and children, rather than as matters of *public* concern for the entire community. But poverty poses the greatest obstacle to young people's successful development and disproportionately affects minority children. Community structure, poverty, and adverse social conditions, in turn, skew the distribution of crime and violence. The association in the public mind of blacks with violence both as perpetrators and as victims, in turn, reinforces the white's resistance to integration and the black's exclusion from the cultural mainstream (Zimring and Hawkins 1997; Massey and Denton 1993).

Social class and racial biases shape public attitudes and policies toward children. A century ago, Progressive reformers used "conscience and convenience" to distinguish between their own children and "other people's children" (Rothman 1980). Politicians and parents tend to make similar distinctions today. They simultaneously invest resources, affection, and high hopes in their own children and view other people's children with suspicion and as potential threats to the well-being of their own.

> Americans are ambivalent toward all children, and ambivalence has sharpened the distinction between one's own children and other people's children. Structural inequalities have affected the balance between positive and negative views of children in a class-divided society: the latent hostility toward children has often become a hostility toward lower-class and minority children—those who are most threatening, most costly, and least like middle-class children. In turn, hostility has undermined public responsibility for such children and has reinforced the efforts to control them. (Grubb and Lazerson 1982:85)

The recent transformation of the juvenile court provides a graphic illustration of the conversion of public fear of and hostility toward other people's children into harsh and punitive social control practices. The mass media depict and the public perceive the "crime problem" and juvenile courts' clientele primarily as poor, urban black males. Politicians have manipulated and exploited these racially tinged perceptions for political advantage with demagogic pledges to "get tough" and "crack down" on youth crime, which has become a "code word" for black males (Beckett 1997).

A generation ago, the National Advisory Commission on Civil Disorders, the Kerner Commission, warned in the aftermath of urban race riots in the 1960s that the United States was "moving toward two societies, one black, one white—separate and unequal" (1968:1). It predicted that continuing current policies would "make permanent the division of our country into two societies; one, largely Negro and poor, located in the central cities; the other, predominantly white and affluent, located in the suburbs" (1968:1). Today, we reap the bitter harvest sown by public policies and social neglect a generation ago of racial segregation, concentrated poverty, urban social disintegration, cultural conflict between blacks and whites, and youth violence (Wilson 1987; Jencks 1992; Hacker 1992). The plight of the urban underclass, the threat that youth violence poses to the entire community, and the inability of the juvenile or criminal justice systems to reduce violence make essential adopting proactive and preventive strategies.

The historical legacy of institutional and personal racism obstructs social policies to reduce child poverty. Many white people and public officials oppose structural programs to aid poor families because African Americans and other minorities who make up so many of the poor inevitably would benefit disproportionately. Although black children suffer from the highest poverty rates, politicians debate child welfare policy issues in terms of their parents' personal failure and welfare dependency, rather than in the context of structural inequality (Murray 1984; Grubb and Lazerson 1982). For some people, concentrated poverty, lower school achievement and school leaving, and youth crime rates demonstrate the need to improve the conditions for minority children and to pursue social justice. For others, these same indicators demonstrate that we already have waged and lost the War on Poverty, provide evidence with which to "blame the victims," and confirm why government should initiate no social action (Murray 1984; Katz 1989; Gans 1995). Like the policies of our Progressive predecessors, our current public policies primarily provide minimal services and compensatory programs to change individuals, rather than to alter structural sources of inequality.

Because we cannot separate children from their families, aiding poor children entails support and assistance for their "undeserving" parents (Katz 1989). Politicians portray and segments of the public perceive poor adults as "welfare queens" who live in idleness and take advantage of the public's generosity. Politicians would, rather, minimize public responsibility for poor children than provide assistance that indirectly might benefit children's caretakers. "Concessions to the needs of these families are made with a tight fist and a mean spirit; day care is not assumed as a community service, and programs to protect the health and diet of these children are among the first to be cut in economy moves" (Douvan 1985:608). Conservatives historically oppose child-care programs yet insist that "welfare mothers" work, count catsup as a vegetable in order to cut school lunch funds and simultaneously subsidize tax cuts for the wealthy, and regard children born into poor families simply as unlucky rather than as a collective responsibility.

The public policy debate systematically excludes socioeconomic *class* from the agenda and thus fails to address another source of inequality. Parental income determines a family's location within a social class system, and variations in class influence the values and attitudes that parents transmit to their children and with which they prepare them for intergenerational mobility. "Class considerations in turn influence the state's relationship to children: through class-biased conceptions of children and of the socialization appropriate for children from different class backgrounds; through the fear of other people's children and the pressure to use public institutions for the advancement of one's own children; through the pressure toward the social control of unruly classes" (Grubb and Lazerson 1982:263–264). The discovery and celebration of diversity among families of different ethnic, racial, and religious backgrounds obscure the reality that parents' location in the social class structure affects many of their child-rearing practices. Social class, rather than private, parental lifestyle choices, in turn, affects children's life chances.

White people, as well as minorities, bear the burdens of a social class structure that denies to all their children access to resources and opportunities. In *The Truly Disadvantaged*, for example, William Julius Wilson (1987) proposes policies to equalize the life chances for all disadvantaged individuals, regardless of race or ethnicity. Wilson (1987, 1996) advocates economic policies to combine growth and full employment with manpower training and educational programs to enhance the employment prospects of the concentrated poor. Unlike affirmative action programs, Wilson argues that universal, comprehensive, and nonracial programs to increase the employability of all economically marginalized and underskilled workers, black and white, would garner greater public support: "[W]hereas poor whites are ignored in programs of reverse discrimination based on the desire to overcome the effects of past discrimination, they would be targeted along with the truly disadvantaged minorities for preferential treatment under programs to equalize life chances by overcoming present class disadvantages" (1987:117). Universal skills, training, education, or apprenticeship programs specifically to improve the life chances of people at the bottom of the social structure would inevitably and disproportionately enhance the employability of inner-city black males. Others advocate similar universal policies to provide job training, raise the minimum wage, enforce child-support orders, and enable the poor to enter labor markets (Katz 1989; Jencks 1992). In *Rethinking Social Policy*, for example, Christopher Jencks (1992) advocates a sliding scale of government-financed "fringe benefits" for all poor working men and women that closely resembles the benefits that the tax code provides upper-income households—housing subsidies, income subsidies—or that private employers give their workers—medical insurance.

Preventing Firearms Violence by Reducing Youths' Access to Guns

A decade ago, youth violence became increasingly lethal as the *proliferation of handguns* transformed adolescent altercations into homicidal encounters. As recalled from chapter 6, youth homicide rates surged in the mid-1980s as a result of the growth of the crack cocaine drug industry and the diffusion of handguns among urban youth. Assaults by guns produce fatal outcomes at a much higher rate than do assaults by any other types of weapons (Zimring and Hawkins 1997). Young people committed more than three-quarters of their homicides with firearms, handguns accounted for 80 percent of all gun homicides, and gun deaths accounted for nearly the entire increase in youth homicides. Communities characterized by concentrated poverty and racial isolation experience higher violence rates and account for young black males' greater risk of homicide victimization (Reiss and Roth 1993; Zimring and Hawkins 1997). In turn, the escalation in gun homicides by urban black males constituted the proximate cause of the get-tough policies that transformed the juvenile court into a scaled-down criminal court.

States prohibit juveniles from purchasing or owning handguns because youths' presumptive immaturity, irresponsibility, and lack of judgment increase the inherent dangers of guns (Zimring 1996). As a result of prohibition, young people obtain their firearms through illegal transactions, for example, by theft, burglary, or barter, rather than through regulated purchases. Strategies to curb homicide and violence must limit youths' access to guns in high-risk situations and reduce the lethality of weapons through restrictions on magazine size or wounding potential (Reiss and Roth 1993; Zimring and Hawkins 1997). And the diffusion of more and powerful weapons within the youth population requires policies to reduce the carnage through an aggressive program of disarmament (Blumstein 1995). Jurisdictions have experimented with a number of different prevention and apprehension strategies to reduce the availability of guns. Aggressive stop-and-frisk practices and offers of rewards for reports of illegal guns may enable police to confiscate some weapons, may inhibit other young people from carrying or brandishing weapons, and indirectly may reduce the felt needs of other youths defensively to arm themselves (Blumstein and Cork 1996). Police may seek parental consent to conduct searches for guns in youths' homes in high-violence neighborhoods with an assurance to parents that any firearms seized will not result in prosecution for illegal possession (Rosenfeld and Decker 1996). Lethal violence prevention strategies require incremental and multiple interventions, including public education, governmental antiviolence campaigns, an end to the glamorization of violence in the media, improved socialization of young people to make resort to violence less efficacious, enhanced gun-safety technology, and criminal law reforms that substantially increase the sentence differential between gun and nongun offenses (Zimring and Hawkins 1997). Ultimately, however, only fundamental changes in public attitudes, social tolerance, and legal policies toward guns will reduce the high rates of death and violent assaults that uniquely distinguish crime in the United States from that in other developed countries.

Conclusion

Many obstacles exist to improving young people's social circumstances and life chances. Child welfare policies implicate complex and value-laden issues of gender, race, political economy, and social class. Despite our claims to be a "child-centered" nation, our public policies reflect a strong cultural antipathy to other people's children. Because our culture defines child rearing as a private matter, many politicians resist public policies that might intrude on family autonomy or disrupt traditional arrangements. While parents make deep commitments and sacrifice for their own children's welfare, no comparable feelings animate the public toward other children. "[W]e lack any sense of 'public love' for children, and we are unwilling to make public commitments to them except when we believe the commitments will pay off" (Grubb and Lazerson 1982:52). At best, public policies take an instrumental view of children as social investments and use cost-benefit criteria to assess the returns on those investments. States do not invest in young people's human capital as an intrinsic end, for example, to improve the quality of their lives or to enable them to become better people, but only as a means to some other public goal, for example, to increase economic productivity and global competitiveness or to reduce expenditures for social welfare or criminal justice programs. Because it is difficult to measure the long-term effect of child welfare or prevention programs using such cost-benefit criteria, evaluation research places public programs on the defensive and sustains calls to do less or to let the private sector provide assistance.

A society incurs substantial human and social costs by allowing young people's adverse circumstances to persist and to worsen. The aphorisms that "an ounce of prevention is worth a pound of cure" and "pay now or pay later" reflect central truths of public policy. "The longer children and parents experience neglect, deprivation, and failure, the more difficult and costly the remedies" (National Commission on Children 1991:73). The polity can adopt public policies to foster real equality of opportunity for all young people and alleviate the social structural sources of child poverty. Or public officials can allow social conditions further to alienate young people, especially poor and minority youth, to deprive many young people of any hope for the future, and to exacerbate the destructive consequences of racial, social, and economic inequality. Many children's programs clearly demonstrate their effectiveness in positive outcomes and social cost savings. The Women, Infant, and Children (WIC) nutrition programs enable children to develop more fully, reduce the numbers of premature and low-birth-weight babies, and save on expensive neonatal intensive care (National Commission on Children 1991). School nutrition programs, housing assistance, and Medicaid mitigate the impacts of poverty by providing basic human necessities, such as food, shelter, and health care. Headstart programs prepare preschool children to take advantage of learning opportunities, stimulate them intellectually, enable them to succeed in school, and reduce long-term costs of welfare dependency and crime (National Commission on Children 1991). "[Q]uality preschool education helps prevent the waste of human potential. Significant benefits to society at large include not only great long-term educational accomplishments but also reduced crime and delinquency, improved productivity of the labor force, reduced welfare dependency, and better health" (Hamburg 1992:146). Despite many such programs' demonstrated efficacy, Congress has never fully funded them to serve even their eligible populations. The price to achieve social justice and a promising future for all young people will be substantial. But far greater costs will appear on the social accounting ledger if we do not do so, which will be in the form of blighted dreams, lost human potential, and increased expenditures for child abuse, foster care, public assistance and dependency, drug treatment programs, escalating crime and violence, overcrowded prisons, lost economic productivity, and social disorder.

Characterizing child poverty as a private family matter consigns the most helpless and vulnerable segments of the population to extreme privation and enables the public to shirk its collective responsibilities. Most child welfare analysts share the common view that the roots of child poverty lie in social structure rather than in simply parental inadequacy. An affluent society that values its own future assures all young people of access to quality education, health care, adequate nutrition, and affordable housing without insisting on either parental failure or youthful criminality as prerequisites of assistance. A society that seeks racial harmony and social justice must address the structural inequality, concentrated poverty, racial segregation, and cultural isolation that excludes many members of minority communities and maintains "two societies, one black, one white, separate and unequal" (Hacker 1992; Massey and Denton 1993).

A nation's children represent its future. Social investments in young people's human capital constitute the long-term national infrastructure. Political responses to three overarching policy issues—creating a promising future for all young people, achieving racial and social justice, and reducing youth's access to firearms—will significantly affect the levels of child poverty and youth violence in the coming generation. Creating a promising future requires us to value and to desire for other people's children the same opportunities and successes that we wish for our own. Promoting racial equality requires a much greater commitment to social justice than white American society previously has evidenced. Because the proliferation and use of guns by youths represents an immediate threat to themselves and to others, political leaders must initiate an aggressive program of disarmament (National Research Council 1993; Blumstein 1995).

Responding to such complex issues pose fundamental challenges to the American future. Although politicians may be unwilling to invest scarce resources in young criminals, particularly those of other colors or cultures, a demographic shift and an aging population give all of us a stake in our young people and encourage us to invest in them for their and our own future well-being and to maintain an intergenerational compact. Social welfare and legal policies to provide all young people with a hopeful future, to reduce racial and social inequality, and to remove guns from the hands of children require a public and political commitment to the welfare of children that extends far beyond the resources and competencies of any juvenile justice system.

References

Abramovitch, Rona, Karen L. Higgins-Biss, and Stephen R. Biss. 1993. "Young Persons' Comprehension of Waivers in Criminal Proceedings." *Canadian Journal of Criminology* 35:309–322.

Aday, David P., Jr. 1986. "Court Structure, Defense Attorney Use, and Juvenile Court Decisions." *Sociological Quarterly* 27:107–119.

Ainsworth, Janet E. 1991. "Re-imagining Childhood and Re-constructing the Legal Order: The Case for Abolishing the Juvenile Court." *North Carolina Law Review* 69:1083–1133.

———. 1993. "In a Different Register: The Pragmatics of Powerlessness in Police Interrogation." *Yale Law Journal* 103:259–322.

———. 1995. "Youth Justice in a Unified Court: Response to Critics of Juvenile Court Abolition." *Boston College Law Review* 36:927–951.

Allen, Francis A. 1964. "Legal Values and the Rehabilitative Ideal." *In The Borderland of the Criminal Law: Essays in Law and Criminology*. Chicago: University of Chicago Press.

———. 1975. "The Judicial Quest for Penal Justice: The Warren Court and the Criminal Cases." *University of Illinois Law Forum* 1975:518–542.

———. 1981. *The Decline of the Rehabilitative Ideal: Penal Policy and Social Purpose*. New Haven: Yale University Press.

Allen-Hagen, Barbara, Melissa Sickmund, and Howard N. Snyder. 1994. *Juveniles and Violence: Juvenile Offending and Victimization*. Washington, D.C.: U.S. Department of Justice, Office of Juvenile Justice and Delinquency Prevention.

Allinson, Richard, ed. 1983. *Status Offenders and the Juvenile Justice System*. Hackensack, N.J.: National Council on Crime and Delinquency.

Alschuler, Albert W. 1983. "Implementing the Criminal Defendant's Right to Trial: Alternatives to the Plea Bargaining System." *University of Chicago Law Review* 50:931–1048.

———. 1986. "Preventive Pretrial Detention and the Failure of Interest-Balancing Approaches to Due Process." *Michigan Law Review* 85:510–569.

Altschuler, David M. 1994. "Tough and Smart Juvenile Incarceration: Reintegrating Punishment, Deterrence and Rehabilitation." *St. Louis University Public Law Review* 14:217–237.

American Bar Association (ABA). 1993. *America's Children at Risk: A National Agenda for Legal Action.* Washington, D.C.: American Bar Association.

————. 1995. *A Call For Justice: An Assessment of Access to Counsel and Quality of Representation in Delinquency Proceedings.* Washington, D.C.: ABA Juvenile Justice Center.

————, and Institute of Judicial Administration. 1980a. *Juvenile Justice Standards Relating to Dispositions.* Cambridge, Mass.: Ballinger.

————. 1980b. *Juvenile Justice Standards Relating to Interim Status.* Cambridge, Mass: Ballinger.

————. 1980c. *Juvenile Justice Standards Relating to Adjudication.* Cambridge, Mass: Ballinger.

————. 1980d. *Juvenile Justice Standards Relating to Juvenile Delinquency and Sanctions.* Cambridge, Mass.: Ballinger.

————. 1980e. *Juvenile Justice Standards Relating to Pretrial Court Proceedings.* Cambridge, Mass.: Ballinger.

————. 1982. *Juvenile Justice Standards Relating to Noncriminal Misbehavior.* Cambridge, Mass.: Ballinger.

American Friends Service Committee. 1971. *Struggle for Justice.* New York: Hill and Wang.

American Law Institute. 1957. *Model Penal Code: Tentative Draft No. 7.* Philadelphia: American Law Institute.

Anderson, Elijah. 1990. *Streetwise: Race, Class, and Change in an Urban Community.* Chicago: University of Chicago Press.

Andrews, D. A., Ivan Zinger, Robert D. Hoge, James Bonta, Paul Gendreau, and Francis T. Cullen. 1990. "Does Correctional Treatment Work? A Clinically Relevant and Psychologically Informed Meta-Analysis." *Criminology* 28:369–404.

Andrews, R. Hale, and Andrew H. Cohn. 1974. "Ungovernability: The Unjustifiable Jurisdiction." *Yale Law Journal* 83:1383–1409.

Archard, David. 1993. *Children: Rights and Childhood.* London: Routledge.

Arenella, Peter. 1977. "The Diminished Capacity and Diminished Responsibility Defenses: Two Children of a Doomed Marriage." *Columbia Law Review* 77:827–865.

————. 1983. "Rethinking the Functions of Criminal Procedure: The Warren and Burger Courts' Competing Ideologies." *Georgetown Law Journal* 72:185–248.

Aries, Philippe. 1962. *Centuries of Childhood: A Social History of Family Life.* New York: Vintage Books.

Arizona Department of Corrections. 1986. *Length of Confinement Guidelines for Juveniles.* Tucson: Arizona Department of Corrections.

Arthur, Lindsay G. 1977. "Status Offenders Need a Court of Last Resort." *Boston University Law Review* 57:631–644.

Bailey, William C. 1981. "Preadjudicatory Detention in a Large Metropolitan Juvenile Court." *Law and Human Behavior* 5:19–43.

Bakal, Yitzhak. 1973. *Closing Correctional Institutions.* Lexington, Mass.: Lexington Books.

Barnes, Carole Wolff, and Randal S. Franz. 1989. "Questionably Adult: Determinants and Effects of the Juvenile Waiver Decision." *Justice Quarterly* 6:117–135.

Bartollas, Clemens, Stuart J. Miller, and Simon Dinitz. 1976. *Juvenile Victimization: The Institutional Paradox.* New York: Wiley.

Barton, William H., and Jeffrey A. Butts. 1991. "Intensive Supervision Alternatives for Adjudicated Juveniles." In *Intensive Interventions with High-Risk Youths: Promising Approaches in Juvenile Probation and Parole,* edited by Troy Armstrong. Monsey, N.Y.: Criminal Justice Press.

Barton, William H., and Ira M. Schwartz. 1994. "Juvenile Detention: No More Hidden Closets." In *Reforming Juvenile Detention: No More Hidden Closets.* Columbus: Ohio State University Press.

Becker, Mary. 1979. "Washington State's New Juvenile Code: An Introduction." *Gonzaga Law Review* 14:289–308.

Beckett, Katherine. 1997. *Making Crime Pay: Law and Order in Contemporary American Politics*. New York: Oxford University Press.

Berger, Peter L., and Thomas Luckmann. 1967. *The Social Construction of Reality*. New York: Anchor Books.

Berger, Brigitte, and Peter L. Berger. 1984. *The War over the Family: Capturing the Middle Ground*. New York: Anchor Books.

Bernard, Thomas J. 1992. *The Cycle of Juvenile Justice*. New York: Oxford University Press.

Bishop, Donna M., and Charles S. Frazier. 1988. "The Influence of Race in Juvenile Justice Processing." *Journal of Research in Crime and Delinquency* 25:242–263.

———. 1991. "Transfer of Juveniles to Criminal Court: A Case Study and Analysis of Prosecutorial Waiver." *Notre Dame Journal of Law, Ethics and Public Policy* 5:281–302.

———. 1992. "Gender Bias in Juvenile Justice Processing: Implications of the JJDP Act." *Journal of Criminal Law and Criminology* 82:1162–1186.

———. 1996. "Race Effects in Juvenile Justice Decision-Making: Findings of a Statewide Analysis." *Journal of Criminal Law and Criminology* 86:392–413.

———, and John Henretta. 1989. "Prosecutorial Waiver: Case Study of a Questionable Reform." *Crime and Delinquency* 35:179–201.

———, Lonn Lanza-Kaduce, and Lawrence Winner. 1996. "The Transfer of Juveniles to Criminal Court: Does It Make a Difference?" *Crime and Delinquency* 42:171–191.

Bledstein, Burton J. 1976. *The Culture of Professionalism: The Middle Class and the Development of Higher Education in America*. New York: Norton.

Blumstein, Alfred. 1993. "Making Rationality Relevant." *Criminology* 31:1–16.

———. 1995. "Youth Violence, Guns, and the Illicit-Drug Industry." *Journal of Criminal Law and Criminology* 86:10–36.

———, Jacqueline Cohen, and Daniel Nagin, eds. 1978. *Deterrence and Incapacitation: Estimating the Effects of Criminal Sanctions on Crime Rates*. Washington, D.C.: National Academy of Sciences.

Blumstein, Alfred, Jacqueline Cohen, Jeffrey A. Roth, and Christy A. Visher, eds. 1986. *Criminal Careers and "Career Criminals."* Washington, D.C.: National Academy Press.

Blumstein, Alfred, and Daniel Cork. 1996. "Linking Gun Availiability to Youth Gun Violence." *Law and Contemporary Problems* 59:5–24.

Blumstein, Alfred, David P. Farrington, and Soumyo Moitra. 1985. "Delinquency Careers: Innocents, Desisters, and Persisters." *Crime and Justice: An Annual Review of Research* 6:187–219.

Boland, Barbara. 1980. "Fighting Crime: The Problem of Adolescents. *Journal of Criminal Law and Criminology* 71:94–97.

———, and James Q. Wilson. 1978. "Age, Crime, and Punishment." *Public Interest* 51:22–34.

Bookin-Weiner, Heidi. 1984. "Assuming Responsibility: Legalizing Preadjudicatory Juvenile Detention." *Crime and Delinquency* 30:39–67.

Bortner, M. A. 1982. *Inside a Juvenile Court*. New York: New York University Press.

———. 1986. "Traditional Rhetoric, Organizational Realities: Remand of Juveniles to Adult Court." *Crime and Delinquency* 32:53–73.

———, and Wornie L. Reed. 1985. "The Preeminence of Process: An Example of Refocused Justice Research." *Social Science Quarterly* 66:413–425.

Boylan, Anne M. 1985. "Growing Up Female in Young America, 1800–1860." In *American Childhood*, edited by Joseph Hawes and N. Ray Hiner. Westport, Conn.: Greenwood.

Brenzel, Barbara. 1980. "Domestication as Reform: A Study of the Socialization of Wayward Girls, 1856–1905." *Harvard Education Review* 50:196–213.

Bridges, George S., Darlene J. Conley, Rodney L. Engen, and Townsand Price-Spratlen. 1995. "Racial Disparities in the Confinement of Juveniles: Effects of Crime and Community Social Structure on Punishment." In *Minorities in Juvenile Justice*, edited by Kimberly Kempf-Leonard, Carl Pope, and William Feyerherm. Thousand Oaks, Calif.: Sage.

Brown, Richard D. 1976. *Modernization: The Transformation of American Life, 1600–1865*. New York: Hill and Wang.

Burch, Charles H., and Kathianne Knaup. 1970. "The Impact of Jury Trials upon the Administration of Juvenile Justice." *Clearinghouse Review* 4:345–349, 366–371.

Butterfield, Fox. 1995. *All God's Children: The Bosket Family and the American Tradition of Violence.* New York: Avon Books.

Button, H. Warren, and Eugene F. Provenzo, Jr. 1981. *History of Education and Culture in America.* Englewood Cliffs, N.J.: Prentice-Hall.

Butts, Jeffrey A., Howard N. Snyder, Terrence A. Finnegan, Anne L. Aughenbaugh, Rowen S. Poole. 1995. *Juvenile Court Statistics, 1994.* Washington, D.C.: U.S. Department of Justice, Office of Juvenile Justice and Delinquency Prevention.

Carnoy, Martin, and Henry M. Levin. 1985. *Schooling and Work in the Democratic State.* Stanford, Calif.: Stanford University Press.

Carrington, Peter J., and Sharon Moyer. 1988a. "Legal Representation and Dispositions in Canadian Juvenile Courts." Ottawa: Department of Justice, Canada.

———. 1988b. "Legal Representation and Workload in Canadian Juvenile Courts." Ottawa: Department of Justice, Canada.

———. 1990. "The Effect of Defence Counsel on Plea and Outcome in Juvenile Court." *Canadian Journal of Criminology* 32:621–637.

Castellano, Thomas C. 1986. "The Justice Model in the Juvenile Justice System: Washington State's Experience." *Law and Policy* 8:397–418.

Cauffman, Elizabeth, and Laurence Steinberg. 1995. "The Cognitive and Affective Influences on Adolesent Decision-Making." *Temple Law Review* 68:1763–1789.

Census of Public and Private Detention, Correctional and Shelter Facilities, 1985–1995. Washington, D.C.: U.S. Department of Justice, Office of Juvenile Justice and Delinquency Prevention.

Chandler, Alfred D., Jr. 1977. *The Visible Hand: The Managerial Revolution in American Business.* Cambridge, Mass.: Belknap.

Chesney-Lind, Meda. 1977. "Judicial Paternalism and the Female Status Offender: Training Women to Know Their Place." *Crime and Delinquency* 23:121–130.

———. 1988. "Girls and Status Offenses: Is Juvenile Justice Still Sexist?" *Criminal Justice Abstracts* 20:144–165.

———, and Randall G. Shelden. 1992. *Girls, Delinquency, and Juvenile Justice.* Pacific Grove, Calif.: Brooks/Cole.

Cicourel, Aaron V. 1968. *The Social Organization of Juvenile Justice.* New York: Wiley.

Clarke, Stevens H., and Gary G. Koch. 1980. "Juvenile Court: Therapy or Crime Control, and Do Lawyers Make a Difference?" *Law and Society Review* 14:263–308.

Clement, Priscilla Ferguson. 1985. "The City and the Child, 1860–1885." In *American Childhood*, edited by Joseph Hawes and N. Ray Hiner. Westport, Conn.: Greenwood.

Coates, Robert, Martin Forst, and Bruce Fisher. 1985. *Institutional Commitment and Release Decision-Making for Juvenile Delinquents: An Assessment of Determinate and Indeterminate Approaches—A Cross-State Analysis.* San Francisco: URSA Institute.

Coates, Robert, Alden Miller, and Lloyd Ohlin. 1978. *Diversity in a Youth Correctional System.* Cambridge, Mass.: Ballinger.

Cochran, Thomas C. 1972. *Business in American Life: A History.* New York: McGraw-Hill.

Cogan, Neil H. 1970. "Juvenile Law, Before and After the Entrance of 'Parens Patriae.' " *South Carolina Law Review* 22:147–181.

Cohen, Fred. 1978. "Juvenile Offenders: Proportionality vs. Treatment." *Children's Rights Reporter* 8:1–16.

Cohen, Lawrence E., and James R. Kluegel. 1978. "Determinants of Juvenile Court Dispositions: Ascriptive and Achieved Factors in Two Metropolitan Courts." *American Sociological Review* 27:162–176.

———. 1979. "The Detention Decision: A Study of the Impact of Social Characteristics and Legal Factors in Two Metropolitan Juvenile Courts." *Social Forces* 58:146–61.

Cohen, Robert D. 1985. "Child-Saving and Progressivism, 1885–1915." In *American Childhood*, edited by Joseph Hawes and N. Ray Hiner. Westport, Conn.: Greenwood.

Coleman, James S., Robert H. Bremner, Burton R. Clark, John B. David, Dorothy H. Eichorn, Zvi Griliches, Joseph F. Kett, Norman B. Ryder, Zahava Blum Doering,

John M. Mays. 1974. *Youth: Transition to Adulthood*. Chicago: University of Chicago Press.

Colomy, Paul, and Martin Kretzmann. 1995. "Projects and Institution Building: Judge Ben B. Lindsey and the Juvenile Court Movement." *Social Problems* 42:191–215.

Cook, Phillip J. 1991. "The Technology of Personal Violence." *Crime and Justice: A Review of Research* 14:1–71.

———, and John H. Laub. 1998. "The Unprecedented Epidemic in Youth Violence." *Crime and Justice: A Review of Research* 24:27–64.

———, Stephanie Molliconi, and Thomas B. Cole. 1995. "Regulating Gun Markets." *Journal of Criminal Law and Criminology* 86:59–91.

Corrado, Raymond R., and Susan D. Turnbull. 1992. "A Comparative Examination of the Modified Justice Model in the United Kingdom and the United States." In *Juvenile Justice in Canada: A Theoretical and Analytical Assessment*, edited by Raymond R. Corrado, Nicholas Bala, Rick Linden, and Marc LeBlanc. Toronto: Butterworths.

Costello, Jan C., and Worthington, Nancy L. 1981. "Incarcerating Status Offenders: Attempts to Circumvent the Juvenile Justice and Delinquency Prevention Act." *Harvard Civil Rights—Civil Liberty Law Review* 16:41–81.

Cottle, Thomas. 1976. *Perceiving Time: A Psychological Investigation with Men and Women*. New York: Wiley.

Cravens, Hamilton. 1985. "Child-Saving in the Age of Professionalism, 1915–1930." In *American Childhood*, edited by Joseph Hawes and N. Ray Hiner Westport, Conn.: Greenwood.

Creekmore, Mark. 1976. "Case Processing: Intake, Adjudication, and Disposition." In *Brought to Justice? Juveniles, the Courts, and the Law*, edited by Rosemary Sarri and Yeheskel Hasenfeld. Ann Arbor: National Assessment of Juvenile Corrections, University of Michigan.

Cremin, Lawrence. 1961. *The Transformation of the School: Progressivism in American Education, 1876–1957*. New York: Vintage Books.

Crime Commission. See President's Commission on Law Enforcement and Administration of Justice.

Cullen, Francis T., and Karen E. Gilbert. 1982. *Reaffirming Rehabilitation*. Cincinnati: Anderson.

Curtis, George B. 1976. "The Checkered Career of Parens Patriae: The State as Parent or Tyrant?" *DePaul Law Review* 25:895– 915.

Dale, Michael J. 1992. "The Supreme Court and the Minimization of Children's Constitutional Rights: Implications for the Juvenile Justice System." *Hamline Journal of Public Law and Policy* 13:199–228.

Damaska, Mirjan. 1973. "Evidentiary Barriers to Conviction and Two Models of Criminal Procedure: A Comparative Study." *University of Pennsylvania Law Review* 121:506–589.

———. 1975. "Structures of Authority and Comparative Criminal Procedure." *Yale Law Journal* 84:480–544.

Dannefer, Dale, and Russell Schutt. 1982. "Race and Juvenile Justice Processing in Court and Police Agencies." *American Journal of Sociology* 87:1113–1132.

Dawson, Robert O. 1988. "The Third Justice System: The New Juvenile Criminal System of Determinate Sentencing for the Youthful Violent Offender in Texas." *St. Mary's Law Journal* 19:943–1016.

———. 1990a. "The Future of Juvenile Justice: Is It Time to Abolish the System?" *Journal of Criminal Law and Criminology* 81:136–155.

———. 1990b. "The Violent Juvenile Offender: An Empirical Study of Juvenile Determinate Sentencing Proceedings as an Alternative to Criminal Prosecution." *Texas Tech Law Review* 21:1897–1939.

Debele, Gary A. 1987. "The Due Process Revolution and the Juvenile Court: The Matter of Race in the Historical Evolution of a Doctrine." *Journal of Law and Inequality* 5:513–548.

Decker, Scott H. 1985. "A Systematic Analysis of Diversion: Net Widening and Beyond." *Journal of Criminal Justice* 13:206–216.

Degler, Carl. 1980. *At Odds: Women and the Family in America from the Revolution to the Present*. New York: Oxford University Press.

Delgado, Richard. 1982. " 'Rotten Social Background': Should Criminal Law Recognize a Defense of Severe Environmental Deprivation?" *Law and Inequality: Journal of Theory and Practice* 3:9–90.

deMause, Lloyd. 1974. "The Evolution of Childhood." In *The History of Childhood*, edited by Lloyd deMaus. New York: Harper Books.

Demos, John. 1970. *A Little Commonwealth: Family Life in Plymouth Colony*. New York: Oxford University Press.

————, and Sarane Spence Boocock. 1978. *Turning Points: Historical and Sociological Essays on the Family*. Chicago: University of Chicago Press.

Douvan, Elizabeth. 1985. "The Age of Narcissism, 1963–1982." In *American Childhood*, edited by Joseph Hawes and N. Ray Hiner. Westport, Conn.: Greenwood.

Driver, Edwin. 1968. "Confessions and the Social Psychology of Coercion." *Harvard Law Review*. 82:42–61.

Duffee, David, and Larry Siegel. 1971. "The Organization Man: Legal Counsel in the Juvenile Court." *Criminal Law Bulletin* 7:544–553.

Edelman, Marian Wright. 1987. *Families in Peril: An Agenda for Social Change*. Cambridge, Mass.: Harvard University Press.

Edwards, Leonard. 1977. "The Case for Abolishing Fitness Hearings in Juvenile Court." *Santa Clara Law Review* 17:595–630.

————. 1992. "The Juvenile Court and the Role of the Juvenile Court Judge." *Juvenile and Family Court Journal* 43:1–45.

————. 1993. "A Comprehensive Approach to the Represenation of Children: The Child Advocacy Coordinating Council." *Family Law Quarterly* 27:417–431.

Eigen, Joel. 1981a. "The Determinants and Impact of Jurisdictional Transfer in Philadelphia." In *Readings in Public Policy*, edited by John Hall, Donna Hamparian, John Pettibone, and Joe White. Columbus, Ohio: Academy for Contemporary Problems.

————. 1981b. "Punishing Youth Homicide Offenders in Philadelphia." *Journal of Criminal Law and Criminology* 72:1072–1093.

Elkind, David. 1988. *The Hurried Child: Growing Up Too Fast Too Soon*. Reading, Mass.: Addison-Wesley.

Ellis, James W. 1974. "Volunteeering Children: Parental Commitment of Minors to Mental Institutions." *California Law Review* 62:840–916.

Emerson, Robert M. 1969. *Judging Delinquents: Context and Process in Juvenile Court*. Chicago: Aldine.

————. 1974. "Role Determinants in Juvenile Court." In *Handbook of Criminology*, edited by Daniel Glaser. Chicago: Rand McNally.

Empey, LaMar T. 1973. "Juvenile Justice Reform: Diversion, Due Process, and Deinstitutionalization." In *Prisoners in America*, edited by Lloyd E. Ohlin. Englewood Cliffs, N.J.: Prentice-Hall.

————. 1979. "The Social Construction of Childhood and Juvenile Justice." In *The Future of Childhood and Juvenile Justice*, edited by LaMar T. Empey. Charlottesville: University Press of Virginia.

Erikson, Erik. 1968. *Identity: Youth and Crisis*. New York: Norton.

Fagan, Jeffrey. 1990. "Social and Legal Policy Dimensions of Violent Juvenile Crime." *Criminal Justice and Behavior* 17:93–133.

————. 1995. "Separating the Men from the Boys: The Comparative Advantage of Juvenile versus Criminal Court Sanctions on Recidivism among Adolescent Felony Offenders." In *A Sourcebook of Serious, Violent, and Chronic Juvenile Offenders*, edited by James C. Howell, Barry Krisberg, J. David Hawkins, and John J. Wilson. Thousand Oaks, Calif.: Sage.

————. 1996. "The Comparative Advantage of Juvenile versus Criminal Court Sanctions on Recidivism among Adolescent Felony Offenders." *Law and Policy* 18:77–114.

————, and Elizabeth Piper Deschenes. 1990. "Determinates of Judicial Waiver Decisions for Violent Juvenile Offenders." *Journal of Criminal Law and Criminology* 81:314–347.

Fagan, Jeffrey, Martin Forst, and Scott Vivona. 1987. "Racial Determinants of the Judicial Transfer Decision: Prosecuting Violent Youth in Criminal Court." *Crime and Delinquency* 33:259–286.

Fagan, Jeffrey, and Martin Guggenheim. 1996. "Preventive Detention and the Judicial Prediction of Dangerousness for Juveniles: A Natural Experiment." *Journal of Criminal Law and Criminology* 86:415–448.

Fagan, Jeffrey, Ellen Slaughter, and Eliot Hartstone. 1987. "Blind Justice? The Impact of Race on the Juvenile Justice Process." *Crime and Delinquency* 33:224–258.

Fagan, Jeffrey A., and Deanna L. Wilkinson. 1998. "Guns, Youth Violence, and Social Identity in Inner Cities."*Crime and Justice: A Review of Research* 24:105–188.

Farrington, David P. 1986. "Age and Crime." In *Crime and Justice: An Annual Review of Research* 7:189–250.

———. 1998. "Predictors, Causes, and Correlates of Youth Violence." *Crime and Justice: A Review of Research* 24:421–476.

———, Lloyd E. Ohlin, and James Q. Wilson. 1986. *Understanding and Controlling Crime: Toward a New Research Strategy.* New York: Springer-Verlag.

Farson, Richard. 1974. *Birthrights.* New York: Macmillan.

Federal Bureau of Investigation. 1992. *Crime in the United States, 1991: Uniform Crime Reports.* Washington D.C.: U.S. Government Printing Office.

———. 1993. *Age-Specific Arrest Rates and Race-Specific Arrest Rates for Selected Offenses, 1965–1992.* Washington, D.C.: Federal Bureau of Investigation.

———. 1996. *Crime in the United States, 1995: Uniform Crime Reports.* Washington, D.C.: U.S. Government Printing Office.

Federle, Katherine H. 1990. "The Abolition of the Juvenile Court: A Proposal for the Preservation of Children's Legal Rights." *Journal of Contemporary Law* 16:23–51.

Feld, Barry C. 1977. *Neutralizing Inmate Violence: Juvenile Offenders in Institutions.* Cambridge, Mass.: Ballinger.

———. 1978. "Reference of Juvenile Offenders for Adult Prosecution: The Legislative Alternative to Asking Unanswerable Questions." *Minnesota Law Review* 62:515–618.

———. 1981a. "A Comparative Analysis of Organizational Structure and Inmate Subcultures in Institutions for Juvenile Offenders." *Crime and Delinquency* 27:336–363.

———. 1981b. "Juvenile Court Legislative Reform and the Serious Young Offender: Dismantling the 'Rehabilitative Ideal.' " *Minnesota Law Review* 69:141–242.

———. 1983. "Delinquent Careers and Criminal Policy: Just Deserts and the Waiver Decision." *Criminology* 21:195–212.

———. 1984. "Criminalizing Juvenile Justice: Rules of Procedure for the Juvenile Court." *Minnesota Law Review* 69:141–276.

———. 1987. "The Juvenile Court Meets the Principle of Offense: Legislative Changes in Juvenile Waiver Statutes." *Journal of Criminal Law and Criminology* 78:471–533.

———. 1988a. "*In re Gault* Revisited: A Cross-State Comparison of the Right to Counsel in Juvenile Court." *Crime and Delinquency* 34:393–424.

———. 1988b. "The Juvenile Court Meets the Principle of Offense: Punishment, Treatment, and the Difference It Makes." *Boston University Law Review* 68:821–915.

———. 1989. "The Right to Counsel in Juvenile Court: An Empirical Study of When Lawyers Appear and the Difference They Make." *Journal of Criminal Law and Criminology* 79:1185–1346.

———. 1990a. "Bad Law Makes Hard Cases: Reflections on Teen-Aged Axe-Murderers, Judicial Activism, and Legislative Default." *Law and Inequality: A Journal of Theory and Practice* 8:1–101.

———. 1990b. "The Punitive Juvenile Court and the Quality of Procedural Justice: Disjunctions Between Rhetoric and Reality." *Crime and Delinquency* 36:443–466.

———. 1991. "Justice by Geography: Urban, Suburban, and Rural Variations in Juvenile Justice Administration." *Journal of Criminal Law and Criminology* 82:156–210.

———. 1993a. "Criminalizing the American Juvenile Court." *Crime and Justice: A Review of Research* 17:197–280.

———. 1993b. *Justice for Children: The Right to Counsel and the Juvenile Court.* Boston: Northeastern University Press.

———. 1995. "Violent Youth and Public Policy: A Case Study of Juvenile Justice Law Reform." *Minnesota Law Review* 79:965–1128.

———. 1997. "Abolish the Juvenile Court: Youthfulness, Criminal Responsibility, and Sentencing Policy." *Journal of Criminal Law and Criminology* 88:68–136.

Ferdinand, Theodore N. 1991. "History Overtakes the Juvenile Justice System." *Crime and Delinquency* 37:204–224.

Ferguson Bruce A., and Alan Charles Douglas. 1970. "A Study of Juvenile Waiver." *San Diego Law Review* 7:39–54.

Ferster, Elyce Zenoff, and Thomas F. Courtless. 1972. "Pre-dispositional Data, Role of Counsel, and Decisions in a Juvenile Court." *Law and Society Review* 7:195–222.

Finestone, Harold. 1976. *Victims of Change: Juvenile Deliquents in American Society.* Westport, Conn.: Greenwood.

Finkelstein, Barbara. 1985. "Casting Networks of Good Influence: The Reconstitution of Childhood in the United States, 1790–1870." In *American Childhood*, edited by Joseph Hawes and N. Ray Hiner. Westport, Conn.: Greenwood.

Fisher, Bruce, Mark Fraser, and Martin Forst. 1985. *Institutional Commitment and Release Decision-Making for Juvenile Delinquents: An Assessment of Determinate and Indeterminate Approaches, Washington State—A Case Study.* San Francisco: URSA Institute.

Flaherty, Michael G. 1980. *An Assessment of the National Incidence of Juvenile Suicide in Adult Jails, Lockups, and Juvenile Detention Centers.* Washington, D.C.: U.S. Department of Justice, Office of Juvenile Justice and Delinquency Prevention.

Flicker, Barbara. 1982. *Standards for Juvenile Justice: A Summary and Analysis.* Cambridge, Mass.: Ballinger.

———. 1983. *Providing Counsel for Accused Juveniles.* New York: Institute of Judicial Administration.

Fogel, David. 1979. *We Are the Living Proof: The Justice Model for Corrections.* 2d ed. Cincinnati: Anderson.

Forst, Martin, and Martha-Elin Blomquist. 1991. "Cracking Down on Juveniles: The Changing Ideology of Youth Corrections." *Notre Dame Journal of Law, Ethics and Public Policy* 5:323–375.

Forst, Martin, Jeffrey, Fagan, and T. Scott Vivona. 1989. "Youth in Prisons and Training Schools: Perceptions and Consequences of the Treatment-Custody Dichotomy." *Juvenile and Family Court Journal* 40:1–14.

Forst, Martin, Elizabeth Friedman, and Robert Coates. 1985. *Institutional Commitment and Release Decision-Making for Juvenile Delinquents: An Assessment of Determinate and Indeterminate Approaches, Georgia—A Case Study.* San Francisco: URSA Institute.

Fox, James Alan. 1996. *Trends in Juvenile Violence: A Report to the United States Attorney General on Current and Future Rates of Juvenile Offending.* Washington, D.C.: U.S. Department of Justice.

Fox, Sanford J. 1970a. "Juvenile Justice Reform: An Historical Perspective." *Stanford Law Review* 22:1187–1239.

———. 1970b. "Responsibility in the Juvenile Court." *William and Mary Law Review* 11: 659–684.

Frase, Richard. 1991. "Sentencing Reform in Minnesota: Ten Years After." *Minnesota Law Review* 75:727–54.

Frazier, Charles E. 1991. *Deep-End Juvenile Justice Placements or Transfer to Adult Court by Direct File?* Tallahassee: Florida Legislature, Commission on Juvenile Justice.

——— and Donna Bishop. 1985. "The Pretrial Detention of Juveniles and Its Impact on Case Dispositions." *Journal of Criminal Law and Criminology* 76:1132–1152.

Frazier, Charles E., and J. K. Cochran. 1986. "Detention of Juveniles: Its Effects on Subsequent Juvenile Court Processing Decisions." *Youth and Society* 17:286–305.

Freeman, Richard B. 1991. "Employment and Earnings of Disadvantaged Youth in a Labor Shortage Economy." In *The Urban Underclass*, edited by Christopher Jencks and Paul Peterson. Washington, D.C.: Brookings Institution.

Friedman, William J. 1982. *The Developmental Psychology of Time.* New York: Academic Press.

Fritsch, Eric, and Craig Hemmens. 1995. "Juvenile Waiver in the United States 1979–1995: A Comparison and Analysis of State Waiver Statutes." *Juvenile and Family Court Judges Journal* 46:17–35.

———and Tory J. Caeti. 1996. "Violent Youth in Juvenile and Adult Court: An Assessment of Sentencing Strategies in Texas." *Law and Policy* 18:115–36.

Furby, Lita, and Ruth Beyth-Marom. 1992. "Risk Taking in Adolescence: A Decision-Making Perspective." *Developmental Review* 12:1–44.

Gans, Herbert J. 1995. *The War against the Poor: The Underclass and Antipoverty Policy.* New York: Basic Books.

Gardner, Martin. 1982. "Punishment and Juvenile Justice: A Conceptual Framework for Assessing Constitutional Rights of Youthful Offenders." *Vanderbilt Law Review* 35:791–847.

———. 1987. "Punitive Juvenile Justice: Some Observations on a Recent Trend." *International Journal of Law and Psychiatry* 10:129–151.

———. 1989. "The Right of Juvenile Offenders to Be Punished: Some Implications of Treating Kids as Persons." *Nebraska Law Review* 68:182–215.

Gardner, William. 1993. "A Life-Span Rational Choice Theory of Risk Taking." In *Adolescent Risk Taking*, edited by Nancy J. Bell and Robert W. Bell. Newbury Park, Calif.: Sage.

———, and Janna Herman. 1990. "Adolescents' AIDS Risk Taking: A Rational Choice Perspective." In *Adolescents and the AIDS Epidemic*, edited by William Gardner, Susan G. Millstein, and Bruce Leroy Wilcox. San Francisco: Jossey-Bass.

Gardner, William, David Scherer, and Maya Tester. 1989. "Asserting Scientific Authority: Cognitive Development and Adolescent Legal Rights." *American Psychologist* 44:895–902.

Garland, David. 1990. *Punishment and Modern Society: A Study in Social Theory.* Chicago: University of Chicago Press.

Garlock, Peter D. 1979. " 'Wayward' Children and the Law, 1820–1900: The Genesis of the Status Offense Jurisdiction of the Juvenile Court." *Georgia Law Review* 13:341–447.

Garrett, Carol J. 1985. "Effects of Residential Treatment on Adjudicated Delinquents: A Meta-Analysis." *Journal of Research in Crime and Delinquency* 22:287–308.

Geimer, William S. 1988. "Juvenileness: A Single-Edged Constitutional Sword." *Georgia Law Review* 22:949–973.

Gendreau, Paul, and Bob Ross. 1979. "Effective Correctional Treatment: Bibliotherapy for Cynics." *Crime and Delinquency* 25:463–489.

———. 1987. "Revivification of Rehabilitation: Evidence from the 1980s." *Justice Quarterly* 4:349–407.

General Accounting Office (GAO). See U.S. General Accounting Office.

Geraghty, Thomas F. 1998. "Justice for Juveniles: How Do We Get There." *Journal of Criminal Law and Criminology* 88:190–241.

Giardino, Linda F. 1997. "Statutory Rhetoric: The Reality behind Juvenile Justice Policies in America." *Journal of Law and Policy* 5:223–276.

Gillespie, L. Kay, and Michael D. Norman. 1984. "Does Certification Mean Prison: Some Preliminary Findings from Utah." *Juvenile and Family Court Journal* 35:23–34.

Glaser, Daniel. 1987. "Classification for Risk." *Crime and Justice: A Review of Research* 9:249–291.

Glassner, Barry, Margaret Ksander, and Bruce Berg. 1983. "A Note on the Deterrent Effect of Juvenile vs. Adult Jurisdiction." *Social Problems* 31:219–221.

Goldstein, Abraham S. 1967. *The Insanity Defense.* New Haven.: Yale University Press.

Goodstein, Lynn, and Henry Sontheimer. 1987. *A Study of the Impact of 10 Pennsylvania Residential Placements on Juvenile Recidivism.* Shippensburg, Pa.: Center for Juvenile Justice Training and Research.

Gottfredson, Don M. 1987. "Prediction and Classification in Criminal Justice Decision Making." *Crime and Justice: A Review of Research* 9:1–20.

Gottfredson, Michael R., and Travis Hirschi. 1990. *A General Theory of Crime.* Stanford, Calif.: Stanford University Press.

Gottfredson, Stephen D. 1987. "Prediction: An Overview of Selected Methodological Issues." *Crime and Justice: A Review of Research* 9:21–51.

Graham, Fred P. 1970. *The Due Process Revolution: The Warren Court's Impact on Criminal Law*. New York: Hayden Books.

Greenberg, David, ed. 1977. *Corrections and Punishment*. Beverly Hills, Calif.: Sage.

Greenwood, Peter. 1986. "Differences in Criminal Behavior and Court Responses among Juvenile and Young Adult Defendants." *In Crime and Justice: An Annual Review of Research* 7:151–188.

———, Allan Abrahamse, and Franklin Zimring. 1984. *Factors Affecting Sentence Severity for Young Adult Offenders*. Santa Monica, Calif.: RAND.

Greenwood, Peter, A. Lipson, A. Abrahamse, and Frank Zimring. 1983. *Youth Crime and Juvenile Justice in California*. Santa Monica, Calif.: RAND.

Greenwood, Peter, Joan Petersilia, and Franklin Zimring. 1980. *Age, Crime, and Sanctions: The Transition from Juvenile to Adult Court*. Santa Monica, Calif.: RAND.

Greenwood, Peter, and Franklin Zimring. 1985. *One More Chance: The Pursuit of Promising Intervention Strategies for Chronic Juvenile Offenders*. Santa Monica, Calif.: RAND.

Grisso, Thomas. 1980. "Juveniles' Capacities to Waive *Miranda* Rights: An Empirical Analysis." *California Law Review* 68:1134–1166.

———. 1981. *Juveniles' Waiver of Rights: Legal and Psychological Competence*. New York: Plenum.

———. 1983. "Juveniles' Consent in Delinquency Proceedings." In *Children's Competence to Consent*, edited by Gary B. Melton, Gerald P. Koocher, and Michael J. Saks. New York: Plenum.

———. 1996. "Society's Retributive Response to Juvenile Violence: A Developmental Perspective." *Law and Human Behavior* 20:229–247.

———, and Linda Vierling. 1978. "Minors' Consent to Treatment: A Developmental Perspective." *Professional Psychology* 9:412–427.

Grubb, W. Norton, and Marvin Lazerson. 1982. *Broken Promises: How Americans Fail Their Children*. New York: Basic Books.

Guarino-Ghezzi, Susan, and Edward J. Loughran. 1996. *Balancing Juvenile Justice*. New Brunswick, N.J.: Transaction.

Guggenheim, Martin. 1977. "Paternalism, Prevention, and Punishment: Pretrial Detention of Juveniles." *New York University Law Review* 52:1064–1092.

———. 1978. "A Call to Abolish the Juvenile Justice System." *Children's Rights Reporter* 2:7–19.

———. 1984. "The Right to Be Represented but Not Heard: Reflections on Legal Representation for Children." *New York University Law Review* 59:76–149.

———. 1985. "Incorrigibility Laws: The State's Role in Resolving Intrafamily Conflict." *Criminal Justice Ethics* 4:11–19.

Hacker, Andrew. 1992. *Two Nations: Black and White, Separate, Hostile, Unequal*. New York: Ballantine Books.

Hagedorn, John M. 1998. "Gang Violence in the Postindustrial Era." *Crime and Justice: A Review of Research* 24:365–420.

Hall, Jerome. 1960. *General Principles of Criminal Law*. 2d ed. New York: Bobbs Merrill.

Hamburg, David A. 1992. *Today's Children: Creating a Future for a Generation in Crisis*. New York: Times Books.

Hamparian, Donna, Linda Estep, Susan Muntean, Ramon Priestino, Robert Swisher, Paul Wallace, and Joseph White. 1982. *Youth in Adult Courts: Between Two Worlds*. Washington, D.C.: U.S. Department of Justice, Office of Juvenile Justice and Delinquency Prevention.

Hamparian, Donna, Joseph M. Davis, Judith M. Jacobson, and Robert E. McGraw. 1985. *The Young Criminal Years of the Violent Few*. Washington, D.C.: U.S. Department of Justice, Office of Juvenile Justice and Delinquency Prevention.

Hamparian, Donna, Richard Schuster, Simon Dinitz, and John Conrad. 1978. *The Violent Few: A Study of Dangerous Juvenile Offenders*. Lexington, Mass.: Lexington Books.

Handler, Joel F. 1965. "The Juvenile Court and the Adversary System: Problems of Function and Form." *Wisconsin Law Review* 1965:7–51.

———, and Julie Zatz, eds. 1982. *Neither Angels nor Thieves: Studies in Deinstitutionalization of Status Offenders*. Washington, D.C.: National Academy Press.

Harris, Donald J. 1994. "Due Process v. Helping Kids in Trouble: Implementing the Right to Appeal from Adjudications of Delinquency in Pennsylvania." *Dickinson Law Review* 98:209–235.

Hart, H. L. A. 1968. *Punishment and Responsibility*. New York: Oxford University Press.

Hasenfeld, Yeheskel, and Paul P. Cheung. 1985. "The Juvenile Court as a People-Processing Organization: A Political Economy Perspective." *American Journal of Sociology* 90:801–824.

Hawes, Joseph. 1971. *Children in Urban Society: Juvenile Delinquency in Nineteenth-Century America*. New York: Oxford University Press.

———. 1991. *The Children's Rights Movement: A History of Advocacy and Protection*. Boston: Twayne.

———, and N. Ray Hiner, eds. 1985. *American Childhood: A Research Guide and Historical Handbook*. Westport, Conn.: Greenwood.

Hays, Samuel P. 1957. *The Response to Industrialism 1885–1914*. Chicago: University of Chicago Press.

Hazard, Geoffrey. 1976. "The Jurisprudence of Juvenile Deviance." In *Pursuing Justice for the Child*, edited by Margaret K. Rosenheim. Chicago: University of Chicago Press.

Hellum, Frank. 1979. "Juvenile Justice: The Second Revolution" *Crime and Delinquency* 25: 299–317.

Henretta, John, Charles Frazier, and Donna Bishop. 1986. "The Effects of Prior Case Outcomes on Juvenile Justice Decision-Making." *Social Forces* 65:554–582.

Herman, Edward S. 1981. *Corporate Control, Corporate Power*. Cambridge: Cambridge University Press.

Heuser, James Paul. 1985. *Juveniles Arrested for Serious Felony Crimes in Oregon and "Remanded" to Adult Criminal Courts: A Statistical Study*. Salem: Oregon Department of Justice Crime Analysis Center.

Higham, John. 1981. *Strangers in the Land: Patterns of American Nativism, 1860–1925*. 2d ed. New Brunswick, N.J.: Rutgers University Press.

Hindelang, Michael. 1978. "Race and Involvement in Common Law Personal Crimes." *American Sociological Review* 43:93–109.

Hirschi, Travis, and Michael Gottfredson. 1983. "Age and the Explanation of Crime." *American Journal of Sociology* 89:552–584.

Hodgson, Godfrey. 1976. *America in Our Time: From World War II to Nixon*. New York: Vintage Books.

Hofstadter, Richard. 1955. *The Age of Reform: From Bryan to F.D.R.* New York: Knopf.

Holt, John. 1974. *Escape from Childhood*. New York: Ballantine Books.

Horowitz, Allan, and Michael Wasserman. 1980. "Some Misleading Conceptions in Sentencing Research: An Example and Reformulation in the Juvenile Court." *Criminology* 18:411–424.

Howell, James C. 1996. "Juvenile Transfers to the Criminal Justice System: State-of the Art." *Law and Policy* 18:17–60.

Huerter, Regina M., and Bonnie E. Saltzman. 1992. "What Do 'They' Think? The Delinquency Court Process in Colorado as Viewed by the Youth." *Denver University Law Review* 69:345–358.

Huizinga, David, and Delbert S. Elliott. 1987. "Juvenile Offenders: Prevalence, Offender Incidence, and Arrest Rates by Race." *Crime and Delinquency* 33:206–223.

Human Rights Watch. 1995. *Children in Confinement in Louisiana*. New York: Human Rights Watch.

Humes, Edward. 1996. *No Matter How Loud I Shout: A Year in the Life of Juvenile Court*. New York: Simon and Schuster.

Illick, Joseph E. 1974. "Child-Rearing in Seventeenth-Century England and America." In *The History of Childhood*, edited by Lloyd deMause. New York: Harper Books.

Izzo, Rhena L., and Robert R. Ross. 1990. "Meta-Analysis of Rehabilitation Programs for Juvenile Delinquents." *Criminal Justice and Behavior* 17:134–142.

Jackson-Beeck, Marilyn. 1985. "Institutionalizing Juveniles for Psychiatric and Chemical Dependency in Minnesota: Ten Years' Experience." Minneapolis: Minnesota Coalition on Health Care Costs.

———, Ira M. Schwartz, and Andrew Rutherford. 1987. "Trends and Issues in Juvenile Confinement for Psychiatric and Chemical Dependency Treatment." *International Journal of Law and Psychiatry* 10:153–165.

Jencks, Christopher. 1992. *Rethinking Social Policy: Race, Poverty, and the Underclass*. New York: Harper Collins.

———, and Paul E. Peterson, eds. 1991. *The Urban Underclass*. Washington, D.C.: Brookings Institution.

Jensen, Eric L., and Linda K. Metsger. 1994. "A Test of the Deterrent Effect of Legislative Waiver on Violence Juvenile Crime." *Crime and Delinquency* 40:96–104.

Kadish, Sanford H. 1968. "The Decline of Innocence." *Cambridge Law Journal* 26:273–290.

———. 1987. "Excusing Crime." *California Law Review* 75:257–289.

Kalven, Harry, and Hans Zeisel. 1966. *The American Jury*. Chicago: University of Chicago Press.

Katz, Al, and Lee Teitelbaum. 1978. "PINS Jurisdiction, the Vagueness Doctrine, and the Rule of Law." *Indiana Law Journal* 53:1–34.

Katz, Michael B. 1968. *The Irony of Early School Reform: Educational Innovation in Mid-Nineteenth Century Massachusetts*. Boston: Beacon.

———. 1971. *Class, Bureaucarcy, & Schools: The Illusion of Educational Change in America*. New York: Praeger.

———. 1986. *In the Shadow of the Poorhouse: A Social History of Welfare in America*. New York: Basic Books.

———. 1989. *The Undeserving Poor: From the War on Poverty to the War on Welfare*. New York: Pantheon Books.

———. 1993. *The "Underclass" Debate: Views from History* (Katz, ed). Princeton.: Princeton University Press.

———, Michael B. Doucet, and Mark Stern. 1982. *The Social Organization of Early Industrial Capitalism*. Cambridge.: Harvard University Press.

Kay, Richard, and Daniel Segal. 1973. "The Role of the Attorney in Juvenile Court Proceedings: A Non-Polar Approach." *Georgetown Law Journal* 61:1401–1424.

Kempf, Kimberly L., Scott H. Decker, and Robert L. Bing. 1990. *An Analysis of Apparent Disparities in the Handling of Black Youth Within Missouri's Juvenile Justice Systems*. St. Louis: University of Missouri Department of Administration of Justice.

Kempf-Leonard, Kimberly, Carl Pope, and William Feyerherm. 1995. *Minorities in Juvenile Justice*. Thousand Oaks, Calif.: Sage.

Kerner Commission. See National Advisory Commission on Civil Disorders.

Kett, Joseph F. 1977. *Rites of Passage: Adolescence in America 1790 to the Present*. New York: Basic Books.

Klein, Malcolm W. 1979. "Deinstitutionalization and Diversion of Juvenile Offenders: A Litany of Impediments." *Crime and Justice: An Annual Review of Research* 1:145–201.

———. 1995. *The American Street Gang: Its Nature, Prevalence, and Control*. New York: Oxford University Press.

Knitzer, Jane, and Merril Sobie. 1984. *Law Guardians in New York State: A Study of the Legal Representation of Children*. New York: New York State Bar Association.

Kohlberg, Lawrence. 1963. "The Development of Children's Orientations toward a Moral Order." *Vita Humana* 6:11–33.

———. 1964. "Development of Moral Character and Moral Ideology." In *Review of Child Development Research*. Vol. 1, edited by Martin Hoffman and Lois Hoffman. Chicago: University of Chicago Press.

———. 1969. "Stage and Sequence: The Cognitive-Developmental Approach to Socialization." In *Handbook of Socialization Theory and Research*, edited by David Goslin. Chicago: Rand McNally.

Kolko, Gabriel. 1963. *The Triumph of Conservatism: A Reinterpretation of American History, 1900–1916*. New York: Free Press.

———. 1965. *Railroads and Regulation, 1877-1916*. Princeton, N.J.: Princeton University Press.

Kozol, Jonathan. 1991. *Savage Inequalities: Children in America's Schools*. New York: Harper Perennial.

Krisberg, Barry, and James Austin. 1993. *Reinventing Juvenile Justice*. Thousand Oaks, Calif.: Sage.

Krisberg, Barry, and Ira Schwartz. 1983. "Rethinking Juvenile Justice." *Crime and Delinquency* 29:333–364.

———, Gideon Fishman, Zvi Eisikovits, Edna Guttman, and Karen Joe. 1987. "The Incarceration of Minority Youth." *Crime and Delinquency* 33:173–205.

Krisberg, Barry, Ira Schwartz, Paul Lisky, and James Austin. 1986. "The Watershed of Juvenile Justice Reform." *Crime and Delinquency* 32:5–38.

Krisberg, Barry, and Patricia Steele. 1991. *Unlocking Juvenile Corrections*. San Francisco: National Council on Crime and Delinquency.

Lab, Steven P., and John T. Whitehead. 1988. "An Analysis of Juvenile Correctional Treatment." *Crime and Delinquency* 34:60–83.

———. 1990. "From 'Nothing Works' to 'The Appropriate Works': The Latest Stop on the Search for the Secular Grail." *Criminology* 28:405–417.

LaFave, Wayne R., and Austin W. Scott, Jr. 1986. *Criminal Law*. 2d ed. St. Paul, Minn.: West.

Lasch, Christopher. 1977. *Haven in a Heartless World: The Family Besieged*. New York: Basic Books.

Lefstein, Norman, Vaughan Stapleton, and Lee Teitelbaum. 1969. "In Search of Juvenile Justice: *Gault* and Its Implementation." *Law and Society Review* 3:491–562.

Lemann, Nicholas. 1992. *The Promised Land: The Great Black Migration and How It Changed America*. New York: Vintage Books.

Lemert, Edwin. 1967. "The Juvenile Court—Quest and Realities." In *Task Force Report: Juvenile Delinquency and Youth Crime*. Washington D.C.

———. 1970. *Social Action and Legal Change: Revolution within the Juvenile Court*. Chicago: Aldine.

———. 1981. "Diversion in Juvenile Court: What Hath Been Wrought." *Journal of Research in Crime and Delinquency* 27:34–46.

Lemmon, John H., Henry Sontheimer, and Keith A. Saylor. 1991. *A Study of Pennsylvania Juveniles Transferred to Criminal Court in 1986*. Harrisburg: Pennsylvania Juvenile Court Judges' Commission.

Lerman, Paul. 1980. "Trends and Issues in the Deinstitutionalization of Youths in Trouble." *Crime and Delinquency* 26:281–298.

———. 1982. *Deinstitutionalization and the Welfare State*. New Brunswick, N.J.: Rutgers University Press.

———. 1984. "Child Welfare, the Private Sector, and Community-Based Corrections." *Crime and Delinquency* 30:5–38.

Lerner, Steven. 1986. *Bodily Harm*. Bolinas, Calif.: Common Knowledge Press.

Lindsey, Duncan. 1994. *The Welfare of Children*. New York: Oxford University Press.

Lipsey, Mark W. 1992. "Juvenile Delinquent Treatment: A Meta-Analytic Inquiry into the Variability of Effects." In *Meta Analysis for Explanation: A Casebook*, edited by Thomas D. Cook. New York: Russell Sage Foundation.

———, and David B. Wilson. 1998. "Effective Intervention for Serious Juvenile Offenders." In *Serious and Violent Juvenile Offenders: Risk Factors and Successful Interventions*, edited by Rolf Loeber and David P. Farrington. Thousand Oaks, Calif.: Sage.

Lipton, Douglas, Robert Martinson, and Judith Wilks. 1975. *The Effectivess of Correctional Treatment*. New York: Praeger.

LIS, Inc. 1995. *Offenders under Age 18 in State Adult Correctional Systems: A National Picture*. Longmont, Colo.: National Institute of Corrections.

Liska, Allen E., and Mark Tausig. 1979. "Theoretical Interpretations of Social Class and

Racial Differentials in Legal Decision-Making for Juveniles." *Sociological Quarterly* 20: 197–207.

Livermore, Joseph, Carl Malmquist, and Paul Meehl. 1968. "On the Justification for Civil Commitment." *University of Pennsylvania Law Review* 117:75–96.

Logan, Charles H., and Gerald G. Gaes. 1993. "Meta-Analysis and the Rehabilitation of Punishment." *Justice Quarterly* 10:245–263.

Lubove, Roy. 1967. *The Professional Altruists: The Emergence of Social Work as a Profession.* Cambridge, Mass.: Harvard University Press.

Ludwig, Frederick J. 1950. "Rationale of Responsibility for Young Offenders." *Nebraska Law Review* 29:521–546.

McCarthy, Belinda. 1987. "Preventive Detention and Pretrial Custody in the Juvenile Court." *Journal of Criminal Justice* 15:185–200.

——, and Brent L. Smith. 1986. "The Conceptualization of Discrimination in the Juvenile Justice Process: The Impact of Administrative Factors and Screening Decisions on Juvenile Court Dispositions." *Criminology* 24:41–64.

McCarthy, Francis Barry. 1977a. "The Role of the Concept of Responsibility in Juvenile Delinquency Proceedings." *University of Michigan Journal of Law Reform* 10:181–219.

——. 1977b. "Should Juvenile Delinquency Be Abolished?" *Crime and Delinquency* 23: 196–203.

——. 1981. "Pre-Adjudicatory Rights in Juvenile Court: An Historical and Constitutional Analysis." *University of Pittsburgh Law Review* 42:457–514.

——. 1994. "The Serious Offender and Juvenile Court Reform: The Case for Prosecutorial Waiver of Juvenile Court Jurisdiction." *St. Louis University Law Journal* 38:629–671.

McCully, Sharon. 1994. "Detention Reform from a Judge's Viewpoint." In *Reforming Juvenile Detention: No More Hidden Closets*, edited by Ira M. Schwartz and William H. Barton. Columbus: Ohio State University Press.

Mack, Julian W. 1909. "The Juvenile Court." *Harvard Law Review* 23:104–122.

McDermott, M. J., and Michael J. Hindelang. 1981. *Juvenile Criminal Behavior in the United States: Its Trends and Patterns.* Washington, D.C.: U.S. Government Printing Office.

McGarrell, Edmund F. 1993. "Trends in Racial Disproportionality in Juvenile Court Processing: 1985–1989." *Crime and Delinquency* 39:29–48.

McNulty, Elizabeth W. 1996. "The Transfer of Juvenile Offenders to Adult Court: Panacea or Problem?" *Law and Policy* 18:61–76.

——, and J. Neil Russel. 1995. *Juvenile Commitment Guidelines Departure Research Project.* Phoenix: Arizona Supreme Court.

McShane, Marilyn D., and Frank P. Williams III. 1989. "The Prison Adjustment of Juvenile Offenders." *Crime and Delinquency* 35:254–269.

Maguire, Kathleen, and Ann L. Pastore, eds. 1994. *Sourcebook of Criminal Justice Statistics— 1993.* Washington, D.C.: U.S. Department of Justice, Bureau of Justice Statistics.

——. 1995. *Sourcebook of Criminal Justice Statistics—1994.* Washington, D.C.: U.S. Department of Justice, Bureau of Justice Statistics.

Mahoney, Anne Rankin. 1974. "The Effect of Labeling upon Youths in the Juvenile Justice System: A Review of the Evidence." *Law and Society Review* 8:583–614.

——. 1987. *Juvenile Justice in Context.* Boston: Northeastern University Press.

——, and Carol Fenster. 1982. "Female Delinquents in a Suburban Court." In *Judge, Lawyer, Victim, Thief: Women, Gender Roles & Criminal Justice.* Edited by Nicole Hahn Rafter and Elizabeth Anne Stanko. Boston: Northeastern University Press.

Martinson, Robert. 1974. "What Works? Questions and Answers about Prison Reform." *The Public Interest* 35:22–54.

Massey, Douglas S. 1995. "Getting Away with Murder: Segregation and Violent Crime in Urban America." *University of Pennsylvania Law Review* 143:1203–1232.

——, and Nancy A. Denton. 1993. *American Apartheid: Segregation and the Making of the Underclass.* Cambridge, Mass.: Harvard University Press.

Matza, David. 1964. *Delinquency and Drift.* New York: Wiley.

Mays, G. Larry, and Peter R. Gregware. 1996. "The Children's Code Reform Movement in New Mexico: The Politics of Expediency." *Law and Policy* 18:179–193.

Meehl, Paul. 1954. *Clinical versus Statistical Prediction: A Theoretical Analysis and a Review of the Evidence.* Minneapolis: University of Minnesota Press.

Melton, Gary B. 1983a. "Children's Competence to Consent: A Problem in Law and Social Science." In *Children's Competence to Consent,* edited by Gary B. Melton, Gerald P. Koocher, and Michael J. Saks. New York: Plenum.

———. 1983b. "Toward 'Personhood' for Adolescents: Autonomy and Privacy as Values in Public Policy." *American Psychologist* 38:99–103.

———. 1989. "Taking *Gault* Seriously: Toward a New Juvenile Court." *Nebraska Law Review* 68:146–181.

———. 1993. "Children, Families, and the Courts in the Twenty-First Century." *Southern California Law Review* 66:1993–2047.

Mennel, Robert. 1973. *Thorns and Thistles: Juvenile Delinquents in the United States, 1825–1940.* Hanover, N.H.: University Press of New England.

———. 1983. "Attitudes and Policies toward Juvenile Delinquency in the United States: A Historiographical Review." *Crime and Justice: A Review of Research* 4:191–224.

Miller, Jerome. 1991. *Last One over the Wall.* Columbus: Ohio State University Press.

Miller, Neal. 1995. *State Laws on Prosecutors' and Judges' Use of Juvenile Records.* Washington, D.C.: U.S. Department of Justice, National Institute of Justice.

Minnesota Department of Corrections. 1980. *Juvenile Release Guidelines.* St. Paul: Minnesota Department of Corrections.

Minnesota Legislative Auditor. 1995. *Residential Facilities for Juvenile Offenders.* St. Paul, Minn.: Office of Legislative Auditor.

Minow, Martha. 1990. *Making All the Difference: Inclusion, Exclusion, and American Law.* Ithaca, N.Y.: Cornell University Press.

———. 1995. "What Ever Happened to Children's Rights?" *Minnesota Law Review* 80:267–298.

Monohan, John. 1981. *Predicting Violent Behavior: An Assessment of Clinical Techniques.* Beverly Hills, Calif.: Sage.

Morris, Norval. 1974. *The Future of Imprisonment.* Chicago: University of Chicago Press.

———. 1982. *Madness and the Criminal Law* Chicago: University of Chicago Press.

———, and Marc Miller. 1985. "Predictions of Dangerousness." *Crime and Justice: An Annual Review of Research* 6:1–50.

Morse, Steven. 1984. "Undiminished Confusion in Diminished Capacity." *Journal of Criminal Law and Criminology* 75:1–55.

———. 1985. "Excusing the Crazy: The Insanity Defense Reconsidered." *Southern California Law Review* 58:779–836.

Mowry, George E., and Blaine A. Brownell. 1981. *The Urban Nation: 1920–1980.* Rev. ed. New York: Hill and Wang.

Moynihan, Daniel P. 1965. *The Negro Family: The Case for National Action.* Washington, D.C.: U.S. Government Printing Office.

Murray, Charles. 1984. *Losing Ground: American Social Policy, 1950–1980.* New York: Basic Books.

Murray, John P. 1983. *Status Offenders: A Sourcebook.* Boys Town, Nebr.: Boys Town Center.

National Advisory Committee on Criminal Justice Standards and Goals. 1976. *Report of the Task Force on Juvenile Justice and Delinqency Prevention.* Washington D.C.: U.S. Government Printing Office.

———. 1980. *Standards for the Administration of Juvenile Justice.* Washington, D.C.: U.S. Government Printing Office.

National Advisory Commission on Civil Disorders (Kerner Commission) 1968. *Report.* Washington, D.C.: U.S. Government Printing Office.

National Center for Juvenile Justice. 1996. *Easy Access to Juvenile Court Statistics.* Pittsburgh: National Center for Juvenile Justice.

National Commission on Children. 1991. *Beyond Rhetoric: A New American Agenda for Children and Families.* Washington, D.C.: U.S. Government Printing Office.

National Council on Crime and Delinquency. 1975. "Jurisdiction over Status Offenses

Should Be Removed from the Juvenile Court: A Policy State." *Crime and Delinquency* 21:97–99.

National Research Council. 1993. *Losing Generations: Adolescents in High-Risk Settings* Washington, D.C.: National Academy Press.

New Jersey Juvenile Delinquency Disposition Commission. 1986. *The Impact of the New Jersey Code of Juvenile Justice: First Annual Report of the Juvenile Delinquency Disposition Commission.* Trenton, N.J.: Juvenile Delinquency Disposition Commission.

Nimick, Ellen, Howard Snyder, Dennis Sullivan, and Nancy Tierney. 1985. *Juvenile Court Statistics, 1982.* Pittsburgh: National Center for Juvenile Justice.

Nimick, Ellen, Linda Szymanski, and Howard Snyder. 1986. *Juvenile Court Waiver: A Study of Juvenile Court Cases Transferred to Criminal Court.* Pittsburgh: National Center for Juvenile Justice.

Nisbet, Robert. 1975. *The Twilight of Authority.* New York: Oxford University Press.

Noble, David F. 1977. *America by Design: Science, Technology, and the Rise of Corporate Capitalism.* New York: Oxford University Press.

Note. 1966. "Juvenile Delinquents, The Police, State Courts, and Individualized Justice." *Harvard Law Review* 79:775–810.

Note. 1983. "The Public Right of Access to Juvenile Delinquency Hearings." *Michigan Law Review* 81:1540–1565.

Office of Juvenile Justice and Delinquency Prevention. 1993. *Comprehensive Strategy for Serious, Violent, and Chronic Juvenile Offenders.* Washington, D.C.: U.S. Government Printing Office.

Packer, Herbert L. 1968. *The Limits of the Criminal Sanction.* Stanford, Calif.: Stanford University Press.

Palmer, Ted. 1991. "The Effectiveness of Intervention: Recent Trends and Current Issues." *Crime and Delinquency* 37:330–350.

Parent, Dale, Terence Dunworth, Douglas McDonald, and William Rhodes. 1997. *Key Legislative Issues in Criminal Justice: Transferring Serious Juvenile Offenders to Adult Courts.* Washington, D.C.: U.S. Department of Justice, National Institute of Justice.

Parent, Dale G., Valierie Lieter, Stephen Kennedy, Lisa Livens, Daniel Wentworth, and Sarah Wilcox. 1994. *Conditions of Confinement: Juvenile Detention and Corrections Facilities.* Washington, D.C.: U.S. Department of Justice, Office of Juvenile Justice and Delinquency Prevention.

Paulsen, Monrad. 1957. "Fairness to the Juvenile Offender." *Minnesota Law Review* 41:547–576.

———. 1967. "The Constitutional Domestication of the Juvenile Court." *Supreme Court Review* 1967:233–266.

Pawlak, Edward J. 1977. "Differential Selection of Juveniles for Detention. *Journal of Research Crime and Delinquency* 14:152–165.

Petersilia, Joan. 1980. "Criminal Career Research: A Review of Recent Evidence." *Crime and Justice An Annual Review of Research* 2:321–379.

———. 1981. "Juvenile Record Use in Adult Court Proceedings: A Survey of Prosecutors." *Journal of Criminal Law and Criminology* 72:1746–1771.

Piaget, Jean. 1932. *The Moral Judgement of the Child.* London: K. Paul, Trench, Trubner.

———. 1969. *The Child's Conception of Time*, translated by A. J. Pomerans. London: Routledge and Kegan Paul.

Pickett, Robert. 1969. *Houses of Refuge: Origins of Juvenile Reform in New York State 1815–1857.* Syracuse, N.Y.: Syracuse University Press.

Pisciotta, Anthony. 1982. "Saving the Children: The Promise and Practice of Parens Patriae, 1838–98." *Crime and Delinquency* 28:410ff.

Platt, Anthony. 1977. *The Child Savers: The Invention of Delinquency.* 2d ed. Chicago: University of Chicago Press.

———, and Ruth Friedman. 1968. "The Limits of Advocacy: Occupational Hazards in Juvenile Court." *University of Pennsylvania Law Review* 116:1156–1184.

Podkopacz, Marcy Rasmussen, and Barry C. Feld. 1995. "Judicial Waiver Policy and Practice:

Persistence, Seriousness, and Race." *Law and Inequality: A Journal of Theory and Practice* 14:73–178.

———. 1996. "The End of the Line: An Empirical Study of Judicial Waiver." *Journal of Criminal Law and Criminology* 86:449–492.

Polk, Kenneth. 1984. "Juvenile Diversion: A Look at the Record." *Crime and Delinquency* 30:648–659.

Pope, Carl E. 1994. "Racial Disparities in Juvenile Justice System." *Overcrowded Times* 5:1–4.

———, and William H. Feyerherm. 1990a. "Minority Status and Juvenile Justice Processing: An Assessment of the Research Literature," pt. 1. *Criminal Justice Abstracts* 22:327–335.

———, 1990b. "Minority Status and Juvenile Justice Processing: An Assessment of the Research Literature," pt. 2. *Criminal Justice Abstracts* 22:527–542.

———. 1992. *Minorities and the Juvenile Justice System*. Washington, D.C.: U.S. Department of Justice, Office of Juvenile Justice and Delinquency Prevention.

Postman, Neil. 1994. *The Disappearance of Childhood*. New York: Vintage Books.

Poulos, Tammy Meredith, and Stan Orchowsky. 1994. "Serious Juvenile Offenders: Predicting the Probability of Transfer to Criminal Court." *Crime and Delinquency* 40:3–17.

President's Commission on Law Enforcement and Administration of Justice. 1967a. *The Challenge of Crime in a Free Society*. Washington, D.C.: U.S. Government Printing Office.

———. 1967b. *Task Force Report: Juvenile Delinquency and Youth Crime*. Washington, D.C.: U.S. Government Printing Office.

Ralph, John H., and Richard Rubinson. 1980. "Immigration and Expansion of Schooling, 1890–1970." *American Sociological Review* 45:943–954.

Reiss, Albert J., Jr., and Jeffrey A. Roth, eds. 1993. *Understanding and Preventing Violence*. Washington, D.C.: National Academy Press.

Rendleman, Douglas R. 1971. "Parens Patriae: From Chancery to the Juvenile Court." *South Carolina Law Review* 23:205–259.

Roberts, Albert R., and Michael J. Camasso. 1991. "The Effects of Juvenile Offender Treatment Programs on Recidivism: A Meta-Analysis of 46 Studies." *Notre Dame Journal of Law, Ethics and Public Policy* 5:421–442.

Rosenberg, Irene M. 1980. "The Constitutional Rights of Children Charged with Crime: Proposal for a Return to the Not So Distant Past." *University of California at Los Angeles Law Review* 27:656–721.

———. 1983. "Juvenile Status Offender Statutes—New Perspectives on an Old Problem." *University of California at Davis Law Review* 16:283–323.

———. 1993. "Leaving Bad Enough Alone: A Reply to the Abolitionists." *Wisconsin Law Review*. 1993:163–185.

———. and Yale L. Rosenberg. 1976. "The Legacy of the Stubborn and Rebellious Son." *Michigan Law Review* 74:1097–1165.

Rosenfeld, Richard, and Scott H. Decker. 1996. "Consent to Search and Seize: Evaluating an Innovative Youth Firearm Suppression Program." *Law and Contemporary Problems* 59:197–220.

Rosenheim, Margaret K. 1976. "Notes on Helping Juvenile Nuisances." In *Pursuing Justice for the Child*, edited by Margaret K. Rosenheim. Chicago: University of Chicago Press.

Rothman, David J. 1971. *The Discovery of the Asylum*. Boston: Little, Brown.

———. 1978. "The State as Parent: Social Policy in the Progressive Era." In *Doing Good: The Limits of Benevolence*, edited by William Gaylin, Ira Glasser, Steven Marcus, and David Rothman. New York: Pantheon Books.

———. 1980. *Conscience and Convenience: The Asylum and Its Alternative in Progressive America*. Boston: Little, Brown.

Rothman, Sheila M. 1978. *Woman's Proper Place: A History of Changing Ideals and Practices, 1870 to the Present*. New York: Basic Books.

Rubin, H. Ted. 1979. "Retain the Juvenile Court? Legislative Developments, Reform Directions, and the Call for Abolition." *Crime and Delinquency* 25:281–298.

———. 1985. *Juvenile Justice: Policy, Practice, and Law*. 2d ed. New York: Random House.

Rudman, Cary, Eliot Hartstone, Jeffrey Fagan, and Melinda Moore. 1986. "Violent Youth in Adult Court: Process and Punishment." *Crime and Delinquency* 36:75–96.

Ruhland, David J., Martin Gold, and Randall J. Hekman. 1982. "Deterring Juvenile Crime: Age of Jurisdiction." *Youth and Society* 13:353–376.

Ryerson, Ellen. 1978. *The Best-Laid Plans: America's Juvenile Court Experiment.* New York: Hill and Wang.

Sampson, Robert J. 1987. "Urban Black Violence: The Effect of Male Joblessness and Family Disruption." *American Journal of Sociology* 93:348–382.

———, and John Laub. 1993. "Structural Variations in Juvenile Court Processing: Inequality, the Underclass, and Social Control." *Law and Society Review* 27:285–311.

Sampson, Robert J. and Janet L. Lauritsen. 1997. "Racial and Ethnic Disparities in Crime and Criminal Justice in the United States." *Crime and Justice: A Review of Research* 23: 311–374.

Sampson, Robert J. and William Julius Wilson. 1995. "Toward a Theory of Race, Crime, and Urban Inequality." In *Crime and Inequality*, edited by John Hagan and Ruth Peterson. Stanford, Calif.: Stanford University Press.

Sanborn, Joseph B., Jr. 1993a. "Philosophical, Legal and Systemic Aspects of Juvenile Court Plea Bargaining." *Crime and Delinquency* 39:509–527.

———. 1993b. "The Right to a Public Jury Trial: A Need for Today's Juvenile Court." *Judicature* 76:230–238.

———. 1994. "Remnants of Parens Patriae in the Adjudicatory Hearing: Is a Fair Trial Possible in Juvenile Court?" *Crime and Delinquency* 40:599–615.

———. 1996. "Policies Regarding the Prosecution of Juvenile Murderers: Which System and Who Should Decide?" *Law and Policy* 18:151–178.

Sarri, Rosemary. 1974. *Under Lock and Key: Juveniles in Jail and Detention.* Ann Arbor: National Assessement of Juvenile Corrections, University of Michigan.

———. 1976. "Service Technologies: Diversion, Probation, and Detention." In *Brought to Justice? Juveniles, the Courts, and the Law*, edited by Rosemary Sarri and Yeheskel Hasenfeld. Ann Arbor: National Assessment of Juvenile Corrections, University of Michigan.

Schlossman, Steven. 1977. *Love and the American Delinquent: The Theory and Practice of "Progressive" Juvenile Justice.* Chicago: University of Chicago Press.

———, and Stephanie Wallach. 1978. "The Crime of Precocious Sexuality: Female Juvenile Delinquency in the Progressive Era." *Harvard Educational Review* 48:65–94.

Schneider, Anne L. 1984a. "Deinstitutionalization of Status Offenders: The Impact on Recidivism and Secure Confinement." *Criminal Justice Abstracts* 16:410–432.

———. 1984b. "Divesting Status Offenses from Juvenile Court Jurisdiction." *Crime and Delinquency* 30:347–370.

———, and Donna Schram. 1983a. *A Justice Philosophy for the Juvenile Court.* Seattle: Urban Policy Research.

———. 1983b. *A Comparison of Intake and Sentencing Decision-Making under Rehabilitation and Justice Models of the Juvenile System.* Seattle: Urban Policy Research.

Schur, Edwin M. 1973. *Radical Nonintervention: Rethinking the Delinquency Problem.* Englewood Cliffs, N.J.: Prentice-Hall.

Schwartz, Ira M. 1989a. "Hospitalization of Adolescents for Psychiatric and Substance Abuse Treatment." *Journal of Adolescent Health Care* 10:1–6.

———. 1989b. *(In)Justice for Juveniles: Rethinking the Best Interests of the Child.* Lexington, MA: Lexington Books.

Schwartz, Ira M. 1991. "Out-of-Home Placement of Children: Selected Issues and Prospects for the Future." *Behavioral Sciences and the Law* 9:189–199.

———. 1992. "Juvenile Crime-Fighting Policies: What the Public Really Wants." In *Juvenile Justice and Public Policy*, edited by Ira M. Schwartz. Lexington Mass.: Lexington Books.

———, and William H. Barton. 1994. *Reforming Juvenile Detention: No More Hidden Closets.* Columbus: Ohio State University Press.

Schwartz, Ira M., Gideon Fishman, Radene Rawson Hatfield, Barry A. Krisberg, and Zvi

Eisikovits. 1987. "Juvenile Detention: The Hidden Closets Revisited." *Justice Quarterly* 4:221–235.

Schwartz, Ira M., Marilyn Jackson-Beeck, and Roger Anderson. 1984. "The Hidden System of Juvenile Control." *Crime and Delinquency* 30:371–385.

Schwartz, Ira M., Linda Harris, and Laurie Levi. 1988. "The Jailing of Juveniles in Minnesota: A Case Study." *Crime and Delinquency* 34:133–149.

Schwartz, Ira M., Martha W. Steketee, and Victoria W. Schneider. 1990. "Federal Juvenile Justice Policy and the Incarceration of Girls." *Crime and Delinquency* 36:511–520.

Scott, Elizabeth S. 1992. "Judgment and Reasoning in Adolescent Decisionmaking." *Villanova Law Review* 37:1607–1669.

———, and Thomas Grisso. 1998. "The Evolution of Adolescence: A Developmental Perspective on Juvenile Justice Reform." *Journal of Criminal Law and Criminology* 88:137–189.

Scott, Elizabeth S., N. Dickon Reppucci, and Jennifer L. Woolard. 1995. "Evaluating Adolescent Decision Making in Legal Contexts." *Law and Human Behavior* 19:221–244.

Sechrest, Lee B. 1987. "Classification for Treatment." *Crime and Justice: A Review of Research* 9:293–322.

———, Susan O. White, and Elizabeth D. Brown, eds. 1979. *The Rehabilitation of Criminal Offenders*. Washington, D.C.: National Academy of Sciences.

Shaughnessy, Patricia L. 1979. "The Right to a Jury under the Juvenile Justice Act of 1977." *Gonzaga Law Review* 14:401–421.

Sheffer, Julianne P. 1995. "Serious and Habitual Juvenile Offender Statutes: Reconciling Punishment and Rehabilitation within the Juvenile Justice System." *Vanderbilt Law Review* 48:479–512.

Shorter, Edward. 1975. *The Making of the Modern Family*. New York: Basic Books.

Sickmund, Melissa, Anne Aughenbaugh, Terrence Finnegan, Howard Snyder, Rowen Poole, and Jeffrey Butts. 1998. *Juvenile Court Statistics, 1995*. Washington, D.C.: U.S. Department of Justice, Office of Juvenile Justice and Delinquency Prevention.

Sickmund, Melissa, Howard N. Snyder, and Eileen Poe-Yamagata. 1997. *Juvenile Offenders and Victims: 1997 Update on Violence*. Washington, D.C.: U.S. Department of Justice, Office of Juvenile Justice and Delinquency Prevention.

Siegler, Robert S. 1986. *Children's Thinking*. Englewood Cliffs, N.J.: Prentice-Hall.

Silberman, Charles. 1978. *Criminal Violence, Criminal Justice*. New York: Random House.

Singer, Simon I. 1996. *Recriminalizing Delinquency: Violent Juvenile Crime and Juvenile Justice Reform*. New York: Cambridge University Press.

———, and David McDowall. 1988. "Criminalizing Delinquency: The Deterrent Effects of the New York Juvenile Offender Law." *Law and Society Review* 22:521–535.

Sizer, Theodore R. 1984. *Horace's Compromise: The Dilemma of the American High School*. Boston: Houghton Mifflin.

Skolnick, Arlene. 1975. "The Limits of Childhood: Conceptions of Child Development and Social Context." *Law and Contemporary Problems* 39:38–79.

Smith, Erin M. 1992. "In a Child's Best Interest: Juvenile Status Offenders Deserve Procedural Due Process." *Law and Inequality* 10:253–284.

Smith, Trudie F. 1985. "Law Talk: Juveniles' Understanding of Legal Language." *Journal of Criminal Justice* 13:339–353.

Snyder, Howard N. 1990. *Growth in Minority Detentions Attributed to Drug Law Violators*. OJJDP Fact Sheet Washington D.C.: U.S. Department of Justice, Office of Juvenile Justice and Delinquency Prevention.

———. 1997. *Juvenile Arrests, 1996*. Washington D.C.: U.S. Department of Justice, Office of Juvenile Justice and Delinquency Prevention.

———, and Terrence A. Finnegan. 1987. *Delinquency in the United States, 1983*. Washington, D.C.: U.S. Department of Justice, Office of Juvenile Justice and Delinquency Prevention.

Snyder, Howard N., and John L. Hutzler. 1981. *The Serious Juvenile Offender: The Scope of the Problem and the Response of Juvenile Courts*. Pittsburgh: National Center for Juvenile Justice.

Snyder, Howard N., and Melissa Sickmund. 1995. *Juvenile Offenders and Victims: A National Report*. Washington, D.C.: U.S. Department of Justice, Office of Juvenile Justice and Delinquency Prevention.

————, and Eileen Poe-Yamagata. 1996. *Juvenile Offenders and Victims: 1996 Update on Violence*. Washington, D.C.: U.S. Department of Justice, Office of Juvenile Justice and Delinquency Prevention.

Sondheim, Stephen. 1956. *West Side Story: A Musical*. New York: Random House.

Spergel, Irving A., Frederic G. Reamer, and James P. Lynch. 1981. "Deinstitutionalization of Status Offenders: Individual Outcome and System Effects." *Journal of Research in Crime and Delinquency* 18:4–33.

Springer, Charles E. 1991. "Rehabilitating the Juvenile Court." *Notre Dame Journal of Law, Ethics and Public Policy* 5:397–420.

Stapleton, W. Vaughan, David P. Aday, Jr., and Jeanne A. Ito. 1982. "An Empirical Typology of American Metropolitan Juvenile Courts." *American Journal of Sociology* 88:549–564.

Stapleton, W. Vaughan, and Lee E. Teitelbaum. 1972. *In Defense of Youth: A Study of the Role of Counsel in American Juvenile Courts*. New York: Russell Sage.

Starr, Paul. 1982. *The Social Transformation of American Medicine*. New York: Basic Books.

Steele, Patricia A., James Austin, and Barry Krisberg. 1989. *Unlocking Juvenile Corrections: Evaluating the Masssachusetts Department of Youth Services*. San Fancisco: National Council on Crime and Delinquency.

Steiger, John C., and Cary Dizon. 1991. *Rehabilitation, Release, and Reoffending: A Report on the Criminal Careers of the Division of Juvenile Rehabilitation "Class of 1982."* Olympia, Wash.: Department of Social and Health Services.

Steinberg, Laurence, and Elizabeth Cauffman. 1996. "Maturity of Judgment in Adolescence: Psychosocial Factors in Adolescent Decision Making." *Law and Human Behavior* 20:249–272.

Stephan, James. 1989. *Prison Rule Violators*. Washington, D.C.: U.S. Department of Justice, Bureau of Justice Statistics.

Stern, David, Sandra Smith, and Fred Doolittle. 1975. "How Children Used to Work." *Law and Contemporary Problems* 39:93–117.

Strasburg, Paul. 1978. *Violent Delinquents: A Report to the Ford Foundation from the Vera Institute of Justice*. New York: Monarch.

Streib, Victor L. 1987. *Death Penalty for Juveniles*. Bloomington and Indianapolis: Indiana University Press.

————. 1998. "The Juvenile Death Penalty Today: Death Sentences and Executions for Juvenile Crimes, January 1973–May 1998." Ada: Ohio Northern University.

Strickland, Charles E., and Andrew M. Ambrose. 1985. "The Changing Worlds of Children, 1945–1963." In *American Childhood*, edited by Joseph Hawes and N. Ray Hiner. Westport, Conn.: Greenwood.

Sullivan, Mercer L. 1989. *"Getting Paid": Youth Crime and Work in the Inner City*. Ithaca, N.Y.: Cornell University Press.

Sussman, Alan. 1977a. "Judicial Control over Noncriminal Behavior." *New York University Law Review* 52:1051–1062.

————. 1977b. "Sex-Based Discrimination and the PINS Jurisdiction." In *Beyond Control*, edited by Lee H. Teitelbaum and Aidan R. Gough. Cambridge, Mass.: Ballinger.

Sutton, John R. 1983. "Social Structure, Institutions, and the Legal Status of Children in the United States." *American Journal of Sociology* 88:915–947.

————. 1988. *Stubborn Children: Controlling Delinquency in the United States*. Berkeley: University of California Press.

Sykes, Charles J. 1992. *A Nation of Victims: The Decay of the American Character*. New York: St. Martin's.

Sykes, Gresham M., and David Matza. 1957. "Techniques of Neutralization: A Theory of Delinquency." *American Sociological Review* 22:664–670.

Tapp, June L. 1976. "Psychology and the Law: An Overture." *Annual Review of Psychology* 27:359–374.

————, and Lawrence Kohlberg. 1977. "Developing Senses of Law and Legal Justice." In *Law, Justice, and the Individual in Society*, edited by June L. Tapp and Felice Levine. New York: Holt, Rinehart and Winston.

Tapp, June L., and Felice Levine. 1974. "Legal Socialization: Strategies for an Ethical Legality." *Stanford Law Review* 27:1–54.

Teilmann, Katherine S., and Malcolm Klein. N.d. *Summary of Interim Findings of the Assessment of the Impact of California's 1977 Juvenile Justice Legislation.* Los Angeles: Social Science Research Institute, University of Southern California.

Teilmann, Katherine S., and Pierre H. Landry, Jr. 1981. "Gender Bias in Juvenile Justice." *Journal of Research in Crime and Delinquency* 18:47–80.

Teitelbaum, Lee E. 1991. "Youth Crime and the Choice between Rules and Standards." *Brigham Young University Law Review* 1991:351–402.

————, and Aidan R. Gough, eds. 1977. *Beyond Control: Status Offenders in the Juvenile Court.* Cambridge, Mass.: Ballinger.

Teitelbaum, Lee E., and Leslie J. Harris. 1977. "Some Historical Perspectives on the Governmental Regulation of Children and Parents." In *Beyond Control: Status Offenders in the Juvenile Court*, edited by Lee E. Teitelbaum and Aidan R. Gough, Cambridge, Mass.: Ballinger.

Thorelli, Hans B. 1954. *The Federal Anti-Trust Policy.* Baltimore, Md.: Johns Hopkins University Press.

Thomas, Charles W., and Shay Bilchik. 1985. "Prosecuting Juveniles in Criminal Courts: A Legal and Empirical Analysis." *Journal of Criminal Law and Criminology* 76:439–479.

Tiffin, Susan. 1982. *In Whose Best Interest? Child Welfare Reform in the Progressive Era.* Westport, Conn.: Greenwood.

Tonry, Michael. 1987. "Prediction and Classification: Legal and Ethical Issues." *Crime and Justice: A Review of Research* 9:367–413.

————. 1995. *Malign Neglect: Race, Crime, and Punishment in America.* New York: Oxford University Press.

————. 1996. *Sentencing Matters.* New York: Oxford University Press.

Torbet, Patricia, Richard Gable, Hunter Hurst, IV, Imogene Montgomery, Linda Szymanski, and Douglas Thomas. 1996. *State Responses to Serious and Violent Juvenile Crime: Research Report.* Washington, D.C.: U.S. Department of Justice, Office of Juvenile Justice and Delinquency Prevention.

Tracy, Paul E., Marvin E. Wolfgang, and Robert M. Figlio. 1990. *Delinquency Careers in Two Birth Cohorts.* New York: Plenum.

Trattner, Walter I. 1970. *Crusade for the Children: A History of the National Child Labor Committee and Child Labor Reform in New York State.* Chicago: Quadrangle.

————. 1984. *From Poor Law to Welfare State: A History of Social Welfare in America.* 3d ed. Westport Conn.: Greenwood.

Twentieth Century Fund Task Force. 1976. *Fair and Certain Punishment.* New York: McGraw-Hill.

Twentieth Century Fund Task Force on Sentencing Policy toward Young Offenders. 1978. *Confronting Youth Crime.* New York: Holmes and Meier.

Tyack, David B. 1974. *The One Best System.* Cambridge, Mass.: Harvard University Press.

U.S. Department of Census, Bureau of Census. 1980. *The Social and Economic Status of the Black Population in the United States: An Historical View, 1790–1978.* Washington, D.C.: U.S. Government Printing Office.

U.S. General Accounting Office. 1983. *Improved Federal Efforts Needed to Change Juvenile Detention Practices.* Washington, D.C.: U.S. General Accounting Office.

————. 1995a. *Juvenile Justice: Juveniles Processed in Criminal Court and Case Dispositions.* Washington, D.C.: U.S. General Accounting Office.

————. 1995b. *Juvenile Justice: Representation Rates Varied As Did Counsel's Impact on Court Outcomes.* Washington, D.C.: U.S. General Accounting Office.

U.S. Sentencing Commission. 1995. *Sentencing Commission Guidelines Manual.* Washington, D.C.: U.S. Sentencing Commission.

van den Haag, Ernest. 1975. *Punishing Criminals: Concerning a Very Old and Painful Question.* New York: Basic Books.

Vereb, Thomas S., and John L. Hutzler. 1981. *Juveniles as Criminals: 1981 Statutes Analysis.* Pittsburgh: National Center for Juvenile Justice.

von Hirsch, Andrew. 1976. *Doing Justice.* New York: Hill and Wang.

———. 1985. *Past vs. Future Crimes.* New Brunswick, N.J.: Rutgers University Press.

———. 1993. *Censure and Sanctions.* Oxford: Oxford University Press.

Wald, Patricia. 1976. "Pretrial Detention for Juveniles." In *Pursuing Justice for the Child,* edited by Margaret K. Rosenheim. Chicago: University of Chicago Press.

Walkover, Andrew. 1984. "The Infancy Defense in the New Juvenile Court." *University of California at Los Angeles Law Review* 31:503–562.

Walter, James D., and Susan A. Ostrander. 1982. "An Observational Study of a Juvenile Court." *Juvenile and Family Court Journal* 33:53–69.

Warner, Sam Bass, Jr. 1978. *Streetcar Suburbs: The Process of Growth in Boston, 1870–1900* 2d ed. Cambridge, Mass.: Harvard University Press.

Warren, Earl. 1964. "Equal Justice for Juveniles." *Juvenile Court Judges Journal* 15:15–16.

Weissman, James C. 1983. "Toward an Integrated Theory of Delinquency Responsibility." *Denver Law Journal* 60:485–518.

Weithorn, Lois A. 1988. "Mental Hospitalization of Troublesome Youth: An Analysis of Skyrocketing Admission Rates." *Stanford Law Review* 40:773–838.

———, and Susan B. Campbell. 1982. "The Competency of Children and Adolescents to Make Informed Treatment Decisions. *Child Development* 53:1589–1598.

Whitehead, John T., and Steven P. Lab. 1989. "A Meta-Analysis of Juvenile Correctional Treatment." *Journal Research Crime and Delinquency* 26:276–295.

Wiebe, Robert H. 1967. *The Search for Order, 1877–1920.* New York: Hill and Wang.

———. 1965. *Businessmen and Reform: A Study of the Progressive Movement.* Cambridge, Mass.: Harvard University Press.

Wilensky, Harold L., and Charles N. Lebeaux. 1958. *Industrial Society and Social Welfare.* New York: The Free Press.

Wilson, James Q. 1975. *Thinking about Crime.* New York: Basic Books.

Wilson, John J., and James C. Howell. 1995. "Comprehensive Strategy for Serious, Violent, and Chronic Juvenile Offenders." In *Serious, Violent and Chronic Juvenile Offenders,* edited by James C. Howell, Barrry Krisberg, J. David Hawkins, John J. Wilson. Thousand Oaks, Calif.: Sage.

Wilson, William J. 1987. *The Truly Disadvantaged.* Chicago: University of Chicago Press.

———. 1996. *When Work Disappears: The World of the New Urban Poor.* New York: Knopf.

Winner, Lawrence, Lonn Lanza-Kaduce, Donna M. Bishop, and Charles E. Frazier. 1997. "The Transfer of Juveniles to Criminal Court: Reexamining Recidivism over the Long Term." *Crime and Delinquency* 43:548–563.

Wishy, Bernard. 1968. *The Child and the Republic.* Philadelphia: University of Pennsylvania Press.

Wizner, Steven, and Mary F. Keller. 1977. "The Penal Model of Juvenile Justice: Is Juvenile Court Delinquency Jurisdiction Obsolete?" *New York University Law Review* 52:1120–1135.

Wolfgang, Marvin, Robert Figlio, and Thorsten Sellin. 1972. *Delinquency in a Birth Cohort.* Chicago: University of Chicago Press.

Wooden, Kenneth. 1976. *Weeping in the Playtime of Others: America's Incarcerated Children.* New York: McGraw-Hill.

Wordes, Madeline, Timothy S. Bynum, and Charles J. Corley. 1994. "Locking Up Youth: The Impact of Race on Detention Decisions." *Journal of Research in Crime and Delinquency* 31:149–165.

Zimring, Franklin E. 1981a. "Kids, Groups, and Crime: Some Implications of a Well-Known Secret." *Journal of Criminal Law and Criminology* 72:867–902.

———. 1981b. "Notes Toward a Jurisprudence of Waiver." In *Readings in Public Policy,* edited by John C. Hall, Donna Martin Hamparian, John M. Pettibone, and Joseph L. White. Columbus, Ohio: Academy for Contemporary Problems.

———. 1982. *The Changing Legal World of Adolescence*. New York: Free Press.

———. 1991. "The Treatment of Hard Cases in American Juvenile Justice: In Defense of Discretionary Waiver." *Notre Dame Journal of Law, Ethics and Public Policy* 5:267–280.

———. 1996. "Kids, Guns, and Homicide: Policy Notes on an Age-Specific Epidemic." *Law and Contemporary Problems* 59:25–37.

———. 1998. *American Youth Violence*. New York: Oxford University Press.

———, and Gordon Hawkins. 1997. *Crime is Not the Problem: Lethal Violence in America*. New York: Oxford University Press.

Index

Rehabilitative ideal. *See also* Punishment
vs. rehabilitation
assumptions underlying, 60–61, 79–80,
211, 254, 328
effectiveness of treatment and, 276, 279–
282
erosion of support for, 89–94, 173, 189,
248, 331
Progressive juvenile court and, 47, 60–
61, 328
return of juvenile court to, 289–297
Roosevelt, Franklin, 81
Rosenheim, Margaret, 188
Rothman, David J., 72, 73, 89
Rousseau, Jean-Jacques, 50
Ryerson, Ellen, 72, 73

Sampson, Robert, 195
Schall v. Martin, 137–140, 145–147, 150,
163, 250
Schlossman, Steven, 65, 72
Scott v. Illinois, 124, 134, 159
Screening cases, 115–116
Self-incrimination, privilege against
adversary system and, 101, 105, 164
confinement and, 249
Gault and, 101–102, 105, 164, 172
waiver of, 110, 117–123
Sentencing
determinate vs. indeterminate, 12, 70,
112, 158, 188, 189, 209, 211, 212, 225,
246–247, 248, 249, 250, 253–261, 283,
284, 292–294, 297–298
graduated scheme for, 188, 260–264,
284, 317–318, 324
guidelines, 225, 234, 239, 255–256, 319
"just deserts," 12, 94, 112, 210, 211, 212,
248, 255–256, 305
length of confinement and, 277
mandatory minimum, 219, 239, 254,
255, 258–260, 284
pretrial detention and, 152
principle of individualized justice and,
14, 73–74, 212, 247, 265, 271–272,
284, 292
principle of offense and, 14, 212, 225,
247, 266–267, 268, 271, 284
proportional vs. nonproportional, 70,
112, 188, 211–212, 238–239, 240, 246–
247, 253–261, 284, 292–294, 297–298,
305

offense-based, 145, 209, 210, 211, 248,
255–261
racial disparities in, 217, 231, 240, 256,
264–272, 284
severity of, for juveniles vs. adults, 213,
220–223, 227–230, 243, 276–277, 301,
304, 314, 324
waiver of jurisdiction and, 208–213, 222–
224, 227–230, 243
"youth discount" and, 289–290, 317–322
youthfulness as mitigating factor and, 9,
112, 154–155, 239–240, 243, 289, 297,
302–317
Shorter, Edward, 23
Smith v. Daily Mail Publishing Co., 160
Spencer, Herbert, 57
Social control
families and, 21–22, 47, 49, 50, 314
formal vs. informal, 47, 50, 174
houses of refuge and, 49–54
ideological assumptions and, 56, 76, 89–
90
minority populations and, 5, 47, 180,
265
Progressive era and, 46
social welfare and, 63, 75, 76–77, 248,
252, 289–297, 327, 328, 332
Social Darwinism, 57–58, 65, 86
Social structure
context of juvenile courts and, 112, 265–
266, 285, 296
crime and, 61, 76, 191–208, 315
Social welfare
child poverty and, 333–334, 335–336,
341
model of juvenile court, 111, 287, 289–
297, 323, 328
social control and, 63, 75, 76–77, 248,
252, 289–297, 327, 332
Solem v. Helms, 238–239
Spencer, Herbert, 57, 86
Spock, Benjamin, 82
Stanford v. Kentucky, 14, 238, 242
Status offenses
criticism of, 168, 169–173
deinstitutionalization and, 13, 150, 177–
179
dispositions and, 167
gender and, 64–65, 67, 170–171, 172,
176, 180, 182–183
noncriminal offenders and, 13, 51–52,
114